INTERNATIONAL DEBT REPORT 2025

This book, along with any associated content or subsequent updates, can be accessed at https://hdl.handle.net/10986/44017.

Data for this book are available in the World Bank's Development Data Hub at https://datacatalog.worldbank.org/int/search/dataset/0038015/international-debt-statistics.

Scan to see this book and prior editions.

INTERNATIONAL DEBT REPORT 2025

WORLD BANK GROUP

1818 H Street NW, Washington, DC 20433
Telephone: 202-473-1000; Internet: www.worldbank.org

1 2 3 4   28 27 26 25

ISBN (paper): 978-1-4648-2262-9
ISBN (electronic): 978-1-4648-2263-6
DOI: 10.1596/978-1-4648-2262-9

Cover photo: Dominic Chavez / World Bank. Further permission required for reuse.
Cover design: Parul Agarwal / World Bank and Bill Pragluski / Critical Stages, LLC.

The Library of Congress Control Number has been requested.

Contents

BOXES

FIGURES

TABLES

Foreword

A paradox is playing out in developing economies. On the bright side, inflation is abating. The oppressive interest rates of the last five years have begun to ease, which implies that the crushing debt service burdens of the last few years might start to shrink. For the right price, foreign bond investors are willing to provide financing again, enabling many countries to stave off default.

For most countries, however, these are small consolations—not enough to overcome the grave setbacks of this decade. As this report documents, the upheavals of the early 2020s produced a financial riptide like no other: between 2022 and 2024, about US$741 billion more flowed out of developing economies in debt repayments and interest than flowed into them in the form of new financing. It was the largest debt-related outflow in more than 50 years. The human toll has been steep: among the 22 most highly indebted countries, one out of every two people today cannot afford the minimum daily diet necessary for lasting health.

It's imperative, therefore, for policy makers everywhere to make the most of the breathing room that exists today, because the luxury could vanish tomorrow. That means putting the debt burdens of developing countries back on a sustainable path—by putting the fiscal house in order and reducing sovereign risks in ways that spur productive investment. It means modernizing the global systems meant to avert debt distress—by sounding the alarm *before* countries stray off the path and by helping them restructure their debts swiftly once the crisis arrives.

In 2024, the total external debt stock of low- and middle-income countries hit a new record: US$8.9 trillion, of which US$1.2 trillion—also a record—was owed by the 78 most vulnerable countries eligible to receive grants and low-cost loans from the World Bank's International Development Association. It was the wrong time for this type of record-breaking: average interest rates for developing countries haven't been higher since just before the great financial crisis of 2008–09. These countries paid a record US$415 billion in interest alone—money that might otherwise have been used to trim the rising ranks of out-of-school children, improve primary health care, and electrify rural villages.

Progress, of course, is occurring, but it is modest, and considerably more is needed. Debt burdens are now growing more slowly. Creditors were in a forgiving mood last year: they agreed to restructure US$90 billion in developing country debt, more than at any time since 2010. Ghana, Haiti, Somalia, and Sri Lanka, for example, secured restructuring agreements that shrank their long-term external debt by anywhere from 4 percent to 70 percent. Because of the work of the Global Sovereign Debt Roundtable, led by the International Monetary Fund and the World Bank, Ghana managed to complete its restructuring with its official bilateral creditors in half the time it took for previous restructurings under the Group of Twenty's Common Framework for Debt Treatments.

Yet it's no easier today for developing countries to stay clear of a debilitating debt trap than it was a decade ago. It would be foolish to expect that the human misery caused by the next debt crisis will be milder than the most recent one. That's because the global machinery for tackling crises has not kept up with the times. It was designed for a time when developing economies owed most of their external debt to the World Bank, the International Monetary Fund, and a handful of high-income economies—all of which provided loans at below-market rates.

That was a long time ago. Today, private creditors—bond investors mostly—account for nearly 60 percent of the long-term public and publicly guaranteed debt of developing economies. Debt owed to Paris Club creditors—the longtime overseers of the global debt-restructuring system—now accounts for about 7 percent.

That imbalance explains why restructurings in the 2020s have been so sluggish. Decision-making authority has shifted beyond the reach of the Paris Club. It is now dispersed among millions of bondholders and a kaleidoscope of governments in high- and middle-income economies. Debt restructurings, as a result, take place through a maze of processes: either via the Common Framework—the emergency mechanism introduced during the COVID-19 period to support debt-distressed countries—or through one-off deals with governments and bondholders.

The early-warning system for managing the debt of low-income countries is equally in need of an update: it was designed for an era when domestic debt markets were undeveloped and foreign private creditors were almost completely out of the picture. The opposite is true today. The system, officially the Low-Income Country Debt Sustainability Framework, is up for review this year. It should be overhauled to account for this new environment.

In 2024, bond investors turned on the spigots: having backed out of developing economies only the year before, they charged back in, pumping in US$80 billion more in new disbursements than they took back in the form of debt repayments.

That allowed some countries to ease their financial squeeze. Several were able to complete multibillion-dollar bond issuances—either to finance budget deficits or to pay off maturing bonds. But this was hardly low-cost borrowing: the interest rate was as much as 10 percent, roughly double the pre-2020 rate.

Not all developing countries, however, are finding it practical to tap foreign bond markets, and other options became scarcer in 2024. Official bilateral creditors—governments and government-related entities—retreated, taking in US$8.8 billion more in principal and interest than they disbursed in new financing. Most developing countries turned to domestic creditors: among the 86 for which domestic debt data are available, more than half—50 in all—saw their domestic government debt grow faster than external government debt. Government borrowing of this type usually comes at the expense of the private sector: local commercial banks load up on government bonds when they should be lending to the private sector. Domestic debt also involves shorter maturities—and therefore greater risk when the loan matures and must be refinanced at a potentially higher interest rate.

The time has come to stop tempting fate. The mismanagement of developing country debt is putting the brakes on economic development, pushing too many countries into a devil's bargain: borrow, at high cost, from foreign bondholders or stifle the domestic private sector by soaking up the assets of domestic commercial banks. The World Bank has remained a major lifeline for the most vulnerable countries: in 2024, it provided US$18.3 billion more in low-cost financing for countries eligible for International Development Association assistance than it received in principal repayments from them. That amount was an all-time high—but the laws of gravity cannot be defied forever.

Debt is still building in pernicious ways. Even if countries had options to climb out of the ditch quickly, governments ought not to be risking debt distress: the long-term human costs are simply unaffordable. But such options are hardly abundant today—and there are few signs that anything will change materially in the near term. Unless it does, the easing of financial conditions today could encourage poor and vulnerable countries to sleepwalk into a larger calamity tomorrow.

Indermit S. Gill
Senior Vice President and Chief Economist
The World Bank Group

Acknowledgments

This volume was prepared by the World Bank's Debt Statistics Program of the Development Data Group, comprising Parul Agarwal, Arzu Aytekin Balibek, Kifaye Didem Bayar, Matthew Benjamin, Sylvie Kabaziga Bishweka, Wendy Huang, Malvina Pollock, Prateek Samal, João Miguel Falcao Pinto Da Silva, Emiriana Stanishja, Rubena Sukaj, Tin Yu To, and Rasiel Vellos. The work was carried out under the management of Evis Rucaj and the direction of Haishan Fu. The team was assisted by Nancy Kebe.

The overview was prepared by the Debt Statistics Team, with contributions from Yan Bai and Eric Metreau from the Real Sector Statistics Unit; Diego Rivetti, Mellany Pintado Vasquez, and Wissam Harake, with guidance from Ewa Joanna Korczyc from the Economic Policy and Global Macro Team; Mike Nyawo and Alvaro Raul Espitia Rueda, with guidance from Sebastien Dessus from the Trade, Investment, and Regional Integration Team; and Hayley Pallen and Naotaka Sugawara, with guidance from M. Ayhan Kose and Carlos Arteta from the Development Economics Prospects Group.

Valuable guidance was provided by Indermit S. Gill, senior vice president and chief economist of the World Bank Group, and Haishan Fu, chief statistician of the World Bank and director of the Development Data Group. Brian R. Pinto, former senior advisor at the World Bank, provided valuable feedback. In addition, the Development Economics Vice Presidency; Macroeconomics, Trade and Investment Global Practice; Development Finance Vice Presidency; and Development Economics Prospects Group of the World Bank provided helpful feedback on the overview section. The final statistics were reviewed by country economists from the Macroeconomics, Trade and Investment Global Practice.

The cover was designed by Parul Agarwal and Bill Pragluski. Mark McClure, Jewel McFadden, and Yaneisy Martinez coordinated the publication and dissemination of this report. Kristen Milhollin, Karolina Ordon, Joseph Rebello, and Shane Kimo managed the communications surrounding the release.

The accompanying International Debt Statistics electronic products were prepared with support from a team led by Kunal Patel, Ramgopal Erabelly, and Sebastian Ariel Dolber, and comprising Yuliyan Nikolaev Bogdanov, Rajesh Kumar Danda, Svetoslava Georgieva Dimitrova, Todor Yordanov Grozdev, and Tsvetelina Nikolova Stefanova.

Key Takeaways

In 2024, slightly easier financial conditions brought some breathing room to low- and middle-income countries (LMICs) struggling with high debt burdens, as interest rates peaked and bond markets opened up once again. Many countries used the opportunity to restructure their debt in order to ease fiscal pressures and improve long-term fiscal sustainability. These actions, however, did not halt the longer-term buildup in public debt burdens, which hit a new record during the year.

Key takeaways from the 2024 data include the following:

- Growth in total external debt stock of LMICs slowed considerably in 2024, rising by only 1.1 percent from 2023 to reach US$8.9 trillion, after more than doubling the 2010 level. A similar trend was observed for countries eligible for International Development Association (IDA) assistance, where external debt stood at US$1.2 trillion in 2024, only 2.0 percent higher than the previous year.
- Net debt inflows (disbursements minus principal repayments) to LMICs increased 40.7 percent to US$210.3 billion in 2024, mainly because of bond issuance and financing from multilateral institutions, which accounted for 38.1 percent and 48.5 percent, respectively, of long-term debt inflows, for a combined share of 86.5 percent. Total net debt inflows to IDA-eligible countries rose 18.6 percent to US$53.1 billion in 2024.
- LMICs saw a reversal in bonds flows, shifting from US$75.4 billion in outflow in 2023 to an inflow of US$55.0 billion in 2024, reflecting renewed investor confidence, stronger economic growth prospects, and lower perceived credit risk. Bondholders were the fastest-growing component of public and publicly guaranteed (PPG) net debt flows to IDA-eligible countries, reversing from an outflow of US$730.4 million in 2023 to an inflow of US$7.1 billion in 2024. The increase, not seen since a US$11.1 billion jump in 2021, was the result of new issuances in 2024, which outpaced the increase in PPG bond principal repayments.
- In 2024, net debt inflows from multilateral creditors were the largest contributing component to PPG net debt flows, accounting for 73.2 percent of PPG net debt flows. They recorded US$70.1 billion in net debt inflows, nearly half of LMICs' net long-term debt inflows. The financial support from this creditor group fell 5.1 percent, easing after the unprecedented support provided during the COVID-19 pandemic.

- Combined World Bank (IDA and International Bank for Reconstruction and Development) lending reached an all-time high of US$36 billion, an increase of 30.4 percent over 2023. The World Bank remained the single-largest provider of financing for IDA-eligible countries, accounting for over one-third of PPG net debt inflows in 2024, an increase of 9.3 percent to US$18.3 billion. In addition, it also provided $7.5 billion in IDA grants in 2024, an increase of 10.9 percent. Conversely, net debt inflows to LMICs from bilateral creditors fell 76 percent to US$4.5 billion during the year, marking their lowest level since net outflows during the 2008 financial crisis. Net debt inflows to IDA-eligible countries from bilateral creditors dropped 84.8 percent in 2024 to US$1.7 billion, barely remaining positive.
- For a second consecutive year, LMICs' interest payments to service their total external debt reached an all-time high, increasing 2.2 percent to US$415.4 billion in 2024. These payments are 2.4 times higher than a decade ago, driven mainly by a 4.5 percent increase from public sector borrowers, to US$161.3 billion. This increase in interest payments has had severe consequences in high-debt countries, where on average more than half the population is already unable to afford a healthy diet.
- In 2024, LMICs paid out US$205.1 billion more in principal and interest than they received in new loans, marking the third consecutive year of net outflows. Long-term net transfers to PPG borrowers, which turned slightly positive in 2024 to US$11.9 billion, were the only positive contributor. Conversely, long-term net debt transfers to private nonguaranteed borrowers continued to remain negative in 2024, deteriorating from US$126.6 billion to US$147.4 billion. Among IDA-eligible countries, net debt transfers to PPG borrowers decreased 14.9 percent, to an inflow of US$24.4 billion in 2024.
- In 2024, debt reorganization by LMICs reached its highest level since 2010. Close to US$90 billion was reorganized, of which more than half was due to agreements with IDA-eligible countries. Reorganizations took several forms, including restructuring agreements in the Group of Twenty Common Framework and other international forums, and with private creditors, notably bondholders, as well as debt swap arrangements with official and private creditors.
- Among many LMICs, a welcome decrease in external indebtedness was offset by an increase in domestic borrowing. Of 86 countries for which domestic public debt data are available, 50 countries (representing more than half of the sample) recorded an increase in domestic debt that outpaced the increase in their external debt from 2023 to 2024.

In addition to the release of the 2024 external debt data from the International Debt Statistics database, this edition of the *International Debt Report* provides

- An analysis of the near-term macroeconomic outlook and risks LMICs face amid changing global financial and trade conditions, and what these shifts imply for these countries' debt burdens and vulnerabilities;
- A breakdown of changing debt patterns by region;
- An analysis of how elevated debt servicing burdens diminish LMICs' resources for other development priorities, including providing food and nutritional security, mitigating vulnerability to crises, and shoring up fiscal and institutional capacity; and
- An update on progress of the debt transparency agenda and the role of the World Bank in advancing sound debt management and policy frameworks, enhancing the accuracy and coverage of debt data, and promoting the reconciliation of borrower and creditor accounts.

Abbreviations

AfDB	African Development Bank
AFESD	Arab Fund for Economic and Social Development
BADEA	Arab Bank for Economic Development in Africa
BCEAO	Central Bank of West African States
BCIE	Central American Bank for Economic Integration
BDEAC	Development Bank of the Central African States
CPIA	Country Policy and Institutional Assessment
DRS	Debtor Reporting System
DSSI	Debt Service Suspension Initiative
EAP	East Asia and Pacific
EBRD	European Bank for Reconstruction and Development
EIB	European Investment Bank
FAO	Food and Agriculture Organization of the United Nations
FCS	fragile and conflict-affected situations
FDI	foreign direct investment
FY	fiscal year
G-7	Group of Seven
G-20	Group of Twenty
GDP	gross domestic product
GNI	gross national income
GSDR	Global Sovereign Debt Roundtable
HIPC	Heavily Indebted Poor Countries
IBRD	International Bank for Reconstruction and Development
IDA	International Development Association
IDB	Inter-American Development Bank
IDR	International Debt Report
IDS	International Debt Statistics
IFAD	International Fund for Agricultural Development
IMF	International Monetary Fund

J-CAP	Joint Capital Market Program
LAC	Latin America and the Caribbean
LICs	low-income countries
LMICs	low- and middle-income countries
MENAAP	Middle East, North Africa, Afghanistan, and Pakistan
MICs	middle-income countries
OCC	official creditor committee
OPEC	Organization of the Petroleum Exporting Countries
PBG	policy-based guarantee
PCO	Program of Creditor Outreach
PPA	Performance and Policy Action
PPG	public and publicly guaranteed
PNG	private nonguaranteed
SDFP	Sustainable Development Finance Policy
SDRs	special drawing rights
SNA	System of National Accounts
SOE	state-owned enterprise
SRBI	Bank Indonesia Rupiah Securities
WGI	Worldwide Governance Indicators

All dollar amounts are in US dollars unless otherwise indicated.

PART 1
Overview

1. Analysis of External Debt Stock and Debt Flows as of End-2024

Trends in External Debt, 2014–24

In 2024, low- and middle-income countries (LMICs) rebalanced their debt portfolios, shifting from new external financing to borrowing in domestic markets, and selectively issuing bonds in order to navigate tight global financial conditions and enhance fiscal resilience. Some countries used liability management operations, and a few restructured their debts. This approach significantly slowed these countries' accumulation of external debt, which increased only marginally by 1.1 percent, to US$8.9 trillion—about US$101 billion above the 2023 level (table 1.1).

Table 1.1 External Debt Stock of Low- and Middle-Income Countries, 2014–24

US$ (billion)

	2014	2015	2016	2017	2018	2019	2020	2021	2022	2023	2024
Debt stock	6,273.0	5,874.7	6,094.5	6,855.4	7,345.0	7,726.2	8,147.3	8,794.2	8,680.5	8,836.3	8,937.0
Long-term	4,252.6	4,346.0	4,613.7	5,048.6	5,320.2	5,679.8	6,088.1	6,535.6	6,422.7	6,501.0	6,542.6
Official creditors	1,000.8	1,018.7	1,076.5	1,178.2	1,249.2	1,314.3	1,481.6	1,682.2	1,714.8	1,812.1	1,834.1
Bilateral creditors	368.4	366.7	394.0	432.8	453.7	462.2	493.1	489.2	480.5	492.9	475.2
Multilateral creditors	632.4	652.0	682.4	745.4	795.5	852.1	988.6	1,193.0	1,234.3	1,319.1	1,358.9
World Bank (IBRD and IDA)	268.6	278.0	288.6	311.7	321.3	339.5	375.2	387.5	405.0	435.7	463.1
IMF (Use of credit and SDR allocations)	97.7	100.5	103.8	114.5	142.0	162.2	214.6	386.4	380.5	380.9	371.6
Private creditors	3,251.8	3,327.3	3,537.3	3,870.3	4,071.0	4,365.5	4,606.5	4,853.4	4,707.9	4,689.0	4,708.5
Bonds	1,205.2	1,230.6	1,343.7	1,634.9	1,752.6	1,971.4	2,192.5	2,375.1	2,237.8	2,154.0	2,175.1
Banks and other private	2,046.6	2,096.7	2,193.5	2,235.4	2,318.4	2,394.1	2,414.0	2,478.2	2,470.1	2,534.9	2,533.4
Short-term	2,020.4	1,528.7	1,480.7	1,806.8	2,024.8	2,046.4	2,059.1	2,258.6	2,257.8	2,335.3	2,394.4
Memorandum item											
Long-term PPG	2,130.8	2,184.4	2,346.0	2,652.9	2,883.1	3,100.6	3,392.0	3,787.3	3,763.2	3,852.1	3,931.2
Long-term PNG	2,121.9	2,161.6	2,267.8	2,395.6	2,437.1	2,579.3	2,696.2	2,748.3	2,659.5	2,648.9	2,611.4

Sources: World Bank International Debt Statistics database; International Monetary Fund; Bank for International Settlements.
Note: IBRD = International Bank for Reconstruction and Development; IDA = International Development Association; IMF = International Monetary Fund; PNG = private nonguaranteed; PPG = public and publicly guaranteed; SDR = special drawing right.

Some LMICs opted to restructure or renegotiate their existing debt in a strategic effort to reduce elevated debt levels. By doing so, these governments attempted to ease fiscal pressures and improve long-term sustainability. New borrowing from commercial banks declined primarily because of unfavorable market conditions: elevated global interest rates in the wake of the global pandemic had increased the cost of securing new loans, rendering commercial financing less attractive. In addition, tighter lending standards and heightened risk aversion among banks further limited access to this source of funding. Notably, LMIC governments increased their reliance on domestic borrowing in 2024 to fill critical financing needs, also in lieu of additional external financing. This shift reflects both short- and long-term factors. In the short term, governments affected by heightened vulnerability concerns reflected a countercyclical adjustment and a more cautious approach to additional borrowing from external sources in a period characterized by persistently elevated interest rates, high debt levels, weak credit ratings, and rising trade uncertainties. The shift also allows for greater control over debt terms and mitigates exposure to foreign exchange risk. In the long term, the substitution of domestic for external borrowing also indicates that the gradual development of domestic capital markets—a long-time goal for the World Bank—is allowing many LMICs to identify and tap internal sources for their financing needs.

Despite the broader shift from external borrowing, many LMICs continued to issue new bonds in international markets in 2024 because of several compelling advantages, including the lower cost (that is, lower interest rates than provided by other private creditors) of bonds compared to other sources of external financing; the longer maturities of bonds that help reduce rollover risk and improve debt sustainability; the larger financing volumes provided by bond issuances, which can provide access to substantial capital to support budgetary needs and development programs; and the rollover potential of bonds that offers refinancing flexibility in managing debt portfolios. The ability of LMICs to resume bond issuance in 2024 at an accelerating pace was a welcome development, as many countries were locked out of global bond markets just a few years ago.

Growth in the total external debt stock slowed in 2024 to 1.1 percent, reaching US$8.9 trillion, after more than doubling the 2010 level. Short-term debt was the fastest-growing component, increasing 2.5 percent in 2024, to US$2.4 trillion. Long-term debt remained steady at US$6.5 trillion, but with an important change in composition. A decade ago (2014) the stock of long-term debt was almost evenly divided between public and publicly guaranteed (PPG) and private nonguaranteed (PNG) debt (figure 1.1). Over the past 10 years, however, the share of long-term debt held by the PPG sector has been on an upward trajectory and reached 60 percent (US$3.9 trillion) in 2024; by contrast, that of the PNG sector has decreased to 40 percent (US$2.6 trillion). The shift was a consequence

Figure 1.1 Creditor Composition of Long-Term External Debt Stock in Low- and Middle-Income Countries, 1970–2024

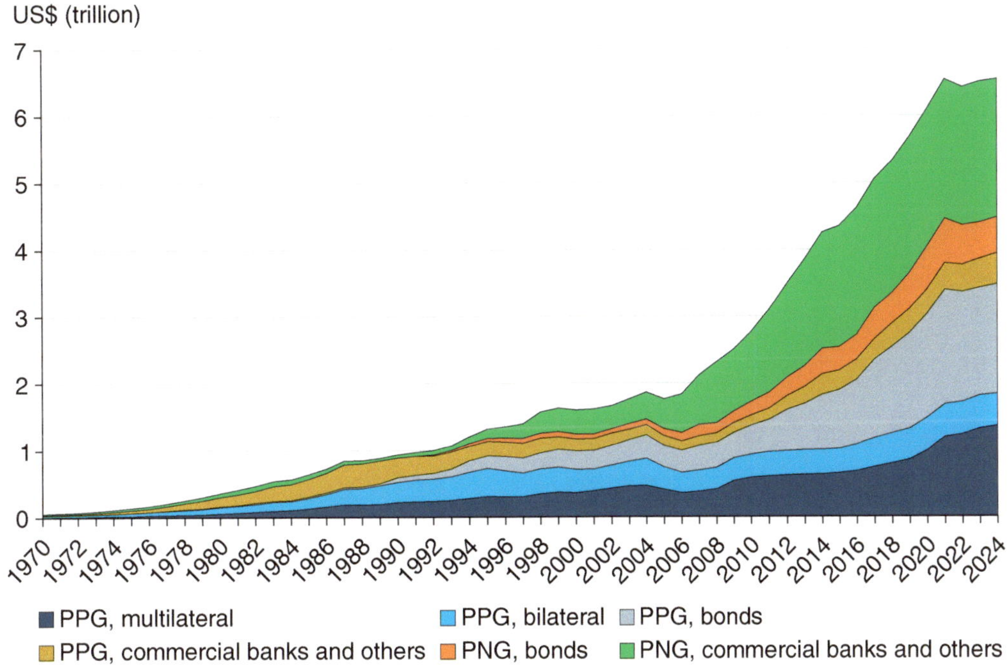

Source: World Bank International Debt Statistics database.
Note: PNG = private nonguaranteed; PPG = public and publicly guaranteed.

of governments stepping in to finance development projects and public services in the aftermath of the COVID-19 pandemic, as borrowing by the private sector declined because of diminished growth prospects and uncertainty. Additionally, as interest rates increased in 2022 following a decade of persistently low rates, investor preferences shifted to safer government debt over private sector lending.

Viewed from the creditor perspective, the composition of long-term debt outstanding varied widely in 2024 and has evolved significantly over the past decade. Public debt owed to multilateral creditors, an important source of concessional financing for LMICs, increased 3.0 percent in 2024, to US$1.4 trillion. Multilateral creditors notably increased their support for LMICs during the COVID-19 pandemic, and they have continued to provide support to these nations as they face limited fiscal space, higher borrowing costs, and fewer sources of financing in the aftermath of the global crisis. This support has become more crucial as funding from private creditors remains steady, whereas support from official bilateral creditors decreased 3.6 percent, to US$475.2 billion, in 2024. Over the past decade, the share of outstanding debt owed to bilateral creditors has decreased 5.2 percentage points, to 12.1 percent in 2024; by contrast, that of multilateral creditors has increased 4.9 percentage points to 34.6 percent. The World Bank accounted for US$463.1 billion, or 34.1 percent, of multilateral debt stock, followed by the International Monetary Fund (IMF) at US$371.6 billion, or 27.3 percent. The notable reduction of debt obligations to official bilateral creditors resulted from a combination of a slowdown in new financing provided by these creditors and the implementation of debt restructuring agreements and forgiveness operations.

In 2024, outstanding debt owed to private creditors remained steady at US$4.7 trillion and accounted for a 72 percent share of long-term debt stock. Over the past decade, the combined share of long-term PPG and PNG debt stock held by private creditors has been on a declining trend, falling 4.5 percentage points since 2014. After decreasing two years in a row, LMICs' PPG debt owed to private creditors resumed an upward trajectory in 2024, increasing 2.8 percent to US$2.1 trillion. The 2024 PPG private debt stock increase was driven by a 1.6 percent rise, to US$1.6 trillion, in debt owed to bondholders, as these creditors returned to lending in international markets. PPG debt stock owed to bondholders has become prominent for LMICs as their financing needs have grown, and the cost of debt has increased. Over the last decade bondholders have accounted for a 41.6 percent share of total PPG debt, a surge driven by a decade of persistently low interest rates, which opened the markets for LMICs. PPG debt outstanding owed to commercial banks and other private entities also increased in 2024, by 7.2 percent, to US$459.9 billion. These creditors' share of total PPG has remained stable over the past decade at 12 percent. Although mostly driven by the borrowing trends of the top 10 LMIC borrowers,[1] the composition of PNG debt over the past decade has averaged a 20.1 percent share held by bondholders and 79.9 percent held by commercial banks and other private lenders. (Refer to box 1.1 for definitions of debt terms used in this report; refer to box 1.2 for income and lending classifications.)

Box 1.1 External Debt Data: Concepts, Sources, and Coverage

This report presents data and analysis on external debt for 119 low- and middle-income countries and Guyana. The primary source for these data is reports to the World Bank's Debtor Reporting System (DRS) from member countries that have received either International Bank for Reconstruction and Development loans or International Development Association credits and that have outstanding obligations to the World Bank. The DRS, instituted in 1951, has its origins in the World Bank's need to monitor and assess the financial position of its borrowers. Comprehensive information on data sources and the methodology used to compile the statistics presented in this report can be found in the appendix under "Data Sources." The following describes the key concepts and data sources.

(Box continues on next page)

Box 1.1 External Debt Data: Concepts, Sources, and Coverage (*continued*)

- The DRS follows international standards and defines *external debt* as the outstanding amount of actual current liabilities in both domestic and foreign currency that require payment(s) of principal and/or interest by the debtor at some point(s) in the future and that are owed to nonresidents by residents of an economy. The sum of principal and interest payments is defined as *debt service*.
- The *total external debt* of a country is the sum of public and publicly guaranteed debt, private nonguaranteed debt, and short-term debt.
- *Public and publicly guaranteed external debt* comprises long-term external obligations (maturities of over one year) of all public debtors, including debt held by the central government and by state-owned enterprises. Data are collected on a loan-by-loan basis through the DRS. Reporting countries submit quarterly reports on new loan commitments and annual reports on loan status and transactions (new commitments, gross disbursements, principal, and interest payments).
- *Private nonguaranteed debt* comprises long-term external obligations of private debtors that are not guaranteed by a public entity. The DRS has covered private nonguaranteed debt since 1973; however, for this category of debt data, the annual status and transactions (gross disbursements, principal, and interest payments) are reported in aggregate.
- *Short-term debt* is defined as debt with an original maturity of one year or less and is not covered under DRS reporting requirements. However, most DRS reporters provide an annual report on outstanding short-term debt stocks on a voluntary basis. For countries that do not provide these data, information on their short-term debt is drawn from the Quarterly External Debt Statistics database, a joint World Bank–International Monetary Fund initiative, wherein data are compiled and reported by countries' central banks, along with data compiled by the Bank for International Settlements.

All debt data reported to the DRS are validated against—and, when appropriate, supplemented by—data from other sources. These additional data include the Balance of Payments and International Investment Position statistics, Quarterly External Debt Statistics, information published on official government websites, reports from the International Monetary Fund, regional development banks, the Organisation for Economic Co-operation and Development, the Bank for International Settlements, and websites and annual publications of lending agencies.

Box 1.2 World Bank Income and Lending Classifications Used in *International Debt Report 2025*

The World Bank classifies economies by income level for analytical purposes (to broadly group countries by level of development) and operational purposes (to determine their Financial Terms and Conditions of Bank Financing). This report presents data for 119 low- and middle-income countries and Guyana (the only high-income country eligible for International Development Association [IDA] resources) reporting to the World Bank Debtor Reporting System. Twenty-four of these countries are classified as low-income, with per capita income of US$1,135 or below; 95 countries are classified as middle-income, with per capita income greater than US$1,135 and less than or equal to US$13,935; and one country, Guyana, is classified as high-income, with per capita income of more than US$13,935.[a]

Income classifications are updated annually at the start of the World Bank fiscal year (July 1) on the basis of gross national income per capita for the previous year. This year Costa Rica was reclassified from a middle-income to a high-income country. Additionally, Equatorial Guinea, a middle-income country, was added to the publication for the first time. Ethiopia is currently in a temporary status of "unclassified" for fiscal year 2026 but, for the effect of this publication, has been retained under its fiscal year 2025 status as a low-income country. The World Bank still considers Ethiopia an IDA-only country, so the terms and conditions of World Bank financing for the country have not changed. Agencies using the World Bank income classification to determine access conditions to their own resources should still consider Ethiopia a low-income country. Gross national income is expressed in US dollars and determined by conversion factors derived according to the Atlas methodology.[b] Forty-seven of the middle-income countries covered in this report are eligible only for nonconcessional loans from the International Bank for Reconstruction and Development (IBRD) and are referred to as IBRD-only countries. The remaining 24 low-income and 48 middle-income countries, and Guyana, reporting to the Debtor Reporting System are either (a) eligible only for concessional lending from IDA and referred to as IDA-only countries; or (b) eligible for a mix of IBRD and IDA lending and referred to as "blend" countries. Together, IDA-only and IBRD-IDA blend countries are referred to as IDA-eligible countries. Figure B1.2.1 shows the distribution of the 119 low- and middle-income countries and Guyana included in *International Debt Report 2025* by income and lending groups. IDA countries receiving their IDA resources only on grant terms, which carry no repayments at all, are not part of the Debtor Reporting System. A comprehensive list of each country's income and lending classifications appears in the appendix of this report under "Country Groups."

(Box continues on next page)

Box 1.2 World Bank Income and Lending Classifications Used in *International Debt Report 2025* (continued)

Regional classifications were also updated at the start of the World Bank fiscal year, moving Afghanistan and Pakistan from the World Bank's South Asia region to the Middle East, North Africa, Afghanistan, and Pakistan region.

Figure B1.2.1 Number of Low- and Middle-Income Countries Covered in *International Debt Report 2025*, by FY2026 Income and Lending Groups

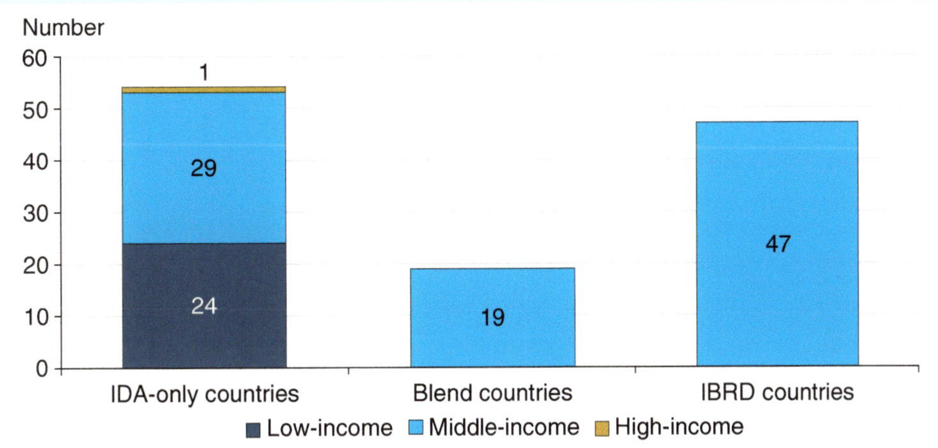

Sources: World Bank, "World Bank Country and Lending Groups," https://datahelpdesk.worldbank.org/knowledgebase/articles/906519-world-bank-country-and-lending-groups; World Bank IDA, https://ida.worldbank.org/en/home.
Note: IBRD = International Bank for Reconstruction and Development; IDA = International Development Association; FY = fiscal year.

a. The country grouping is held fixed when data are compared over time in the International Debt Report. For example, the aggregate for low-income countries from 2010 to 2024 consists of the same group of countries that are classified as low-income countries according to the latest World Bank income classification as of end-2024.
b. For more information on the Atlas methodology, refer to World Bank, "The World Bank Atlas Method—Detailed Methodology," https://datahelpdesk.worldbank.org/knowledgebase/articles/378832-what-is-the-world-bank-atlas-method.

Trends in Domestic Debt, 2014–24

Among many LMICs, a decrease or containment of the growth of external indebtedness has been offset by increases in domestic borrowing. This trend has been developing over the past decade as the expansion of domestic debt markets has allowed countries to fund fiscal deficits amid repeated shocks, growing development needs, and sluggish revenue growth (and, although the increase in domestic debt in 2024 may reflect some short-term and cyclical factors, the longer-term structural trend is clear). Debt from domestic sources of financing has grown rapidly in LMICs, leading to increases in overall domestic public debt burdens. Consequently, concerns over the sustainability of the total (external plus domestic) public debt position among some LMICs persist.

Among 86 LMICs for which domestic government debt data are available, 50 countries (representing about 58 percent of the sample) recorded an increase in domestic debt that outpaced the increase in their external debt from 2023 to 2024. The remaining countries displayed more mixed patterns, with some experiencing declines in both external and domestic debt and others showing a sharper reduction in external debt relative to the domestic portion. Although this sample of 86 countries is limited because the World Bank does not require reporting on domestic debt, the findings nonetheless indicate a clear shift to a greater reliance on domestic borrowing among LMICs in 2024.

The development of domestic capital markets has enabled LMICs to reduce their dependence on external financing, contributing to macroeconomic resilience and allowing governments to borrow in local currency and mitigate their exposure to exchange rate volatility, global interest rate volatility, and currency mismatches between assets and liabilities. This ability is particularly important for issuers trying to hedge against exchange rate risks, or for borrowers that operate in nontradable sectors of the economy. As domestic financial markets deepen and investor bases broaden, governments increasingly lean on domestic borrowing, which builds a domestic yield curve that anchors financial markets and gives governments more control over financing conditions because they often act as the primary price-setters in their own markets. On the instrument side, issuance of bonds in domestic markets has not just been a source of liquidity for LMICs but also provided governments with tools to conduct monetary policy to target inflation and manage shocks. Domestic debt rose more rapidly than external public debt from 2023 to 2024. In figure 1.2, the dashed line represents an equal increase in domestic and external debt, and the clustering of points above the line indicates that domestic borrowing outpaced external financing in many countries.

Governments, however, seek to also participate in international bond markets (Eurobonds, global bonds, and so on) in order to diversify funding sources, to signal credibility to investors, and sometimes to raise large volumes of foreign exchange in a single operation, which may not be possible domestically.

Figure 1.2 Change in Domestic and External Government Debt, Selected Low- and Middle-Income Countries, 2023–24

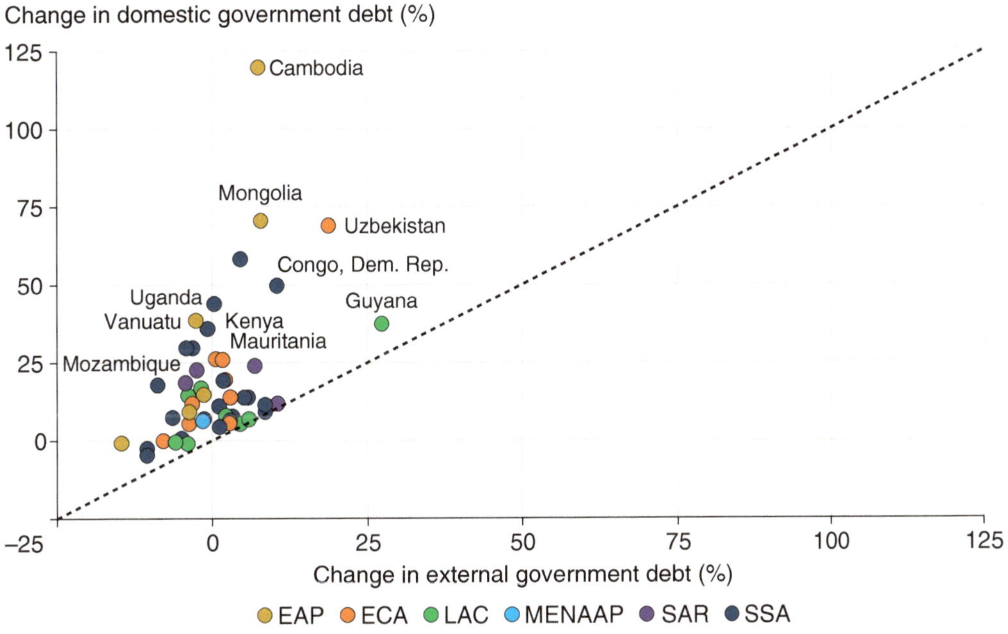

Sources: Country reports to the World Bank–International Monetary Fund Quarterly Public Sector Debt database; publicly available country debt bulletins; market sources.
Note: The World Bank's Debtor Reporting System does not collect data on domestic debt; domestic debt figures presented in this report are derived from the sources listed. EAP = East Asia and Pacific; ECA = Europe and Central Asia; LAC = Latin America and the Caribbean; LMICs = low- and middle-income countries; MENAAP = Middle East, North Africa, Afghanistan, and Pakistan; SAR = South Asia; SSA = Sub-Saharan Africa.

The shift to domestic financing, although generally a positive development, has also introduced new challenges for LMICs, because they need to manage the simultaneous use of domestic and external debt financing. Strong legal and regulatory frameworks are essential for proper public debt management and the overall soundness of the domestic financial system. Consequently, borrowing decisions should be balanced with a country's overall debt management objectives of ensuring debt sustainability, lowering cost and risk, and managing domestic and external shock absorption mechanisms. Domestic debt tends to be of a shorter maturity than external debt and is consequently more susceptible to rollover risk. Heavy reliance on domestic debt increases this risk, as well as the risk associated with increased interest rates. Government credibility is critical to managing and minimizing these risks and is enhanced by the availability of timely and reliable information on domestic and external debt financing. Government support is also crucial, especially in the early stages of developing domestic markets, for providing liquidity and guarantees and setting benchmarks on the pricing of the instruments and in the adoption of flexible exchange rate regimes. However, as domestic markets become more established, greater government borrowing and rising interest rates can crowd out private borrowing and investment. With domestic banks preferring to (or being pressured to) lend to the government, their exposure to the sovereign grows and creates a balance sheet interconnectedness referred to as the "sovereign-bank nexus" that can amplify macroeconomic risks when public debt sustainability problems arise. Additionally, heavy government borrowing can limit and reshape private sector financing and investment, resulting in the public debt–private finance nexus.

Domestic markets in LMICs have not only attracted resident investors but also become attractive to international investors. Their development has led to nonresidents borrowing in domestic currency in countries with well-established access to capital markets, such as in Argentina, Indonesia, Mauritius, Mexico, and South Africa, as well as newer issuances in Colombia, the Dominican Republic, Jamaica, the Philippines, and Türkiye. The liberalization of capital markets in these economies has played an important role in deepening domestic markets and attracting international investors. Such participation can benefit the depth and liquidity of domestic financial markets, increase investor competition, and promote international standards. Multilateral organizations, including the World Bank, have played an important role in assisting countries with the development of their domestic financial markets (box 1.3).

Box 1.3 The World Bank's Role in Developing Domestic Financial Markets

Deep and efficient domestic debt markets help build resilience to shocks in times of financial turbulence and convey multiple additional economic benefits. They can mitigate currency risk, help price risk appropriately, allow financial market participants to better manage their portfolios, and provide a more effective conduit for monetary policy. They can also attract vital capital when the appetite of international bond holders dwindles.

The World Bank Group has introduced multiple resources and programs to support the development of local currency bond markets (LCBMs) in low- and middle-income countries. One such resource, the *Guidance Note for Developing Government Local Currency Bond Markets* published in 2021 by the International Monetary Fund and World Bank, provides a comprehensive and systematic framework for LCBM development (Hashimoto et al. 2021). The note identifies the enabling conditions, diagnostic frameworks, and basic building blocks that countries can implement to develop and expand LCBMs, while emphasizing the critical roles of risk management and transparency.

(Box continues on next page)

Box 1.3 The World Bank's Role in Developing Domestic Financial Markets (*continued*)

Apart from providing guidance, the World Bank has also participated directly in developing borrowers' domestic debt markets. Bhutan is an example. A 2022 joint International Monetary Fund–World Bank mission assisted the South Asian nation's government in assessing the development of its domestic government debt market and provided inputs for a master plan to deepen that market. Recommended policies focused mainly on the primary market, including introduction of a more regular issuance calendar, a gradual maturity lengthening, and a buildup of benchmark securities.

The World Bank and the International Finance Corporation also launched the Joint Capital Market Program (J-CAP) in 2017 to support the development of strong local capital markets. The program mobilizes experts across the World Bank Group to advance deep, efficient, and well-regulated local capital markets that create access to long-term, local-currency finance. J-CAP initially focused on six priority countries and one region: Bangladesh, Indonesia, Kenya, Morocco, Peru, Viet Nam, and the West African Economic and Monetary Union. Since then, it has added several more countries where it works to support local capital markets development. In Bangladesh, regulatory reforms enabled by J-CAP led to a US$50 million International Finance Corporation investment in the country's first low-income housing bond. In Colombia, J-CAP advisory enabled the issuance of two private bonds to fund biodiversity projects. In Côte d'Ivoire, J-CAP helped create a bond that raised money to bring electricity to up to 800,000 low-income households.

In addition, the World Bank's Sustainable Development Finance Policy has targeted the development of domestic debt markets through the issuance of guidelines and calendars for issuing domestic securities in alignment with annual borrowing plans, among other actions.

Low- and middle-income countries tend to have relatively small local capital markets, but those markets can still serve as alternative mechanisms for finance when external funding from international bondholders dries up. When economic uncertainties dampen international investor demand for sovereign bonds and effectively shut low- and middle-income countries out of financing, local capital markets can step in and fill the role.

From a policy perspective, domestic debt accumulations have been driven by two factors: crisis-response policies following the retrenchment of credit during the COVID-19 pandemic and, more recently, policies designed to reduce external debt reliance. Consequently, the extent of the switch from external to domestic debt has varied across countries and regions.[2] In countries such as China, Gabon, Kenya, Mozambique, and Vanuatu, improvements in external debt were offset by increases in domestic debt (figure 1.3). In Cambodia, Guyana, Malawi, Mongolia, and Uzbekistan, external and domestic debt both increased, with the rise in domestic debt being relatively larger than that of external debt. Conversely, Ghana, Jamaica, and Mexico recorded decreases in both their domestic and external indebtedness in 2024.

Figure 1.3 Change in External vs. Domestic Government Debt, Selected Low- and Middle-Income Countries, 2023–24

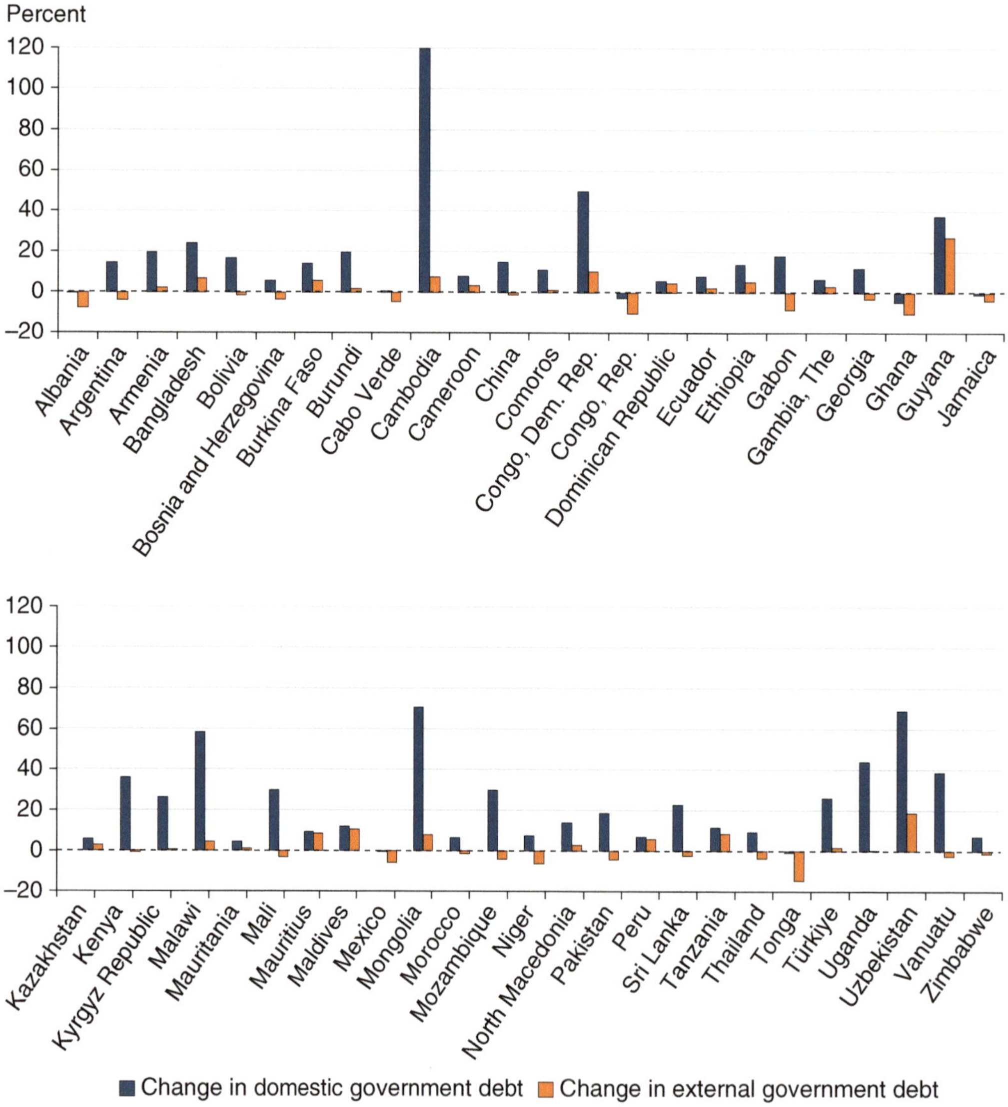

Sources: Country reports to the World Bank–International Monetary Fund Quarterly Public Sector Debt database; publicly available country debt bulletins; market sources.

Even if external sources of financing remain stable for LMICs, their economies' vulnerability to global shocks such as interest rate increases and currency risks remains high. Each year, movements in the value of the US dollar against other global currencies affect the value of LMICs' debt. These fluctuations can typically be quite volatile and have important implications for LMICs with large dollar-denominated external debt portfolios. As the US dollar climbed in 2024 against the euro, the British pound, the Chinese yuan, the Japanese yen, and many other currencies, the debt stock denominated in those currencies shrank when converted into US dollars. However, when considering this effect only on the liabilities side, an appreciation of the dollar increases countries' debt burdens (measured in domestic currency), because it increases the value of outstanding debt and the cost of servicing their dollar-denominated debt. On a bilateral basis in 2024, the dollar appreciated 9.4 percent against the Japanese yen, 6 percent against the euro, 2.8 percent against the special drawing rights, and 2.1 percent against the Chinese yuan, with these four currencies making up the largest portion of LMICs' debt stock after the US dollar–denominated portion. Nevertheless, this effect was reversed in the first half of 2025, when the dollar experienced its biggest depreciation since 1973.

Debt Servicing Burdens of LMICs, 2014–24

For the second year in a row, LMICs' interest payments to service their external debt reached an all-time high. Total interest payments on external debt stock of LMICs increased 2.2 percent in 2024, to US$415.4 billion. Debt servicing costs became more expensive because of persistently high interest rates that continued into 2024, combined with LMICs' elevated debt stock positions. As core inflation remained elevated in many countries, central banks continued to adhere to a tight monetary policy and kept interest rates high for a longer period of time. Such policies, implemented to contain inflation, also amplified fragilities for countries already facing tight fiscal space as they emerged from the COVID-19 pandemic.

Whereas interest payments on servicing short-term debt remained stable, interest payments on long-term external debt increased 3.0 percent in 2024, to US$280.1 billion. These payments are 2.1 times higher than they were a decade earlier. The increase in long-term interest payments in 2024 was primarily driven by a 4.5 percent increase in interest payments on PPG debt, to US$161.3 billion; the relative increase in payments from the PNG sector was moderate at 0.9 percent, to US$118.8 billion (figure 1.4). As interest rates remained elevated in 2024, the increase in long-term PPG interest expenses followed the same trend as the outstanding debt obligations of this borrower group, which increased 2.1 percent to US$3.9 trillion in 2024. Conversely, although the long-term outstanding debt of PNG borrowers decreased 1.4 percent in 2024, to US$2.6 trillion, interest payments on these obligations increased slightly in 2024.

Figure 1.4 Low- and Middle-Income Countries' Interest Payments on External Debt, by Debtor Type, 2014–24

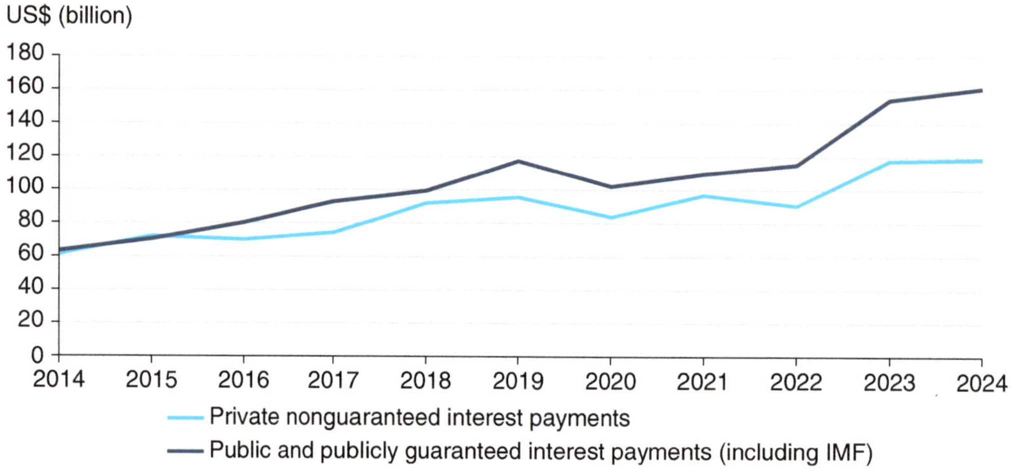

Source: World Bank International Debt Statistics database.
Note: IMF = International Monetary Fund.

China, the largest debtor country among LMICs, accounted for 30.1 percent of LMICs' interest payments on total debt stock. In 2024, the country's interest cost on short-term debt stock increased marginally by 1.4 percent to US$82.9 billion, whereas interest payments on long-term debt obligations decreased substantially by 21.3 percent, to US$41.9 billion. The decrease was associated with a 4 percent fall, to US$1.1 billion, in long-term debt obligations in 2024. Excluding China, total interest costs of other LMICs increased 7.1 percent, to US$290.6 billion. Interest payments from this group of countries on short-term debt remained almost unchanged, at US$52.4 billion, whereas interest payments on long-term debt increased 8.9 percent to US$238.2 billion. PPG borrowers drove the trend, paying 12.9 percent higher interest payments on long-term debt than they did a year earlier, amounting to US$145 billion. Bondholders were the largest recipients of these payments, at US$61.6 billion, followed by multilateral creditors at US$52 billion. Long-term interest payments from PNG borrowers also increased to US$93.2 billion, but at a smaller pace of 3.1 percent.

As high global interest rates persist and countries face elevated debt levels, the risks and costs of debt rollovers for LMICs have become significant and a financial burden for governments, many of which are diverting essential resources to service debt obligations. During the past two decades, the risks associated with rolling over debt were relatively low because countries could continue securing favorable financing terms to pay off maturing debt instruments in a period characterized by predominantly low global interest rates. However, since global interest rates began to increase in early 2022, the risks and costs of rollovers also increased substantially, because of markedly higher interest rates on newly contracted instruments than on maturing ones. In February 2024, Kenya successfully issued a new US$1.5 billion bond and used the proceeds to refinance a portion of its maturing external debt by paying off its June 2024 maturing US$2 billion Eurobond. Although the operation successfully extended the maturity profile of Kenya's debt portfolio by extending the maturity of the new instrument until 2031, it did so at a higher cost: the new bond issuance offered a coupon and yield of 9.75 percent and 10.375 percent, respectively, compared to the 6.875 percent coupon of the maturing instrument.

Higher interest rates have not only affected the cost of rollovers but also increased the overall cost of all new borrowing, which continues to be contracted at much higher rates. Since global interest rates began to increase rapidly in 2022 to tame inflation, LMICs' average interest rate on new external commitments continued to remain high in 2024 at 5.89 percent for lending from private creditors and 3.8 percent for lending from official creditor sources (figure 1.5). The last time LMICs' average interest rate on debt commitments from private creditors exceeded the 2023–24 level was in 2007, right before the 2008 financial crisis, at 6.14 percent; the equivalent rate from official creditors was last recorded as higher than 3.8 percent in year 2000 at 4.72 percent.

Figure 1.5 Average Terms on New External Debt Commitments for Low- and Middle-Income Countries, by Creditor Type, 2014–24

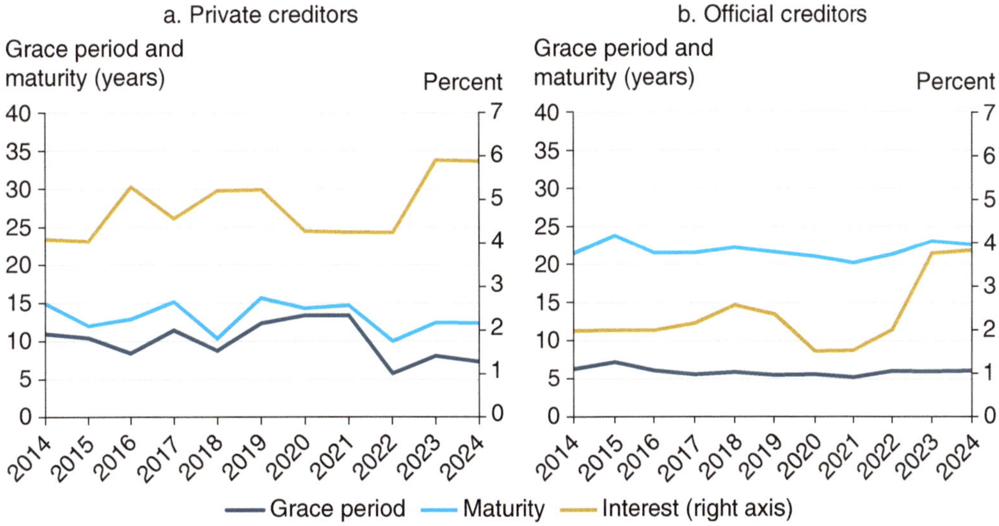

Source: World Bank International Debt Statistics database.

Favorable lending terms can be acquired through the combination of low interest rates, longer maturity structures, and a longer grace period, which can provide stability for borrowers. Lending from official creditor sources such as bilateral and multilateral institutions has historically provided borrowers with more favorable terms, lowering their cost of borrowing, freeing up their fiscal space, and reducing their financial risk exposure through longer maturities and longer grace periods. Consequently, the average maturity on new commitments from official and private creditors remained steady in 2024, with official creditors offering almost twice the length of maturity offered by private creditors, at 22 years.

Higher global interest rates also continued to elevate the interest payments on debt previously contracted at variable rates. As the underlying benchmark rates increased, servicing already contracted obligations became more expensive and continued to pose serious challenges for governments' budgeting forecasts. Variable debt financing offered cost saving options during the period of predominantly low interest rates; however, its fluctuations over time have become risky and costly as interest rates remain elevated. LMICs' share of total outstanding PPG debt (excluding IMF obligations) contracted at variable interest rates has decreased slightly over the past decade, from 36 percent in 2014 to 33 percent in 2024. However, the share of interest payments on PPG debt contracted at variable interest rates has increased by 16.1 percentage points over the same period, accounting for a 41.0 percent share in 2024, equivalent to US$59.2 billion in nominal US dollar terms (figure 1.6).

Figure 1.6 Interest Payments on Public and Publicly Guaranteed Debt for Low- and Middle-Income Countries, by Type of Interest Rate, 2014–24

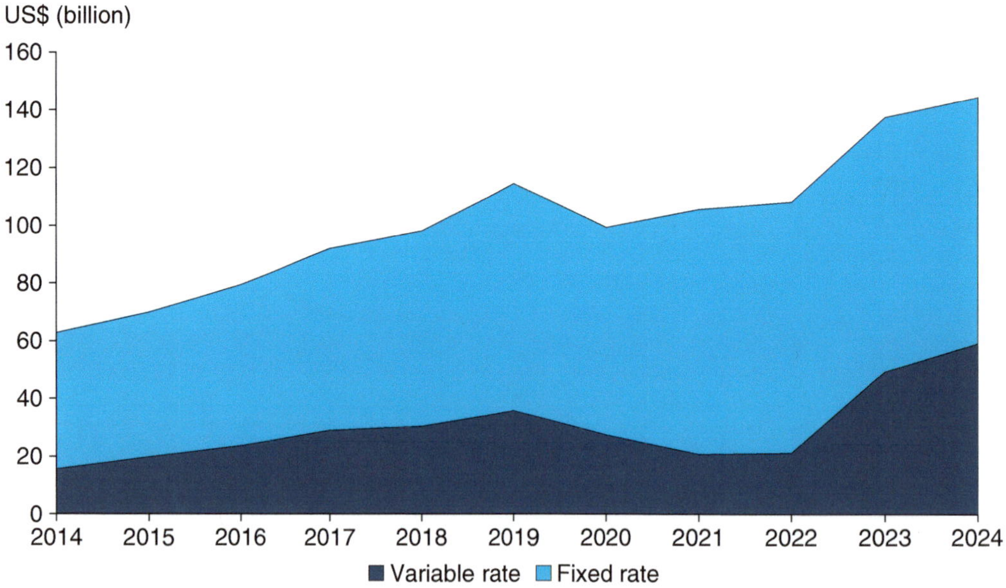

Source: World Bank International Debt Statistics database.

At the regional level, interest payments on PPG debt increased in all regions except East Asia and Pacific. Interest payments in the East Asia and Pacific region decreased 16.8 percent in 2024, to US$36.5 billion (figure 1.7). Interest payments on PPG debt owed to official creditors increased 11.6 percent in 2024, to US$11.2 billion in the region, and interest payments on PPG debt owed to private creditors decreased 25.3 percent to US$25.3 billion. China, the largest borrower in the region, is the driver for the overall regional decrease, with the country's PPG debt payments to private creditors almost halving in 2024. The South Asia region experienced the fastest growth in PPG debt interest payments, 19.2 percent in 2024; however, in nominal terms it accounted for the smallest volume, US$11.6 billion. The increase was attributed to increases in PPG debt interest payments to both official and private creditor entities, with Sri Lanka and Bangladesh driving the trend. Latin America and the Caribbean accounted for the largest volume of interest payments in 2024 among all the regions. Interest payments on PPG debt increased 12.3 percent in 2024, to US$53.3 billion. Mexico and Brazil recorded the highest PPG payments at US$15.1 billion and US$11.5 billion, respectively.

Figure 1.7 Interest Payments on Public and Publicly Guaranteed Debt of Low- and Middle-Income Countries, by Region and Creditor Type, 2022–24

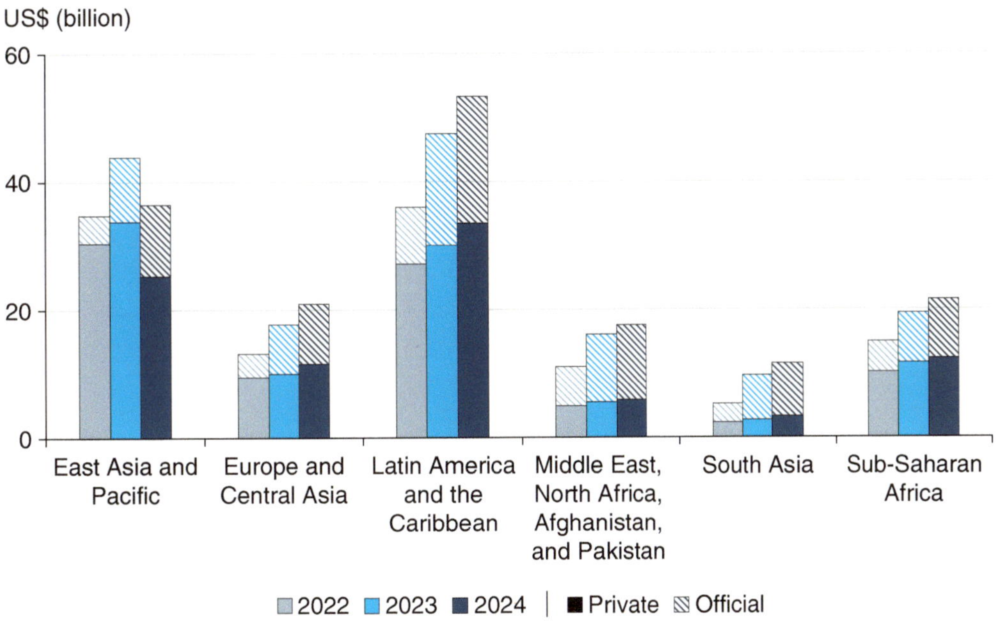

Source: World Bank International Debt Statistics database.

Trends in External Debt Flows, 2014–24

Net debt flows (disbursements minus principal repayments) to LMICs increased 40.7 percent in 2024, to US$210.3 billion (figure 1.8). Short-term debt net flows contracted 8.7 percent to US$65.8 billion; long-term debt net flows nearly doubled in 2024, from US$77.5 billion to US$144.6 billion. The increase in long-term flows resulted from a twofold increase in inflows to PPG borrowers, which was offset by higher outflows from PNG borrowers.

Figure 1.8 Net Debt Inflows, by Maturity, Low- and Middle-Income Countries, 2014–24

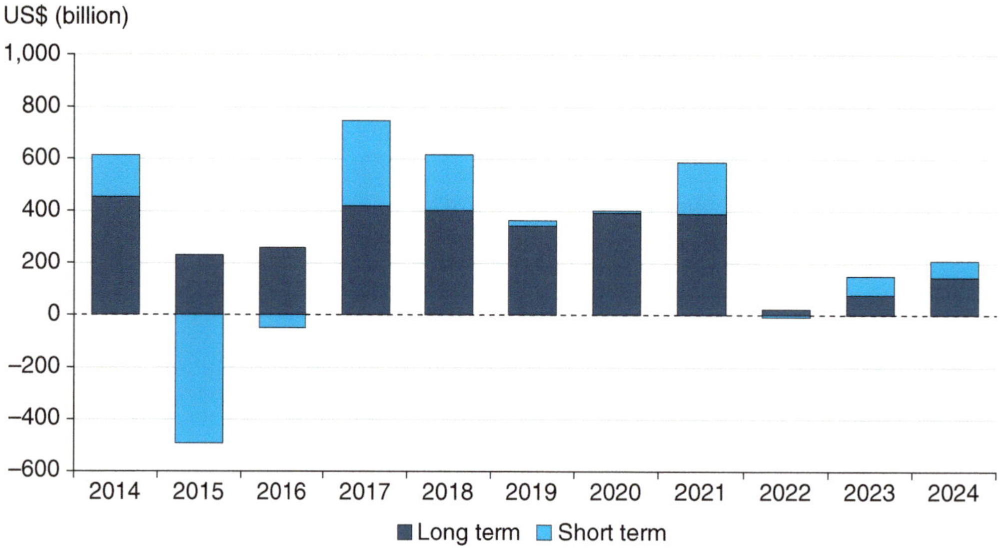

Source: World Bank International Debt Statistics database.

The volume and trend of 2024 net debt flows, specifically those to private creditors, were dominated and distorted by a third consecutive year of net debt outflows from China. China's total net debt inflows of US$366.9 billion in 2021, equivalent to a 62.6 percent share of total LMIC net flows, were followed by three consecutive years of outflows. In 2024, China's net debt flows remained negative, at US$19.5 billion, but these outflows were small compared to the massive contraction of US$544.1 billion recorded in 2022. The improvement was a consequence of an increase in long-term debt flows from private creditors. Net flows to bondholders dropped from an outflow of US$101.4 billion to an outflow of US$16.1 billion, and net debt flows to banks and other private creditors decreased US$17.6 billion to an outflow of US$19.4 billion in 2024. Short-term net inflows decreased 16.9 percent to US$18.5 billion.

China's net debt inflows from private creditors improved by US$67.7 billion in 2024, reversing the substantial outflows experienced by LMICs in 2022 and 2023, US$70.7 billion and US$15.1 billion respectively (figure 1.9).

Figure 1.9 Long-Term External Debt Flows to Low- and Middle-Income Countries, by Borrower Type, 2022–24

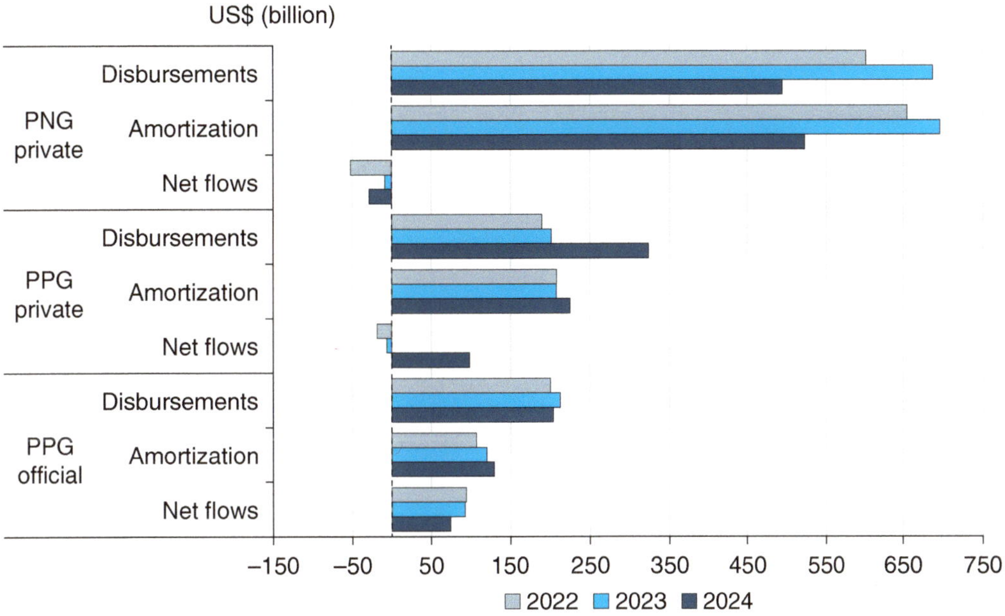

Source: World Bank International Debt Statistics database.
Note: PNG = private nonguaranteed; PPG = public and publicly guaranteed.

This rebound was notably more pronounced for China than for the rest of LMIC borrowers. When China is excluded, total net debt flows to LMICs remained stable in 2024, increasing only 0.9 percent to US$229.9 billion, and long-term net debt inflows remained almost unchanged at US$182.6 billion. Viet Nam, Kazakhstan, the Arab Republic of Egypt, Argentina, and Azerbaijan recorded the largest net outflows in 2024; the Philippines, Türkiye, Indonesia, Ukraine, and India recorded the largest net inflows.

Bondholders and multilateral institutions were the source of over 86.5 percent of long-term debt inflows to LMICs in 2024, accounting for 38.1 percent and 48.5 percent, respectively. The most significant shift in the creditor composition of debt inflows in 2024 was the surge in inflows from bondholders, which reversed from a net debt outflow of US$75.4 billion in 2023 to an inflow of US$55.0 billion in 2024. Bondholders' share of net long-term debt inflows to LMICs in 2024 was 38.1 percent, a marked divergence from the negative contribution in 2023. The change in debt outstanding owed to bondholders in 2024 was positively affected by the increase in net debt flows, but negatively affected by currency valuation effects as a result of the appreciation of the US dollar and the restructuring agreements implemented during the year when they included an up-front haircut. These agreements have no impact on current net flows calculations, which measure the provision of new financing minus repayments during that period. The reversal reflected a turnaround in renewed investor confidence, improvements in economic growth prospects, and reduced credit risk perceptions.

Bond financing was very responsive to changes in investor sentiment, as the external financing environment and domestic economic conditions in LMICs improved in the aftermath of the COVID-19 pandemic. Additionally, expectations about US monetary policy gradually shifted in 2024 as the Federal Reserve ended its tightening cycle and began to move from a restrictive stance to a more accommodative one. Consequently, investors anticipated a decline in global interest rates, which would raise bond prices. This prospect of capital gains, combined with still-elevated yields on LMIC sovereign bonds, made bond holdings increasingly attractive, prompting a strong investor demand and oversubscription in LMICs bond issuances and a surge in bond inflows. Overall, in 2024, gross bond financing for both the PPG and PNG sectors of the economy increased 76.5 percent over 2023. PPG borrowers led the recovery in new bond financing, accounting for over two-thirds of the total US$268.7 billion in new issuance by LMICs. Bond financing for PNG sector borrowers also grew in 2024, more than doubling to US$85.7 billion (figure 1.10). China, the largest LMIC borrower, accounted for 21.1 percent of new bond disbursements. China led the recovery of LMIC's PPG bond issuances, which more than doubled in 2024 to US$32.6 billion. These increases highlighted not only the recovery and growth of investor confidence and appetite in LMICs but also the capacity to adapt to changes in external financing conditions from borrowing governments and public sector entities of LMICs.

Figure 1.10 Bond Flows to Low- and Middle-Income Countries, by Borrower Type, 2023–24

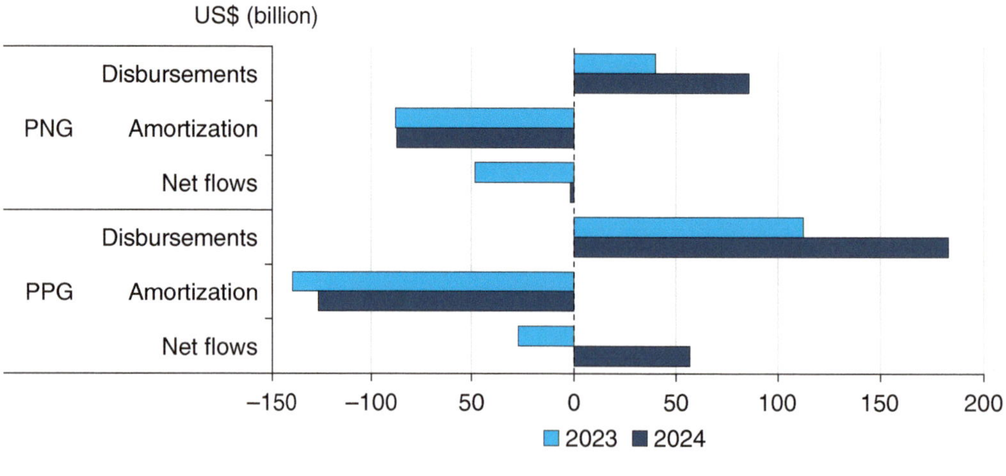

Source: World Bank International Debt Statistics database.
Note: PNG = private nonguaranteed; PPG = public and publicly guaranteed.

LMICs' principal repayments to bondholders decreased 6.1 percent in 2024 to US$213.7 billion. China, which accounted for 34.1 percent of these payments, was the primary reason behind the decrease, recording a 43 percent drop, to US$72.8 billion. When China is excluded, principal repayments to bondholders increased 40.8 percent in 2024 to US$140.9 billion. Net flows to bondholders from this group of countries increased close to threefold in 2024, to US$71.1 billion.

Multilateral creditors continued to provide the most support to LMICs, albeit at a much slower pace following the unprecedented support provided during the COVID-19 pandemic, recording US$70.1 billion in net debt inflows in 2024. Net debt flows from multilateral creditors decreased 5.1 percent in 2024 and accounted for 48.5 percent of net long-term debt inflows to LMICs. Despite the overall decrease, net flows from the World Bank (International Bank for Reconstruction and Development [IBRD] and International Development Association [IDA] lending) reached an all-time high of US$36 billion, increasing 30.4 percent in 2024. They accounted for 51.3 percent of net flows from multilateral institutions. Bangladesh, Kenya, Nigeria, the Philippines, and Ukraine were the largest recipients of these funds. The second-largest net debt flows by volume in 2024 came from the European Union, at US$15.5 billion, driven largely by support provided to Ukraine.

Conversely, net debt inflows from bilateral creditors decreased 76 percent to a nominal volume of US$4.5 billion, lows not seen since the net outflows during the 2008 financial crisis. The bilateral restructuring agreements implemented in 2024 reduce debt outstanding when they include an element of debt forgiveness but have no impact on the current year's net flows calculations. Consequently, the decrease in bilateral net debt flows is a direct consequence of a fall in new financing provided by these creditors. New bilateral creditor disbursements decreased 22.1 percent in 2024 to US$44.3 billion, comparable to lows not seen since 2015. During the same period, principal repayments increased 4.2 percent to US$39.8 billion. Thus, LMICs have been under pressure to find alternative sources of financing, which are typically more costly when sourced from external private creditors.

Additionally, LMICs' net debt flows from banks and other private creditors experienced a reduction in 2024, decreasing by 75.1 percent to US$15.0 billion after bouncing back and more than doubling in 2023. PPG net flows from banks and other private creditors more than doubled to US$41.8 billion in 2024, indicating the return to lending by private creditors to sovereigns and other public sector entities. PNG net flows from the same group of creditors diverged from the upward trend and turned negative in 2024. One-third of the decrease was attributed to China, which recorded a net outflow of US$45.5 billion, and two-thirds resulted from decreases experienced in the rest of LMICs. PNG net flows from banks and other private creditors to LMICS, excluding China, decreased 69.3 percent in 2024 but remained positive at US$18.7 billion.

Trends in Net Transfers on External Debt, 2014–24

LMICs' total net debt transfers (disbursement minus total debt service payments) were negative for a third consecutive year in 2024, albeit at an improving pace and equivalent to a US$205.1 billion outflow in 2024. Negative net transfers, which indicate that a country's new disbursements are lower than what it pays in interest and principal payments to service its debt obligations, commenced in the aftermath of the COVID-19 pandemic and have persisted for the past three years. Net transfers on long-term debt improved in 2024 but remained negative at US$135.5 billion amid a change in composition (figure 1.11). The improvement was due to net transfers to PPG borrowers, which turned slightly positive in 2024 to US$11.9 billion. Conversely, net debt transfers to PNG borrowers continued to remain negative in 2024, deteriorating from US$126.6 billion to US$147.4 billion. The combination of suppressed new gross financing and persistently high interest payments has resulted in negative net transfers to LMICs. This behavior is even more evident at the creditor-composition level.

Figure 1.11 Long-Term Net Transfers on External Debt in Low-and Middle-Income Countries, by Debtor Type, 2014–24

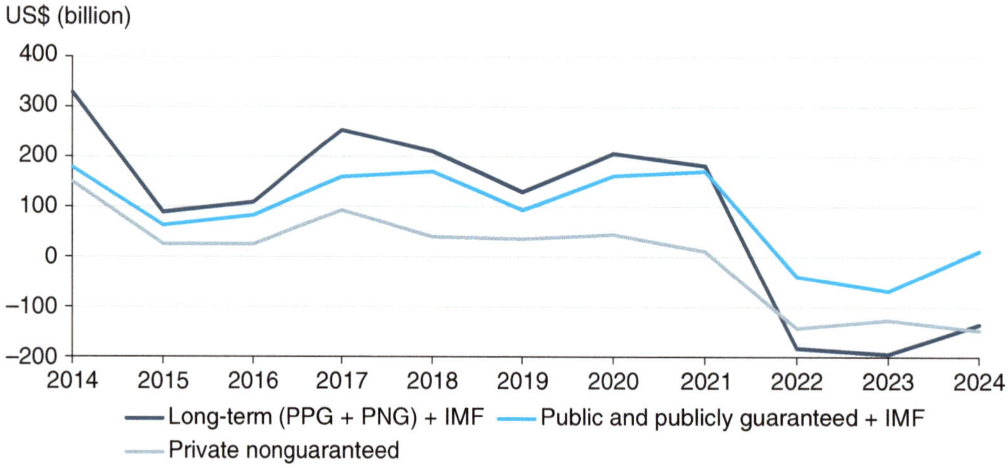

Source: World Bank International Debt Statistics database.
Note: IMF = International Monetary Fund; PPG = public and publicly guaranteed; PNG = private nonguaranteed.

In 2024, net transfers from multilateral institutions and commercial banks and other private creditors to PPG borrowers were the only two positive contributors to long-term net transfers (figure 1.12). Multilateral institutions have provided positive support since 2007, providing financing at concessional terms and interest-free loans in critical sectors, as well as budget support to LMIC governments to help achieve sustainable development, shared growth, and poverty reduction. Multilateral institutions provided US$14.1 billion more in financing during the year than they received in principal and interest payments, and the World Bank Group provided US$18.9 more than it received. Still, overall multilateral lending to LMICs has been on a downward trend since 2022, falling by 43.8 percent in 2024. Commercial banks and other private creditors were the other source of positive net transfers to PPG borrowers, which reversed from an outflow of US$613.12 million in 2023 to an inflow of US$17.9 billion in 2024. China was the primary reason behind this reversal: net transfers from this creditor base increased from an inflow of US$15.2 billion to US$20.7 billion in 2024. When China is excluded, LMICs' PPG net transfers from this creditor base turned into an outflow of US$2.8 billion. Multilateral institutions remain the only creditor base that provided more in new disbursements than it received in interest and principal repayments from LMICs excluding China.

Figure 1.12 Long-Term Net Transfers on Public and Publicly Guaranteed External Debt in Low- and Middle-Income Countries, by Creditor Type, 2014–24

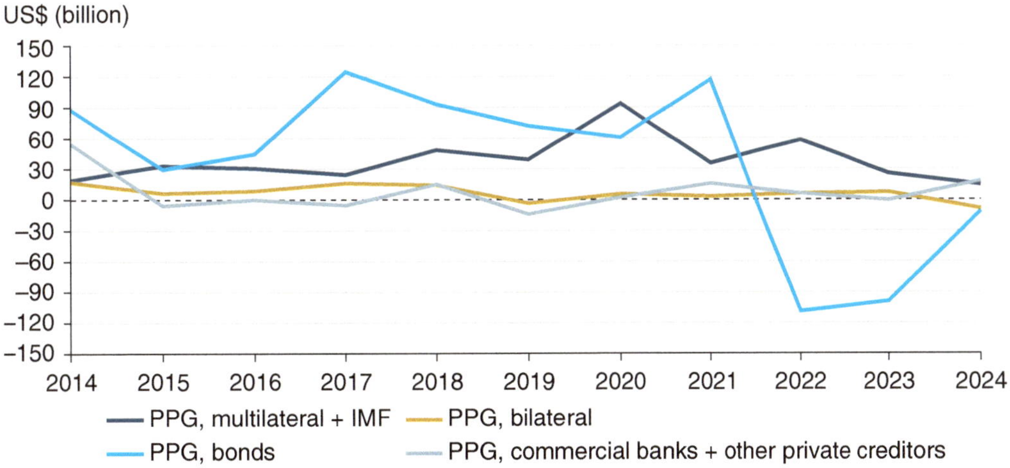

Source: World Bank International Debt Statistics database.
Note: IMF = International Monetary Fund; PPG = public and publicly guaranteed.

Net transfers from bilateral creditors to LMICs turned sharply negative in 2024, completely reversing from a US$7.0 billion inflow in 2023 to a US$8.8 billion outflow in 2024. As new gross financing from this creditor base decreased in 2024, LMICs' higher principal payments and record interest payments intensified the increase in outflows on net transfers. The reversal in net transfers can become highly detrimental to sustainable development finance and its ability to promote economic growth and welfare, because this creditor base often provides direct financing on concessional terms. Net transfers from bondholders to PPG borrowers in 2024 improved because of the increase in new bond issuance, but the cost of servicing bonds (principal plus interest) continued to exceed new disbursements, resulting in outflows of US$11.3 billion in 2024. Although higher yields have made LMIC bonds more attractive to investors, this situation has resulted in LMIC issuers making higher interest payments to attract investors and consequently increasing the cost of financing.

Key Debt Indicators, 2014–24

LMICs' external debt indicators, measured in terms of gross national income (GNI) and export earnings, have improved markedly since the COVID-19 pandemic, with most LMICs seeing their economies rebound strongly. The resumption of economic activity and a sharp rise in export volumes in the aftermath of the pandemic were the most important factors contributing to improvements in the debt ratios. Despite the volatility of export revenue and global economic uncertainty, LMICs' export revenues expanded by 6.6 percent to US$9.9 trillion in 2024, and GNI grew 3.8 percent to US$38.2 trillion. Both of these increases outpaced the 1.1 percent rise to US$8.9 trillion in outstanding external debt obligations and the corresponding increase in interest payment levels. Over this period, the combined stock of LMICs' external debt measured in terms of GNI fell to 23.4 percent, 2.4 percentage points lower than the 2021 level. The corresponding ratio of external debt stock to export earnings fell from 103.8 percent in 2021 to 90.2 percent in 2024 (figure 1.13; box 1.4).

Figure 1.13 External Debt-to-GNI and Interest Payments-to-GNI Ratios for Low- and Middle-Income Countries and IDA-Eligible Countries, 2014–24

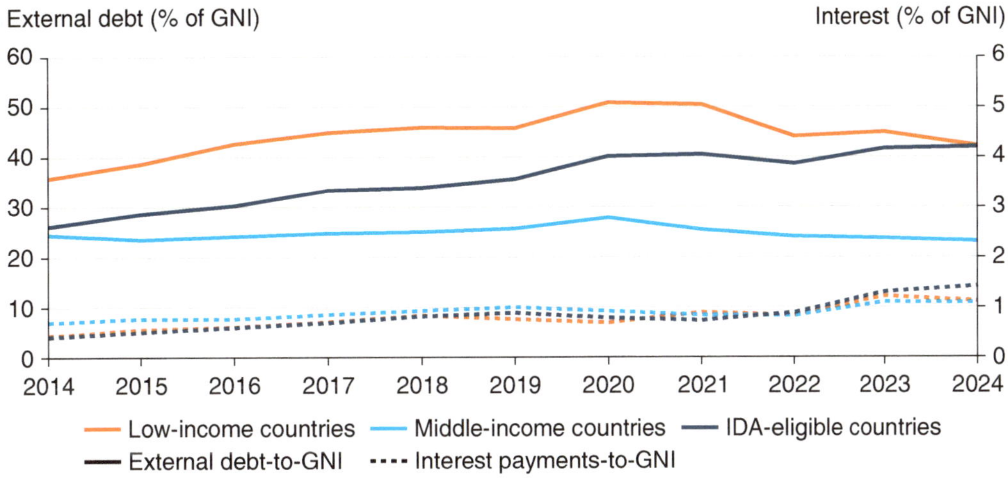

Source: World Bank International Debt Statistics database.
Note: For each country group, solid lines show the ratio of external debt to GNI (left axis) and dashed lines of the same colors show the ratio of interest payments to GNI (right axis). GNI = gross national income; IDA = International Development Association.

Box 1.4 Debt-to-GDP and Debt-to-GNI Ratios, and Accounts Rebasing

Debt-to-GDP versus Debt-to-GNI Ratios

Gross domestic product (GDP) and gross national income (GNI) both measure a country's income, but GDP counts only income received from domestic sources, whereas GNI includes net income received from abroad. The World Bank favors the use of GNI for operational purposes. Member countries' relative poverty is measured in relation to GNI per capita, and this measure underpins the annual income classification published by the International Bank for Reconstruction and Development and the International Development Association operational cutoff (US$1,135 per capita for fiscal year 2026) and both entities' lending terms (interest rate and maturity) for specified borrowers. The International Debt Statistics database follows this convention and provides users with GNI data for each reporting country and the relevant external ratios of debt stock and debt service to GNI. The International Monetary Fund uses the concept of GDP in Article IV consultation reports and its programs to measure macroeconomic outcomes. The practice is carried forward to the joint World Bank–International Monetary Fund Debt Sustainability Analysis, with debt stocks and debt service measured in relation to GDP. Conceptually, GDP may be regarded as a more accurate measure of a national government's capacity to raise domestic resources from which debt-related obligations must be serviced. For most countries, the difference between GDP and GNI is minimal. For example, the World Bank calculates the United States' GNI to be only 0.2 percent higher than GDP in 2024. GNI may be lower

(Box continues on next page)

Box 1.4 Debt-to-GDP and Debt-to-GNI Ratios, and Accounts Rebasing (*continued*)

than GDP if nonresidents control a sizable proportion of a country's production, or it may be higher than GDP if, for example, a country receives a large amount of foreign aid. For most low- and middle-income countries, the difference between end-2024 GDP and GNI was small, but there were some outliers: aid-dependent Pacific islands such as Kiribati and Nauru had a GNI significantly higher than their GDP. Conversely, in countries such as Equatorial Guinea and Guyana, GDP surpassed GNI by 40 percent.

What Is the Base Year?

In general, the *base period* tends to be defined as the period against which quantities and prices of a given period are compared. It is not to be confused with *weight period*, the period whose weights are used (for instance, for the Laspeyres formulation, the weight period is the base period, whereas, in the Paasche index formula, the weight period is the current period).

In national accounts, the base period (year) is also the weight period. It is the year whose prices are used to derive estimates of national accounts variables in real terms and also provides national accounts compilers with the structure used to ultimately extrapolate economic growth.

Why Do Countries Rebase Their National Accounts?

Countries rebase their national accounts to reflect the current structure and evolution of their economy by updating weights for prices and production, incorporating new or previously uncounted economic activities, and adopting international standards. This process provides a more accurate and up-to-date picture of the economy, enabling policy makers to make evidence-based decisions and track structural changes. It also improves comparability across countries.

Rebasing is necessary to reflect economic evolution: new products and industries emerge while others decline, different production technologies arise, user preferences change, and relative prices diverge from those of the base year, affecting economic growth calculations. Rebasing updates the economic data to align with these structural shifts, preventing outdated information from misrepresenting the economy's true nature. Doing so may imply the following:

- *Choosing a new base year.* A new base year should be a recent "normal" economic period without major shocks.
- *Updating weights.* National accounts use weights to reflect the relative importance of different economic activities. Rebasing updates these weights to match the current economic reality, ensuring that calculations of GDP and other aggregates are more relevant and accurate.

(Box continues on next page)

Box 1.4 Debt-to-GDP and Debt-to-GNI Ratios, and Accounts Rebasing (*continued*)

- *Incorporating new data and activities.* Rebasing allows for the inclusion of previously uncounted economic activities, such as illegal transactions, to provide a more comprehensive picture of the economy.
- *Adopting new standards and compilation methods.* This process can include the implementation of the latest standard for national accounts, international classifications for economic activities and products, and improved compilation techniques. The latest standard for national accounts is currently the 2008 version, but the United Nations Statistical Commission has just adopted a new version (2025 SNA) with first implementations expected by 2030. Some features in that new version will have an impact on GDP levels.

Accurate and current national account data are crucial for effective economic analysis and policy formulation. Policy makers can better understand economic trends, identify growth drivers, and allocate public resources more effectively by using up-to-date information.

Rebasing is only one type of revision. The accuracy of national accounts estimates and their comparability across countries also depend on timely revisions to GDP and its components. The frequency of revisions varies, with some countries revising numbers each month, others quarterly or annually, and others less frequently.

Routine revisions are usually small and based on additional information received throughout the year. Comprehensive revisions, such as a rebasing exercise, often (but not always) result in upward adjustments as improved data sources increase coverage of the economy and as new weights for growing industries more accurately reflect their contributions. These revisions will cause breaks in series unless applied consistently to historical data.

Frequency and Impact of Rebasing National Accounts

Rebasing occurrences are not rare: the 2008 SNA recommends rebasing national accounts at least every five years.[a] If this standard were strictly implemented, about 40 countries would undergo such exercise every year. However, many countries do not rebase their national accounts that often. Over the past five years, an estimated 89 countries rebased their national accounts.

The magnitude of the revision after a rebasing exercise may vary significantly from one country to another. The average GDP revision is about 10 percent, and the distribution of revisions is shown in figure B1.4.1. Very large revisions (50 percent and more) are associated with weak statistical systems and long delays between successive rebasing exercises (10 to 25 years for the three countries concerned).

(Box continues on next page)

Box 1.4 Debt-to-GDP and Debt-to-GNI Ratios, and Accounts Rebasing (*continued*)

Figure B1.4.1 Variation in GDP levels

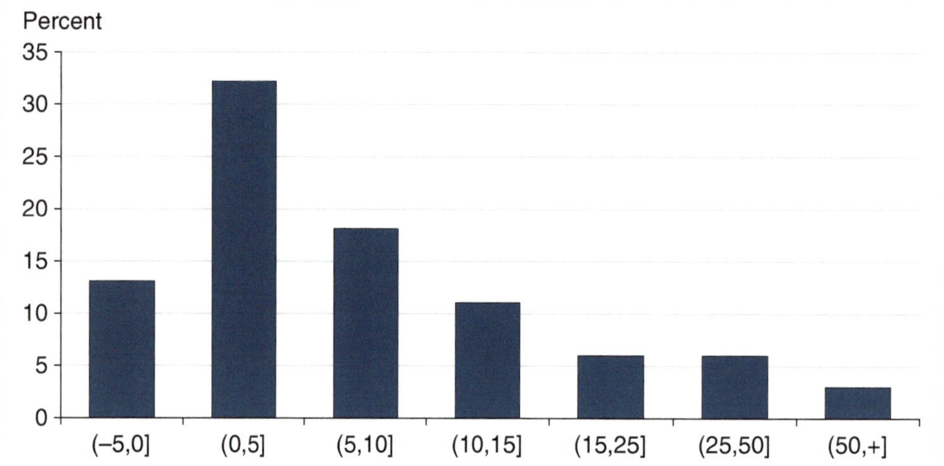

Source: World Bank World Development Indicators database.

a. Moreover, the actual recommendation is to produce the so-called chain-linked volume measures, which consists of changing the base year (or rebasing) every year and linking the results to be comparable in real terms.

LMICs also saw an improvement in their overall external debt payment capacity, measured in terms of total debt service (interest plus principal) payments relative to GNI and export earnings. After recording an all-time high in 2023, LMICs' total debt service payments decreased 9.7 percent in 2024, to US$1.3 trillion. The combined effect of the decrease in debt service payments and improvement in economic growth and increased export earnings led to an improvement in debt service ratios. The ratio of total debt service payments to export earnings improved 2.4 percentage points in 2024, to 13 percent, and the debt service ratio in terms of GNI improved from 3.9 to 3.4 percent over the same period.

When China is excluded, LMICs' total debt service payments in 2024 decreased at a smaller rate of 4.1 percent, to US$940.5 billion. The ratio of total debt service payments to export earnings for this group of countries improved 1.7 percentage points to 16.2 percent in 2024; the corresponding ratio in terms of GNI improved by a smaller margin of 0.4 percentage point to 4.8 percent over the same period.

Total debt service ratios should be interpreted with caution, because they mask a divergence between lower principal repayments and increased interest burdens arising from persistent high interest rates in 2024. LMICs' interest payments reached an all-time high in 2024, increasing 2.2 percent to US$415.4 billion. However, the increase in interest payments was much smaller than the accumulation rate of export earnings and growth in economic activity. Consequently, LMICs' ratio of interest payments to export earnings improved slightly in 2024, to 4.2 percent, and the equivalent payments in terms of GNI remained stable at 1.1 percent, respectively. When China is excluded, LMICs' ratios of interest payments to exports earnings and to GNI remain almost stable at 5.0 and 1.5 percent, respectively.

The increase in interest payments on external debt obligations was more pronounced among middle-income countries excluding China than among low-income countries. As middle-income countries' interest payments increased 7.3 percent to US$284.1 billion in 2024, their interest payments relative to export earnings and GNI remained relatively stable at 5.0 percent and 1.5 percent, respectively. By contrast, low-income countries saw improvements in their respective ratios, with the ratio of interest payments to export earnings decreasing from 5.5 percent to 5.0 percent in 2024 and the ratio of interest payments to GNI decreasing slightly to 1.1 percent. Because low-income countries rely more heavily on concessional financing, their interest payment costs remained almost unchanged in 2024 at US$6.4 billion. Interest costs for middle-income countries (excluding China) were more dependent on market financing and recorded a higher increase in 2024. The five countries recording the highest interest payments on external debt relative to export earnings in 2024 were Mozambique, Senegal, Mongolia, Egypt, and Colombia; the five countries that recorded the highest interest payments relative to GNI were Mozambique, Mongolia, Angola, Senegal, and Lebanon.

Trends in External Debt of IDA-Eligible Countries, 2014–24

The external debt stock of countries eligible for IDA assistance increased to an all-time high of US$1.2 trillion in 2024, 2.0 percent higher than the previous year. Over the past decade, the external debt stock of IDA-eligible countries has more than doubled, raising concerns about sustainability. Official creditors continue to account for a large share of long-term debt, equivalent to 63 percent of that stock. However, the fastest-growing component of public and publicly guaranteed external debt stock for these countries has been borrowing from bondholders, which rose to US$91.4 billion in 2024, equivalent to 9 percent of long-term debt stock (figure 1.14). Large-scale forgiveness of external debt obligations was also an important contributing factor to the outstanding debt of IDA-eligible

Figure 1.14 Creditor Composition of IDA-Eligible Countries' Long-Term Public and Publicly Guaranteed External Debt during Crises, 2014–24

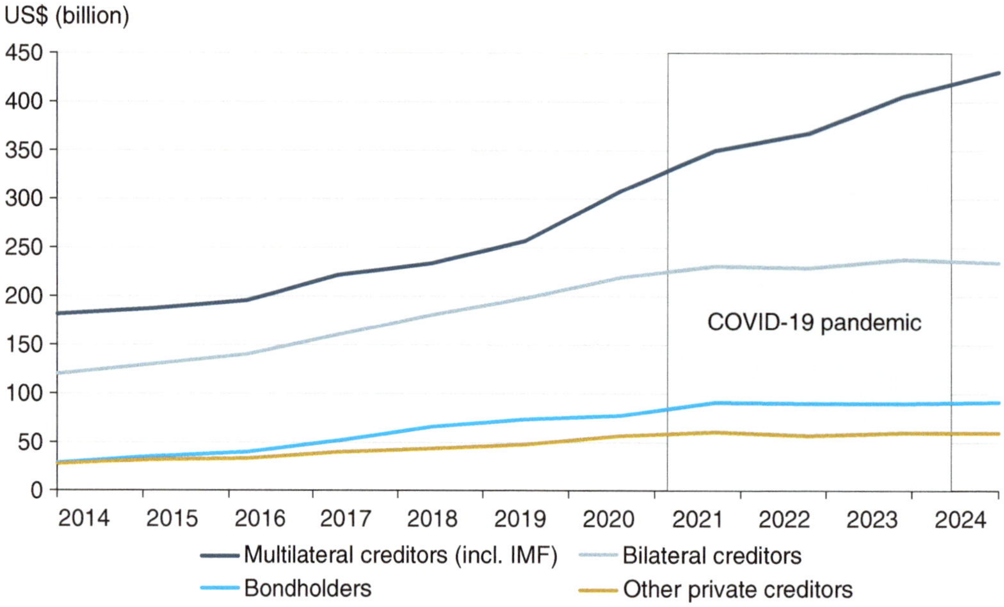

Source: World Bank International Debt Statistics database.
Note: IDA = International Development Association; IMF = International Monetary Fund.

countries in 2024. Ghana, Haiti, the Federal Republic of Somalia, and Sri Lanka were among the IDA-eligible countries that implemented debt reorganization agreements with their bilateral creditors and bondholders, resulting in reductions in their 2024 debt outstanding positions in nominal terms in addition to the net present value reductions. For all countries involved, these agreements were significant; in specific cases like Haiti, they resulted in 70.5 percent reductions of long-term public debt.

Viewed from the borrower perspective, the composition of long-term debt stock, 75 percent PPG debt and 25 percent PNG debt, has remained relatively stable over the past decade. Whereas the debt stock of PPG borrowers increased 2.8 percent to US$816.5 billion in 2024, the debt stock of PNG borrowers decreased slightly to US$241.9 billion. The total external debt stock of IDA-eligible countries is quite concentrated, with the top seven borrowers accounting for over half of total IDA-eligible debt stock. Bangladesh, Nigeria, and Pakistan together account for close to 30 percent of IDA-eligible countries' debt stock; Mozambique, Senegal, Sri Lanka, and Uzbekistan together account for another 21 percent.

Total net debt inflows to IDA-eligible countries rose 18.6 percent to US$53.1 billion in 2024, driven by an increase in short-term net debt inflows (table 1.2). Short-term debt flows turned from an outflow of US$10.6 billion in 2023 to

Table 1.2 Net Debt Inflows to IDA-Eligible Countries, 2014–24

US$ (billion)

	2014	2015	2016	2017	2018	2019	2020	2021	2022	2023	2024
Net debt inflows	62.1	50.3	45.2	81.1	66.4	73.4	77.5	84.7	48.8	44.7	53.1
Long-term	61.8	49.8	46.2	62.1	70.6	60.3	78.3	68.3	44.7	55.4	47.4
Official creditors	25.2	26.9	24.4	31.0	38.9	41.9	55.9	37.0	39.3	46.0	36.8
Bilateral creditors	14.4	12.8	11.9	14.7	22.0	17.7	14.9	15.0	8.0	11.1	1.7
Multilateral creditors	10.8	14.1	12.6	16.3	16.9	24.2	41.0	22.0	31.3	34.9	35.1
World Bank	6.8	7.2	6.7	7.9	9.4	11.7	13.3	11.1	15.2	16.7	18.3
IMF	−0.2	1.6	1.0	0.5	0.2	1.7	15.2	3.2	3.7	5.3	6.9
Private creditors	36.6	22.9	21.8	31.1	31.7	18.4	22.4	31.4	5.4	9.3	10.6
Bonds	15.6	7.2	4.7	13.7	13.0	8.4	3.0	15.3	−0.9	−0.9	7.2
Banks and other private	21.0	15.6	17.0	17.4	18.8	10.0	19.5	16.1	6.3	10.2	3.4
Short-term	0.3	0.5	−1.0	19.0	−4.2	13.1	−0.7	16.3	4.0	−10.6	5.6
Memorandum item											
Long-term PPG	40.5	37.7	30.4	47.4	56.8	52.2	65.8	54.9	36.9	48.1	48.0
Long-term PNG	21.3	12.1	15.8	14.6	13.9	8.1	12.5	13.5	7.8	7.3	−0.6

Sources: World Bank Debtor Reporting System, International Monetary Fund, and Bank for International Settlements.
Note: World Bank includes IBRD and IDA; IMF includes use of credit only; IBRD = International Bank for Reconstruction and Development; IDA = International Development Association; IMF = International Monetary Fund; PNG = private nonguaranteed; PPG = public and publicly guaranteed.

an inflow of US$5.6 billion in 2024. Although long-term debt flows decreased 14.4 percent in 2024, they remained positive at US$47.4 billion—and higher than their comparable 2022 figure. From a borrower perspective, long-term debt flows to PNG borrowers decreased and turned negative in 2024, from an inflow of US$7.3 billion to an outflow of US$567 million, driven by net flows to commercial banks and other private creditors that turned negative for the first time since 1999. Net flows to PPG borrowers remained constant at US$48.0 billion. Net debt inflows from multilateral creditors were the largest contributing component to PPG net debt flows in 2024, accounting for a 73 percent share of PPG net debt flows. The World Bank was the single largest provider of financing for IDA-eligible countries, accounting for over one-third of PPG net debt inflows in 2024. In volume terms, World Bank (IBRD and IDA) inflows were US$18.3 billion, up from US$16.7 billion the previous year. Additionally, the World Bank also provided US$7.5 billion in IDA grants in 2024, an increase of 10.9 percent.

Net debt inflows from bilateral creditors declined 84.8 percent in 2024 to US$1.7 billion, barely remaining positive and reaching a historic low not seen since 2007. Inflows from private creditors accounted for a 23.3 percent share of PPG net debt inflows, up sharply from 4.3 percent in 2023 but well below the

29 percent average share recorded during the first half of the last decade, from 2014 to 2019. Net flows from banks and other private creditors increased one and half times in 2024, to US$4.1 billion. Bondholders were the fastest-growing component of PPG net debt flows, reversing from an outflow of US$730.4 million in 2023 to an inflow of US$7.1 billion in 2024. The increase, not seen since the US$11.1 billion jump in 2021, was the result of new issuances in 2024, which outpaced the rate of increase in PPG bond principal repayments (figure 1.15).

Public sector entities of nine IDA-eligible countries issued bonds in international markets in 2024, recording a total of US$12.9 billion in new bond disbursements and marking a significant improvement in investor confidence combined with sovereigns' renewed objectives to fund investment needs and support budget operations. The increase is significant compared to 2022 and 2023, but still lower than the US$19 billion issuance recorded in 2021. Côte d'Ivoire was the first IDA-eligible country to issue a bond in 2024 and to reopen issuance in international markets after a one-year pause for IDA-eligible countries in the Sub-Saharan Africa region. In 2024, Uzbekistan issued a record US$4.1 billion of PPG bonds from the government and state-owned enterprises. The combined issuance was the highest for IDA-eligible countries in 2024 and a record for the country's bond market. The sovereign Eurobond issue was diversified in euros and US dollars,

Figure 1.15 Net Flows to IDA-Eligible Countries, by Region and Creditor Type, 2024

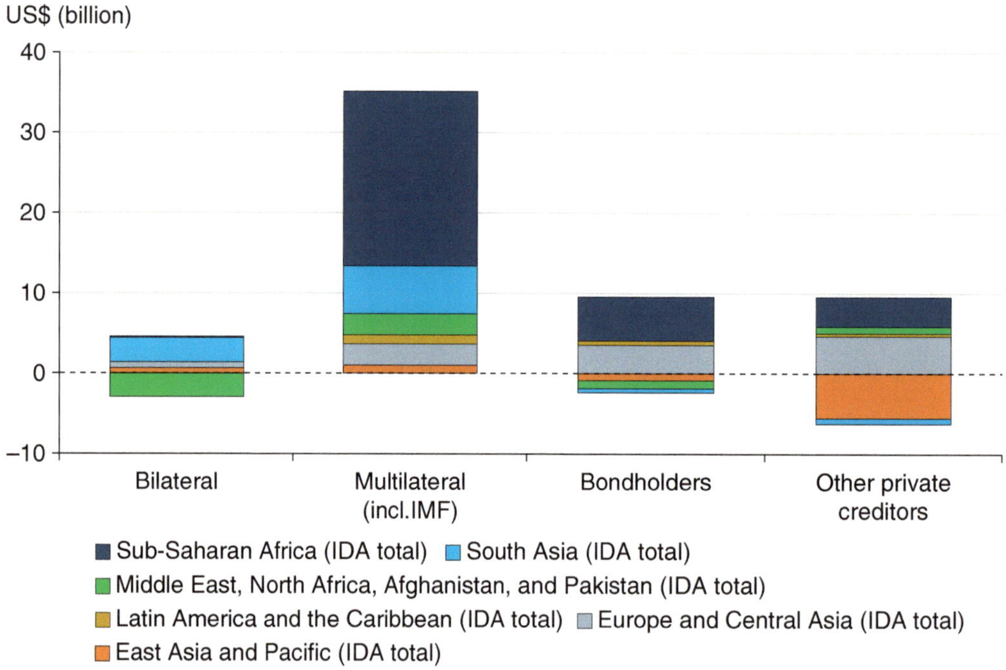

Source: World Bank International Debt Statistics database.
Note: IDA = International Development Association; IMF = International Monetary Fund.

and a portion was also issued in local currency of Uzbek som. In 2024, Nigeria and Kenya also returned to international markets after one- and two-year pauses, respectively. Nigeria successfully raised US$2.2 billion in Eurobonds to help fund its budget deficit; Kenya issued a US$1.5 billion Eurobond to partially pay back its maturing 2024 bond. Both countries' issuances were at higher interest rates than in the past, with Nigeria's tranches issued at 9.625 and 10.375 percent, respectively, and Kenya's issuance recording a high coupon rate of 9.75 percent. Benin, Dominica, Eswatini, Honduras, and Senegal were the other IDA-eligible countries accessing international markets in 2024.

New external loan commitments to public sector entities in IDA-eligible countries totaled US$74.9 billion in 2024, 16.1 percent lower than the comparable 2023 figure. New commitments from official creditors, which offer loans on concessional terms or more favorable terms than the market, decreased 32 percent to US$52.6 billion. The average interest rate on new commitments from this creditor base decreased slightly to 2.78 percent in 2024, and the average maturity increased by one year to an average of 25 years (figure 1.16). Meanwhile, new external commitments to public sector entities from private creditors, bonds, and syndicated commercial bank loans almost doubled in 2024, to US$22.3 billion. Overall, they accounted for 30 percent of the total new commitments to public entity borrowers. Financing from this creditor base is more costly and of shorter maturity than that provided by official creditors. The average interest rate of new financing from private creditors increased 1.24 percentage points in 2024, to 7.45 percent, and the average maturity was shortened by two years, to an average

Figure 1.16 Average Terms on New External Debt Commitments for IDA-Eligible Countries, by Creditor Type, 2014–24

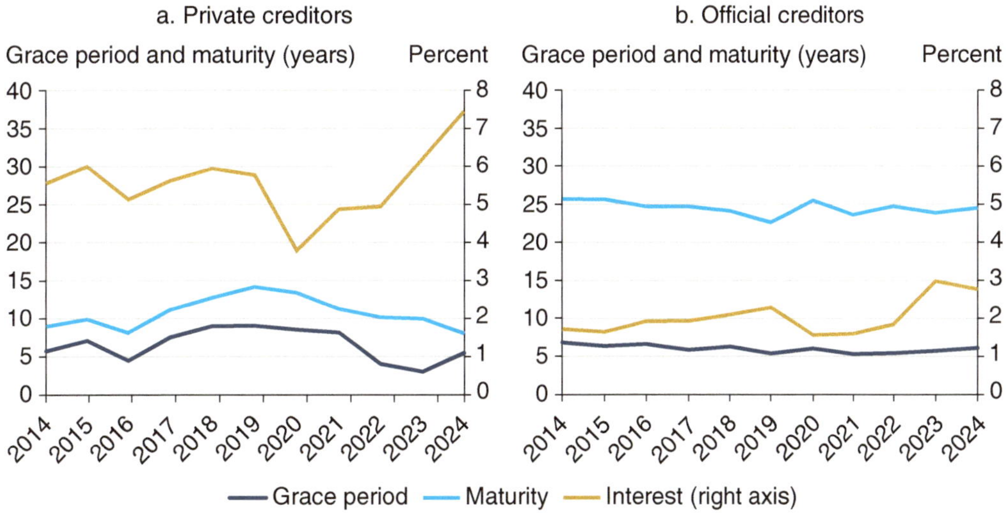

Source: World Bank International Debt Statistics database.

of eight years. Extended borrowing from this creditor group underscores debt sustainability concerns for IDA-eligible countries given that the terms of these obligations have on average become more costly to finance.

The cost of servicing debt recorded an all-time high for the second year in a row for IDA-eligible countries. Total debt service payments (interest plus principal) increased 16.5 percent in 2024, to US$118.1 billion. Interest payments accounted for 33.5 percent of these payments, also at an all-time high of US$39.5 billion (a 10.5 percent increase); principal payments accounted for 66.5 percent of the payments, recording an all-time high of US$78.5 billion (a 19.8 percent increase from the previous year).

The principal repayment, driven by both PPG and PNG borrowers, increased 18.9 percent to US$45.8 billion and by 21.0 percent to US$32.7 billion, respectively, in 2024. PPG bond principal repayments increased from US$1.9 billion to US$5.9 billion in 2024. Kenya's US$2 billion bond repayment in 2024 accounted for 34 percent of these payments. PPG borrowers' principal repayments to commercial banks and other private creditors decreased 10.2 percent in 2024, to US$6.9 billion. Principal repayments to PPG borrowing from official creditors increased 14 percent in 2024, with bilateral creditors receiving US$14.0 billion of these payments, a 1.1 percent increase, and multilateral creditors receiving US$19 billion, a 25.8 percent increase.

As interest rates remained elevated in 2024, the cost of financing existing and new obligations negatively affected IDA-eligible borrowers. The increase in total interest payments on external debt obligations was driven by increases in borrowing by the PPG sector, which rose 21.4 percent to US$23.6 billion. The biggest volume of interest payments went from PPG borrowers to multilateral creditors, at US$10.6 billion in 2024, reflecting the significant increases in lending by the World Bank's IDA during the pandemic when other creditors were retreating; however, the interest rate paid to this lender was a modest 1.1 percent in 2024, compared with a much larger average of 8.2 percent for bondholders. Consequently, interest payments to private creditors also affected the increase in overall PPG interest payments. Interest payments to bondholders, which accounted for 22 percent of the payments, increased 23.1 percent in 2024 to US$5.1 billion, and interest payments to commercial banks and other private creditors increased 33 percent to US$2.3 billion.

Among IDA-eligible countries, net debt transfers to PPG borrowers decreased 14.9 percent, to US$24.4 billion in 2024. The overall increase in debt service payments and decrease in new disbursements led to a decrease in official net transfers to PPG borrowers of IDA-eligible countries in 2024. Net transfers from this creditor base remained positive at US$20.7 billion but decreased 36.4 percent from the previous year (figure 1.17). Conversely, net transfers from private creditors to PPG borrowers reversed from a net outflow of US$3.8 billion to a net inflow of US$3.7 billion in 2024. This reversal was driven by a more than twofold increase in new disbursements from this creditor base, which increased at a much faster pace than total debt service payments.

Total debt service of IDA-eligible countries, measured relative to GNI and export earnings, deteriorated in 2024. The 16.5 percent growth in total debt service payments to US$118.1 billion outpaced the 7.7 percent increase in export earnings to US$656.3 billion, and 1.2 percent growth in GNI to US$2.8 trillion. Consequently, the ratio of total debt service to GNI increased to 4.2 percent, compared to 3.7 percent the previous year, and the ratio of total debt service to export earnings increased 1.4 percentage points to 18 percent. Because the cost of servicing total debt remains large, countries eligible for IDA support face growing challenges of fiscal space for shock absorption and financing of development needs. Haiti, the Lao People's Democratic Republic, Mozambique, Pakistan, Papua New Guinea, and Senegal had the largest total debt service-to-export ratios in 2024; Mozambique, Papua New Guinea, Suriname, and Zambia had the largest total debt service-to-GNI ratios.

Figure 1.17 Net Transfers on Public and Publicly Guaranteed Debt in IDA-Eligible Countries, by Creditor Type, 2022–24

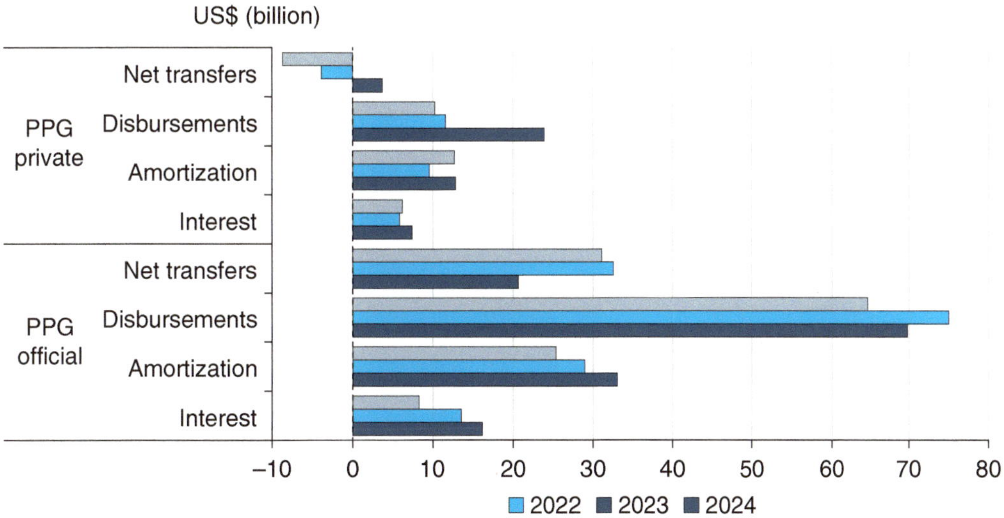

Source: World Bank International Debt Statistics database.
Note: IDA = International Development Association; PPG = public and publicly guaranteed.

Regional Perspectives

EAST ASIA AND PACIFIC

Net debt inflows to the region increased to US$9.9 billion in 2024 (table 1.3), driven by a combined improvement in China's net long-term debt outflows to US$38 billion and a 159.7 percent increase in net debt flows of the region's other countries to US$29.4 billion.

China, the largest borrower among LMICs, accounted for 71 percent of the combined end-2024 external debt of countries in the East Asia and Pacific (EAP) region. China's external debt stock fell a further 1.1 percent in 2024 to US$2.42 trillion. In other countries in the region, external debt stock rose on

Table 1.3 External Debt Stock and Net Financial Flows and Transfers, East Asia and Pacific, 2014–24

US$ (billion)

	2014	2015	2016	2017	2018	2019	2020	2021	2022	2023	2024
External debt stocks	**2,444.8**	**2,004.5**	**2,111.8**	**2,489.0**	**2,798.1**	**2,993.0**	**3,263.9**	**3,697.0**	**3,496.6**	**3,416.7**	**3,409.4**
as % of GNI	19.4	15.2	15.7	16.9	17.0	17.6	18.9	17.9	16.7	16.2	15.7
Net debt inflows	**288.5**	**−374.8**	**47.0**	**396.2**	**340.8**	**186.2**	**260.5**	**394.9**	**−158.7**	**−71.1**	**9.9**
Official creditors	4.8	3.9	1.0	1.0	4.3	2.1	14.5	7.1	5.5	6.2	3.1
Bilateral	2.2	−1.9	−2.9	−2.8	−1.0	−2.9	1.8	−0.6	0.0	0.5	−0.4
Multilateral	2.6	5.8	3.8	3.8	5.3	5.0	12.7	7.7	5.5	5.7	3.5
Private creditors	124.9	62.0	61.1	137.3	152.5	196.6	203.4	247.9	−75.5	−99.2	-34.1
Long-term	129.7	65.9	62.1	138.2	156.9	198.7	217.9	255.0	−70.0	−93.0	-31.0
Public and publicly guaranteed	41.1	21.4	26.5	66.1	98.6	85.9	91.0	175.1	−17.6	−33.0	39.8
Private nonguaranteed	88.6	44.4	35.5	72.1	58.3	112.9	126.9	79.9	−52.4	−60.1	−70.8
Short-term	158.8	−440.6	−15.1	258.0	183.9	−12.6	42.6	139.9	−88.7	21.9	40.9
Net debt transfers	**228.8**	**−444.6**	**−9.5**	**312.2**	**234.9**	**64.8**	**143.5**	**264.9**	**−289.8**	**−243.8**	**−156.1**
Official creditors	1.0	0.1	−2.7	−2.9	−0.2	−3.5	10.4	4.2	1.1	−3.9	−8.1
Bilateral	−0.2	−4.4	−5.0	−4.7	−3.0	−5.1	0.1	−2.0	−1.4	−0.9	−1.9
Multilateral	1.3	4.6	2.3	1.8	2.8	1.7	10.4	6.2	2.5	−3.0	−6.2
Private creditors	29.5	9.6	16.9	54.6	80.5	66.5	57.3	142.2	−53.5	−73.0	11.4
Long-term	105.2	31.0	33.0	102.9	109.1	140.5	164.7	190.9	−138.3	−174.6	-104.8
Public and publicly guaranteed	30.5	9.7	14.1	51.8	80.3	63.0	67.7	146.4	−52.4	−76.8	3.3
Private nonguaranteed	74.7	21.3	18.9	51.2	28.9	77.5	97.0	44.6	−85.9	−97.7	-108.1

Source: World Bank International Debt Statistics database.
Note: GNI = gross national income.

average 2.1 percent to US$989.5 billion. The long-term debt stock in other EAP countries declined marginally, but short-term debt rose 12.7 percent to US$201.7 billion, driven by a 29.1 percent rise in Indonesia's short-term debt to US$65.1 billion, equivalent to 15.5 percent of the country's end-2024 external debt stock. The sharp jump reflects the Bank of Indonesia's issuance of short-term securities (Bank Indonesia Rupiah Securities or SRBI) introduced in August 2023 as a measure to support monetary policy, defend the value of the rupiah during periods of market volatility, and attract foreign capital. These securities are issued with variable interest rates at 6-, 9-, and 12-month tenors and offered to domestic and nonresident investors.

Net debt inflows to the EAP region totaled US$9.9 billion in 2024, a sharp reversal from the net outflow of US$71.1 billion recorded in 2023. The turnaround was driven by a sharp increase in inflows to the Chinese bond markets from nonresident investors and borrowing from other private creditors by Chinese public and private sector entities. Consequently, net long-term outflows from China fell to US$38 billion in 2024 from US$104.6 billion in 2023. Excluding China, net debt inflows to the region were US$29.4 billion in 2024, 159.7 percent higher than the US$11.3 billion recorded in 2023 (figure 1.18). Close to half of the 2024 inflows were short-term debt inflows to Indonesia, which rose to US$14.3 billion, from an average of US$1.6 billion in 2022 and 2023. Long-term debt inflows fell 39.9 percent to US$7 billion in 2024 because of a 66.3 percent fall in net inflows from private creditors, to US$1.4 billion. Inflows from official creditors (US$5.6 billion) accounted for 80.6 percent of net long-term inflows to the EAP region in 2024 and were all from multilateral creditors.

Figure 1.18 Net Debt Flows for East Asia and Pacific Countries (Excluding China), by Creditor Type, 2022–24

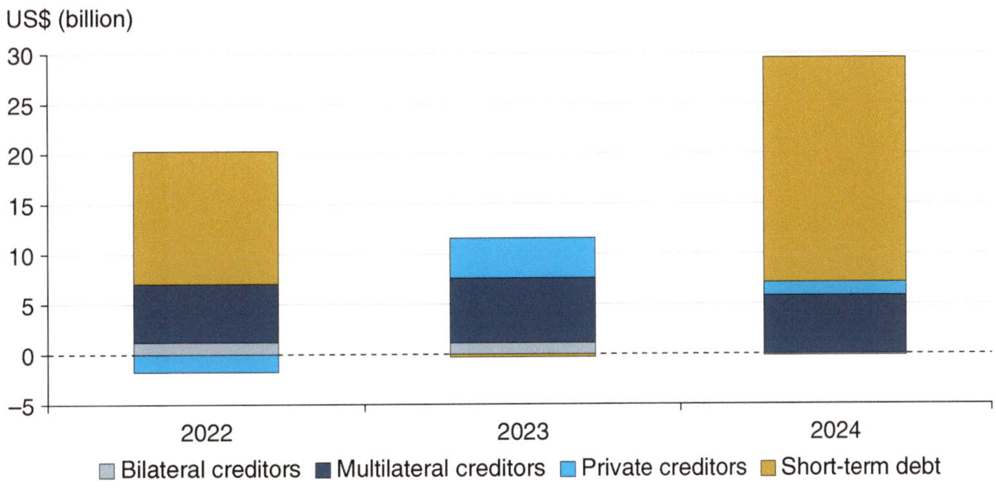

Source: World Bank International Debt Statistics database.

The sharp 66.3 percent fall in net long-term debt inflows from private creditors to the region in 2024, excluding China, masked divergent trends in inflows from bondholders and other private creditors in aggregate and for individual countries. Net inflows from bondholders more than doubled in 2024 to US$6.8 billion from US$3.2 billion in 2023, with inflows to the Philippines and Indonesia, the largest recipients, of US$5.2 billion and US$3.5 billion, respectively, offset by outflows of US$2 billion to Thailand (figure 1.19). In contrast to bonds, flows from other private creditors registered an outflow of US$5.5 billion in 2024 compared to an inflow of US$0.8 billion in 2023. This turnaround was largely explained by Viet Nam, which recorded outflows from other private creditors of US$7.2 billion in 2024. The Philippines also recorded a sharp contraction in inflows from private creditors in 2024, but these inflows remained positive at US$985 million, down from US$4.7 billion in 2023. In Indonesia, inflows from other private creditors of US$3.8 billion in 2024 were in marked contrast to outflows of US$2.5 billion in 2023.

Figure 1.19 Net Long-Term Debt Inflows from Private Creditors to Select East Asia and Pacific Countries, 2023 and 2024

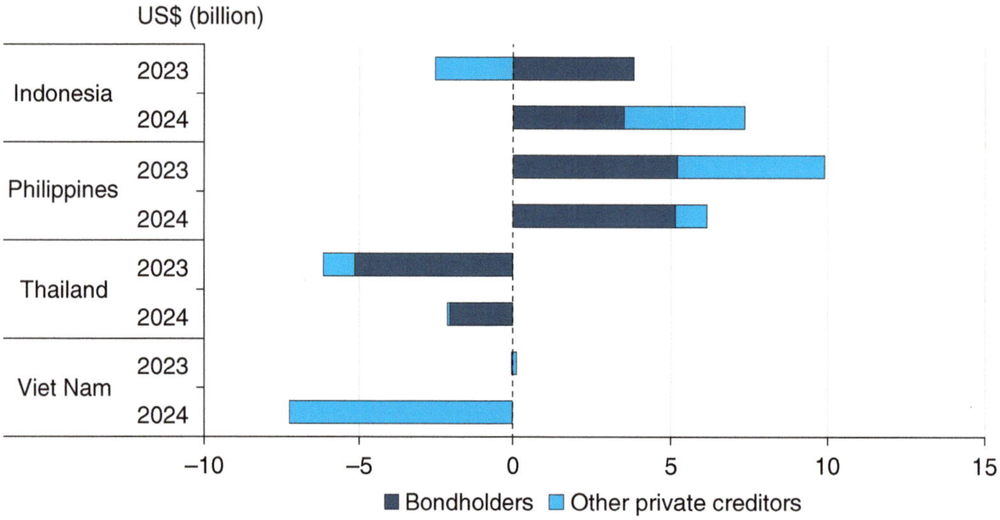

Source: World Bank International Debt Statistics database.

EUROPE AND CENTRAL ASIA

Net debt flows recorded an inflow of US$53.1 billion, a 38 percent drop from the previous year, whereas net transfers turned into a US$91.3 million outflow in 2024 (table 1.4).

Short-term debt flows in the Europe and Central Asia (ECA) region decreased by a factor of seven in 2024, to US$4.5 billion, and long-term debt flows decreased by 10 percent to US$48.6 billion. Much of this shift was attributable to ECA's largest borrower, Türkiye, which accounted for 44 percent of the region's total outstanding external debt and where net short-term debt flows plunged 87.9 percent to US$3.3 billion in 2024. The decrease was the result of a milestone liability management transaction, involving the swap of short-term treasury bonds for a new 10-year bond issuance of US$3.5 billion. Net short-term debt

Table 1.4 External Debt Stock and Net Financial Flows and Transfers, Europe and Central Asia, 2014–24

US$ (billion)

	2014	2015	2016	2017	2018	2019	2020	2021	2022	2023	2024
External debt stocks	**883.6**	**854.1**	**866.7**	**933.9**	**913.2**	**926.7**	**980.5**	**1,003.7**	**1,040.8**	**1,135.8**	**1,169.3**
as % of GNI	52.2	57.4	61.0	63.9	63.9	63.5	69.4	61.9	58.4	54.3	49.2
Net debt inflows	**34.7**	**–43.2**	**19.3**	**58.4**	**–3.9**	**13.2**	**40.7**	**19.7**	**47.1**	**85.6**	**53.1**
Official creditors	10.5	12.4	8.3	8.2	3.3	1.0	7.6	5.0	24.2	30.8	33.9
Bilateral	4.9	2.6	2.9	3.9	2.2	2.3	0.1	0.9	4.8	1.1	5.7
Multilateral	5.6	9.8	5.4	4.3	1.1	–1.3	7.5	4.1	19.4	29.8	28.3
Private creditors	39.6	–8.4	25.8	28.5	9.1	5.5	15.1	4.2	–11.2	23.2	14.7
Long-term	50.2	4.0	34.2	36.7	12.4	6.5	22.7	9.2	13.0	54.0	48.6
Public and publicly guaranteed	19.3	19.2	15.0	15.1	10.5	12.4	21.8	16.9	23.6	39.3	45.2
Private nonguaranteed	30.8	–15.2	19.2	21.6	1.9	–6.0	0.9	–7.6	–10.6	14.7	3.4
Short-term	–15.5	–47.2	–14.9	21.7	–16.4	6.7	18.1	10.4	34.1	31.7	4.5
Net debt transfers	**3.6**	**–70.2**	**–6.9**	**28.5**	**–33.2**	**–18.1**	**9.5**	**–11.6**	**12.8**	**40.0**	**–0.1**
Official creditors	8.1	10.0	5.6	5.0	–0.3	–3.1	4.1	1.9	20.5	23.1	24.6
Bilateral	3.9	1.6	1.7	2.6	0.8	0.7	–1.5	–0.6	3.3	–1.0	3.5
Multilateral	4.2	8.4	3.9	2.4	–1.0	–3.7	5.5	2.5	17.1	24.1	21.1
Private creditors	1.8	0.1	–0.5	–0.7	–0.5	2.5	4.7	1.6	–10.1	–1.6	–0.3
Long-term	27.4	–18.5	12.1	13.0	–11.3	–19.4	–3.2	–16.7	–13.0	19.5	6.6
Public and publicly guaranteed	9.9	10.1	5.1	4.3	–0.8	–0.6	8.8	3.4	10.4	21.5	24.3
Private nonguaranteed	17.5	–28.6	7.0	8.7	–10.5	–18.7	–12.0	–20.1	–23.4	–2.0	–17.7

Source: World Bank International Debt Statistics database.
Note: GNI = gross national income.

flows also fell in Uzbekistan, where they reversed from an inflow of US$657.6 million to an outflow of US$1.2 billion in 2024.

Long-term net flows to public sector borrowers increased 15.2 percent in 2024, to US$45.2 billion, reflecting increased multilateral support for Ukraine and increases in debt flows from bilateral creditors and bondholders. Net flows from multilateral creditors to public sector entities in the region decreased 7.6 percent to US$25.9 billion in 2024 but remained the largest source of inflows at 58 percent of long-term obligations (figure 1.20). Ukraine accounted for most of these net inflows, equivalent to 89.8 percent of multilateral net inflows. Multilateral financial support for Ukraine has reached unprecedented levels since the start of its invasion by the Russian Federation in February 2022. The European Union has provided a cumulative US$41.7 billion in disbursements of new financing during the 2022–24 period, followed by the World Bank (IBRD and IDA combined support) at US$17.7 billion, and the IMF at US$12.5 billion. During this period, the World Bank Group has offered a range of financial instruments and support to help the government of Ukraine sustain essential public services, rebuild critical infrastructure, and support the private sector, such as through trust funds, financial intermediaries, guarantees, co- and parallel financing, and other financial instruments.[3]

After being hit hard by the COVID-19 pandemic and its aftermath, ECA saw strong recovery of bond issuance by public and private sectors in 2024. Bondholders were the second largest positive contributors to long-term net flows in the region, increasing more than threefold to US$18.4 billion in 2024, and

Figure 1.20 Net Debt Flows to Europe and Central Asia, by Creditor Type, 2014–24

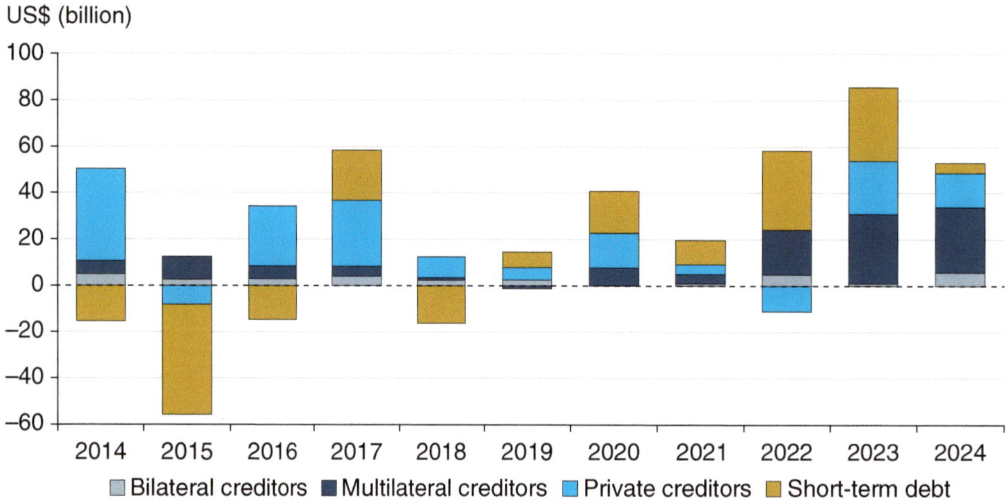

Source: World Bank International Debt Statistics database.

accounting for 37.8 percent of the region's long-term inflows. The increase was driven by new bond issuances from both public sector borrowers, which increased 55.6 percent to US$27.7 billion in 2024, and issuances from PNG borrowers, which more than doubled to US$19.8 billion (figure 1.21). Türkiye was ECA's largest new issuer, recording a 43.9 percent increase to US$19.8 billion in 2024 from public sector borrowers and an almost threefold increase to US$16.6 billion from PNG borrowers. Türkiye's 2024 new bond issuances included the country's first ever blue and green bond package, and a milestone maturity swap operation of short-term bonds for the new 10-year, US$3.5 billion issuance.

The region also had the sharpest increase among all regions in net debt flows from official creditors, up nearly 10.1 percent to US$33.9 billion. This rise occurred in large part because of the increase in bilateral creditors, which rose fivefold to US$5.7 billion. The principal driver was Türkiye, where disbursements almost doubled in 2024 to US$4.1 billion and principal repayments from maturing obligations decreased 71.5 percent to US$686.3 million.

Figure 1.21 Bond Flows to Europe and Central Asia, by Borrower Type, 2023 and 2024

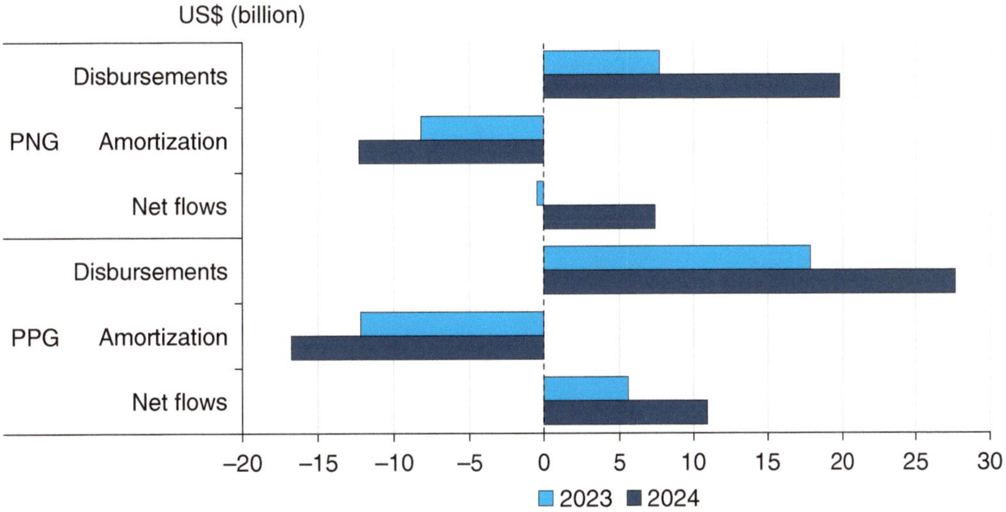

Source: World Bank International Debt Statistics database.
Note: PNG = private nonguaranteed; PPG = public and publicly guaranteed.

LATIN AMERICA AND THE CARIBBEAN

Net debt flows fell 70.5 percent in 2024, to US$19.4 billion, the lowest level since 2007, as net debt transfers plunged to an outflow of US$78.0 billion in 2024 (table 1.5).

At the creditor level in Latin America and the Caribbean (LAC), the decline of long-term net debt flows was most pronounced in public sector borrowing from bondholders, which nearly halved to US$12.9 billion in 2024, and public and private sector borrowing from commercial banks and other private creditors, which decreased 82.1 percent to US$2.1 billion (figure 1.22). Mexico was the primary driver of the decline in public sector borrowing from bondholders,

Table 1.5 External Debt Stock and Net Financial Flows and Transfers, Latin America and the Caribbean, 2014–24

US$ (billion)

	2014	2015	2016	2017	2018	2019	2020	2021	2022	2023	2024
External debt stocks	**1,579.1**	**1,599.5**	**1,632.9**	**1,728.2**	**1,837.1**	**1,879.7**	**1,878.6**	**1,922.1**	**1,942.1**	**2,007.3**	**2,000.4**
as % of GNI	30.4	36.4	38.5	36.5	40.2	41.8	49.7	44.0	38.6	35.4	34.5
Net debt inflows	**168.5**	**78.6**	**72.8**	**109.6**	**176.3**	**37.6**	**26.7**	**58.5**	**62.4**	**65.5**	**19.4**
Official creditors	10.8	5.6	5.5	8.3	33.7	17.4	26.4	8.5	20.3	7.6	2.9
Bilateral	5.6	−1.4	−0.6	5.8	−2.1	−6.0	−0.6	−0.4	0.0	2.6	−3.3
Multilateral	5.2	7.0	6.1	2.4	35.8	23.4	26.9	8.9	20.3	5.0	6.3
Private creditors	142.7	69.5	97.9	90.2	98.5	10.1	45.6	35.1	35.2	30.4	20.4
Long-term	153.5	75.2	103.3	98.4	132.2	27.5	72.0	43.6	55.5	38.0	23.4
Public and publicly guaranteed	92.9	37.5	67.0	60.1	82.3	25.9	72.6	15.3	35.5	23.6	20.3
Private nonguaranteed	60.6	37.6	36.3	38.3	49.9	1.6	−0.7	28.3	20.0	14.4	3.1
Short-term	15.0	3.4	−30.6	11.2	44.1	10.1	−45.3	15.0	6.9	27.5	−4.0
Net debt transfers	**114.9**	**19.3**	**2.2**	**32.0**	**96.5**	**−49.5**	**−41.7**	**−19.2**	**−6.0**	**−30.9**	**−78.0**
Official creditors	6.0	0.8	−0.1	2.1	27.1	8.0	19.1	1.6	11.5	−9.8	−16.9
Bilateral	4.0	−3.1	−2.4	3.9	−3.7	−7.8	−1.7	−2.1	−1.3	1.3	−5.1
Multilateral	2.0	3.9	2.3	−1.8	30.8	15.7	20.8	3.7	12.7	−11.1	−11.7
Private creditors	58.9	3.6	28.5	10.7	12.0	−32.4	15.4	−24.8	−12.0	−14.1	−16.1
Long-term	104.1	20.2	37.5	26.3	60.0	−51.5	8.5	−29.0	−4.5	−44.8	−61.3
Public and publicly guaranteed	64.9	4.4	28.4	12.8	39.1	−24.4	34.6	−23.2	−0.5	−23.9	−33.0
Private nonguaranteed	39.2	15.8	9.1	13.5	20.9	−27.0	−26.1	−5.9	−4.0	−20.9	−28.3

Source: World Bank International Debt Statistics database.
Note: GNI = gross national income.

Figure 1.22 Net Debt Flows to Latin America and the Caribbean, by Creditor Type, 2014–24

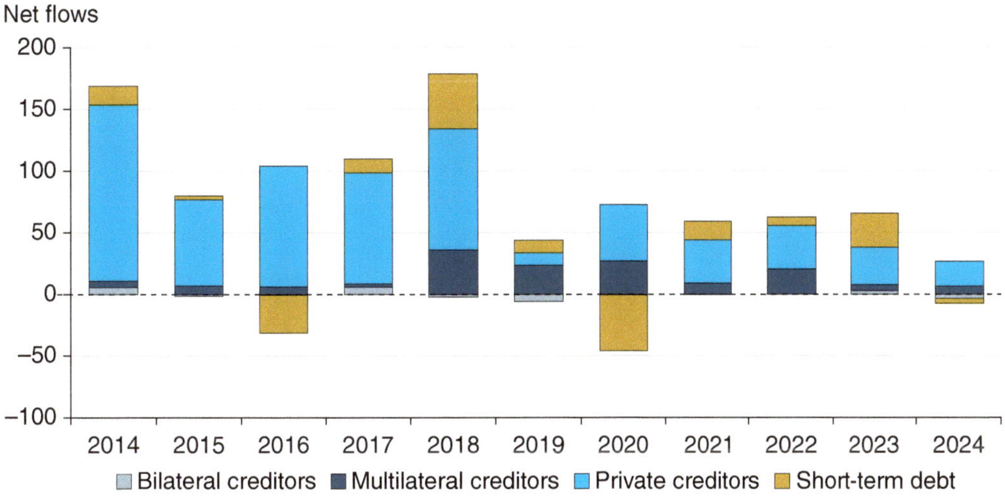

Source: World Bank International Debt Statistics database.

which despite a strong issuance start in January 2024 saw disbursements of new financing almost halved to US$13.3 billion in 2024; maturing obligations raised principal payments by almost fourfold to US$18.1 billion. The decrease in borrowing from commercial banks and other private creditors was driven by Brazil, which recorded a drop in new disbursements by more than a factor of three, from a high of US$191.7 billion to US$60.1 billion in 2024. Principal repayments to the country also decreased, by a smaller volume, to US$73.7 billion.

Net debt flows of private sector borrowers from bondholders in the LAC region bounced back in 2024, reversing from an outflow of US$5.6 billion to an inflow of US$5.4 billion (figure 1.23). Disbursements from new financing more than doubled in 2024, outpacing the 17.5 percent increase in principal repayments, driven by net debt flows improvements in Brazil, Mexico, and Peru. Multilateral creditors were the only other category of creditors to post an increase in 2024, up 26 percent over the 2023 level. Most of the increase was attributable to the World Bank's IBRD and the Inter-American Development Bank. With regard to bilateral creditors, 2024 marked a sharp reversal of the upward trajectory of flows observed in 2023, instead registering an outflow of US$3.3 billion.

The LAC region recorded the second largest interest payments on total external debt obligations in 2024, at US$97.3 billion, second only to the EAP region at US$166.0 billion, and the overall largest interest payments made by public sector borrowers. The LAC region also accounted for the largest total payments of any region, when China is excluded from the EAP region. Whereas interest payments from private nonguaranteed borrowers in the region declined 11.6 percent to US$31.3 billion in 2024, public sector entities paid 12.4 percent more than they did in 2023, at US$53.2 billion. The largest payments were made by public sector borrowers in Argentina, Brazil, and Mexico, which together accounted for 65.4 percent of interest payments in the region made by this borrower base.

The region's creditors received an all-time high of US$78.0 billion more in debt service payments than they disbursed in new financing in 2024. Net transfers to public and private sector entities continued to deteriorate in 2024, recording net outflows for the fourth year in a row because of the combined effect of decreasing net flows to the region and large and increasing interest payments for public sector borrowers. Brazil recorded the largest net outflow in net transfers of US$27.5 billion in 2024, accounting for 35.3 percent of the region's outflows. The 2024 increase in outflows was driven by borrowing by the PNG sector from private creditors, through the combined effect of a 76.5 percent decrease in new disbursements to US$44.2 billion, the lowest since 2008 financial crisis, and a 69.7 percent decrease in principal repayments to US$52.7 billion. Mexico and Argentina recorded the region's next largest outflows in net transfers at US$20 billion and US$16 billion, respectively.

Figure 1.23 Bond Flows to Latin America and the Caribbean, by Borrower Type, 2023 and 2024

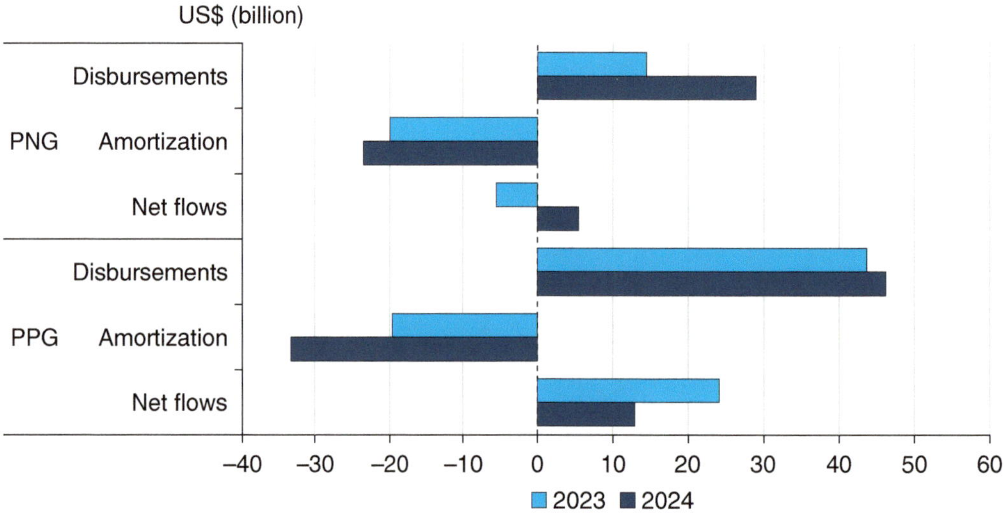

Source: World Bank International Debt Statistics database.
Note: PNG = private nonguaranteed; PPG = public and publicly guaranteed.

MIDDLE EAST, NORTH AFRICA, AFGHANISTAN, AND PAKISTAN

Note: In June 2025 the World Bank reclassified Afghanistan and Pakistan from its South Asia region to the Middle East, North Africa, Afghanistan, and Pakistan region.

Net debt flows reversed to an outflow of US$4.1 billion in 2024, from an inflow of US$11.9 billion the previous year, the lowest level since the 2008 financial crisis (table 1.6). Net debt transfers plunged even more, to an outflow of US$29.0 billion in 2024.

Net debt flows to the Middle East, North Africa, Afghanistan, and Pakistan region turned negative in 2024, from an inflow of US$11.9 billion in 2023 to an outflow of US$4.1 billion. These flows were heavily concentrated in Egypt,

Table 1.6 External Debt Stock and Net Financial Flows and Transfers, Middle East, North Africa, Afghanistan, and Pakistan, 2014–24

US$ (billion)

	2014	2015	2016	2017	2018	2019	2020	2021	2022	2023	2024
External debt stocks	**310.8**	**331.0**	**368.9**	**424.4**	**453.0**	**482.6**	**520.2**	**556.6**	**563.1**	**578.7**	**561.2**
as % of GNI	17.0	19.5	21.1	24.2	25.9	28.3	33.3	30.3	27.6	29.7	27.3
Net debt inflows	**17.3**	**29.0**	**40.5**	**42.0**	**31.7**	**31.2**	**25.7**	**25.0**	**17.2**	**11.9**	**−4.1**
Official creditors	4.7	13.6	23.7	16.2	13.2	16.0	22.6	6.1	7.6	5.5	−2.0
Bilateral	0.5	5.2	9.4	6.6	8.9	5.6	2.5	1.2	0.4	3.9	−3.7
Multilateral	4.2	8.3	14.3	9.6	4.3	10.4	20.1	4.9	7.2	1.6	1.6
Private creditors	7.9	13.1	4.9	23.2	24.4	8.8	1.3	9.5	−9.4	4.5	−3.6
Long-term	12.6	26.7	28.6	39.4	37.6	24.7	23.9	15.6	−1.7	10.0	−5.7
Public and publicly guaranteed	10.2	23.0	24.7	33.0	28.9	25.8	33.0	19.6	1.2	11.0	−6.5
Private nonguaranteed	2.4	3.7	3.9	6.5	8.7	−1.0	−9.1	−3.9	−3.0	−1.0	0.9
Short-term	4.8	2.3	11.9	2.6	−5.9	6.5	1.8	9.4	19.0	1.9	1.5
Net debt transfers	**10.4**	**21.6**	**31.7**	**31.6**	**18.2**	**16.2**	**14.3**	**13.6**	**0.8**	**−12.1**	**−29.0**
Official creditors	1.9	10.9	20.8	12.7	8.6	10.2	17.6	1.5	1.5	−5.1	−13.7
Bilateral	−1.1	3.8	7.8	4.8	6.5	2.7	0.0	−1.0	−2.4	0.6	−7.4
Multilateral	2.9	7.1	13.0	7.9	2.1	7.6	17.6	2.5	3.9	−5.6	−6.3
Private creditors	2.6	6.4	−2.5	12.9	10.7	4.1	6.5	9.0	−11.3	−0.0	−10.4
Long-term	6.3	20.1	21.1	30.6	25.7	11.3	13.9	5.4	−14.5	−8.5	−25.4
Public and publicly guaranteed	4.5	17.3	18.4	25.6	19.3	14.4	24.2	10.4	−9.8	−5.1	−24.1
Private nonguaranteed	1.8	2.8	2.8	5.0	6.4	−3.0	−10.3	−5.0	−4.6	−3.4	−1.3

Source: World Bank International Debt Statistics database.
Note: GNI = gross national income.

where net flows reversed from an inflow of US$5.2 billion to an outflow of US$3.4 billion in 2024, followed by Pakistan, where net flows decreased by more than a factor of 10 to US$354.4 million. Morocco and Tunisia also recorded significant drops in their net debt inflows, to US$206.5 million and an outflow of US$867.9 million, respectively. However, despite the drop, the pattern of financial instruments and debt composition used across countries diverged widely.

Net debt flows from bilateral creditors turned negative for the first time since 2011, from an inflow of US$3.9 billion to an outflow of US$3.7 billion (figure 1.24). Net bilateral debt flows to Pakistan and Iraq drove the trend, led by reductions of more than 75 percent in disbursements from new financing to US$1.5 billion and US$320.7 million, respectively. Egypt's debt-swap agreement did not affect the country's net flows; consequently, it also did not affect the region's net flows operations from bilateral creditors, which measure the provision of new financing minus repayments during that period. Multilateral creditors were the only creditor base that provided positive flows to public sector borrowers in 2024. Most of the region's increase was attributable to the World Bank's IBRD. At the country level, increases were largest in Tunisia, Jordan, and Pakistan (primarily because of the 2024 IMF disbursement), but they were offset by Egypt's surge in principal repayments, primarily to the IMF.

Bond issuance by public and private sector borrowers in the region fell sharply in 2024, to US$3.0 billion. Most of the issuance in the region is incurred by public sector borrowers (figure 1.25). In May 2024, Morocco's OCP Group issued a US$2 billion Eurobond to finance green investments, structured in two tranches—a US$1.25 billion tranche of 10-year maturity and a US$750 million tranche of 30-year maturity—with corresponding interest rates of 6.75 percent and 7.5 percent, respectively. The combined effect of a decline in new issuance and a marked increase in the share of maturing bonds reduced the net flow to public sector borrowers to an outflow of US$2.3 billion from an inflow of US$4.2 billion in 2023. Egypt, Pakistan, and Tunisia accounted for 80 percent of these principal payments.

As the cost of servicing debt has increased in the region, the ratio of total debt service payments to GNI and export revenues increased in 2024 to 3.7 percent and 13.7 percent, respectively. The increased cost of servicing debt caused net transfers in the region to turn even more negative in 2024, from an outflow of US$12.1 billion to an outflow of US$29 billion. Remarkably, net transfers from all creditor bases in 2024 registered an outflow for the region.

Figure 1.24 Net Debt Flows to the Middle East, North Africa, Afghanistan, and Pakistan, by Creditor Type, 2014–24

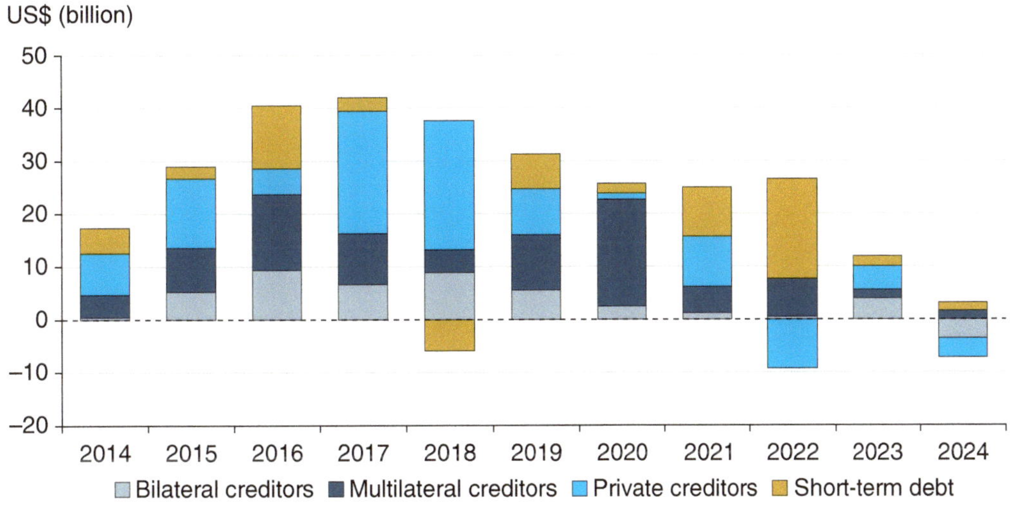

Source: World Bank International Debt Statistics database.

Figure 1.25 Bond Flows to the Middle East, North Africa, Afghanistan, and Pakistan, by Borrower Type, 2023 and 2024

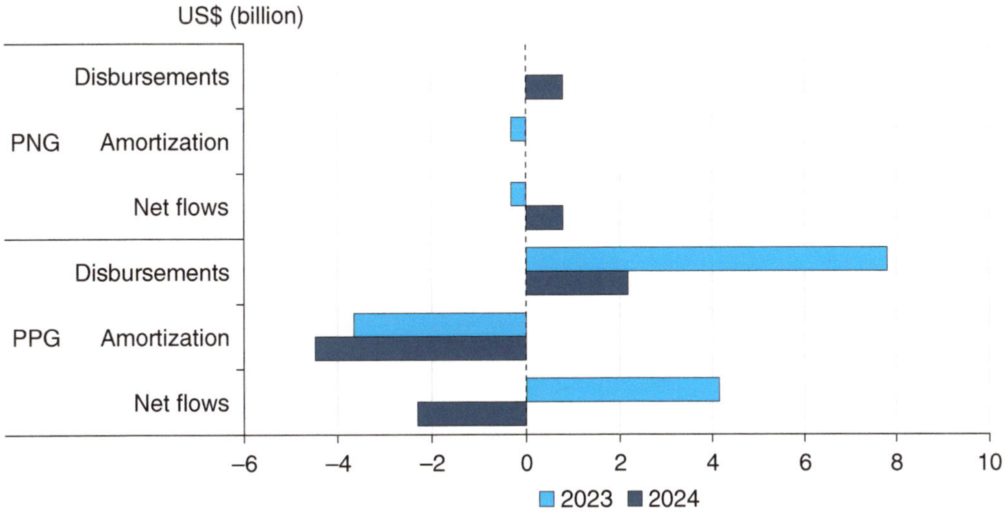

Source: World Bank International Debt Statistics database.
Note: PNG = private nonguaranteed; PPG = public and publicly guaranteed.

SOUTH ASIA

Net debt inflows rose 106 percent in 2024 to US$83.5 billion (table 1.7), the highest level of the decade, driven by the almost 100 percent increase in net long-term inflows from private creditors to US$57.5 billion, directed entirely to India.

The external debt stock of countries in the region rose on average 8.4 percent in 2024 to US$896 billion, a much faster pace of accumulation than the 5 percent increase recorded in 2023. This rise in external debt stock, the largest of any region in 2024, was driven by a 10.6 percent increase in India, which accounts for 80 percent of the region's external debt stock. For other countries in the region, the combined external debt stock at end-2024, US$179.6 billion, was broadly unchanged from the prior year. For India, 2024 was marked by a significant

Table 1.7 External Debt Stock and Net Financial Flows and Transfers, South Asia, 2014–24

US$ (billion)

	2014	2015	2016	2017	2018	2019	2020	2021	2022	2023	2024
External debt stocks	**542.1**	**568.7**	**551.6**	**622.5**	**641.7**	**691.6**	**710.2**	**778.4**	**787.5**	**826.7**	**896.0**
as % of GNI	23.5	23.7	20.7	20.4	20.4	20.9	22.5	21.0	20.2	19.8	20.0
Net debt inflows	**47.8**	**30.4**	**−15.1**	**64.5**	**22.1**	**49.8**	**12.7**	**53.3**	**19.8**	**40.4**	**83.5**
Official creditors	4.3	3.4	5.5	7.7	11.1	10.0	19.2	16.2	17.1	19.5	14.6
Bilateral	2.5	1.3	2.6	4.2	6.0	4.1	7.1	8.0	9.6	9.0	6.5
Multilateral	1.8	2.1	2.9	3.5	5.1	6.0	12.1	8.2	7.6	10.5	8.1
Private creditors	49.5	28.2	−23.9	39.7	6.3	35.7	−4.4	18.6	−10.2	28.8	57.5
Long-term	53.8	31.6	−18.5	47.4	17.4	45.7	14.8	34.8	6.9	48.4	72.1
Public and publicly guaranteed	37.9	14.8	−3.2	34.3	7.8	20.5	7.6	26.4	14.4	23.8	36.2
Private nonguaranteed	16.0	16.8	−15.3	13.1	9.6	25.2	7.2	8.4	−7.5	24.5	35.9
Short-term	−6.1	−1.2	3.3	17.1	4.7	4.1	−2.0	18.5	12.8	−7.9	11.4
Net debt transfers	**34.4**	**18.1**	**−27.9**	**49.8**	**1.7**	**30.2**	**−3.1**	**36.9**	**−1.6**	**5.2**	**43.4**
Official creditors	2.8	2.1	3.9	5.8	8.8	7.3	16.7	14.1	14.2	12.5	6.3
Bilateral	1.7	0.6	1.9	3.5	5.2	3.2	6.3	7.1	8.8	7.9	5.0
Multilateral	1.1	1.4	2.1	2.3	3.6	4.1	10.5	7.0	5.4	4.6	1.3
Private creditors	32.1	9.7	−10.6	24.8	−5.5	7.7	−13.3	7.4	−5.0	1.6	18.3
Long-term	41.7	20.6	−29.5	35.3	1.1	30.2	0.9	19.9	−10.6	21.8	41.9
Public and publicly guaranteed	34.9	11.8	−6.6	30.5	3.2	14.9	3.5	21.5	9.2	14.2	24.7
Private nonguaranteed	6.8	8.9	−22.8	4.8	−2.2	15.3	−2.6	−1.6	−19.8	7.7	17.2

Source: World Bank International Debt Statistics database.
Note: GNI = gross national income.

increase in bond issuance by the government and private entities, reflecting lower borrowing costs and rising investor demand aided by the inclusion of India in global bond indexes. From mid-2024 India was included in the J. P. Morgan Government Bond Index-Emerging Markets; in 2025, it was added to the FTSE Russell Emerging Markets Government Bond Index. Lending from financial institutions to Indian private sector entities also hit record levels in 2024. At end-2024, 77.3 percent of India's long-term external debt stock was owed to private creditors. In contrast, in other countries in the region, all classified as IDA-only borrowers, 76.5 percent was owed to official creditors.

Net debt inflows to the region rose 106 percent in 2024 to US$83.5 billion, the highest level of the decade, driven by a sharp increase in new long-term financing from private creditors to both public and private sector borrowers. Disbursements from private creditors of US$110.5 billion in 2024 were 95.5 percent higher than average disbursements of US$56.5 billion in 2022 and 2023. In contrast, principal payments to private creditors, US$52.9 billion in 2024, increased by only 12.3 percent over the same period (figure 1.26). Consequently, net long-term inflows from private creditors rose almost 100 percent in 2024 to US$57.5 billion, equivalent to 80 percent of long-term net debt inflows to the region and directed entirely to India. Other South Asian countries received only 20 percent of net long-term inflows to the region in 2024. These inflows all came from official creditors, and two-thirds of them were concessional financing from multilateral creditors.

Figure 1.26 Net Inflows of Long-Term Public and Publicly Guaranteed and Private Nonguaranteed External Debt to South Asia, by Borrower Type, 2022–24

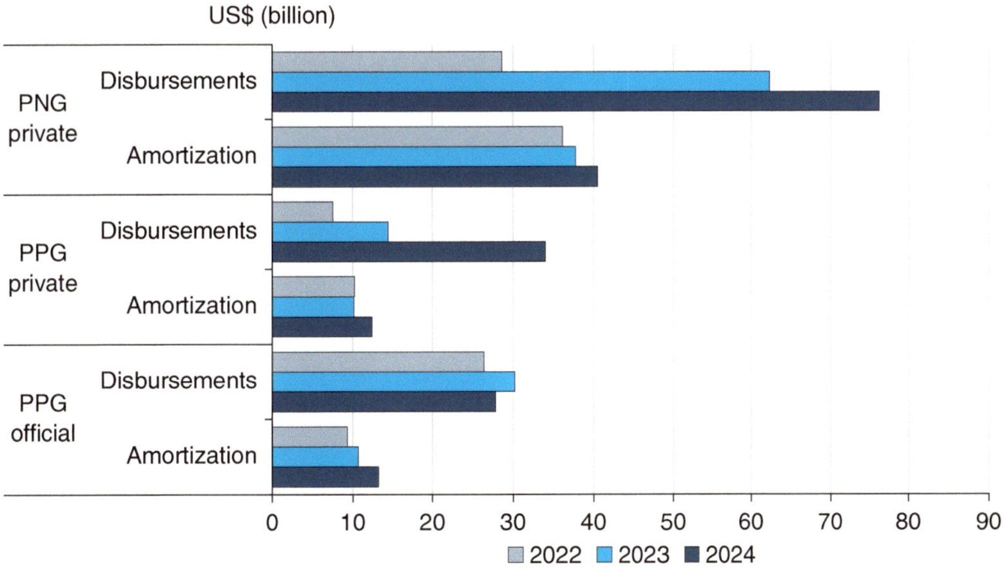

Source: World Bank International Debt Statistics database.
Note: PNG = private nonguaranteed; PPG = public and publicly guaranteed.

The ratio of external debt stock to GNI for the region, 20 percent in 2024, and the ratio of external debt stock to exports, 92.9 percent, worsened slightly over the comparable ratios for 2023. They also correlate to those for India—debt-to-GNI of 18.6 percent and debt-to-exports of 82.1 percent in 2024 (figure 1.27)—given the size of the Indian economy relative to other South Asian countries. Although debt indicators for the region as a whole are moderate for individual countries, they differ considerably in relation to both GNI and exports. Bhutan had the highest ratio of debt to GNI in 2024, 110.1 percent, followed by Maldives, 75.6 percent, and Sri Lanka, 58.9 percent. In Bhutan, the ratio of debt to exports was 349.3 percent, and in Sri Lanka it was 280.1 percent. The ratio of debt service to exports ranged from 9.2 percent in Maldives to 23.7 percent in Sri Lanka. Sri Lanka's rise in this ratio from 16.1 percent in 2023 reflects clearance of arrears to external creditors.

Figure 1.27 External Debt Stocks as a Share of Exports of Goods, Services, and Primary Income and GNI, South Asia, 2023 and 2024

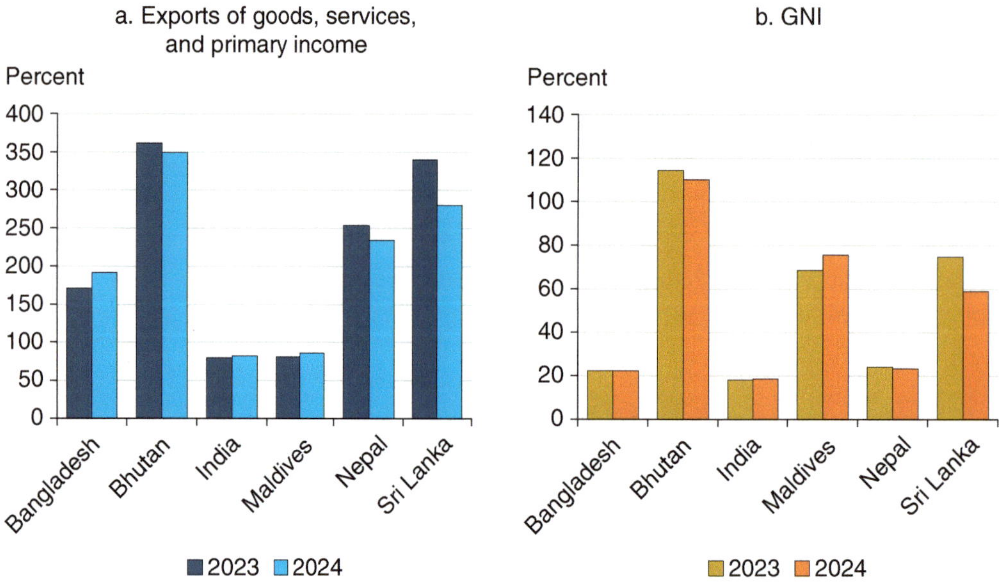

Source: World Bank International Debt Statistics database.
Note: GNI = gross national income.

SUB-SAHARAN AFRICA

Net debt inflows almost tripled in 2024 to US$48.7 billion (table 1.8)—propelled by South Africa, which accounted for 21 percent of the region's net debt flows; net transfers of external public sector borrowers, excluding South Africa, rose 69.2 percent to US$15.6 billion in 2024.

The external debt stock of countries in the Sub-Saharan Africa region rose on average 3.4 percent in 2024, to US$900.8 billion, propelled by a 6.1 percent rise in the external debt stock of South Africa, which was driven by a 4.4 percent rise in long-term debt and 10.9 percent increase in short-term debt. The pace of external debt stock accumulation in countries in the region, excluding

Table 1.8 External Debt Stock and Net Financial Flows and Transfers, Sub-Saharan Africa, 2014–24

US$ (billion)

	2014	2015	2016	2017	2018	2019	2020	2021	2022	2023	2024
External debt stocks	**512.7**	**517.0**	**562.5**	**657.4**	**701.8**	**752.6**	**793.8**	**836.4**	**850.4**	**871.0**	**900.8**
as % of GNI	28.7	32.3	38.1	41.1	40.8	42.4	47.2	44.6	42.4	46.1	49.5
Net debt inflows	**55.1**	**17.8**	**44.3**	**75.5**	**48.1**	**44.8**	**34.7**	**35.0**	**28.6**	**17.1**	**48.7**
Official creditors	18.3	17.8	14.2	20.5	22.1	21.1	35.0	20.1	19.3	22.9	22.0
Bilateral	9.9	9.2	6.4	7.7	10.4	5.5	4.0	3.1	0.4	1.5	-0.3
Multilateral	8.3	8.6	7.8	12.8	11.7	15.6	31.0	17.0	18.9	21.4	22.3
Private creditors	34.4	9.5	34.7	38.5	22.7	17.6	5.6	10.4	0.3	-2.8	15.2
Long-term	52.7	27.3	48.8	59.0	44.8	38.7	40.6	30.5	19.7	20.1	37.2
Public and publicly guaranteed	39.9	17.6	33.1	43.5	41.5	40.0	37.7	27.2	18.4	21.6	38.1
Private nonguaranteed	12.8	9.7	15.7	15.5	3.3	-1.4	2.9	3.3	1.3	-1.5	-1.0
Short-term	2.4	-9.5	-4.6	16.5	3.3	6.1	-6.0	4.5	8.9	-3.0	11.6
Net debt transfers	**43.7**	**3.7**	**28.1**	**58.6**	**26.7**	**21.6**	**13.3**	**14.1**	**4.0**	**-15.0**	**14.7**
Official creditors	16.3	15.4	11.3	17.5	18.5	16.5	30.8	15.0	14.6	15.2	12.9
Bilateral	8.9	7.9	4.6	6.0	8.4	3.0	2.1	1.7	-1.4	-0.9	-2.9
Multilateral	7.4	7.5	6.7	11.5	10.1	13.6	28.7	13.3	16.0	16.1	15.8
Private creditors	17.1	-5.5	12.5	16.9	10.6	9.4	-8.1	-3.1	-11.2	-13.0	3.8
Long-term	43.4	14.9	34.2	44.0	25.6	17.5	21.0	11.2	-1.7	-8.0	7.4
Public and publicly guaranteed	33.5	9.9	23.9	34.3	29.1	25.9	22.7	11.9	3.4	2.2	16.6
Private nonguaranteed	9.9	5.0	10.3	9.7	-3.5	-8.4	-1.8	-0.8	-5.1	-10.2	-9.2

Source: World Bank International Debt Statistics database.
Note: GNI = gross national income.

South Africa, continued to slow, rising on average just 2.8 percent in 2024, to US$724.9 billion, compared to a 3.9 percent increase in 2023 and an average increase of 4.8 percent in 2021 and 2022. The slowdown in the growth of external debt stocks in 2024 is in part explained by debt restructuring agreements with bondholders and other debt reorganizations implemented in 2024. The most significant of these were the up-front haircuts included in the debt restructuring agreements with bondholders for Ghana and Zambia, and implementation of debt forgiveness granted to Somalia in the context of the Heavily Indebted Poor Countries (HIPC) Initiative Completion Point reached in 2023. Taken together, these measures reduced end-2024 long-term debt stocks by US$5.0 billion.

Net debt inflows to countries in Sub-Saharan Africa, excluding South Africa, rose 66.1 percent in 2024 to US$38.3 billion (figure 1.28). This increase was accompanied by a marked change in borrowing patterns and creditor composition. Short-term debt inflows turned from an outflow of US$2.2 billion in 2023 to an inflow of US$6.9 billion in 2024, equivalent to 18 percent of total debt inflows. Long-term debt inflows rose 23.9 percent to US$31.3 billion, driven by inflows from bondholders of US$7 billion, as compared to an outflow of US$1.4 billion in 2023. This reversal reflects renewed access to international capital markets for countries like Benin, Côte d'Ivoire, and Kenya. Net inflows from multilateral creditors rose 6.1 percent in 2024 to US$22.7 billion, of which the World Bank accounted for 63.5 percent. Bilateral creditors recorded an outflow of US$0.7 billion.

Figure 1.28 Net Debt Flows to Sub-Saharan Africa (Excluding South Africa), by Creditor Type, 2022–24

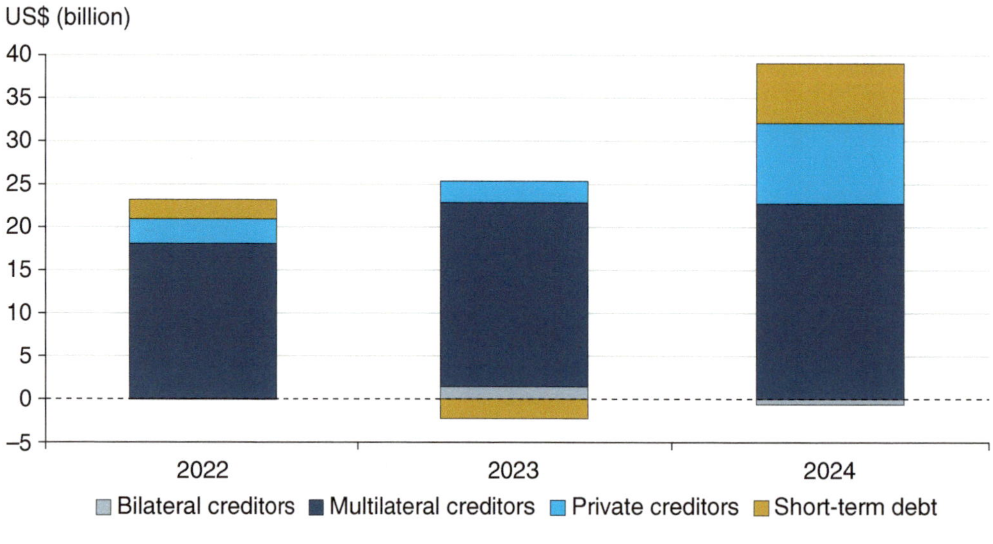

Source: World Bank International Debt Statistics database.

Net transfers of external public debt to the region, excluding South Africa, rose to US$13.1 billion in 2024, from US$7.8 billion in 2023 (figure 1.29). The primary reason for this rebound was increased disbursements to public sector entities, which rose 20.5 percent to US$54.6 billion, compared to a much smaller, 13.2 percent increase in debt service payments to US$47.2 billion. The rise in disbursements was driven by an 80.1 percent increase in those from private creditors, notably from bond issuance in international capital markets. Consequently, the net transfer from private creditors turned positive in 2024 to an inflow of US$1.4 billion, from the prior year outflow of US$7 billion. Net transfers from official creditors, US$14.2 billion in 2024, equivalent to 91 percent of total net transfers on external public debt, remained the primary source of financing.

Figure 1.29 Net Transfers to Sub-Saharan Africa (Excluding South Africa), by Borrower Type, 2014–24

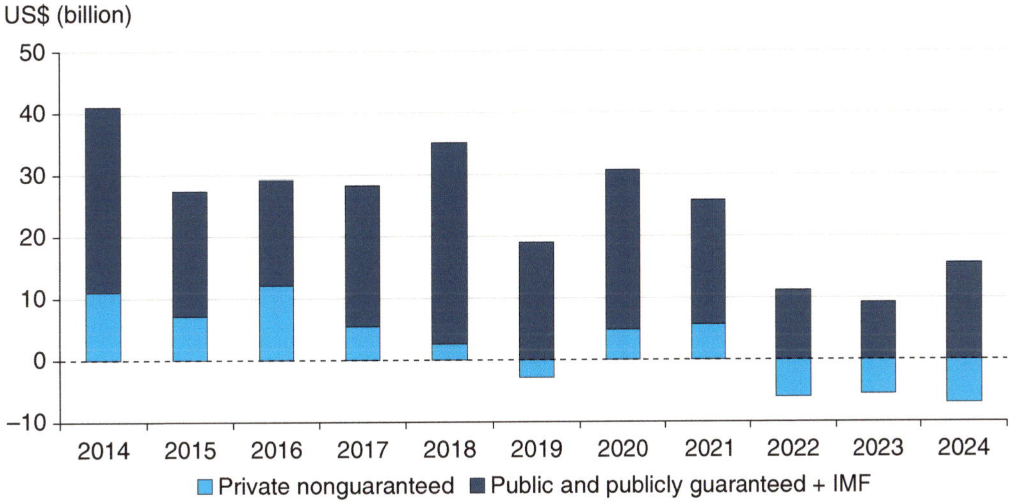

Source: World Bank International Debt Statistics database.
Note: IMF = International Monetary Fund.

Debt Restructuring, 2024

This section presents an overview of debt reorganization by LMICs in 2024 and outcomes against the backdrop of slower global growth, high real interest rates, increased trade restrictions and heightened uncertainty, and real and acute concerns about sovereign defaults.

In 2024, debt reorganization by LMICs reached its highest level since 2010. Close to US$90 billion was reorganized, of which about 58 percent was due to agreements with IDA-eligible countries. The debt reorganization took several forms, including restructuring agreements in the Group of Twenty (G-20) Common Framework and other international forums, and with private creditors, notably bondholders. In addition, outright debt forgiveness and several debt swaps occurred. LMICs, including several IDA-eligible countries, also took advantage of improved market conditions to reprofile the public debt portfolio through new bond issuance in international capital markets or borrowing from private creditors to refinance more costly loans, including with support from multilateral institutions.

Debt Restructuring Agreements

A significant development in 2024 was the accelerated pace of debt restructuring in the G-20 Common Framework. Following their agreement with Zambia in 2023, bilateral creditors concluded an agreement with Ghana in January 2024. Both countries reached agreement with bondholders in 2024. In addition, Ethiopia, which was granted a debt service suspension under the framework for 2023–24, secured a new IMF-supported program in July 2024. This program led to an agreement in principle with the Official Creditor Committee in March 2025 that rescheduled over US$8 billion in bilateral claims with an estimated US$3.5 billion in debt relief and paves the way for restructuring with bondholders and other private creditors.

Zambia concluded the Eurobond exchange in May of 2024, restructuring US$3.9 billion, including US$3 billion outstanding on its three sovereign bonds and US$890 million of past due interest. The bonds were exchanged for two new bonds with a combined value of US$3.05 billion, and US$840 million of past due interest was forgiven, providing a 40 percent reduction in present value terms in the baseline scenario. The agreement includes an upside case treatment that accelerates the amortizations and increases the interest rate if the Zambian economy performs better than projected under the IMF program.

Ghana followed its successful Domestic Debt Exchange Program in 2023 with an agreement on a comprehensive restructuring of external obligations to bilateral creditors in January 2024. The agreement, formalized by Paris Club creditors in a Memorandum of Understanding of June 11, 2024, rescheduled about US$5.4 billion in debt service falling due in December 2022, and that due during the January 1, 2023, to December 31, 2026, period. It extended the weighted average maturity from 2029 to 2038 and reduced interest rates, commensurate with the contractual interest rate of each claim. The agreement with bilateral creditors paved the way for the one with bondholders in October 2024, which restructured US$13.0 billion on 15 separate issues. The old bonds were exchanged for five new bonds totaling US$9.4 billion. The up-front haircut of US$3.5 billion, coupled with extended maturities and lower coupon (interest rate) on the new bonds, delivered an overall reduction of 37 percent in present value terms.

Outside the Common Framework, **Sri Lanka** restructured about US$26 billion with external creditors in 2024, including US$10.3 billion with bilateral creditors, of which US$4 billion was owed to China Eximbank; US$14.2 billion with bondholders, including overdue interest; and US$2.2 billion with private creditors, specifically the China Development Bank.[4] In addition, the domestic debt program restructured another US$9.9 billion. The agreement with bilateral creditors included a four-year grace period, an extension of maturities to 2043, and a reduction in interest rates. Bondholders agreed to an up-front US$3 billion haircut, extended maturities, and lower coupon (interest rate). The new bonds, tied to macroeconomic and governance performance, allow for a reduction in the concessions offered by bondholders if the Sri Lankan economy outperforms IMF program targets.

The Paris Club signed a Memorandum of Understanding with **Suriname** in October 2024 to implement the second phase of the 2022 agreement. It restructured US$88 million in end-2024 debt stock owed to France, Israel, Italy, and the Netherlands. Concessional loans will be repaid over 17 years including 4 years of grace, and nonconcessional loans will be repaid over 12 years including 5 years of grace.

Two of the world's poorest countries, **Haiti** and **Somalia,** benefited from debt forgiveness of US$6.2 billion from official creditors following Somalia's attainment of the HIPC Completion Point in late 2023, the first country to do so since 2015, and forgiveness of Haiti's oil-related debt by República Bolivariana de Venezuela.

Haiti's US$2.2 billion oil-related obligations to República Bolivariana de Venezuela under the Petrocaribe program were extinguished, with US$500 million settled by Haiti from funds previously paid into a blocked account and US$1.7 billion written off by República Bolivariana de Venezuela.

Petrocaribe—an oil alliance established by República Bolivariana de Venezuela in 2005 to provide member countries in the Caribbean and Central America with oil on concessionary financial terms, including long-term payment options at low interest rates—provided energy security for participating countries and served to strengthen República Bolivariana de Venezuela's geopolitical influence in the region. In recent years, however, the program has largely collapsed because of the decline in República Bolivariana de Venezuela's oil production and the country's turbulent political situation.

Somalia reached the HIPC Completion Point in December 2023, with total debt service savings of US$4.5 billion, of which US$1.5 billion came from multilateral creditors, including US$448.5 million from the World Bank (IDA) and US$343 million from the IMF. In their Memorandum of Understanding of March 2024, Paris Club creditors canceled US$1.2 billion and confirmed their willingness to forgive a further US$815 million on a voluntary, bilateral basis.

Turning to middle-income countries, the bond restructuring for **Ukraine** in September 2024 was the largest among LMICs aside from that of Argentina in 2021. It followed the two-year repayment deferral implemented in 2022 and restructured about US$24 billion, including US$3.5 billion of accrued interest. The agreement, which covers sovereign bonds and sovereign-guaranteed bonds of the State Agency for Restoration and Development of Infrastructure, canceled about US$9 billion; it included an up-front haircut that reduced immediate debt service payments by 93 percent and provided a significant extension of maturities and reduction in coupon (interest) rates. It was implemented through an exchange of existing bonds for eight new bonds totaling US$15.2 billion: four Step-Up A bonds with an interest rate of 1.75 percent starting in 2025 and increasing to 7.75 percent after 2034, and four Step-Up B bonds with an interest rate of 7 percent beginning in 2027 and gradually increasing to 7.75 percent after 2034. The agreement provides for an increase in the principal amount of each series in February 2030 if the Ukrainian economy outperforms IMF expectations, which allows bondholders to recoup 12 percent of the principal haircut provided by the restructuring agreement.

The G-20 Common Framework: Recent Developments

Since its creation in 2020, the G-20 Common Framework has served as the coordinating mechanism for the provision of comprehensive debt restructuring for low-income IDA-eligible countries. It brings together all G-20 bilateral creditors and coordinates with private creditor groups to provide a debt treatment, tailored to each borrower's debt structure, that will restore medium-term debt sustainability. As discussed in the previous section, 2024 saw the delivery of concrete results for Ghana and Zambia, and acceleration of the restructuring process for Ethiopia. This progress reflects a continuous effort on the part of G-20 creditors and their key international partners to strengthen the Common Framework, streamline the restructuring process, and enhance creditor coordination.

In early 2024 the IMF, World Bank, and Presidency of the Group of Twenty set up the Global Sovereign Debt Roundtable (GSDR) to serve as a forum for creditor dialogue, among and across creditor groups, and to foster consensus on key technical questions such as comparability of treatment, as well as challenging issues that arise during the restructuring process. The GSDR has helped overcome disagreement, enhanced information sharing, and speeded decision-making as reflected in the accelerated pace of the agreement with Ghana. That agreement was completed in half the time of the prior ones with Chad and Zambia. Additionally, in April 2025, the IMF adopted important reforms to its debt policies that will facilitate faster engagement with the borrower, a critical improvement because delays are likely to exacerbate a debt crisis. The reforms cut the approval time for an IMF program (a prerequisite for the debt restructuring), created new procedures for financing assurances aimed at providing greater flexibility, and laid the groundwork for a smoother, faster process in the future.

Consensus reached by the GSDR on key technical issues is now available in a one-stop Compendium of Common Understanding on Technical Issues, which covers several important topics of key concern to debtors, including comparability of treatment, anticipated timelines for the restructuring process, and how to approach domestic debt restructuring. Creditors recognize the need, however, to strengthen the predictability and timeliness of the restructuring process, and to address some other important issues. These issues include (a) accelerating the restructuring of debt owed to commercial creditors, other than bondholders; (b) incentivizing parallel rather than sequential negotiation when it accords with the debtor's strategy; (c) galvanizing support for early post-restructuring credit rating upgrades; and (d) tackling the complex topic of restructuring collateralized claims, or commercial loans backed by export credit agencies.

There is also a need to strengthen debt transparency, including restructuring outcomes. In this context, early and continuous information sharing between the debtor, creditors or creditor groups (Official Creditor Committee, bondholders' committees, and so on), and the IMF and World Bank is seen as a key factor in a timely and efficient restructuring process. Participants in the GSDR have also reaffirmed support for a debtor-convened meeting of all official bilateral and private creditors early in the restructuring process to explain the context and goals of the restructuring, and for further engagements, as appropriate, to facilitate information sharing as the process advances. Such meetings would also provide an opportunity for the IMF and the World Bank to share information on the macroeconomic framework and debt sustainability analysis, consistent with policies on information sharing, and to explain their policy frameworks, including with regard to IMF debt and financing assurances policies and World Bank requirements for providing financing through budget support operations.

Debt Swaps

Debt swaps continued to serve as an important liability management tool for LMICs in 2024. Debt-for-development swaps, a subcategory of debt swaps, reduce external debt obligations or lower financing in return for a commitment from borrowers to use the savings to fund investment in development projects, expenditures in the social sector, or measures to protect the natural environment and mitigate the impact of climate change. In 2024, seven countries implemented a debt swap agreement: Côte d'Ivoire, Ecuador, Egypt, El Salvador, Indonesia, Kenya, and Mongolia. Collectively these swaps unlocked over US$12 billion in financing to support various sectors, including the natural environment, education, and health. The swaps encompassed debt owed to bilateral creditors, market-based operations, and an innovative refinancing-cum-swap agreement pioneered by the World Bank and supported by an IBRD policy-based guarantee that combined improving debt sustainability management and support for a country's development and investment in human capital (box 1.5).

By far the largest of the 2024 swap operations was the swap concluded between Egypt and the United Arab Emirates. Under the agreement, the United Arab Emirates converted US$11 billion of the outstanding term deposits it had extended to Egypt to equity investment as part of a US$35 billion investment package to develop Egypt's Ras El-Hekma peninsula. The US$11 billion subject to conversion to equity comprised US$5.65 billion in medium-term deposits and US$5.35 billion in short-term deposits.[5]

In LAC, Ecuador and El Salvador implemented debt-for-climate swaps. Ecuador followed its successful 2023 swap to conserve the Galapagos with a similar operation in 2024 aimed at preservation of the Ecuadorian Amazon. Supported by a loan from the Amazon Conservation Designated Activity Company, Ecuador paid US$1 billion, or on average 35 cents on the dollar, to buy back US$1.527 billion of its sovereign bonds, thereby realizing an immediate reduction in its external obligations of US$527 million, plus savings in future interest costs. El Salvador's debt-for-nature swap, its first, which aimed at conservation of the Rio Lempa watershed, was financed by a US$1 billion loan from J. P. Morgan. The par value and secondary market price of El Salvador's sovereign bonds closely aligned, and it paid US$1 billion to buy back bonds valued at US$1.031 billion. However, after taking account of the more advantageous terms on the loan from J. P. Morgan and interest savings on the sovereign bonds bought back, El Salvador expects the debt swap to generate overall savings of about US$352 million for conservation of the Rio Lempa watershed.

With regard to bilateral creditors, in 2024, Germany—a leading and long-time supporter of the Global Fund's Debt2Health program—signed swap agreements with Indonesia and Mongolia to convert €75 million and €29 million, respectively, of its concessional bilateral claims into public health investments. Under these arrangements external debt is swapped for local currency and the creditor, in this case Germany, forgoes debt service payments in euros in return for a commitment from the borrower to invest the equivalent amount in local currency in agreed health service projects. Germany also concluded a €60 million debt-for-climate swap with Kenya that operates in the same way as the health projects but in this case in return for a commitment to invest in climate and renewable energy projects.

Box 1.5 Côte d'Ivoire: World Bank–Supported Debt-for-Development Swap

In December 2024, Côte d'Ivoire announced a debt-for-development swap designed to improve the public debt profile and free up resources for investment in education. This innovative debt swap-cum-liability management operation, facilitated by the World Bank, is the first of its kind to explicitly combine improving debt sustainability management and supporting a country's development objectives and investment in human capital. A €240 million policy-based guarantee (PBG) extended by the World Bank's International Bank for Reconstruction and Development is designed to enable Côte d'Ivoire to access long-term commercial financing in euros on more favorable terms. It will be used to redeem the equivalent amount of the country's costly external debt obligations to private creditors, thereby freeing resources for development initiatives. The PBG serves to lower borrowing costs and provide protection to commercial lenders in the event of nonpayment of debt service by Côte d'Ivoire.

The swap-cum-liability management operation is part of the World Bank's €800 million Third Investment for Growth Development Policy Financing loan approved in December 2024. It includes, in addition to the €240 million PBG, a €260 million guarantee to support a sustainability-linked commercial bank loan to finance Côte d'Ivoire's green transition, and €300 million in direct budget support.

The new €400 million loan extended at end-December 2024 to implement the debt-for-development swap, supported by the PBG at 60 percent coverage, has

(Box continues on next page)

Box 1.5 Côte d'Ivoire: World Bank–Supported Debt-for-Development Swap (*continued*)

a 15-year maturity, including a 7-year grace period. The buyback targets external commercial loans maturing between 2029 and 2033 carrying variable interest rates, with a current annual cost as high as 8 percent. Refinancing these loans with the new loan from MFUG Bank is expected to free up about €330 million in debt service payments in the near term and realize an overall net debt reduction of about €60 million. These fiscal savings will provide the incentive for the authorities to meet the increased target of a World Bank Program for Results, notably by building 30 new primary schools benefiting some 30,000 children.

Tangible benefits in terms of debt service savings and improved fiscal space are important given the challenging external financing conditions facing LMICs. Côte d'Ivoire has market access, but the buyback allows it to further improve its public debt profile, to solidify the downward trajectory in the volume of outstanding public debt, and to smooth the future debt service curve. Additionally, unlike other commercial debt-for-climate swaps which required high legal and transaction costs, this debt-for-development operation is implemented by the government of Côte d'Ivoire, which not only eliminated costly overheads but also signals confidence in the capacity and integrity of the country's administrative processes.

2. Debt Dynamics: Policy Implications and Future Outlook

Debt Dynamics: Policy Implications

Over the past decade, debt accumulation in developing economies has become increasingly disconnected from economic growth. In many countries, recent trends may reflect short-term stabilization needs rather than growth-oriented investment, particularly in low-income countries (LICs) where official financing plays a countercyclical role. External debt has grown faster than exports, while slowing trade, tighter financial conditions, and policy uncertainties have further constrained fiscal space. In several cases, rising debt service costs are absorbing a growing share of public revenues, potentially decreasing spending on health, education, and infrastructure—and eroding prospects for inclusive growth. High external debt burdens are also associated with broader systemic fragility, because countries with weaker institutions and limited resilience face elevated vulnerability and reduced fiscal flexibility.

Current Debt-Growth Dynamics

Regional averages reveal a divergence between real gross domestic product (GDP) growth and external debt burden dynamics over the past decade, particularly after the COVID-19 pandemic (IMF 2024, chapter 1). Figure 2.1 tracks regional trends from 2015 to 2024, comparing real GDP growth with year-on-year percentage growth in total external debt for 119 countries. Before 2020, most regions experienced steady GDP growth alongside accelerating external debt accumulation. The COVID-19 crisis disrupted that balance: growth weakened across nearly all regions in 2019 and contracted sharply in 2020. Although output rebounded in 2021, recovery has remained uneven. External debt stocks rose markedly during 2020 and 2021 in regions such as East Asia and Pacific, Europe and Central Asia, and South Asia, but the growth has since declined in most regions. Sub-Saharan Africa stands out as an exception; both debt levels and servicing burdens have continued to rise even as growth remains subdued, underscoring persistent fiscal stress and limited progress in debt reduction (World Bank 2024).

Figure 2.1 GDP Growth and Year-on-Year Percentage Growth in External Debt Stock, by Region, 2015–24

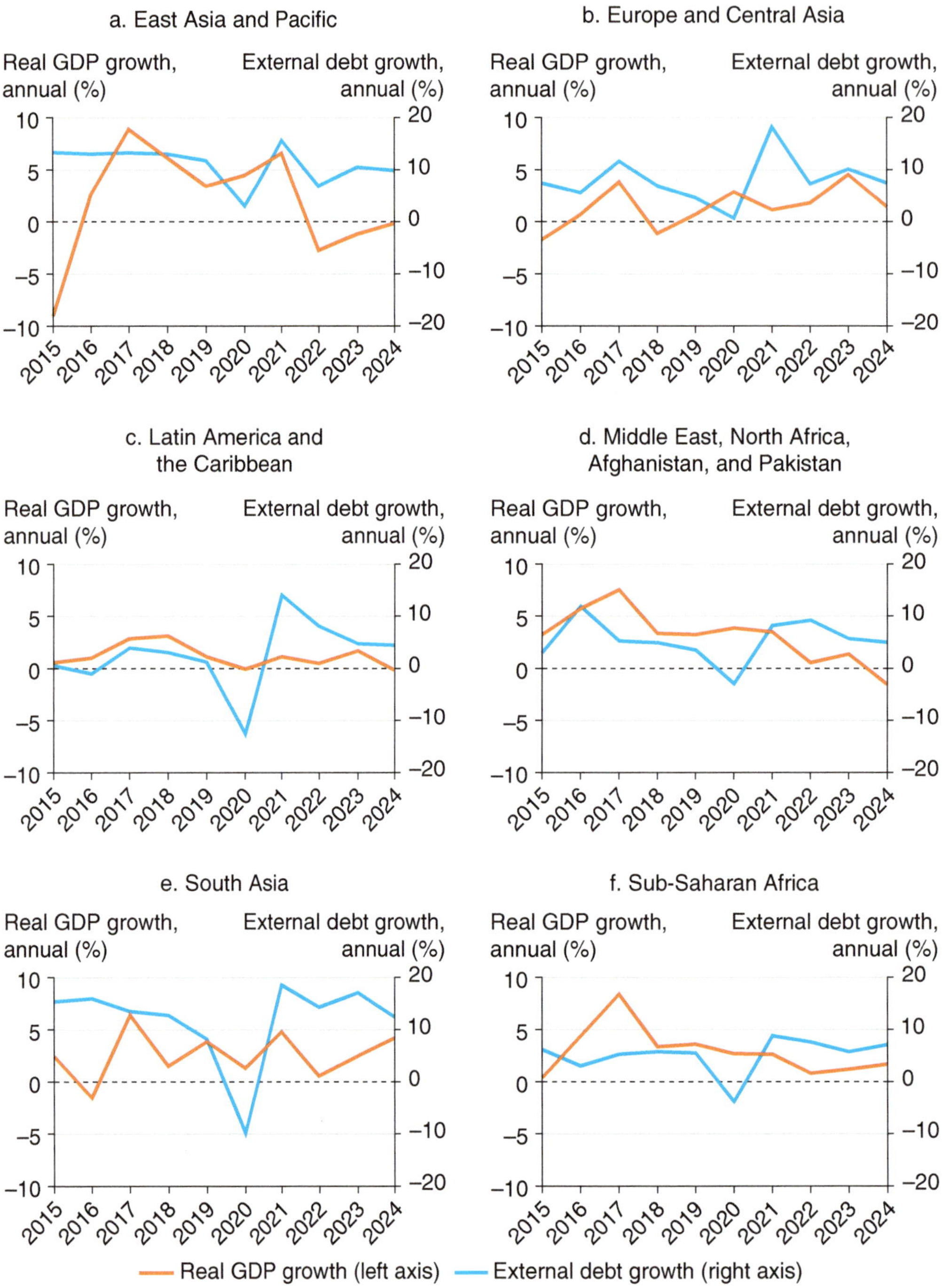

Sources: Original calculations based on data from the World Bank's International Debt Statistics and World Development Indicators databases.
Note: Each panel displays regional GDP growth rates, calculated as weighted averages, based on real GDP in constant 2015 prices, expressed in US dollars, and external debt stock year-on-year percentage growth from 2015 to 2024. The sample includes 119 countries: 16 in East Asia and Pacific; 18 in Europe and Central Asia; 22 in Latin America and the Caribbean; 13 in the Middle East, North Africa, Afghanistan, and Pakistan; 6 in South Asia; and 44 in Sub-Saharan Africa.

The relationship between debt accumulation and economic growth may vary across countries and periods, reflecting differences in economic structures, policy responses, and institutional quality. Nevertheless, historical evidence shows that past waves of debt buildup have often coincided with slower growth and rising macroeconomic vulnerabilities, particularly in emerging and developing economies (El Khalfi et al. 2024; Heimberger 2023; Kose et al. 2021). Figure 2.2 further summarizes regional dynamics by plotting the correlation between GDP growth and the year-on-year growth in external debt stocks, calculated separately for 2015–19 and 2020–24. The share of economies with a negative correlation increased from 51 out of 119 (about 43 percent) during 2015–19 to 76 out of 118 (about 64 percent) during 2020–24. This increase is observed across all regions, notably in the Europe and Central Asia, South Asia, and Sub-Saharan Africa regions, suggesting that higher debt growth has increasingly coincided with slower output performance.

Figure 2.2 Correlation between GDP Growth and External Debt Stock Year-on-Year Percentage Growth, by Region, 2015–19 vs. 2020–24

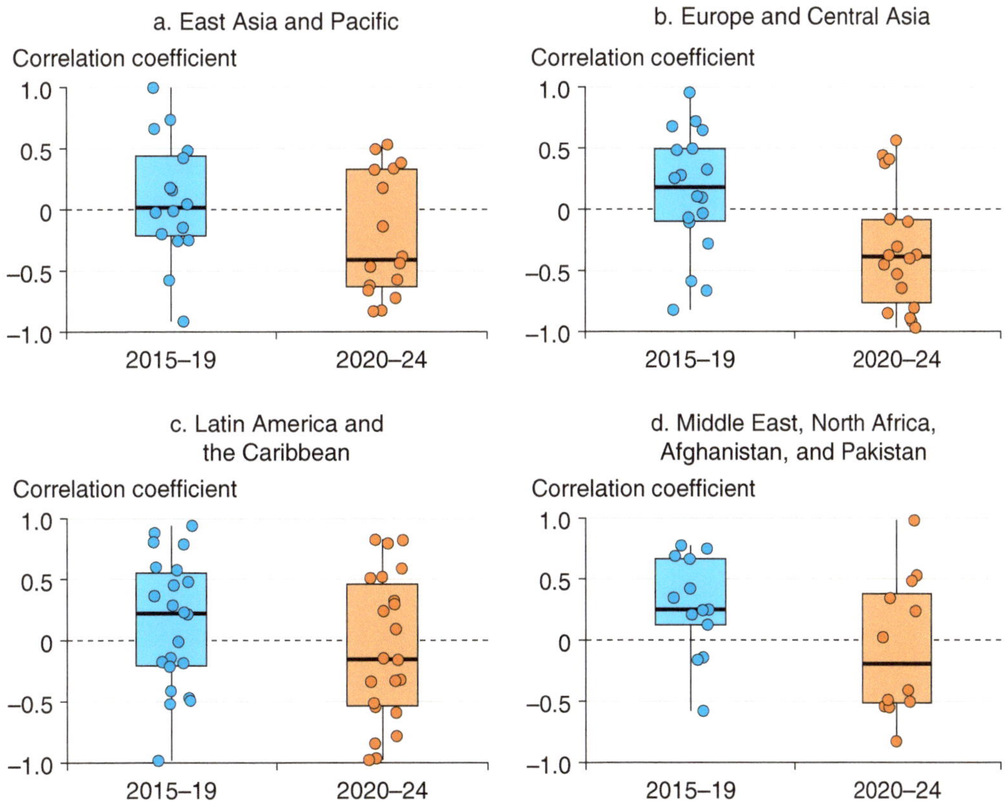

(Figure continues on next page)

Figure 2.2 Correlation between GDP Growth and External Debt Stock Year-on-Year Percentage Growth, by Region, 2015–19 vs. 2020–24 *(continued)*

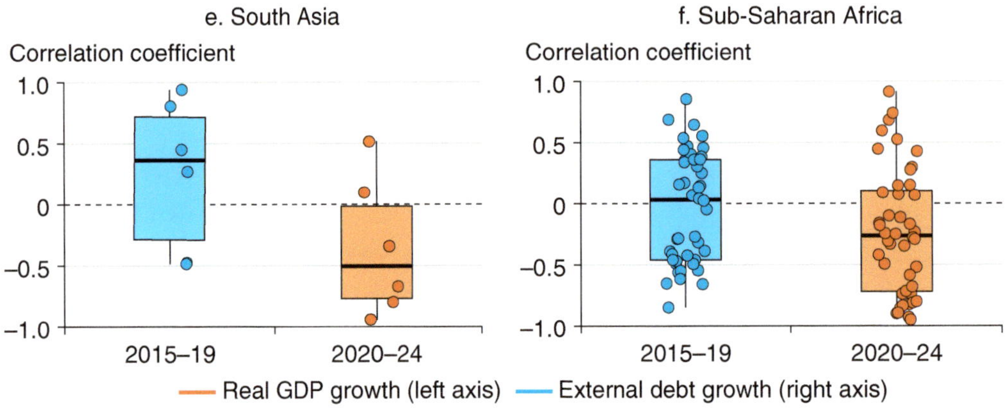

Sources: Original calculations based on data from the World Bank's International Debt Statistics and World Development Indicators databases.
Note: Each panel represents a region and plots the distribution of Pearson correlation coefficients between real GDP growth rates and year-on-year percentage growth in external debt stock, calculated separately for 2015–19 and 2020–24. Points represent country-level observations; boxes show the interquartile range (25th–75th percentiles), with the horizontal line showing the median; whiskers extend to the most extreme values within 1.5 times the interquartile range.

The wider prevalence of negative correlations during 2020–24 partly reflects the exceptional impact of the pandemic and subsequent policy responses, when economic contractions and emergency spending led to rapid increases in public borrowing. Nonetheless, the evidence still points to a broader, though preliminary, pattern of divergence between rising debt and economic expansion across many countries. Recent trends suggest that debt accumulation might have been driven less by growth-oriented investment and more by short-term stabilization, rollover, and essential expenditure needs, reflecting the countercyclical nature of official financing in many LICs. At the same time, the negative correlation may partly reflect reverse causality, because stronger growth can also reduce the need for new borrowing, leading to slower debt accumulation.

Growth Outlook in Low- and Middle-Income Countries

Growth in low- and middle-income countries (LMICs) is expected to soften in the short term, primarily because of increased trade restrictions and heightened uncertainty related to global trade, which will increase debt service burdens. Weakening growth will likely contribute to an increase in public debt-to-GDP ratios in LMICs and exacerbate debt dynamics. In addition, compared to the past couple of years, the pace of government revenue collection is projected to slow in

LMICs, particularly when China is excluded, with softening activity, which will constrain the debt service capacity of governments.

GDP growth in LMICs is estimated to inch down to 4.3 percent in 2025 from 4.4 percent in 2024, mainly reflecting an export slowdown that offsets resilient domestic activity supported by the loosening of financial conditions and benign credit expansion (figure 2.3). In China, slowing export growth, alongside elevated uncertainty, is estimated to lead to a marginal decline in growth in 2025. Excluding China, growth in LMICs is set to remain stable at 3.9 percent between 2024 and 2025.The decline in growth in 2025 will be broad-based, with more than half of LMICs expected to experience lower growth than in 2024, and will mark the fourth consecutive year (2022–25) of growth deceleration taking place in more than half of LMICs.

In 2026–27, growth is projected to slow further to an average of 4.1 percent per year in LMICs because of the continued impacts of trade restrictions and heightened uncertainty, including in China. Excluding China, growth in LMICs is forecasted to increase to 4.1 percent annually, on average, in 2026–27, primarily driven by strengthening domestic demand backed by easing financial conditions that lower borrowing costs, falling inflation, and improving business and consumer confidence. In addition, the share of LMICs with slowing growth is set to decline over 2026–27.

Figure 2.3 Growth in Low- and Middle-Income Countries, 2022–27

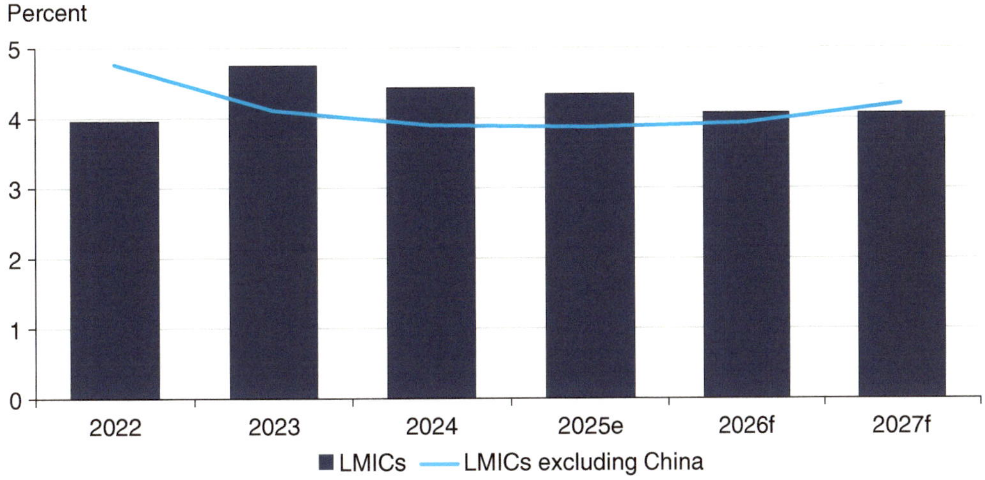

Source: Original calculations based on data from the World Bank's Macro Poverty Outlook (October 2025), https://www.worldbank.org/en/publication/macro-poverty-outlook.
Note: Aggregate GDP growth rates are calculated as weighted averages, based on real GDP in constant 2015 prices, expressed in US dollars, as weights. e = estimated; f = forecasted; LMICs = low- and middle-income countries.

Further moderation of growth in LMICs is expected to contribute to a continued increase in the public debt-to-GDP ratio by the end of 2027, and lower interest rates on public debt will marginally improve the interest rate-growth differentials over 2026–27. Excluding China, an increase in the debt ratio is expected to be modest, partly because of rising growth. However, growth in government revenues is projected to stay lower in 2026–27 than in 2023–24, reflecting that debt service capacity will remain limited.

In LICs as well as in economies eligible for International Development Association (IDA) assistance, growth is projected to increase in 2026–27, with an assumed improvement in security, leading to a recovery in several fragile and conflict-affected situations, alongside easing inflation. Despite accelerated growth projections, fiscal buffers will remain constrained in many LICs, partly reflecting reductions in foreign aid, including official development assistance. Depleted fiscal space will continue to undermine resilience and constrain the ability to absorb shocks.

Risks to the outlook in LMICs remain tilted to the downside. The materialization of these risks could weaken economic activity, increase borrowing costs, and worsen the debt service capacity. Key downside risks include a further escalation of trade tensions and heightened policy uncertainty, tighter financial conditions and financial stress, and increased conflict and geopolitical stress.

Further escalation of trade tensions and persistently high trade policy uncertainty could weigh more heavily on business and investor sentiments, and have adverse impacts on output and employment in LMICs. A sharp rise in uncertainty, particularly for an extended period, could raise the costs of borrowing and lower investment through, for example, delays in investing in productive capacity. Weaker investor sentiment and a lack of clarity over future trading arrangements could curtail the flow of foreign direct investment (FDI) linked to establishing supply chains in LMICs.

Financial market disruptions and tighter financial conditions could weaken global growth and lead to capital outflows from LMICs, with particularly adverse impacts in countries with limited fiscal and external buffers. In LMICs with weak credit ratings and high debt levels, market access for refinancing maturing debt could be disrupted, requiring sharp fiscal adjustments or debt restructuring. Higher borrowing costs would raise debt servicing burdens and worsen fiscal pressures in many LMICs.

The risk of continued or escalating conflict remains high, which could worsen economic and social conditions in economies directly involved and spill over to neighboring economies. Private activity could be constrained, with persistent output losses in the affected economies. Neighboring countries could also see weaker private investment due to heightened uncertainty and reduced economic stability.

Declines in productive capacity induced by conflicts could lower future expected incomes, raise risk premiums, and increase the probability of debt default.

Easing Inflation in LMICs amid Heightened Uncertainty

Inflationary pressures are projected to continue to soften in LMICs in the short term, partly because of loosening labor markets and softening wage growth. Although monetary authorities in LMICs have maintained a cautious stance amid elevated uncertainty, monetary policy is expected to ease gradually in 2026–27, contributing to a decline in debt service costs.

Headline inflation in LMICs is estimated to decrease to 3.7 percent in 2025 from 4.9 percent in the previous year, partly reflecting easing labor markets with softer wage growth (figure 2.4). When China is excluded, the deceleration of inflation is projected to be faster, from 9.6 percent in 2024 to 7.3 percent in 2025. In several LICs, food prices fell in the second half of 2025 following strong harvests.

However, declining inflation will be driven by major LMICs, as inflation is estimated to increase in about half of LMICs in 2025, compared to about one-fifth of these economies in 2024. Given heightened global economic and trade policy uncertainty and fragile economic situations, central banks in LMICs are still cautious about lowering policy rates although rates have been on a declining path. In LMICs excluding China and in LICs, policy rates have remained elevated, near the level of mid-2023 (figure 2.5).

Figure 2.4 Inflation in Low- and Middle-Income Countries, 2024–27

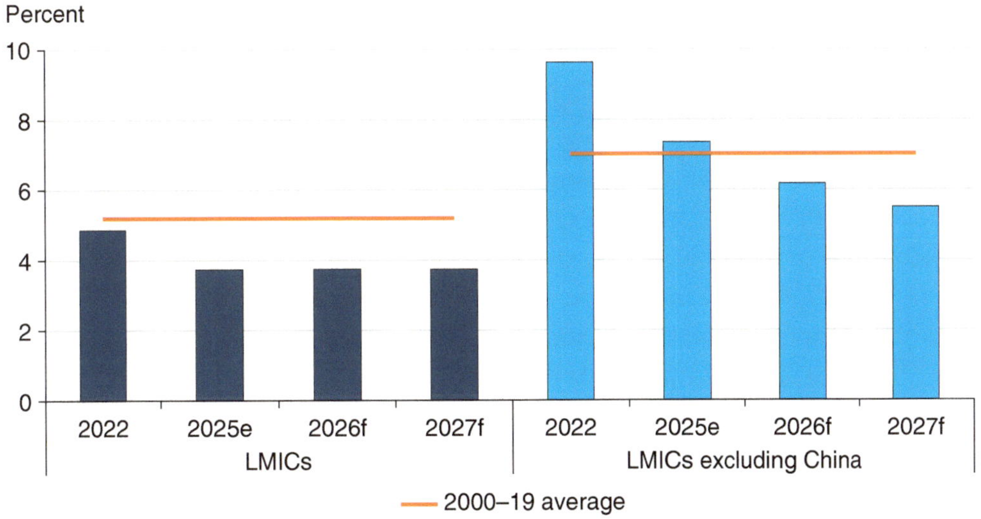

Source: Original calculations based on data from the World Bank's Macro Poverty Outlook (October 2025), https://www.worldbank.org/en/publication/macro-poverty-outlook.
Note: Aggregate consumer price index inflation rates are calculated as geometric weighted averages, based on nominal GDP in US dollars, as weights. e = estimated; f = forecasted; LMICs = low- and middle-income countries.

Figure 2.5 Policy Rates in Low- and Middle-Income Countries, 2022–25

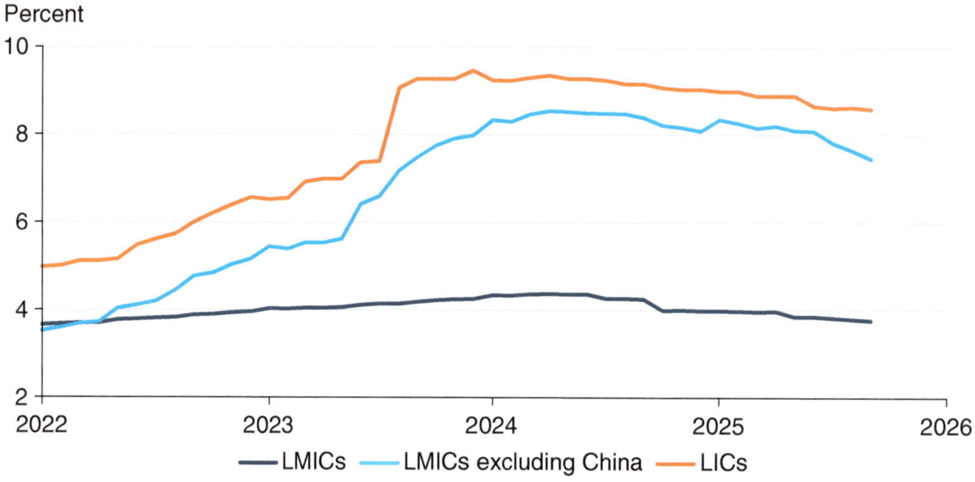

Source: Original calculations based on data from Haver Analytics.
Note: The last observation is September 2025. Aggregate monetary policy rates are calculated as geometric weighted averages, based on nominal GDP in US dollars, as weights, using data up to 59 LMICs, including 12 LICs. LICs = low-income countries; LMICs = low- and middle-income countries.

In 2026–27, inflation in LMICs is expected to stabilize further as labor markets approach balance. Excluding China, inflation in the group is set to decline to an average of 5.8 percent a year in 2026–27. Inflation is projected to decelerate in about 60 percent of LMICs in 2026. A further reduction in price pressures is also expected in LICs and IDA-eligible countries, assuming that normal weather conditions continue without any disruptions to supply chains. With softening inflationary pressures alongside easing financial conditions, monetary policies in LMICs are projected to loosen gradually; therefore, the cost of servicing debt is expected to decline.

Projected softening of inflationary pressures is set to coincide with easing debt service burdens in LMICs. In 2025, total external debt service is estimated to decline by 10 percent to US$1.2 trillion. The declining trend is expected to continue in 2026–27, with debt service payments decreasing to US$918 billion in 2027. In particular, amid the expected easing of financial conditions and financing costs, interest payments on total external debt are forecasted to shrink further. Between 2024 and 2027, interest payment burdens are expected to decline by 42 percent in LMICs, 41 percent in LICs, and 32 percent in IDA-eligible countries. Consequently, the share of interest payments in total debt service in LMICs will decrease to 27 percent a year, on average, in 2025–27, from 34 percent in 2024. Excluding China, the share of interest payments is also projected to fall in LMICs over the same period.

Multiple drivers could, however, heighten inflationary pressures in LMICs in 2026–27, potentially leading to a tightening of monetary policies and a rise in debt service burdens. Those drivers include escalated tension and uncertainty in global trade policy, tighter global financial conditions, the intensification of conflicts, and adverse weather conditions.

Heightened tensions and uncertainty in global trade policy uncertainty, especially if sustained for an extended period of time, could increase consumer prices and inflation expectations in LMICs. Disruptions in global supply chains caused by further escalation of trade tensions and heightened uncertainty could lead firms to delay investment and raise prices, particularly when facing a surge in production expenses, in order to maintain profit margins. A rise in producer prices could translate into higher consumer prices and inflation expectations, resulting in shifts in monetary policy stances, especially if inflation expectations show signs of de-anchoring.

Tighter global financial conditions could increase inflationary pressures, mainly resulting from currency depreciation in LMICs. Inflation in LMICs could also rise if cross-border conflicts or domestic violence damages the supply network, putting upward pressure on commodity prices by increasing production and transportation costs. In addition, adverse weather conditions, including extreme droughts or excess rainfall, could result in a surge in food prices, especially in LICs or economies reliant on agricultural output.

Rising debt levels in LMICs could reverse recent progress on inflation in these countries. An unanticipated increase in government debt-to-GDP in emerging markets and developing economies is associated with a rise in long-term inflation expectations (Brandão-Marques et al. 2023).

Persistent Current Account Pressures: Increased Borrowing Costs and Low Growth Rates

About three-quarters of LMICs had current account deficits in 2024. Such deficits have been persistent in LMICs, with these economies (excluding China) continuously running deficits since 2008. These deficits have contributed to the accumulation of external debt over the years, particularly in LICs, where the current account deficit was about 8 percent of GDP in the early 2020s (figure 2.6a). Current accounts in LMICs excluding China are expected to remain in deficit in the short run, partly reflecting heightened geopolitical tensions and elevated global trade policy uncertainty, reducing export revenues and raising vulnerability to external shocks in several economies. As of 2024, 23 LMICs had current account surpluses—the largest were in Africa (Djibouti, Nigeria, and Angola), followed by several countries in Europe and Central Asia (Azerbaijan and Tajikistan).

Figure 2.6 Current Account Balance and Foreign Direct Investment, Low- and Middle-Income Countries, 2000–24

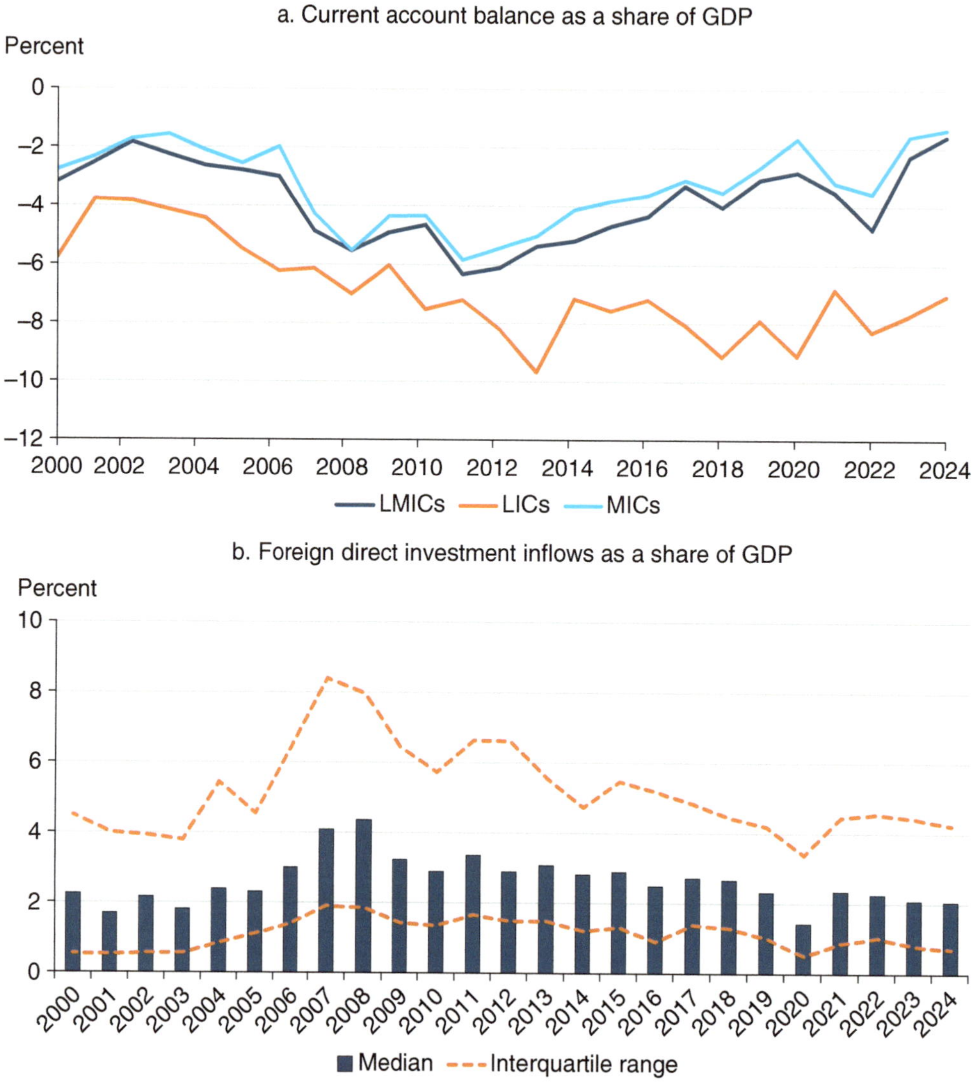

Source: World Bank World Development Indicators database.
Note: Panel a: median current account balance in percent of GDP for LMICs, LICs, or MICs per year. Panel b: median and interquartile range of foreign direct investment net inflows in percent of GDP for LMICs. LICs = low-income countries; LMICs = low- and middle-income countries; MICs = middle-income countries.

Current account pressures can weaken investor confidence, contributing to an increase in borrowing costs and weaker output growth. Interest payments on external public and publicly guaranteed debt in LMICs rose by 33 percent between 2022 and 2024. This trend is expected to continue at a more modest rate: interest payments are projected to increase by 2.2 and 12.4 percent between 2024 and 2026 in middle- and low-income countries, respectively. Persistently elevated debt servicing, including interest, can crowd out spending in other areas important to development. Moreover, when output growth falls below interest rates, it puts government debt on an unsustainable path and further erodes investor confidence. Low confidence can make countries more vulnerable to external shocks, which could trigger capital outflows, further erode confidence, and weaken debt sustainability, with currency depreciation making it more costly to service external debt.

Persistently elevated geopolitical and trade tensions can depress export activity and discourage capital flows to LMICs. Tensions could put pressure on migrant workers, leaving LMICs that are dependent upon cross-border remittances vulnerable to a deterioration in international liquidity. FDI has already been declining (relative to GDP) in most economies over the past decade (figure 2.6b). FDI is a particularly important source of external capital for LMICs: beyond its role in financing imports, it can lead to technology spillovers, job creation, and productivity improvements (Adarov and Pallan 2025). LMICs need to make efforts to create a favorable climate for FDI, thereby boosting capital mobilization and investor confidence, and supporting debt sustainability. Geo-economic fragmentation of trade and capital flows also poses a risk to government debt sustainability by negatively affecting output and raising borrowing costs.

Trade-Off Challenges amid Global Trade Tensions and Uncertainty on Countries' Fiscal Space, Expenditures, and Debt Management

Trade tensions can further affect the debt outlook by damping growth prospects, because policy uncertainty may erode investor confidence. These spillovers from trade tensions can reduce fiscal space. Growth of trade in goods and services in LMICs is projected to slow in 2025 because of the introduction of tariffs in the United States and then to remain subdued in 2026. Moreover, heightened trade tensions and policy uncertainty could raise spending pressures in LMICs to mitigate the social consequences of economic volatility, resulting in the reduction of debt service capacity at a time when LMICs already face elevated interest payments on government debt. Fiscal support could be needed for vulnerable populations and sectors directly affected by tariff hikes or by supply chain disruptions. In addition, principal repayments on public and publicly guaranteed debt have complicated liquidity management. Between 2022 and 2024, principal repayments rose by 11.7 percent. Even though principal repayments are expected to fall in LMICs by 5.4 percent between 2024 and 2026, low-income and IDA-eligible countries are expected to see increases in principal repayments of 87.5 and 54.2 percent, respectively.

Weak domestic revenue mobilization in many LMICs compounds the fiscal situation. In LMICs, median government revenue (relative to GDP) improved only modestly between the 2010s and 2020s (figure 2.7). But government revenues are substantially lower in LICs, which also tend to have persistent current account deficits and elevated sensitivity to external shocks because of accumulation of external debt. Heightened spending on the green transition, infrastructure, and health and education for young populations could increase debt stocks in the near and medium terms.

Financial instability could rise because of increased risk premiums, tightened financial conditions, and higher debt service. Financial sector stress could force governments to provide fiscal support to banks and other financial institutions, increasing government debt and worsening fiscal positions. In addition, the link between the financial sector and the fiscal health of governments is even stronger when domestic financial institutions hold a significant amount of sovereign debt.

If global tariff wars and elevated policy uncertainty lead to lower-than-expected global disinflation and monetary easing, it could further raise the stock of government debt in LMICs (figure 2.8). Interest payments are already high, and a further rise in borrowing costs would add to fiscal strains. In addition, currency depreciation could increase the burden of US dollar–denominated debt in LMICs.

The current context is similar to past circumstances in which sovereign defaults have occurred. Historically, many sovereign defaults have occurred in countries that have above-median ratios of government debt to GDP (World Bank 2023). Given preexisting debt levels, more countries may be at risk of debt distress in the near and medium terms. Between 2019 and 2024, the share of LMICs in debt distress nearly doubled, to half. If the situation worsens, lengthy debt resolution processes may be required, leading to large output decreases, losses of market access, and deteriorating development outcomes. Restructuring government debt in a timely, coordinated way should be a policy priority.

At the country level, improving fiscal space and debt management is critical (box 2.1). Countries should urgently implement medium-term budget frameworks and fiscal reforms to strengthen domestic revenue mobilization and expenditure efficiency. They should also spur domestic debt market development. The latter can encourage local currency financing to lessen exposure to currency risk. They should use caution, however, because rollover risks are often larger in the domestic market because of shorter maturities (refer to the discussion on domestic debt in the next section). Fiscal rules and councils can also support prudent debt management.

Figure 2.7 Government Revenues as a Share of GDP, 2010s and 2020s

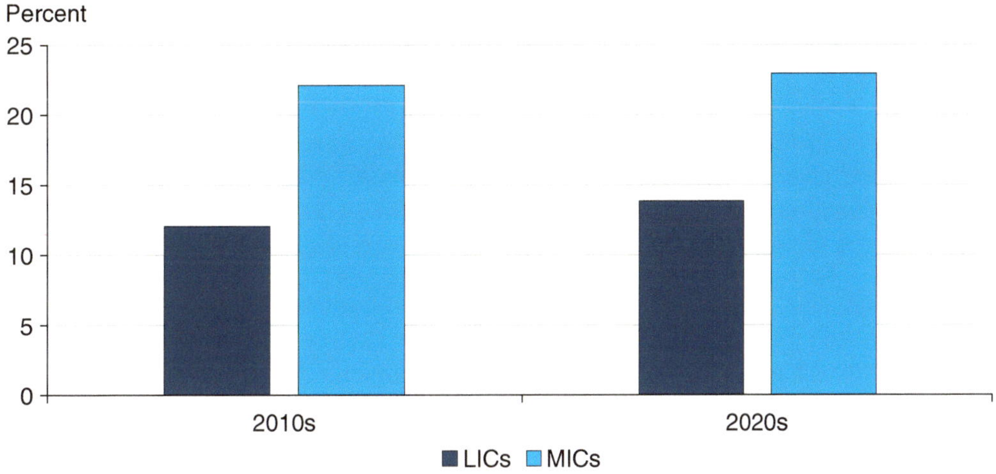

Source: Original figure for this publication based on World Bank World Development Indicators database.
Note: Period average of median government revenue (excluding grants) in percent of GDP in low- and middle-income countries. 2010s = 2010–19; 2020s = 2020–23; LICs = low-income countries; MICs = middle-income countries.

Figure 2.8 Economic Policy Uncertainty, 2000–09, 2010–19, and 2020–25

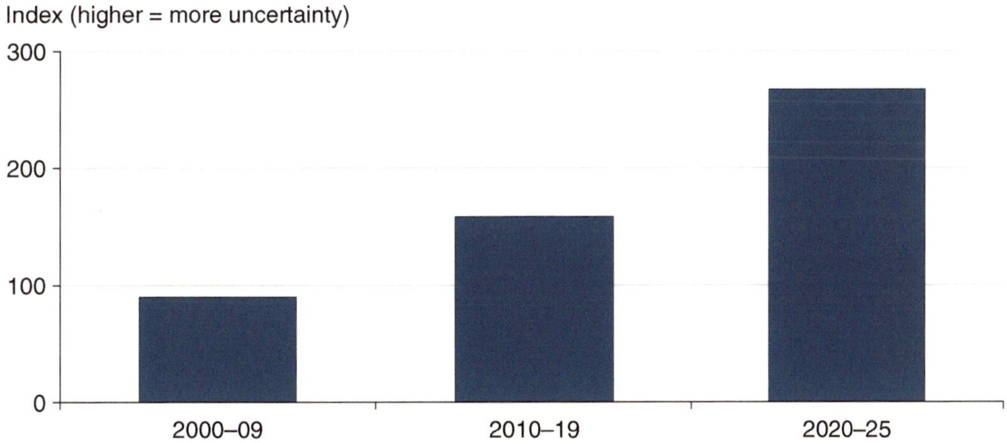

Sources: Original figure for this publication based on Baker, Bloom, and Davis 2016 and World Bank World Development Indicators.
Note: Period averages of the monthly Baker, Bloom, and Davis economic policy uncertainty index. Last observation is March 2025.

Box 2.1 Trade Volatility and Debt Sustainability in Low-Income Countries

As external debt of low-income countries (LICs) continues to grow, understanding how trade volatility interacts with debt sustainability is crucial for sound fiscal planning and trade reforms. Recent World Bank analysis suggests that volatility in export earnings is closely associated with risks of debt distress in LICs, underscoring the need to better integrate trade resilience considerations into debt sustainability frameworks and the broader macroeconomic policy dialogue.

External debt stocks in LICs have grown much faster than export earnings over the last decade. Between 2014 and 2024, LICs' total external debt nearly doubled, from US$139.0 billion to US$242.4 billion; export earnings grew from US$76.0 billion to US$130.0 billion (figure B2.1.1). Over the same period, LICs' debt service payments, including principal and interest, increased sharply, absorbing more than 9 percent of export earnings in 2024, up from 7 percent in 2014 (figure B2.1.2). As such, LICs increasingly face a significantly higher debt repayment burden relative to their capacity to earn through exports.

Figure B2.1.1 Export Earnings and External Debt Stock, Low-Income Countries, 2005–24

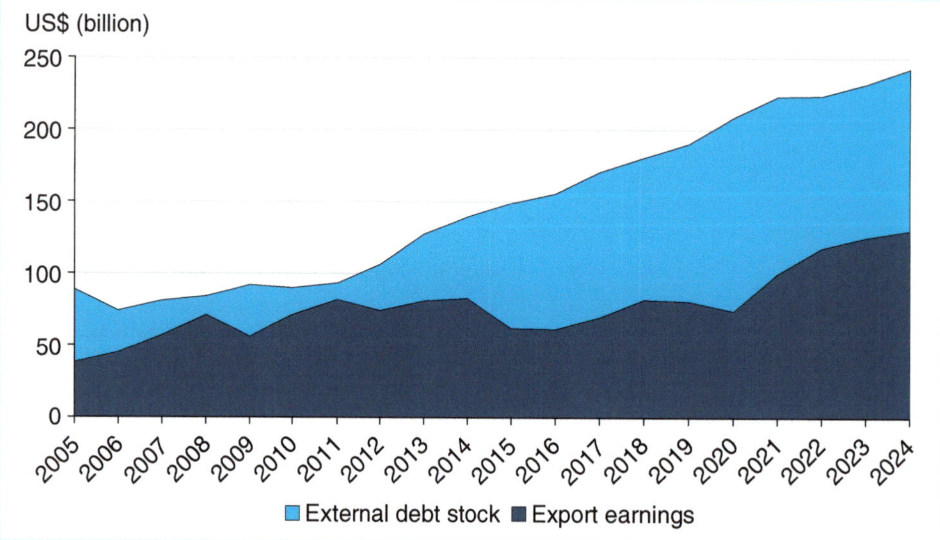

Source: World Bank International Debt Statistics database.
Note: Low-income country grouping based on fiscal year 2025 World Bank Group Income Classification.

(Box continues on next page)

Box 2.1 Trade Volatility and Debt Sustainability in Low-Income Countries (*continued*)

Figure B2.1.2 Ratio of Debt Service to Exports, 2014 vs. 2024

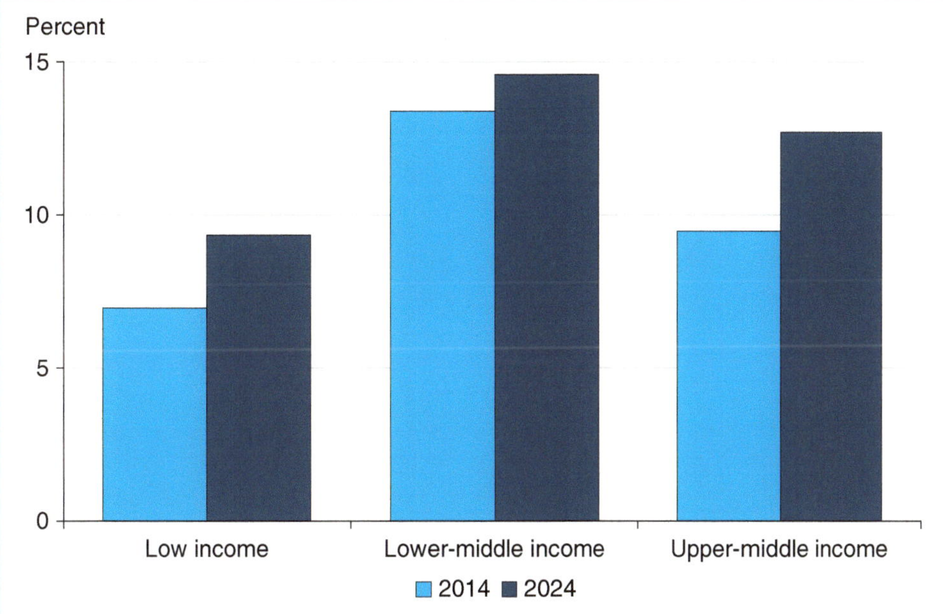

Source: World Bank International Debt Statistics database.
Note: Country groupings based on fiscal year 2025 World Bank Group Income Classification.

Meanwhile, the share of LICs classified as facing high debt risk or in debt distress has more than doubled, from 24 percent in 2013 to 54 percent in 2024.[a] Export volatility in LICs—measured by year-to-year changes in export earnings—has risen sharply since 2019 (figure B2.1.3). Much of the increase was driven primarily by commodity price fluctuations, which remain the dominant source of trade instability for many LICs (Dessus and Constantinescu 2024). Notably, countries at high risk of or in debt distress in 2023 are among those experiencing the highest trade volatility (figure B2.1.4).

(Box continues on next page)

Box 2.1 Trade Volatility and Debt Sustainability in Low-Income Countries (*continued*)

Figure B2.1.3 Five-Year Rolling Volatility of Exports Earnings, 2009–24

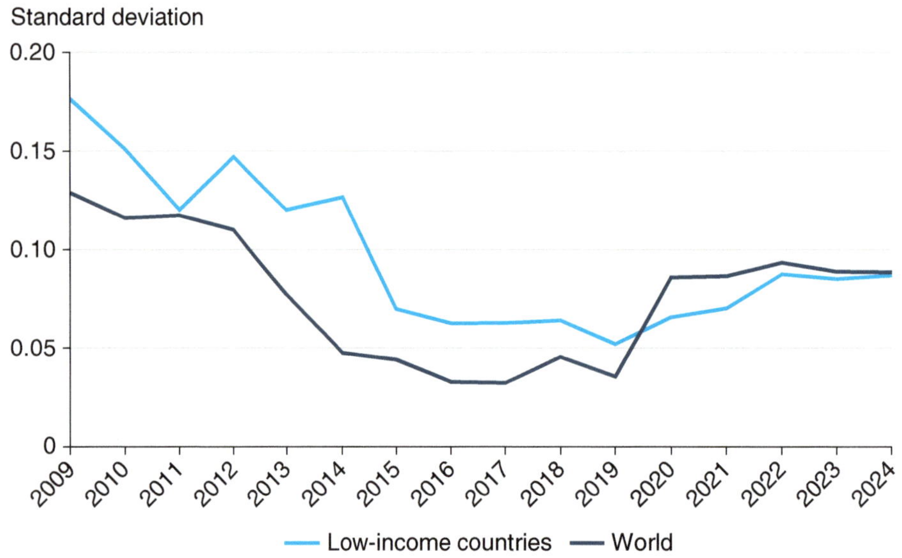

Sources: World Bank Debt Sustainability Analysis and World Development Indicators databases.
Note: Low-income country grouping based on fiscal year 2025 World Bank Group Income Classification. Export volatility is measured as short-term, year-to-year fluctuations in export values of goods, services, and primary income, net of long-term growth trends. Volatility is calculated over five-year rolling periods.

In the current global trade policy environment, volatility is expected to remain high and possibly rise even higher. Rising protectionism and frequent shifts in trade policies increase uncertainty, threatening demand for LIC exports and foreign exchange earnings. Climate change is also expected to intensify trade volatility by amplifying the frequency and severity of supply shocks, especially for commodity-dependent exporters. As previously shown, countries with higher debt risks or in debt distress are among those with greater volatility, suggesting a potential link between trade volatility and debt unsustainability. This correlation does not necessarily imply causality, but it highlights the importance of a better and more systematic consideration of trade volatility in debt sustainability analysis.

To build resilience, LICs need policies that directly address the structural sources of vulnerability in their trade sectors. Strengthening trade resilience can both stabilize external revenues and broaden the export base, reducing the probability that temporary shocks undermine debt sustainability.

(Box continues on next page)

Box 2.1 Trade Volatility and Debt Sustainability in Low-Income Countries (*continued*)

Figure B2.1.4 Export Volatility in Low-Income Countries, by Debt Risk Category, 2014–24

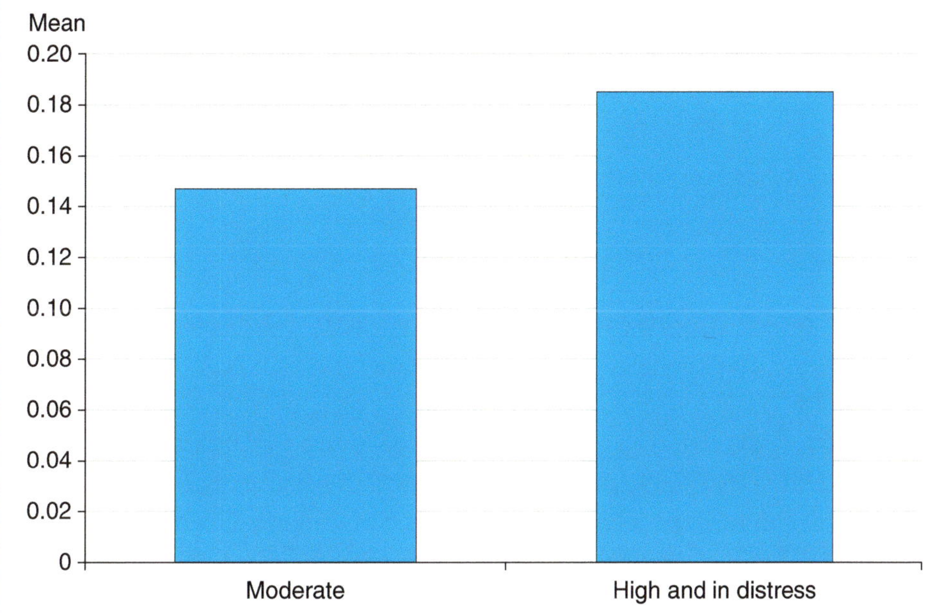

Sources: World Bank Debt Sustainability Analysis and World Development Indicators databases.
Note: Low-income country grouping based on fiscal year 2025 World Bank Group Income Classification. Export volatility is measured as short-term, year-to-year fluctuations in export values of goods, services, and primary income, net of long-term growth trends. Volatility is measured as the simple average of the log volatility, defined as the standard deviation of residuals from a linear trend in the natural logarithm of export values (2014–24).

Key areas for policy action:

- *Promotion of export diversification.* Reduces reliance on a narrow set of products and partners while broadening opportunities in digital trade and services.
- *Strengthening of logistics systems.* Improves supply chain reliability and lowers costs, making exports more resilient.
- *Deepening of trade agreements.* Enhances stable market access through stronger legal and institutional frameworks.

(*Box continues on next page*)

Box 2.1 Trade Volatility and Debt Sustainability in Low-Income Countries (*continued*)

- *Increasing export responsiveness to currency movements.* Strengthens the ability of firms to expand exports when faced with exchange rate depreciation, increasing resilience to external shocks (Stojanov, Engel, and Varela 2024).

Systematically integrating trade volatility into debt sustainability analysis frameworks, alongside structural reforms to enhance export resilience, will be essential to safeguarding debt sustainability in LICs.

a. Reflects published debt sustainability analysis ratings as of end-August 2025.

Domestic Debt in Low-Income Countries: Recent Developments

Many countries covered under the Low-Income Country Debt Sustainability Framework (LIC DSF)[6] have increased their domestic financing over the past decade in order to meet pressing financing needs and manage debt vulnerabilities. This expansion of domestic debt markets has helped these countries finance widening fiscal deficits amid repeated shocks, growing development needs, and sluggish revenue growth, while reducing exposure to exchange rate risks. The World Bank continues to support countries in strengthening these markets, with a new focus on capital market development. However, rising domestic debt burdens and a tightening sovereign-bank nexus in several LIC DSF countries highlights the need for close monitoring and risk management.

Public domestic debt in LIC DSF countries has risen steadily over the last decade. Between 2014 and 2024, their public domestic debt-to-GDP ratio rose from 8 percent to 17 percent, with about half of this increase occurring before the COVID-19 pandemic (12 percent in 2019).[7] Over the same period, the median LIC DSF country expanded its public domestic debt share by 10 percentage points (figure 2.9a). Moreover, the share of countries with public domestic debt that is more than half of their total public and publicly guaranteed debt more than doubled from 10 percent in 2014 to 21 percent in 2024 (figure 2.9b). During this period, some frontier LIC DSF countries such as Ghana, Kenya, and Tanzania were able to issue local currency bonds at maturities greater than 15 years (IMF and World Bank 2020).

Figure 2.9 Share of Domestic Public Debt in Low-Income Country Debt Sustainability Framework Countries, 2014 and 2024

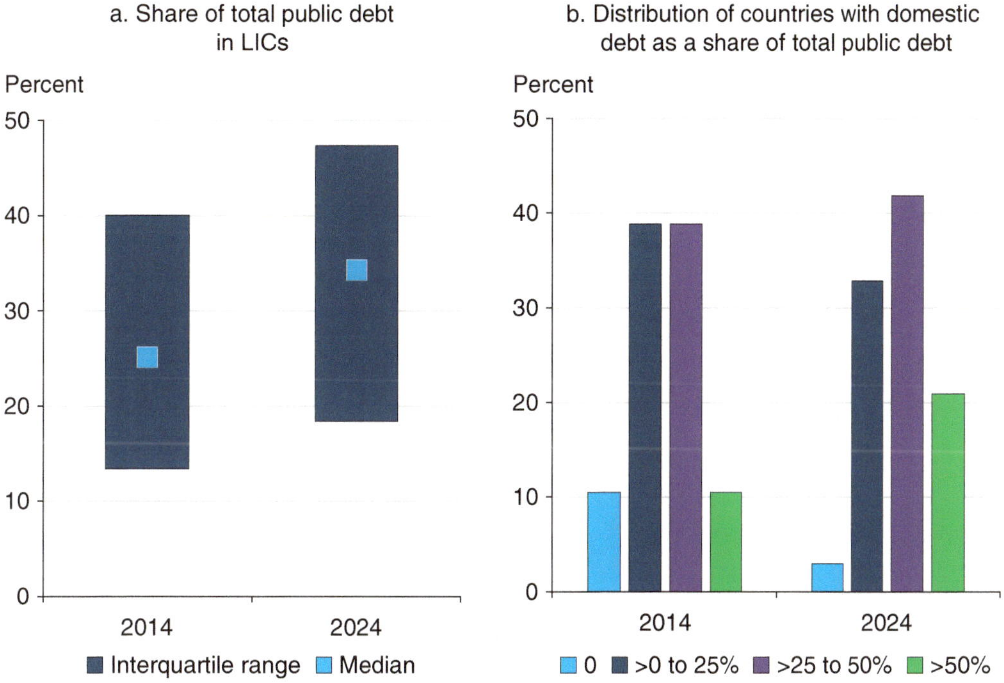

Source: International Monetary Fund–World Bank Low-Income Country Debt Sustainability Framework database as of June 2025.
Note: IMF = International Monetary Fund; LIC = low-income country.

Domestic debt in LIC DSF countries is dominated by marketable instruments, though nonmarketable debt remains important, especially in certain regions. As of end-2024, about 59 percent of the stock of public domestic debt is in marketable securities (mainly treasury bills and treasury bonds, with a marginal share of sukuk), 24 percent is in nonmarketable debt such as loans and central bank financing, and 17 percent is in arrears (figure 2.10).[8] Among the 60 countries considered, 80 percent issue marketable debt. About two-thirds of the remaining countries are countries affected by fragility, conflict and violence, and the rest are small states. The increasing reliance on marketable debt has been accompanied in some cases by improvements in debt transparency.[9]

Figure 2.10 Composition of Public Domestic Debt in Low-Income Country Debt Sustainability Framework Countries, 2024

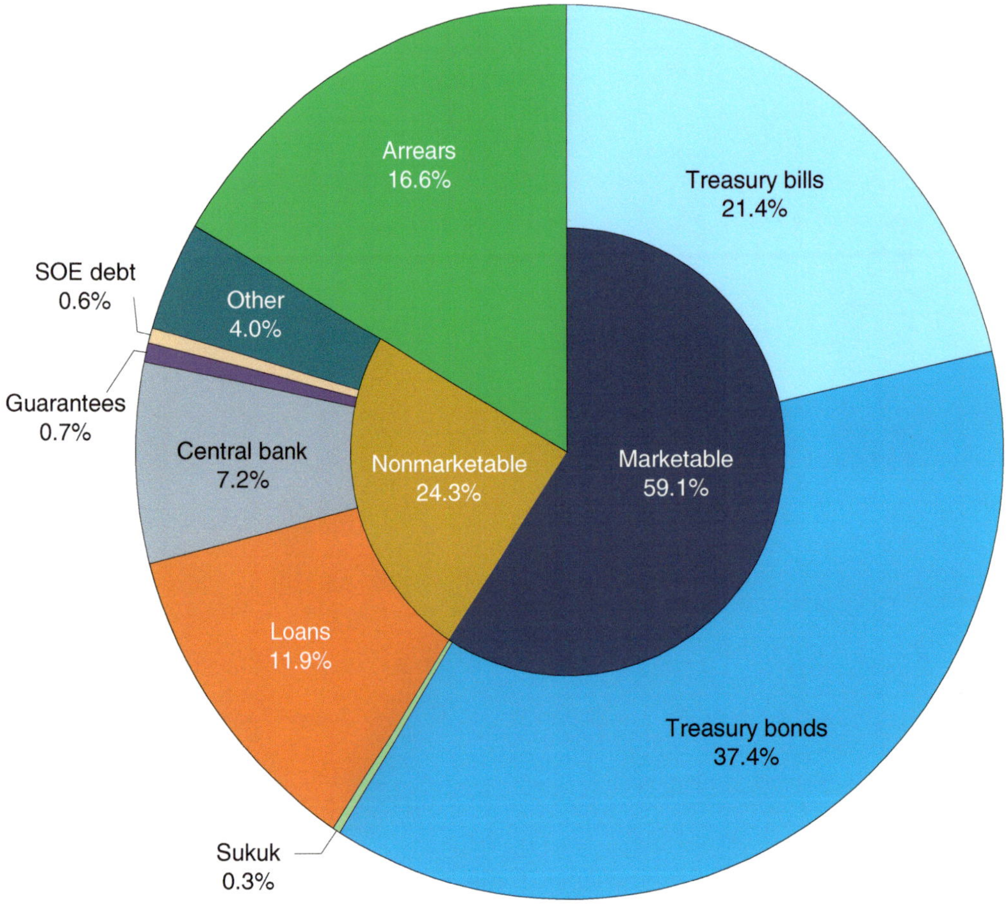

Sources: Low-Income Country Debt Sustainability Analyses, debt bulletins of national authorities; Bank of Canada–Bank of England database of sovereign defaults.
Note: SOE = state-owned enterprise.

The increased reliance on domestic debt has helped mobilize resources during shocks and has reduced exchange rate risks, but it comes at the cost of heightened refinancing and interest rate risks. Whereas the 2024 stock of domestic debt was predominantly medium- and long-term (79 percent), new issuance in 2025 shows a shift to short-term borrowing, with 41 percent of new debt (including central bank financing) issued at short maturities. The median maturity of new longer-term debt is 4.5 years for LIC DSF countries and 5.0 years for frontier LIC DSF countries, but it is significantly shorter for small economies (2.9 years) and countries affected by fragility, conflict, and violence (3.6 years).

Nominal costs for domestic borrowing are generally higher than for external concessional borrowing and may be obscured by nonmarketable instruments and financial repression. The effective costs of external borrowing, however, depend not only on nominal interest rates but also on exchange rate movements. High nominal rates on domestic debt—reaching 25 percent in some LIC DSF countries, with the median at about 5 percent in 2024—combined with increased volumes have driven domestic public debt service costs higher, which increases rollover risks. The median ratio of domestic debt service-to- revenues (including grants) has increased more than sixfold over the past decade, from 3 percent in 2014 to 19 percent in 2024. More critically, countries with the highest ratios of interest payments to revenue also face low revenue-generating capacity. Further, nearly half of LIC DSF countries continue to record negative real domestic interest rates (figure 2.11), with the median close to zero in 2024, partly reflecting the global inflationary spike that inflated away the real value of existing debts. In some cases, however, persistently negative real rates reflect financial repression, as regulatory requirements or policy incentives push domestic financial institutions to absorb government securities at below-market returns.

Figure 2.11 Distribution of Real Interest Rate on Domestic Debt, 2024

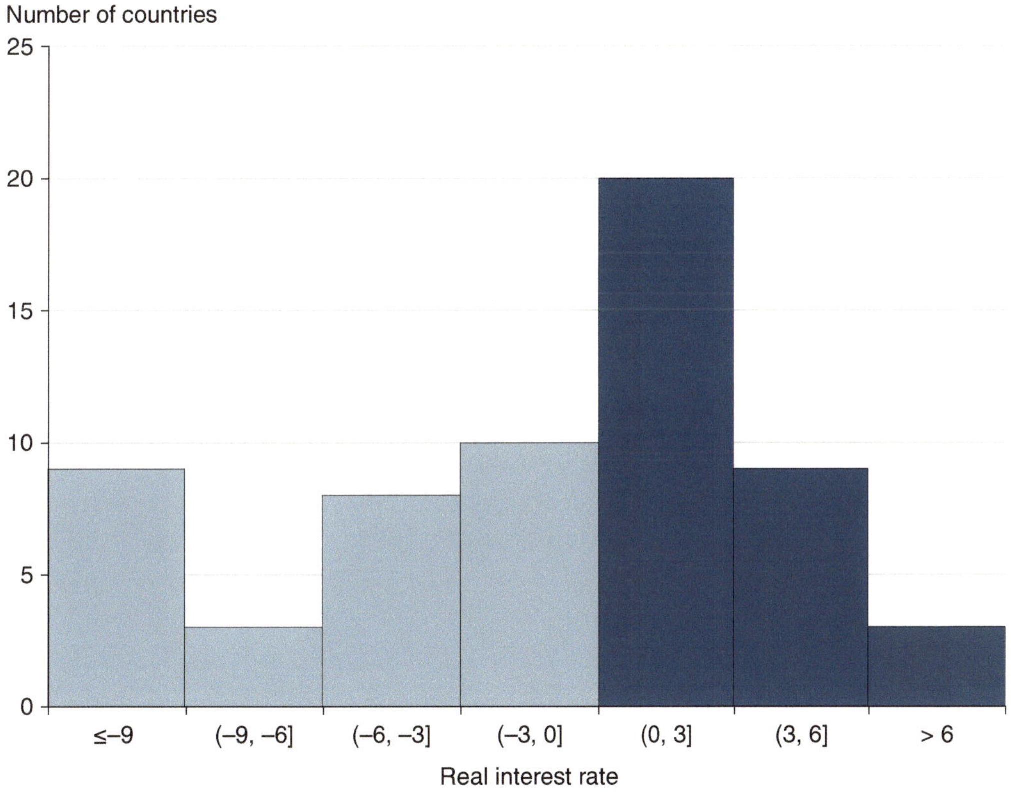

Source: International Monetary Fund–World Bank Low-Income Country Debt Sustainability Framework database as of end-June 2025.

Domestic debt poses distinct risks compared to external debt, reflecting differences in creditor bases and macrofinancial links. External debt pressures aggravate balance-of-payments pressures with broader macroeconomic risks, reflecting the impact on external creditors and the prospects of future access to external financing. Meanwhile, domestic debt is primarily held by the local financial system, which creates links across sovereign-bank-central bank balance sheets with bidirectional risk. Banking crises can put pressure on sovereign financing as demand for domestic debt recedes, and sovereign defaults imply asset losses on the balance sheet of the local financial sector, which could risk citizens' deposits. Both can impede credit creation and constrain growth.

In addition, central banks' exposures to the sovereign across LIC DSF countries have risen over the last decade, with central bank interventions in response to COVID-19 contributing to the increase. Monetary financing can distort the pricing of domestic debt, artificially lowering costs and concealing sovereign risks. In large volumes, it can also be a source of vulnerability on the balance sheet of the central bank itself. More generally, monetary financing has well-known implications for price stability across the economy.

The sovereign-banking nexus in LIC DSF countries has also strengthened over the recent past, mirroring governments' growing dependence on domestic financing. Since 2014, domestic commercial banks in LIC DSF countries have increased their exposure to the sovereign. Over the last decade, the number of LIC DSF countries with domestic banks that had more than a quarter of their assets with the sovereign more than doubled (figure 2.12a). Over the same period, the number of these countries that had more than a quarter of their banks' assets with the private sector declined (figure 2.12b).

Domestic nonbank investors in LIC DSF countries have also become larger players in the domestic debt market over the last decade. Domestic pension funds and other nonbank domestic investors increased their share of domestic debt in more LIC DSF countries over the period 2015–24 than in 2000–10. This situation reflects the role that pension funds play in many countries as a source of unchecked financing for governments.

Figure 2.12 Low-Income Debt Sustainability Framework Countries with Claims Exceeding 25 Percent of Balance Sheet, by Type of Investor, 2014 vs. 2023

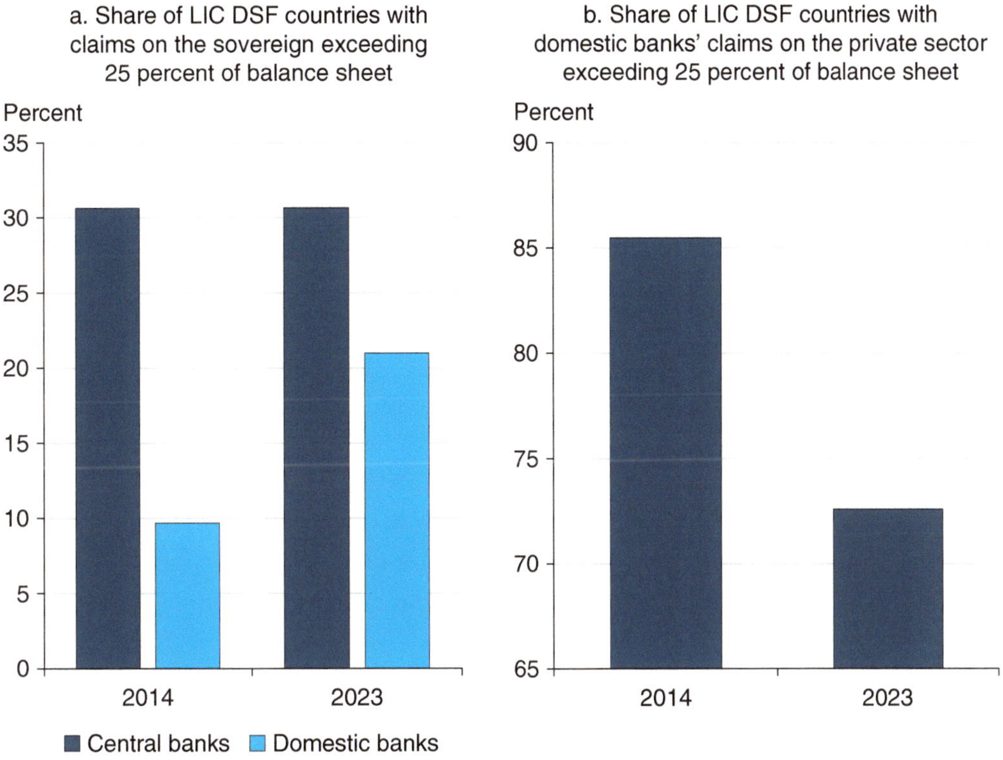

Source: Original calculations based on data from the International Monetary Fund International Financial Statistics database.
Note: In panel a, exposure to the sovereign includes central banks' claims on the central government, nonfinancial public institutions, and state and local governments. DSF = Debt Sustainability Framework; LIC = low-income country.

High Debt, High Fragility: Interlinked Risks to Development

External debt stocks across many LMICs have accumulated substantially over the past decade, approaching or exceeding historical highs (refer to chapter 1 of this report). Although the pace of new borrowing has recently slowed, this debt buildup, along with long-standing structural fragilities, continues to constrain development progress.

External debt burdens and systemic fragility are interconnected (Kraay and Nehru 2006; World Bank 2025a). In this analysis, fragility spans a broad spectrum of persistent weaknesses, including underperforming food systems, limited preparedness for shocks, and institutional weaknesses that undermine effective governance and policy implementation. Countries facing such challenges often resort to external borrowing during crises, primarily from official creditors in lower-income countries, given their limited market access. Once accumulated, however, high debt burdens may further constrain fiscal space and policy flexibility, crowding out critical investments in infrastructure, agriculture, health, social protection, and crisis response capacities. This dynamic can become self-reinforcing: elevated debt restricts a country's ability to invest in development and resilience, thereby increasing its vulnerability to future shocks and the likelihood of further borrowing until it reaches financing ceilings (AfriCatalyst 2025; Federspiel, Borghi, and Martinez-Alvarez 2022; IMF and World Bank 2022).

To examine these interlinkages, this section applies a set of complementary global indicators capturing various development dimensions. The affordability of a healthy diet serves as an indicator reflecting population-level vulnerability and constraints within food systems and income distribution. The INFORM Risk Index, developed by the European Commission and United Nations agencies, captures exposure and vulnerability to shocks such as natural disasters and conflict; institutional capacity is measured through the World Bank's Country Policy and Institutional Assessment and Worldwide Governance Indicators. These indicators are analyzed with the most recent debt data from the 2025 International Debt Statistics database to ensure data recency and cross-country consistency.

The latest data from 106 LMICs in the 2025 International Debt Statistics reveal consistent associations between high external debt burdens (relative to exports of goods, services, and primary income) and adverse conditions, including unaffordability of healthy diets, structural vulnerability, and limited institutional capacity. On average, IDA-only countries face external debt stocks that represent about 189 percent of their export revenue, compared to 130 percent in non-IDA countries. Similarly, on average, 58 percent of the population in IDA-only countries cannot afford a healthy diet, versus 24 percent in non-IDA countries. IDA-only countries also score substantially worse on vulnerability metrics and institutional indicators compared to their non-IDA peers.

These findings indicate a pressing need to integrate debt statistics and diagnostics with broader development risk monitoring. Doing so can support policy makers in anticipating crises, prioritizing interventions, and designing timely and coordinated policy responses.

Food and Nutrition Security under Debt Pressure

Access to affordable and healthy diets is a core development priority, reflecting concerns about both population-level vulnerability and constraints in food systems and income structures. Persistently unaffordable healthy diets not only signal economic hardship but also undermine nutrition and health outcomes, which in turn impair learning and productivity, posing serious long-term risks to development.

Drawing on the Cost and Affordability of a Healthy Diet indicators jointly produced by the United Nations Food and Agriculture Organization and the World Bank (FAO et al. 2025; Fu et al. 2025), recent data reveal that countries experiencing significant debt distress also face acute challenges in ensuring nutrition security for their populations. These data underscore the need to align debt relief and concessional financing with institutional and growth-oriented reforms, as well as with investments in nutrition-sensitive food systems.

As illustrated in figure 2.13, external debt exposure is closely linked to the affordability of a healthy diet. Among the 22 countries with external debt stock exceeding 200 percent of export revenue, 15 are IDA-only countries. This country group classification includes eligible countries that receive the most concessional IDA financing, including grants and highly subsidized loans depending on the risk of debt distress, and does not include IDA-blend countries, which use a mix of IDA and IBRD resources. Across these 22 high-debt countries, an average of 56 percent of the population cannot afford a healthy diet. This figure rises to 65 percent in the IDA-only group, underscoring how debt distress and nutrition security challenges frequently overlap in the most vulnerable contexts. In 17 of these 22 countries, the share exceeds 40 percent, meaning more than 40 percent of the population in a country cannot afford a healthy diet, a threshold that signals high risk of nutrition insecurity in this analysis. Even calorie-adequate diets, a lower-cost benchmark that meets basic dietary energy needs using the cheapest starchy staple foods, are unaffordable for over 20 percent of the population in many of these countries. This finding signals severe deprivation and further underscores the compounding effects of limited purchasing power and inefficiencies in food systems.

Countries such as Kenya, Mozambique, and Zambia, located in Eastern and Southern Africa, are identified as high-risk across all panels in figure 2.13. In Mozambique, for example, nearly 90 percent of the population cannot afford even the lowest-cost healthy diet, and nearly 60 percent are priced out of a calorie-adequate diet. At the same time, the country faces external debt stocks exceeding 700 percent of exports and debt service ratios above 46 percent of exports as of 2024.

Figure 2.13 Food and Nutrition Security, by Country Debt Level

Prevalence of unaffordability: healthy diets vs. caloric adequacy

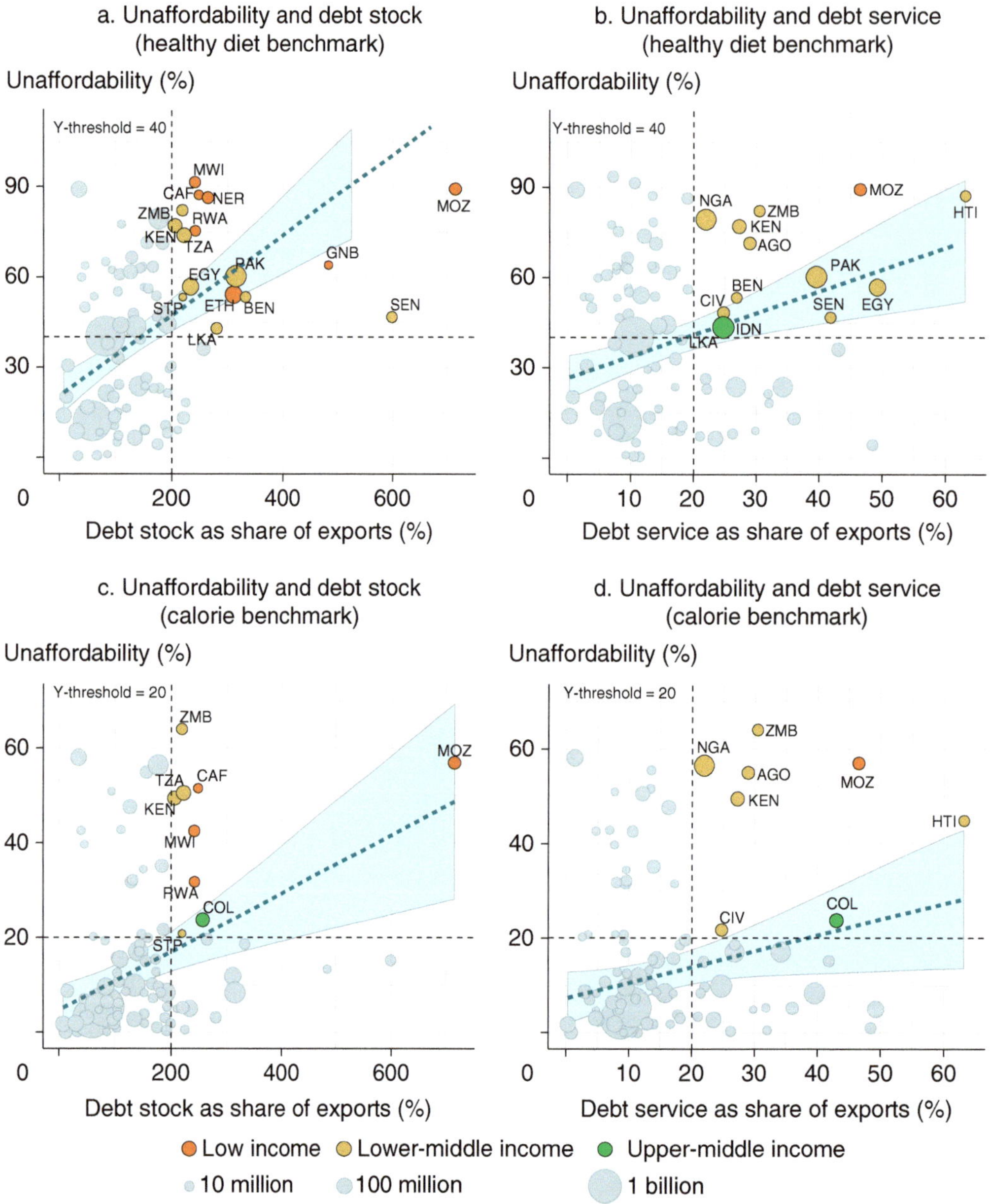

Sources: World Bank Food Prices for Nutrition, International Debt Statistics, and World Development Indicators databases.

Note: Bubble size and regression weights reflect 2024 populations. Trend lines represent population-weighted ordinary least squares regressions with 95 percent confidence intervals shaded. Panels a and b show the share of the population unable to afford a healthy diet; panels c and d show the share unable to afford a calorie-adequate diet. The analysis covers 90 countries for the healthy diet indicator and 91 for the calorie benchmark. Countries are flagged as high risk if over 40 percent (healthy diet benchmark) or 20 percent (calorie benchmark) of people cannot afford the diets. Thresholds correspond to the upper end of the global distribution in 2024 and 2021 as the most recent estimates, respectively. Debt distress thresholds, defined as external debt stock exceeding 200 percent of exports and debt service exceeding 20 percent, apply across all figures. Gray bubbles represent countries that do not fall into the high-risk quadrant.

Compounding Risk and Vulnerability

Beyond nutritional deprivation, countries with high levels of external debt often face multiple, interrelated risks that heighten their vulnerability to crises. In resource-constrained settings, financial stress frequently overlaps with exposure to shocks and disasters, societal vulnerability, and limited coping capacity. Understanding these interlinked dynamics is essential for assessing how debt amplifies broader development risks and undermines resilience.

To illustrate how these risks manifest across countries, figure 2.14 uses the INFORM Risk Index,[10] which captures a country's exposure to shocks such as conflict and natural disasters, as well as its underlying societal vulnerability and coping capacity. This analysis highlights the country's overall INFORM score and its vulnerability subscore, which reflects structural development fragilities such as chronic poverty, limited access to essential services, and economic marginalization.

Both indicators show positive associations with external debt burdens, especially the vulnerability score. Countries such as Benin, Colombia, Kenya, Mozambique, and Pakistan are consistently identified as high-risk across all panels, exhibiting both high debt and high compounding vulnerability. Although many of these countries are in the Sub-Saharan Africa region, high-risk countries are also found in Asia and Latin America and include upper-middle-income economies such as Ukraine and Türkiye.

These findings reinforce the fact that debt and fragility are deeply intertwined. Financial stress can be both a symptom and a driver of broader vulnerability, reinforcing cycles of underinvestment, weak resilience, and stalled development progress. The next section turns to one of the most critical underlying factors sustaining this cycle: institutional capacity.

Figure 2.14 Risk and Vulnerability, by Country Debt Level

INFORM risk and vulnerability indices

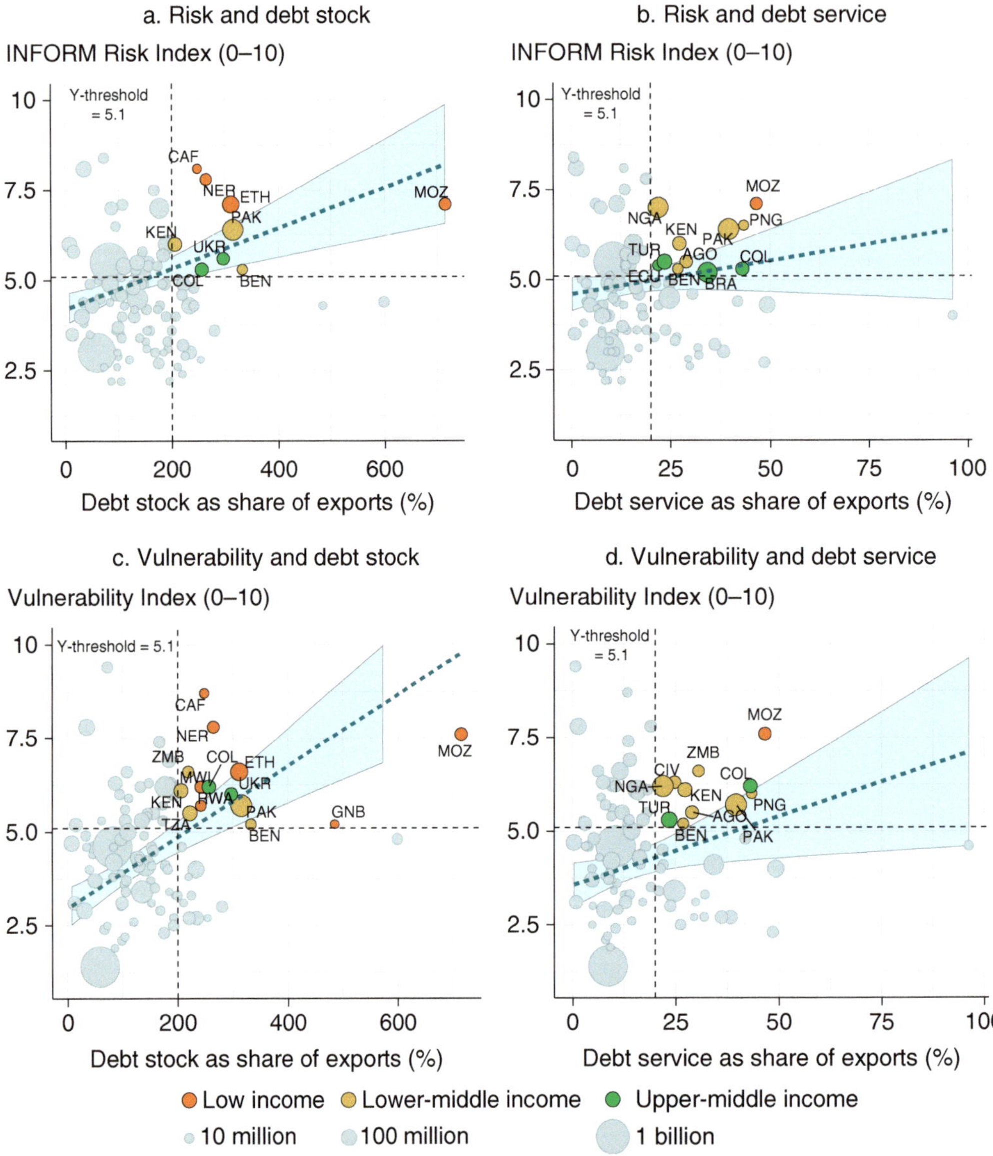

Sources: European Commission and Inter-Agency Standing Committee Reference Group on Risk, Early Warning and Preparedness, "DRMKC–INFORM," https://drmkc.jrc.ec.europa.eu/inform-index; Joint Research Centre, European Commission and United Nations agencies; World Bank International Debt Statistics and World Development Indicators databases.

Note: Bubble size and regression weights reflect 2024 populations. Trend lines represent population-weighted ordinary least squares regressions with 95 percent confidence intervals shaded. The analysis covers 105 countries with data on external debt and risk indexes. Panels a and b show INFORM Risk Index; panels c and d show vulnerability subscores. Countries are flagged as high risk if their index value exceeds 5.1. Latest INFORM data published in mid-2025, with underlying data up to 2025. Gray bubbles represent countries that do not fall into the high-risk quadrant.

Weak Fiscal and Institutional Capacity

A country's institutional capacity plays a critical role in shaping how debt burdens translate into development risks. A governments' ability to maintain macrofiscal stability, respond effectively to crises, and deliver essential public services depends heavily on the strength of its institutions, particularly the quality of public administration and the credibility of fiscal policy frameworks.

Figure 2.15 illustrates a strong relationship between external debt burdens and two global indicators of institutional capacity, underscoring the systemic link between financial pressures and the effectiveness of institutions. The Fiscal Policy score from the World Bank's Country Policy and Institutional Assessment evaluates the quality of fiscal policy in its stabilization and allocation functions. The score reflects how well a country uses public expenditure and revenue instruments to maintain macroeconomic stability and provide essential public goods—such as infrastructure and agricultural services—to support growth.[11] The Government Effectiveness score from the Worldwide Governance Indicators reflects perceptions of the quality of public services, the independence and professionalism of the civil service, and the government's ability to formulate and implement sound policies (Kaufmann, Kraay, and Mastruzzi 2010).

Fiscal Policy scores show a modest negative association with external debt levels. Although these scores are available only for IDA-eligible countries, the pattern suggests that several highly indebted countries also exhibit weak fiscal policy performance. Government Effectiveness scores, covering all 106 countries, display a stronger negative relationship with external debt. Many countries with elevated debt burdens register lower-than-average scores on governance quality—not only among LMICs but also in some upper-middle-income economies such as Argentina, Colombia, and Mongolia. Notably, Mozambique, Pakistan, Sri Lanka, and Zambia are consistently identified across multiple measures—underscoring their limited institutional capacity to respond effectively to emerging development challenges.

Figure 2.15 Institutional Capacity, by Country Debt Level

Fiscal Policy and Government Effectiveness scores

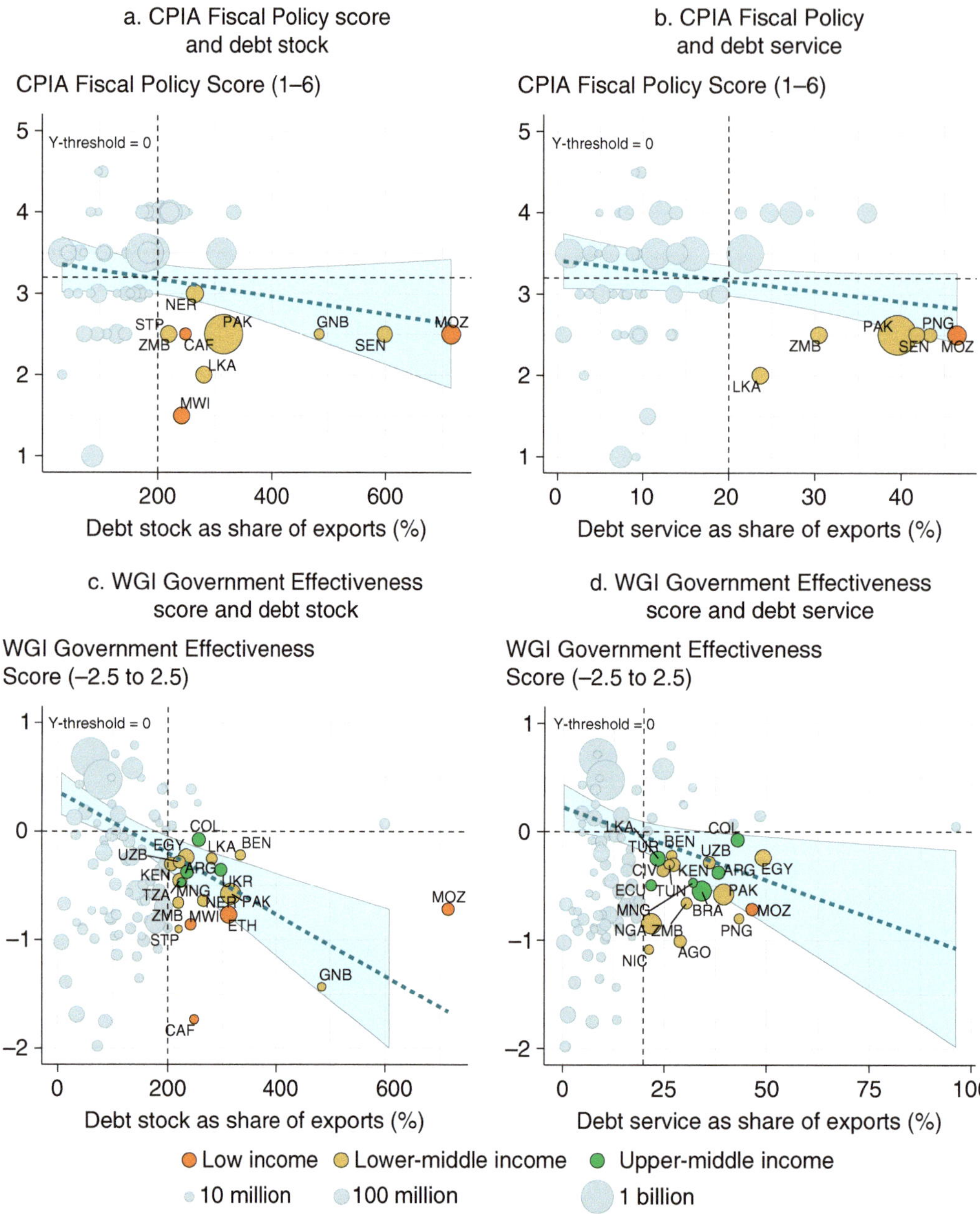

Sources: World Bank International Debt Statistics and World Development Indicators databases.
Note: Bubble size and regression weights reflect 2024 populations. Trend lines represent population-weighted ordinary least squares regressions with 95 percent confidence intervals shaded. Countries are flagged as institutionally weak if their CPIA Fiscal Policy score is below 3.2 or their WGI Government Effectiveness score is below 0. The 3.2 cutoff is based on related World Bank practice for identifying fragile and conflict-affected situations. The CPIA data set includes 63 countries (2024), and the WGI data set includes 106 countries (2023). Gray bubbles represent countries that do not fall into the high-risk quadrant. CPIA = Country Policy and Institutional Assessment; WGI = Worldwide Governance Indicators.

Taken together, the evidence presented in this section shows that external debt is not merely a fiscal metric but also a broader signal of development stress, one closely linked to nutrition insecurity, structural vulnerability, and institutional weakness. Countries with high debt burdens often face interlocking challenges across governance, fiscal capacity, and human development, creating feedback loops that reinforce fragility. At the same time, data gaps and incomplete reporting—particularly on domestic and private liabilities—can mask the true scale of risk, especially in countries with weaker statistical systems. These findings underscore the need for an integrated diagnostic approach that embeds debt data analysis within a wider development-risk framework, linking fiscal indicators with social, institutional, and human outcomes to inform more timely and effective policy responses.

3. Advancing Debt Transparency

Introduction

The World Bank has been collecting external debt data from borrowers since the 1950s and has disseminated those data to the public for over 50 years. The rationale for this annual collection of data from World Bank borrowers is to support both the institution's operational needs and debt transparency. Debt transparency is increasingly recognized as an unconditional public good and one that underpins sustainable development and financial stability. Transparent disclosure of public debt reduces the risk of hidden liabilities, fosters investor confidence, strengthens fiscal management, and allows citizens of borrowing countries and their development partners to hold governments accountable. By contrast, a lack of transparency raises uncertainty and borrowing costs, and complicates debt restructuring. In recent years, that driving force has become more concrete, sustained, and measured—a debt transparency agenda that seeks not only to strengthen the integrity of debtor-creditor relations but also to safeguard development outcomes.

Each year, the World Bank's International Debt Report makes significant progress in expanding the coverage, timeliness, and consistency of the debt data it disseminates. Over the past three years in particular, debt transparency has accelerated because of the coordinated efforts of borrower countries, bilateral and multilateral creditors, the international community, and academia.

The new Debtor Reporting System (DRS) reporting requirements, set to launch in 2026, will further advance the debt transparency agenda by compelling both debtors and creditors to disclose more granular information and additional information on collateralization and restructuring agreements. Meanwhile, the recent World Bank report "Radical [Debt] Transparency" calls for the implementation of stronger audit and oversight systems to ensure accountability and data reliability (World Bank 2025b). This chapter describes those coordinated actions and quantifies their impact to show the following: how data-sharing exercises have closed data gaps, how concerted reconciliation efforts and technical assistance missions have improved consistency, how debtor coverage and timeliness have improved, and how upgraded debt management systems can increase the accuracy of debt commitments and disbursements, expand instrument coverage, and reduce inconsistencies across sources. The World Bank is strongly committed to continuing to quantify how transparency has advanced and what the data now allow us to see.

Borrower Countries

The World Bank requires that all member countries that borrow from International Bank for Reconstruction and Development and the International Development Association (IDA) provide regular detailed reports at a debt instrument level on long-term external debt with an original maturity of over one year owed by a public agency or a private agency with a public guarantee. It also requires borrowers to report aggregate data on long-term external debt owed by the private sector with no public guarantee. Currently, 119 low- and middle-income countries (LMICs) and Guyana report to the DRS.

Borrower countries bear the primary responsibility for debt transparency, and the goal for these countries—with significant support from the World Bank—is comprehensive and timely disclosure of public debt commitments, repayment terms, and transactions sufficiently granular to facilitate scrutiny of government borrowing and public accountability. Achieving this goal, however, requires both the willingness to disclose and the capacity to do so.

Borrowers have made measurable strides in expanding their debt disclosure, particularly in recent years, with progress particularly visible in the accessibility, comprehensiveness, and timeliness of published public debt data. Although practices remain uneven across countries, regions, and income groups, the overall trend since 2020 reflects a growing recognition among borrower governments that complete and transparent reporting is in both their interests and those of their citizens.

Progress in Direct Public Debt Disclosure

Public debt data are disseminated in two forms: *direct*, when they are made public by national authorities in dedicated bulletins, and *indirect*, through their reporting to the World Bank's DRS. The World Bank regularly tracks and assesses the extent and progress of borrowing countries' public debt dissemination practices, presenting its assessment of these outcomes in an annual heat map[12] that measures the strengths and weaknesses of direct reporting in IDA-eligible countries across nine key indicators: data accessibility, instrument coverage, sectoral coverage, information on recently contracted external loans, periodicity, time lag, debt management strategy, annual borrowing plan, and additional statistics and memo items.

The Debt Reporting Heat Map shows significant improvement in public debt disclosure from 2020 to 2024. Of the 76 countries covered, the share of countries that do not publish any reports fell from close to 40 percent in 2020 to less than 25 percent, and now mostly includes fragile and conflict-afflicted countries or countries with severe capacity constraints.

In 2020, only 36 countries (47.4 percent) published fully accessible public debt data, whereas by 2023 this figure had risen to 51 countries (67.1 percent), representing a gain of close to 20 percentage points. The 2024 Heat Map found a 5-percentage-point improvement over the previous year: 55 countries (72.3 percent) had fully accessible public debt data (figure 3.1). Data accessibility in Sub-Saharan African nations remains lower than other regions, but it too continues to improve, rising from 19 nations publishing fully accessible data in 2020 to 30 in 2024, a 57.9 percent increase.

Policy Reforms and Institutionalization

IDA's Sustainable Development Finance Policy (SDFP) has been instrumental in embedding debt transparency reforms into national policy frameworks. The SDFP aims to incentivize countries to move toward transparent, sustainable financing and to promote coordination between IDA and other creditors in support of recipient countries' efforts. The SDFP recognizes that, although the implementation of transparent and sustainable financing practices requires actions by both creditors and borrowers, sound debt management—including debt transparency—remains the primary responsibility of borrowers.

Figure 3.1 Public Debt Disclosures by IDA-Eligible Countries, Access and Coverage, 2020 and 2024

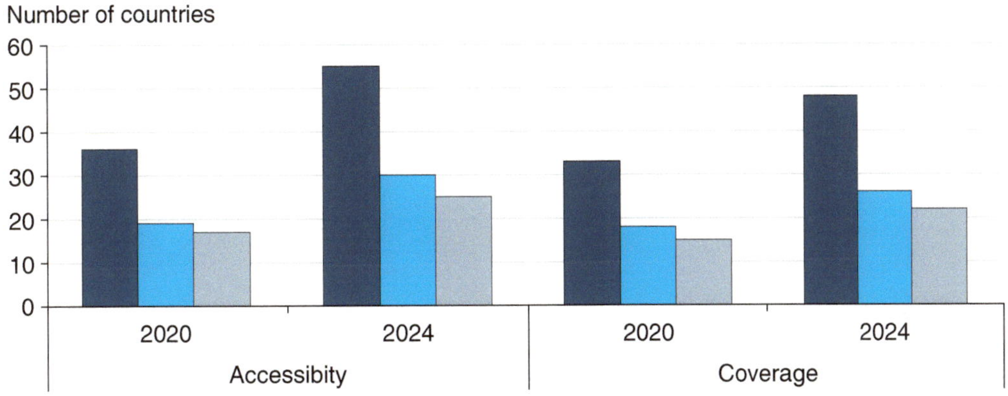

Sources: World Bank Debt Reporting Heat Maps 2020 and 2024.
Note: IDA = International Development Association.

Performance and policy actions (PPAs) are concrete actions and processes that borrowers adopt to enhance debt transparency, fiscal sustainability, and debt management. Since 2020, countries have implemented more than 700 PPAs, with one-fifth targeting transparency. In fiscal year 2024, almost half of IDA borrowers implemented at least one transparency-related policy action, ranging from expanded debt coverage (especially for state-owned enterprises [SOEs]) to the institutionalization of regular debt reports or bulletins. In fiscal year 2025, 61 IDA-eligible countries prepared a total of 152 PPAs.

SDFP conditionalities have driven measurable gains in debt transparency, with countries that implement more PPAs achieving higher disclosure standards, as measured by the Debt Reporting Heat Map. Countries implementing more PPAs under the SDFP achieved stronger gains in debt transparency: 80 percent of countries with three or more PPAs improved their heat map scores, compared to 58 percent with one to two PPAs and 60 percent with none (figure 3.2).

Reporting to the World Bank Debtor Reporting System

Reporting to the World Bank's DRS has also improved. Borrowers are increasingly submitting data on time, broadening coverage to include more debt instruments and sectors, and aligning reporting with international standards. These advances reduce gaps and asymmetries in global debt statistics, strengthen cross-country comparability, and enhance the system's role as a cornerstone of global debt transparency.

Figure 3.2 Share of Countries Improving or Backsliding on Debt Reporting Heat Map, by Number of Debt Transparency PPAs Implemented, 2021–24

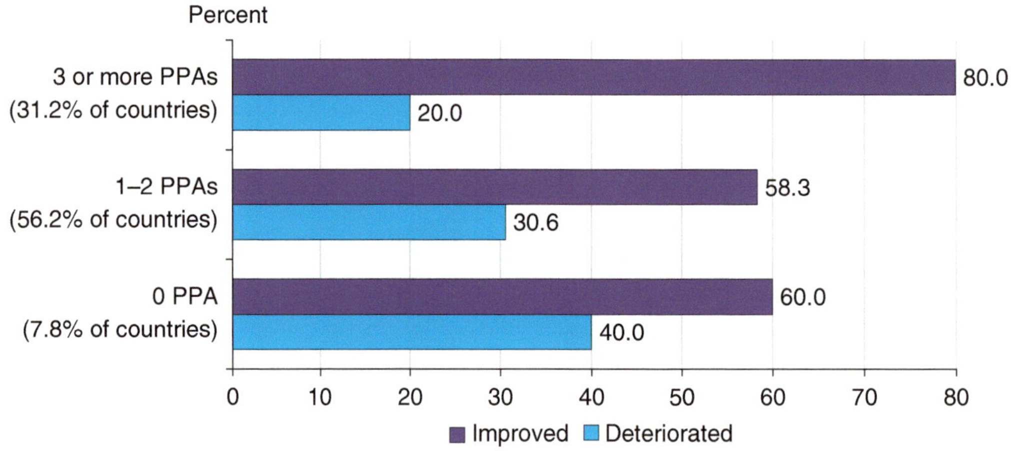

Sources: World Bank Debt Reporting Heat Map; World Bank Sustainable Development Finance Policy database.
Note: An improved country improved its average heat map scores in 2024 as compared to 2020; a deteriorated country's heat map scores deteriorated over the same period. Group labels show the percent of countries in each PPA group as a share of the total sample. PPA = performance and policy action.

The accuracy and coverage of reporting to the DRS have improved markedly over the past five years. To disclose public debt data on a regular basis in debt reports and bulletins, national debt offices must implement effective mechanisms to record and validate public debt data. In turn, these mechanisms lead to improvements in the coverage, accuracy, and timeliness of borrowers' reports to the DRS. The number of late reporters and nonreporters to the DRS fell from 28 in 2019 to just 8 in 2024, a 71.4 percent decrease. In addition, more countries are reporting earlier in the cycle, as shown in figure 3.3.

Reconciling Borrower and Creditor Data

Although borrower countries continue to improve debt data collection and reporting to the DRS, asymmetries persist between debt stock and flow data reported to the DRS and comparable creditor data. To address the issue of reconciling differences between borrower and creditor data, and to validate the accuracy of data reported to the DRS that are disseminated annually in the International Debt Report, the World Bank has cooperated with Group of Twenty (G-20) bilateral creditors since 2022 to harmonize their records of loans to IDA-eligible countries with the information submitted by those borrowers to the DRS. This cooperation has resulted in the World Bank Group of Seven (G-7)/Paris Club data-sharing exercise for end-2021 data, the first large-scale effort of its kind to systematically compare creditor- and debtor-reported data at the loan-by-loan level. Eighteen countries participated in the first exercise, including all G-7 countries plus 11 other members of the Paris Club.

Figure 3.3 Debtor Reporting System Reporting Timetable, 2019–24

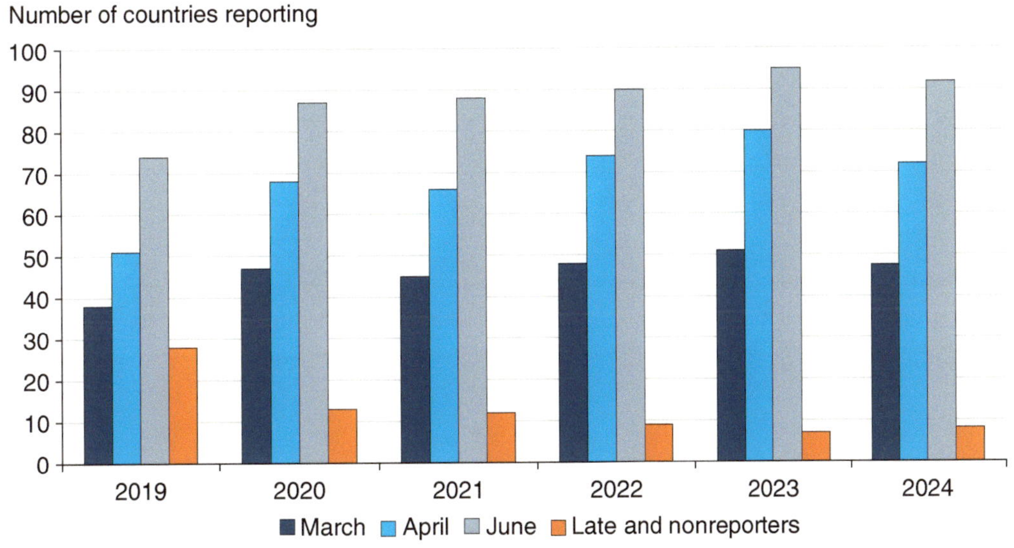

Source: World Bank Debtor Reporting System database.

The second round of data sharing and reconciliation, conducted in 2024 with end-2023 data, built on the success of the first round and focused on replicating the original comparison and improving post-reconciliation communication with both creditors and debtors. Seventeen creditor countries (all of the G-7 plus 10 Paris Club members) participated. Creditors reported 4,692 individual loans or tranches—over 1,000 more items than in the first round—reflecting both new loans extended in 2022 and 2023 and the inclusion of Sri Lanka. Of the loans reported by creditors, 73 percent were matched to a DRS counterpart. The matched loans accounted for the majority (94 percent) of end-2023 outstanding debt reported by creditors, and the overall difference between creditor claims and the amount outstanding reported by debtors to the DRS was less than 1 percent. Unmatched items (1,255 loans) represented about 6 percent of creditor claims, suggesting that the gap between borrower and creditor data is narrow and resolvable through agreements on methodology and follow-up discussions.

The differences reflect technical issues rather than missing data and have two major reasons: (a) the practice of some creditors to report each disbursement tranche as a separate loan whereas most debtors report one consolidated loan; and (b) the indemnification of export credit guarantees that convert contingent liabilities of an official export credit agency into a direct bilateral claim. In principle, borrowers are asked to report to the DRS if a loan from a private creditor benefits from an export credit guarantee. This information is not systematically reported by borrowers, however, and most bilateral creditors do not publish information on loans they have guaranteed.

The World Bank is confident that, with appropriate input from debtors and creditors, all loans can eventually be matched and any discrepancies between end-2023 creditor claims and debt outstanding reported by debtors to the DRS eliminated—a milestone achievement. To a large extent, the gap has already been closed, as evidenced by a comparison of the results from the first round of the data-sharing exercises with those of the second round. Between the 2022 and 2024 reconciliation exercises, coverage of legacy (pre-2022) obligations improved materially. In total, 723 additional loans accounting for US$8.8 billion were matched (figure 3.4), largely because of improved communications with borrowers and creditor countries, and reporting of additional information, particularly with regard to borrowers' reporting of loan tranches.

Figure 3.4 Debt Stock of Newly Matched Loans between End-2021 and End-2023, G-7/Paris Club Data-Sharing Exercise

US$ (billion)

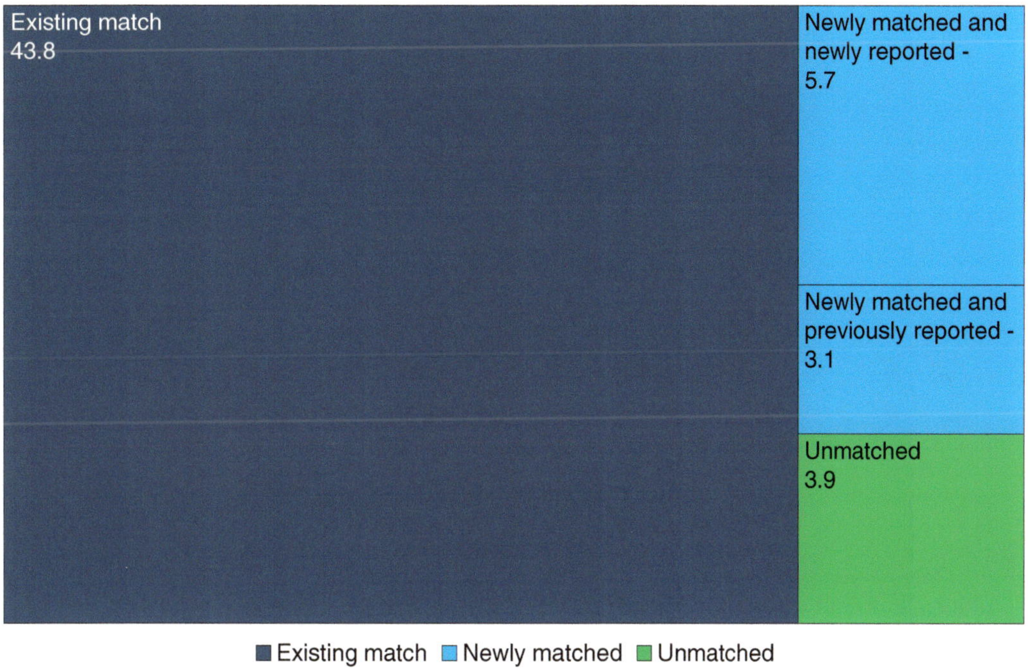

Sources: G7/Paris Club creditor files; World Bank Debtor Reporting System.
Note: Excludes loans contracted in 2022–23. G7 = Group of Seven.

The latest data reconciliation exercise also shows that the gap between borrower and creditor data has narrowed for individual creditors. For 10 of the 17 participating creditors, the end-2023 claims align closely with the comparable figure reported by borrowers to the DRS. For 7 creditors, a larger difference with DRS data is observed and stems in part from issues discussed earlier with regard to loan tranches and indemnification of claims on guaranteed export credits. Other factors include misclassification by borrowers of direct and guaranteed export credits, loans extended by creditors to private sector companies that are not reported to the DRS at the loan level, or methodological differences in borrower/creditor accounting of debt swaps. Figure 3.5 compares the total end-2023 claims reported by each of the 17 creditors as outstanding with the total debt owed to those same creditors reported to the DRS by the borrowers. Points on the dashed line indicate perfect alignment between debtor and creditor reporting.

Figure 3.5 Asymmetries between Creditor and Borrower Claims on Debt Outstanding Position at End-2023

Total reported by creditors (US$, million)

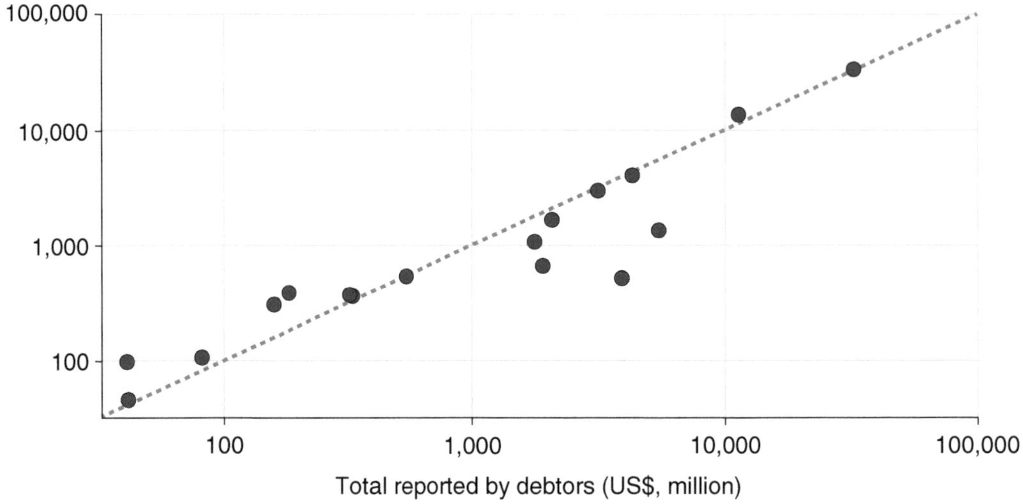

Sources: G-7/Paris Club creditor files; World Bank Debtor Reporting System.
Note: Data for selected International Development Association debtors and G-7/Paris Club creditors. Both axes are on a logarithmic scale. G7 = Group of Seven.

The World Bank and creditors are committed to addressing these issues by refining the data-sharing template, institutionalizing an annual sharing exercise, and expanding participation beyond the G-7 and Paris Club creditors to the broader group of G-20 countries. These steps, combined with bilateral dialogue with both creditors and borrowers, are designed to make reconciliation faster, more replicable, and more complete in future rounds.

The World Bank is also testing innovative information technology solutions to digitalize and automatically reconcile debt records. In 2025, the World Bank launched a pilot project in Indonesia, funded by the Japanese Ministry of Finance, for the development of a digital platform facilitating information sharing between borrowers and official creditors. Both parties would connect to the platform to transfer or receive digital information related to loan contracts and related transactions. For each new transaction (that is, new loan signed, payment, disbursement, or modification), the originator would create a new data file electronically transmitted to the platform according to standardized templates. The counterpart would validate the information and automatically transfer the data as needed into its own debt recording system. The platform will restrict access to individual loan data to the respective borrower and creditor, and will generate aggregated statistics only. In Indonesia, the debt office can now automatically transfer World Bank loan data for validation and upload the data into the local debt system, and efforts are under way to cover other official creditors.

Measuring Progress: Data Revisions and Transparency Outcomes

Progress in improving debt data transparency is evidenced by the introduction of new data sets and revisions to the DRS database to improve accuracy and coverage as additional or more comprehensive data become available. In 2021, the Bank introduced a new four-dimensional database that incorporates the breakdown by individual creditor country and multilateral institution in published data. Previously, the database had three dimensions: debtor country, type of borrower and type of creditor series, and time. The new database facilitates creditor-by-creditor reconciliation of data reported to the DRS with information published by borrowers in debt bulletins, as illustrated in the case of Guinea-Bissau (box 3.1), or made available by creditors. It also allows the World Bank to make more comprehensive analyses of the systematic improvements in the accuracy and coverage of the database on a continuous basis as new data become available.

Box 3.1 Guinea-Bissau: A Commitment to Debt Transparency

[*Note:* This box was prepared before the government transition that occurred in November 2025.]

Guinea-Bissau is one of the world's poorest and most fragile countries, with a history of political and institutional fragility dating back to independence from Portugal in 1974. It is characterized by significant economic vulnerabilities, high risk of debt distress, and limited institutional capacity and human resources.

Despite those and other challenges, the government is committed to transparent disclosure of public debt data. A National Committee on Debt Policy was instituted in 2021, and decrees were issued to establish the responsibilities of the Debt Directorate. Monitoring and recording of public debt were strengthened with support from the International Monetary Fund and the World Bank. In 2023, a Ministerial Order expanded the coverage of the debt bulletin and mandated quarterly publication.

Accurate and timely reporting to the World Bank Debtor Reporting System (DRS) is key to debt transparency. In this context, the Debt Directorate and the World Bank recently collaborated on a comprehensive review of the data reported to the DRS since 2007 to determine that they (a) captured borrowing from all external creditors, and (b) mirrored the data in the national record and published in debt bulletins. For a small country, Guinea-Bissau has a relatively complex external debt portfolio, with 19 creditors and 98 active loans as of end-2024.

The review improved the coverage and accuracy of DRS data. From 2020 to 2024, it added a total of US$160 million to external public debt stocks. Most of the increase (US$129 million, or 81 percent) resulted from the reconciliation of the DRS database

(Box continues on next page)

Box 3.1 Guinea-Bissau: A Commitment to Debt Transparency (*continued*)

with the records of the Debt Directorate and the availability of more detailed information. The inclusion of loans from the Economic Community of West African States and from Spain, previously omitted from the DRS reports, added US$31 million, or 19 percent. The overall difference in the 2024 debt stock was reduced to less than 1 percent, largely because of small exchange rate differences.

Classification, rather than a lack of transparency, accounts for the seemingly large difference between DRS data and information in the debt bulletin. Guinea-Bissau considers debt owed to the Central Bank of West African States and bonds raised in the regional market as domestic public debt, whereas the DRS classifies them as external debt in line with the international, residency-based definition (figure B3.1.1).[a] The difference in classification has no impact on total public debt, which remains unchanged.

Figure B3.1.1 External Debt Stock: Comparison of DRS and Debt Bulletins, 2023 and 2024

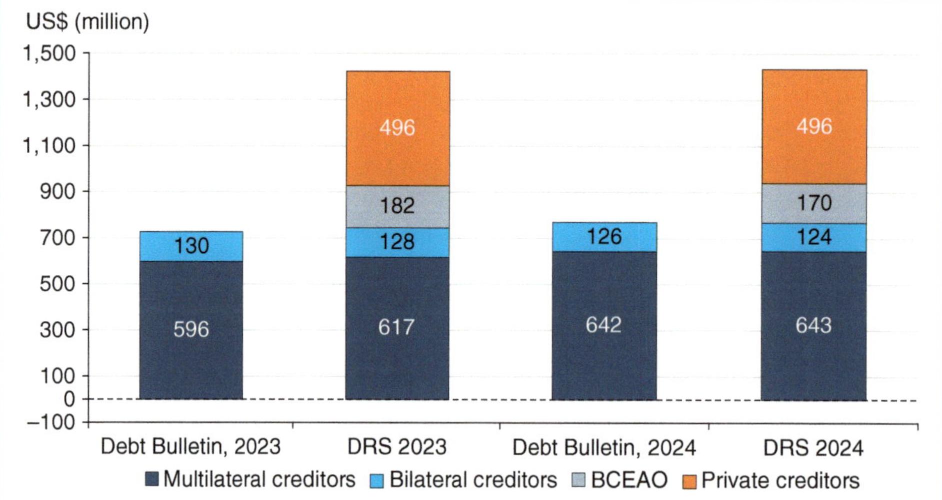

Sources: Ministério das Finanças 2024, 2025; World Bank International Debt Statistics database.
Note: BCEAO = Central Bank of West African States; DRS = World Bank Debtor Reporting System.

Going forward, continuous monitoring of external borrowing and accurate reporting to the DRS remain critical to the dissemination of transparent and accurate data that are essential for sound public debt management and maintaining the support and confidence of stakeholders.

(Box continues on next page)

Box 3.1 Guinea-Bissau: A Commitment to Debt Transparency (*continued*)

a. Expansion and quarterly publication of the Debt Bulletin reflected an IDA Sustainable Development Finance Policy fiscal year 2023 policy performance action. The DRS definition of external debt accords with the international standards of the System of National Accounts and the Balance of Payments, which is based on residency. The Central Bank of West African States, the regional central bank for eight states, including Guinea-Bissau, is classified as a nonresident international institution.

An analysis of five vintages of International Debt Statistics, including the one accompanying this report, reveals for LMICs excluding China an upward revision of US$229.4 billion in previously unrecorded external public and publicly guaranteed commitments contracted over the past decade because of systematic improvements in accuracy and expansion in coverage of the database. This revision equates to, on average, a 5.6 percent increase in annual commitments to LMICs from 2014 to 2024, with the newly recorded commitments divided almost equally between official creditors (US$113.6 billion) and private creditors (US$115.8 billion) (figure 3.6).

Figure 3.6 Ex Post Revision of Commitments, Low- and Middle-Income Countries (Excluding China), 2014–24

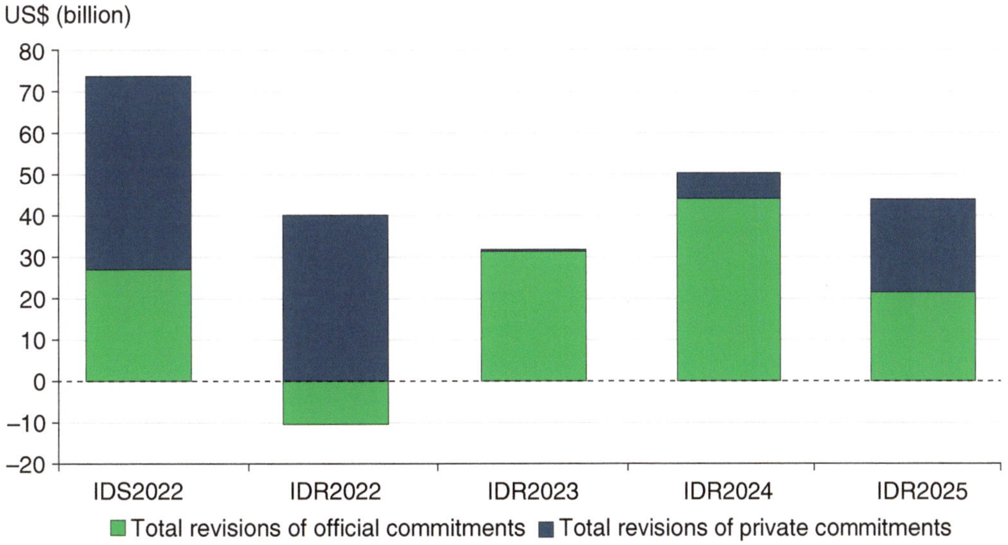

Sources: World Bank International Debt Statistics database, 2022–25.
Note: The figure quantifies the revisions as a result of the analysis using International Debt Statistics data to review public and publicly guaranteed commitments reported in IDS2022 and IDR2022 through 2025. IDR = International Debt Report; IDS = International Debt Statistics.

Several factors account for these ex post revisions of the commitment figures. From the borrower perspective, first and foremost, there is often a lag of one to two years in reporting on loan commitments to the DRS because borrowers often do not record loan commitments in the loan accounting system until a disbursement occurs. Second, measures taken by LMICs to strengthen the capacity to monitor and record external borrowing or to upgrade debt management software will invariably improve the accuracy and coverage of the national database and lead to more timely and comprehensive reporting to the DRS. For example, Angola added US$29.3 billion in commitments from private creditors, and Tanzania added US$4.3 billion divided roughly equally between official and private creditors. Large-scale data revisions occurred in South Africa when it transitioned to loan-level reporting to the DRS, having previously reported in aggregate. Although this shift did not materially affect the overall level of outstanding debt, the more granular data provided information on US$19.2 billion in commitments from private creditors. Occasionally a country may pay off all loans to the World Bank and be removed from the DRS database, only to subsequently resume borrowing and reporting to the DRS. A case in point is Turkmenistan, which returned to the database in 2021 after a four-year hiatus, adding US$6.9 billion in commitments, most of which were from official creditors.

A major reason for the upward revision of commitments is the concerted effort by the World Bank Group's Debt Statistics Team to ensure that external public debt recorded in the DRS captures borrowing by central banks, including bilateral currency swaps and borrowing of SOEs, which often constitute an important component of external debt. Bilateral currency swaps with the People's Bank of China—and, for countries in South Asia, the Reserve Bank of India—have been a key factor in the upward revision of commitments to Argentina, Bhutan, the Arab Republic of Egypt, the Lao People's Democratic Republic, Maldives, Pakistan, and Sri Lanka. Deposits from China and the Gulf States have also led to revised commitment data for several countries including Egypt and Pakistan.

The steady rise in the number of borrowers that include the external obligations of SOEs in the data reported to the DRS often accounts for the largest share of the ex post increase in commitments, because this borrowing is often significant. In 2022, Türkiye reported additional commitments of US$5.8 billion spread over several years to SOEs, primarily public banks. Similarly, in 2023, Viet Nam provided information on US$5 billion in commitments to SOEs from official and private creditors not previously reported to the DRS.

Improved Debt Management Capacity, Standards, and Methodology

Capacity building and standard setting have been essential enablers of transparency gains. Regular World Bank training workshops and technical assistance have strengthened the ability of national authorities to produce higher-quality debt data. At the same time, harmonization of definitions and the adoption of reconciliation templates have fostered greater consistency across countries and creditors.

In this context, the World Bank Group's Debt Statistics Team held two recent workshops—the first in Perugia, Italy, in June 2024 and the second in Chiba, Japan, in April 2025—that brought together a group of debt management professionals and central bankers for a technical deep dive and strategic dialogue on the evolving debt ecosystem. Participants explored the gaps and discrepancies that undermine debt sustainability and complicate restructuring efforts, and they examined the rationale to improve transparency and resilience in their own debt reporting processes. The workshops also looked at important debt-related issues such as how to improve debt sustainability, increase transparency, and facilitate swifter restructuring.

In addition, the World Bank continues to offer direct, hands-on assistance to DRS reporting countries in the form of technical assistance missions. These missions typically entail World Bank staff traveling to reporting countries to work side by side with government officials to improve their databases, reporting, and understanding of DRS methodology. Such assistance can help resolve issues and overcome challenges in obtaining the best possible data.

Debt transparency is also a key component of the broader debt-management technical assistance that the World Bank, together with the International Monetary Fund and international and regional implementing partners, provides through the Debt Management Facility Program. This program provides technical assistance to 89 developing countries as of fiscal year 2025 in areas such as Debt Management Performance Assessments, the Medium-Term Debt Management Strategy, and the formulation of Debt Reform Plans. The third phase of the Debt Management Facility Program, launched in 2019, has also focused on debt transparency by offering technical assistance in reviewing the legal framework and institutional arrangements related to debt reporting, assessing quality of back-office functions, identifying gaps in publication of debt reports, and making recommendations aligned with sound practices.

Next Steps: Institutionalizing Debt Transparency Gains

Looking ahead, the priority is to ensure that recent transparency gains are consolidated and institutionalized. Achieving this goal will require several initiatives.

Data-sharing exercises. The World Bank plans to extend its annual data-sharing exercise to all G-20 countries, plus any other lending nations that want to participate. It will also work more closely with the G-7 and other lending countries to address discrepancies and request appropriate corrections to DRS data. It will follow up with debtors about anomalies or lags that the sharing exercise identifies in their reports to the DRS, and it will keep exploring innovative solutions to facilitate debt reconciliation.

The World Bank will also continue its efforts to expand the coverage of SOE debt and private sector debt to gain a more comprehensive picture of what borrower countries, including the private sector, owe and to whom they owe it.

Policy reforms. Through the SDFP, currently in its sixth year of implementation, the World Bank will continue to incentivize IDA-eligible countries to move toward transparent, sustainable financing. Under the SDFP's Program of Creditor Outreach, the World Bank will continue to leverage its role as a convener and enabler to promote stronger collective action, greater debt transparency, and closer coordination among borrowers and creditors to mitigate debt-related risks. Effective collective action by creditors—including multilateral development banks, other international financial institutions, bilateral lenders, and private sector creditors—can help mitigate debt-related risks pertaining to supply-side factors. As part of the Program of Creditor Outreach, IDA will broaden and strengthen its engagement with international financial institutions, including through the development and promotion of sustainable financing principles. IDA will also enhance transparency and communication on sustainable financing with a broad range of creditors, including through dialogue on the SDFP, and other information-sharing initiatives.

Technical assistance missions will also remain vital to sustaining momentum on debt transparency gains. Under the fourth phase of the Debt Management Facility Program, to be launched in 2025, technical assistance and training will continue to be provided on debt recording, investor relations, monitoring, and reporting to increase the number of countries that perform satisfactorily in this area of government debt management. Activities will also focus on enshrining debt transparency in legislation and improving policies and procedures, including through the rollout of the new, automated real-time debt reconciliation tool and other tools for managing loans and bonds.

Finally, leveraging modern debt management systems for integrated, real-time reporting and maintaining international and academic scrutiny of LMIC debt will help to ensure that transparency gains already made are locked into place and that further gains are enabled.

Notes

1. Top 10 borrowers in 2024 comprised China, India, Brazil, Mexico, Türkiye, Indonesia, Argentina, Colombia, Ukraine, and Thailand.
2. Because the World Bank's Debtor Reporting System does not collect data on domestic debt, domestic debt figures presented in this report are derived from country reports to the World Bank–IMF Quarterly Public Sector Debt database, publicly available country debt bulletins, and market sources.
3. For further information please visit World Bank, "Donor Financing Mechanisms for Ukraine," https://www.worldbank.org/en/country/ukraine/brief/world-bank-group-donor-financing-mechanisms-for-supporting-ukraine.
4. Sri Lanka was not eligible for the Debt Service Suspension Initiative or the Common Framework because it was not classified as IDA-only when they were initiated.
5. The conversion of medium-term deposits to equity is reflected as forgiveness of external debt in International Debt Statistics. The conversion of short-term deposits is recorded as a reduction in the stock of short-term debt but is indistinguishable from other changes in the stock of short-term debt.
6. The Low-Income Country Debt Sustainability Framework covers 69 countries.
7. The pandemic amplified the reliance on domestic borrowing, particularly for Sub-Saharan Africa, frontier LIC DSF countries, and LIC DSF countries characterized by fragile and conflict-affected situations; LIC DSF governments borrowed more heavily in domestic markets to meet the sudden increase in financing needs.
8. Data on public domestic debt composition cover 60 out of the 69 countries under the LIC DSF. The analysis excludes 9 countries because of the lack of published data or of sufficiently detailed data: Afghanistan, Eritrea, Myanmar, Sudan, and the Republic of Yemen due to the lack of a recent LIC Debt Sustainability Analysis and Samoa, Solomon Islands, Tonga, and Tuvalu due to lack of sufficiently detailed data.
9. Domestic debt transparency in LICs has improved since 2020 according to the World Bank's annual assessment of the transparency of domestic debt issuance, with notable advances among active issuers. More countries have adopted market-based instruments, with the share of LICs relying on auctions for more than half of their domestic borrowing rising by 15 percent (to 30 countries by 2023). The number of countries publishing issuance calendars also increased by 20 percent, to 30 out of 69 LICs. These advances have improved predictability and communication with market participants. However, weak implementation and gaps in post-issuance transparency continue to constrain market development.
10. European Commission and Inter-Agency Standing Committee Reference Group on Risk, Early Warning and Preparedness, "DRMKC–INFORM," https://drmkc.jrc.ec.europa.eu/inform-index.
11. Using data from the World Bank's World Development Indicators, https://databank.worldbank.org/source/world-development-indicators.
12. World Bank, "Debt Reporting Heat Map—2024," https://www.worldbank.org/en/topic/debt/brief/debt-transparency-report/2024.

References

Adarov, A., and H. Pallan. 2025. "Foreign Direct Investment in Retreat: Policies to Turn the Tide." Conference Edition, World Bank, Washington, DC. https://openknowledge.worldbank.org/server/api/core/bitstreams/7c3cf4fc-7fea-4e17-9d52-0aa7ed15fd15/content.

AfriCatalyst. 2025. "Debt over Development? New Report Reveals Debt Trap Draining Developing Nations of Vital Services." *AfriCatalyst* (blog), June 30, 2025. https://africatalyst.com/debt-over-development-new-report-reveals-debt-trap-draining-developing-nations-of-vital-services/.

Baker, S. R., N. Bloom, and S. J. Davis. 2016. "Measuring Economic Policy Uncertainty." *Quarterly Journal of Economics* 131 (4): 1593–636. https://academic.oup.com/qje/article-abstract/131/4/1593/2468873?redirectedFrom=fulltext.

Brandão-Marques, L., M. Casiraghi, G. Gelos, O. Harrison, and G. Kamber. 2023. "Is High Debt Constraining Monetary Policy? Evidence from Inflation Expectations." IMF Working Paper WP/23/143, International Monetary Fund, Washington, DC. https://www.imf.org/en/-/media/files/publications/wp/2023/english/wpiea2023143-print-pdf.pdf.

Dessus, S., and C. Constantinescu. 2024. "Trade and Development Chart—Increasingly Volatile Exports Amplify Supply Uncertainty." *The Trade Post* (blog), March 28, 2024. https://blogs.worldbank.org/en/trade/trade-and-development-chart--increasingly-volatile-exports-ampli.

El Khalfi, O., R. Chaâbita, M. Benboubker, M. Ghoujdam, K. Zahraoui, H. El Alaoui, S. Laalam, I. Belhaj, and H. Hammouch. 2024. "The Impact of External Debt on Economic Growth: The Case of Emerging Countries." *Research in Globalization* 9: 100248. https://doi.org/10.1016/j.resglo.2024.100248.

FAO (Food and Agriculture Organization of the United Nations), IFAD (International Fund for Agricultural Development), UNICEF (United Nations Children's Fund), WFP (World Food Programme), and WHO (World Health Organization). 2025. *The State of Food Security and Nutrition in the World 2025: Addressing High Food Price Inflation for Food Security and Nutrition*. Rome: FAO, IFAD, UNICEF, WFP, and WHO. https://doi.org/10.4060/cd6008en.

Federspiel, F., J. Borghi, and M. Martinez-Alvarez. 2022. "Growing Debt Burden in Low- and Middle-Income Countries during COVID-19 May Constrain Health Financing." *Global Health Action* 15 (1): 2072461. https://doi.org/10.1080/16549716.2022.2072461.

Fu, H., J. Rosero Moncayo, Y. Bai, C. Cafiero, V. Conti, and M. Rissanen. 2025. "Can Everyone Afford to Eat Healthy? New Data Show Progress, but Not Everywhere." *Data Blog*, August 6, 2025. https://blogs.worldbank.org/en/opendata/can-everyone-afford-to-eat-healthy--new-data-show-progress--but-.

Hashimoto, H., Y. Mooi, G. Pedras, A. Roy, K. Chung, T. Galeza, M. G. Papaioannou, P. Katz, Z. Bango, J. A. Gragnani, B. Gurhy, and C. Paladines. 2021. *Guidance Note for Developing Government Local Currency Bond Markets*. Washington, DC: International Monetary Fund and World Bank. https://doi.org/10.5089/9781513573922.064.

Heimberger, P. 2023. "Do Higher Public Debt Levels Reduce Economic Growth? A Meta-regression Analysis." *Journal of Economic Surveys* 37 (4): 1101–33. https://doi.org/10.1111/joes.12536.

IMF (International Monetary Fund). 2024. *Fiscal Monitor: Putting a Lid on Public Debt*. Washington, DC: IMF. https://www.imf.org/en/publications/fm/issues/2024/10/23/fiscal-monitor-october-2024.

IMF (International Monetary Fund) and World Bank. 2020. "Staff Note for the G20 International Financial Architecture Working Group (IFAWG): Recent Developments On Local Currency Bond Markets In Emerging Economies." IMF and World Bank, Washington, DC. https://documents.worldbank.org/pt/publication/documents-reports/documentdetail/129961580334830825.

IMF (International Monetary Fund) and World Bank. 2022. *Making Debt Work for Development and Macroeconomic Stability*. Policy Papers 2022 (019). Washington, DC: IMF and World Bank. https://doi.org/10.5089/9798400208591.007.

Kaufmann, D., A. Kraay, and M. Mastruzzi. 2010. "The Worldwide Governance Indicators: Methodology and Analytical Issues." Policy Research Working Paper 5430, World Bank, Washington, DC. http://hdl.handle.net/10986/3913.

Kose, M. A., P. Nagle, F. Ohnsorge, and N. Sugawara. 2021. *Global Waves of Debt: Causes and Consequences*. Washington, DC: World Bank. https://documents1.worldbank.org/curated/en/121251614759884881/pdf/Global-Waves-of-Debt-Causes-and-Consequences.pdf.

Kraay, A., and V. Nehru. 2006. "When Is External Debt Sustainable?" *World Bank Economic Review* 20 (3): 341–65. https://doi.org/10.1093/wber/lhl006.

Ministério das Finanças, Guiné-Bissau. 2024. *Boletim Anual de Estatisticas da Dívida Pública 2023*. Governo da Guiné-Bissau. https://www.mef.gw/boletim-estatistico-da-divida-publica/boletim-anual-de-estatistica-da-divida-publica-2023/viewdocument/112.

Ministério das Finanças, Guiné-Bissau. 2025. *Boletim Anual de Estatisticas da Dívida Pública 2024*. Governo da Guiné-Bissau. https://mef.gw/boletim-estatistico-da-divida-publica/boletim-estatistico-da-divida-publica-anual-2024/viewdocument/164.

Stojanov, A., J. Engel, and G. Varela. 2024. "How Exports React to Exchange Rate Fluctuations—and What It Means for Low- and Middle-Income Countries." *The Trade Post* (blog), April 24, 2024 https://blogs.worldbank.org/en/trade/how-exports-react-to-exchange-rate-fluctuations--and-what-it-mea.

World Bank. 2023. "An Ounce of Prevention, a Pound of Cure: Averting and Dealing with Sovereign Debt Default." Spotlight, South Asia Development Update, October, Washington, DC. https://openknowledge.worldbank.org/server/api/core/bitstreams/7df29a1f-5a5e-46b5-a497-f24736daad00/content.

World Bank. 2024. "Tackling Inequality to Revitalize Growth and Reduce Poverty in Africa." Africa's Pulse, No. 29 (Spring 2024). World Bank, Washington, DC. https://doi.org/10.1596/978-1-4648-2109-7.

World Bank. 2025a. *Fragile and Conflict-Affected Situations: Intertwined Crises, Multiple Vulnerabilities*. Washington, DC: World Bank. https://openknowledge.worldbank.org/server/api/core/bitstreams/35bb4b31-e9b0-4a1e-8c6c-df4336558673/content.

World Bank. 2025b. "Radical [Debt] Transparency." World Bank, Washington, DC. https://documents1.worldbank.org/curated/en/099439106192540687/pdf/IDU-a86e3bb4-3446-4716-9131-085141b81950.pdf.

PART 2
Aggregate and Country Tables

Note:
0 or 0.0 means zero or small enough that the number would round to zero at the displayed number of decimal places.
.. means that data are not available or that aggregates cannot be calculated because of missing data in the years shown.
Percent share may not add up to 100 percent because of rounding.

ALL LOW- AND MIDDLE-INCOME COUNTRIES

(US$ billion, unless otherwise indicated)

Snapshot	**2024**
Total external debt stocks	**8,937**
External debt stocks as % of:	
Exports	90
GNI	23
Debt service as % of:	
Exports	13
GNI	3
Net financial flows, debt and equity	569
Net debt inflows	210
Net equity inflows	359
GNI	**38,192**
Population (million)	**6,595**

Figure 1 Public and publicly guaranteed debt, by creditor and creditor type in 2024, including IMF credit

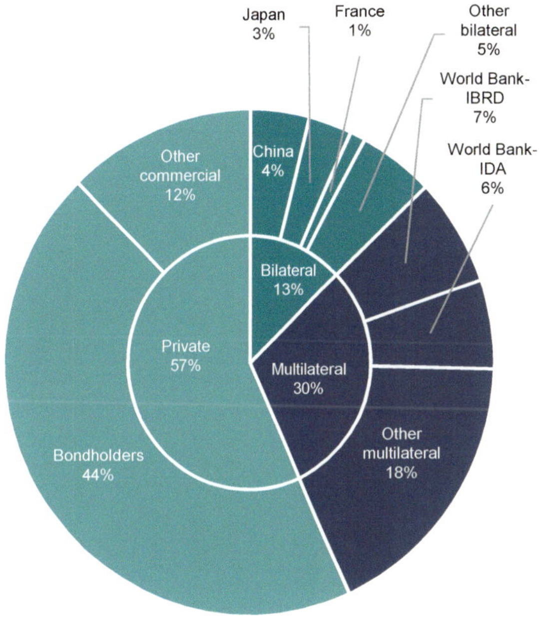

Figure 2 Average terms on new debt commitments from official and private creditors

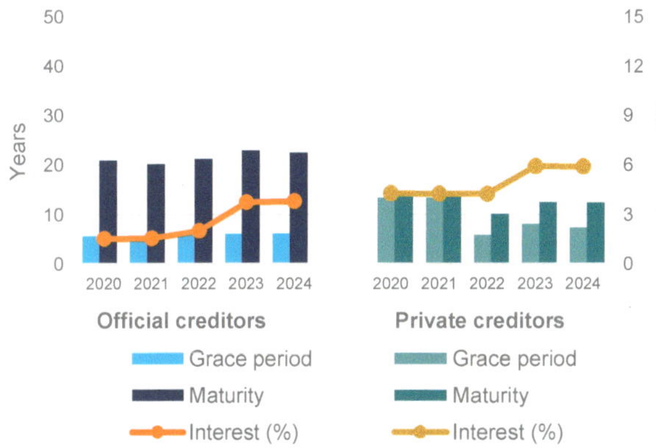

Summary External Debt Data	**2010**	**2020**	**2021**	**2022**	**2023**	**2024**
Total external debt stocks	**3,857**	**8,147**	**8,794**	**8,681**	**8,836**	**8,937**
Long-term external debt stocks	**2,640**	**5,873**	**6,149**	**6,042**	**6,120**	**6,171**
Public and publicly guaranteed debt from:	*1,390*	*3,177*	*3,401*	*3,383*	*3,471*	*3,560*
Official creditors	809	1,267	1,296	1,334	1,431	1,463
Multilateral	460	774	807	854	938	987
of which: World Bank	235	375	387	405	436	463
Bilateral	349	493	489	480	493	475
Private creditors	582	1,910	2,105	2,048	2,040	2,097
Bondholders	434	1,548	1,711	1,643	1,611	1,637
Commercial banks and others	148	363	394	405	429	460
Private nonguaranteed debt from:	*1,249*	*2,696*	*2,748*	*2,660*	*2,649*	*2,611*
Bondholders	207	645	664	594	543	538
Commercial banks and others	1,042	2,051	2,085	2,065	2,106	2,073
Use of IMF credit and SDR allocations	**125**	**215**	**386**	**381**	**381**	**372**
IMF credit	49	144	141	147	145	143
SDR allocations	75	71	246	233	235	229
Short-term external debt stocks	**1,092**	**2,059**	**2,259**	**2,258**	**2,335**	**2,394**
Disbursements, long-term	**576**	**1,142**	**1,237**	**959**	**1,076**	**993**
Public and publicly guaranteed sector	235	460	541	355	388	499
Private sector not guaranteed	342	682	695	604	688	494
Principal repayments, long-term	**314**	**794**	**849**	**948**	**996**	**850**
Public and publicly guaranteed sector	105	240	262	293	299	327
Private sector not guaranteed	210	554	587	656	697	523
Interest payments, long-term	**85**	**183**	**203**	**199**	**255**	**263**
Public and publicly guaranteed sector	44	99	106	108	138	145
Private sector not guaranteed	41	84	97	91	118	119

EAST ASIA AND PACIFIC

(US$ billion, unless otherwise indicated)

Snapshot	2024
Total external debt stocks	**3,409**
External debt stocks as % of:	
Exports	63
GNI	16
Debt service as % of:	
Exports	9
GNI	2
Net financial flows, debt and equity	119
Net debt inflows	10
Net equity inflows	109
GNI	**21,664**
Population (million)	**2,079**

Figure 1 Public and publicly guaranteed debt, by creditor and creditor type in 2024, including IMF credit

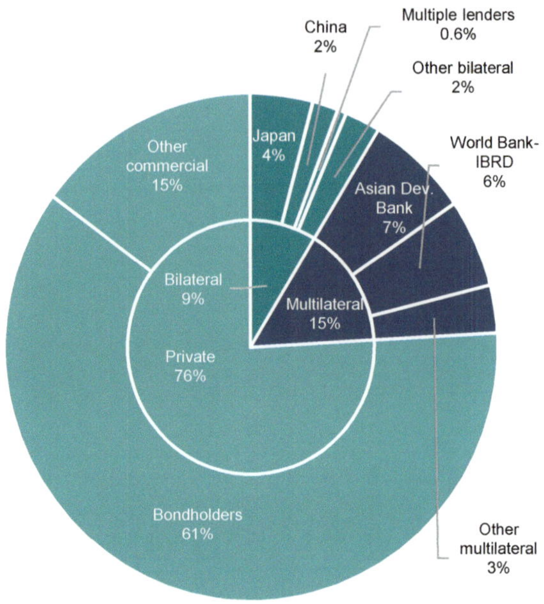

Figure 2 Average terms on new debt commitments from official and private creditors

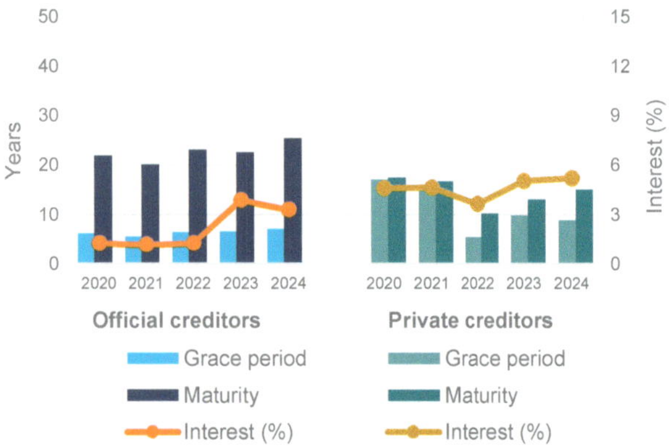

Summary External Debt Data	2010	2020	2021	2022	2023	2024
Total external debt stocks	**1,193**	**3,264**	**3,697**	**3,497**	**3,417**	**3,409**
Long-term external debt stocks	**558**	**1,853**	**2,086**	**1,978**	**1,878**	**1,831**
Public and publicly guaranteed debt from:	*319*	*838*	*997*	*960*	*923*	*951*
Official creditors	217	236	234	229	232	228
Multilateral	87	130	135	138	144	145
of which: World Bank	47	66	68	69	71	71
Bilateral	130	105	99	91	88	83
Private creditors	102	603	762	731	691	723
Bondholders	73	534	677	634	575	581
Commercial banks and others	29	68	86	96	116	142
Private nonguaranteed debt from:	*240*	*1,015*	*1,089*	*1,018*	*955*	*881*
Bondholders	20	371	394	361	318	299
Commercial banks and others	220	644	695	657	637	581
Use of IMF credit and SDR allocations	**18**	**18**	**75**	**72**	**72**	**70**
IMF credit	0	1	1	1	1	1
SDR allocations	18	17	74	70	71	69
Short-term external debt stocks	**616**	**1,393**	**1,536**	**1,447**	**1,466**	**1,508**
Disbursements, long-term	**117**	**500**	**590**	**403**	**347**	**320**
Public and publicly guaranteed sector	48	150	245	101	92	147
Private sector not guaranteed	69	350	345	302	255	173
Principal repayments, long-term	**65**	**283**	**335**	**473**	**440**	**351**
Public and publicly guaranteed sector	29	60	70	118	125	107
Private sector not guaranteed	36	223	265	355	315	244
Interest payments, long-term	**16**	**53**	**64**	**67**	**79**	**71**
Public and publicly guaranteed sector	9	23	29	34	41	34
Private sector not guaranteed	7	30	35	33	38	37

EUROPE AND CENTRAL ASIA

(US$ billion, unless otherwise indicated)

Snapshot	2024
Total external debt stocks	**1,169**
External debt stocks as % of:	
Exports	139
GNI	49
Debt service as % of:	
Exports	23
GNI	8
Net financial flows, debt and equity	80
Net debt inflows	53
Net equity inflows	27
GNI	**2,376**
Population (million)	**250**

Figure 1 Public and publicly guaranteed debt, by creditor and creditor type in 2024, including IMF credit

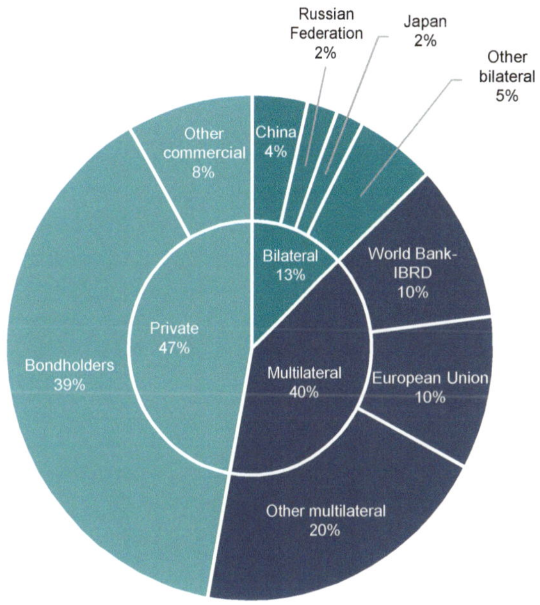

Figure 2 Average terms on new debt commitments from official and private creditors

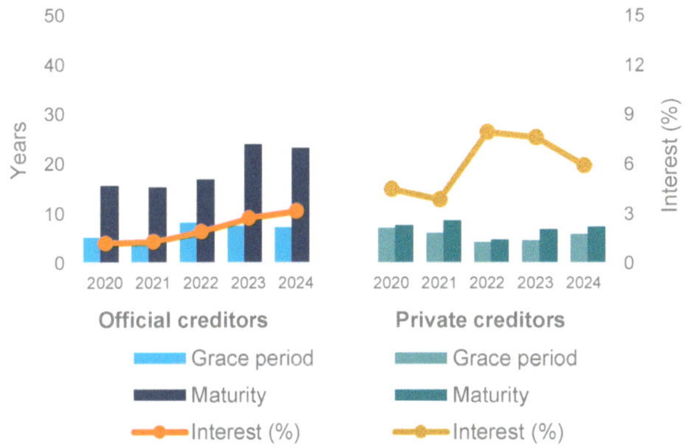

Summary External Debt Data	2010	2020	2021	2022	2023	2024
Total external debt stocks	**697**	**981**	**1,004**	**1,041**	**1,136**	**1,169**
Long-term external debt stocks	**508**	**784**	**783**	**784**	**842**	**874**
Public and publicly guaranteed debt from:	*170*	*343*	*354*	*369*	*411*	*440*
Official creditors	85	149	150	168	199	224
Multilateral	57	96	97	112	143	163
of which: World Bank	29	41	41	44	51	61
Bilateral	28	53	53	56	56	60
Private creditors	85	193	204	201	212	216
Bondholders	58	161	171	168	174	178
Commercial banks and others	27	32	33	33	37	38
Private nonguaranteed debt from:	*338*	*441*	*429*	*416*	*431*	*434*
Bondholders	32	52	51	41	41	49
Commercial banks and others	306	389	378	374	390	386
Use of IMF credit and SDR allocations	**36**	**22**	**37**	**37**	**39**	**40**
IMF credit	28	15	14	15	17	19
SDR allocations	8	7	23	22	22	21
Short-term external debt stocks	**153**	**175**	**184**	**220**	**255**	**255**
Disbursements, long-term	**147**	**150**	**129**	**137**	**177**	**183**
Public and publicly guaranteed sector	34	51	51	54	72	84
Private sector not guaranteed	114	99	78	84	105	99
Principal repayments, long-term	**113**	**131**	**119**	**126**	**125**	**137**
Public and publicly guaranteed sector	10	32	33	32	34	41
Private sector not guaranteed	103	99	86	94	91	96
Interest payments, long-term	**19**	**26**	**26**	**25**	**33**	**40**
Public and publicly guaranteed sector	6	13	13	13	16	19
Private sector not guaranteed	13	13	12	13	17	21

LATIN AMERICA AND THE CARIBBEAN

(US$ billion, unless otherwise indicated)

Snapshot	2024
Total external debt stocks	**2,000**
External debt stocks as % of:	
Exports	128
GNI	34
Debt service as % of:	
Exports	20
GNI	5
Net financial flows, debt and equity	130
Net debt inflows	19
Net equity inflows	111
GNI	**5,799**
Population (million)	**583**

Figure 1 Public and publicly guaranteed debt, by creditor and creditor type in 2024, including IMF credit

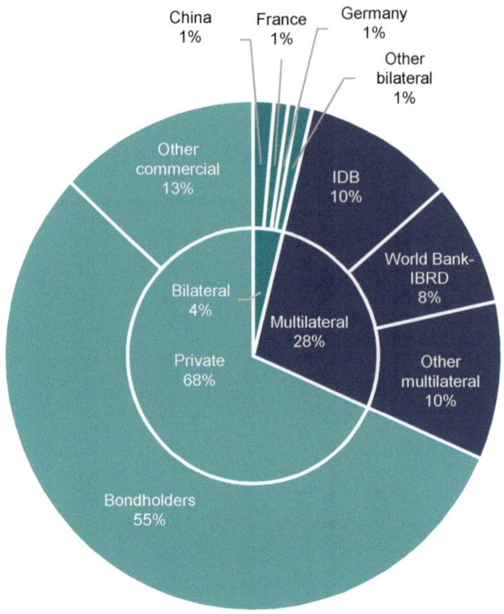

Figure 2 Average terms on new debt commitments from official and private creditors

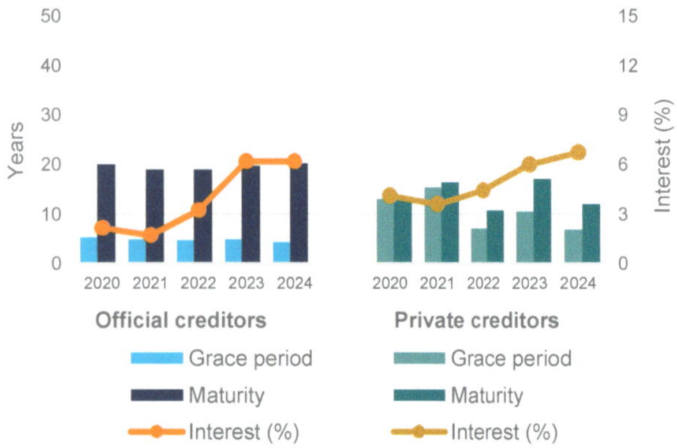

Summary External Debt Data	2010	2020	2021	2022	2023	2024
Total external debt stocks	**1,005**	**1,879**	**1,922**	**1,942**	**2,007**	**2,000**
Long-term external debt stocks	**837**	**1,606**	**1,599**	**1,609**	**1,651**	**1,652**
Public and publicly guaranteed debt from:	*422*	*880*	*888*	*890*	*917*	*918*
Official creditors	155	221	230	241	256	255
Multilateral	120	179	190	201	213	218
of which: World Bank	48	66	70	75	77	80
Bilateral	36	41	40	40	43	37
Private creditors	266	660	657	649	662	663
Bondholders	226	533	527	517	536	536
Commercial banks and others	40	126	131	132	126	127
Private nonguaranteed debt from:	*415*	*725*	*712*	*719*	*734*	*735*
Bondholders	133	185	175	149	143	148
Commercial banks and others	282	540	536	570	590	587
Use of IMF credit and SDR allocations	**19**	**77**	**112**	**115**	**110**	**106**
IMF credit	2	61	56	61	57	54
SDR allocations	17	16	56	53	53	52
Short-term external debt stocks	**149**	**196**	**211**	**218**	**246**	**242**
Disbursements, long-term	**189**	**284**	**294**	**239**	**332**	**228**
Public and publicly guaranteed sector	82	131	95	84	91	108
Private sector not guaranteed	107	153	199	155	242	120
Principal repayments, long-term	**82**	**224**	**247**	**191**	**289**	**204**
Public and publicly guaranteed sector	39	71	77	57	62	87
Private sector not guaranteed	43	153	170	135	227	117
Interest payments, long-term	**34**	**62**	**71**	**57**	**77**	**79**
Public and publicly guaranteed sector	19	37	37	33	42	47
Private sector not guaranteed	15	25	34	24	35	31

MIDDLE EAST, NORTH AFRICA, AFGHANISTAN, AND PAKISTAN

(US$ billion, unless otherwise indicated)

Snapshot	2024
Total external debt stocks	**561**
External debt stocks as % of:	
Exports	103
GNI	27
Debt service as % of:	
Exports	14
GNI	4
Net financial flows, debt and equity	45
Net debt inflows	-4
Net equity inflows	49
GNI	**2,057**
Population (million)	**729**

Figure 1 Public and publicly guaranteed debt, by creditor and creditor type in 2024, including IMF credit

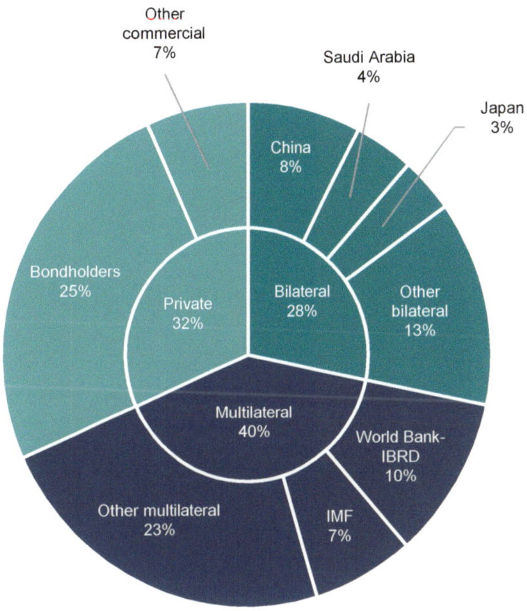

Figure 2 Average terms on new debt commitments from official and private creditors

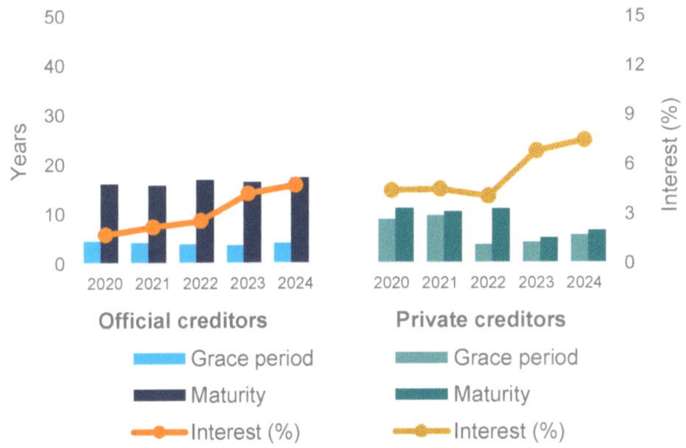

Summary External Debt Data	2010	2020	2021	2022	2023	2024
Total external debt stocks	**276**	**520**	**557**	**563**	**579**	**561**
Long-term external debt stocks	**212**	**406**	**413**	**401**	**416**	**400**
Public and publicly guaranteed debt from:	*176*	*348*	*359*	*350*	*365*	*348*
Official creditors	136	230	231	230	240	230
Multilateral	63	110	113	116	122	125
of which: World Bank	25	51	52	53	57	58
Bilateral	73	119	118	114	117	105
Private creditors	41	118	128	120	125	119
Bondholders	29	92	99	93	96	92
Commercial banks and others		26	29	27	29	26
Private nonguaranteed debt from:	*12*	*58*	*54*	*51*	*51*	*52*
Bondholders	1	1	1	1	0	1
Commercial banks and others	34	58	53	51	51	51
Use of IMF credit and SDR allocations	**22**	**46**	**64**	**61**	**58**	**53**
IMF credit	10	35	33	32	29	25
SDR allocations	12	11	30	29	29	28
Short-term external debt stocks	**43**	**68**	**80**	**101**	**105**	**108**
Disbursements, long-term	**27**	**51**	**57**	**38**	**47**	**39**
Public and publicly guaranteed sector	16	47	53	35	42	33
Private sector not guaranteed	11	4	4	2	5	6
Principal repayments, long-term	**21**	**37**	**41**	**40**	**34**	**41**
Public and publicly guaranteed sector	13	24	33	35	27	36
Private sector not guaranteed	8	13	8	5	6	5
Interest payments, long-term	**6**	**9**	**9**	**11**	**16**	**17**
Public and publicly guaranteed sector	5	8	8	10	13	15
Private sector not guaranteed	1	1	1	2	2	2

SOUTH ASIA

(US$ billion, unless otherwise indicated)

Snapshot	2024
Total external debt stocks	**896**
External debt stocks as % of:	
Exports	93
GNI	20
Debt service as % of:	
Exports	11
GNI	2
Net financial flows, debt and equity	109
Net debt inflows	83
Net equity inflows	25
GNI	**4,475**
Population (million)	**1,677**

Figure 1 Public and publicly guaranteed debt, by creditor and creditor type in 2024, including IMF credit

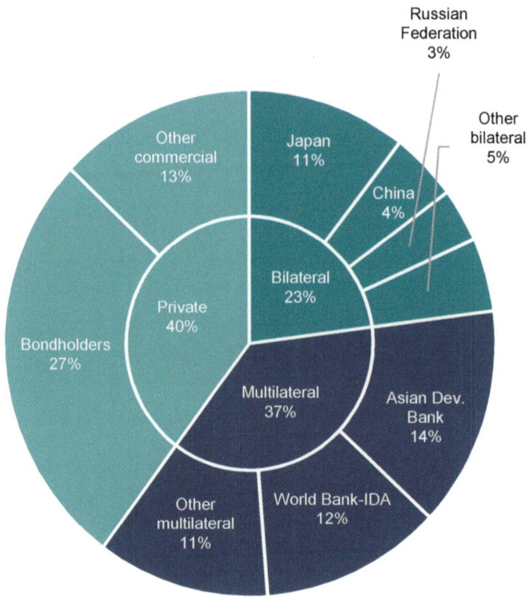

Figure 2 Average terms on new debt commitments from official and private creditors

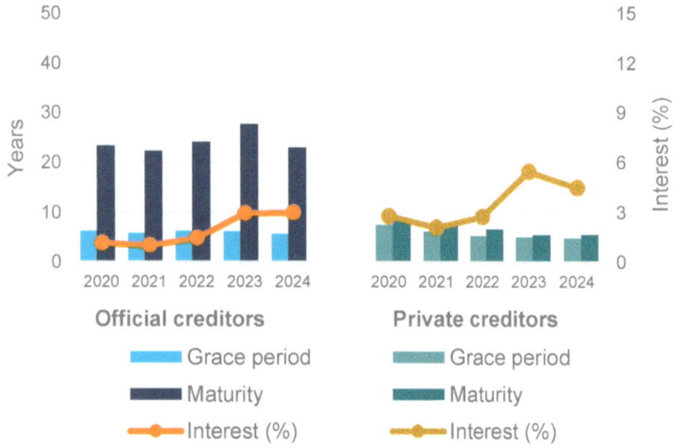

Summary External Debt Data	2010	2020	2021	2022	2023	2024
Total external debt stocks	**344**	**710**	**778**	**788**	**827**	**896**
Long-term external debt stocks	**273**	**576**	**606**	**604**	**648**	**707**
Public and publicly guaranteed debt from:	*143*	*298*	*320*	*325*	*346*	*372*
Official creditors	112	179	189	198	214	224
Multilateral	75	112	119	124	133	138
of which: World Bank	52	65	66	65	68	69
Bilateral	37	66	71	74	81	85
Private creditors	31	120	131	128	132	149
Bondholders	17	87	91	86	88	100
Commercial banks and others	15	32	40	41	43	48
Private nonguaranteed debt from:	*129*	*278*	*286*	*278*	*302*	*335*
Bondholders	13	27	33	34	32	33
Commercial banks and others	116	251	254	244	271	302
Use of IMF credit and SDR allocations	**10**	**10**	**30**	**28**	**30**	**30**
IMF credit	2	3	3	2	4	5
SDR allocations	8	7	27	26	26	25
Short-term external debt stocks	**62**	**124**	**142**	**156**	**149**	**159**
Disbursements, long-term	**48**	**84**	**82**	**63**	**105**	**137**
Public and publicly guaranteed sector	29	36	46	34	43	60
Private sector not guaranteed	20	48	36	29	62	76
Principal repayments, long-term	**21**	**70**	**47**	**55**	**58**	**66**
Public and publicly guaranteed sector	7	29	19	19	20	25
Private sector not guaranteed	14	41	28	36	38	41
Interest payments, long-term	**6**	**14**	**15**	**17**	**25**	**29**
Public and publicly guaranteed sector	2	4	5	5	9	10
Private sector not guaranteed	4	10	10	12	17	19

SUB-SAHARAN AFRICA

(US$ billion, unless otherwise indicated)

Snapshot	2024
Total external debt stocks	**901**
External debt stocks as % of:	
Exports	164
GNI	49
Debt service as % of:	
Exports	17
GNI	5
Net financial flows, debt and equity	86
Net debt inflows	49
Net equity inflows	37
GNI	**1,821**
Population (million)	**1,276**

Figure 1 Public and publicly guaranteed debt, by creditor and creditor type in 2024, including IMF credit

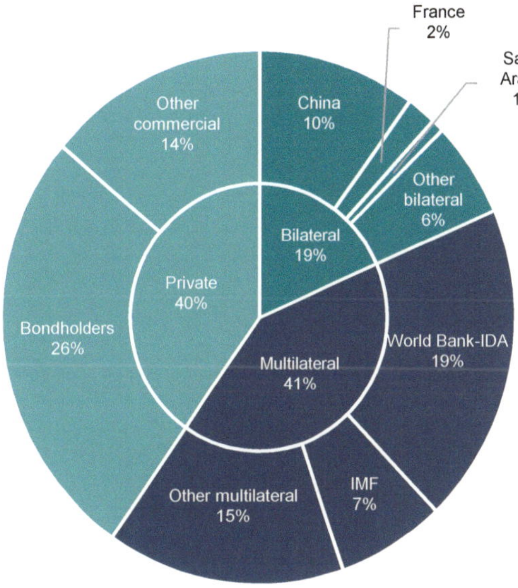

Figure 2 Average terms on new debt commitments from official and private creditors

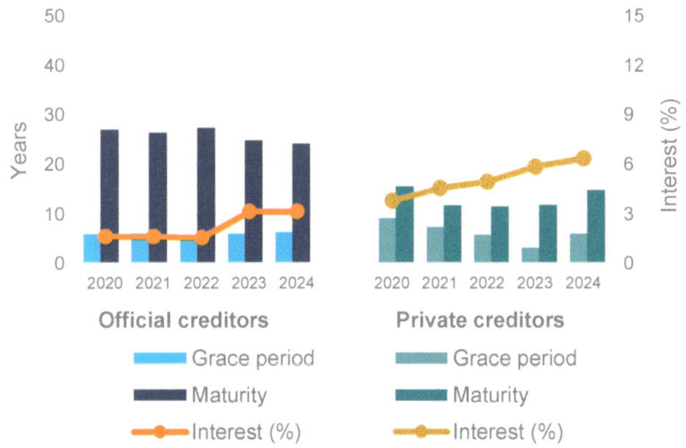

Summary External Debt Data	2010	2020	2021	2022	2023	2024
Total external debt stocks	**341**	**794**	**836**	**850**	**871**	**901**
Long-term external debt stocks	**253**	**649**	**662**	**666**	**685**	**706**
Public and publicly guaranteed debt from:	*160*	*470*	*484*	*488*	*509*	*531*
Official creditors	104	253	261	269	290	302
Multilateral	59	146	152	162	183	198
of which: World Bank	34	86	91	99	112	124
Bilateral	44	107	109	107	107	104
Private creditors	57	217	222	220	219	229
Bondholders	32	140	147	144	141	149
Commercial banks and others	24	78	75	76	78	79
Private nonguaranteed debt from:	*93*	*179*	*178*	*177*	*176*	*175*
Bondholders	9	10	10	9	8	8
Commercial banks and others	84	169	168	168	168	167
Use of IMF credit and SDR allocations	**20**	**41**	**69**	**68**	**71**	**72**
IMF credit	6	29	33	35	37	38
SDR allocations	14	13	36	34	34	33
Short-term external debt stocks	**69**	**103**	**105**	**116**	**114**	**123**
Disbursements, long-term	**48**	**73**	**84**	**79**	**68**	**87**
Public and publicly guaranteed sector	27	45	51	48	49	67
Private sector not guaranteed	21	28	33	32	18	20
Principal repayments, long-term	**12**	**49**	**60**	**63**	**50**	**52**
Public and publicly guaranteed sector	7	24	30	32	30	31
Private sector not guaranteed	5	25	30	30	20	21
Interest payments, long-term	**4**	**19**	**18**	**21**	**26**	**28**
Public and publicly guaranteed sector	3	15	14	14	17	19
Private sector not guaranteed	1	5	4	6	9	8

AFGHANISTAN

(US$ million, unless otherwise indicated)

Snapshot	2024
Total external debt stocks	**3,344**
External debt stocks as % of:	
Exports	..
GNI	..
Debt service as % of:	
Exports	..
GNI	..
Net financial flows, debt and equity	-33
Net debt inflows	-33
Net equity inflows	..
GNI	..
Population (million)	**43**

Figure 1 Public and publicly guaranteed debt, by creditor and creditor type in 2024, including IMF credit

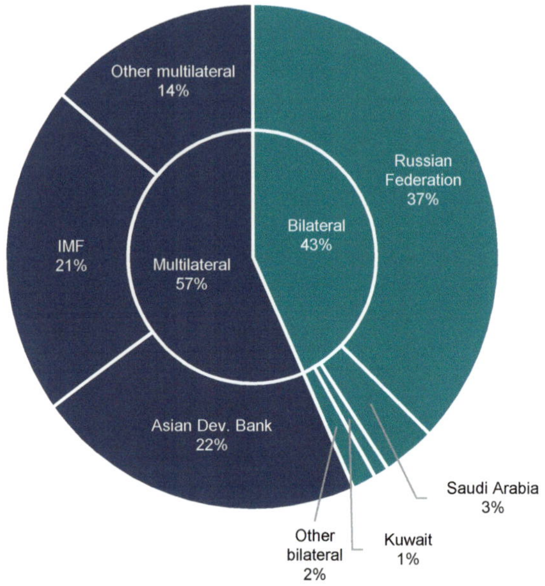

Figure 2 Average terms on new debt commitments from official and private creditors

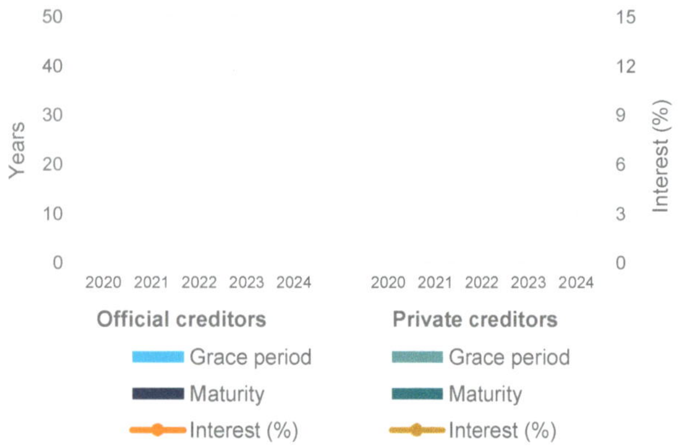

Summary External Debt Data	2010	2020	2021	2022	2023	2024
Total external debt stocks	**2,436**	**3,040**	**3,556**	**3,393**	**3,428**	**3,344**
Long-term external debt stocks	**1,976**	**1,976**	**1,926**	**1,877**	**1,874**	**1,812**
Public and publicly guaranteed debt from:	*1,976*	*1,958*	*1,908*	*1,859*	*1,857*	*1,795*
Official creditors	1,976	1,958	1,908	1,859	1,857	1,795
Multilateral	1,016	968	919	872	869	808
of which: World Bank	406	344	329	303	297	280
Bilateral	959	991	989	987	988	986
Private creditors	0	..	..	..	..	..
Bondholders	..	..	..	..	..	..
Commercial banks and others	..	..	..	..	..	..
Private nonguaranteed debt from:	..	*18*	*18*	*18*	*18*	*18*
Bondholders	..	..	..	..	..	..
Commercial banks and others	..	18	18	18	18	18
Use of IMF credit and SDR allocations	**355**	**629**	**1,185**	**1,122**	**1,127**	**1,089**
IMF credit	116	405	534	502	502	482
SDR allocations	239	224	652	620	625	607
Short-term external debt stocks	**105**	**435**	**445**	**394**	**427**	**443**
Disbursements, long-term	**76**	**0**	**..**	**..**	**0**	**0**
Public and publicly guaranteed sector	76	0	..	..	0	0
Private sector not guaranteed	..	..	..	..	..	..
Principal repayments, long-term	**1**	**26**	**14**	**9**	**10**	**27**
Public and publicly guaranteed sector	1	22	14	9	10	27
Private sector not guaranteed	..	5	..	..	..	..
Interest payments, long-term	**8**	**8**	**5**	**3**	**3**	**8**
Public and publicly guaranteed sector	8	7	5	3	3	8
Private sector not guaranteed	..	1	..	..	..	..

Note: Figure 2 shows no data values because the country did not have new commitments from 2020 to 2024.

ALBANIA

(US$ million, unless otherwise indicated)

Snapshot	2024
Total external debt stocks	**10,713**
External debt stocks as % of:	
Exports	98
GNI	40
Debt service as % of:	
Exports	8
GNI	3
Net financial flows, debt and equity	1,971
Net debt inflows	288
Net equity inflows	1,683
GNI	**26,971**
Population (million)	**3**

Figure 1 Public and publicly guaranteed debt, by creditor and creditor type in 2024, including IMF credit

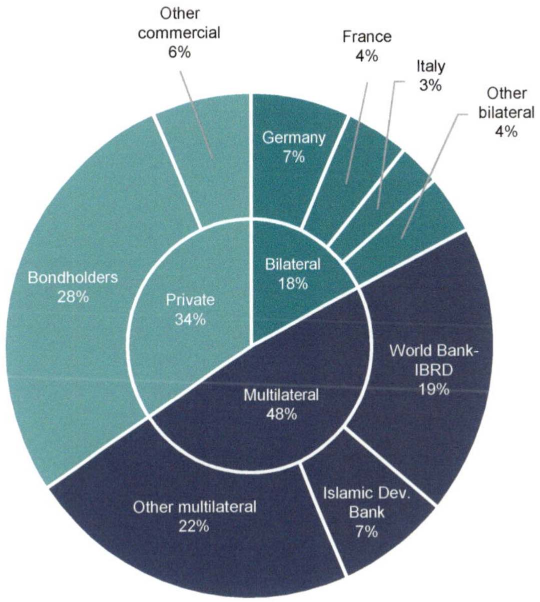

Figure 2 Average terms on new debt commitments from official and private creditors

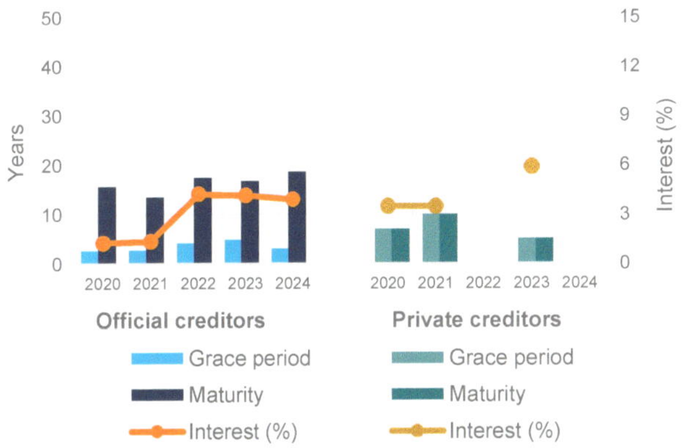

Summary External Debt Data	2010	2020	2021	2022	2023	2024
Total external debt stocks	**5,438**	**10,478**	**11,055**	**10,420**	**11,315**	**10,713**
Long-term external debt stocks	**4,565**	**8,887**	**9,095**	**8,505**	**9,585**	**9,112**
Public and publicly guaranteed debt from:	*3,211*	*4,897*	*5,303*	*4,859*	*5,553*	*5,082*
Official creditors	2,176	3,255	3,411	3,327	3,451	3,291
Multilateral	1,522	2,547	2,639	2,537	2,590	2,381
of which: World Bank	875	1,418	1,409	1,310	1,400	1,305
Bilateral	654	708	773	790	861	910
Private creditors	1,035	1,642	1,892	1,533	2,103	1,791
Bondholders	477	1,116	1,441	1,142	1,733	1,453
Commercial banks and others	558	526	451	391	369	338
Private nonguaranteed debt from:	*1,354*	*3,990*	*3,792*	*3,646*	*4,032*	*4,030*
Bondholders	69	284	267	248	254	247
Commercial banks and others	1,285	3,706	3,525	3,397	3,778	3,783
Use of IMF credit and SDR allocations	**129**	**627**	**734**	**632**	**525**	**360**
IMF credit	58	560	482	393	283	125
SDR allocations	72	67	252	240	241	235
Short-term external debt stocks	**743**	**964**	**1,226**	**1,283**	**1,205**	**1,241**
Disbursements, long-term	**866**	**1,162**	**1,532**	**604**	**1,476**	**889**
Public and publicly guaranteed sector	631	880	1,234	318	921	291
Private sector not guaranteed	235	283	298	286	555	599
Principal repayments, long-term	**250**	**948**	**693**	**499**	**539**	**484**
Public and publicly guaranteed sector	174	537	369	283	311	312
Private sector not guaranteed	76	410	323	216	228	171
Interest payments, long-term	**110**	**146**	**116**	**126**	**170**	**213**
Public and publicly guaranteed sector	66	96	101	101	146	191
Private sector not guaranteed	44	50	15	25	24	21

ALGERIA

(US$ million, unless otherwise indicated)

Snapshot	2024
Total external debt stocks	**6,898**
External debt stocks as % of:	
Exports	12
GNI	3
Debt service as % of:	
Exports	1
GNI	0
Net financial flows, debt and equity	917
Net debt inflows	-267
Net equity inflows	1,184
GNI	**258,580**
Population (million)	**47**

Figure 1 Public and publicly guaranteed debt, by creditor and creditor type in 2024, including IMF credit

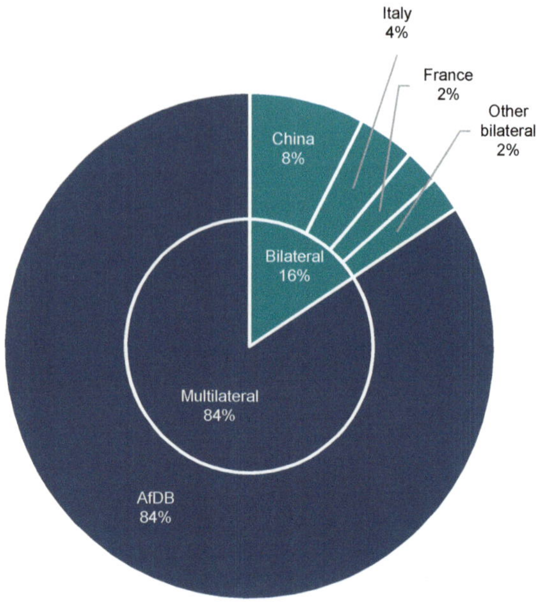

Figure 2 Average terms on new debt commitments from official and private creditors

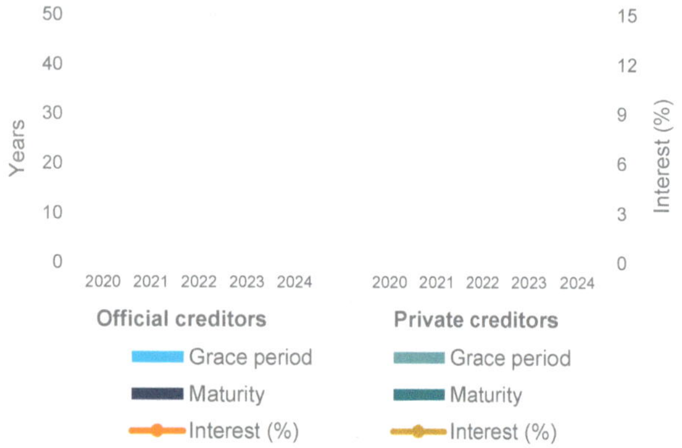

Summary External Debt Data	2010	2020	2021	2022	2023	2024
Total external debt stocks	**7,253**	**5,178**	**7,379**	**7,129**	**7,315**	**6,898**
Long-term external debt stocks	**3,630**	**1,669**	**1,476**	**1,291**	**1,275**	**1,130**
Public and publicly guaranteed debt from:	*2,662*	*1,436*	*1,240*	*1,056*	*993*	*852*
Official creditors	1,986	1,433	1,239	1,056	993	852
Multilateral	10	1,095	984	860	826	717
of which: World Bank	9	..	..	..	..	..
Bilateral	1,976	338	256	195	166	134
Private creditors	676	3	1	0	0	..
Bondholders	..	..	..	..	..	..
Commercial banks and others	676	3	1	0	..	..
Private nonguaranteed debt from:	*968*	*232*	*236*	*235*	*282*	*278*
Bondholders	..	..	..	..	..	..
Commercial banks and others	968	232	236	235	282	278
Use of IMF credit and SDR allocations	**1,845**	**1,726**	**4,306**	**4,095**	**4,128**	**4,012**
IMF credit	0	0	0	0	0	0
SDR allocations	1,845	1,726	4,306	4,095	4,128	4,012
Short-term external debt stocks	**1,778**	**1,784**	**1,597**	**1,744**	**1,913**	**1,756**
Disbursements, long-term	**42**	**98**	**70**	**53**	**137**	**62**
Public and publicly guaranteed sector	40	0	0	0	0	0
Private sector not guaranteed	2	98	70	53	137	62
Principal repayments, long-term	**557**	**119**	**147**	**147**	**172**	**173**
Public and publicly guaranteed sector	324	77	101	107	98	89
Private sector not guaranteed	234	41	46	39	74	84
Interest payments, long-term	**95**	**23**	**22**	**18**	**17**	**15**
Public and publicly guaranteed sector	64	22	22	18	17	15
Private sector not guaranteed	31	1	1	..	..	..

Note: Figure 2 shows no data values because the country did not have new commitments from 2020 to 2024.

ANGOLA

(US$ million, unless otherwise indicated)

Snapshot	2024
Total external debt stocks	**58,733**
External debt stocks as % of:	
Exports	156
GNI	80
Debt service as % of:	
Exports	29
GNI	15
Net financial flows, debt and equity	471
Net debt inflows	1,935
Net equity inflows	-1,463
GNI	**73,811**
Population (million)	**38**

Figure 1 Public and publicly guaranteed debt, by creditor and creditor type in 2024, including IMF credit

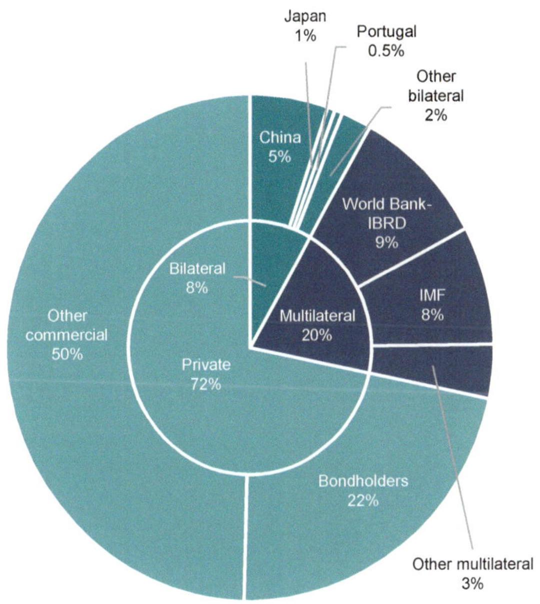

Figure 2 Average terms on new debt commitments from official and private creditors

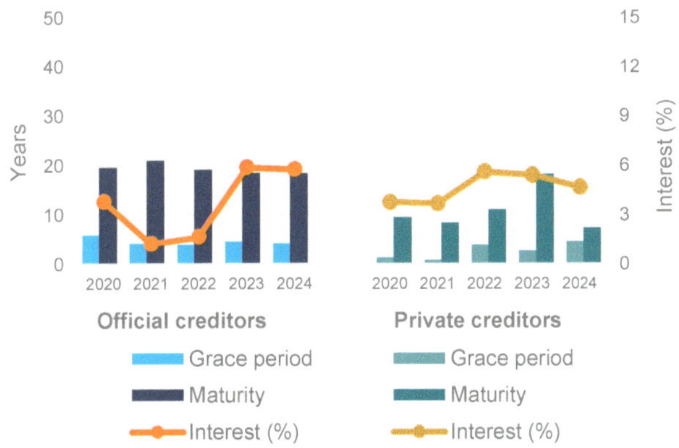

Summary External Debt Data	2010	2020	2021	2022	2023	2024
Total external debt stocks	**26,796**	**65,405**	**66,020**	**60,446**	**57,273**	**58,733**
Long-term external debt stocks	**20,926**	**57,062**	**55,508**	**50,669**	**46,893**	**47,861**
Public and publicly guaranteed debt from:	*15,662*	*47,384*	*46,646*	*48,157*	*45,457*	*46,110*
Official creditors	4,746	9,925	10,551	10,517	10,089	10,315
Multilateral	445	3,069	3,857	4,559	5,216	6,199
of which: World Bank	378	1,746	2,481	3,235	3,885	4,775
Bilateral	4,301	6,856	6,694	5,958	4,872	4,117
Private creditors	10,916	37,459	36,095	37,640	35,368	35,794
Bondholders	..	8,000	8,000	9,114	9,114	11,042
Commercial banks and others	10,916	29,459	28,095	28,525	26,254	24,752
Private nonguaranteed debt from:	*5,264*	*9,679*	*8,862*	*2,513*	*1,436*	*1,751*
Bondholders	..	..	..	..	..	..
Commercial banks and others	5,264	9,679	8,862	2,513	1,436	1,751
Use of IMF credit and SDR allocations	**1,302**	**2,992**	**5,872**	**5,584**	**5,449**	**5,064**
IMF credit	882	2,599	4,497	4,277	4,131	3,783
SDR allocations	420	393	1,375	1,307	1,318	1,281
Short-term external debt stocks	**4,568**	**5,351**	**4,639**	**4,193**	**4,931**	**5,809**
Disbursements, long-term	**6,714**	**3,966**	**6,194**	**7,945**	**4,056**	**7,626**
Public and publicly guaranteed sector	4,082	3,966	6,194	7,945	4,056	7,311
Private sector not guaranteed	2,632	..	..	..	..	315
Principal repayments, long-term	**2,639**	**5,129**	**7,611**	**12,520**	**8,028**	**6,333**
Public and publicly guaranteed sector	2,113	4,557	6,795	6,170	6,951	6,333
Private sector not guaranteed	526	572	816	6,350	1,077	..
Interest payments, long-term	**257**	**2,571**	**2,234**	**2,526**	**3,782**	**3,636**
Public and publicly guaranteed sector	177	2,408	2,128	2,477	3,701	3,525
Private sector not guaranteed	80	163	106	48	81	111

ARGENTINA

(US$ million, unless otherwise indicated)

Snapshot	2024
Total external debt stocks	**242,357**
External debt stocks as % of:	
Exports	235
GNI	39
Debt service as % of:	
Exports	38
GNI	6
Net financial flows, debt and equity	5,636
Net debt inflows	-3,294
Net equity inflows	8,929
GNI	**620,500**
Population (million)	**46**

Figure 1 Public and publicly guaranteed debt, by creditor and creditor type in 2024, including IMF credit

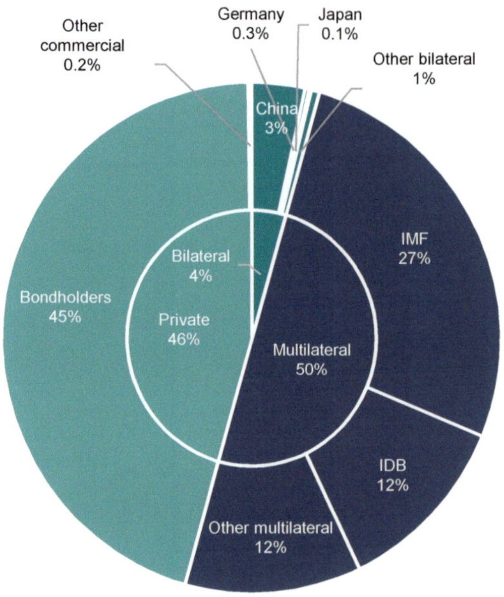

Figure 2 Average terms on new debt commitments from official and private creditors

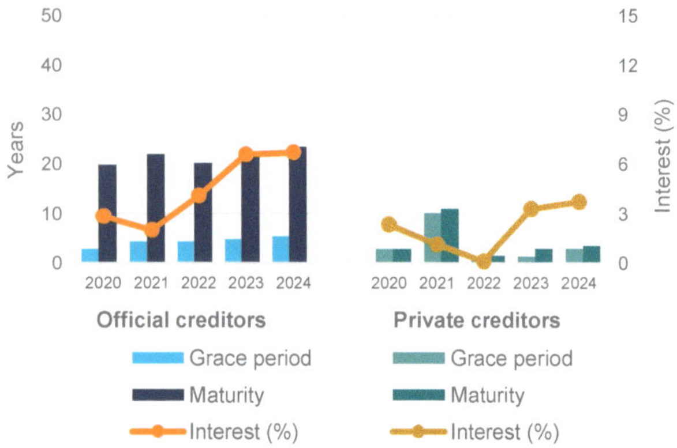

Summary External Debt Data	2010	2020	2021	2022	2023	2024
Total external debt stocks	**126,642**	**255,603**	**246,114**	**248,977**	**252,794**	**242,357**
Long-term external debt stocks	**107,118**	**164,123**	**154,324**	**147,337**	**150,066**	**146,597**
Public and publicly guaranteed debt from:	*69,183*	*118,080*	*114,797*	*110,319*	*112,886*	*110,608*
Official creditors	22,874	30,306	31,459	36,090	42,917	41,603
Multilateral	17,016	25,301	27,107	29,787	33,292	34,906
of which: World Bank	5,349	7,721	8,517	9,205	9,889	10,738
Bilateral	5,859	5,005	4,352	6,303	9,625	6,697
Private creditors	46,309	87,774	83,338	74,229	69,969	69,005
Bondholders	44,344	86,537	82,219	73,775	69,561	68,693
Commercial banks and others	1,965	1,237	1,119	454	408	312
Private nonguaranteed debt from:	*37,934*	*46,042*	*39,527*	*37,018*	*37,180*	*35,989*
Bondholders	7,855	15,742	15,354	13,617	12,322	10,634
Commercial banks and others	30,080	30,300	24,173	23,401	24,858	25,355
Use of IMF credit and SDR allocations	**3,111**	**48,874**	**48,055**	**52,290**	**47,612**	**47,177**
IMF credit	0	45,964	40,953	45,536	40,804	40,559
SDR allocations	3,111	2,909	7,103	6,754	6,809	6,618
Short-term external debt stocks	**16,413**	**42,607**	**43,735**	**49,350**	**55,115**	**48,583**
Disbursements, long-term	**6,923**	**23,201**	**16,167**	**10,215**	**21,438**	**24,458**
Public and publicly guaranteed sector	2,623	12,372	4,907	8,254	11,525	11,646
Private sector not guaranteed	4,300	10,830	11,260	1,961	9,913	12,812
Principal repayments, long-term	**11,690**	**21,685**	**17,860**	**10,048**	**15,762**	**22,233**
Public and publicly guaranteed sector	6,035	8,200	4,472	6,071	6,061	9,231
Private sector not guaranteed	5,655	13,485	13,388	3,977	9,701	13,002
Interest payments, long-term	**3,789**	**5,608**	**4,152**	**3,066**	**6,046**	**7,238**
Public and publicly guaranteed sector	2,700	2,484	1,290	1,929	3,593	5,015
Private sector not guaranteed	1,089	3,124	2,863	1,137	2,453	2,224

ARMENIA

(US$ million, unless otherwise indicated)

Snapshot	2024
Total external debt stocks	**16,396**
External debt stocks as % of:	
Exports	83
GNI	66
Debt service as % of:	
Exports	9
GNI	7
Net financial flows, debt and equity	771
Net debt inflows	704
Net equity inflows	66
GNI	**24,848**
Population (million)	3

Figure 1 Public and publicly guaranteed debt, by creditor and creditor type in 2024, including IMF credit

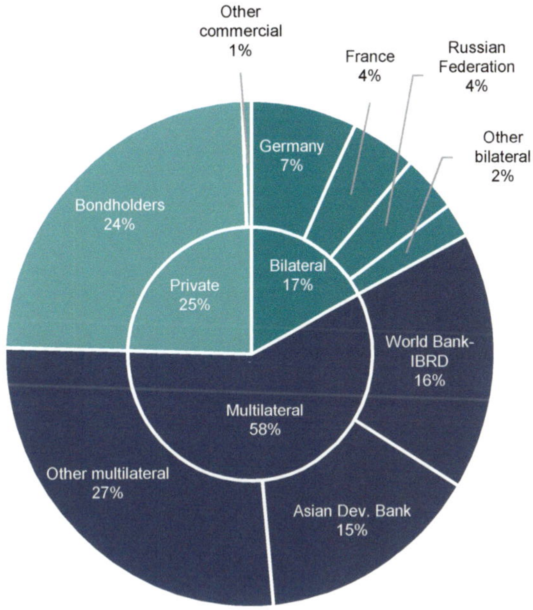

Figure 2 Average terms on new debt commitments from official and private creditors

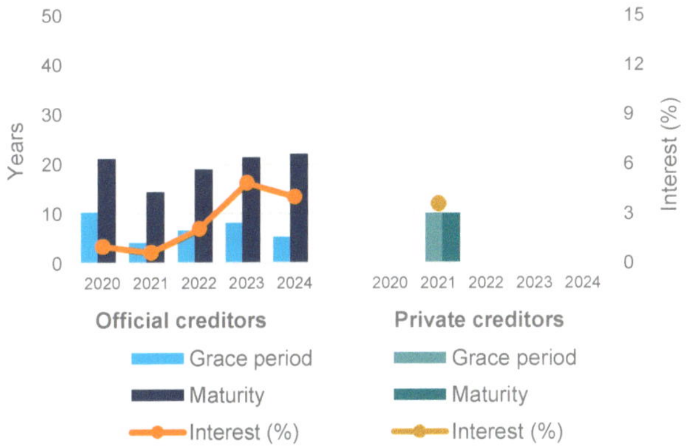

Summary External Debt Data	2010	2020	2021	2022	2023	2024
Total external debt stocks	**6,307**	**13,062**	**14,040**	**15,931**	**15,839**	**16,396**
Long-term external debt stocks	**4,775**	**10,813**	**11,781**	**11,931**	**12,062**	**12,414**
Public and publicly guaranteed debt from:	*2,560*	*5,616*	*6,246*	*6,320*	*6,241*	*6,314*
Official creditors	2,556	4,555	4,460	4,539	4,633	4,713
Multilateral	1,513	3,401	3,334	3,297	3,438	3,587
of which: World Bank	1,267	1,830	1,763	1,659	1,717	1,723
Bilateral	1,042	1,154	1,125	1,242	1,195	1,126
Private creditors	4	1,061	1,786	1,780	1,608	1,601
Bondholders	..	1,000	1,733	1,733	1,563	1,563
Commercial banks and others	4	61	53	47	45	38
Private nonguaranteed debt from:	*2,216*	*5,197*	*5,535*	*5,612*	*5,821*	*6,100*
Bondholders	..	300	300	300	300	300
Commercial banks and others	2,216	4,897	5,235	5,312	5,521	5,800
Use of IMF credit and SDR allocations	**876**	**646**	**735**	**758**	**670**	**483**
IMF credit	741	519	439	476	386	208
SDR allocations	136	127	296	281	284	276
Short-term external debt stocks	**656**	**1,603**	**1,524**	**3,242**	**3,107**	**3,499**
Disbursements, long-term	**1,734**	**2,136**	**2,552**	**1,681**	**1,979**	**1,431**
Public and publicly guaranteed sector	198	129	1,092	471	355	519
Private sector not guaranteed	1,536	2,007	1,460	1,210	1,624	912
Principal repayments, long-term	**857**	**1,386**	**1,368**	**1,388**	**1,887**	**948**
Public and publicly guaranteed sector	24	313	246	256	473	315
Private sector not guaranteed	833	1,073	1,122	1,132	1,414	633
Interest payments, long-term	**60**	**443**	**446**	**417**	**560**	**450**
Public and publicly guaranteed sector	35	167	145	162	238	254
Private sector not guaranteed	25	276	302	256	322	195

AZERBAIJAN

(US$ million, unless otherwise indicated)

Snapshot	2024
Total external debt stocks	**12,199**
External debt stocks as % of:	
Exports	33
GNI	17
Debt service as % of:	
Exports	11
GNI	6
Net financial flows, debt and equity	-2,408
Net debt inflows	-2,627
Net equity inflows	219
GNI	**71,581**
Population (million)	**10**

Figure 1 Public and publicly guaranteed debt, by creditor and creditor type in 2024, including IMF credit

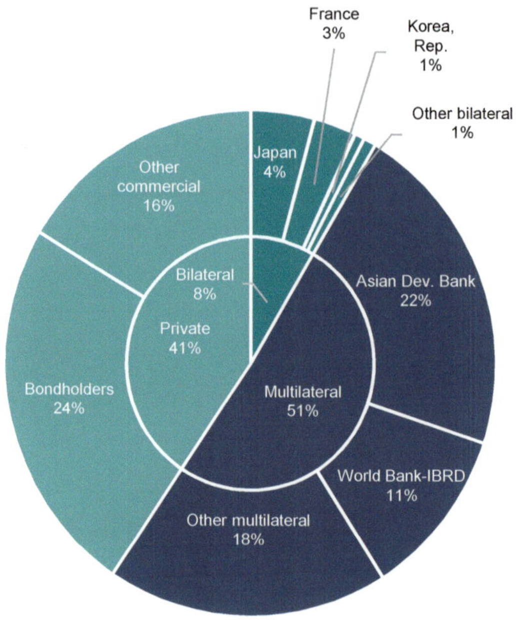

Figure 2 Average terms on new debt commitments from official and private creditors

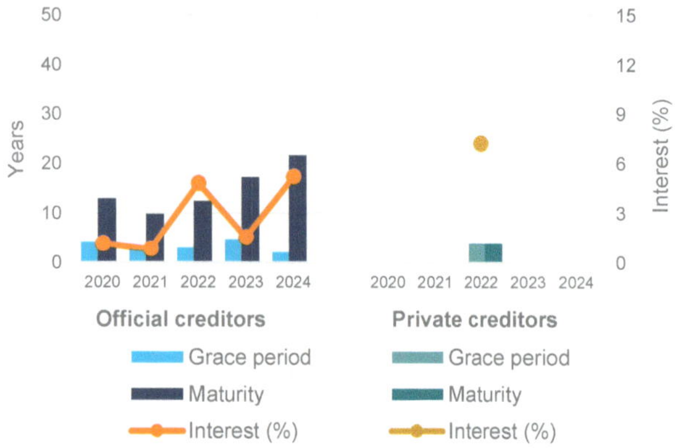

Summary External Debt Data	2010	2020	2021	2022	2023	2024
Total external debt stocks	**7,286**	**16,385**	**15,577**	**15,457**	**14,990**	**12,199**
Long-term external debt stocks	**6,004**	**15,711**	**14,837**	**14,247**	**13,667**	**11,291**
Public and publicly guaranteed debt from:	*3,846*	*14,667*	*13,623*	*12,911*	*12,233*	*9,476*
Official creditors	2,661	7,838	7,266	6,657	6,238	5,626
Multilateral	1,738	6,484	6,084	5,641	5,294	4,825
of which: World Bank	1,063	2,098	1,681	1,487	1,333	1,166
Bilateral	922	1,354	1,182	1,016	944	801
Private creditors	1,186	6,829	6,358	6,254	5,994	3,850
Bondholders	..	3,750	3,750	4,050	4,050	2,300
Commercial banks and others	1,186	3,079	2,608	2,204	1,944	1,550
Private nonguaranteed debt from:	*2,158*	*1,044*	*1,213*	*1,336*	*1,434*	*1,815*
Bondholders	..	500	500	513	515	530
Commercial banks and others	2,158	544	713	823	920	1,285
Use of IMF credit and SDR allocations	**282**	**221**	**740**	**704**	**710**	**690**
IMF credit	46	0	0	0	0	0
SDR allocations	237	221	740	704	710	690
Short-term external debt stocks	**999**	**452**	**0**	**506**	**613**	**218**
Disbursements, long-term	**2,643**	**1,080**	**1,094**	**513**	**773**	**1,211**
Public and publicly guaranteed sector	729	553	653	503	155	111
Private sector not guaranteed	1,914	527	442	11	618	1,100
Principal repayments, long-term	**306**	**1,282**	**1,687**	**1,089**	**1,402**	**3,443**
Public and publicly guaranteed sector	234	866	1,408	969	880	2,712
Private sector not guaranteed	72	416	280	120	522	732
Interest payments, long-term	**78**	**548**	**437**	**493**	**727**	**696**
Public and publicly guaranteed sector	65	496	403	448	635	594
Private sector not guaranteed	13	52	34	45	92	103

BANGLADESH

(US$ million, unless otherwise indicated)

Snapshot	2024
Total external debt stocks	**104,487**
External debt stocks as % of:	
Exports	192
GNI	22
Debt service as % of:	
Exports	16
GNI	2
Net financial flows, debt and equity	7,095
Net debt inflows	5,769
Net equity inflows	1,326
GNI	**469,503**
Population (million)	**174**

Figure 1 Public and publicly guaranteed debt, by creditor and creditor type in 2024, including IMF credit

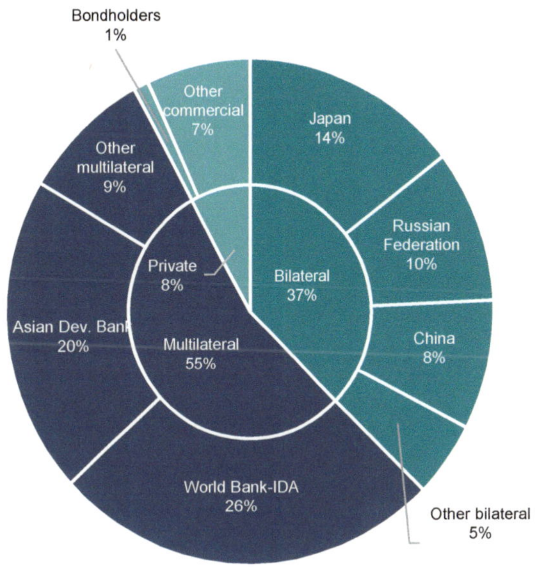

Figure 2 Average terms on new debt commitments from official and private creditors

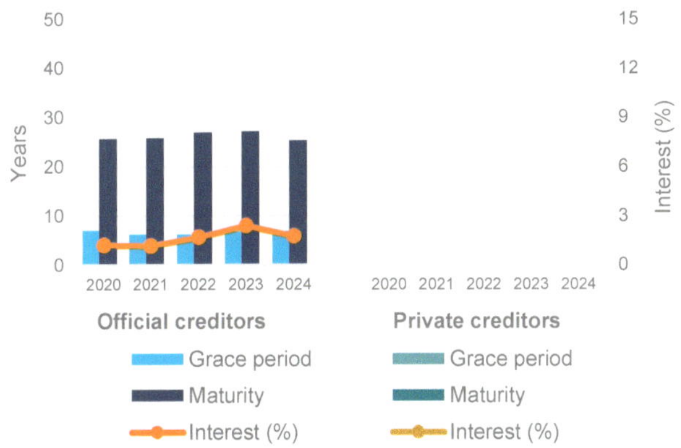

Summary External Debt Data	2010	2020	2021	2022	2023	2024
Total external debt stocks	**26,572**	**73,551**	**91,478**	**96,944**	**101,371**	**104,487**
Long-term external debt stocks	**22,222**	**60,455**	**70,088**	**75,434**	**83,208**	**86,875**
Public and publicly guaranteed debt from:	*21,146*	*54,830*	*62,473*	*67,541*	*74,055*	*77,582*
Official creditors	21,129	49,518	54,880	60,316	67,168	71,243
Multilateral	18,463	31,181	33,382	35,101	39,022	41,223
of which: World Bank	10,653	17,572	17,832	18,226	19,772	20,731
Bilateral	2,666	18,337	21,498	25,215	28,146	30,020
Private creditors	16	5,313	7,594	7,226	6,886	6,339
Bondholders	..	1,736	1,675	1,266	952	770
Commercial banks and others	16	3,577	5,919	5,959	5,934	5,569
Private nonguaranteed debt from:	*1,076*	*5,625*	*7,615*	*7,892*	*9,153*	*9,293*
Bondholders	..	..	..	..	..	..
Commercial banks and others	1,076	5,625	7,615	7,892	9,153	9,293
Use of IMF credit and SDR allocations	**1,403**	**2,109**	**3,301**	**2,981**	**3,932**	**4,667**
IMF credit	617	1,374	1,156	941	1,876	2,668
SDR allocations	786	735	2,145	2,040	2,056	1,999
Short-term external debt stocks	**2,947**	**10,986**	**18,088**	**18,530**	**14,231**	**12,945**
Disbursements, long-term	**1,355**	**10,220**	**13,975**	**13,309**	**12,844**	**11,099**
Public and publicly guaranteed sector	968	7,931	9,564	10,474	9,870	9,264
Private sector not guaranteed	388	2,289	4,410	2,835	2,973	1,835
Principal repayments, long-term	**821**	**2,871**	**4,401**	**5,141**	**4,560**	**4,904**
Public and publicly guaranteed sector	724	1,307	1,981	2,583	2,847	3,209
Private sector not guaranteed	97	1,565	2,420	2,558	1,713	1,695
Interest payments, long-term	**203**	**863**	**900**	**1,037**	**1,721**	**2,443**
Public and publicly guaranteed sector	195	707	798	819	1,578	1,899
Private sector not guaranteed	8	155	102	218	143	544

BELARUS

(US$ million, unless otherwise indicated)

Snapshot	2024
Total external debt stocks	**34,217**
External debt stocks as % of:	
Exports	67
GNI	46
Debt service as % of:	
Exports	10
GNI	7
Net financial flows, debt and equity	-954
Net debt inflows	-2,562
Net equity inflows	1,608
GNI	**74,151**
Population (million)	**9**

Figure 1 Public and publicly guaranteed debt, by creditor and creditor type in 2024, including IMF credit

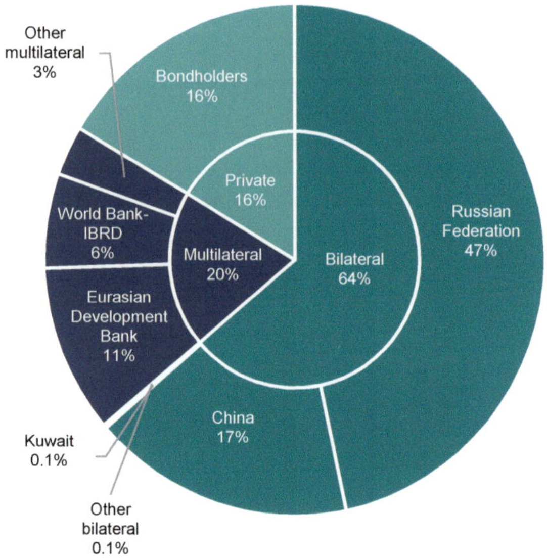

Figure 2 Average terms on new debt commitments from official and private creditors

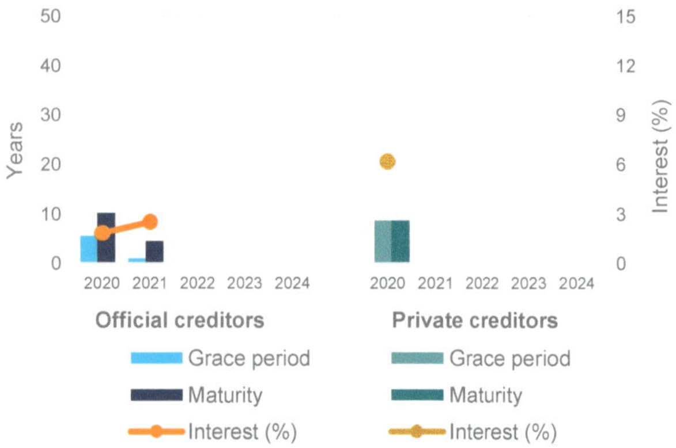

Summary External Debt Data	2010	2020	2021	2022	2023	2024
Total external debt stocks	**28,412**	**41,792**	**41,654**	**39,859**	**36,775**	**34,217**
Long-term external debt stocks	**12,486**	**31,180**	**29,859**	**28,355**	**24,953**	**22,956**
Public and publicly guaranteed debt from:	*8,014*	*20,270*	*19,979*	*19,208*	*17,500*	*16,325*
Official creditors	5,729	16,710	16,437	15,803	14,823	13,642
Multilateral	295	3,595	3,678	3,620	3,519	3,224
of which: World Bank	291	955	1,002	993	1,005	975
Bilateral	5,434	13,115	12,759	12,183	11,304	10,418
Private creditors	2,286	3,560	3,543	3,405	2,678	2,683
Bondholders	1,019	3,521	3,519	3,392	2,673	2,683
Commercial banks and others	1,266	39	23	13	5	..
Private nonguaranteed debt from:	*4,471*	*10,910*	*9,880*	*9,147*	*7,452*	*6,630*
Bondholders	..	368	367	371	356	358
Commercial banks and others	4,471	10,542	9,512	8,776	7,097	6,272
Use of IMF credit and SDR allocations	**4,063**	**531**	**1,430**	**1,360**	**1,371**	**1,333**
IMF credit	3,495	0	0	0	0	0
SDR allocations	568	531	1,430	1,360	1,371	1,333
Short-term external debt stocks	**11,864**	**10,082**	**10,365**	**10,144**	**10,451**	**9,929**
Disbursements, long-term	**3,810**	**4,099**	**1,691**	**3,767**	**2,611**	**1,260**
Public and publicly guaranteed sector	2,679	3,533	1,691	1,935	1,921	1,260
Private sector not guaranteed	1,132	566	..	1,832	690	0
Principal repayments, long-term	**1,265**	**2,881**	**2,968**	**5,226**	**5,641**	**3,245**
Public and publicly guaranteed sector	463	2,712	1,938	2,658	3,272	2,421
Private sector not guaranteed	802	169	1,030	2,568	2,369	825
Interest payments, long-term	**208**	**1,282**	**1,240**	**1,356**	**1,579**	**1,484**
Public and publicly guaranteed sector	128	892	853	906	1,162	1,141
Private sector not guaranteed	80	391	387	451	417	343

BELIZE

(US$ million, unless otherwise indicated)

Snapshot	2024
Total external debt stocks	**1,559**
External debt stocks as % of:	
Exports	94
GNI	46
Debt service as % of:	
Exports	8
GNI	4
Net financial flows, debt and equity	171
Net debt inflows	43
Net equity inflows	128
GNI	**3,386**
Population (thousand)	**417**

Figure 1 Public and publicly guaranteed debt, by creditor and creditor type in 2024, including IMF credit

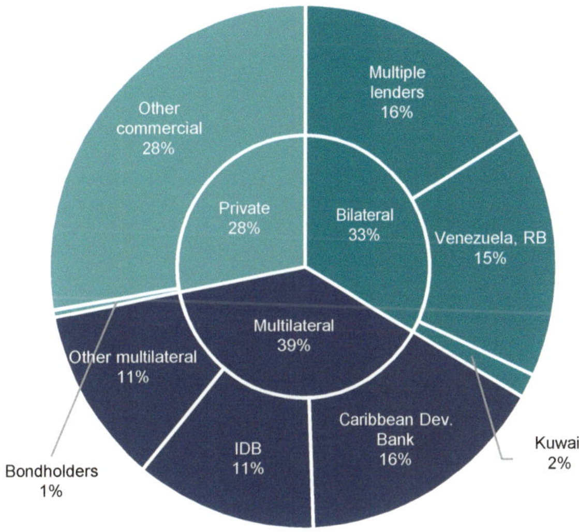

Figure 2 Average terms on new debt commitments from official and private creditors

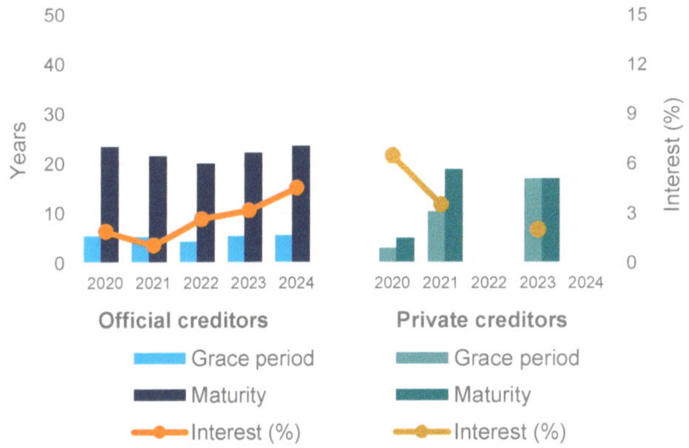

Summary External Debt Data	2010	2020	2021	2022	2023	2024
Total external debt stocks	**1,304**	**1,528**	**1,452**	**1,471**	**1,518**	**1,559**
Long-term external debt stocks	**1,262**	**1,494**	**1,381**	**1,403**	**1,448**	**1,489**
Public and publicly guaranteed debt from:	*1,019*	*1,410*	*1,278*	*1,305*	*1,355*	*1,399*
Official creditors	425	823	874	901	956	1,006
Multilateral	254	430	487	512	525	540
of which: World Bank	13	28	38	36	36	41
Bilateral	171	393	387	389	432	466
Private creditors	594	587	404	404	399	393
Bondholders	21	563	17	17	12	7
Commercial banks and others	573	24	387	387	387	386
Private nonguaranteed debt from:	*243*	*84*	*103*	*98*	*93*	*90*
Bondholders	..	..	..	..	..	..
Commercial banks and others	243	84	103	98	93	90
Use of IMF credit and SDR allocations	**35**	**26**	**61**	**58**	**58**	**57**
IMF credit	7	0	0	0	0	0
SDR allocations	28	26	61	58	58	57
Short-term external debt stocks	**7**	**8**	**10**	**10**	**12**	**13**
Disbursements, long-term	**39**	**154**	**482**	**69**	**107**	**106**
Public and publicly guaranteed sector	32	148	458	69	107	106
Private sector not guaranteed	7	7	24	..	0	..
Principal repayments, long-term	**69**	**45**	**599**	**43**	**61**	**63**
Public and publicly guaranteed sector	49	43	597	41	56	62
Private sector not guaranteed	20	2	2	2	4	1
Interest payments, long-term	**58**	**34**	**19**	**33**	**51**	**62**
Public and publicly guaranteed sector	47	32	17	31	50	62
Private sector not guaranteed	11	2	3	2	1	1

BENIN

(US$ million, unless otherwise indicated)

Snapshot	2024
Total external debt stocks	**14,163**
External debt stocks as % of:	
Exports	332
GNI	67
Debt service as % of:	
Exports	27
GNI	5
Net financial flows, debt and equity	2,549
Net debt inflows	2,115
Net equity inflows	434
GNI	**21,280**
Population (million)	**14**

Figure 1 Public and publicly guaranteed debt, by creditor and creditor type in 2024, including IMF credit

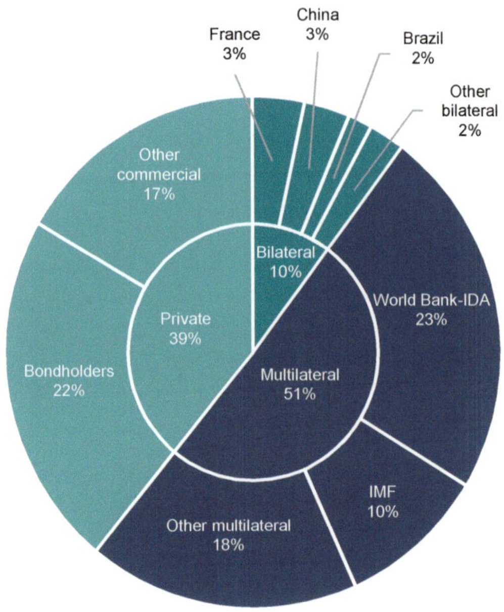

Figure 2 Average terms on new debt commitments from official and private creditors

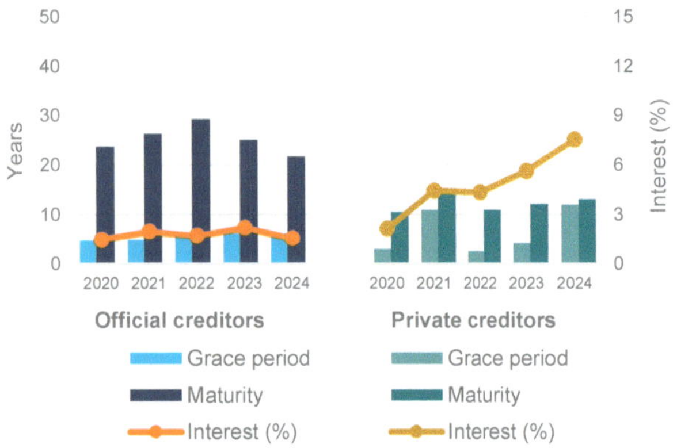

Summary External Debt Data	2010	2020	2021	2022	2023	2024
Total external debt stocks	**2,284**	**8,516**	**10,441**	**10,927**	**12,540**	**14,163**
Long-term external debt stocks	**1,481**	**6,483**	**7,933**	**8,327**	**10,104**	**11,711**
Public and publicly guaranteed debt from:	*1,112*	*4,465*	*5,836*	*6,040*	*7,313*	*8,921*
Official creditors	1,112	3,205	3,335	3,614	4,191	5,061
Multilateral	937	2,627	2,675	2,895	3,437	4,053
of which: World Bank	383	1,309	1,369	1,555	1,977	2,317
Bilateral	175	579	660	719	755	1,009
Private creditors	..	1,259	2,501	2,427	3,122	3,859
Bondholders	..	614	1,898	1,788	1,852	2,222
Commercial banks and others	..	646	603	639	1,270	1,637
Private nonguaranteed debt from:	*368*	*2,018*	*2,097*	*2,287*	*2,791*	*2,791*
Bondholders	..	..	..	..	..	..
Commercial banks and others	368	2,018	2,097	2,287	2,791	2,791
Use of IMF credit and SDR allocations	**146**	**563**	**699**	**944**	**1,142**	**1,182**
IMF credit	55	477	450	707	903	950
SDR allocations	91	85	249	237	239	232
Short-term external debt stocks	**658**	**1,471**	**1,808**	**1,656**	**1,295**	**1,270**
Disbursements, long-term	**218**	**942**	**2,369**	**984**	**2,163**	**2,704**
Public and publicly guaranteed sector	175	681	2,290	795	1,658	2,704
Private sector not guaranteed	43	261	79	189	505	..
Principal repayments, long-term	**26**	**99**	**623**	**292**	**569**	**637**
Public and publicly guaranteed sector	26	99	623	292	569	637
Private sector not guaranteed	..	..	..	..	..	..
Interest payments, long-term	**13**	**112**	**116**	**172**	**195**	**320**
Public and publicly guaranteed sector	13	111	105	163	191	315
Private sector not guaranteed	0	1	10	8	4	4

BHUTAN

(US$ million, unless otherwise indicated)

Snapshot	2024
Total external debt stocks	**3,400**
External debt stocks as % of:	
Exports	349
GNI	..
Debt service as % of:	
Exports	17
GNI	..
Net financial flows, debt and equity	**246**
Net debt inflows	223
Net equity inflows	23
GNI	**..**
Population (thousand)	**792**

Figure 1 Public and publicly guaranteed debt, by creditor and creditor type in 2024, including IMF credit

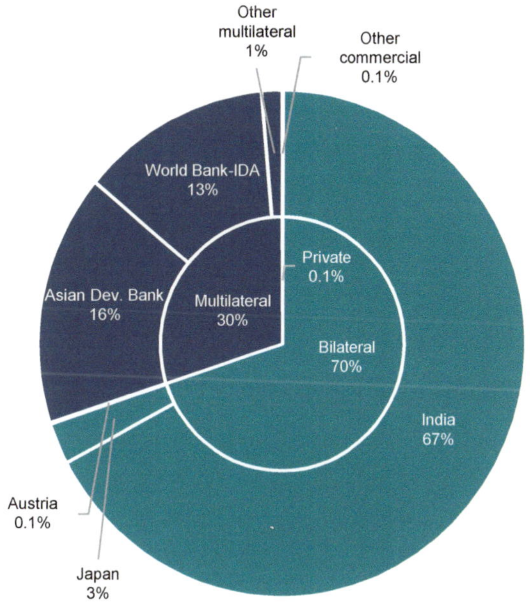

Figure 2 Average terms on new debt commitments from official and private creditors

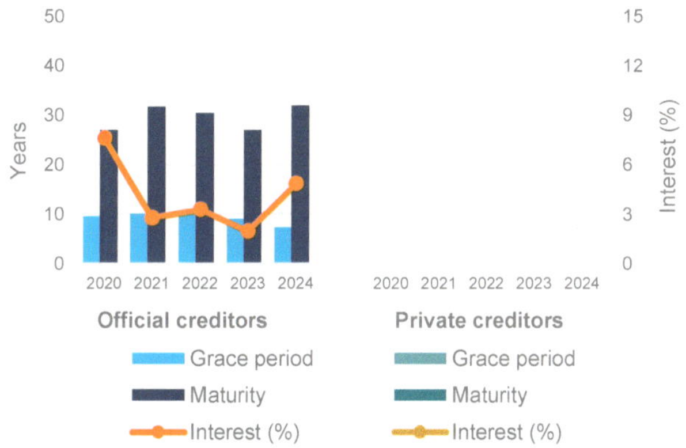

Summary External Debt Data	2010	2020	2021	2022	2023	2024
Total external debt stocks	**935**	**3,237**	**3,269**	**3,160**	**3,267**	**3,400**
Long-term external debt stocks	**919**	**3,227**	**3,230**	**3,121**	**3,232**	**3,367**
Public and publicly guaranteed debt from:	*919*	*3,185*	*3,186*	*3,077*	*3,188*	*3,323*
Official creditors	899	3,164	3,171	3,066	3,181	3,321
Multilateral	330	789	829	905	967	996
of which: World Bank	112	337	353	390	438	420
Bilateral	568	2,374	2,341	2,161	2,214	2,325
Private creditors	21	22	16	10	7	2
Bondholders	..	..	..	..	..	..
Commercial banks and others	21	22	16	10	7	2
Private nonguaranteed debt from:	..	*41*	*44*	*44*	*44*	*44*
Bondholders	..	..	..	..	..	..
Commercial banks and others	..	41	44	44	44	44
Use of IMF credit and SDR allocations	**9**	**9**	**36**	**34**	**34**	**33**
IMF credit	0	0	0	0	0	0
SDR allocations	9	9	36	34	34	33
Short-term external debt stocks	**6**	**1**	**3**	**6**	**1**	**0**
Disbursements, long-term	**178**	**508**	**138**	**215**	**194**	**320**
Public and publicly guaranteed sector	178	508	135	215	194	320
Private sector not guaranteed	..	..	3	..	..	..
Principal repayments, long-term	**47**	**37**	**73**	**71**	**77**	**96**
Public and publicly guaranteed sector	47	27	73	71	77	96
Private sector not guaranteed	..	10	..	..	..	..
Interest payments, long-term	**41**	**34**	**59**	**60**	**63**	**64**
Public and publicly guaranteed sector	41	33	57	58	61	62
Private sector not guaranteed	..	1	2	2	2	2

BOLIVIA

(US$ million, unless otherwise indicated)

Snapshot	2024
Total external debt stocks	**15,718**
External debt stocks as % of:	
Exports	152
GNI	33
Debt service as % of:	
Exports	18
GNI	4
Net financial flows, debt and equity	-27
Net debt inflows	-503
Net equity inflows	476
GNI	**48,306**
Population (million)	**12**

Figure 1 Public and publicly guaranteed debt, by creditor and creditor type in 2024, including IMF credit

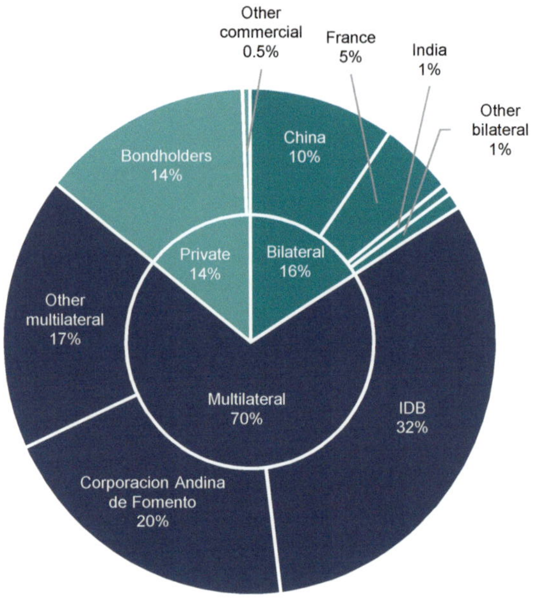

Figure 2 Average terms on new debt commitments from official and private creditors

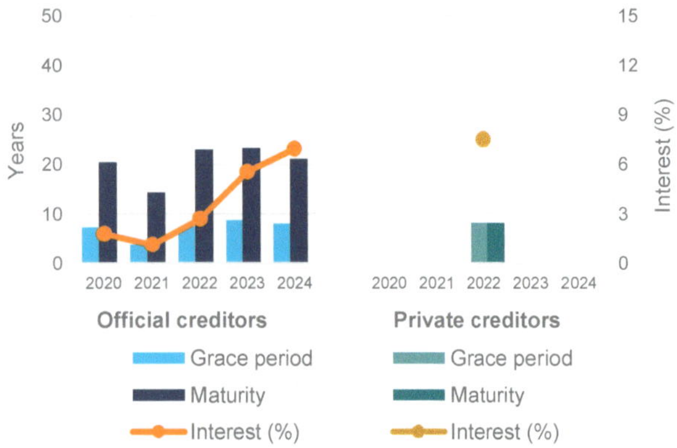

Summary External Debt Data	2010	2020	2021	2022	2023	2024
Total external debt stocks	**5,777**	**15,420**	**16,026**	**15,930**	**16,311**	**15,718**
Long-term external debt stocks	**5,187**	**14,260**	**14,714**	**14,775**	**14,989**	**14,568**
Public and publicly guaranteed debt from:	*2,830*	*11,877*	*12,773*	*13,372*	*13,665*	*13,420*
Official creditors	2,806	9,818	10,673	11,253	11,736	11,506
Multilateral	2,285	8,248	8,669	9,136	9,422	9,345
of which: World Bank	355	1,300	1,416	1,445	1,535	1,626
Bilateral	521	1,569	2,003	2,118	2,314	2,160
Private creditors	24	2,060	2,100	2,118	1,928	1,915
Bondholders	..	2,000	2,000	2,033	1,850	1,850
Commercial banks and others	24	60	100	85	78	65
Private nonguaranteed debt from:	*2,358*	*2,383*	*1,942*	*1,403*	*1,325*	*1,148*
Bondholders	..	..	..	..	..	..
Commercial banks and others	2,358	2,383	1,942	1,403	1,325	1,148
Use of IMF credit and SDR allocations	**253**	**582**	**552**	**525**	**529**	**514**
IMF credit	0	346	0	0	0	0
SDR allocations	253	236	552	525	529	514
Short-term external debt stocks	**336**	**577**	**759**	**631**	**793**	**635**
Disbursements, long-term	**548**	**1,445**	**1,453**	**2,123**	**1,123**	**683**
Public and publicly guaranteed sector	518	1,244	1,453	2,123	1,123	683
Private sector not guaranteed	30	201	..	..	..	..
Principal repayments, long-term	**569**	**764**	**936**	**1,959**	**935**	**1,028**
Public and publicly guaranteed sector	247	458	495	1,420	857	851
Private sector not guaranteed	322	306	441	539	78	177
Interest payments, long-term	**76**	**391**	**332**	**410**	**714**	**751**
Public and publicly guaranteed sector	54	363	307	389	630	685
Private sector not guaranteed	22	29	26	21	84	65

BOSNIA AND HERZEGOVINA

(US$ million, unless otherwise indicated)

Snapshot	**2024**
Total external debt stocks	**13,888**
External debt stocks as % of:	
Exports	103
GNI	49
Debt service as % of:	
Exports	11
GNI	5
Net financial flows, debt and equity	1,095
Net debt inflows	323
Net equity inflows	772
GNI	**28,254**
Population (million)	**3**

Figure 1 Public and publicly guaranteed debt, by creditor and creditor type in 2024, including IMF credit

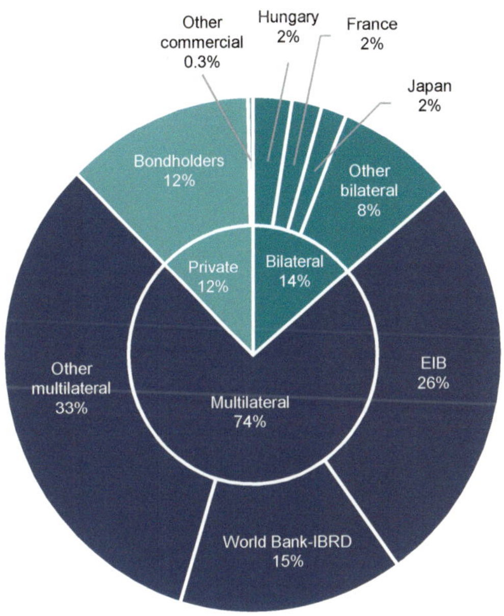

Figure 2 Average terms on new debt commitments from official and private creditors

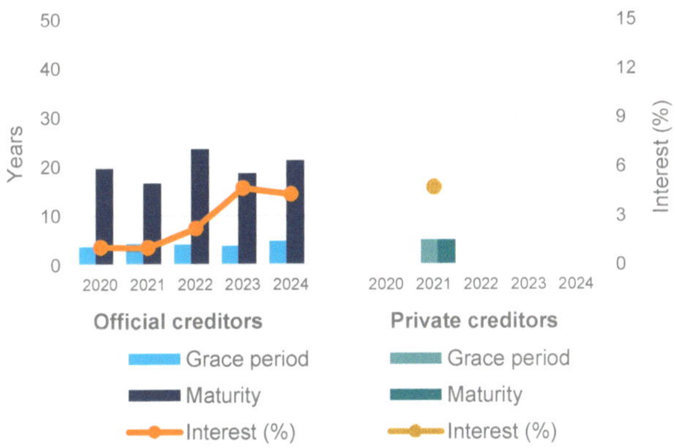

Summary External Debt Data	**2010**	**2020**	**2021**	**2022**	**2023**	**2024**
Total external debt stocks	**14,357**	**13,980**	**13,747**	**13,440**	**13,868**	**13,888**
Long-term external debt stocks	**12,439**	**10,405**	**10,027**	**9,769**	**10,047**	**10,112**
Public and publicly guaranteed debt from:	*3,801*	*5,106*	*5,469*	*5,065*	*5,063*	*4,927*
Official creditors	3,323	4,827	4,563	4,220	4,380	4,289
Multilateral	2,483	3,923	3,766	3,529	3,612	3,582
of which: World Bank	1,626	1,670	1,586	1,423	1,319	1,251
Bilateral	840	904	797	690	767	707
Private creditors	478	278	905	845	683	638
Bondholders	273	229	868	818	661	622
Commercial banks and others	204	50	37	28	22	16
Private nonguaranteed debt from:	*8,638*	*5,299*	*4,558*	*4,704*	*4,985*	*5,184*
Bondholders	..	..	..	..	..	..
Commercial banks and others	8,638	5,299	4,558	4,704	4,985	5,184
Use of IMF credit and SDR allocations	**769**	**796**	**1,115**	**1,039**	**930**	**704**
IMF credit	521	565	534	487	373	162
SDR allocations	248	232	581	552	557	541
Short-term external debt stocks	**1,149**	**2,779**	**2,605**	**2,632**	**2,891**	**3,073**
Disbursements, long-term	**566**	**1,239**	**1,518**	**640**	**1,258**	**1,213**
Public and publicly guaranteed sector	441	390	1,261	270	553	572
Private sector not guaranteed	125	849	257	370	705	641
Principal repayments, long-term	**375**	**516**	**1,298**	**600**	**1,117**	**868**
Public and publicly guaranteed sector	147	393	421	376	693	427
Private sector not guaranteed	227	123	877	224	424	441
Interest payments, long-term	**177**	**101**	**130**	**238**	**328**	**164**
Public and publicly guaranteed sector	56	82	79	85	135	141
Private sector not guaranteed	121	19	51	153	193	23

BOTSWANA

(US$ million, unless otherwise indicated)

Snapshot	2024
Total external debt stocks	**2,318**
External debt stocks as % of:	
Exports	40
GNI	12
Debt service as % of:	
Exports	5
GNI	1
Net financial flows, debt and equity	96
Net debt inflows	156
Net equity inflows	-60
GNI	**19,434**
Population (million)	**3**

Figure 1 Public and publicly guaranteed debt, by creditor and creditor type in 2024, including IMF credit

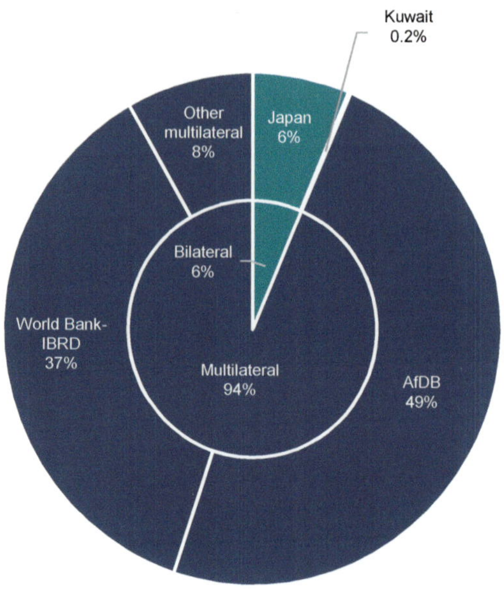

Figure 2 Average terms on new debt commitments from official and private creditors

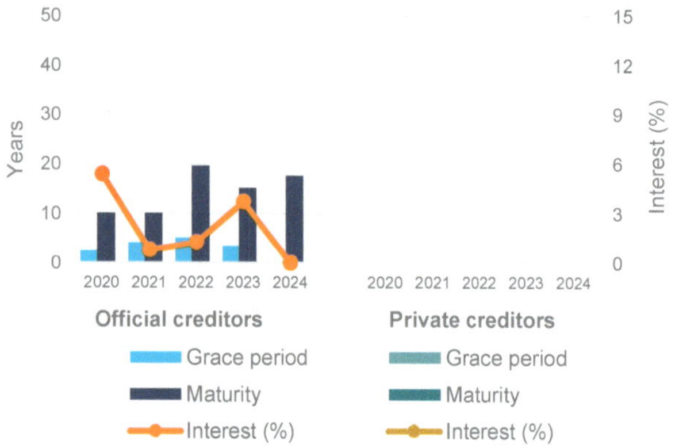

Summary External Debt Data	2010	2020	2021	2022	2023	2024
Total external debt stocks	**1,807**	**1,603**	**1,997**	**2,003**	**2,185**	**2,318**
Long-term external debt stocks	**1,358**	**1,303**	**1,497**	**1,563**	**1,564**	**1,852**
Public and publicly guaranteed debt from:	*1,358*	*1,284*	*1,482*	*1,558*	*1,564*	*1,852*
Official creditors	1,357	1,284	1,482	1,558	1,564	1,852
Multilateral	1,219	1,240	1,447	1,529	1,429	1,732
of which: World Bank	11	194	470	521	540	678
Bilateral	138	44	36	29	134	120
Private creditors	1	..	..	..	..	..
Bondholders	..	..	..	..	..	..
Commercial banks and others	1	..	..	..	..	..
Private nonguaranteed debt from:	..	*19*	*14*	*4*	*0*	..
Bondholders	..	..	..	..	..	..
Commercial banks and others	..	19	14	4	0	..
Use of IMF credit and SDR allocations	**88**	**83**	**345**	**328**	**331**	**321**
IMF credit	0	0	0	0	0	0
SDR allocations	88	83	345	328	331	321
Short-term external debt stocks	**360**	**218**	**156**	**112**	**290**	**145**
Disbursements, long-term	**17**	**96**	**348**	**221**	**153**	**452**
Public and publicly guaranteed sector	17	80	341	221	153	452
Private sector not guaranteed	..	16	7	..	..	..
Principal repayments, long-term	**58**	**147**	**145**	**149**	**150**	**150**
Public and publicly guaranteed sector	58	138	135	140	146	150
Private sector not guaranteed	..	10	10	9	4	..
Interest payments, long-term	**18**	**32**	**15**	**20**	**69**	**103**
Public and publicly guaranteed sector	18	31	14	20	69	103
Private sector not guaranteed	..	1	0	0	0	..

BRAZIL

(US$ million, unless otherwise indicated)

Snapshot	2024
Total external debt stocks	**605,464**
External debt stocks as % of:	
Exports	142
GNI	29
Debt service as % of:	
Exports	27
GNI	5
Net financial flows, debt and equity	46,071
Net debt inflows	2,943
Net equity inflows	43,129
GNI	**2,112,481**
Population (million)	**212**

Figure 1 Public and publicly guaranteed debt, by creditor and creditor type in 2024, including IMF credit

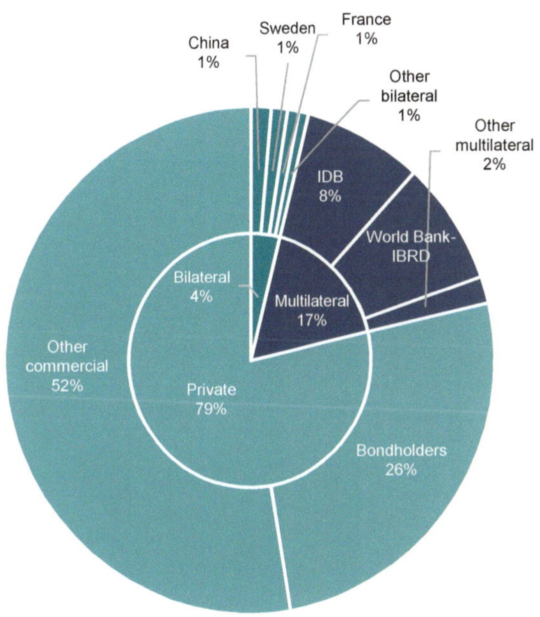

Figure 2 Average terms on new debt commitments from official and private creditors

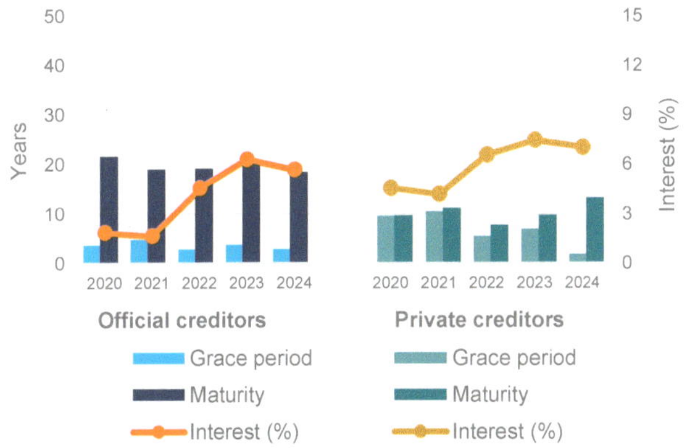

Summary External Debt Data	2010	2020	2021	2022	2023	2024
Total external debt stocks	**352,364**	**549,329**	**571,194**	**579,258**	**607,387**	**605,464**
Long-term external debt stocks	**282,426**	**476,188**	**473,588**	**493,559**	**508,823**	**503,614**
Public and publicly guaranteed debt from:	*97,486*	*194,332*	*193,849*	*190,347*	*191,025*	*194,369*
Official creditors	41,553	44,003	44,520	43,338	44,397	43,915
Multilateral	29,980	33,716	35,174	35,214	36,417	36,531
of which: World Bank	13,523	15,682	15,419	16,061	15,579	15,131
Bilateral	11,573	10,287	9,346	8,124	7,980	7,384
Private creditors	55,933	150,329	149,329	147,010	146,629	150,454
Bondholders	46,806	49,385	46,520	43,132	44,925	49,634
Commercial banks and others	9,127	100,943	102,809	103,877	101,704	100,819
Private nonguaranteed debt from:	*184,940*	*281,856*	*279,739*	*303,212*	*317,797*	*309,245*
Bondholders	83,032	35,903	31,375	27,194	30,054	37,668
Commercial banks and others	101,908	245,953	248,364	276,018	287,744	271,577
Use of IMF credit and SDR allocations	**4,446**	**4,158**	**18,853**	**17,927**	**18,073**	**17,567**
IMF credit	0	0	0	0	0	0
SDR allocations	4,446	4,158	18,853	17,927	18,073	17,567
Short-term external debt stocks	**65,492**	**68,983**	**78,753**	**67,772**	**80,492**	**84,282**
Disbursements, long-term	**85,379**	**126,735**	**155,701**	**133,964**	**208,596**	**82,789**
Public and publicly guaranteed sector	19,957	39,465	16,294	23,654	20,293	38,618
Private sector not guaranteed	65,422	87,270	139,408	110,310	188,303	44,172
Principal repayments, long-term	**32,026**	**109,830**	**132,321**	**106,163**	**195,334**	**83,637**
Public and publicly guaranteed sector	9,628	23,167	20,397	22,860	21,584	30,914
Private sector not guaranteed	22,398	86,663	111,924	83,303	173,750	52,724
Interest payments, long-term	**13,157**	**19,055**	**28,690**	**17,788**	**24,509**	**24,526**
Public and publicly guaranteed sector	5,172	7,764	8,520	7,985	9,625	10,779
Private sector not guaranteed	7,985	11,292	20,169	9,803	14,884	13,747

BURKINA FASO

(US$ million, unless otherwise indicated)

Snapshot	2024
Total external debt stocks	**10,845**
External debt stocks as % of:	
Exports	167
GNI	49
Debt service as % of:	
Exports	14
GNI	4
Net financial flows, debt and equity	697
Net debt inflows	614
Net equity inflows	83
GNI	**22,241**
Population (million)	**24**

Figure 1 Public and publicly guaranteed debt, by creditor and creditor type in 2024, including IMF credit

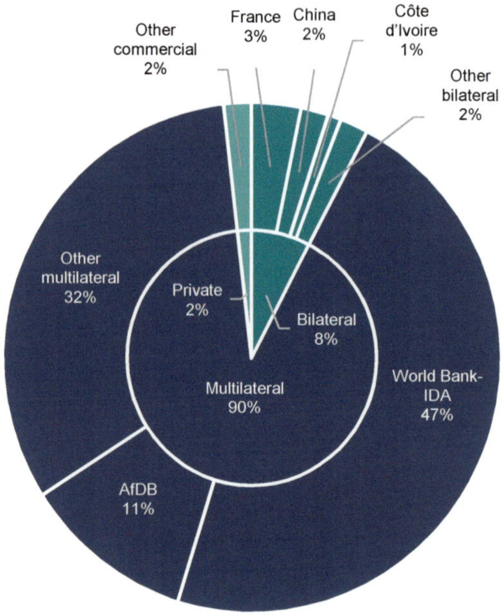

Figure 2 Average terms on new debt commitments from official and private creditors

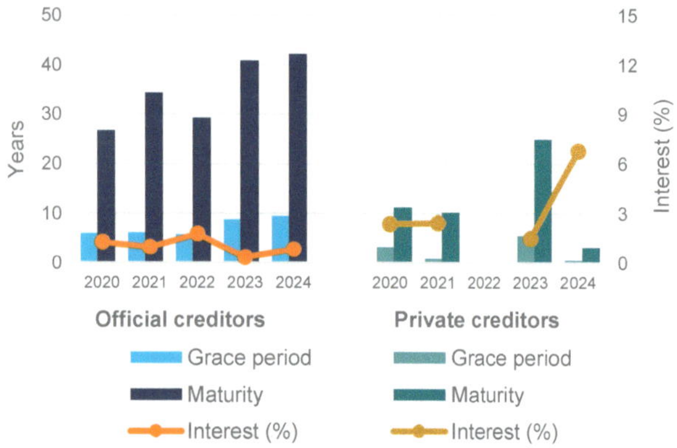

Summary External Debt Data	2010	2020	2021	2022	2023	2024
Total external debt stocks	**4,808**	**9,769**	**10,333**	**9,906**	**10,478**	**10,845**
Long-term external debt stocks	**4,590**	**9,303**	**9,747**	**9,372**	**9,846**	**10,189**
Public and publicly guaranteed debt from:	*1,968*	*4,032*	*4,365*	*4,440*	*4,846*	*5,121*
Official creditors	1,927	4,022	4,354	4,431	4,806	5,023
Multilateral	1,619	3,559	3,873	3,946	4,347	4,598
of which: World Bank	776	2,014	2,146	2,187	2,417	2,616
Bilateral	308	463	481	485	460	426
Private creditors	41	10	11	9	40	98
Bondholders	..	..	..	..	..	..
Commercial banks and others	41	10	11	9	40	98
Private nonguaranteed debt from:	*2,622*	*5,271*	*5,382*	*4,932*	*4,999*	*5,068*
Bondholders	..	..	..	..	..	..
Commercial banks and others	2,622	5,271	5,382	4,932	4,999	5,068
Use of IMF credit and SDR allocations	**217**	**466**	**586**	**534**	**632**	**656**
IMF credit	129	383	344	304	400	431
SDR allocations	89	83	242	230	232	226
Short-term external debt stocks	**0**	**0**	**0**	**0**	**0**	**0**
Disbursements, long-term	**1,393**	**2,094**	**1,076**	**839**	**719**	**1,074**
Public and publicly guaranteed sector	287	534	655	443	465	719
Private sector not guaranteed	1,106	1,560	421	396	254	354
Principal repayments, long-term	**293**	**1,868**	**414**	**984**	**355**	**502**
Public and publicly guaranteed sector	31	103	104	138	168	216
Private sector not guaranteed	262	1,764	310	846	187	286
Interest payments, long-term	**149**	**274**	**55**	**65**	**345**	**352**
Public and publicly guaranteed sector	18	36	41	47	64	80
Private sector not guaranteed	131	238	14	18	281	272

BURUNDI

(US$ million, unless otherwise indicated)

Snapshot	2024
Total external debt stocks	**1,024**
External debt stocks as % of:	
Exports	..
GNI	47
Debt service as % of:	
Exports	..
GNI	2
Net financial flows, debt and equity	41
Net debt inflows	10
Net equity inflows	32
GNI	**2,173**
Population (million)	**14**

Figure 1 Public and publicly guaranteed debt, by creditor and creditor type in 2024, including IMF credit

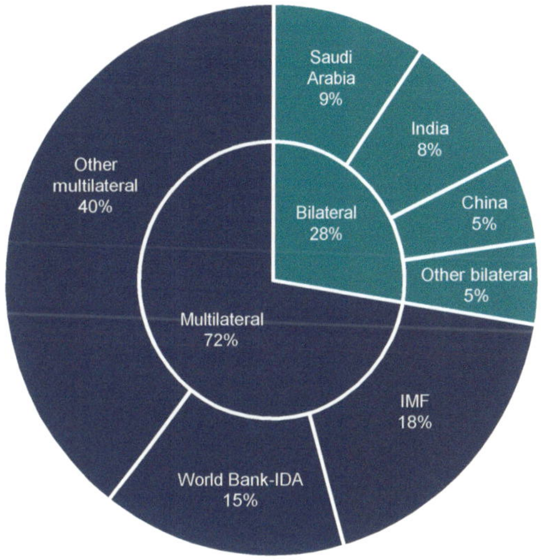

Figure 2 Average terms on new debt commitments from official and private creditors

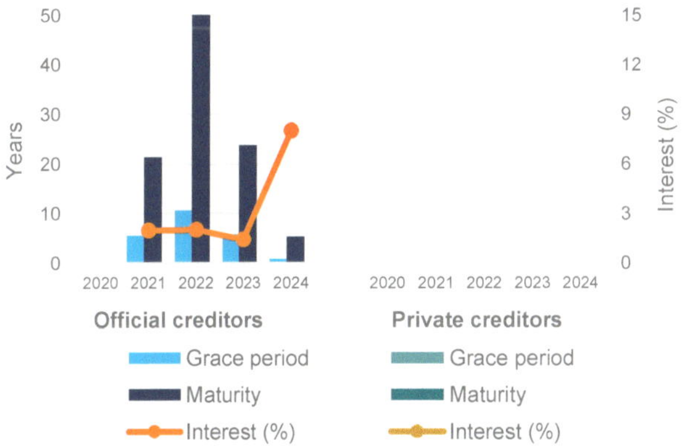

Summary External Debt Data	2010	2020	2021	2022	2023	2024
Total external debt stocks	**621**	**665**	**976**	**947**	**1,034**	**1,024**
Long-term external debt stocks	**382**	**532**	**576**	**570**	**598**	**601**
Public and publicly guaranteed debt from:	*382*	*532*	*576*	*570*	*598*	*601*
Official creditors	382	532	576	570	598	601
Multilateral	325	361	390	388	411	399
of which: World Bank	163	140	132	122	118	109
Bilateral	57	171	186	182	187	202
Private creditors	..	..	..	..	..	..
Bondholders	..	..	..	..	..	..
Commercial banks and others	..	..	..	..	..	..
Private nonguaranteed debt from:	..	..	..	..	..	..
Bondholders	..	..	..	..	..	..
Commercial banks and others	..	..	..	..	..	..
Use of IMF credit and SDR allocations	**223**	**132**	**400**	**376**	**435**	**420**
IMF credit	110	26	90	82	138	131
SDR allocations	114	106	310	295	297	289
Short-term external debt stocks	**16**	**0**	**0**	**0**	**0**	**3**
Disbursements, long-term	**32**	**50**	**62**	**32**	**48**	**31**
Public and publicly guaranteed sector	32	50	62	32	48	31
Private sector not guaranteed	..	..	..	..	..	..
Principal repayments, long-term	**2**	**10**	**13**	**20**	**22**	**18**
Public and publicly guaranteed sector	2	10	13	20	22	18
Private sector not guaranteed	..	..	..	..	..	..
Interest payments, long-term	**1**	**4**	**6**	**5**	**5**	**3**
Public and publicly guaranteed sector	1	4	6	5	5	3
Private sector not guaranteed	..	..	..	..	..	..

CABO VERDE

(US$ million, unless otherwise indicated)

Snapshot	2024
Total external debt stocks	**2,360**
External debt stocks as % of:	
Exports	195
GNI	87
Debt service as % of:	
Exports	13
GNI	6
Net financial flows, debt and equity	95
Net debt inflows	-10
Net equity inflows	105
GNI	**2,716**
Population (thousand)	**525**

Figure 1 Public and publicly guaranteed debt, by creditor and creditor type in 2024, including IMF credit

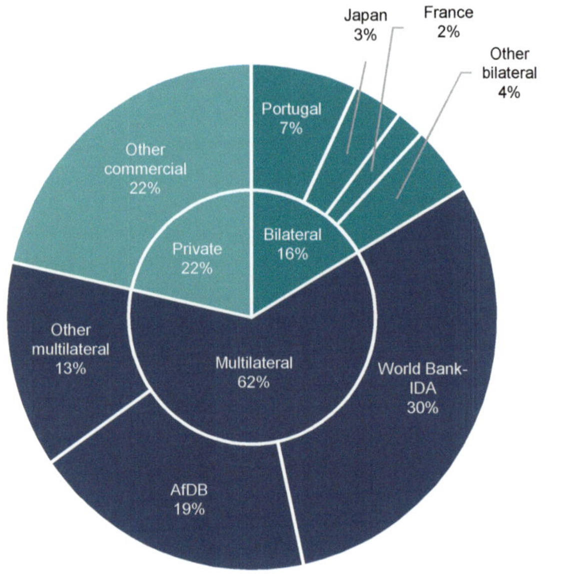

Figure 2 Average terms on new debt commitments from official and private creditors

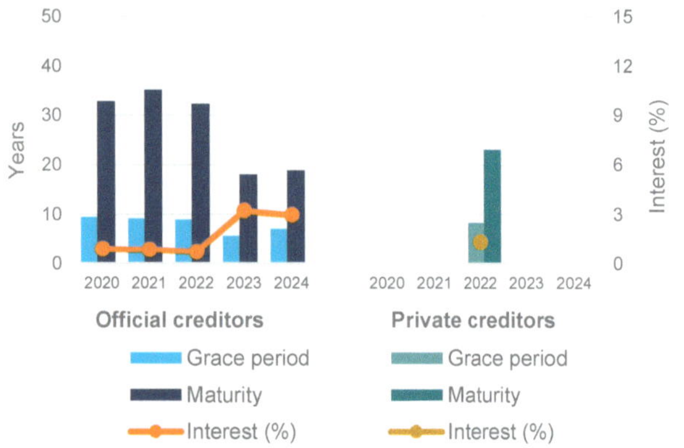

Summary External Debt Data	2010	2020	2021	2022	2023	2024
Total external debt stocks	**885**	**2,429**	**2,457**	**2,403**	**2,463**	**2,360**
Long-term external debt stocks	**862**	**2,032**	**1,994**	**1,918**	**1,940**	**1,845**
Public and publicly guaranteed debt from:	*862*	*2,032*	*1,994*	*1,918*	*1,940*	*1,845*
Official creditors	778	1,474	1,478	1,443	1,475	1,429
Multilateral	598	1,014	1,043	1,058	1,113	1,111
of which: World Bank	303	482	523	547	601	616
Bilateral	181	459	435	385	362	318
Private creditors	84	558	515	475	465	416
Bondholders	..	..	..	..	..	..
Commercial banks and others	84	558	515	475	465	416
Private nonguaranteed debt from:	..	..	..	..	..	..
Bondholders	..	..	..	..	..	..
Commercial banks and others	..	..	..	..	..	..
Use of IMF credit and SDR allocations	**23**	**47**	**78**	**89**	**111**	**126**
IMF credit	9	34	33	47	68	85
SDR allocations	14	13	45	42	43	42
Short-term external debt stocks	**0**	**350**	**385**	**396**	**412**	**388**
Disbursements, long-term	**203**	**125**	**120**	**105**	**80**	**89**
Public and publicly guaranteed sector	203	125	120	105	80	89
Private sector not guaranteed	..	..	..	..	..	..
Principal repayments, long-term	**25**	**43**	**44**	**66**	**95**	**94**
Public and publicly guaranteed sector	25	43	44	66	95	94
Private sector not guaranteed	..	..	..	..	..	..
Interest payments, long-term	**8**	**17**	**11**	**20**	**30**	**35**
Public and publicly guaranteed sector	8	17	11	20	30	35
Private sector not guaranteed	..	..	..	..	..	..

CAMBODIA

(US$ million, unless otherwise indicated)

Snapshot	2024
Total external debt stocks	**20,977**
External debt stocks as % of:	
Exports	65
GNI	46
Debt service as % of:	
Exports	11
GNI	7
Net financial flows, debt and equity	3,163
Net debt inflows	-1,232
Net equity inflows	4,395
GNI	**45,493**
Population (million)	**18**

Figure 1 Public and publicly guaranteed debt, by creditor and creditor type in 2024, including IMF credit

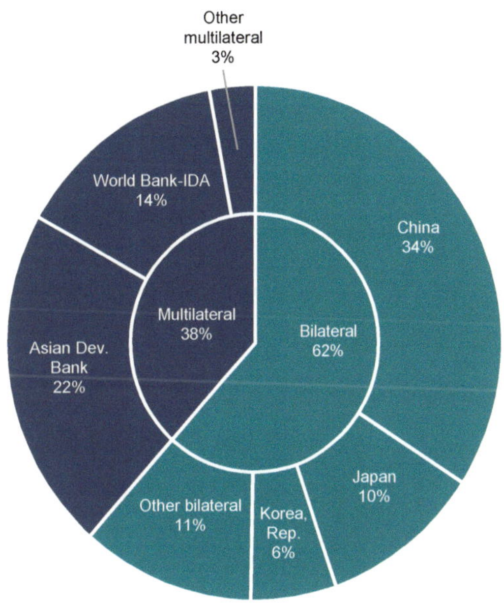

Figure 2 Average terms on new debt commitments from official and private creditors

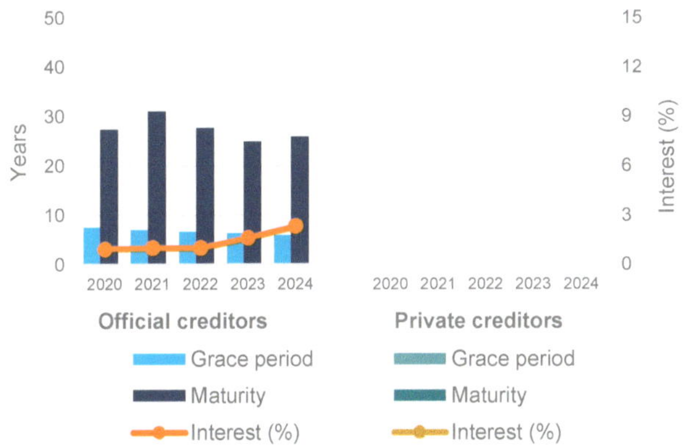

Summary External Debt Data	2010	2020	2021	2022	2023	2024
Total external debt stocks	**4,010**	**17,594**	**20,050**	**22,474**	**22,534**	**20,977**
Long-term external debt stocks	**3,502**	**13,691**	**15,261**	**17,529**	**17,824**	**16,353**
Public and publicly guaranteed debt from:	*3,060*	*8,789*	*9,481*	*10,067*	*11,098*	*11,918*
Official creditors	3,060	8,789	9,481	10,067	11,098	11,918
Multilateral	1,529	2,717	2,874	3,232	3,988	4,579
of which: World Bank	565	685	727	936	1,315	1,654
Bilateral	1,531	6,073	6,608	6,835	7,111	7,339
Private creditors	..	..	..	..	..	..
Bondholders	..	..	..	..	..	..
Commercial banks and others	..	..	..	..	..	..
Private nonguaranteed debt from:	*442*	*4,902*	*5,779*	*7,462*	*6,725*	*4,435*
Bondholders	..	650	550	550	550	0
Commercial banks and others	442	4,252	5,229	6,912	6,175	4,435
Use of IMF credit and SDR allocations	**129**	**121**	**352**	**335**	**338**	**328**
IMF credit	0	0	0	0	0	0
SDR allocations	129	121	352	335	338	328
Short-term external debt stocks	**379**	**3,782**	**4,437**	**4,610**	**4,372**	**4,297**
Disbursements, long-term	**596**	**2,945**	**3,687**	**4,778**	**2,317**	**1,553**
Public and publicly guaranteed sector	348	1,215	1,155	1,352	1,476	1,553
Private sector not guaranteed	248	1,729	2,532	3,426	841	..
Principal repayments, long-term	**33**	**1,344**	**1,946**	**2,095**	**1,958**	**2,709**
Public and publicly guaranteed sector	33	264	291	352	379	419
Private sector not guaranteed	..	1,079	1,654	1,743	1,578	2,290
Interest payments, long-term	**27**	**170**	**301**	**416**	**478**	**442**
Public and publicly guaranteed sector	26	95	103	113	118	126
Private sector not guaranteed	1	76	198	303	360	316

CAMEROON

(US$ million, unless otherwise indicated)

Snapshot	2024
Total external debt stocks	**15,771**
External debt stocks as % of:	
Exports	..
GNI	31
Debt service as % of:	
Exports	..
GNI	3
Net financial flows, debt and equity	1,827
Net debt inflows	901
Net equity inflows	925
GNI	**50,406**
Population (million)	**29**

Figure 1 Public and publicly guaranteed debt, by creditor and creditor type in 2024, including IMF credit

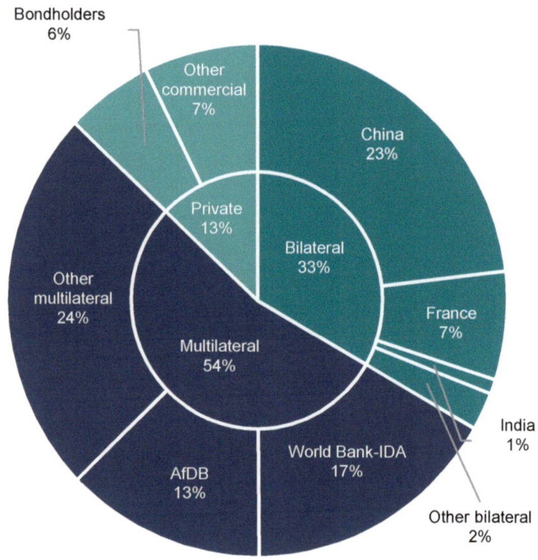

Figure 2 Average terms on new debt commitments from official and private creditors

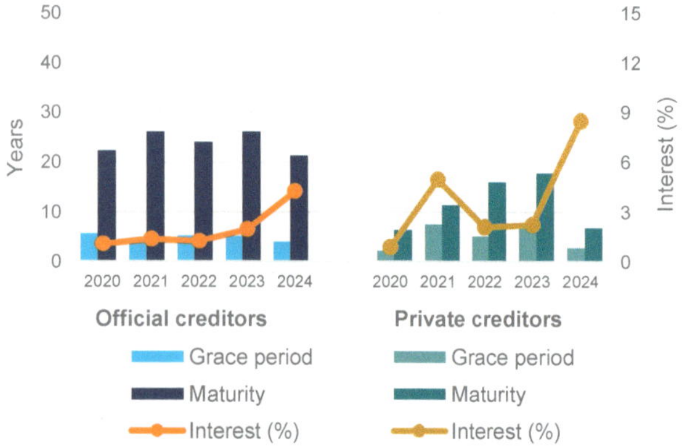

Summary External Debt Data	2010	2020	2021	2022	2023	2024
Total external debt stocks	**3,190**	**14,723**	**15,378**	**15,123**	**15,402**	**15,771**
Long-term external debt stocks	**2,737**	**13,086**	**12,951**	**12,370**	**12,489**	**12,788**
Public and publicly guaranteed debt from:	*2,160*	*11,391*	*12,380*	*11,866*	*12,128*	*12,517*
Official creditors	2,143	9,951	10,293	10,434	10,720	10,718
Multilateral	787	4,319	4,720	5,042	5,630	6,069
of which: World Bank	374	1,915	2,068	2,234	2,543	2,865
Bilateral	1,356	5,631	5,572	5,392	5,090	4,649
Private creditors	17	1,440	2,087	1,432	1,409	1,799
Bondholders	..	750	1,526	891	870	777
Commercial banks and others	17	690	561	542	539	1,021
Private nonguaranteed debt from:	*577*	*1,695*	*571*	*504*	*360*	*271*
Bondholders	..	..	..	..	..	..
Commercial banks and others	577	1,695	571	504	360	271
Use of IMF credit and SDR allocations	**445**	**1,269**	**1,777**	**1,874**	**2,055**	**2,032**
IMF credit	172	1,014	1,159	1,286	1,463	1,456
SDR allocations	273	255	618	588	593	576
Short-term external debt stocks	**9**	**368**	**650**	**879**	**858**	**951**
Disbursements, long-term	**278**	**1,724**	**1,851**	**1,363**	**1,015**	**1,835**
Public and publicly guaranteed sector	278	1,091	1,851	1,321	1,004	1,819
Private sector not guaranteed	..	633	0	42	11	16
Principal repayments, long-term	**160**	**964**	**1,648**	**1,480**	**1,107**	**1,061**
Public and publicly guaranteed sector	122	623	523	1,371	938	992
Private sector not guaranteed	38	341	1,125	109	169	69
Interest payments, long-term	**42**	**343**	**283**	**280**	**473**	**434**
Public and publicly guaranteed sector	27	330	276	275	468	405
Private sector not guaranteed	15	13	8	4	5	29

CENTRAL AFRICAN REPUBLIC

(US$ million, unless otherwise indicated)

Snapshot	2024
Total external debt stocks	**1,046**
External debt stocks as % of:	
Exports	248
GNI	36
Debt service as % of:	
Exports	13
GNI	2
Net financial flows, debt and equity	20
Net debt inflows	-20
Net equity inflows	40
GNI	**2,917**
Population (million)	**5**

Figure 1 Public and publicly guaranteed debt, by creditor and creditor type in 2024, including IMF credit

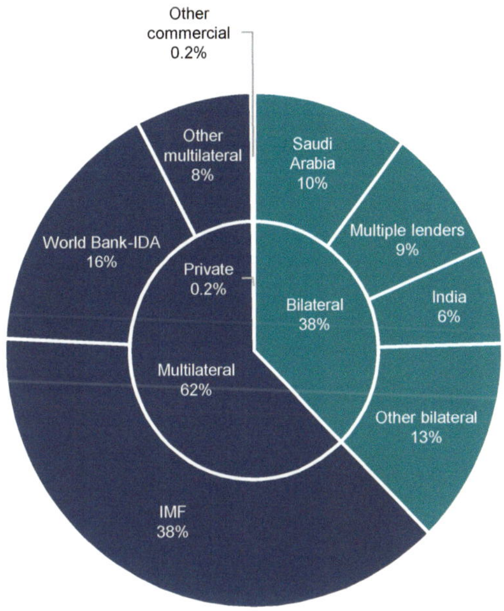

Figure 2 Average terms on new debt commitments from official and private creditors

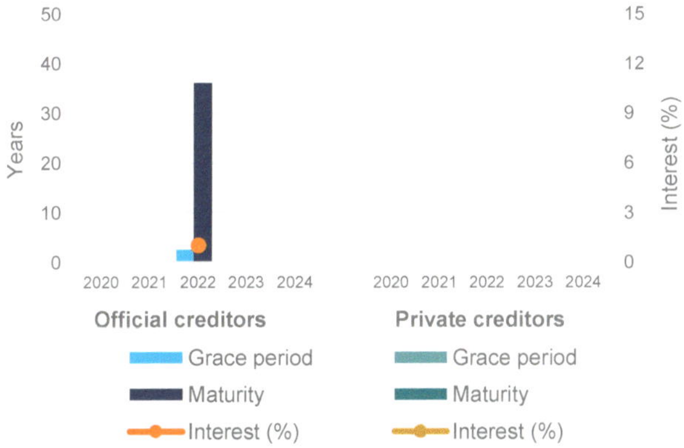

Summary External Debt Data	2010	2020	2021	2022	2023	2024
Total external debt stocks	**655**	**908**	**1,111**	**1,046**	**1,083**	**1,046**
Long-term external debt stocks	**375**	**429**	**433**	**445**	**456**	**439**
Public and publicly guaranteed debt from:	*375*	*429*	*433*	*445*	*456*	*439*
Official creditors	336	426	428	441	453	437
Multilateral	56	189	187	182	182	170
of which: World Bank	14	130	133	126	124	117
Bilateral	280	237	241	259	271	267
Private creditors	39	3	5	4	3	2
Bondholders	..	..	..	..	..	..
Commercial banks and others	39	3	5	4	3	2
Private nonguaranteed debt from:	..	..	..	..	..	..
Bondholders	..	..	..	..	..	..
Commercial banks and others	..	..	..	..	..	..
Use of IMF credit and SDR allocations	**173**	**355**	**518**	**483**	**504**	**481**
IMF credit	90	279	294	270	289	272
SDR allocations	82	77	224	213	215	209
Short-term external debt stocks	**107**	**124**	**160**	**118**	**123**	**126**
Disbursements, long-term	**35**	**26**	**33**	**8**	**15**	**1**
Public and publicly guaranteed sector	35	26	33	8	15	1
Private sector not guaranteed	..	..	..	..	..	..
Principal repayments, long-term	**1**	**4**	**6**	**4**	**6**	**12**
Public and publicly guaranteed sector	1	4	6	4	6	12
Private sector not guaranteed	..	..	..	..	..	..
Interest payments, long-term	**1**	**2**	**2**	**3**	**2**	**2**
Public and publicly guaranteed sector	1	2	2	3	2	2
Private sector not guaranteed	..	..	..	..	..	..

CHAD

(US$ million, unless otherwise indicated)

Snapshot	2024
Total external debt stocks	**3,348**
External debt stocks as % of:	
Exports	..
GNI	16
Debt service as % of:	
Exports	..
GNI	2
Net financial flows, debt and equity	1,236
Net debt inflows	217
Net equity inflows	1,019
GNI	**20,415**
Population (million)	**20**

Figure 1 Public and publicly guaranteed debt, by creditor and creditor type in 2024, including IMF credit

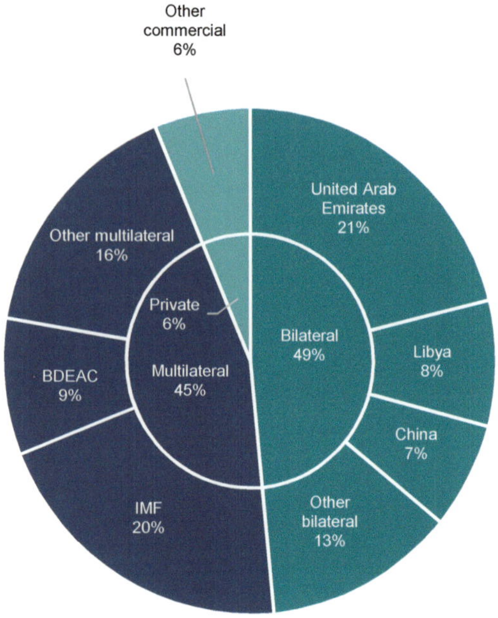

Figure 2 Average terms on new debt commitments from official and private creditors

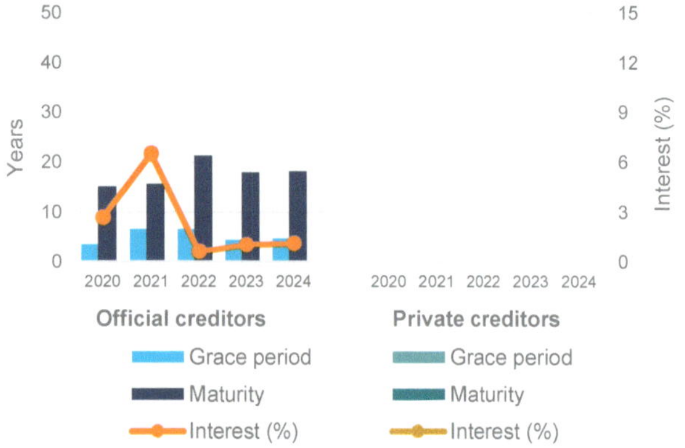

Summary External Debt Data	2010	2020	2021	2022	2023	2024
Total external debt stocks	**2,158**	**3,488**	**3,585**	**3,270**	**3,192**	**3,348**
Long-term external debt stocks	**2,049**	**2,781**	**2,641**	**2,244**	**2,198**	**2,444**
Public and publicly guaranteed debt from:	*2,049*	*2,781*	*2,641*	*2,244*	*2,198*	*2,444*
Official creditors	2,032	1,705	1,713	1,616	1,831	2,250
Multilateral	1,529	716	759	717	823	760
of which: World Bank	865	180	169	155	151	140
Bilateral	504	990	954	899	1,008	1,490
Private creditors	17	1,076	929	628	366	193
Bondholders	..	..	..	..	..	..
Commercial banks and others	17	1,076	929	628	366	193
Private nonguaranteed debt from:	..	..	..	..	..	..
Bondholders	..	..	..	..	..	..
Commercial banks and others	..	..	..	..	..	..
Use of IMF credit and SDR allocations	**99**	**678**	**914**	**996**	**964**	**875**
IMF credit	17	601	651	746	712	630
SDR allocations	83	77	263	250	252	245
Short-term external debt stocks	**9**	**28**	**29**	**30**	**30**	**29**
Disbursements, long-term	**366**	**132**	**174**	**15**	**281**	**530**
Public and publicly guaranteed sector	366	132	174	15	281	530
Private sector not guaranteed	..	..	..	..	..	..
Principal repayments, long-term	**45**	**137**	**271**	**346**	**346**	**250**
Public and publicly guaranteed sector	45	137	271	346	346	250
Private sector not guaranteed	..	..	..	..	..	..
Interest payments, long-term	**17**	**50**	**49**	**49**	**52**	**43**
Public and publicly guaranteed sector	17	50	49	49	52	43
Private sector not guaranteed	..	..	..	..	..	..

CHINA

(US$ million, unless otherwise indicated)

Snapshot	2024
Total external debt stocks	**2,419,835**
External debt stocks as % of:	
Exports	59
GNI	13
Debt service as % of:	
Exports	9
GNI	2
Net financial flows, debt and equity	33,059
Net debt inflows	-19,514
Net equity inflows	52,573
GNI	**18,613,042**
Population (million)	**1,409**

Figure 1 Public and publicly guaranteed debt, by creditor and creditor type in 2024, including IMF credit

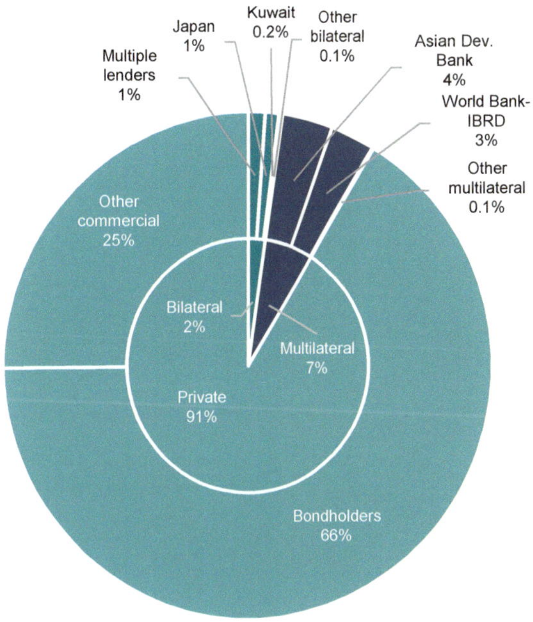

Figure 2 Average terms on new debt commitments from official and private creditors

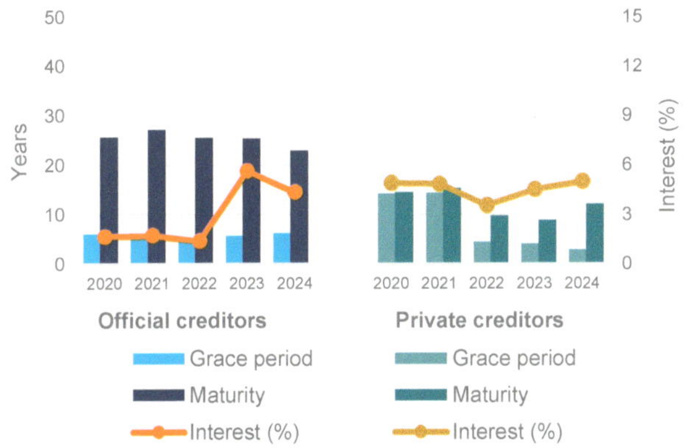

Summary External Debt Data	2010	2020	2021	2022	2023	2024
Total external debt stocks	**742,737**	**2,326,233**	**2,724,354**	**2,530,502**	**2,447,537**	**2,419,835**
Long-term external debt stocks	**219,650**	**1,079,933**	**1,306,580**	**1,217,127**	**1,111,558**	**1,066,746**
Public and publicly guaranteed debt from:	*102,275*	*391,682*	*554,292*	*538,307*	*487,486*	*504,113*
Official creditors	75,476	52,994	51,622	48,897	47,246	44,016
Multilateral	35,527	36,007	36,424	35,840	35,189	32,708
of which: World Bank	22,135	16,236	16,585	16,067	15,447	14,687
Bilateral	39,949	16,987	15,198	13,057	12,057	11,308
Private creditors	26,799	338,688	502,670	489,410	440,240	460,096
Bondholders	12,398	288,234	431,520	406,384	338,401	333,548
Commercial banks and others	14,401	50,454	71,150	83,026	101,839	126,548
Private nonguaranteed debt from:	*117,375*	*688,252*	*752,287*	*678,820*	*624,072*	*562,634*
Bondholders	5,561	323,512	340,314	309,315	275,845	262,210
Commercial banks and others	111,814	364,739	411,974	369,505	348,227	300,424
Use of IMF credit and SDR allocations	**10,764**	**10,067**	**50,674**	**48,185**	**48,577**	**47,218**
IMF credit	0	0	0	0	0	0
SDR allocations	10,764	10,067	50,674	48,185	48,577	47,218
Short-term external debt stocks	**512,323**	**1,236,232**	**1,367,100**	**1,265,190**	**1,287,403**	**1,305,872**
Disbursements, long-term	**39,167**	**361,370**	**462,392**	**272,633**	**210,895**	**189,670**
Public and publicly guaranteed sector	12,421	95,258	202,131	65,693	44,423	84,795
Private sector not guaranteed	26,746	266,112	260,262	206,940	166,472	104,875
Principal repayments, long-term	**18,782**	**181,917**	**226,388**	**347,905**	**315,522**	**227,653**
Public and publicly guaranteed sector	11,978	25,312	33,310	75,119	94,763	64,831
Private sector not guaranteed	6,803	156,605	193,078	272,786	220,759	162,821
Interest payments, long-term	**5,484**	**31,593**	**46,492**	**47,296**	**51,394**	**40,051**
Public and publicly guaranteed sector	1,819	8,506	17,050	21,110	24,013	14,443
Private sector not guaranteed	3,665	23,087	29,442	26,187	27,381	25,608

COLOMBIA

(US$ million, unless otherwise indicated)

Snapshot	2024
Total external debt stocks	**201,764**
External debt stocks as % of:	
Exports	256
GNI	49
Debt service as % of:	
Exports	43
GNI	8
Net financial flows, debt and equity	19,877
Net debt inflows	6,739
Net equity inflows	13,138
GNI	**410,056**
Population (million)	**53**

Figure 1 Public and publicly guaranteed debt, by creditor and creditor type in 2024, including IMF credit

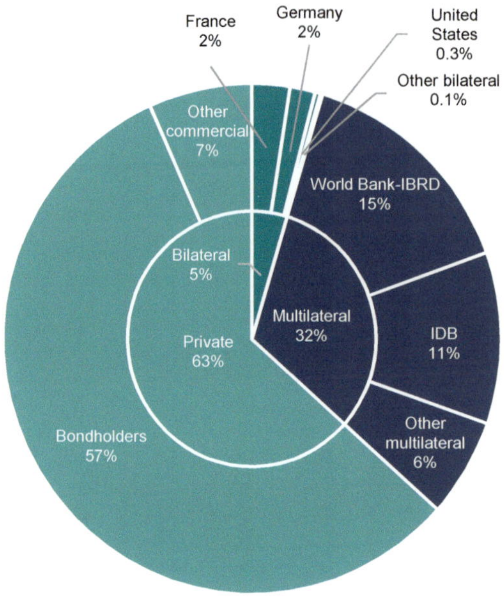

Figure 2 Average terms on new debt commitments from official and private creditors

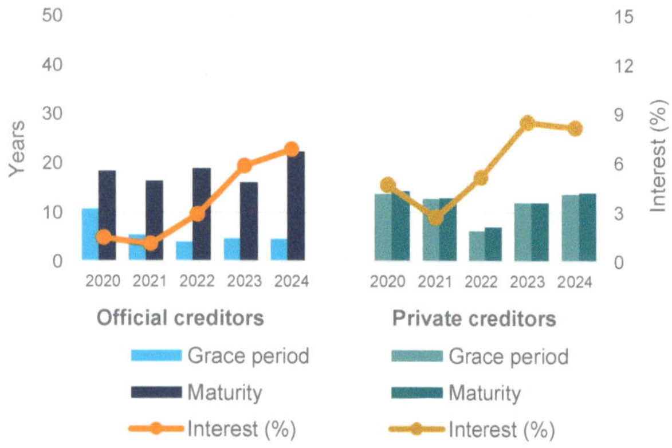

Summary External Debt Data	2010	2020	2021	2022	2023	2024
Total external debt stocks	**64,432**	**155,866**	**172,249**	**184,496**	**196,166**	**201,764**
Long-term external debt stocks	**55,383**	**135,502**	**147,366**	**156,551**	**169,021**	**176,747**
Public and publicly guaranteed debt from:	*37,058*	*85,692*	*94,072*	*97,743*	*103,538*	*106,625*
Official creditors	16,483	31,368	33,780	35,905	37,223	37,476
Multilateral	15,898	25,539	28,047	30,163	32,038	32,439
of which: World Bank	7,504	11,989	13,515	15,122	15,797	16,238
Bilateral	585	5,829	5,733	5,742	5,185	5,037
Private creditors	20,574	54,324	60,292	61,838	66,315	69,149
Bondholders	17,965	48,536	52,916	52,448	57,982	61,781
Commercial banks and others	2,609	5,788	7,376	9,390	8,333	7,368
Private nonguaranteed debt from:	*18,325*	*49,810*	*53,294*	*58,808*	*65,483*	*70,122*
Bondholders	3,329	8,954	9,604	8,249	7,140	6,840
Commercial banks and others	14,996	40,856	43,689	50,558	58,344	63,283
Use of IMF credit and SDR allocations	**1,137**	**6,464**	**9,024**	**8,581**	**8,651**	**5,964**
IMF credit	0	5,401	5,248	4,991	5,031	2,445
SDR allocations	1,137	1,063	3,776	3,590	3,620	3,518
Short-term external debt stocks	**7,912**	**13,900**	**15,858**	**19,364**	**18,494**	**19,053**
Disbursements, long-term	**12,970**	**27,645**	**31,053**	**30,004**	**30,509**	**29,217**
Public and publicly guaranteed sector	3,629	13,525	18,768	9,698	13,573	13,057
Private sector not guaranteed	9,340	14,120	12,286	20,306	16,936	16,160
Principal repayments, long-term	**6,566**	**15,060**	**18,335**	**19,717**	**18,937**	**20,548**
Public and publicly guaranteed sector	2,318	3,591	9,533	4,925	8,676	9,026
Private sector not guaranteed	4,248	11,469	8,802	14,792	10,261	11,521
Interest payments, long-term	**2,839**	**5,995**	**6,230**	**6,446**	**8,336**	**9,555**
Public and publicly guaranteed sector	2,121	3,483	3,812	3,885	4,918	5,845
Private sector not guaranteed	717	2,513	2,418	2,561	3,417	3,710

COMOROS

(US$ million, unless otherwise indicated)

Snapshot	2024
Total external debt stocks	**385.6**
External debt stocks as % of:	
Exports	271.4
GNI	24.8
Debt service as % of:	
Exports	17.3
GNI	1.6
Net financial flows, debt and equity	19.8
Net debt inflows	12.7
Net equity inflows	7.1
GNI	**1,554.0**
Population (thousand)	**867**

Figure 1 Public and publicly guaranteed debt, by creditor and creditor type in 2024, including IMF credit

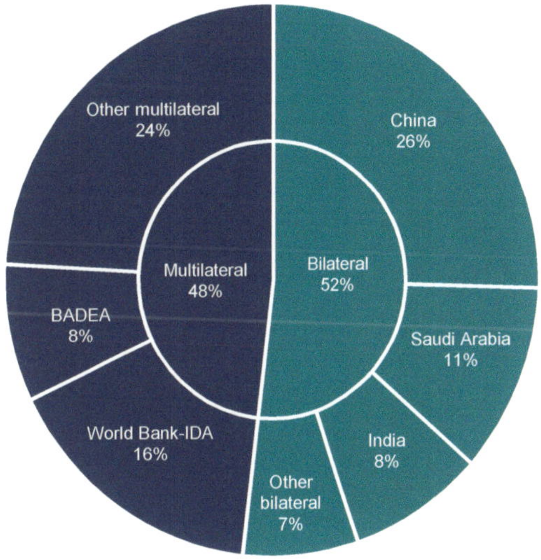

Figure 2 Average terms on new debt commitments from official and private creditors

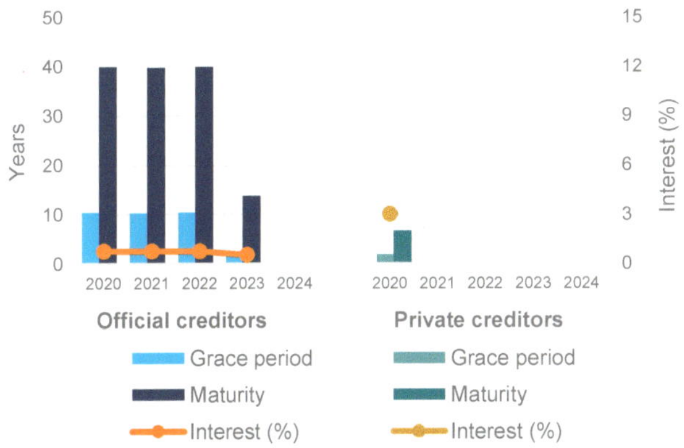

Summary External Debt Data	2010	2020	2021	2022	2023	2024
Total external debt stocks	**278.4**	**304.8**	**351.5**	**362.1**	**381.7**	**385.6**
Long-term external debt stocks	**248.5**	**261.4**	**287.1**	**303.2**	**320.5**	**324.0**
Public and publicly guaranteed debt from:	*248.5*	*261.4*	*287.1*	*303.2*	*320.5*	*324.0*
Official creditors	248.5	261.4	287.1	303.2	320.5	324.0
Multilateral	201.6	85.2	93.5	105.3	126.3	141.5
of which: World Bank	115.5	16.7	21.8	33.1	45.4	56.8
Bilateral	46.9	176.2	193.6	197.9	194.2	182.5
Private creditors	..	0.0	0.0	0.0	0.0	0.0
Bondholders	..	..	..	..	..	..
Commercial banks and others	..	0.0	0.0	0.0	0.0	0.0
Private nonguaranteed debt from:	..	..	..	..	..	..
Bondholders	..	..	..	..	..	..
Commercial banks and others	..	..	..	..	..	..
Use of IMF credit and SDR allocations	**25.4**	**41.9**	**62.9**	**57.3**	**60.8**	**61.6**
IMF credit	12.3	29.7	27.1	23.3	26.5	28.3
SDR allocations	13.1	12.2	35.8	34.0	34.3	33.3
Short-term external debt stocks	**4.4**	**1.5**	**1.5**	**1.6**	**0.5**	**0.0**
Disbursements, long-term	**0.0**	**17.7**	**27.3**	**30.9**	**24.3**	**23.7**
Public and publicly guaranteed sector	0.0	17.7	27.3	30.9	24.3	23.7
Private sector not guaranteed	..	..	..	..	..	..
Principal repayments, long-term	**3.1**	**4.6**	**1.1**	**1.2**	**6.3**	**13.5**
Public and publicly guaranteed sector	3.1	4.6	1.1	1.2	6.3	13.5
Private sector not guaranteed	..	..	..	..	..	..
Interest payments, long-term	**1.1**	**3.3**	**0.5**	**0.5**	**4.1**	**2.6**
Public and publicly guaranteed sector	1.1	3.3	0.5	0.5	4.1	2.6
Private sector not guaranteed	..	..	..	..	..	..

CONGO, DEMOCRATIC REPUBLIC OF

(US$ million, unless otherwise indicated)

Snapshot	2024
Total external debt stocks	**12,485**
External debt stocks as % of:	
Exports	35
GNI	18
Debt service as % of:	
Exports	1
GNI	1
Net financial flows, debt and equity	3,764
Net debt inflows	651
Net equity inflows	3,113
GNI	**68,396**
Population (million)	**109**

Figure 2 Average terms on new debt commitments from official and private creditors

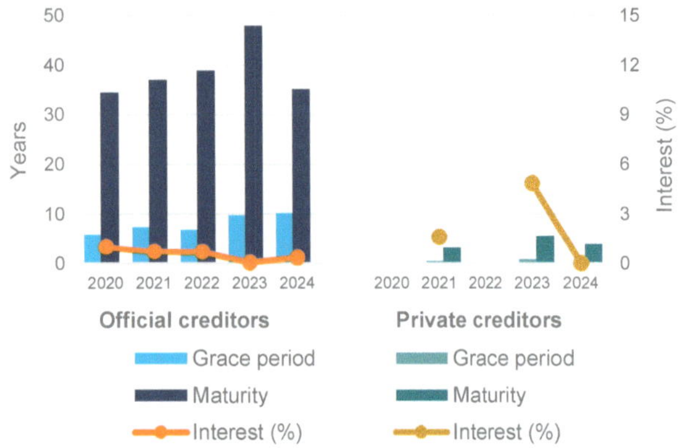

Figure 1 Public and publicly guaranteed debt, by creditor and creditor type in 2024, including IMF credit

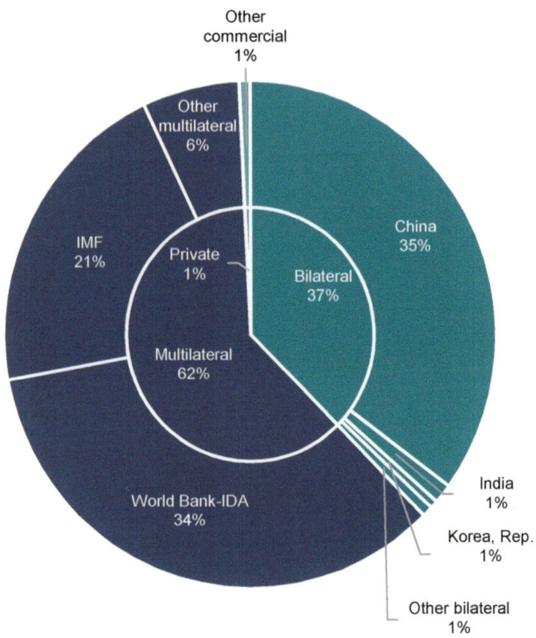

Summary External Debt Data	2010	2020	2021	2022	2023	2024
Total external debt stocks	**5,682**	**8,476**	**10,484**	**10,683**	**12,008**	**12,485**
Long-term external debt stocks	**4,137**	**6,707**	**6,872**	**6,536**	**7,437**	**7,925**
Public and publicly guaranteed debt from:	*4,137*	*6,707*	*6,872*	*6,536*	*7,437*	*7,925*
Official creditors	4,060	6,609	6,773	6,460	7,357	7,854
Multilateral	2,585	2,290	2,448	2,689	3,542	4,087
of which: World Bank	849	1,521	1,772	2,125	2,997	3,453
Bilateral	1,474	4,320	4,325	3,771	3,815	3,767
Private creditors	77	97	99	76	80	71
Bondholders	..	..	..	..	..	..
Commercial banks and others	77	97	99	76	80	71
Private nonguaranteed debt from:	..	..	..	..	..	..
Bondholders	..	..	..	..	..	..
Commercial banks and others	..	..	..	..	..	..
Use of IMF credit and SDR allocations	**1,110**	**1,511**	**3,317**	**3,560**	**3,997**	**4,084**
IMF credit	323	775	1,172	1,520	1,941	2,085
SDR allocations	787	736	2,145	2,040	2,056	1,999
Short-term external debt stocks	**435**	**259**	**294**	**588**	**574**	**476**
Disbursements, long-term	**732**	**1,019**	**484**	**590**	**1,156**	**754**
Public and publicly guaranteed sector	732	1,019	484	590	1,156	754
Private sector not guaranteed	..	..	..	..	..	..
Principal repayments, long-term	**89**	**161**	**257**	**806**	**262**	**206**
Public and publicly guaranteed sector	89	161	257	806	262	206
Private sector not guaranteed	..	..	..	..	..	..
Interest payments, long-term	**124**	**59**	**54**	**49**	**137**	**180**
Public and publicly guaranteed sector	124	59	54	49	137	180
Private sector not guaranteed	..	..	..	..	..	..

CONGO, REPUBLIC OF

(US$ million, unless otherwise indicated)

Snapshot	2024
Total external debt stocks	**6,728**
External debt stocks as % of:	
Exports	84
GNI	45
Debt service as % of:	
Exports	14
GNI	7
Net financial flows, debt and equity	559
Net debt inflows	-45
Net equity inflows	604
GNI	**14,986**
Population (million)	**6**

Figure 1 Public and publicly guaranteed debt, by creditor and creditor type in 2024, including IMF credit

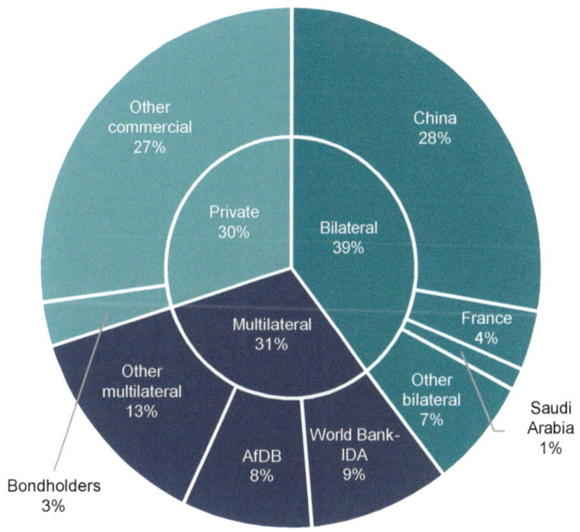

Figure 2 Average terms on new debt commitments from official and private creditors

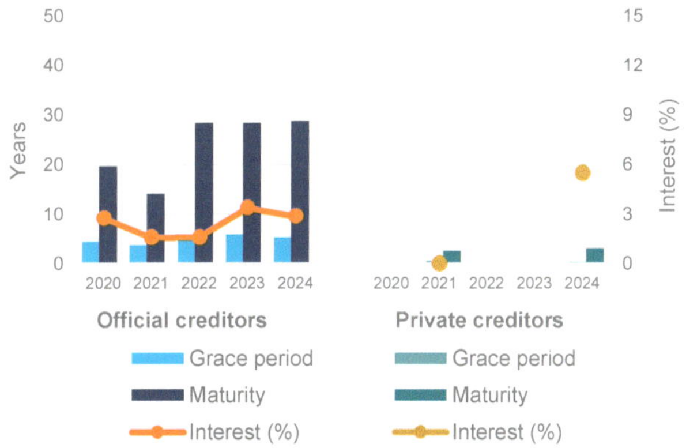

Summary External Debt Data	2010	2020	2021	2022	2023	2024
Total external debt stocks	**2,796**	**8,224**	**8,151**	**7,330**	**6,870**	**6,728**
Long-term external debt stocks	**2,450**	**7,778**	**7,487**	**6,609**	**5,966**	**5,343**
Public and publicly guaranteed debt from:	*2,450*	*7,772*	*7,478*	*6,599*	*5,956*	*5,334*
Official creditors	1,023	4,081	4,061	3,922	3,805	3,615
Multilateral	182	985	1,022	1,108	1,274	1,338
of which: World Bank	84	342	413	543	629	745
Bilateral	842	3,096	3,039	2,814	2,531	2,277
Private creditors	1,426	3,691	3,417	2,677	2,151	1,719
Bondholders	454	268	241	213	186	159
Commercial banks and others	973	3,423	3,176	2,464	1,964	1,561
Private nonguaranteed debt from:	..	*6*	*9*	*10*	*11*	*8*
Bondholders	..	..	..	..	..	..
Commercial banks and others	..	6	9	10	11	8
Use of IMF credit and SDR allocations	**150**	**162**	**374**	**528**	**706**	**729**
IMF credit	27	48	45	216	391	423
SDR allocations	123	115	329	313	315	306
Short-term external debt stocks	**197**	**284**	**290**	**193**	**197**	**657**
Disbursements, long-term	**882**	**189**	**204**	**317**	**245**	**396**
Public and publicly guaranteed sector	882	183	198	313	243	396
Private sector not guaranteed	..	6	5	3	2	0
Principal repayments, long-term	**95**	**542**	**426**	**1,146**	**922**	**922**
Public and publicly guaranteed sector	95	542	424	1,145	920	920
Private sector not guaranteed	..	..	2	2	2	2
Interest payments, long-term	**24**	**94**	**69**	**173**	**125**	**126**
Public and publicly guaranteed sector	24	93	68	172	124	126
Private sector not guaranteed	..	0	1	1	1	1

CÔTE D'IVOIRE

(US$ million, unless otherwise indicated)

Snapshot	2024
Total external debt stocks	**40,561**
External debt stocks as % of:	
Exports	186
GNI	49
Debt service as % of:	
Exports	25
GNI	6
Net financial flows, debt and equity	9,552
Net debt inflows	5,750
Net equity inflows	3,802
GNI	**83,065**
Population (million)	**32**

Figure 1 Public and publicly guaranteed debt, by creditor and creditor type in 2024, including IMF credit

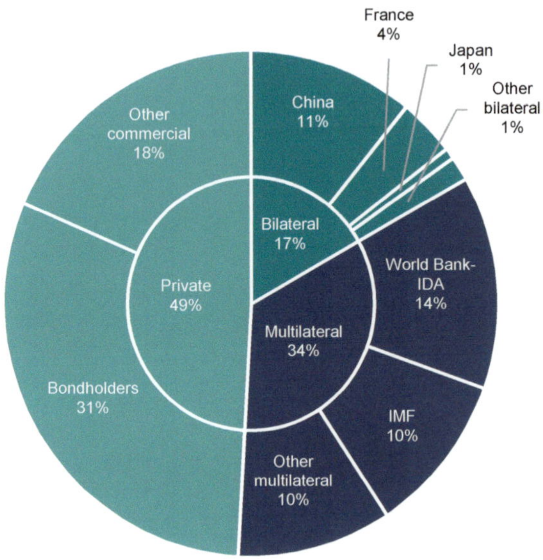

Figure 2 Average terms on new debt commitments from official and private creditors

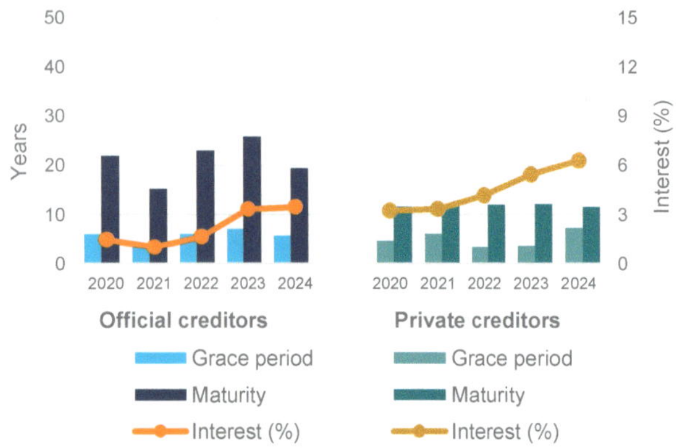

Summary External Debt Data	2010	2020	2021	2022	2023	2024
Total external debt stocks	**11,702**	**25,111**	**29,773**	**31,623**	**36,356**	**40,561**
Long-term external debt stocks	**10,430**	**21,008**	**23,937**	**26,633**	**29,370**	**31,489**
Public and publicly guaranteed debt from:	*9,412*	*20,017*	*23,189*	*26,109*	*28,977*	*31,249*
Official creditors	9,300	7,966	10,082	11,527	13,612	14,055
Multilateral	2,372	4,014	4,758	5,851	7,502	8,225
of which: World Bank	1,763	1,882	2,488	3,117	4,189	4,878
Bilateral	6,928	3,952	5,324	5,676	6,110	5,830
Private creditors	112	12,051	13,106	14,582	15,365	17,194
Bondholders	0	8,532	9,010	8,592	8,747	10,613
Commercial banks and others	112	3,519	4,097	5,991	6,618	6,581
Private nonguaranteed debt from:	*1,018*	*991*	*749*	*524*	*393*	*240*
Bondholders	..	..	..	..	..	..
Commercial banks and others	1,018	991	749	524	393	240
Use of IMF credit and SDR allocations	**861**	**3,047**	**3,647**	**3,303**	**4,002**	**4,788**
IMF credit	383	2,600	2,339	2,060	2,749	3,569
SDR allocations	479	448	1,308	1,243	1,253	1,218
Short-term external debt stocks	**411**	**1,056**	**2,188**	**1,687**	**2,984**	**4,284**
Disbursements, long-term	**599**	**4,307**	**4,989**	**5,172**	**3,975**	**6,747**
Public and publicly guaranteed sector	244	4,307	4,989	5,172	3,975	6,747
Private sector not guaranteed	355	..	..	..	..	..
Principal repayments, long-term	**623**	**1,565**	**803**	**1,420**	**1,969**	**3,210**
Public and publicly guaranteed sector	438	1,226	603	1,223	1,828	3,069
Private sector not guaranteed	185	340	200	197	141	141
Interest payments, long-term	**114**	**701**	**700**	**642**	**1,052**	**1,299**
Public and publicly guaranteed sector	58	671	683	630	1,026	1,281
Private sector not guaranteed	56	29	17	12	26	18

DJIBOUTI

(US$ million, unless otherwise indicated)

Snapshot	2024
Total external debt stocks	**3,424**
External debt stocks as % of:	
Exports	62
GNI	83
Debt service as % of:	
Exports	3
GNI	3
Net financial flows, debt and equity	113
Net debt inflows	45
Net equity inflows	68
GNI	**4,124**
Population (million)	**1**

Figure 1 Public and publicly guaranteed debt, by creditor and creditor type in 2024, including IMF credit

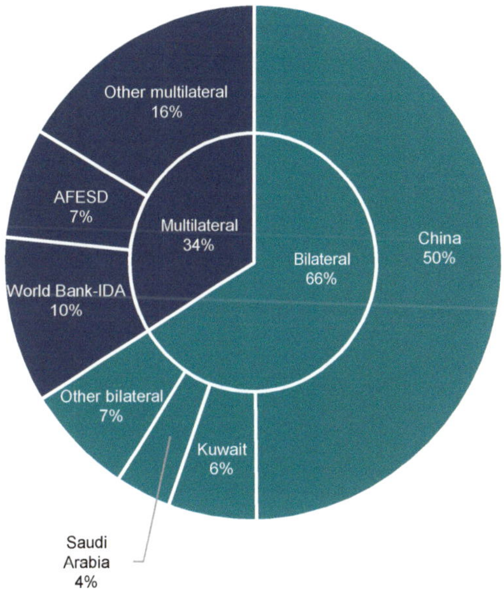

Figure 2 Average terms on new debt commitments from official and private creditors

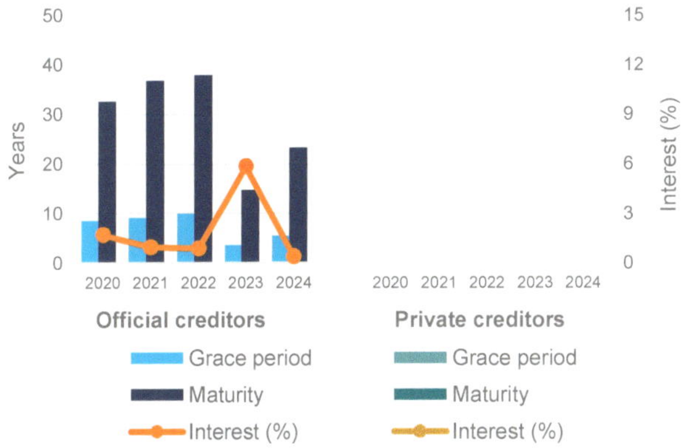

Summary External Debt Data	2010	2020	2021	2022	2023	2024
Total external debt stocks	**769**	**2,900**	**3,207**	**3,170**	**3,429**	**3,424**
Long-term external debt stocks	**612**	**2,575**	**2,427**	**2,439**	**2,847**	**2,805**
Public and publicly guaranteed debt from:	*612*	*2,354*	*2,407*	*2,409*	*2,837*	*2,795*
Official creditors	595	2,354	2,407	2,409	2,837	2,795
Multilateral	406	660	692	708	898	917
of which: World Bank	155	191	215	230	274	296
Bilateral	189	1,694	1,715	1,701	1,938	1,877
Private creditors	16	..	..	..	..	..
Bondholders	..	..	..	..	..	..
Commercial banks and others	16	..	..	..	..	..
Private nonguaranteed debt from:	..	*221*	*21*	*30*	*10*	*10*
Bondholders	..	219	20	20	0	0
Commercial banks and others	..	2	1	10	10	10
Use of IMF credit and SDR allocations	**35**	**72**	**109**	**103**	**104**	**101**
IMF credit	12	51	45	42	43	41
SDR allocations	23	22	64	61	61	60
Short-term external debt stocks	**122**	**253**	**670**	**628**	**478**	**518**
Disbursements, long-term	**35**	**435**	**86**	**75**	**306**	**83**
Public and publicly guaranteed sector	35	214	86	66	306	83
Private sector not guaranteed	..	221	..	9	..	..
Principal repayments, long-term	**22**	**28**	**30**	**33**	**45**	**68**
Public and publicly guaranteed sector	22	28	28	33	25	68
Private sector not guaranteed	..	..	1	..	20	0
Interest payments, long-term	**8**	**34**	**21**	**21**	**26**	**42**
Public and publicly guaranteed sector	8	25	20	19	24	41
Private sector not guaranteed	..	8	1	1	1	0

DOMINICA

(US$ million, unless otherwise indicated)

Snapshot	2024
Total external debt stocks	**569.5**
External debt stocks as % of:	
Exports	254.1
GNI	82.4
Debt service as % of:	
Exports	29.4
GNI	9.5
Net financial flows, debt and equity	18.8
Net debt inflows	-18.3
Net equity inflows	37.0
GNI	**691.5**
Population (thousand)	**66**

Figure 1 Public and publicly guaranteed debt, by creditor and creditor type in 2024, including IMF credit

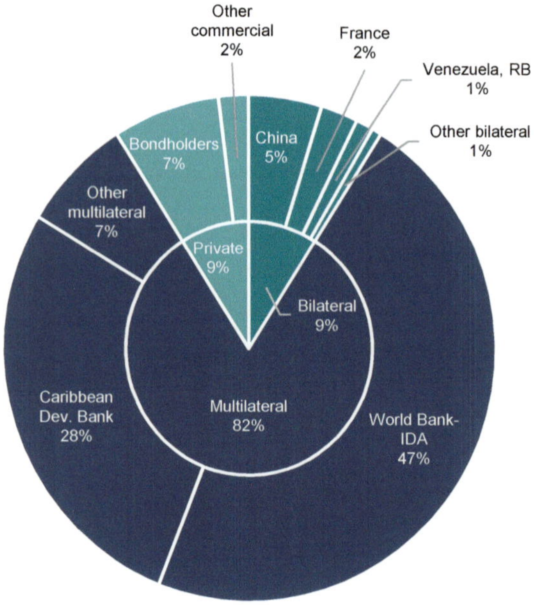

Figure 2 Average terms on new debt commitments from official and private creditors

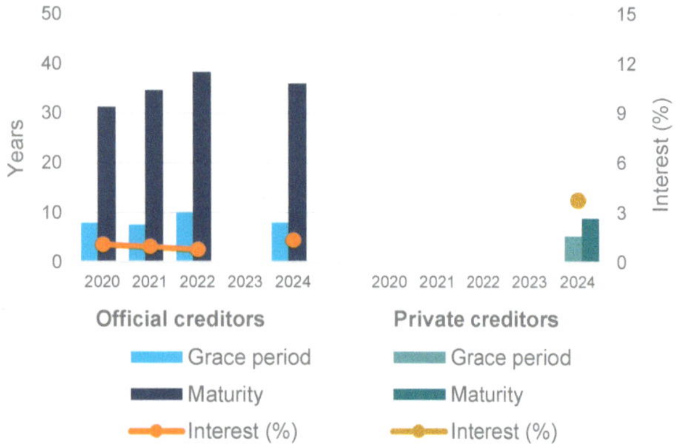

Summary External Debt Data	2010	2020	2021	2022	2023	2024
Total external debt stocks	**271.4**	**480.9**	**510.0**	**599.2**	**592.2**	**569.5**
Long-term external debt stocks	**235.6**	**302.6**	**335.5**	**357.4**	**380.9**	**356.3**
Public and publicly guaranteed debt from:	*235.6*	*279.4*	*314.8*	*339.0*	*364.0*	*339.6*
Official creditors	172.4	225.6	263.8	292.0	320.4	307.6
Multilateral	117.0	159.6	197.1	236.4	274.3	275.7
of which: World Bank	27.8	51.4	88.2	121.4	158.2	166.6
Bilateral	55.4	66.0	66.6	55.5	46.1	31.9
Private creditors	63.2	53.8	51.0	47.0	43.6	32.0
Bondholders	57.1	40.2	39.0	36.4	34.9	25.1
Commercial banks and others	6.0	13.5	12.1	10.6	8.7	6.9
Private nonguaranteed debt from:	..	*23.3*	*20.7*	*18.4*	*16.9*	*16.6*
Bondholders	..	..	..	..	..	..
Commercial banks and others	..	23.3	20.7	18.4	16.9	16.6
Use of IMF credit and SDR allocations	**30.2**	**35.8**	**48.0**	**43.7**	**42.4**	**39.6**
IMF credit	18.2	24.5	21.6	18.6	17.1	15.0
SDR allocations	12.1	11.3	26.4	25.1	25.3	24.6
Short-term external debt stocks	**5.5**	**142.5**	**126.5**	**198.1**	**168.9**	**173.7**
Disbursements, long-term	**29.7**	**45.0**	**47.7**	**50.8**	**47.0**	**23.4**
Public and publicly guaranteed sector	29.7	39.3	47.7	50.8	47.0	23.4
Private sector not guaranteed	..	5.7	..	..	..	..
Principal repayments, long-term	**9.8**	**20.4**	**14.4**	**22.8**	**24.0**	**44.5**
Public and publicly guaranteed sector	9.8	20.4	11.9	20.5	22.4	44.2
Private sector not guaranteed	..	..	2.6	2.2	1.6	0.2
Interest payments, long-term	**5.4**	**7.1**	**6.9**	**8.8**	**8.7**	**8.5**
Public and publicly guaranteed sector	5.4	6.6	6.4	8.2	8.3	8.0
Private sector not guaranteed	..	0.4	0.4	0.5	0.4	0.5

DOMINICAN REPUBLIC

(US$ million, unless otherwise indicated)

Snapshot	2024
Total external debt stocks	**53,294**
External debt stocks as % of:	
Exports	178
GNI	45
Debt service as % of:	
Exports	22
GNI	6
Net financial flows, debt and equity	5,755
Net debt inflows	1,365
Net equity inflows	4,390
GNI	**117,559**
Population (million)	**11**

Figure 1 Public and publicly guaranteed debt, by creditor and creditor type in 2024, including IMF credit

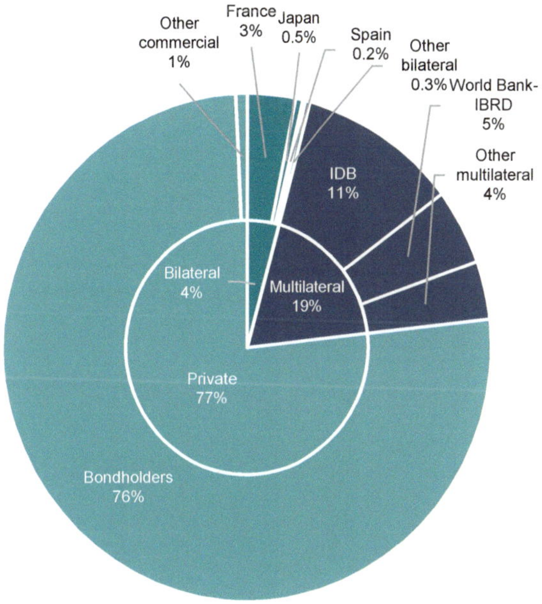

Figure 2 Average terms on new debt commitments from official and private creditors

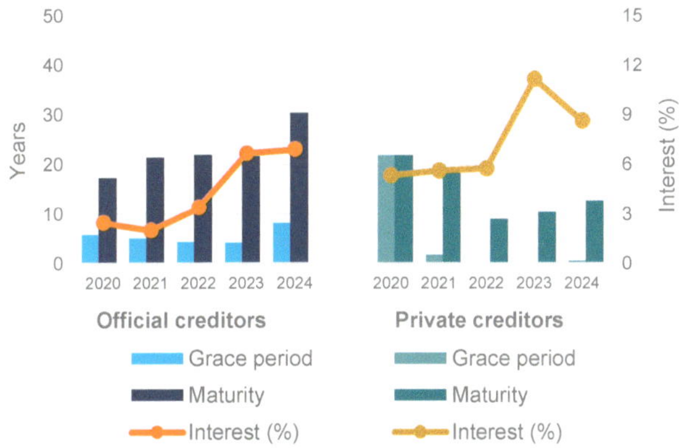

Summary External Debt Data	2010	2020	2021	2022	2023	2024
Total external debt stocks	**13,499**	**40,560**	**43,885**	**48,290**	**52,188**	**53,294**
Long-term external debt stocks	**10,283**	**37,400**	**39,973**	**43,553**	**46,849**	**48,121**
Public and publicly guaranteed debt from:	*9,441*	*29,856*	*32,507*	*35,559*	*38,209*	*39,906*
Official creditors	6,343	7,089	7,134	7,491	8,672	9,153
Multilateral	3,079	5,900	5,779	6,042	7,053	7,473
of which: World Bank	872	1,183	1,185	1,174	1,528	1,930
Bilateral	3,264	1,189	1,356	1,448	1,619	1,680
Private creditors	3,098	22,767	25,372	28,069	29,537	30,753
Bondholders	1,134	22,158	24,893	27,671	29,199	30,459
Commercial banks and others	1,964	609	479	398	338	294
Private nonguaranteed debt from:	*843*	*7,544*	*7,467*	*7,994*	*8,640*	*8,216*
Bondholders	843	707	1,007	1,007	1,007	1,007
Commercial banks and others	0	6,837	6,460	6,987	7,633	7,209
Use of IMF credit and SDR allocations	**1,461**	**988**	**1,601**	**1,522**	**1,374**	**1,025**
IMF credit	1,139	688	668	635	480	156
SDR allocations	322	301	933	887	894	869
Short-term external debt stocks	**1,754**	**2,172**	**2,311**	**3,214**	**3,965**	**4,148**
Disbursements, long-term	**2,111**	**9,769**	**3,510**	**4,981**	**5,395**	**3,826**
Public and publicly guaranteed sector	2,111	9,769	3,210	4,352	4,710	3,676
Private sector not guaranteed	..	..	300	629	685	150
Principal repayments, long-term	**799**	**4,531**	**926**	**1,413**	**2,019**	**2,327**
Public and publicly guaranteed sector	798	2,789	549	1,311	1,980	1,753
Private sector not guaranteed	0	1,742	377	102	39	574
Interest payments, long-term	**444**	**1,662**	**1,870**	**2,086**	**2,621**	**3,637**
Public and publicly guaranteed sector	336	1,415	1,668	1,851	2,187	2,502
Private sector not guaranteed	108	247	203	235	433	1,134

ECUADOR

(US$ million, unless otherwise indicated)

Snapshot	2024
Total external debt stocks	**60,365**
External debt stocks as % of:	
Exports	155
GNI	50
Debt service as % of:	
Exports	22
GNI	7
Net financial flows, debt and equity	18
Net debt inflows	-486
Net equity inflows	504
GNI	**121,339**
Population (million)	**18**

Figure 1 Public and publicly guaranteed debt, by creditor and creditor type in 2024, including IMF credit

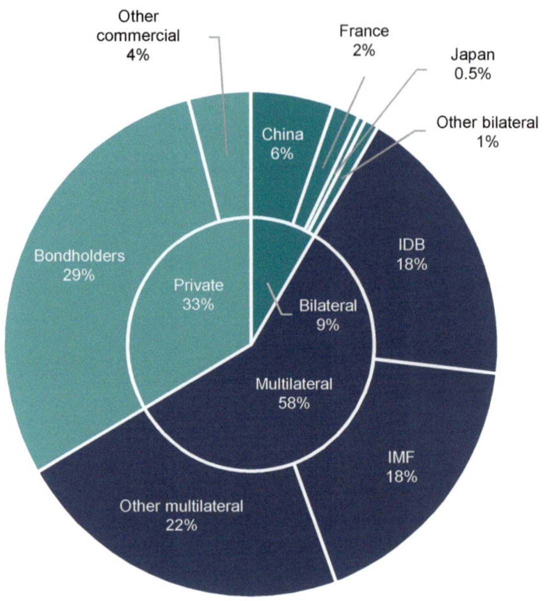

Figure 2 Average terms on new debt commitments from official and private creditors

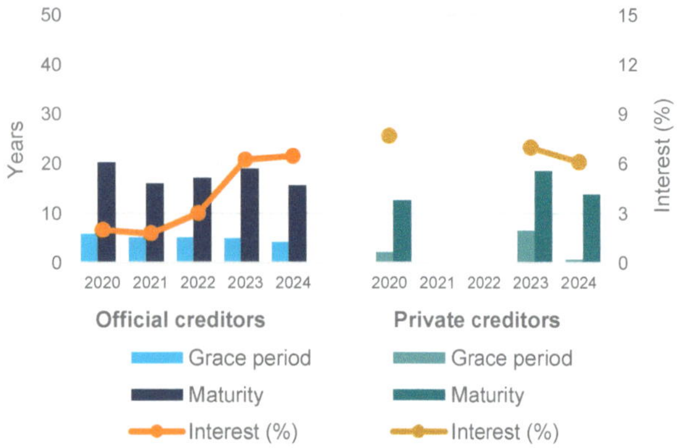

Summary External Debt Data	2010	2020	2021	2022	2023	2024
Total external debt stocks	**15,389**	**56,397**	**58,116**	**60,683**	**61,658**	**60,365**
Long-term external debt stocks	**13,881**	**48,488**	**48,680**	**49,373**	**50,349**	**49,818**
Public and publicly guaranteed debt from:	*8,800*	*37,785*	*38,753*	*39,482*	*39,702*	*40,755*
Official creditors	7,559	19,646	20,996	21,873	22,875	24,236
Multilateral	5,207	13,258	14,813	16,613	18,021	19,959
of which: World Bank	456	2,596	2,897	4,353	5,240	6,285
Bilateral	2,352	6,388	6,183	5,260	4,855	4,277
Private creditors	1,241	18,139	17,757	17,609	16,827	16,519
Bondholders	1,082	17,694	17,494	17,440	16,053	14,497
Commercial banks and others	159	445	263	169	774	2,022
Private nonguaranteed debt from:	*5,082*	*10,703*	*9,928*	*9,890*	*10,647*	*9,063*
Bondholders	..	..	..	..	..	..
Commercial banks and others	5,082	10,703	9,928	9,890	10,647	9,063
Use of IMF credit and SDR allocations	**444**	**6,781**	**8,183**	**9,387**	**9,233**	**9,921**
IMF credit	0	6,365	6,843	8,113	7,949	8,673
SDR allocations	444	415	1,340	1,274	1,284	1,248
Short-term external debt stocks	**1,064**	**1,128**	**1,253**	**1,923**	**2,076**	**626**
Disbursements, long-term	**2,977**	**7,629**	**4,650**	**4,150**	**6,872**	**5,107**
Public and publicly guaranteed sector	2,307	3,649	2,735	2,690	3,295	4,286
Private sector not guaranteed	670	3,981	1,916	1,460	3,577	821
Principal repayments, long-term	**1,259**	**7,548**	**4,441**	**3,379**	**5,226**	**5,076**
Public and publicly guaranteed sector	636	3,813	1,750	1,882	2,406	2,671
Private sector not guaranteed	623	3,735	2,691	1,498	2,820	2,405
Interest payments, long-term	**470**	**1,517**	**1,858**	**1,629**	**2,150**	**2,262**
Public and publicly guaranteed sector	332	1,173	1,360	1,353	1,580	1,837
Private sector not guaranteed	139	344	497	276	570	425

EGYPT, ARAB REPUBLIC OF

(US$ million, unless otherwise indicated)

Snapshot	2024
Total external debt stocks	**155,973**
External debt stocks as % of:	
Exports	233
GNI	42
Debt service as % of:	
Exports	49
GNI	9
Net financial flows, debt and equity	42,928
Net debt inflows	-3,381
Net equity inflows	46,309
GNI	**371,523**
Population (million)	**117**

Figure 1 Public and publicly guaranteed debt, by creditor and creditor type in 2024, including IMF credit

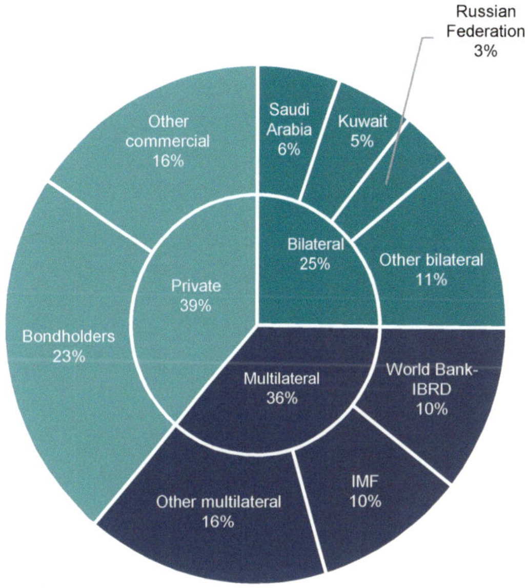

Figure 2 Average terms on new debt commitments from official and private creditors

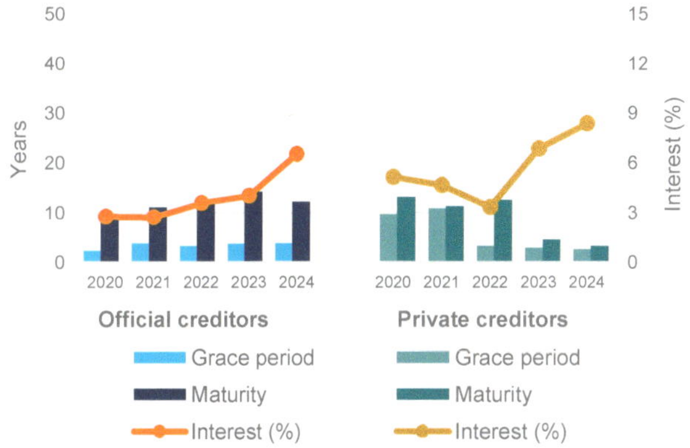

Summary External Debt Data	2010	2020	2021	2022	2023	2024
Total external debt stocks	**36,804**	**132,539**	**145,998**	**163,111**	**168,182**	**155,973**
Long-term external debt stocks	**32,271**	**100,218**	**109,475**	**111,112**	**119,380**	**109,860**
Public and publicly guaranteed debt from:	*32,218*	*99,816*	*108,692*	*110,213*	*117,500*	*106,927*
Official creditors	28,033	62,977	62,687	64,069	67,048	60,319
Multilateral	9,293	26,322	28,442	29,986	31,111	30,753
of which: World Bank	3,881	11,993	12,037	12,318	12,314	12,295
Bilateral	18,741	36,655	34,244	34,083	35,937	29,566
Private creditors	4,184	36,838	46,005	46,144	50,452	46,608
Bondholders	3,333	25,905	31,457	29,080	29,798	27,308
Commercial banks and others	851	10,933	14,548	17,064	20,655	19,300
Private nonguaranteed debt from:	*54*	*402*	*784*	*899*	*1,879*	*2,933*
Bondholders	..	..	100	100	100	599
Commercial banks and others	54	402	684	799	1,779	2,334
Use of IMF credit and SDR allocations	**1,384**	**20,362**	**23,681**	**21,753**	**19,319**	**15,118**
IMF credit	0	19,068	19,691	17,959	15,494	11,400
SDR allocations	1,384	1,294	3,990	3,794	3,825	3,718
Short-term external debt stocks	**3,149**	**11,959**	**12,842**	**30,246**	**29,483**	**30,995**
Disbursements, long-term	**3,625**	**17,824**	**25,481**	**14,561**	**17,894**	**16,553**
Public and publicly guaranteed sector	3,620	17,631	24,771	14,355	16,607	15,386
Private sector not guaranteed	5	193	710	206	1,287	1,167
Principal repayments, long-term	**2,164**	**8,216**	**13,283**	**10,677**	**9,340**	**17,719**
Public and publicly guaranteed sector	2,139	8,065	13,054	10,486	9,033	17,605
Private sector not guaranteed	25	151	229	191	307	114
Interest payments, long-term	**770**	**3,389**	**3,702**	**4,192**	**6,272**	**6,797**
Public and publicly guaranteed sector	769	3,378	3,623	4,153	6,166	6,660
Private sector not guaranteed	1	12	79	39	106	137

EL SALVADOR

(US$ million, unless otherwise indicated)

Snapshot	2024
Total external debt stocks	**24,962**
External debt stocks as % of:	
Exports	207
GNI	75
Debt service as % of:	
Exports	96
GNI	35
Net financial flows, debt and equity	2,741
Net debt inflows	2,158
Net equity inflows	582
GNI	**33,109**
Population (million)	**6**

Figure 1 Public and publicly guaranteed debt, by creditor and creditor type in 2024, including IMF credit

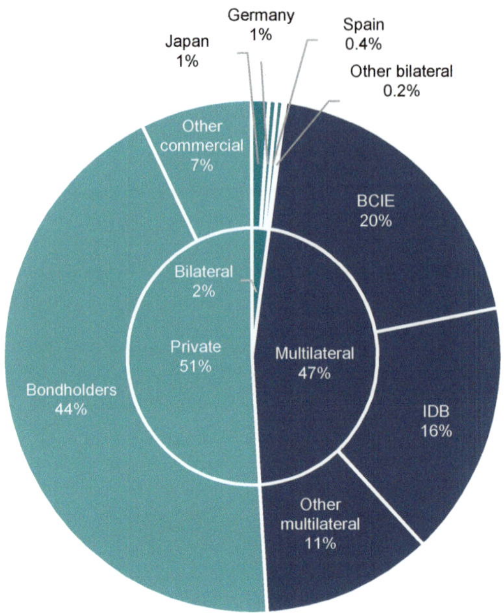

Figure 2 Average terms on new debt commitments from official and private creditors

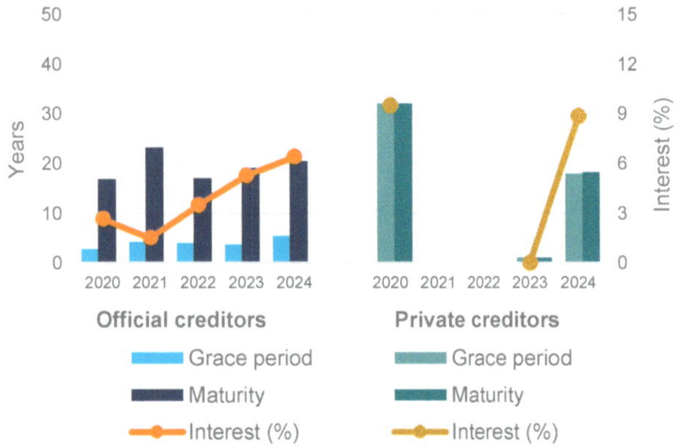

Summary External Debt Data	2010	2020	2021	2022	2023	2024
Total external debt stocks	**11,496**	**18,485**	**20,342**	**21,188**	**22,862**	**24,962**
Long-term external debt stocks	**10,408**	**15,965**	**17,068**	**17,853**	**19,072**	**21,647**
Public and publicly guaranteed debt from:	*6,839*	*10,797*	*11,560*	*12,144*	*12,650*	*14,130*
Official creditors	4,211	4,539	5,335	5,551	6,651	6,886
Multilateral	3,549	4,158	4,987	5,234	6,308	6,572
of which: World Bank	922	786	768	879	875	919
Bilateral	661	382	348	317	343	314
Private creditors	2,628	6,258	6,225	6,593	5,999	7,244
Bondholders	2,596	6,223	6,194	6,564	5,960	6,217
Commercial banks and others	32	35	31	28	39	1,026
Private nonguaranteed debt from:	*3,569*	*5,167*	*5,508*	*5,709*	*6,422*	*7,517*
Bondholders	..	0	0	20	17	12
Commercial banks and others	3,569	5,167	5,508	5,689	6,405	7,505
Use of IMF credit and SDR allocations	**252**	**650**	**1,016**	**967**	**878**	**666**
IMF credit	0	414	402	382	289	94
SDR allocations	252	236	615	584	589	573
Short-term external debt stocks	**836**	**1,871**	**2,258**	**2,369**	**2,912**	**2,649**
Disbursements, long-term	**1,455**	**5,297**	**5,683**	**1,873**	**8,148**	**12,490**
Public and publicly guaranteed sector	1,107	1,379	1,232	667	1,607	3,660
Private sector not guaranteed	348	3,918	4,451	1,206	6,541	8,830
Principal repayments, long-term	**605**	**4,205**	**4,524**	**2,062**	**7,664**	**9,878**
Public and publicly guaranteed sector	456	421	413	1,046	1,100	2,163
Private sector not guaranteed	149	3,785	4,111	1,015	6,564	7,715
Interest payments, long-term	**495**	**927**	**1,241**	**1,187**	**1,213**	**1,325**
Public and publicly guaranteed sector	380	625	696	737	806	897
Private sector not guaranteed	115	302	545	450	408	428

EQUATORIAL GUINEA

(US$ million, unless otherwise indicated)

Snapshot	2024
Total external debt stocks	**1,220**
External debt stocks as % of:	
Exports	..
GNI	14
Debt service as % of:	
Exports	..
GNI	2
Net financial flows, debt and equity	65
Net debt inflows	-123
Net equity inflows	188
GNI	**8,957**
Population (million)	**2**

Figure 2 Average terms on new debt commitments from official and private creditors

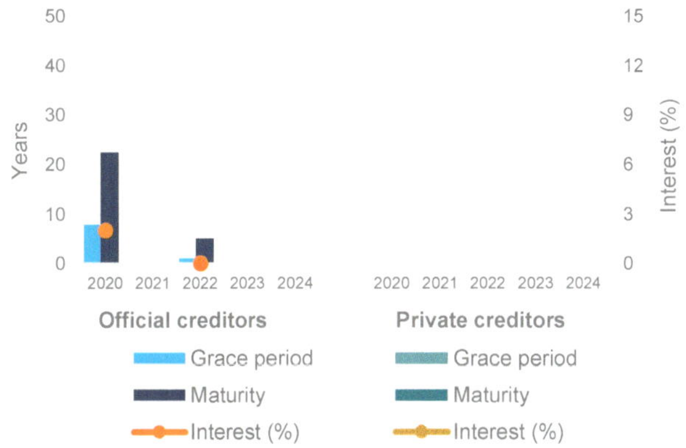

Figure 1 Public and publicly guaranteed debt, by creditor and creditor type in 2024, including IMF credit

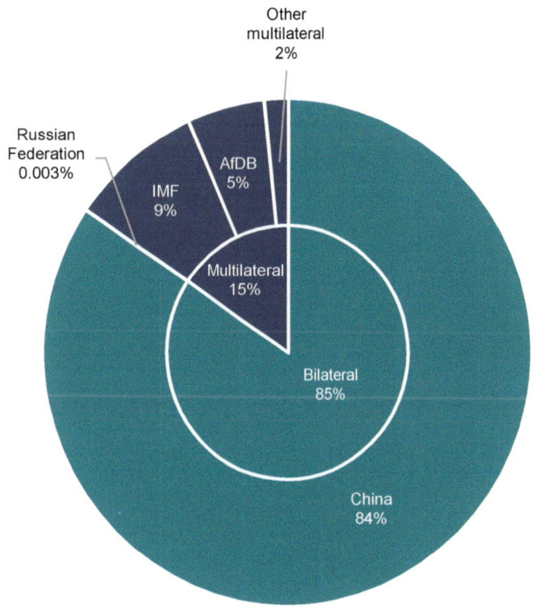

Summary External Debt Data	2010	2020	2021	2022	2023	2024
Total external debt stocks	..	**1,326**	**1,495**	**1,484**	**1,365**	**1,220**
Long-term external debt stocks	..	**1,218**	**1,133**	**1,139**	**1,018**	**896**
Public and publicly guaranteed debt from:	..	*1,218*	*1,133*	*1,139*	*1,018*	*896*
Official creditors	..	1,218	1,133	1,139	1,018	896
Multilateral	..	76	72	67	68	66
of which: World Bank	..	20	17	15	14	12
Bilateral	..	1,142	1,062	1,073	950	829
Private creditors	..	..	..	..	..	..
Bondholders	..	..	..	..	..	..
Commercial banks and others	..	..	..	..	..	..
Private nonguaranteed debt from:	..	..	..	..	..	..
Bondholders	..	..	..	..	..	..
Commercial banks and others	..	..	..	..	..	..
Use of IMF credit and SDR allocations	..	**87**	**362**	**344**	**347**	**323**
IMF credit	..	42	107	102	103	86
SDR allocations	..	45	255	243	245	238
Short-term external debt stocks	..	**21**	**0**	**0**	**0**	**0**
Disbursements, long-term	..	**28**	**64**	**175**	**2**	**7**
Public and publicly guaranteed sector	..	28	64	175	2	7
Private sector not guaranteed	..	..	..	..	..	..
Principal repayments, long-term	..	**155**	**136**	**150**	**125**	**116**
Public and publicly guaranteed sector	..	155	136	150	125	116
Private sector not guaranteed	..	..	..	..	..	..
Interest payments, long-term	..	**39**	**35**	**29**	**30**	**30**
Public and publicly guaranteed sector	..	39	35	29	30	30
Private sector not guaranteed	..	..	..	..	..	..

ERITREA

(US$ million, unless otherwise indicated)

Snapshot	2024
Total external debt stocks	**667.3**
External debt stocks as % of:	
Exports	..
GNI	..
Debt service as % of:	
Exports	..
GNI	..
Net financial flows, debt and equity	-44.9
Net debt inflows	-17.0
Net equity inflows	-27.9
GNI	..
Population (million)	4

Figure 1 Public and publicly guaranteed debt, by creditor and creditor type in 2024, including IMF credit

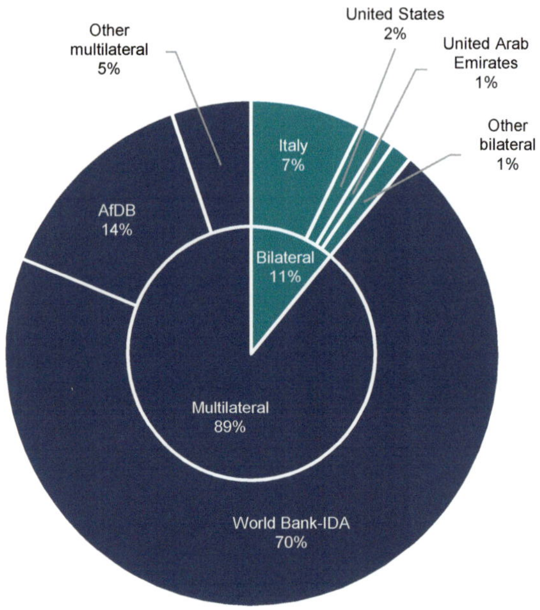

Figure 2 Average terms on new debt commitments from official and private creditors

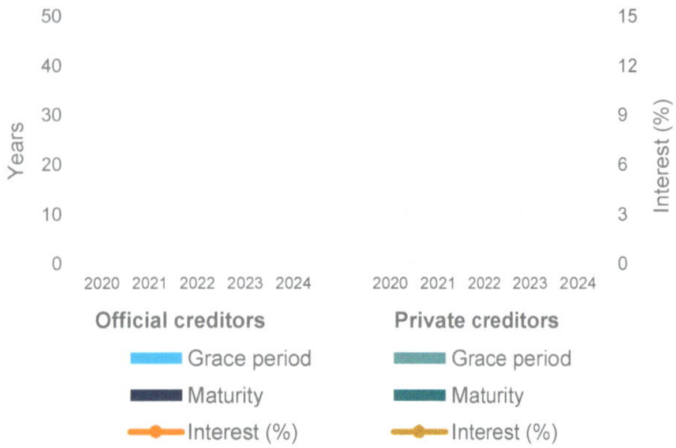

Summary External Debt Data	2010	2020	2021	2022	2023	2024
Total external debt stocks	**1,037.3**	**798.7**	**772.1**	**727.1**	**725.9**	**667.3**
Long-term external debt stocks	**998.4**	**739.5**	**690.7**	**646.3**	**641.3**	**581.9**
Public and publicly guaranteed debt from:	*998.4*	*739.5*	*690.7*	*646.3*	*641.3*	*581.9*
Official creditors	998.4	739.5	690.7	646.3	641.3	581.9
Multilateral	651.4	587.8	565.4	533.2	535.9	517.4
of which: World Bank	467.9	449.9	437.2	415.7	419.3	407.4
Bilateral	347.1	151.7	125.3	113.1	105.3	64.5
Private creditors	..	..	..	..	..	..
Bondholders	..	..	..	..	..	..
Commercial banks and others	..	..	..	..	..	..
Private nonguaranteed debt from:	..	..	..	..	..	..
Bondholders	..	..	..	..	..	..
Commercial banks and others	..	..	..	..	..	..
Use of IMF credit and SDR allocations	**23.3**	**21.8**	**42.5**	**40.5**	**40.8**	**39.6**
IMF credit	0.0	0.0	0.0	0.0	0.0	0.0
SDR allocations	23.3	21.8	42.5	40.5	40.8	39.6
Short-term external debt stocks	**15.6**	**37.4**	**38.9**	**40.4**	**43.9**	**45.7**
Disbursements, long-term	**8.6**	**2.8**	**0.9**	**0.8**	**4.2**	**1.6**
Public and publicly guaranteed sector	8.6	2.8	0.9	0.8	4.2	1.6
Private sector not guaranteed	..	..	..	..	..	..
Principal repayments, long-term	**16.9**	**16.5**	**17.0**	**13.4**	**13.1**	**18.6**
Public and publicly guaranteed sector	16.9	16.5	17.0	13.4	13.1	18.6
Private sector not guaranteed	..	..	..	..	..	..
Interest payments, long-term	**9.7**	**2.3**	**2.3**	**1.7**	**1.4**	**1.6**
Public and publicly guaranteed sector	9.7	2.3	2.3	1.7	1.4	1.6
Private sector not guaranteed	..	..	..	..	..	..

Note: Figure 2 shows no data values because the country did not have new commitments from 2020 to 2024.

ESWATINI

(US$ million, unless otherwise indicated)

Snapshot	2024
Total external debt stocks	**1,239**
External debt stocks as % of:	
Exports	46
GNI	28
Debt service as % of:	
Exports	8
GNI	5
Net financial flows, debt and equity	118
Net debt inflows	26
Net equity inflows	93
GNI	**4,463**
Population (million)	1

Figure 1 Public and publicly guaranteed debt, by creditor and creditor type in 2024, including IMF credit

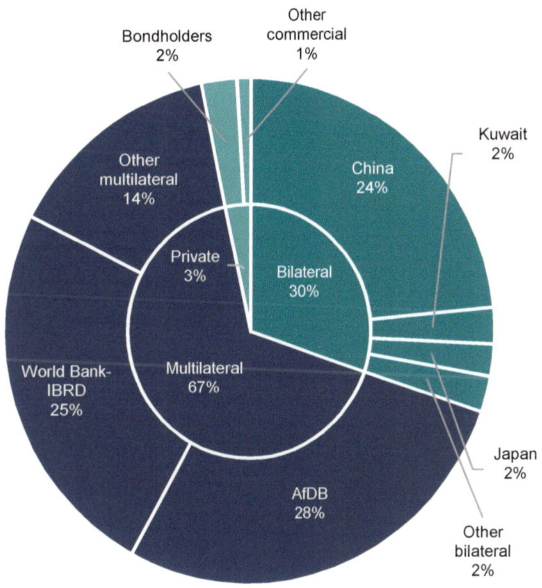

Figure 2 Average terms on new debt commitments from official and private creditors

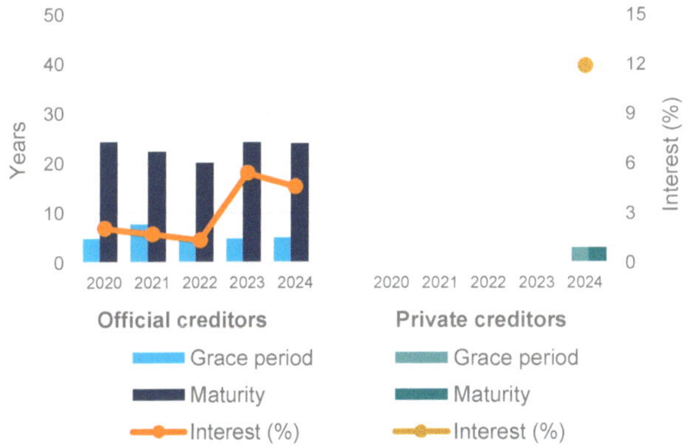

Summary External Debt Data	2010	2020	2021	2022	2023	2024
Total external debt stocks	**1,017**	**958**	**1,179**	**1,248**	**1,228**	**1,239**
Long-term external debt stocks	**734**	**749**	**857**	**967**	**914**	**969**
Public and publicly guaranteed debt from:	*432*	*585*	*620*	*758*	*773*	*867*
Official creditors	391	574	611	749	765	838
Multilateral	239	274	341	497	523	564
of which: World Bank	5	43	87	175	192	222
Bilateral	152	300	270	252	242	273
Private creditors	41	10	9	9	8	29
Bondholders	..	..	..	..	..	21
Commercial banks and others	41	10	9	9	8	8
Private nonguaranteed debt from:	*302*	*164*	*237*	*209*	*140*	*102*
Bondholders	..	..	..	..	..	..
Commercial banks and others	302	164	237	209	140	102
Use of IMF credit and SDR allocations	**74**	**183**	**283**	**269**	**258**	**199**
IMF credit	0	113	110	104	92	38
SDR allocations	74	70	173	164	166	161
Short-term external debt stocks	**208**	**26**	**40**	**12**	**57**	**70**
Disbursements, long-term	**320**	**78**	**170**	**192**	**55**	**147**
Public and publicly guaranteed sector	18	78	97	192	55	147
Private sector not guaranteed	302	..	73	..	..	..
Principal repayments, long-term	**34**	**82**	**49**	**64**	**105**	**83**
Public and publicly guaranteed sector	34	39	49	37	36	45
Private sector not guaranteed	..	43	..	27	69	38
Interest payments, long-term	**17**	**20**	**15**	**17**	**48**	**58**
Public and publicly guaranteed sector	17	20	15	17	39	50
Private sector not guaranteed	..	..	..	..	9	8

ETHIOPIA

(US$ million, unless otherwise indicated)

Snapshot	2024
Total external debt stocks	**36,548**
External debt stocks as % of:	
Exports	311
GNI	..
Debt service as % of:	
Exports	12
GNI	..
Net financial flows, debt and equity	6,801
Net debt inflows	2,817
Net equity inflows	3,984
GNI	..
Population (million)	132

Figure 1 Public and publicly guaranteed debt, by creditor and creditor type in 2024, including IMF credit

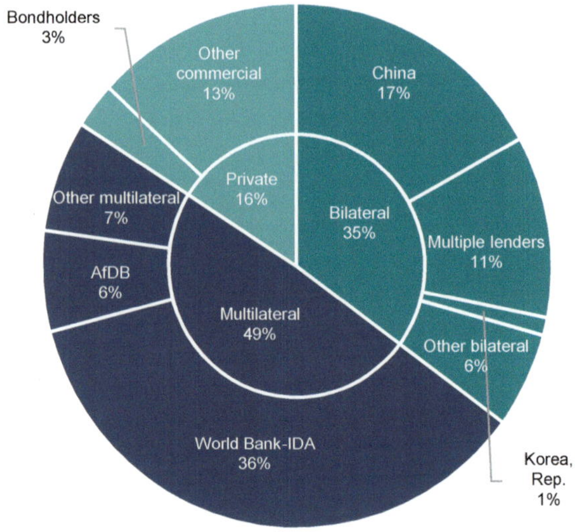

Figure 2 Average terms on new debt commitments from official and private creditors

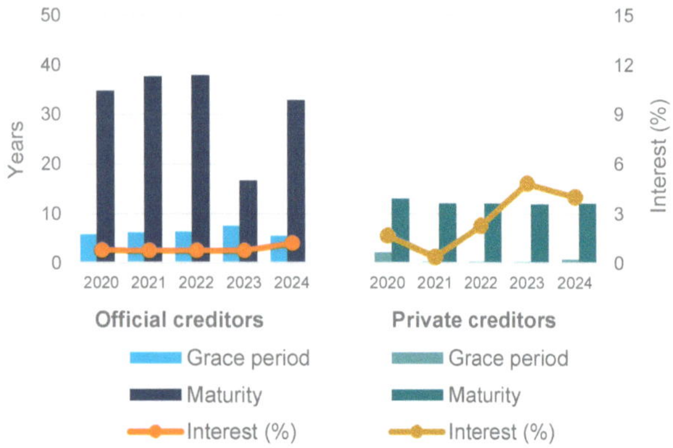

Summary External Debt Data	2010	2020	2021	2022	2023	2024
Total external debt stocks	**7,287**	**32,364**	**32,000**	**30,621**	**33,274**	**36,548**
Long-term external debt stocks	**6,500**	**31,016**	**30,152**	**29,044**	**31,910**	**33,950**
Public and publicly guaranteed debt from:	*6,500*	*31,016*	*30,152*	*29,044*	*31,910*	*33,950*
Official creditors	4,613	24,506	24,225	23,795	26,526	28,261
Multilateral	2,812	14,024	14,194	14,244	14,990	15,735
of which: World Bank	1,804	10,991	11,170	11,211	11,984	12,762
Bilateral	1,800	10,482	10,031	9,551	11,536	12,526
Private creditors	1,887	6,511	5,927	5,249	5,384	5,690
Bondholders	..	1,000	1,000	1,000	1,000	1,000
Commercial banks and others	1,887	5,511	4,927	4,249	4,384	4,690
Private nonguaranteed debt from:	..	..	..	..	..	..
Bondholders	..	..	..	..	..	..
Commercial banks and others	..	..	..	..	..	..
Use of IMF credit and SDR allocations	**485**	**940**	**1,317**	**1,252**	**1,161**	**2,246**
IMF credit	288	755	734	698	603	1,704
SDR allocations	197	184	582	554	558	543
Short-term external debt stocks	**302**	**408**	**531**	**325**	**202**	**352**
Disbursements, long-term	**1,763**	**2,194**	**1,082**	**1,132**	**3,824**	**2,312**
Public and publicly guaranteed sector	1,763	2,194	1,082	1,132	3,824	2,312
Private sector not guaranteed	..	..	..	..	..	..
Principal repayments, long-term	**129**	**1,371**	**1,544**	**1,523**	**1,036**	**717**
Public and publicly guaranteed sector	129	1,371	1,544	1,523	1,036	717
Private sector not guaranteed	..	..	..	..	..	..
Interest payments, long-term	**46**	**620**	**460**	**460**	**379**	**370**
Public and publicly guaranteed sector	46	620	460	460	379	370
Private sector not guaranteed	..	..	..	..	..	..

FIJI

(US$ million, unless otherwise indicated)

Snapshot	**2024**
Total external debt stocks	**3,869**
External debt stocks as % of:	
Exports	151
GNI	71
Debt service as % of:	
Exports	10
GNI	5
Net financial flows, debt and equity	759
Net debt inflows	555
Net equity inflows	204
GNI	**5,420**
Population (thousand)	**929**

Figure 1 Public and publicly guaranteed debt, by creditor and creditor type in 2024, including IMF credit

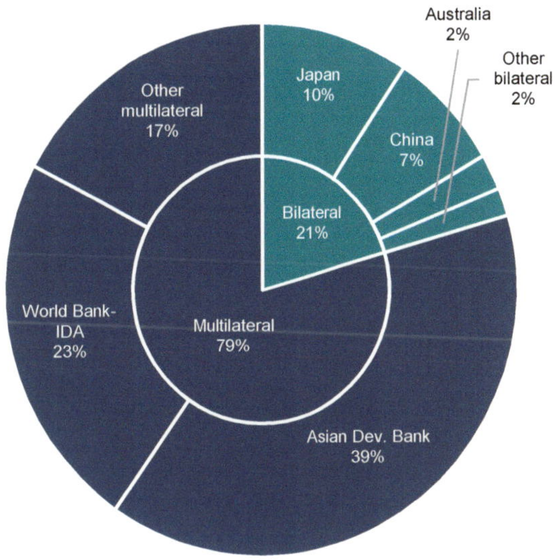

Figure 2 Average terms on new debt commitments from official and private creditors

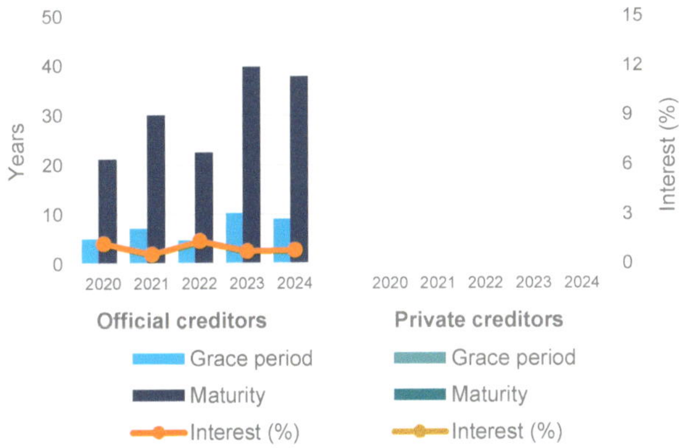

Summary External Debt Data	**2010**	**2020**	**2021**	**2022**	**2023**	**2024**
Total external debt stocks	**1,107**	**2,047**	**2,498**	**2,988**	**3,348**	**3,869**
Long-term external debt stocks	**926**	**1,628**	**1,905**	**2,265**	**2,338**	**2,605**
Public and publicly guaranteed debt from:	*426*	*904*	*1,213*	*1,603*	*1,595*	*1,696*
Official creditors	276	904	1,213	1,603	1,595	1,696
Multilateral	113	638	828	1,203	1,207	1,347
of which: World Bank	0	142	326	468	479	575
Bilateral	162	265	384	400	388	349
Private creditors	150	0	..	..	..	..
Bondholders	150	0	..	..	..	..
Commercial banks and others	..	..	..	..	..	..
Private nonguaranteed debt from:	*500*	*724*	*692*	*662*	*743*	*909*
Bondholders	..	..	..	..	..	..
Commercial banks and others	500	724	692	662	743	909
Use of IMF credit and SDR allocations	**103**	**97**	**226**	**215**	**217**	**210**
IMF credit	0	0	0	0	0	0
SDR allocations	103	97	226	215	217	210
Short-term external debt stocks	**78**	**323**	**367**	**509**	**794**	**1,053**
Disbursements, long-term	**50**	**433**	**399**	**511**	**153**	**378**
Public and publicly guaranteed sector	38	403	326	481	72	212
Private sector not guaranteed	13	30	73	30	81	166
Principal repayments, long-term	**36**	**250**	**120**	**105**	**66**	**83**
Public and publicly guaranteed sector	9	231	15	44	66	83
Private sector not guaranteed	27	19	106	60	..	..
Interest payments, long-term	**23**	**24**	**9**	**62**	**94**	**87**
Public and publicly guaranteed sector	15	24	9	59	75	80
Private sector not guaranteed	7	0	0	3	19	7

GABON

(US$ million, unless otherwise indicated)

Snapshot	2024
Total external debt stocks	**6,817**
External debt stocks as % of:	
Exports	..
GNI	36
Debt service as % of:	
Exports	..
GNI	6
Net financial flows, debt and equity	549
Net debt inflows	-595
Net equity inflows	1,145
GNI	**18,960**
Population (million)	**3**

Figure 2 Average terms on new debt commitments from official and private creditors

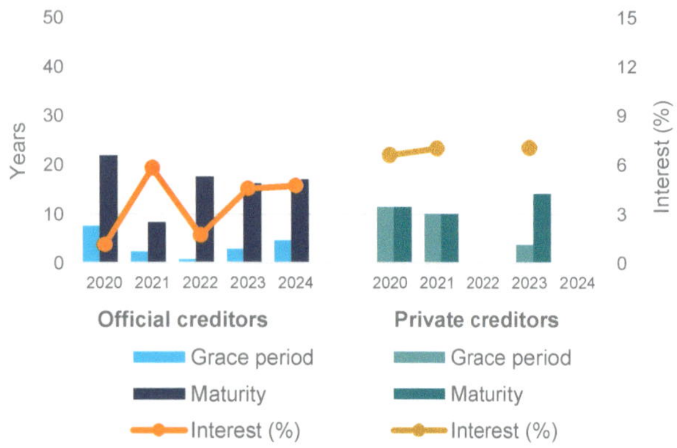

Figure 1 Public and publicly guaranteed debt, by creditor and creditor type in 2024, including IMF credit

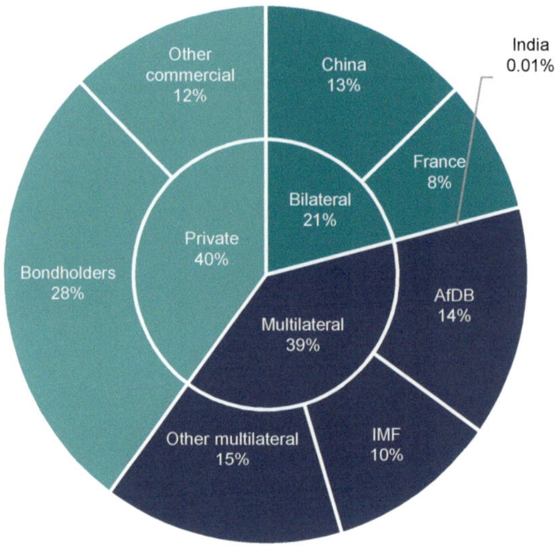

Summary External Debt Data	2010	2020	2021	2022	2023	2024
Total external debt stocks	**2,915**	**7,730**	**7,834**	**7,991**	**7,576**	**6,817**
Long-term external debt stocks	**2,519**	**6,592**	**6,389**	**6,186**	**6,078**	**5,551**
Public and publicly guaranteed debt from:	*2,519*	*6,592*	*6,389*	*6,186*	*6,078*	*5,551*
Official creditors	1,122	3,650	3,405	3,309	3,249	3,074
Multilateral	466	2,082	1,936	1,910	1,906	1,771
of which: World Bank	22	680	654	649	660	620
Bilateral	656	1,568	1,469	1,399	1,343	1,303
Private creditors	1,397	2,942	2,984	2,877	2,829	2,478
Bondholders	879	2,436	2,573	2,549	2,024	1,710
Commercial banks and others	518	506	411	328	804	768
Private nonguaranteed debt from:	..	..	..	..	..	..
Bondholders	..	..	..	..	..	..
Commercial banks and others	..	..	..	..	..	..
Use of IMF credit and SDR allocations	**226**	**1,063**	**1,427**	**1,480**	**1,374**	**1,113**
IMF credit	0	851	932	1,009	899	652
SDR allocations	226	211	495	471	475	461
Short-term external debt stocks	**170**	**76**	**17**	**324**	**124**	**152**
Disbursements, long-term	**509**	**1,273**	**905**	**293**	**654**	**173**
Public and publicly guaranteed sector	509	1,273	905	293	654	173
Private sector not guaranteed	..	..	..	..	..	..
Principal repayments, long-term	**313**	**1,135**	**909**	**320**	**783**	**548**
Public and publicly guaranteed sector	313	1,135	909	320	783	548
Private sector not guaranteed	..	..	..	..	..	..
Interest payments, long-term	**137**	**274**	**217**	**188**	**567**	**280**
Public and publicly guaranteed sector	137	274	217	188	567	280
Private sector not guaranteed	..	..	..	..	..	..

GAMBIA, THE

(US$ million, unless otherwise indicated)

Snapshot	2024
Total external debt stocks	**1,643**
External debt stocks as % of:	
Exports	173
GNI	66
Debt service as % of:	
Exports	8
GNI	3
Net financial flows, debt and equity	571
Net debt inflows	339
Net equity inflows	232
GNI	**2,476**
Population (million)	**3**

Figure 1 Public and publicly guaranteed debt, by creditor and creditor type in 2024, including IMF credit

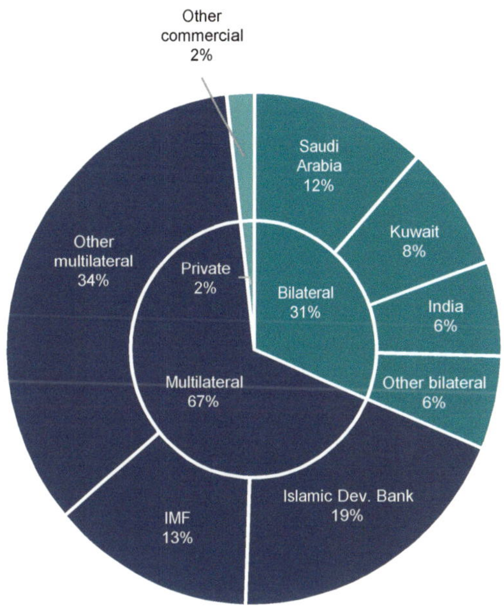

Figure 2 Average terms on new debt commitments from official and private creditors

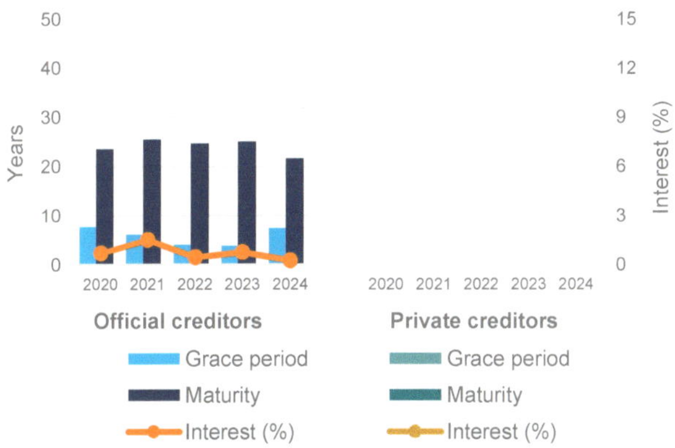

Summary External Debt Data	2010	2020	2021	2022	2023	2024
Total external debt stocks	**544**	**964**	**1,113**	**1,180**	**1,325**	**1,643**
Long-term external debt stocks	**422**	**832**	**847**	**891**	**982**	**1,310**
Public and publicly guaranteed debt from:	*422*	*832*	*847*	*891*	*982*	*1,010*
Official creditors	416	796	816	864	959	990
Multilateral	296	530	533	551	619	625
of which: World Bank	65	128	131	126	128	122
Bilateral	120	266	283	313	340	365
Private creditors	6	36	31	27	24	20
Bondholders	..	..	..	..	..	..
Commercial banks and others	6	36	31	27	24	20
Private nonguaranteed debt from:	..	..	..	..	..	*300*
Bondholders	..	..	..	..	..	300
Commercial banks and others	..	..	..	..	..	..
Use of IMF credit and SDR allocations	**77**	**103**	**228**	**248**	**251**	**271**
IMF credit	31	61	103	129	131	155
SDR allocations	46	43	125	119	120	117
Short-term external debt stocks	**45**	**29**	**38**	**40**	**91**	**62**
Disbursements, long-term	**43**	**92**	**50**	**89**	**115**	**378**
Public and publicly guaranteed sector	43	92	50	89	115	78
Private sector not guaranteed	..	..	..	..	..	300
Principal repayments, long-term	**18**	**26**	**26**	**26**	**30**	**37**
Public and publicly guaranteed sector	18	26	26	26	30	37
Private sector not guaranteed	..	..	..	..	..	..
Interest payments, long-term	**7**	**8**	**11**	**9**	**10**	**27**
Public and publicly guaranteed sector	7	8	11	9	10	11
Private sector not guaranteed	..	..	..	..	..	16

GEORGIA

(US$ million, unless otherwise indicated)

Snapshot	2024
Total external debt stocks	**25,163**
External debt stocks as % of:	
Exports	139
GNI	80
Debt service as % of:	
Exports	27
GNI	15
Net financial flows, debt and equity	2,892
Net debt inflows	1,238
Net equity inflows	1,654
GNI	**31,581**
Population (million)	**4**

Figure 1 Public and publicly guaranteed debt, by creditor and creditor type in 2024, including IMF credit

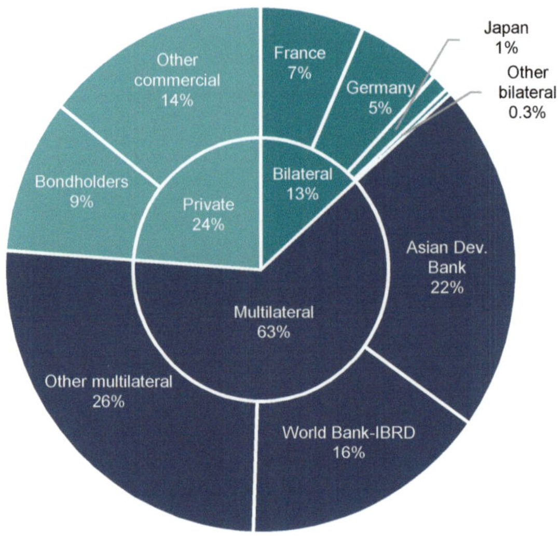

Figure 2 Average terms on new debt commitments from official and private creditors

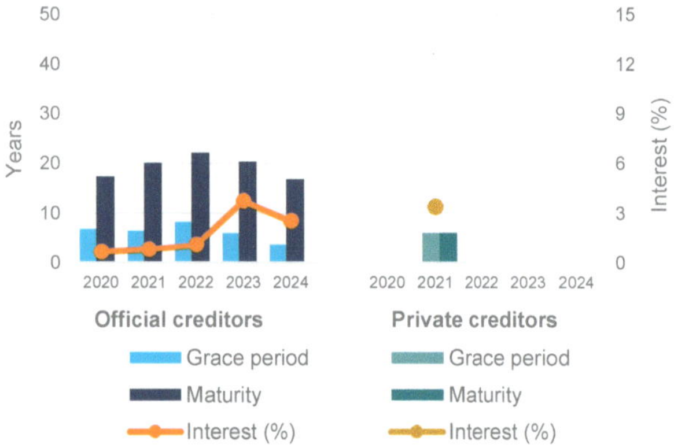

Summary External Debt Data	2010	2020	2021	2022	2023	2024
Total external debt stocks	**8,790**	**20,084**	**21,993**	**23,320**	**24,123**	**25,163**
Long-term external debt stocks	**6,418**	**16,969**	**18,463**	**18,427**	**18,894**	**19,454**
Public and publicly guaranteed debt from:	*3,274*	*7,968*	*9,082*	*9,723*	*10,263*	*9,980*
Official creditors	2,448	6,332	6,944	7,149	7,726	7,473
Multilateral	1,802	4,801	5,378	5,627	6,197	6,071
of which: World Bank	1,359	2,054	2,043	2,009	2,125	2,115
Bilateral	645	1,531	1,567	1,522	1,529	1,402
Private creditors	827	1,635	2,138	2,575	2,537	2,507
Bondholders	750	750	1,000	1,000	1,000	1,000
Commercial banks and others	77	885	1,138	1,575	1,537	1,507
Private nonguaranteed debt from:	*3,143*	*9,001*	*9,381*	*8,703*	*8,631*	*9,474*
Bondholders	..	3,372	3,535	2,881	2,641	3,323
Commercial banks and others	3,143	5,629	5,846	5,823	5,990	6,151
Use of IMF credit and SDR allocations	**1,272**	**792**	**1,158**	**1,084**	**1,063**	**978**
IMF credit	1,050	585	674	624	599	527
SDR allocations	222	207	484	460	464	451
Short-term external debt stocks	**1,101**	**2,322**	**2,372**	**3,809**	**4,167**	**4,731**
Disbursements, long-term	**1,026**	**2,508**	**3,793**	**2,574**	**2,425**	**4,078**
Public and publicly guaranteed sector	651	1,452	2,543	846	822	551
Private sector not guaranteed	375	1,056	1,250	1,729	1,603	3,527
Principal repayments, long-term	**510**	**1,820**	**2,002**	**2,220**	**2,406**	**3,474**
Public and publicly guaranteed sector	169	799	1,079	364	429	473
Private sector not guaranteed	342	1,022	923	1,855	1,977	3,001
Interest payments, long-term	**247**	**587**	**655**	**693**	**844**	**930**
Public and publicly guaranteed sector	87	135	100	131	260	337
Private sector not guaranteed	160	452	554	562	584	594

GHANA

(US$ million, unless otherwise indicated)

Snapshot	2024
Total external debt stocks	**37,415**
External debt stocks as % of:	
Exports	129
GNI	47
Debt service as % of:	
Exports	9
GNI	3
Net financial flows, debt and equity	2,260
Net debt inflows	628
Net equity inflows	1,632
GNI	**79,746**
Population (million)	**34**

Figure 1 Public and publicly guaranteed debt, by creditor and creditor type in 2024, including IMF credit

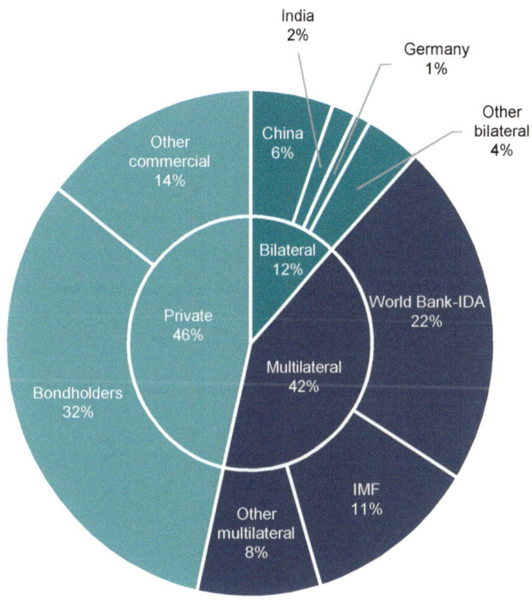

Figure 2 Average terms on new debt commitments from official and private creditors

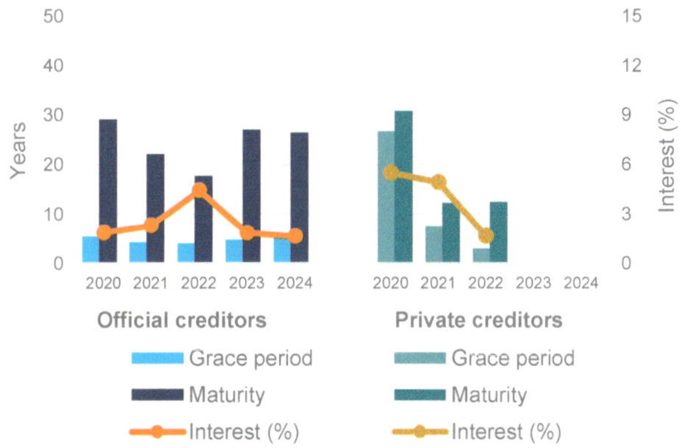

Summary External Debt Data	2010	2020	2021	2022	2023	2024
Total external debt stocks	**17,985**	**40,295**	**46,584**	**43,607**	**41,701**	**37,415**
Long-term external debt stocks	**14,956**	**32,511**	**38,031**	**35,830**	**34,309**	**30,132**
Public and publicly guaranteed debt from:	*5,399*	*22,915*	*26,610*	*27,610*	*28,526*	*25,584*
Official creditors	4,270	9,366	9,725	10,534	11,186	12,153
Multilateral	2,749	6,080	6,306	7,142	7,782	8,751
of which: World Bank	1,868	4,477	4,663	4,747	5,393	6,373
Bilateral	1,521	3,287	3,418	3,393	3,403	3,402
Private creditors	1,130	13,548	16,885	17,075	17,341	13,431
Bondholders	..	10,215	13,120	13,104	13,104	9,236
Commercial banks and others	1,130	3,333	3,765	3,971	4,237	4,195
Private nonguaranteed debt from:	*9,556*	*9,596*	*11,421*	*8,220*	*5,783*	*4,548*
Bondholders	0	831	253	253	253	253
Commercial banks and others	9,556	8,765	11,168	7,967	5,530	4,295
Use of IMF credit and SDR allocations	**937**	**2,612**	**3,411**	**3,124**	**3,630**	**4,663**
IMF credit	392	2,102	1,926	1,711	2,206	3,279
SDR allocations	545	510	1,485	1,412	1,424	1,384
Short-term external debt stocks	**2,092**	**5,173**	**5,142**	**4,653**	**3,761**	**2,620**
Disbursements, long-term	**4,582**	**7,299**	**8,295**	**2,435**	**1,251**	**1,402**
Public and publicly guaranteed sector	1,321	4,417	5,892	2,435	999	1,321
Private sector not guaranteed	3,261	2,882	2,403	..	252	81
Principal repayments, long-term	**171**	**1,692**	**1,791**	**4,167**	**3,057**	**1,720**
Public and publicly guaranteed sector	171	1,538	1,791	966	367	404
Private sector not guaranteed	0	154	..	3,201	2,690	1,316
Interest payments, long-term	**243**	**1,064**	**1,337**	**1,363**	**491**	**692**
Public and publicly guaranteed sector	96	915	1,196	989	149	441
Private sector not guaranteed	147	149	141	374	342	251

GRENADA

(US$ million, unless otherwise indicated)

Snapshot	2024
Total external debt stocks	**863.3**
External debt stocks as % of:	
Exports	96.9
GNI	68.6
Debt service as % of:	
Exports	4.9
GNI	3.4
Net financial flows, debt and equity	210.1
Net debt inflows	-23.5
Net equity inflows	233.6
GNI	**1,258.5**
Population (thousand)	**117**

Figure 2 Average terms on new debt commitments from official and private creditors

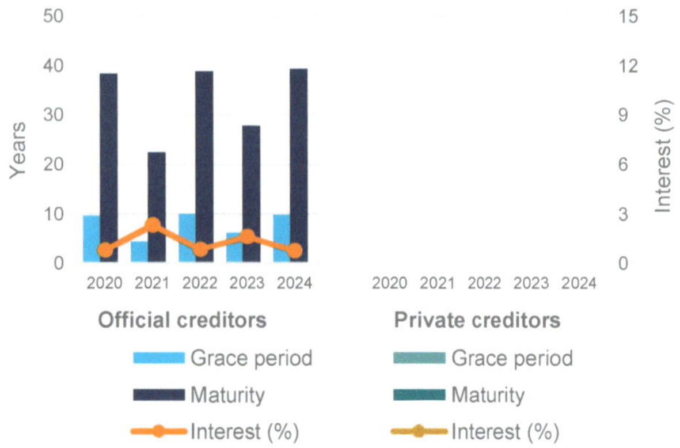

Figure 1 Public and publicly guaranteed debt, by creditor and creditor type in 2024, including IMF credit

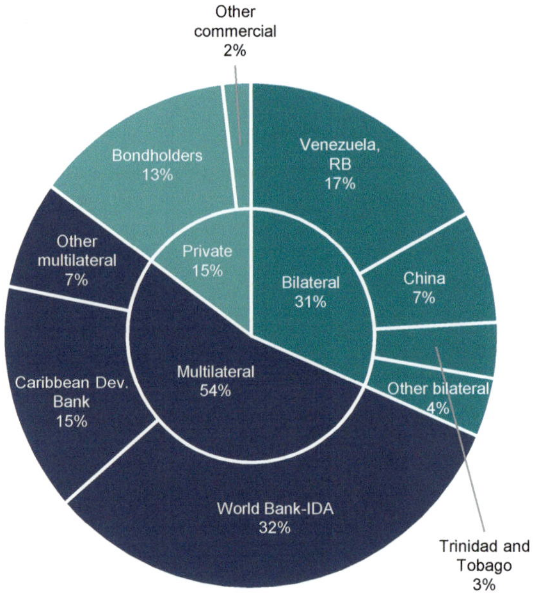

Summary External Debt Data	2010	2020	2021	2022	2023	2024
Total external debt stocks	**560.6**	**834.2**	**898.7**	**853.7**	**881.5**	**863.3**
Long-term external debt stocks	**476.7**	**673.3**	**701.8**	**719.7**	**760.1**	**787.0**
Public and publicly guaranteed debt from:	*476.7*	*673.3*	*701.8*	*719.7*	*760.1*	*787.0*
Official creditors	278.2	530.7	572.1	593.5	643.5	665.4
Multilateral	187.8	317.5	341.2	365.3	392.8	409.5
of which: World Bank	58.2	161.4	187.0	211.6	248.9	273.0
Bilateral	90.4	213.2	231.0	228.1	250.7	256.0
Private creditors	198.5	142.5	129.7	126.3	116.6	121.6
Bondholders	193.2	128.5	122.7	111.7	102.4	106.7
Commercial banks and others	5.3	14.1	7.0	14.6	14.2	14.9
Private nonguaranteed debt from:	..	..	..	..	..	..
Bondholders	..	..	..	..	..	..
Commercial banks and others	..	..	..	..	..	..
Use of IMF credit and SDR allocations	**46.3**	**58.8**	**76.6**	**69.3**	**66.1**	**60.6**
IMF credit	29.1	42.7	38.9	33.6	30.1	25.6
SDR allocations	17.2	16.1	37.6	35.8	36.1	35.1
Short-term external debt stocks	**37.6**	**102.2**	**120.3**	**64.7**	**55.3**	**15.7**
Disbursements, long-term	**21.1**	**44.9**	**65.8**	**56.7**	**71.0**	**45.2**
Public and publicly guaranteed sector	21.1	44.9	65.8	56.7	71.0	45.2
Private sector not guaranteed	..	..	..	..	..	..
Principal repayments, long-term	**15.1**	**28.8**	**37.9**	**31.3**	**31.6**	**24.1**
Public and publicly guaranteed sector	15.1	28.8	37.9	31.3	31.6	24.1
Private sector not guaranteed	..	..	..	..	..	..
Interest payments, long-term	**10.5**	**16.2**	**15.7**	**15.7**	**16.7**	**13.9**
Public and publicly guaranteed sector	10.5	16.2	15.7	15.7	16.7	13.9
Private sector not guaranteed	..	..	..	..	..	..

GUATEMALA

(US$ million, unless otherwise indicated)

Snapshot	2024
Total external debt stocks	**27,059**
External debt stocks as % of:	
Exports	132
GNI	24
Debt service as % of:	
Exports	10
GNI	2
Net financial flows, debt and equity	3,289
Net debt inflows	1,433
Net equity inflows	1,857
GNI	**111,608**
Population (million)	**18**

Figure 1 Public and publicly guaranteed debt, by creditor and creditor type in 2024, including IMF credit

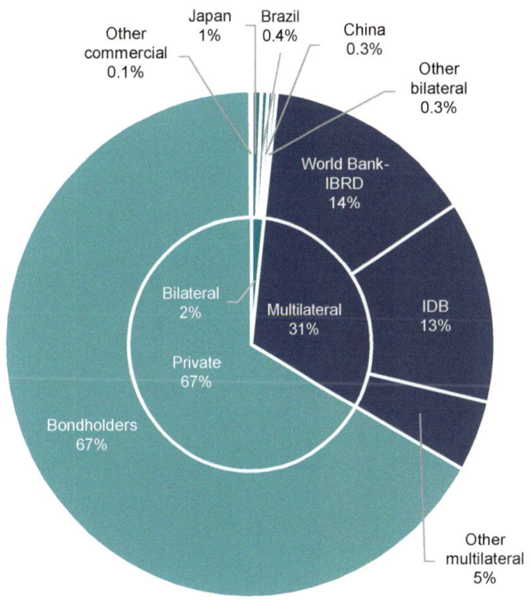

Figure 2 Average terms on new debt commitments from official and private creditors

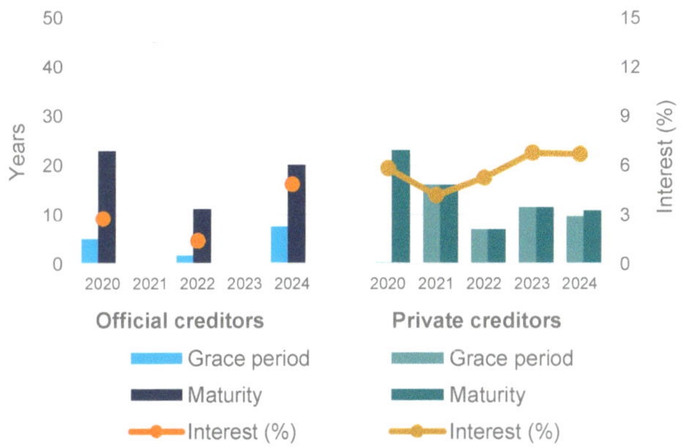

Summary External Debt Data	2010	2020	2021	2022	2023	2024
Total external debt stocks	**15,043**	**24,357**	**26,313**	**25,269**	**25,662**	**27,059**
Long-term external debt stocks	**13,149**	**22,681**	**24,094**	**24,153**	**24,652**	**26,090**
Public and publicly guaranteed debt from:	*5,559*	*10,561*	*11,210*	*11,201*	*12,554*	*13,642*
Official creditors	4,600	5,209	4,861	5,052	4,841	4,532
Multilateral	4,241	4,820	4,509	4,754	4,573	4,303
of which: World Bank	1,372	1,758	1,689	2,114	2,061	1,921
Bilateral	359	389	352	298	268	229
Private creditors	959	5,353	6,349	6,149	7,713	9,110
Bondholders	955	5,330	6,330	6,130	7,695	9,095
Commercial banks and others	4	23	19	19	18	15
Private nonguaranteed debt from:	*7,589*	*12,119*	*12,884*	*12,952*	*12,098*	*12,449*
Bondholders	5	700	1,700	3,700	3,700	3,700
Commercial banks and others	7,584	11,419	11,184	9,252	8,398	8,749
Use of IMF credit and SDR allocations	**309**	**289**	**856**	**814**	**821**	**798**
IMF credit	0	0	0	0	0	0
SDR allocations	309	289	856	814	821	798
Short-term external debt stocks	**1,585**	**1,388**	**1,364**	**302**	**189**	**171**
Disbursements, long-term	**1,472**	**1,957**	**2,092**	**3,146**	**1,727**	**1,938**
Public and publicly guaranteed sector	881	1,745	1,061	1,096	1,717	1,541
Private sector not guaranteed	592	212	1,030	2,050	10	397
Principal repayments, long-term	**949**	**2,269**	**659**	**3,063**	**1,212**	**487**
Public and publicly guaranteed sector	264	539	393	1,081	359	440
Private sector not guaranteed	685	1,730	266	1,981	854	47
Interest payments, long-term	**636**	**1,195**	**1,013**	**1,053**	**1,309**	**1,429**
Public and publicly guaranteed sector	284	490	466	484	599	698
Private sector not guaranteed	352	705	547	570	710	731

GUINEA

(US$ million, unless otherwise indicated)

Snapshot	2024
Total external debt stocks	**5,388**
External debt stocks as % of:	
Exports	46
GNI	23
Debt service as % of:	
Exports	4
GNI	2
Net financial flows, debt and equity	497
Net debt inflows	345
Net equity inflows	152
GNI	**23,228**
Population (million)	**15**

Figure 1 Public and publicly guaranteed debt, by creditor and creditor type in 2024, including IMF credit

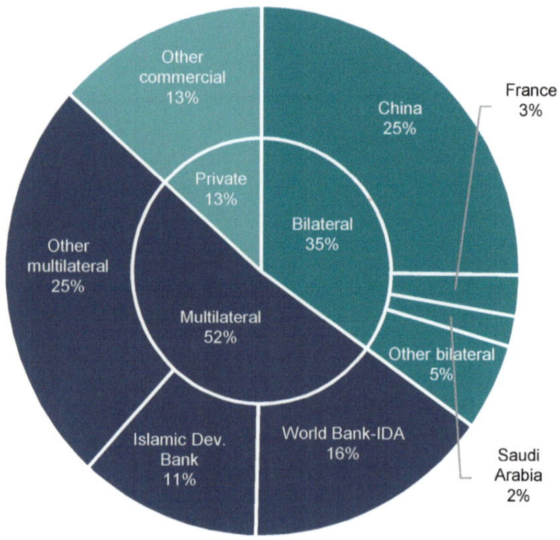

Figure 2 Average terms on new debt commitments from official and private creditors

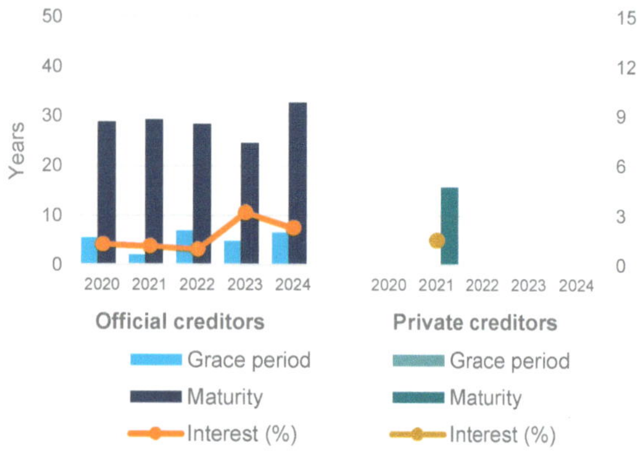

Summary External Debt Data	2010	2020	2021	2022	2023	2024
Total external debt stocks	**3,239**	**4,117**	**4,642**	**4,904**	**5,163**	**5,388**
Long-term external debt stocks	**2,926**	**3,306**	**3,540**	**3,773**	**4,020**	**4,168**
Public and publicly guaranteed debt from:	*2,926*	*3,306*	*3,540*	*3,668*	*3,930*	*4,093*
Official creditors	2,900	3,077	3,256	3,270	3,337	3,484
Multilateral	1,875	1,242	1,409	1,461	1,636	1,905
of which: World Bank	1,248	572	621	616	655	700
Bilateral	1,025	1,836	1,847	1,809	1,701	1,580
Private creditors	26	229	284	397	593	609
Bondholders	..	..	..	..	..	..
Commercial banks and others	26	229	284	397	593	609
Private nonguaranteed debt from:	..	..	..	*105*	*90*	*75*
Bondholders	..	..	..	..	..	..
Commercial banks and others	..	..	..	105	90	75
Use of IMF credit and SDR allocations	**205**	**668**	**886**	**884**	**845**	**843**
IMF credit	48	520	455	475	432	441
SDR allocations	158	148	431	410	413	401
Short-term external debt stocks	**108**	**143**	**217**	**247**	**298**	**378**
Disbursements, long-term	**36**	**371**	**343**	**433**	**393**	**507**
Public and publicly guaranteed sector	36	371	343	328	393	507
Private sector not guaranteed	..	..	..	105	..	..
Principal repayments, long-term	**48**	**37**	**50**	**106**	**158**	**260**
Public and publicly guaranteed sector	48	37	50	106	143	245
Private sector not guaranteed	..	..	..	..	15	15
Interest payments, long-term	**21**	**41**	**52**	**58**	**74**	**93**
Public and publicly guaranteed sector	21	41	52	58	69	89
Private sector not guaranteed	..	..	..	0	4	5

GUINEA-BISSAU

(US$ million, unless otherwise indicated)

Snapshot	2024
Total external debt stocks	**1,433**
External debt stocks as % of:	
Exports	485
GNI	67
Debt service as % of:	
Exports	13
GNI	2
Net financial flows, debt and equity	74
Net debt inflows	47
Net equity inflows	27
GNI	**2,136**
Population (million)	**2**

Figure 1 Public and publicly guaranteed debt, by creditor and creditor type in 2024, including IMF credit

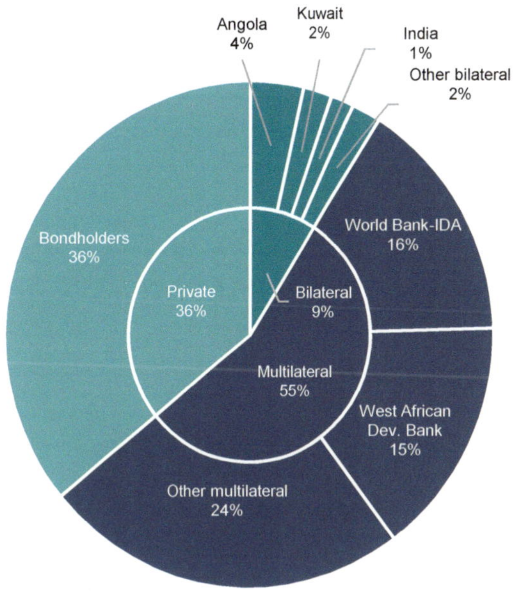

Figure 2 Average terms on new debt commitments from official and private creditors

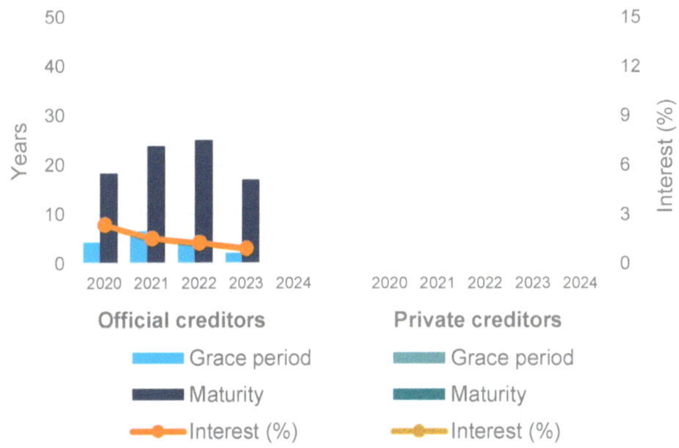

Summary External Debt Data	2010	2020	2021	2022	2023	2024
Total external debt stocks	**1,074**	**1,118**	**1,258**	**1,251**	**1,423**	**1,433**
Long-term external debt stocks	**958**	**1,037**	**1,115**	**1,154**	**1,313**	**1,310**
Public and publicly guaranteed debt from:	*957*	*1,037*	*1,115*	*1,154*	*1,313*	*1,310*
Official creditors	957	801	810	782	817	815
Multilateral	502	706	676	651	690	691
of which: World Bank	289	164	182	187	214	215
Bilateral	454	95	134	131	127	124
Private creditors	..	236	305	372	495	495
Bondholders	..	236	305	372	495	495
Commercial banks and others	..	..	..	..	..	..
Private nonguaranteed debt from:	*1*	*0*	*0*	*0*	*0*	*0*
Bondholders	..	..	..	..	..	..
Commercial banks and others	1	0	0	0	0	0
Use of IMF credit and SDR allocations	**25**	**49**	**103**	**95**	**108**	**122**
IMF credit	4	29	46	41	54	69
SDR allocations	21	20	57	54	55	53
Short-term external debt stocks	**92**	**32**	**40**	**1**	**2**	**1**
Disbursements, long-term	**6**	**98**	**48**	**38**	**45**	**45**
Public and publicly guaranteed sector	6	98	48	38	45	45
Private sector not guaranteed	..	..	..	..	..	..
Principal repayments, long-term	**9**	**41**	**29**	**28**	**26**	**14**
Public and publicly guaranteed sector	6	17	29	28	26	14
Private sector not guaranteed	3	24	..	..	..	..
Interest payments, long-term	**4**	**23**	**29**	**32**	**22**	**18**
Public and publicly guaranteed sector	4	23	29	32	22	18
Private sector not guaranteed	..	..	..	..	..	..

GUYANA

(US$ million, unless otherwise indicated)

Snapshot	2024
Total external debt stocks	**3,682**
External debt stocks as % of:	
Exports	18
GNI	23
Debt service as % of:	
Exports	3
GNI	4
Net financial flows, debt and equity	11,170
Net debt inflows	769
Net equity inflows	10,401
GNI	**16,261**
Population (thousand)	**831**

Figure 1 Public and publicly guaranteed debt, by creditor and creditor type in 2024, including IMF credit

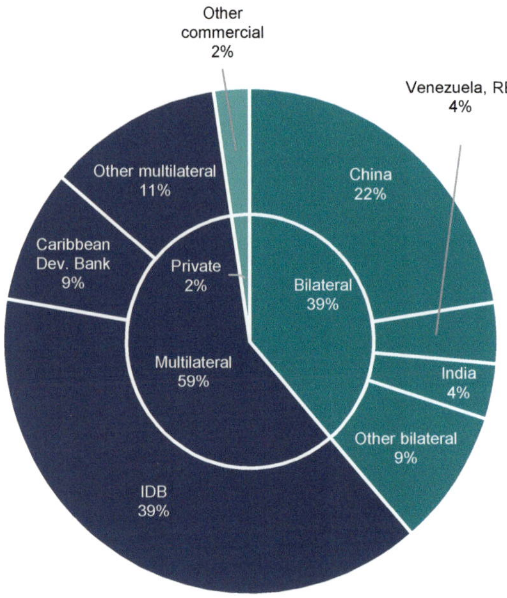

Figure 2 Average terms on new debt commitments from official and private creditors

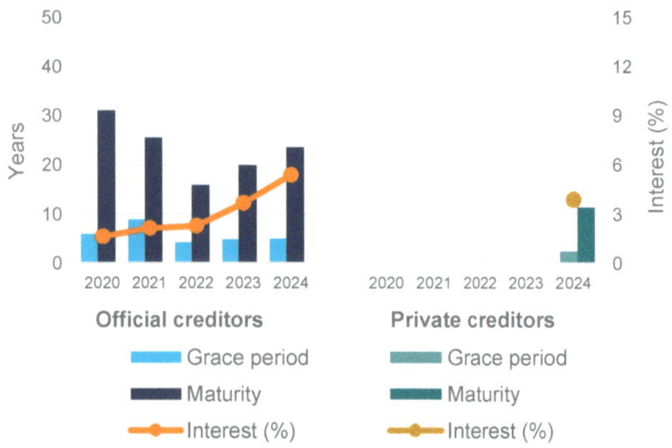

Summary External Debt Data	2010	2020	2021	2022	2023	2024
Total external debt stocks	**1,408**	**1,507**	**1,890**	**2,070**	**2,953**	**3,682**
Long-term external debt stocks	**885**	**1,327**	**1,467**	**1,668**	**2,542**	**3,277**
Public and publicly guaranteed debt from:	*885*	*1,271*	*1,342*	*1,520*	*1,726*	*2,187*
Official creditors	869	1,240	1,312	1,491	1,698	2,137
Multilateral	533	825	910	1,092	1,202	1,290
of which: World Bank	9	90	92	117	172	186
Bilateral	336	415	402	398	496	846
Private creditors	16	31	30	29	28	51
Bondholders	0	0	0	0	0	0
Commercial banks and others	16	31	30	29	28	51
Private nonguaranteed debt from:	*0*	*56*	*125*	*148*	*816*	*1,090*
Bondholders	..	..	..	..	..	..
Commercial banks and others	0	56	125	148	816	1,090
Use of IMF credit and SDR allocations	**190**	**125**	**366**	**348**	**351**	**341**
IMF credit	56	0	0	0	0	0
SDR allocations	134	125	366	348	351	341
Short-term external debt stocks	**333**	**54**	**57**	**54**	**60**	**64**
Disbursements, long-term	**123**	**48**	**218**	**336**	**1,142**	**1,206**
Public and publicly guaranteed sector	123	48	121	262	270	569
Private sector not guaranteed	0	..	97	74	872	637
Principal repayments, long-term	**16**	**103**	**85**	**110**	**268**	**440**
Public and publicly guaranteed sector	16	52	57	60	64	77
Private sector not guaranteed	..	51	28	50	204	363
Interest payments, long-term	**11**	**30**	**25**	**27**	**85**	**145**
Public and publicly guaranteed sector	11	24	23	24	35	45
Private sector not guaranteed	..	6	3	3	50	100

HAITI

(US$ million, unless otherwise indicated)

Snapshot	2024
Total external debt stocks	**944.7**
External debt stocks as % of:	
Exports	109.9
GNI	3.7
Debt service as % of:	
Exports	63.2
GNI	2.2
Net financial flows, debt and equity	-496.7
Net debt inflows	-537.6
Net equity inflows	40.9
GNI	**25,227.8**
Population (million)	**12**

Figure 1 Public and publicly guaranteed debt, by creditor and creditor type in 2024, including IMF credit

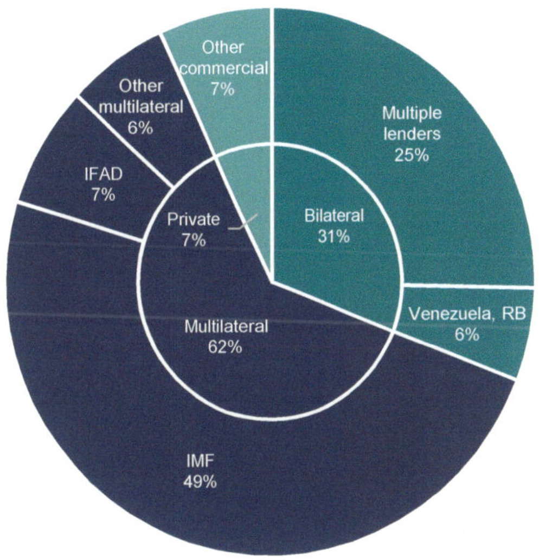

Figure 2 Average terms on new debt commitments from official and private creditors

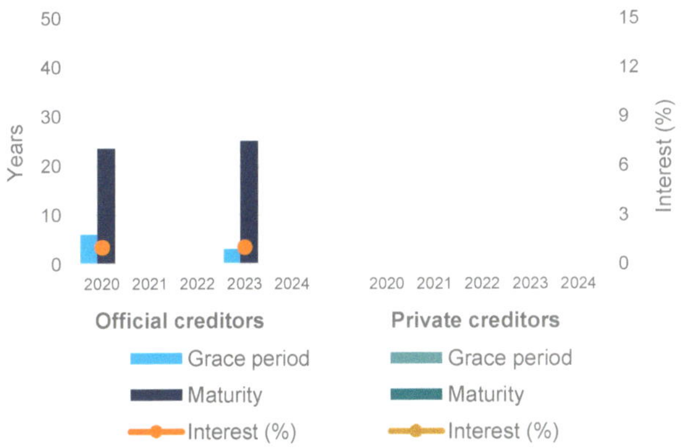

Summary External Debt Data	2010	2020	2021	2022	2023	2024
Total external debt stocks	**1,045.0**	**2,619.4**	**2,970.1**	**2,965.3**	**3,156.5**	**944.7**
Long-term external debt stocks	**824.0**	**2,035.0**	**2,110.0**	**2,145.1**	**2,212.3**	**256.3**
Public and publicly guaranteed debt from:	*824.0*	*2,035.0*	*2,106.0*	*2,139.4*	*2,206.6*	*250.6*
Official creditors	774.0	1,992.0	2,065.3	2,102.2	2,171.7	216.9
Multilateral	557.0	92.1	85.9	77.6	71.3	65.5
of which: World Bank	0.0	..	..	..	..	..
Bilateral	217.0	1,899.8	1,979.4	2,024.5	2,100.4	151.4
Private creditors	50.0	43.0	40.7	37.2	34.9	33.7
Bondholders	..	..	..	..	..	..
Commercial banks and others	50.0	43.0	40.7	37.2	34.9	33.7
Private nonguaranteed debt from:	..	*0.0*	*4.0*	*5.7*	*5.7*	*5.7*
Bondholders	..	..	..	..	..	..
Commercial banks and others	..	0.0	4.0	5.7	5.7	5.7
Use of IMF credit and SDR allocations	**134.9**	**291.1**	**502.5**	**444.7**	**552.7**	**559.2**
IMF credit	12.7	180.5	170.7	143.3	243.0	239.8
SDR allocations	122.2	110.5	331.8	301.4	309.7	319.4
Short-term external debt stocks	**86.1**	**293.4**	**357.6**	**375.5**	**391.5**	**129.2**
Disbursements, long-term	**287.6**	**22.5**	**86.5**	**33.9**	**1.7**	**..**
Public and publicly guaranteed sector	287.6	22.5	82.5	32.3	..	..
Private sector not guaranteed	..	..	4.0	1.7	1.7	..
Principal repayments, long-term	**122.4**	**7.3**	**9.0**	**10.9**	**32.6**	**507.1**
Public and publicly guaranteed sector	122.4	7.3	9.0	10.9	32.6	507.1
Private sector not guaranteed	..	..	..	..	..	..
Interest payments, long-term	**8.0**	**2.5**	**2.9**	**4.9**	**8.4**	**5.0**
Public and publicly guaranteed sector	8.0	2.5	2.9	4.9	8.4	5.0
Private sector not guaranteed	..	..	..	..	..	..

HONDURAS

(US$ million, unless otherwise indicated)

Snapshot	2024
Total external debt stocks	**14,300**
External debt stocks as % of:	
Exports	145
GNI	42
Debt service as % of:	
Exports	18
GNI	5
Net financial flows, debt and equity	2,358
Net debt inflows	1,427
Net equity inflows	931
GNI	**34,191**
Population (million)	**11**

Figure 1 Public and publicly guaranteed debt, by creditor and creditor type in 2024, including IMF credit

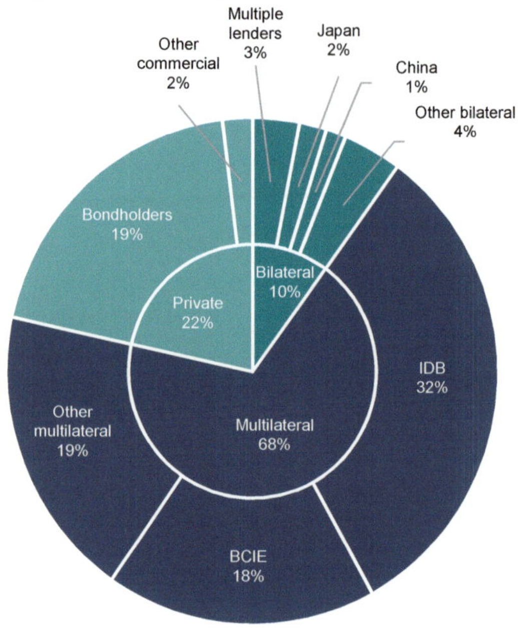

Figure 2 Average terms on new debt commitments from official and private creditors

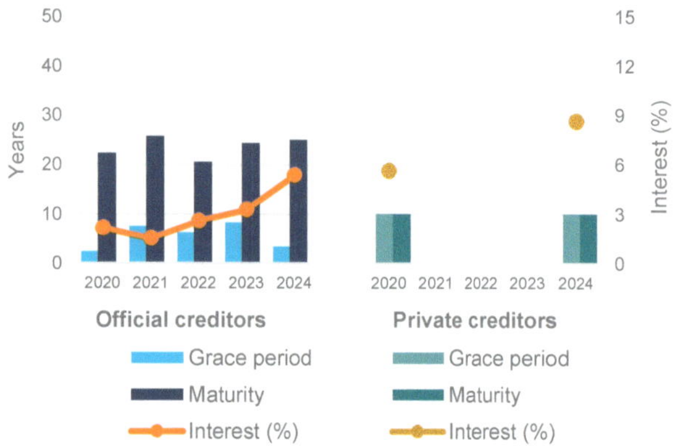

Summary External Debt Data	2010	2020	2021	2022	2023	2024
Total external debt stocks	**4,008**	**11,074**	**12,508**	**12,639**	**12,944**	**14,300**
Long-term external debt stocks	**3,413**	**9,782**	**10,392**	**10,601**	**10,346**	**11,456**
Public and publicly guaranteed debt from:	*2,834*	*8,598*	*8,641*	*9,013*	*8,817*	*9,565*
Official creditors	2,704	6,401	6,503	7,067	7,085	7,367
Multilateral	1,907	5,404	5,554	6,076	6,106	6,349
of which: World Bank	602	1,034	1,015	936	970	1,114
Bilateral	796	997	949	991	979	1,018
Private creditors	131	2,197	2,138	1,946	1,732	2,198
Bondholders	..	1,800	1,800	1,633	1,467	2,000
Commercial banks and others	131	397	338	312	265	198
Private nonguaranteed debt from:	*579*	*1,184*	*1,751*	*1,588*	*1,529*	*1,891*
Bondholders	..	..	300	300	300	300
Commercial banks and others	579	1,184	1,451	1,288	1,229	1,591
Use of IMF credit and SDR allocations	**220**	**664**	**1,103**	**1,049**	**1,103**	**1,082**
IMF credit	30	486	594	565	615	609
SDR allocations	191	178	508	483	487	474
Short-term external debt stocks	**374**	**628**	**1,013**	**989**	**1,496**	**1,761**
Disbursements, long-term	**906**	**2,096**	**1,351**	**1,576**	**878**	**2,192**
Public and publicly guaranteed sector	454	1,603	389	872	316	1,351
Private sector not guaranteed	452	494	962	704	562	841
Principal repayments, long-term	**453**	**1,194**	**873**	**1,311**	**1,139**	**1,041**
Public and publicly guaranteed sector	63	822	297	444	517	562
Private sector not guaranteed	390	372	576	867	621	479
Interest payments, long-term	**56**	**321**	**313**	**337**	**422**	**423**
Public and publicly guaranteed sector	46	302	247	256	349	362
Private sector not guaranteed	10	19	66	81	72	61

INDIA

(US$ million, unless otherwise indicated)

Snapshot	2024
Total external debt stocks	**716,456**
External debt stocks as % of:	
Exports	82
GNI	19
Debt service as % of:	
Exports	10
GNI	2
Net financial flows, debt and equity	98,722
Net debt inflows	76,738
Net equity inflows	21,984
GNI	**3,856,153**
Population (million)	**1,451**

Figure 1 Public and publicly guaranteed debt, by creditor and creditor type in 2024, including IMF credit

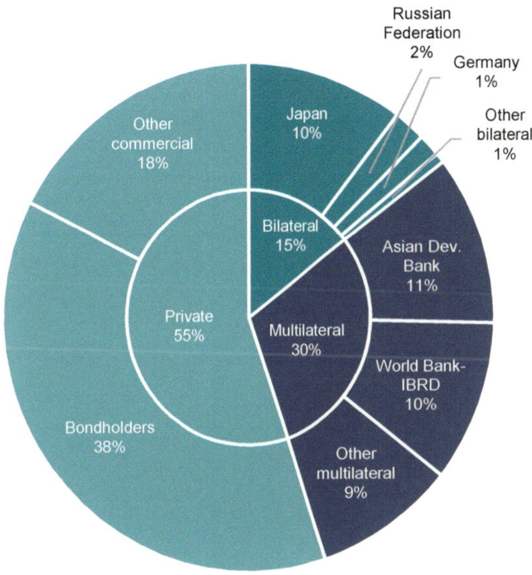

Figure 2 Average terms on new debt commitments from official and private creditors

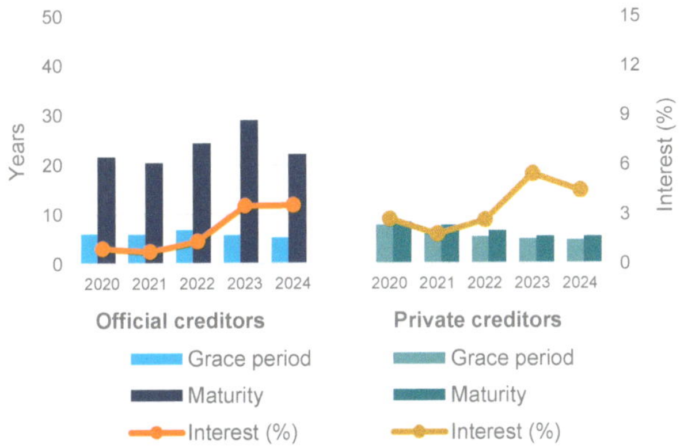

Summary External Debt Data	2010	2020	2021	2022	2023	2024
Total external debt stocks	**290,428**	**564,979**	**611,987**	**615,515**	**647,556**	**716,456**
Long-term external debt stocks	**227,853**	**455,716**	**474,183**	**465,621**	**498,261**	**555,307**
Public and publicly guaranteed debt from:	*100,563*	*192,805*	*205,282*	*205,217*	*214,912*	*238,950*
Official creditors	72,499	96,151	99,657	101,850	107,184	109,627
Multilateral	46,513	64,454	67,713	70,145	73,705	75,355
of which: World Bank	37,068	39,577	39,742	38,257	39,284	38,740
Bilateral	25,986	31,696	31,944	31,705	33,479	34,273
Private creditors	28,065	96,654	105,625	103,367	107,728	129,322
Bondholders	14,700	71,333	75,093	72,077	74,172	88,352
Commercial banks and others	13,364	25,322	30,531	31,291	33,556	40,970
Private nonguaranteed debt from:	*127,290*	*262,911*	*268,902*	*260,404*	*283,350*	*316,358*
Bondholders	13,217	26,822	32,393	33,698	31,478	32,377
Commercial banks and others	114,073	236,089	236,509	226,706	251,871	283,981
Use of IMF credit and SDR allocations	**6,127**	**5,730**	**23,160**	**22,023**	**22,202**	**21,581**
IMF credit	0	0	0	0	0	0
SDR allocations	6,127	5,730	23,160	22,023	22,202	21,581
Short-term external debt stocks	**56,448**	**103,533**	**114,644**	**127,871**	**127,094**	**139,568**
Disbursements, long-term	**43,406**	**67,698**	**61,278**	**44,213**	**86,283**	**121,030**
Public and publicly guaranteed sector	24,337	22,418	30,078	19,359	27,004	47,410
Private sector not guaranteed	19,069	45,280	31,201	24,854	59,279	73,621
Principal repayments, long-term	**19,018**	**63,444**	**38,650**	**47,385**	**51,518**	**56,767**
Public and publicly guaranteed sector	5,164	24,346	13,693	14,367	15,874	19,446
Private sector not guaranteed	13,854	39,098	24,957	33,018	35,644	37,321
Interest payments, long-term	**4,675**	**11,197**	**12,229**	**15,078**	**22,540**	**25,294**
Public and publicly guaranteed sector	1,063	1,655	2,517	3,246	6,253	7,342
Private sector not guaranteed	3,612	9,543	9,712	11,832	16,287	17,952

INDONESIA

(US$ million, unless otherwise indicated)

Snapshot	2024
Total external debt stocks	**421,059**
External debt stocks as % of:	
Exports	135
GNI	31
Debt service as % of:	
Exports	25
GNI	6
Net financial flows, debt and equity	45,474
Net debt inflows	23,909
Net equity inflows	21,565
GNI	**1,359,440**
Population (million)	**283**

Figure 1 Public and publicly guaranteed debt, by creditor and creditor type in 2024, including IMF credit

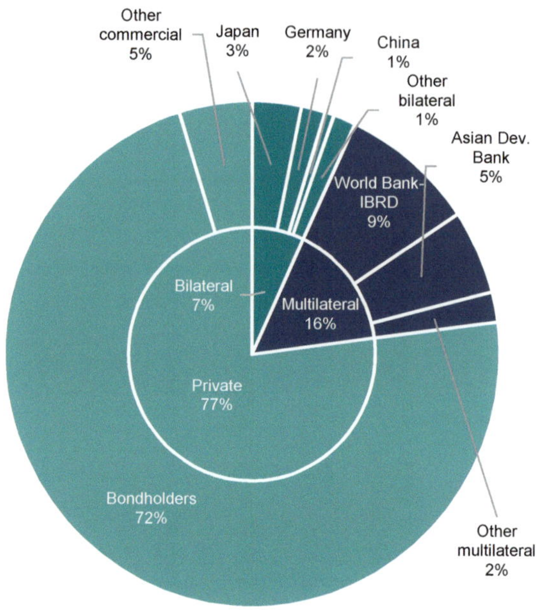

Figure 2 Average terms on new debt commitments from official and private creditors

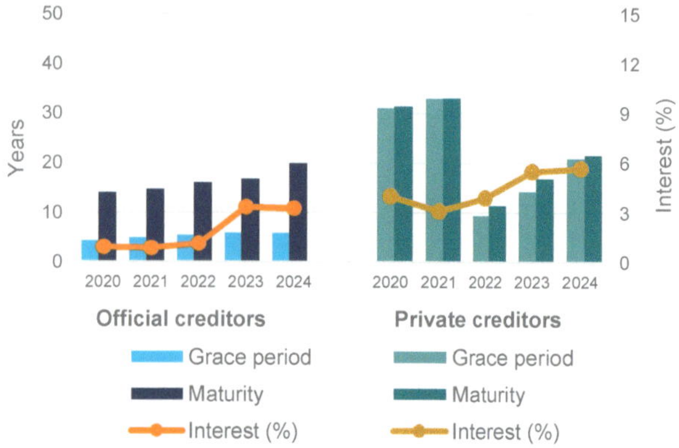

Summary External Debt Data	2010	2020	2021	2022	2023	2024
Total external debt stocks	**198,278**	**417,036**	**417,845**	**395,986**	**399,613**	**421,059**
Long-term external debt stocks	**162,181**	**369,696**	**361,509**	**339,405**	**340,525**	**347,543**
Public and publicly guaranteed debt from:	*102,748*	*247,923*	*242,631*	*226,179*	*235,114*	*245,497*
Official creditors	66,180	57,958	55,065	53,915	56,287	56,293
Multilateral	22,567	34,326	34,259	35,742	38,551	39,437
of which: World Bank	11,367	19,669	19,622	20,627	22,216	21,568
Bilateral	43,613	23,632	20,806	18,172	17,736	16,856
Private creditors	36,568	189,966	187,566	172,265	178,826	189,203
Bondholders	28,698	182,704	181,413	165,859	170,806	177,448
Commercial banks and others	7,870	7,261	6,153	6,405	8,020	11,755
Private nonguaranteed debt from:	*59,433*	*121,773*	*118,878*	*113,226*	*105,411*	*102,047*
Bondholders	8,437	18,208	20,214	19,999	16,227	13,054
Commercial banks and others	50,996	103,565	98,664	93,227	89,184	88,993
Use of IMF credit and SDR allocations	**3,050**	**2,852**	**9,007**	**8,565**	**8,635**	**8,393**
IMF credit	0	0	0	0	0	0
SDR allocations	3,050	2,852	9,007	8,565	8,635	8,393
Short-term external debt stocks	**33,047**	**44,488**	**47,329**	**48,016**	**50,454**	**65,123**
Disbursements, long-term	**34,335**	**64,993**	**50,291**	**52,950**	**48,534**	**68,044**
Public and publicly guaranteed sector	13,695	30,155	21,249	18,080	25,799	40,576
Private sector not guaranteed	20,640	34,838	29,042	34,869	22,735	27,467
Principal repayments, long-term	**26,202**	**52,629**	**55,227**	**61,475**	**44,251**	**58,454**
Public and publicly guaranteed sector	8,072	18,521	23,292	31,171	16,451	27,272
Private sector not guaranteed	18,129	34,108	31,935	30,304	27,800	31,182
Interest payments, long-term	**4,944**	**13,682**	**10,944**	**11,602**	**12,897**	**14,284**
Public and publicly guaranteed sector	3,034	9,512	7,914	8,433	9,598	10,935
Private sector not guaranteed	1,910	4,170	3,030	3,169	3,300	3,349

IRAN, ISLAMIC REPUBLIC OF

(US$ million, unless otherwise indicated)

Snapshot	2024
Total external debt stocks	**9,654**
External debt stocks as % of:	
Exports	8
GNI	2
Debt service as % of:	
Exports	0
GNI	0
Net financial flows, debt and equity	1,405
Net debt inflows	-44
Net equity inflows	1,449
GNI	**436,292**
Population (million)	**92**

Figure 1 Public and publicly guaranteed debt, by creditor and creditor type in 2024, including IMF credit

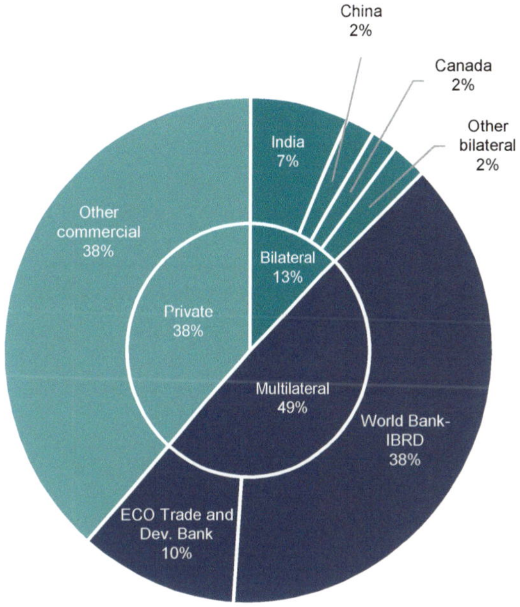

Figure 2 Average terms on new debt commitments from official and private creditors

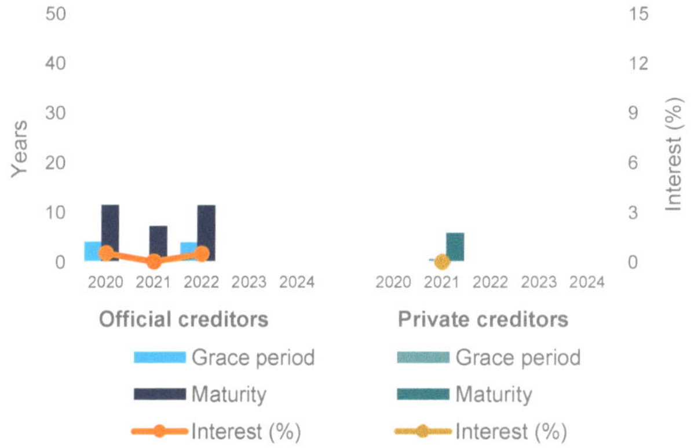

Summary External Debt Data	2010	2020	2021	2022	2023	2024
Total external debt stocks	**19,769**	**5,433**	**10,349**	**9,460**	**9,901**	**9,654**
Long-term external debt stocks	**5,960**	**1,313**	**1,060**	**1,124**	**1,116**	**1,051**
Public and publicly guaranteed debt from:	*5,960*	*419*	*332*	*397*	*388*	*323*
Official creditors	2,068	300	225	249	235	199
Multilateral	833	190	119	168	173	158
of which: World Bank	801	132	76	129	135	124
Bilateral	1,234	110	106	81	61	41
Private creditors	3,892	118	107	148	154	125
Bondholders	..	..	..	..	..	..
Commercial banks and others	3,892	118	107	148	154	125
Private nonguaranteed debt from:	*0*	*894*	*727*	*727*	*727*	*727*
Bondholders	..	..	..	..	..	..
Commercial banks and others	0	894	727	727	727	727
Use of IMF credit and SDR allocations	**2,196**	**2,054**	**6,781**	**6,448**	**6,500**	**6,318**
IMF credit	0	0	0	0	0	0
SDR allocations	2,196	2,054	6,781	6,448	6,500	6,318
Short-term external debt stocks	**11,613**	**2,067**	**2,508**	**1,888**	**2,285**	**2,285**
Disbursements, long-term	**249**	**116**	**21**	**141**	**43**	**18**
Public and publicly guaranteed sector	249	116	21	141	43	18
Private sector not guaranteed	..	..	..	..	..	..
Principal repayments, long-term	**1,532**	**263**	**254**	**52**	**63**	**63**
Public and publicly guaranteed sector	1,532	84	88	52	63	63
Private sector not guaranteed	..	178	167	..	..	..
Interest payments, long-term	**136**	**26**	**46**	**7**	**13**	**14**
Public and publicly guaranteed sector	136	15	7	7	13	14
Private sector not guaranteed	..	11	39	..	..	..

IRAQ

(US$ million, unless otherwise indicated)

Snapshot	2024
Total external debt stocks	**17,517**
External debt stocks as % of:	
Exports	15
GNI	6
Debt service as % of:	
Exports	3
GNI	1
Net financial flows, debt and equity	-9,812
Net debt inflows	-2,163
Net equity inflows	-7,649
GNI	**281,334**
Population (million)	**46**

Figure 1 Public and publicly guaranteed debt, by creditor and creditor type in 2024, including IMF credit

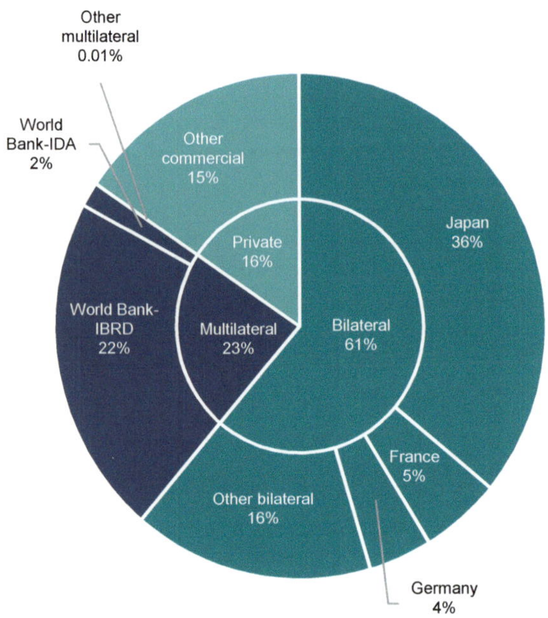

Figure 2 Average terms on new debt commitments from official and private creditors

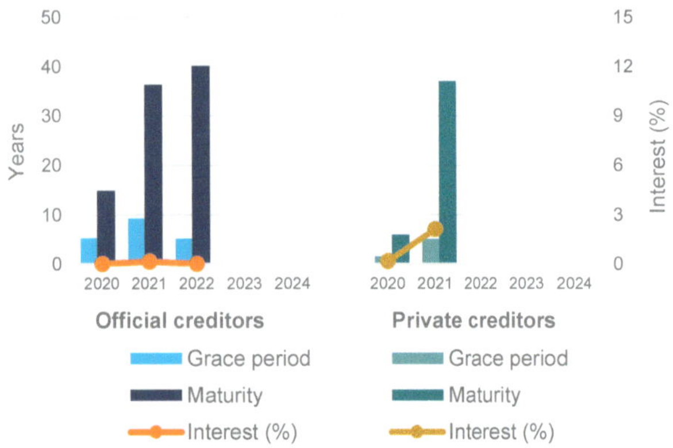

Summary External Debt Data	2010	2020	2021	2022	2023	2024
Total external debt stocks	..	**26,328**	**25,360**	**22,723**	**20,318**	**17,517**
Long-term external debt stocks	..	**22,805**	**20,614**	**17,936**	**15,686**	**13,232**
Public and publicly guaranteed debt from:	..	*22,805*	*20,614*	*17,936*	*15,686*	*12,932*
Official creditors	..	16,832	15,069	13,774	13,012	10,927
Multilateral	..	3,623	3,607	3,463	3,294	3,014
of which: World Bank	..	3,618	3,606	3,460	3,291	3,013
Bilateral	..	13,209	11,462	10,311	9,718	7,913
Private creditors	..	5,973	5,545	4,162	2,674	2,005
Bondholders	..	2,000	2,000	1,000	0	..
Commercial banks and others	..	3,973	3,545	3,162	2,674	2,005
Private nonguaranteed debt from:	..	..	..	..	..	*300*
Bondholders	..	..	..	..	..	300
Commercial banks and others	..	..	..	..	..	..
Use of IMF credit and SDR allocations	..	**2,944**	**4,126**	**3,632**	**3,662**	**3,559**
IMF credit	..	1,310	307	0	0	0
SDR allocations	..	1,634	3,820	3,632	3,662	3,559
Short-term external debt stocks	..	**580**	**620**	**1,155**	**971**	**726**
Disbursements, long-term	..	**1,709**	**826**	**1,622**	**1,662**	**784**
Public and publicly guaranteed sector	..	1,709	826	1,622	1,662	484
Private sector not guaranteed	..	..	..	..	..	300
Principal repayments, long-term	..	**1,983**	**2,450**	**3,648**	**3,692**	**2,702**
Public and publicly guaranteed sector	..	1,983	2,450	3,648	3,692	2,702
Private sector not guaranteed	..	..	..	..	..	..
Interest payments, long-term	..	**803**	**675**	**591**	**606**	**562**
Public and publicly guaranteed sector	..	803	675	591	606	542
Private sector not guaranteed	..	..	..	..	..	20

JAMAICA

(US$ million, unless otherwise indicated)

Snapshot	2024
Total external debt stocks	**14,837**
External debt stocks as % of:	
Exports	193
GNI	76
Debt service as % of:	
Exports	32
GNI	13
Net financial flows, debt and equity	-245
Net debt inflows	-504
Net equity inflows	259
GNI	**19,504**
Population (million)	**3**

Figure 1 Public and publicly guaranteed debt, by creditor and creditor type in 2024, including IMF credit

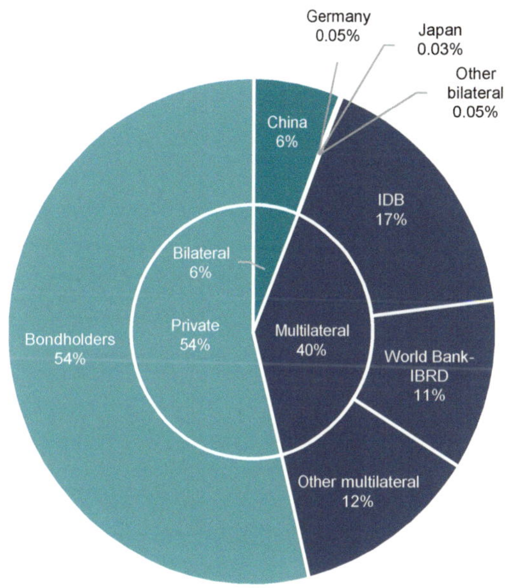

Figure 2 Average terms on new debt commitments from official and private creditors

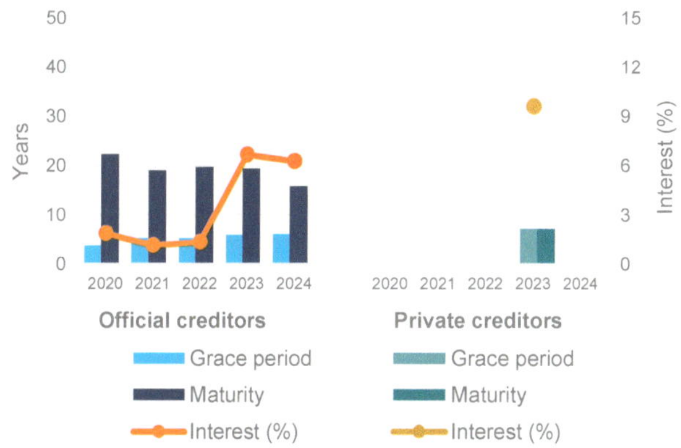

Summary External Debt Data	2010	2020	2021	2022	2023	2024
Total external debt stocks	**14,187**	**14,489**	**16,036**	**15,812**	**15,395**	**14,837**
Long-term external debt stocks	**11,910**	**10,924**	**11,996**	**12,029**	**11,148**	**10,695**
Public and publicly guaranteed debt from:	*7,603*	*9,155*	*9,024*	*8,764*	*8,397*	*7,944*
Official creditors	3,265	3,570	3,638	3,598	3,415	3,164
Multilateral	2,352	2,947	3,012	2,968	2,798	2,620
of which: World Bank	579	945	1,062	1,032	988	966
Bilateral	913	623	626	630	617	544
Private creditors	4,338	5,585	5,386	5,165	4,982	4,780
Bondholders	3,786	5,585	5,386	5,165	4,982	4,780
Commercial banks and others	552	0	..	..	..	..
Private nonguaranteed debt from:	*4,307*	*1,769*	*2,972*	*3,265*	*2,751*	*2,751*
Bondholders	4,290	1,750	1,750	1,750	825	225
Commercial banks and others	17	19	1,222	1,515	1,926	2,526
Use of IMF credit and SDR allocations	**1,188**	**1,449**	**1,792**	**1,580**	**1,611**	**1,743**
IMF credit	785	1,072	912	743	768	923
SDR allocations	403	377	880	837	843	820
Short-term external debt stocks	**1,088**	**2,116**	**2,248**	**2,203**	**2,636**	**2,399**
Disbursements, long-term	**2,360**	**683**	**1,583**	**543**	**829**	**659**
Public and publicly guaranteed sector	1,285	270	380	250	419	59
Private sector not guaranteed	1,075	413	1,203	293	410	600
Principal repayments, long-term	**345**	**996**	**503**	**503**	**1,708**	**1,106**
Public and publicly guaranteed sector	337	521	503	503	783	506
Private sector not guaranteed	9	475	..	..	925	600
Interest payments, long-term	**829**	**690**	**720**	**800**	**801**	**804**
Public and publicly guaranteed sector	489	552	519	582	612	613
Private sector not guaranteed	341	138	201	219	189	191

JORDAN

(US$ million, unless otherwise indicated)

Snapshot	2024
Total external debt stocks	**46,966**
External debt stocks as % of:	
Exports	189
GNI	90
Debt service as % of:	
Exports	18
GNI	9
Net financial flows, debt and equity	4,324
Net debt inflows	2,773
Net equity inflows	1,552
GNI	**52,106**
Population (million)	**12**

Figure 1 Public and publicly guaranteed debt, by creditor and creditor type in 2024, including IMF credit

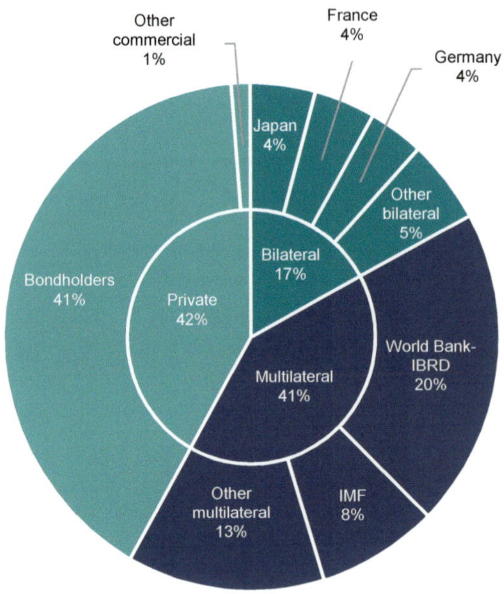

Figure 2 Average terms on new debt commitments from official and private creditors

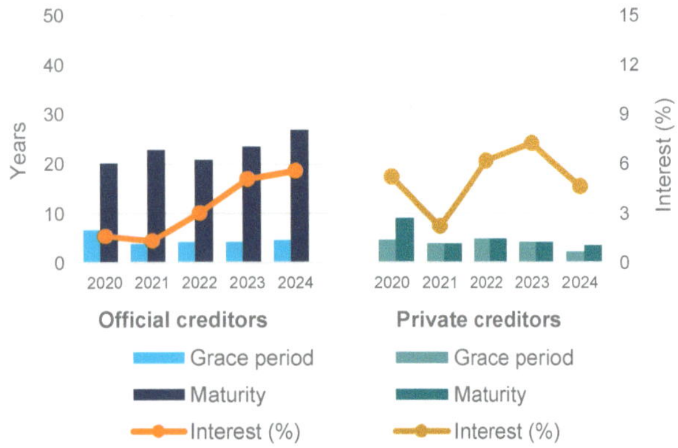

Summary External Debt Data	2010	2020	2021	2022	2023	2024
Total external debt stocks	**16,894**	**38,038**	**41,757**	**41,170**	**44,559**	**46,966**
Long-term external debt stocks	**7,588**	**22,684**	**23,936**	**22,834**	**26,058**	**26,417**
Public and publicly guaranteed debt from:	*6,323*	*18,778*	*19,866*	*19,227*	*22,489*	*23,708*
Official creditors	5,284	9,449	10,419	10,581	11,932	12,946
Multilateral	2,526	5,491	6,468	6,526	7,448	8,542
of which: World Bank	1,040	3,329	3,723	3,970	4,457	5,422
Bilateral	2,757	3,958	3,951	4,055	4,484	4,404
Private creditors	1,040	9,330	9,447	8,646	10,558	10,762
Bondholders	881	9,198	9,340	8,550	10,470	10,450
Commercial banks and others	159	132	107	96	88	312
Private nonguaranteed debt from:	*1,265*	*3,905*	*4,070*	*3,607*	*3,568*	*2,710*
Bondholders	..	..	..	..	..	..
Commercial banks and others	1,265	3,905	4,070	3,607	3,568	2,710
Use of IMF credit and SDR allocations	**257**	**1,271**	**2,215**	**2,609**	**2,528**	**2,650**
IMF credit	8	1,038	1,528	1,955	1,869	2,010
SDR allocations	250	233	687	653	659	640
Short-term external debt stocks	**9,049**	**14,084**	**15,606**	**15,728**	**15,974**	**17,898**
Disbursements, long-term	**1,508**	**4,044**	**3,820**	**2,641**	**4,665**	**2,375**
Public and publicly guaranteed sector	1,358	3,440	3,405	2,641	4,665	2,375
Private sector not guaranteed	150	604	415	..	..	..
Principal repayments, long-term	**506**	**2,089**	**2,272**	**3,441**	**1,490**	**1,724**
Public and publicly guaranteed sector	480	1,775	2,022	2,978	1,452	865
Private sector not guaranteed	26	313	251	463	38	859
Interest payments, long-term	**161**	**580**	**645**	**805**	**1,147**	**1,362**
Public and publicly guaranteed sector	145	523	604	639	920	1,208
Private sector not guaranteed	16	56	41	167	227	154

KAZAKHSTAN

(US$ million, unless otherwise indicated)

Snapshot	2024
Total external debt stocks	**167,535**
External debt stocks as % of:	
Exports	175
GNI	63
Debt service as % of:	
Exports	48
GNI	17
Net financial flows, debt and equity	-5,430
Net debt inflows	-5,251
Net equity inflows	-179
GNI	**267,616**
Population (million)	**21**

Figure 1 Public and publicly guaranteed debt, by creditor and creditor type in 2024, including IMF credit

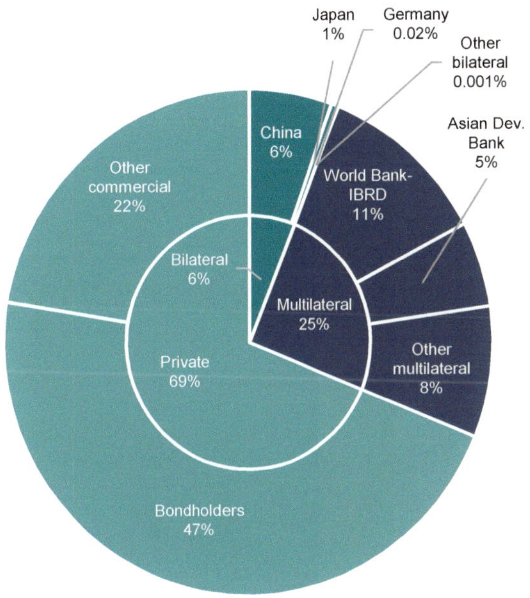

Figure 2 Average terms on new debt commitments from official and private creditors

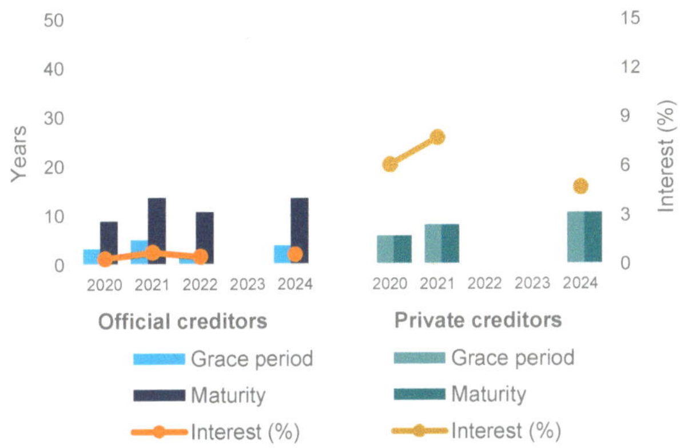

Summary External Debt Data	2010	2020	2021	2022	2023	2024
Total external debt stocks	**119,151**	**172,889**	**173,390**	**169,570**	**171,484**	**167,535**
Long-term external debt stocks	**109,757**	**162,879**	**159,298**	**151,251**	**150,158**	**146,045**
Public and publicly guaranteed debt from:	*3,845*	*37,637*	*40,369*	*35,407*	*32,829*	*34,032*
Official creditors	3,845	9,027	9,756	9,640	9,817	10,588
Multilateral	2,785	7,195	7,717	7,673	7,841	8,528
of which: World Bank	1,830	3,615	3,463	3,576	3,383	3,831
Bilateral	1,060	1,833	2,039	1,967	1,976	2,059
Private creditors	0	28,609	30,612	25,767	23,012	23,444
Bondholders	..	21,575	23,503	19,059	16,368	15,826
Commercial banks and others	0	7,035	7,109	6,708	6,644	7,618
Private nonguaranteed debt from:	*105,912*	*125,242*	*118,929*	*115,844*	*117,329*	*112,013*
Bondholders	21,044	6,361	5,917	3,500	3,478	3,482
Commercial banks and others	84,868	118,881	113,012	112,345	113,851	108,531
Use of IMF credit and SDR allocations	**529**	**495**	**2,035**	**1,935**	**1,951**	**1,896**
IMF credit	0	0	0	0	0	0
SDR allocations	529	495	2,035	1,935	1,951	1,896
Short-term external debt stocks	**8,864**	**9,516**	**12,058**	**16,384**	**19,375**	**19,594**
Disbursements, long-term	**45,054**	**34,737**	**22,369**	**35,272**	**37,249**	**31,325**
Public and publicly guaranteed sector	1,522	2,119	1,909	718	501	3,448
Private sector not guaranteed	43,532	32,618	20,460	34,554	36,748	27,876
Principal repayments, long-term	**34,639**	**28,789**	**28,093**	**43,737**	**39,840**	**36,790**
Public and publicly guaranteed sector	278	2,746	1,264	6,093	4,598	3,594
Private sector not guaranteed	34,361	26,042	26,829	37,644	35,242	33,196
Interest payments, long-term	**4,517**	**3,988**	**4,484**	**5,266**	**6,504**	**8,354**
Public and publicly guaranteed sector	54	1,657	1,753	1,531	1,656	1,958
Private sector not guaranteed	4,463	2,331	2,732	3,735	4,847	6,396

KENYA

(US$ million, unless otherwise indicated)

Snapshot	2024
Total external debt stocks	**42,886**
External debt stocks as % of:	
Exports	206
GNI	35
Debt service as % of:	
Exports	27
GNI	5
Net financial flows, debt and equity	1,275
Net debt inflows	1,006
Net equity inflows	269
GNI	**122,557**
Population (million)	**56**

Figure 1 Public and publicly guaranteed debt, by creditor and creditor type in 2024, including IMF credit

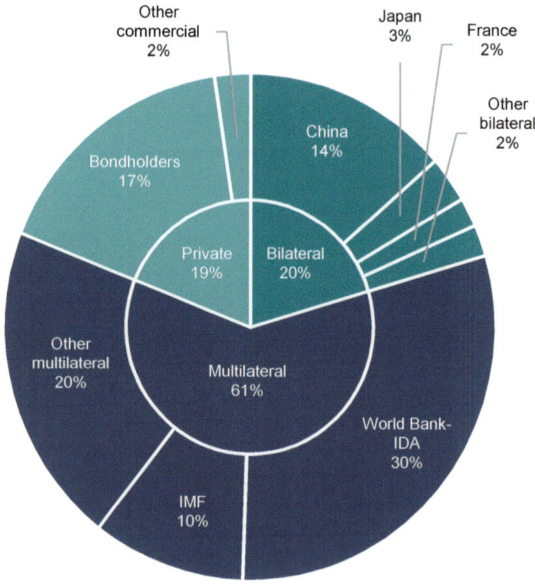

Figure 2 Average terms on new debt commitments from official and private creditors

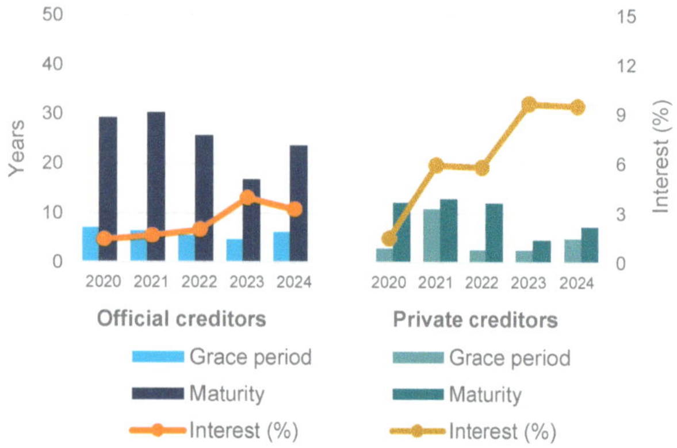

Summary External Debt Data	2010	2020	2021	2022	2023	2024
Total external debt stocks	**8,885**	**38,038**	**41,219**	**41,556**	**42,910**	**42,886**
Long-term external debt stocks	**7,027**	**34,355**	**35,871**	**35,606**	**36,295**	**35,920**
Public and publicly guaranteed debt from:	*7,027*	*33,534*	*35,228*	*35,037*	*35,864*	*35,583*
Official creditors	6,754	26,135	26,898	26,840	27,445	28,061
Multilateral	4,110	15,111	15,780	16,720	18,594	19,995
of which: World Bank	3,238	9,334	10,228	11,053	12,465	13,820
Bilateral	2,644	11,024	11,118	10,120	8,851	8,066
Private creditors	273	7,399	8,330	8,197	8,419	7,522
Bondholders	..	6,100	7,100	7,100	7,100	6,600
Commercial banks and others	273	1,299	1,230	1,097	1,319	922
Private nonguaranteed debt from:	..	*821*	*644*	*569*	*432*	*338*
Bondholders	..	..	..	..	..	..
Commercial banks and others	..	821	644	569	432	338
Use of IMF credit and SDR allocations	**817**	**1,391**	**2,913**	**3,389**	**3,799**	**4,958**
IMF credit	417	1,017	1,821	2,351	2,753	3,941
SDR allocations	400	374	1,092	1,038	1,046	1,017
Short-term external debt stocks	**1,041**	**2,293**	**2,435**	**2,561**	**2,815**	**2,008**
Disbursements, long-term	**532**	**3,417**	**3,405**	**2,957**	**3,111**	**4,424**
Public and publicly guaranteed sector	532	3,273	3,405	2,881	3,110	4,409
Private sector not guaranteed	..	144	..	76	1	15
Principal repayments, long-term	**260**	**1,465**	**1,334**	**2,016**	**2,195**	**3,918**
Public and publicly guaranteed sector	260	1,310	1,165	1,872	2,056	3,812
Private sector not guaranteed	..	154	169	143	140	106
Interest payments, long-term	**90**	**1,195**	**952**	**1,118**	**1,391**	**1,513**
Public and publicly guaranteed sector	90	1,150	916	1,088	1,348	1,477
Private sector not guaranteed	..	45	36	29	42	36

KOSOVO

(US$ million, unless otherwise indicated)

Snapshot	2024
Total external debt stocks	**4,395**
External debt stocks as % of:	
Exports	84
GNI	39
Debt service as % of:	
Exports	7
GNI	3
Net financial flows, debt and equity	1,164
Net debt inflows	292
Net equity inflows	872
GNI	**11,385**
Population (million)	**2**

Figure 1 Public and publicly guaranteed debt, by creditor and creditor type in 2024, including IMF credit

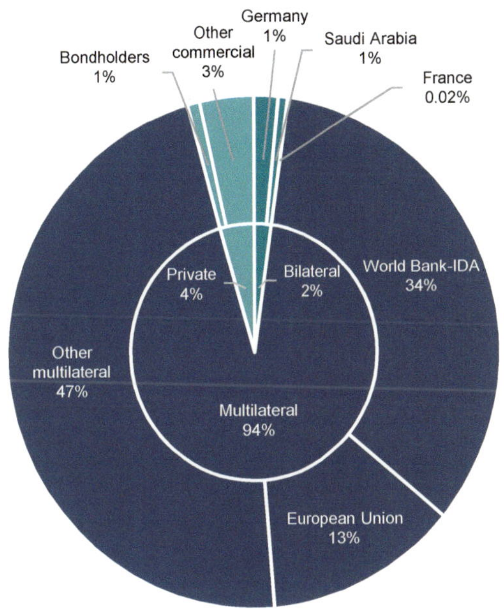

Figure 2 Average terms on new debt commitments from official and private creditors

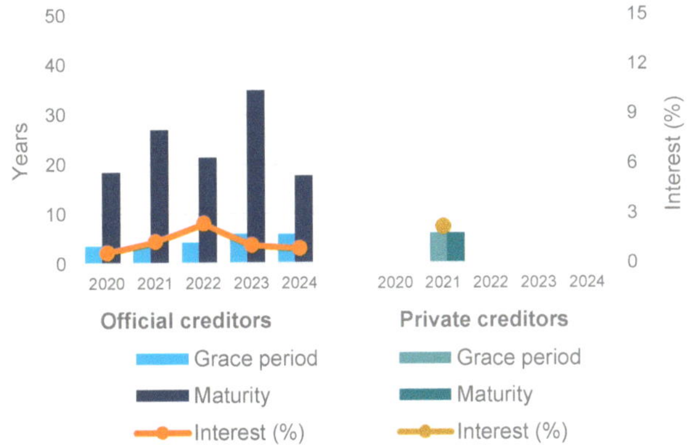

Summary External Debt Data	2010	2020	2021	2022	2023	2024
Total external debt stocks	**1,701**	**3,088**	**3,346**	**3,660**	**4,241**	**4,395**
Long-term external debt stocks	**886**	**1,911**	**1,982**	**2,175**	**2,524**	**2,572**
Public and publicly guaranteed debt from:	*319*	*517*	*596*	*642*	*694*	*732*
Official creditors	319	488	557	605	656	697
Multilateral	319	441	521	578	637	679
of which: World Bank	319	314	313	342	373	359
Bilateral	0	46	36	26	19	18
Private creditors	..	30	39	37	38	35
Bondholders	..	..	7	7	7	7
Commercial banks and others	..	30	32	31	31	29
Private nonguaranteed debt from:	*567*	*1,394*	*1,386*	*1,533*	*1,830*	*1,840*
Bondholders	..	..	..	..	..	..
Commercial banks and others	567	1,394	1,386	1,533	1,830	1,840
Use of IMF credit and SDR allocations	**114**	**216**	**260**	**234**	**264**	**260**
IMF credit	29	136	72	55	83	84
SDR allocations	85	80	188	179	181	175
Short-term external debt stocks	**700**	**962**	**1,103**	**1,251**	**1,453**	**1,564**
Disbursements, long-term	**169**	**567**	**647**	**558**	**513**	**482**
Public and publicly guaranteed sector	0	192	152	118	68	114
Private sector not guaranteed	169	375	495	441	445	369
Principal repayments, long-term	**76**	**251**	**327**	**267**	**213**	**305**
Public and publicly guaranteed sector	14	27	33	39	38	36
Private sector not guaranteed	61	224	293	229	175	269
Interest payments, long-term	**34**	**47**	**18**	**15**	**24**	**28**
Public and publicly guaranteed sector	11	11	11	10	12	14
Private sector not guaranteed	23	36	7	5	12	14

KYRGYZ REPUBLIC

(US$ million, unless otherwise indicated)

Snapshot	2024
Total external debt stocks	**11,690**
External debt stocks as % of:	
Exports	200
GNI	69
Debt service as % of:	
Exports	14
GNI	5
Net financial flows, debt and equity	2,219
Net debt inflows	1,609
Net equity inflows	610
GNI	**16,882**
Population (million)	**7**

Figure 1 Public and publicly guaranteed debt, by creditor and creditor type in 2024, including IMF credit

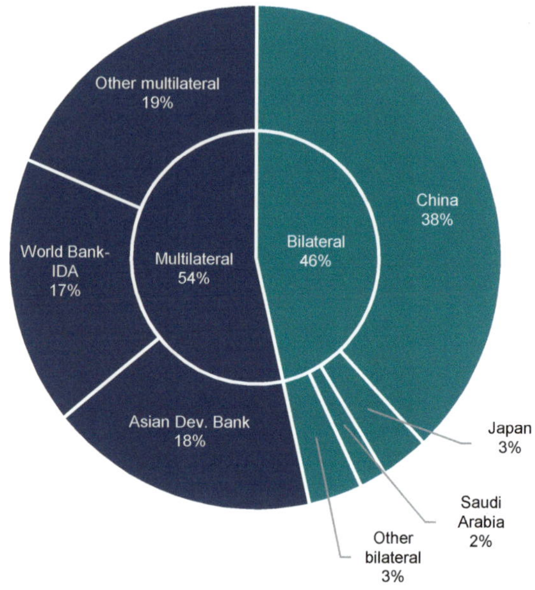

Figure 2 Average terms on new debt commitments from official and private creditors

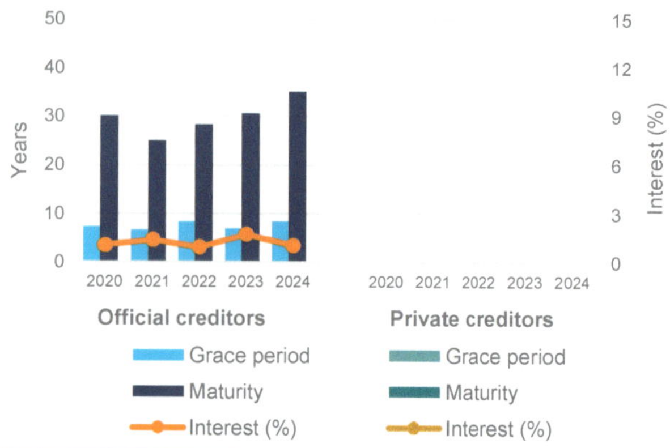

Summary External Debt Data	2010	2020	2021	2022	2023	2024
Total external debt stocks	**4,118**	**8,676**	**9,061**	**9,746**	**10,168**	**11,690**
Long-term external debt stocks	**3,616**	**7,652**	**7,825**	**8,132**	**8,415**	**9,626**
Public and publicly guaranteed debt from:	*2,446*	*3,843*	*3,958*	*4,031*	*4,192*	*4,217*
Official creditors	2,446	3,843	3,958	4,031	4,192	4,217
Multilateral	1,296	1,588	1,704	1,839	2,098	2,197
of which: World Bank	649	677	653	636	721	750
Bilateral	1,150	2,255	2,255	2,192	2,094	2,020
Private creditors	..	..	..	..	..	..
Bondholders	..	..	..	..	..	..
Commercial banks and others	..	..	..	..	..	..
Private nonguaranteed debt from:	*1,171*	*3,809*	*3,866*	*4,101*	*4,222*	*5,410*
Bondholders	..	0	0	0	0	0
Commercial banks and others	1,171	3,809	3,866	4,101	4,222	5,410
Use of IMF credit and SDR allocations	**307**	**498**	**697**	**642**	**575**	**466**
IMF credit	177	376	340	302	233	133
SDR allocations	130	122	357	339	342	333
Short-term external debt stocks	**195**	**525**	**539**	**972**	**1,178**	**1,598**
Disbursements, long-term	**672**	**390**	**626**	**755**	**970**	**1,509**
Public and publicly guaranteed sector	151	166	289	380	375	321
Private sector not guaranteed	521	224	336	375	595	1,187
Principal repayments, long-term	**462**	**509**	**464**	**327**	**689**	**224**
Public and publicly guaranteed sector	38	125	117	186	216	224
Private sector not guaranteed	424	384	347	141	474	..
Interest payments, long-term	**39**	**104**	**93**	**210**	**328**	**390**
Public and publicly guaranteed sector	23	55	40	57	60	64
Private sector not guaranteed	15	49	53	153	268	326

LAO PEOPLE'S DEMOCRATIC REPUBLIC

(US$ million, unless otherwise indicated)

Snapshot	2024
Total external debt stocks	**17,837**
External debt stocks as % of:	
Exports	159
GNI	115
Debt service as % of:	
Exports	19
GNI	14
Net financial flows, debt and equity	877
Net debt inflows	-111
Net equity inflows	988
GNI	**15,456**
Population (million)	**8**

Figure 1 Public and publicly guaranteed debt, by creditor and creditor type in 2024, including IMF credit

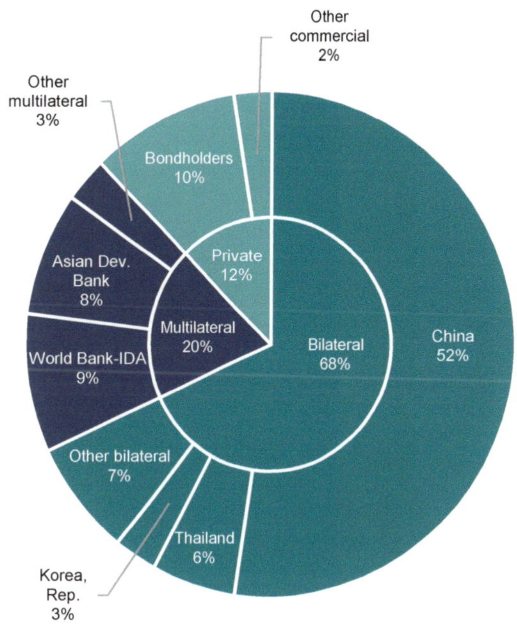

Figure 2 Average terms on new debt commitments from official and private creditors

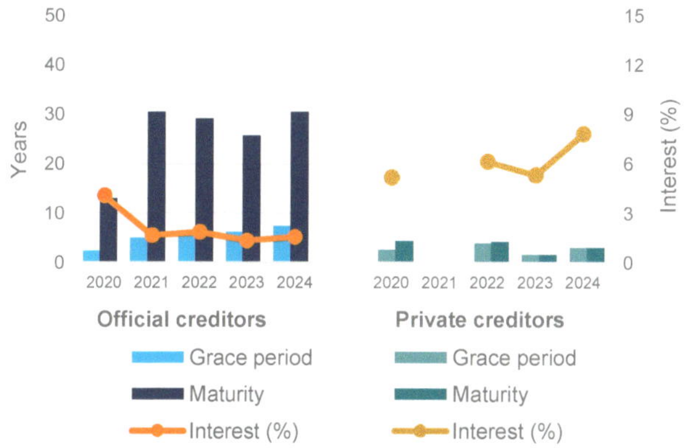

Summary External Debt Data	2010	2020	2021	2022	2023	2024
Total external debt stocks	**6,348**	**20,435**	**18,712**	**18,495**	**18,057**	**17,837**
Long-term external debt stocks	**6,204**	**19,377**	**17,638**	**17,542**	**17,712**	**16,541**
Public and publicly guaranteed debt from:	*3,545*	*10,720*	*10,321*	*10,517*	*10,321*	*10,025*
Official creditors	3,542	8,623	8,666	8,912	8,881	8,788
Multilateral	2,084	1,845	1,831	1,830	1,925	1,963
of which: World Bank	655	717	740	756	836	887
Bilateral	1,459	6,778	6,835	7,082	6,956	6,825
Private creditors	3	2,097	1,655	1,606	1,440	1,237
Bondholders	..	1,368	981	1,076	1,088	996
Commercial banks and others	3	730	674	529	352	241
Private nonguaranteed debt from:	*2,659*	*8,657*	*7,317*	*7,025*	*7,391*	*6,517*
Bondholders	..	692	779	1,041	1,149	955
Commercial banks and others	2,659	7,965	6,538	5,983	6,242	5,562
Use of IMF credit and SDR allocations	**88**	**73**	**213**	**202**	**204**	**198**
IMF credit	10	0	0	0	0	0
SDR allocations	78	73	213	202	204	198
Short-term external debt stocks	**56**	**985**	**861**	**750**	**140**	**1,097**
Disbursements, long-term	**460**	**1,376**	**553**	**1,075**	**783**	**315**
Public and publicly guaranteed sector	267	709	358	807	379	315
Private sector not guaranteed	193	668	196	268	403	..
Principal repayments, long-term	**217**	**576**	**2,062**	**902**	**619**	**1,383**
Public and publicly guaranteed sector	59	447	550	347	575	505
Private sector not guaranteed	159	129	1,512	555	44	879
Interest payments, long-term	**78**	**335**	**236**	**409**	**622**	**686**
Public and publicly guaranteed sector	28	203	130	124	174	316
Private sector not guaranteed	50	132	106	285	448	369

LEBANON

(US$ million, unless otherwise indicated)

Snapshot	2024
Total external debt stocks	**67,389**
External debt stocks as % of:	
Exports	570
GNI	..
Debt service as % of:	
Exports	21
GNI	..
Net financial flows, debt and equity	1,314
Net debt inflows	-636
Net equity inflows	1,951
GNI	**..**
Population (million)	**6**

Figure 1 Public and publicly guaranteed debt, by creditor and creditor type in 2024, including IMF credit

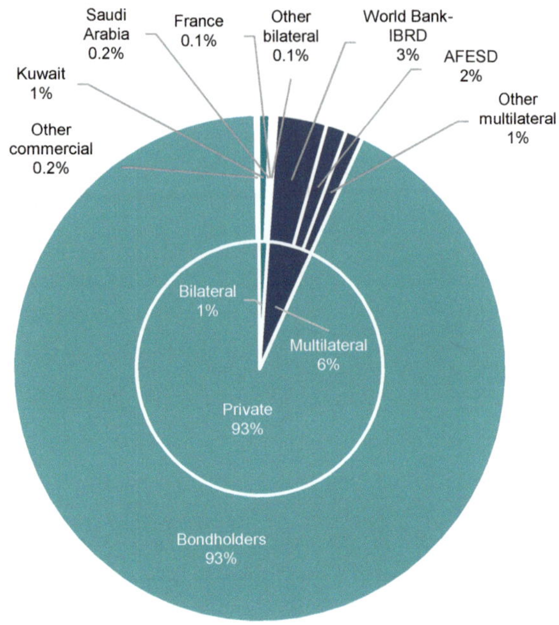

Figure 2 Average terms on new debt commitments from official and private creditors

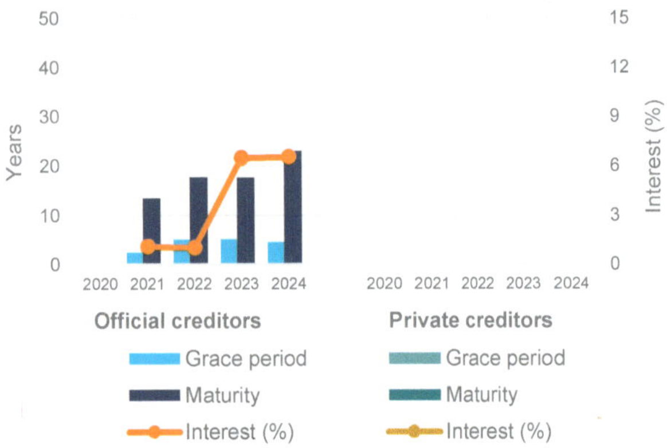

Summary External Debt Data	2010	2020	2021	2022	2023	2024
Total external debt stocks	**47,829**	**68,900**	**66,924**	**67,101**	**66,329**	**67,389**
Long-term external debt stocks	**43,867**	**58,468**	**52,947**	**50,516**	**48,099**	**47,300**
Public and publicly guaranteed debt from:	*20,396*	*33,386*	*33,301*	*33,392*	*33,568*	*33,728*
Official creditors	2,368	1,963	1,916	2,011	2,183	2,348
Multilateral	1,378	1,487	1,493	1,621	1,769	1,940
of which: World Bank	321	615	663	846	1,011	1,207
Bilateral	990	476	423	390	414	408
Private creditors	18,028	31,423	31,385	31,381	31,385	31,380
Bondholders	17,422	31,314	31,314	31,314	31,314	31,314
Commercial banks and others	606	109	71	67	71	66
Private nonguaranteed debt from:	*23,471*	*25,081*	*19,646*	*17,124*	*14,531*	*13,572*
Bondholders	500	600	600	600	300	300
Commercial banks and others	22,971	24,481	19,046	16,524	14,231	13,272
Use of IMF credit and SDR allocations	**395**	**278**	**1,120**	**1,065**	**1,074**	**1,044**
IMF credit	98	0	0	0	0	0
SDR allocations	298	278	1,120	1,065	1,074	1,044
Short-term external debt stocks	**3,567**	**10,154**	**12,857**	**15,519**	**17,156**	**19,045**
Disbursements, long-term	**9,625**	**203**	**145**	**242**	**289**	**282**
Public and publicly guaranteed sector	2,196	203	145	242	289	282
Private sector not guaranteed	7,430	..	..	..	..	..
Principal repayments, long-term	**8,395**	**10,458**	**5,639**	**2,635**	**2,711**	**1,060**
Public and publicly guaranteed sector	2,477	196	203	114	118	101
Private sector not guaranteed	5,918	10,262	5,436	2,521	2,593	959
Interest payments, long-term	**1,792**	**510**	**342**	**721**	**1,020**	**854**
Public and publicly guaranteed sector	1,406	157	47	33	82	75
Private sector not guaranteed	386	353	295	689	937	778

LESOTHO

(US$ million, unless otherwise indicated)

Snapshot	2024
Total external debt stocks	**1,773**
External debt stocks as % of:	
Exports	111
GNI	65
Debt service as % of:	
Exports	7
GNI	4
Net financial flows, debt and equity	-2
Net debt inflows	30
Net equity inflows	-32
GNI	**2,713**
Population (million)	**2**

Figure 1 Public and publicly guaranteed debt, by creditor and creditor type in 2024, including IMF credit

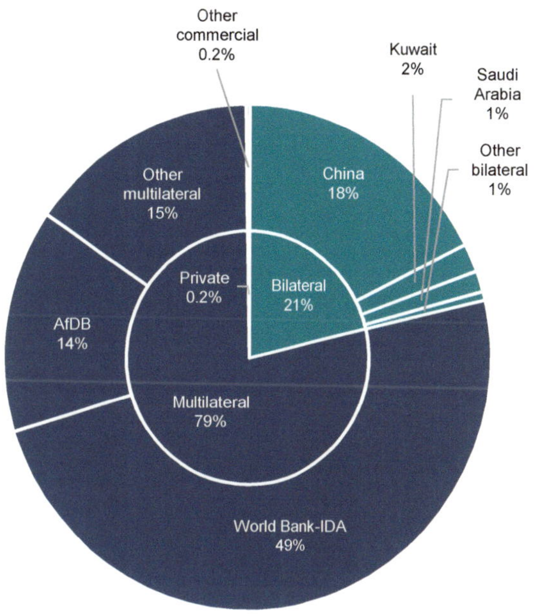

Figure 2 Average terms on new debt commitments from official and private creditors

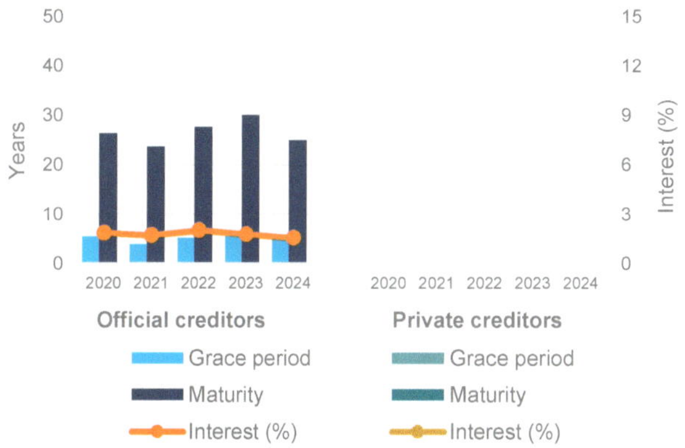

Summary External Debt Data	2010	2020	2021	2022	2023	2024
Total external debt stocks	**788**	**1,738**	**1,833**	**1,809**	**1,776**	**1,773**
Long-term external debt stocks	**709**	**1,616**	**1,633**	**1,613**	**1,595**	**1,625**
Public and publicly guaranteed debt from:	*709*	*931*	*978*	*968*	*999*	*1,016*
Official creditors	688	927	974	965	996	1,014
Multilateral	633	755	760	742	765	794
of which: World Bank	330	400	424	427	457	505
Bilateral	55	171	215	222	230	220
Private creditors	21	4	4	3	3	2
Bondholders	..	..	..	..	..	..
Commercial banks and others	21	4	4	3	3	2
Private nonguaranteed debt from:	..	*685*	*655*	*645*	*597*	*609*
Bondholders	..	..	..	..	..	..
Commercial banks and others	..	685	655	645	597	609
Use of IMF credit and SDR allocations	**79**	**119**	**198**	**182**	**177**	**145**
IMF credit	28	72	58	49	43	15
SDR allocations	51	47	140	133	134	130
Short-term external debt stocks	**0**	**2**	**3**	**14**	**3**	**3**
Disbursements, long-term	**45**	**117**	**106**	**84**	**79**	**115**
Public and publicly guaranteed sector	45	79	106	84	79	103
Private sector not guaranteed	..	38	..	..	..	12
Principal repayments, long-term	**19**	**44**	**66**	**54**	**99**	**58**
Public and publicly guaranteed sector	19	44	35	45	51	58
Private sector not guaranteed	..	..	31	9	49	..
Interest payments, long-term	**8**	**16**	**17**	**18**	**19**	**19**
Public and publicly guaranteed sector	8	16	17	18	19	19
Private sector not guaranteed	..	..	..	..	..	..

LIBERIA

(US$ million, unless otherwise indicated)

Snapshot	2024
Total external debt stocks	**2,235**
External debt stocks as % of:	
Exports	148
GNI	50
Debt service as % of:	
Exports	9
GNI	3
Net financial flows, debt and equity	918
Net debt inflows	171
Net equity inflows	747
GNI	**4,429**
Population (million)	**6**

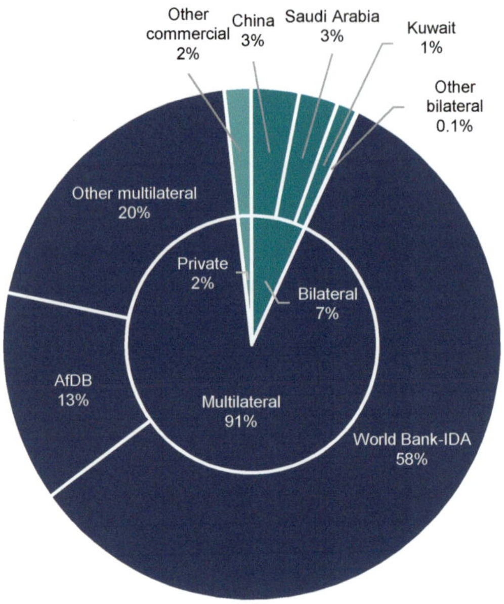

Figure 1 Public and publicly guaranteed debt, by creditor and creditor type in 2024, including IMF credit

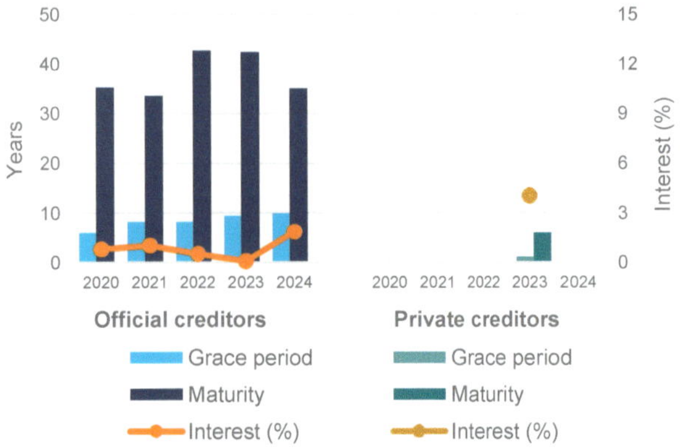

Figure 2 Average terms on new debt commitments from official and private creditors

Summary External Debt Data	2010	2020	2021	2022	2023	2024
Total external debt stocks	**419**	**1,460**	**1,848**	**1,922**	**2,106**	**2,235**
Long-term external debt stocks	**183**	**987**	**1,050**	**1,164**	**1,379**	**1,554**
Public and publicly guaranteed debt from:	*183*	*946*	*1,017*	*1,109*	*1,283*	*1,409*
Official creditors	183	946	1,017	1,109	1,276	1,381
Multilateral	63	828	898	995	1,160	1,269
of which: World Bank	0	550	616	703	828	929
Bilateral	120	118	119	114	116	113
Private creditors	0	..	..	..	7	27
Bondholders	..	..	..	..	..	..
Commercial banks and others	0	..	..	..	7	27
Private nonguaranteed debt from:	..	*41*	*33*	*56*	*96*	*146*
Bondholders	..	..	..	..	..	..
Commercial banks and others	..	41	33	56	96	146
Use of IMF credit and SDR allocations	**235**	**473**	**798**	**757**	**727**	**680**
IMF credit	44	294	278	263	228	196
SDR allocations	191	179	520	495	499	485
Short-term external debt stocks	**0**	**0**	**0**	**0**	**0**	**0**
Disbursements, long-term	**8**	**112**	**100**	**192**	**261**	**264**
Public and publicly guaranteed sector	8	110	100	148	193	169
Private sector not guaranteed	..	1	..	44	68	95
Principal repayments, long-term	**4**	**24**	**18**	**40**	**53**	**66**
Public and publicly guaranteed sector	4	16	10	19	24	22
Private sector not guaranteed	..	8	8	21	29	44
Interest payments, long-term	**1**	**11**	**10**	**13**	**16**	**21**
Public and publicly guaranteed sector	1	10	9	12	10	13
Private sector not guaranteed	..	1	0	1	5	8

MADAGASCAR

(US$ million, unless otherwise indicated)

Snapshot	2024
Total external debt stocks	**6,654**
External debt stocks as % of:	
Exports	163
GNI	39
Debt service as % of:	
Exports	7
GNI	2
Net financial flows, debt and equity	817
Net debt inflows	403
Net equity inflows	413
GNI	**16,969**
Population (million)	**32**

Figure 1 Public and publicly guaranteed debt, by creditor and creditor type in 2024, including IMF credit

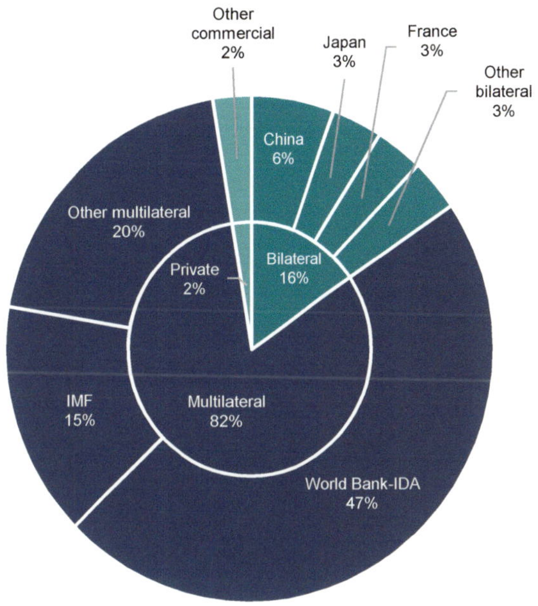

Figure 2 Average terms on new debt commitments from official and private creditors

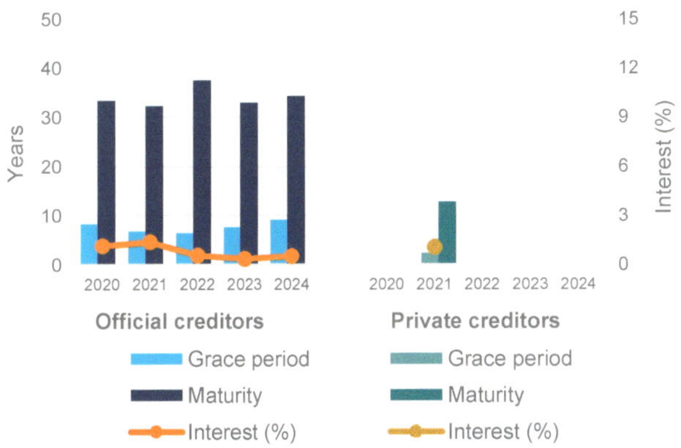

Summary External Debt Data	2010	2020	2021	2022	2023	2024
Total external debt stocks	**2,756**	**4,841**	**5,345**	**5,935**	**6,429**	**6,654**
Long-term external debt stocks	**2,054**	**3,612**	**3,811**	**4,439**	**4,957**	**5,255**
Public and publicly guaranteed debt from:	*2,039*	*3,508*	*3,715*	*3,932*	*4,459*	*4,766*
Official creditors	2,031	3,362	3,598	3,833	4,341	4,628
Multilateral	1,575	2,809	2,986	3,059	3,472	3,760
of which: World Bank	1,161	1,874	2,010	2,043	2,388	2,650
Bilateral	456	553	612	774	869	868
Private creditors	8	146	118	99	118	138
Bondholders	..	..	..	..	..	..
Commercial banks and others	8	146	118	99	118	138
Private nonguaranteed debt from:	*15*	*104*	*95*	*507*	*498*	*489*
Bondholders	..	..	..	420	420	420
Commercial banks and others	15	104	95	87	78	69
Use of IMF credit and SDR allocations	**278**	**956**	**1,304**	**1,317**	**1,344**	**1,297**
IMF credit	97	788	812	850	872	839
SDR allocations	180	169	492	468	471	458
Short-term external debt stocks	**425**	**273**	**230**	**180**	**128**	**102**
Disbursements, long-term	**198**	**347**	**413**	**905**	**635**	**600**
Public and publicly guaranteed sector	198	336	413	485	635	600
Private sector not guaranteed	..	11	..	420	..	..
Principal repayments, long-term	**39**	**82**	**105**	**109**	**143**	**161**
Public and publicly guaranteed sector	37	73	96	100	135	152
Private sector not guaranteed	1	9	9	9	9	9
Interest payments, long-term	**16**	**37**	**39**	**72**	**48**	**50**
Public and publicly guaranteed sector	16	31	32	36	43	46
Private sector not guaranteed	0	6	6	37	5	5

MALAWI

(US$ million, unless otherwise indicated)

Snapshot	2024
Total external debt stocks	**3,744**
External debt stocks as % of:	
Exports	241
GNI	35
Debt service as % of:	
Exports	11
GNI	2
Net financial flows, debt and equity	448
Net debt inflows	228
Net equity inflows	220
GNI	**10,621**
Population (million)	22

Figure 1 Public and publicly guaranteed debt, by creditor and creditor type in 2024, including IMF credit

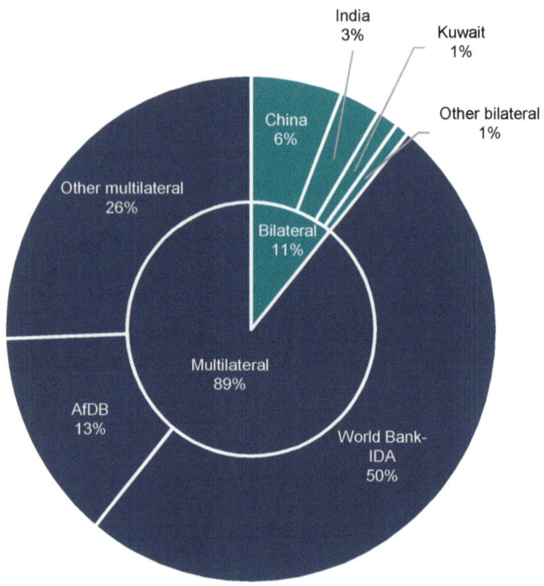

Figure 2 Average terms on new debt commitments from official and private creditors

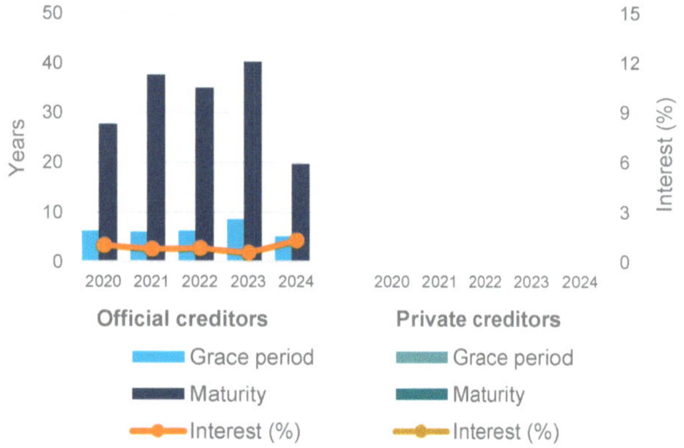

Summary External Debt Data	2010	2020	2021	2022	2023	2024
Total external debt stocks	**1,021**	**2,962**	**3,197**	**3,340**	**3,604**	**3,744**
Long-term external debt stocks	**730**	**2,255**	**2,379**	**2,546**	**2,876**	**3,004**
Public and publicly guaranteed debt from:	*730*	*2,255*	*2,379*	*2,546*	*2,876*	*3,004*
Official creditors	724	2,255	2,379	2,546	2,876	3,004
Multilateral	586	1,818	1,929	2,119	2,486	2,631
of which: World Bank	243	1,104	1,177	1,319	1,550	1,702
Bilateral	138	438	450	427	390	372
Private creditors	5	..	..	..	..	..
Bondholders	..	..	..	..	..	..
Commercial banks and others	5	..	..	..	..	..
Private nonguaranteed debt from:	..	..	..	..	..	..
Bondholders	..	..	..	..	..	..
Commercial banks and others	..	..	..	..	..	..
Use of IMF credit and SDR allocations	**248**	**528**	**673**	**704**	**715**	**664**
IMF credit	146	432	394	438	447	404
SDR allocations	102	96	279	265	268	260
Short-term external debt stocks	**43**	**178**	**145**	**91**	**14**	**75**
Disbursements, long-term	**81**	**211**	**229**	**342**	**397**	**285**
Public and publicly guaranteed sector	81	211	229	342	397	285
Private sector not guaranteed	..	..	..	..	..	..
Principal repayments, long-term	**13**	**51**	**63**	**77**	**83**	**88**
Public and publicly guaranteed sector	13	51	63	77	83	88
Private sector not guaranteed	..	..	..	..	..	..
Interest payments, long-term	**7**	**21**	**22**	**24**	**26**	**31**
Public and publicly guaranteed sector	7	21	22	24	26	31
Private sector not guaranteed	..	..	..	..	..	..

MALDIVES

(US$ million, unless otherwise indicated)

Snapshot	2024
Total external debt stocks	**4,692**
External debt stocks as % of:	
Exports	86
GNI	76
Debt service as % of:	
Exports	9
GNI	8
Net financial flows, debt and equity	1,548
Net debt inflows	742
Net equity inflows	806
GNI	**6,210**
Population (thousand)	**528**

Figure 1 Public and publicly guaranteed debt, by creditor and creditor type in 2024, including IMF credit

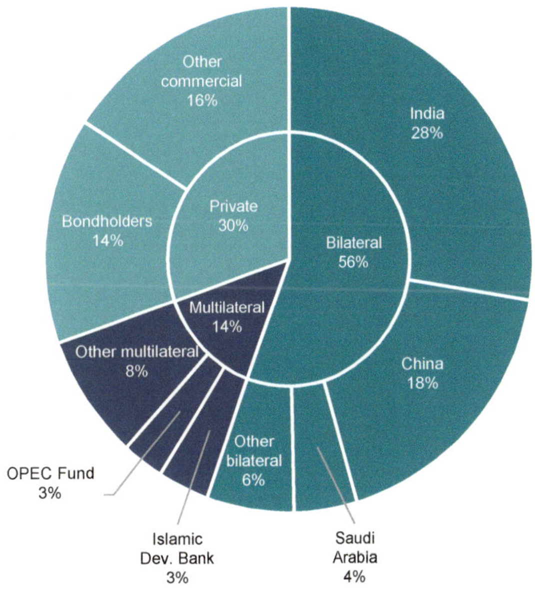

Figure 2 Average terms on new debt commitments from official and private creditors

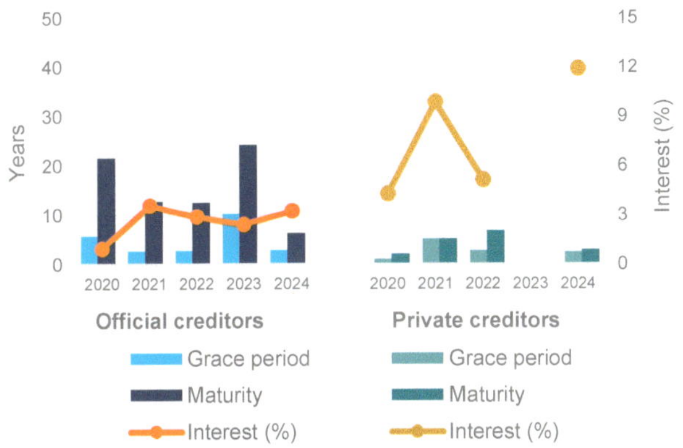

Summary External Debt Data	2010	2020	2021	2022	2023	2024
Total external debt stocks	**914**	**3,661**	**4,099**	**3,993**	**4,000**	**4,692**
Long-term external debt stocks	**743**	**3,211**	**3,545**	**3,476**	**3,835**	**4,468**
Public and publicly guaranteed debt from:	*628*	*2,852*	*3,134*	*3,067*	*3,418*	*4,116*
Official creditors	536	1,988	1,824	1,907	2,272	2,860
Multilateral	301	413	443	440	574	558
of which: World Bank	99	106	101	95	98	93
Bilateral	236	1,575	1,381	1,466	1,699	2,302
Private creditors	92	864	1,311	1,161	1,145	1,255
Bondholders	..	350	850	600	600	600
Commercial banks and others	92	514	461	561	545	655
Private nonguaranteed debt from:	*115*	*359*	*411*	*409*	*418*	*353*
Bondholders	..	..	..	..	..	..
Commercial banks and others	115	359	411	409	418	353
Use of IMF credit and SDR allocations	**28**	**42**	**69**	**65**	**66**	**64**
IMF credit	16	31	30	28	28	28
SDR allocations	12	11	39	37	38	37
Short-term external debt stocks	**143**	**409**	**485**	**451**	**98**	**160**
Disbursements, long-term	**168**	**1,070**	**1,037**	**501**	**663**	**987**
Public and publicly guaranteed sector	142	775	935	450	604	987
Private sector not guaranteed	26	295	102	51	59	..
Principal repayments, long-term	**60**	**231**	**706**	**524**	**302**	**306**
Public and publicly guaranteed sector	51	191	656	470	251	262
Private sector not guaranteed	9	40	50	53	51	44
Interest payments, long-term	**11**	**78**	**91**	**150**	**190**	**185**
Public and publicly guaranteed sector	9	74	85	134	164	165
Private sector not guaranteed	1	5	5	16	27	20

MALI

(US$ million, unless otherwise indicated)

Snapshot	2024
Total external debt stocks	**6,440**
External debt stocks as % of:	
Exports	108
GNI	25
Debt service as % of:	
Exports	6
GNI	1
Net financial flows, debt and equity	900
Net debt inflows	192
Net equity inflows	709
GNI	**25,818**
Population (million)	**24**

Figure 2 Average terms on new debt commitments from official and private creditors

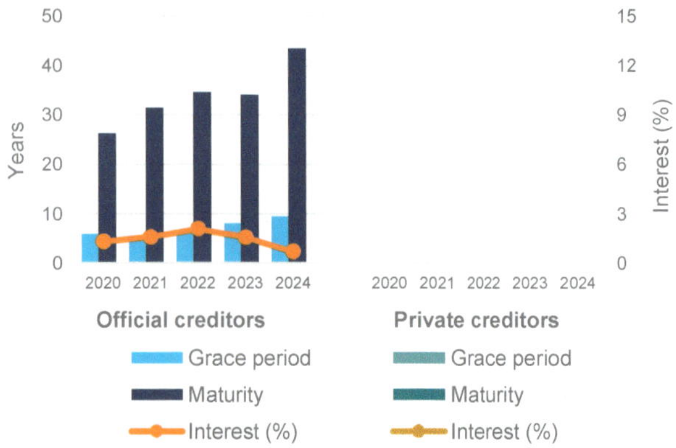

Figure 1 Public and publicly guaranteed debt, by creditor and creditor type in 2024, including IMF credit

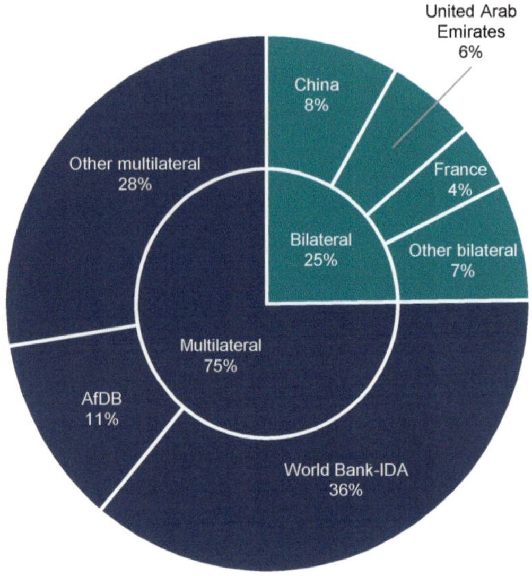

Summary External Debt Data	2010	2020	2021	2022	2023	2024
Total external debt stocks	**2,439**	**5,813**	**6,380**	**6,234**	**6,471**	**6,440**
Long-term external debt stocks	**2,246**	**5,060**	**5,349**	**5,302**	**5,555**	**5,618**
Public and publicly guaranteed debt from:	*2,246*	*5,060*	*5,349*	*5,302*	*5,555*	*5,618*
Official creditors	2,241	5,060	5,349	5,302	5,555	5,618
Multilateral	1,788	3,790	3,766	3,749	4,041	4,118
of which: World Bank	840	2,146	2,131	2,033	2,166	2,190
Bilateral	453	1,270	1,583	1,552	1,513	1,501
Private creditors	5	..	..	..	..	..
Bondholders	..	..	..	..	..	..
Commercial banks and others	5	..	..	..	..	..
Private nonguaranteed debt from:	..	..	..	..	..	..
Bondholders	..	..	..	..	..	..
Commercial banks and others	..	..	..	..	..	..
Use of IMF credit and SDR allocations	**187**	**681**	**946**	**880**	**851**	**780**
IMF credit	49	552	571	523	491	430
SDR allocations	138	129	375	357	360	350
Short-term external debt stocks	**6**	**72**	**85**	**53**	**65**	**42**
Disbursements, long-term	**310**	**555**	**707**	**424**	**411**	**501**
Public and publicly guaranteed sector	310	555	707	424	411	501
Private sector not guaranteed	..	..	..	..	..	..
Principal repayments, long-term	**47**	**195**	**211**	**224**	**232**	**238**
Public and publicly guaranteed sector	47	195	211	224	232	238
Private sector not guaranteed	..	..	..	..	..	..
Interest payments, long-term	**21**	**37**	**59**	**59**	**65**	**67**
Public and publicly guaranteed sector	21	37	59	59	65	67
Private sector not guaranteed	..	..	..	..	..	..

MAURITANIA

(US$ million, unless otherwise indicated)

Snapshot	2024
Total external debt stocks	**4,460**
External debt stocks as % of:	
Exports	105
GNI	42
Debt service as % of:	
Exports	10
GNI	4
Net financial flows, debt and equity	1,366
Net debt inflows	-75
Net equity inflows	1,440
GNI	**10,662**
Population (million)	**5**

Figure 1 Public and publicly guaranteed debt, by creditor and creditor type in 2024, including IMF credit

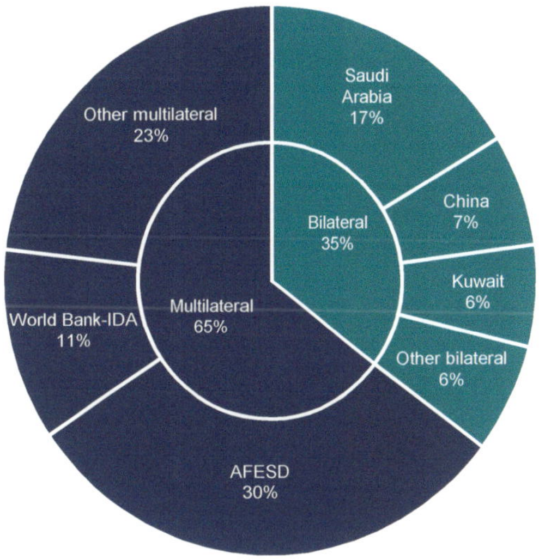

Figure 2 Average terms on new debt commitments from official and private creditors

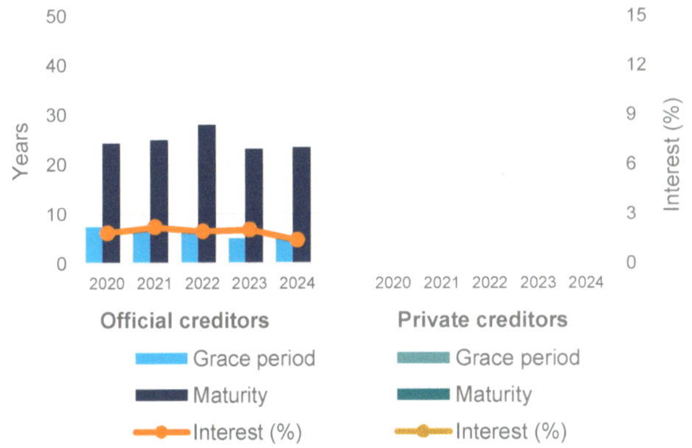

Summary External Debt Data	2010	2020	2021	2022	2023	2024
Total external debt stocks	**3,556**	**5,685**	**4,786**	**4,559**	**4,588**	**4,460**
Long-term external debt stocks	**2,326**	**4,186**	**4,011**	**3,797**	**3,734**	**3,607**
Public and publicly guaranteed debt from:	*2,326*	*4,186*	*4,011*	*3,797*	*3,734*	*3,607*
Official creditors	2,325	4,186	4,011	3,797	3,734	3,607
Multilateral	1,501	2,458	2,327	2,211	2,214	2,194
of which: World Bank	316	418	415	385	424	451
Bilateral	824	1,727	1,684	1,586	1,520	1,413
Private creditors	1	..	..	..	..	..
Bondholders	..	..	..	..	..	..
Commercial banks and others	1	..	..	..	..	..
Private nonguaranteed debt from:	..	..	..	..	..	..
Bondholders	..	..	..	..	..	..
Commercial banks and others	..	..	..	..	..	..
Use of IMF credit and SDR allocations	**145**	**424**	**594**	**556**	**596**	**639**
IMF credit	50	336	335	310	348	398
SDR allocations	95	89	259	246	248	241
Short-term external debt stocks	**1,086**	**1,075**	**180**	**206**	**258**	**213**
Disbursements, long-term	**412**	**223**	**130**	**135**	**214**	**204**
Public and publicly guaranteed sector	412	223	130	135	214	204
Private sector not guaranteed	..	..	..	..	..	..
Principal repayments, long-term	**77**	**212**	**335**	**260**	**277**	**294**
Public and publicly guaranteed sector	77	212	335	260	277	294
Private sector not guaranteed	..	..	..	..	..	..
Interest payments, long-term	**35**	**59**	**57**	**66**	**83**	**79**
Public and publicly guaranteed sector	35	59	57	66	83	79
Private sector not guaranteed	..	..	..	..	..	..

MAURITIUS

(US$ million, unless otherwise indicated)

Snapshot	2024
Total external debt stocks	**20,364**
External debt stocks as % of:	
Exports	104
GNI	123
Debt service as % of:	
Exports	8
GNI	10
Net financial flows, debt and equity	5,194
Net debt inflows	1,358
Net equity inflows	3,836
GNI	**16,534**
Population (million)	1

Figure 1 Public and publicly guaranteed debt, by creditor and creditor type in 2024, including IMF credit

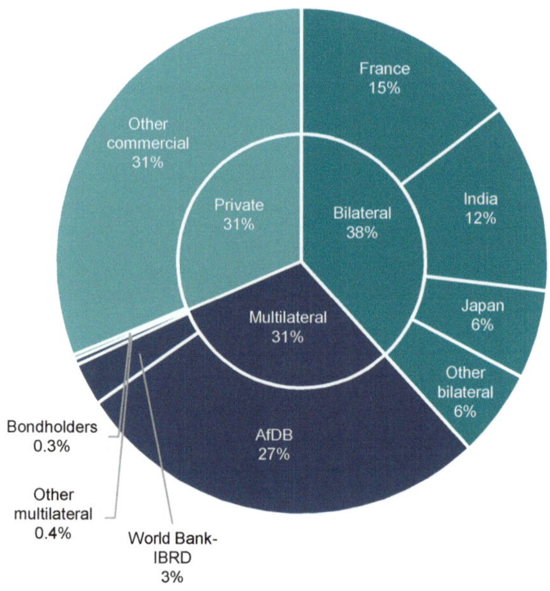

Figure 2 Average terms on new debt commitments from official and private creditors

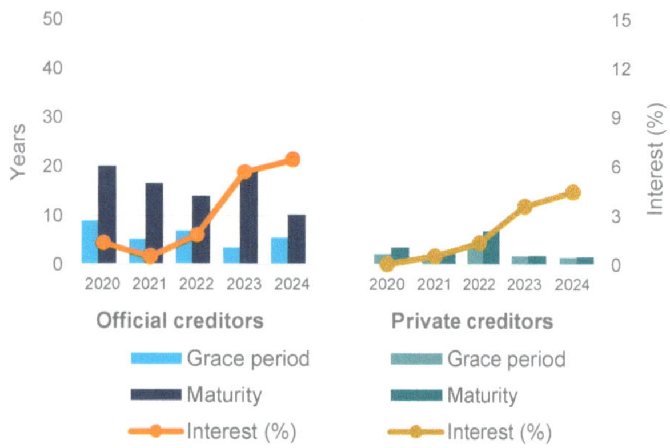

Summary External Debt Data	2010	2020	2021	2022	2023	2024
Total external debt stocks	**7,929**	**12,402**	**14,700**	**17,653**	**19,079**	**20,364**
Long-term external debt stocks	**6,294**	**5,996**	**6,965**	**9,004**	**9,323**	**8,905**
Public and publicly guaranteed debt from:	*1,007*	*1,917*	*2,826*	*3,350*	*3,675*	*3,399*
Official creditors	888	1,883	2,004	1,943	2,215	2,333
Multilateral	501	790	702	633	864	1,037
of which: World Bank	204	189	158	131	113	93
Bilateral	387	1,093	1,302	1,310	1,351	1,297
Private creditors	119	33	822	1,407	1,461	1,066
Bondholders	..	8	9	7	8	9
Commercial banks and others	119	26	814	1,400	1,452	1,056
Private nonguaranteed debt from:	*5,287*	*4,079*	*4,139*	*5,654*	*5,647*	*5,505*
Bondholders	..	399	381	666	815	756
Commercial banks and others	5,287	3,681	3,757	4,988	4,832	4,749
Use of IMF credit and SDR allocations	**149**	**139**	**326**	**310**	**313**	**304**
IMF credit	0	0	0	0	0	0
SDR allocations	149	139	326	310	313	304
Short-term external debt stocks	**1,485**	**6,267**	**7,409**	**8,339**	**9,444**	**11,155**
Disbursements, long-term	**2,568**	**1,636**	**3,164**	**2,418**	**1,830**	**709**
Public and publicly guaranteed sector	356	784	1,163	772	1,530	709
Private sector not guaranteed	2,212	851	2,001	1,646	300	..
Principal repayments, long-term	**2,118**	**2,243**	**2,390**	**278**	**1,530**	**1,055**
Public and publicly guaranteed sector	69	341	164	147	1,223	914
Private sector not guaranteed	2,049	1,902	2,227	131	307	142
Interest payments, long-term	**73**	**314**	**286**	**483**	**270**	**400**
Public and publicly guaranteed sector	17	27	20	38	103	112
Private sector not guaranteed	56	287	267	444	167	288

MEXICO

(US$ million, unless otherwise indicated)

Snapshot	2024
Total external debt stocks	**591,255**
External debt stocks as % of:	
Exports	84
GNI	33
Debt service as % of:	
Exports	10
GNI	4
Net financial flows, debt and equity	31,353
Net debt inflows	3,867
Net equity inflows	27,486
GNI	**1,797,562**
Population (million)	**131**

Figure 1 Public and publicly guaranteed debt, by creditor and creditor type in 2024, including IMF credit

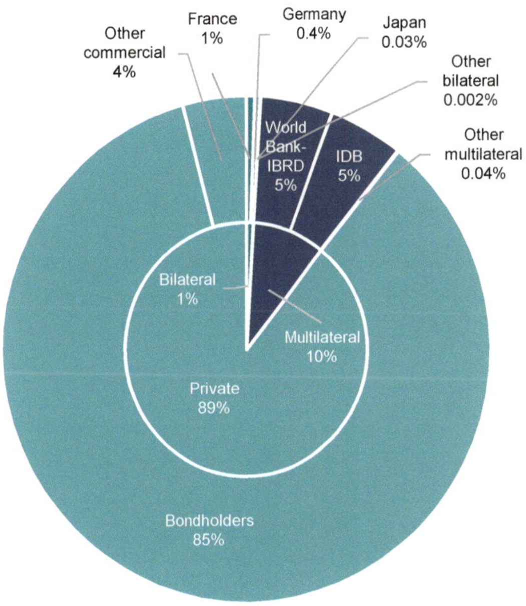

Figure 2 Average terms on new debt commitments from official and private creditors

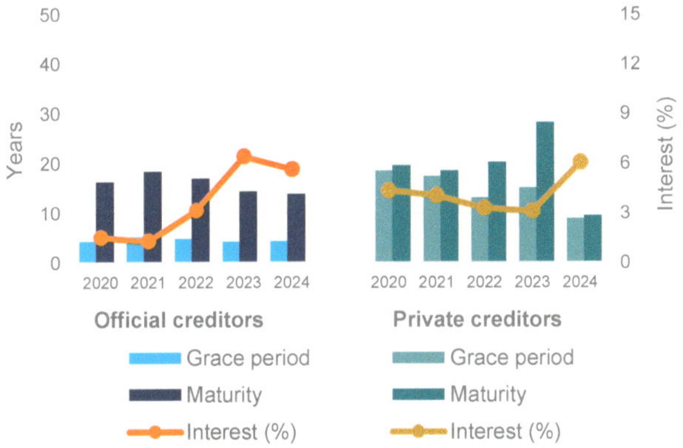

Summary External Debt Data	2010	2020	2021	2022	2023	2024
Total external debt stocks	**312,338**	**616,686**	**601,472**	**585,862**	**595,981**	**591,255**
Long-term external debt stocks	**264,887**	**566,202**	**538,484**	**515,932**	**520,479**	**515,222**
Public and publicly guaranteed debt from:	*145,925*	*309,061*	*290,868*	*289,397*	*301,048*	*289,465*
Official creditors	25,389	34,877	33,844	33,597	32,291	31,195
Multilateral	21,433	32,215	31,144	31,234	29,778	28,441
of which: World Bank	12,462	15,714	15,237	15,596	14,618	14,265
Bilateral	3,956	2,662	2,699	2,363	2,513	2,754
Private creditors	120,536	274,184	257,024	255,800	268,756	258,270
Bondholders	97,656	259,213	241,284	241,168	257,410	246,046
Commercial banks and others	22,880	14,971	15,740	14,633	11,346	12,223
Private nonguaranteed debt from:	*118,961*	*257,141*	*247,616*	*226,534*	*219,431*	*225,757*
Bondholders	32,898	102,661	95,854	75,126	71,244	68,959
Commercial banks and others	86,063	154,480	151,762	151,408	148,187	156,798
Use of IMF credit and SDR allocations	**4,391**	**4,106**	**15,946**	**15,163**	**15,286**	**14,859**
IMF credit	0	0	0	0	0	0
SDR allocations	4,391	4,106	15,946	15,163	15,286	14,859
Short-term external debt stocks	**43,061**	**46,378**	**47,041**	**54,767**	**60,216**	**61,174**
Disbursements, long-term	**62,651**	**57,419**	**45,700**	**34,519**	**34,743**	**46,032**
Public and publicly guaranteed sector	41,812	31,660	27,421	24,259	26,624	20,621
Private sector not guaranteed	20,839	25,759	18,278	10,260	8,119	25,411
Principal repayments, long-term	**21,683**	**47,968**	**55,816**	**34,880**	**28,274**	**43,123**
Public and publicly guaranteed sector	13,941	25,548	35,863	13,015	13,496	24,345
Private sector not guaranteed	7,742	22,420	19,953	21,866	14,778	18,778
Interest payments, long-term	**8,658**	**21,676**	**21,393**	**18,215**	**23,120**	**20,478**
Public and publicly guaranteed sector	5,859	16,415	16,155	11,509	13,563	14,468
Private sector not guaranteed	2,799	5,261	5,238	6,707	9,557	6,010

MOLDOVA

(US$ million, unless otherwise indicated)

Snapshot	2024
Total external debt stocks	**10,491**
External debt stocks as % of:	
Exports	153
GNI	57
Debt service as % of:	
Exports	17
GNI	6
Net financial flows, debt and equity	408
Net debt inflows	15
Net equity inflows	393
GNI	**18,358**
Population (million)	**2**

Figure 1 Public and publicly guaranteed debt, by creditor and creditor type in 2024, including IMF credit

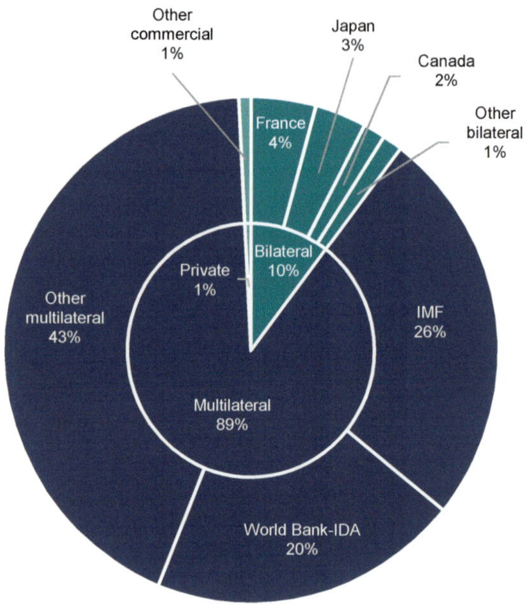

Figure 2 Average terms on new debt commitments from official and private creditors

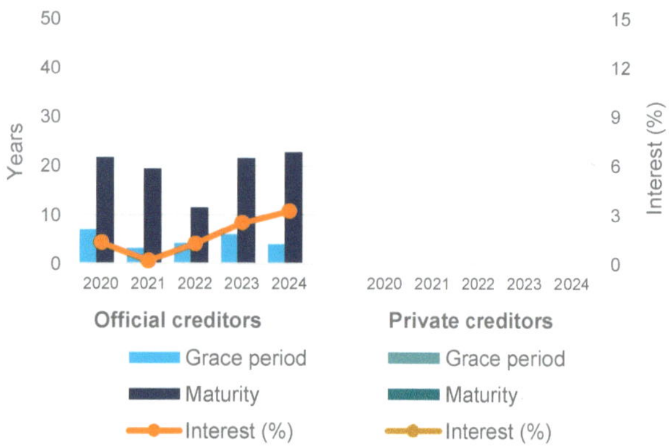

Summary External Debt Data	2010	2020	2021	2022	2023	2024
Total external debt stocks	**4,725**	**7,948**	**9,068**	**9,752**	**10,663**	**10,491**
Long-term external debt stocks	**2,745**	**5,283**	**5,805**	**6,296**	**6,662**	**6,893**
Public and publicly guaranteed debt from:	*839*	*1,794*	*1,852*	*2,289*	*2,654*	*2,914*
Official creditors	816	1,736	1,799	2,244	2,615	2,883
Multilateral	565	1,574	1,700	2,058	2,293	2,478
of which: World Bank	479	792	813	928	1,067	1,083
Bilateral	251	163	99	186	322	405
Private creditors	23	57	53	45	39	31
Bondholders	..	..	..	..	..	..
Commercial banks and others	23	57	53	45	39	31
Private nonguaranteed debt from:	*1,906*	*3,490*	*3,953*	*4,008*	*4,008*	*3,979*
Bondholders	..	..	500	500	500	500
Commercial banks and others	1,906	3,490	3,453	3,508	3,508	3,479
Use of IMF credit and SDR allocations	**509**	**669**	**912**	**1,008**	**1,178**	**1,364**
IMF credit	327	499	516	631	798	995
SDR allocations	181	170	396	377	380	369
Short-term external debt stocks	**1,471**	**1,996**	**2,350**	**2,448**	**2,823**	**2,235**
Disbursements, long-term	**464**	**837**	**1,198**	**1,015**	**1,209**	**1,088**
Public and publicly guaranteed sector	94	335	312	643	773	686
Private sector not guaranteed	370	503	886	372	436	402
Principal repayments, long-term	**306**	**548**	**513**	**435**	**904**	**697**
Public and publicly guaranteed sector	55	127	145	118	468	265
Private sector not guaranteed	251	422	368	317	436	431
Interest payments, long-term	**49**	**65**	**110**	**109**	**162**	**180**
Public and publicly guaranteed sector	16	20	21	23	51	75
Private sector not guaranteed	33	45	89	86	111	104

MONGOLIA

(US$ million, unless otherwise indicated)

Snapshot	2024
Total external debt stocks	**38,017**
External debt stocks as % of:	
Exports	225
GNI	182
Debt service as % of:	
Exports	32
GNI	26
Net financial flows, debt and equity	4,190
Net debt inflows	3,599
Net equity inflows	591
GNI	**20,905**
Population (million)	**4**

Figure 1 Public and publicly guaranteed debt, by creditor and creditor type in 2024, including IMF credit

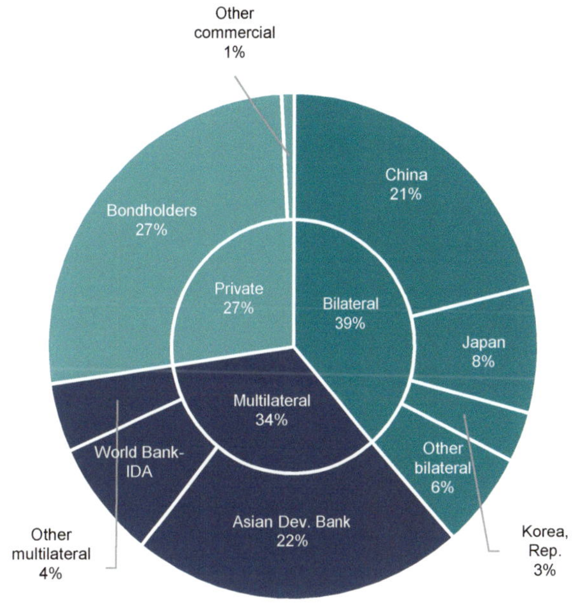

Figure 2 Average terms on new debt commitments from official and private creditors

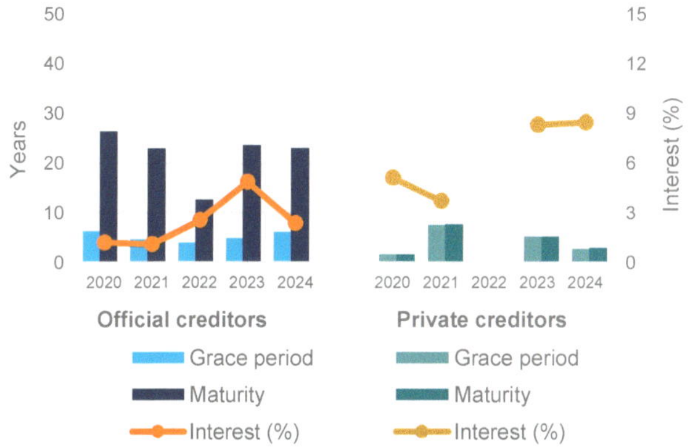

Summary External Debt Data	2010	2020	2021	2022	2023	2024
Total external debt stocks	**5,928**	**32,635**	**34,963**	**33,701**	**35,039**	**38,017**
Long-term external debt stocks	**5,290**	**30,953**	**33,063**	**31,348**	**32,746**	**35,381**
Public and publicly guaranteed debt from:	*1,782*	*11,086*	*11,524*	*9,802*	*9,730*	*9,863*
Official creditors	1,776	7,588	7,783	7,655	7,651	7,129
Multilateral	1,073	2,692	2,875	3,010	3,154	3,275
of which: World Bank	403	760	809	798	816	804
Bilateral	703	4,897	4,908	4,645	4,497	3,855
Private creditors	7	3,498	3,741	2,147	2,079	2,733
Bondholders	0	3,432	3,637	2,100	2,000	2,652
Commercial banks and others	7	66	104	47	79	82
Private nonguaranteed debt from:	*3,508*	*19,866*	*21,538*	*21,546*	*23,016*	*25,518*
Bondholders	..	1,696	2,024	1,467	800	1,187
Commercial banks and others	3,508	18,171	19,515	20,079	22,217	24,331
Use of IMF credit and SDR allocations	**273**	**401**	**483**	**436**	**380**	**288**
IMF credit	198	331	318	279	221	134
SDR allocations	75	70	165	157	158	154
Short-term external debt stocks	**365**	**1,281**	**1,417**	**1,917**	**1,913**	**2,348**
Disbursements, long-term	**2,929**	**3,480**	**4,444**	**3,483**	**5,260**	**5,943**
Public and publicly guaranteed sector	67	1,670	1,568	460	1,619	1,302
Private sector not guaranteed	2,863	1,810	2,875	3,024	3,641	4,640
Principal repayments, long-term	**139**	**2,176**	**2,256**	**3,370**	**3,951**	**2,696**
Public and publicly guaranteed sector	121	817	1,053	1,779	1,602	1,004
Private sector not guaranteed	18	1,359	1,204	1,591	2,348	1,691
Interest payments, long-term	**89**	**464**	**397**	**511**	**894**	**2,491**
Public and publicly guaranteed sector	20	320	270	358	309	355
Private sector not guaranteed	70	145	127	153	585	2,136

MONTENEGRO

(US$ million, unless otherwise indicated)

Snapshot	2024
Total external debt stocks	**8,741**
External debt stocks as % of:	
Exports	211
GNI	109
Debt service as % of:	
Exports	30
GNI	15
Net financial flows, debt and equity	686
Net debt inflows	272
Net equity inflows	414
GNI	**8,046**
Population (thousand)	**624**

Figure 1 Public and publicly guaranteed debt, by creditor and creditor type in 2024, including IMF credit

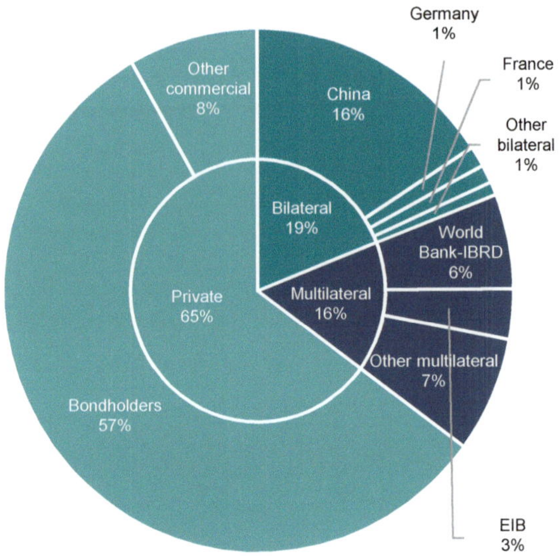

Figure 2 Average terms on new debt commitments from official and private creditors

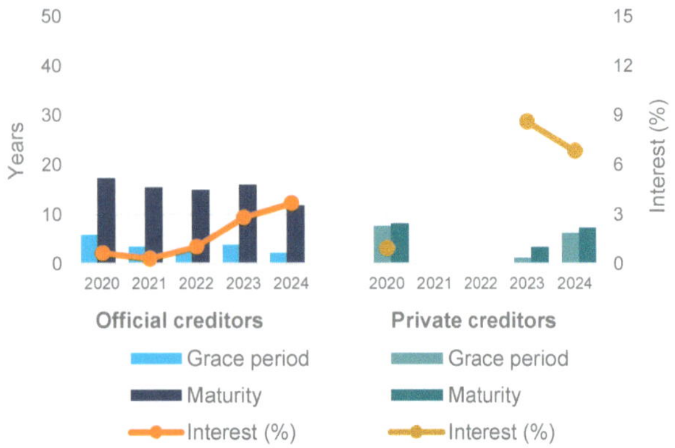

Summary External Debt Data	2010	2020	2021	2022	2023	2024
Total external debt stocks	**4,503**	**10,524**	**9,638**	**8,806**	**8,665**	**8,741**
Long-term external debt stocks	**4,277**	**9,988**	**8,972**	**8,403**	**8,320**	**8,377**
Public and publicly guaranteed debt from:	*1,349*	*4,826*	*4,294*	*3,940*	*3,968*	*4,513*
Official creditors	818	1,658	1,658	1,597	1,521	1,573
Multilateral	546	637	650	613	621	708
of which: World Bank	306	252	232	208	204	268
Bilateral	271	1,021	1,008	984	900	865
Private creditors	531	3,168	2,636	2,344	2,448	2,940
Bondholders	267	2,427	1,982	1,867	1,934	2,568
Commercial banks and others	264	741	654	477	514	372
Private nonguaranteed debt from:	*2,928*	*5,162*	*4,678*	*4,462*	*4,352*	*3,864*
Bondholders	..	..	..	..	..	..
Commercial banks and others	2,928	5,162	4,678	4,462	4,352	3,864
Use of IMF credit and SDR allocations	**40**	**124**	**202**	**192**	**173**	**129**
IMF credit	0	87	85	81	61	20
SDR allocations	40	37	117	112	112	109
Short-term external debt stocks	**186**	**411**	**464**	**212**	**171**	**235**
Disbursements, long-term	**676**	**2,063**	**222**	**160**	**179**	**1,055**
Public and publicly guaranteed sector	383	1,313	213	150	177	1,039
Private sector not guaranteed	293	750	9	10	3	16
Principal repayments, long-term	**59**	**530**	**934**	**522**	**375**	**808**
Public and publicly guaranteed sector	59	517	452	304	259	306
Private sector not guaranteed	..	13	482	219	116	501
Interest payments, long-term	**33**	**173**	**165**	**301**	**394**	**368**
Public and publicly guaranteed sector	33	108	108	97	121	150
Private sector not guaranteed	..	64	57	203	273	218

MOROCCO

(US$ million, unless otherwise indicated)

Snapshot	2024
Total external debt stocks	**67,994**
External debt stocks as % of:	
Exports	99
GNI	45
Debt service as % of:	
Exports	13
GNI	6
Net financial flows, debt and equity	1,329
Net debt inflows	206
Net equity inflows	1,122
GNI	**152,048**
Population (million)	**38**

Figure 1 Public and publicly guaranteed debt, by creditor and creditor type in 2024, including IMF credit

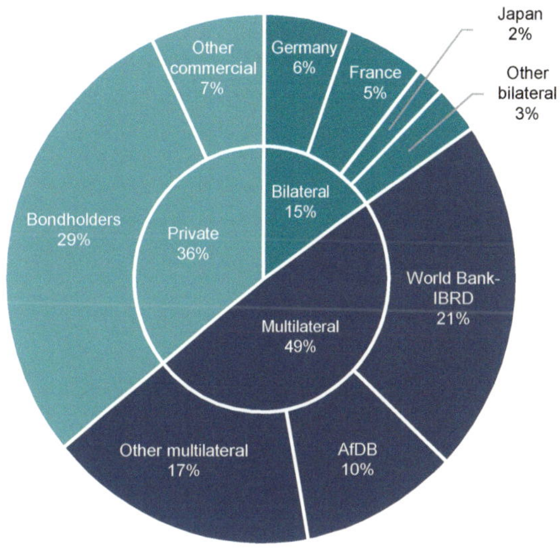

Figure 2 Average terms on new debt commitments from official and private creditors

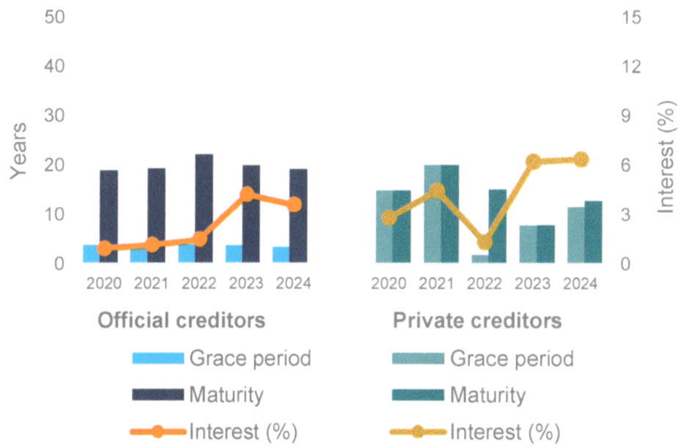

Summary External Debt Data	2010	2020	2021	2022	2023	2024
Total external debt stocks	**27,348**	**66,010**	**65,687**	**64,972**	**69,632**	**67,994**
Long-term external debt stocks	**23,736**	**53,957**	**52,524**	**51,137**	**55,557**	**57,205**
Public and publicly guaranteed debt from:	*21,148*	*43,949*	*42,422*	*41,286*	*45,117*	*45,727*
Official creditors	17,296	27,404	26,167	27,020	28,260	28,776
Multilateral	10,186	19,816	19,204	19,965	21,093	21,528
of which: World Bank	2,518	7,886	8,118	8,669	9,423	10,202
Bilateral	7,110	7,588	6,963	7,056	7,167	7,248
Private creditors	3,852	16,545	16,255	14,265	16,857	16,951
Bondholders	1,336	10,912	11,602	9,897	12,516	13,578
Commercial banks and others	2,515	5,633	4,653	4,368	4,341	3,374
Private nonguaranteed debt from:	*2,589*	*10,008*	*10,102*	*9,851*	*10,440*	*11,477*
Bondholders	..	..	..	..	..	..
Commercial banks and others	2,589	10,008	10,102	9,851	10,440	11,477
Use of IMF credit and SDR allocations	**865**	**3,906**	**4,085**	**3,884**	**3,916**	**3,285**
IMF credit	0	3,098	2,099	1,996	2,012	1,435
SDR allocations	865	809	1,986	1,888	1,903	1,850
Short-term external debt stocks	**2,747**	**8,146**	**9,079**	**9,951**	**10,160**	**7,504**
Disbursements, long-term	**4,999**	**9,315**	**5,401**	**4,550**	**6,430**	**8,616**
Public and publicly guaranteed sector	3,882	8,197	4,241	4,144	5,195	6,862
Private sector not guaranteed	1,116	1,117	1,160	407	1,235	1,754
Principal repayments, long-term	**2,430**	**4,062**	**4,323**	**4,395**	**3,569**	**5,224**
Public and publicly guaranteed sector	1,276	3,386	3,533	3,710	2,240	4,413
Private sector not guaranteed	1,154	677	790	686	1,328	811
Interest payments, long-term	**851**	**1,045**	**1,161**	**1,102**	**1,421**	**1,792**
Public and publicly guaranteed sector	820	939	1,020	1,003	1,308	1,653
Private sector not guaranteed	31	106	141	99	113	139

MOZAMBIQUE

(US$ million, unless otherwise indicated)

Snapshot	2024
Total external debt stocks	**69,765**
External debt stocks as % of:	
Exports	715
GNI	351
Debt service as % of:	
Exports	47
GNI	23
Net financial flows, debt and equity	3,411
Net debt inflows	3,038
Net equity inflows	373
GNI	**19,900**
Population (million)	**35**

Figure 1 Public and publicly guaranteed debt, by creditor and creditor type in 2024, including IMF credit

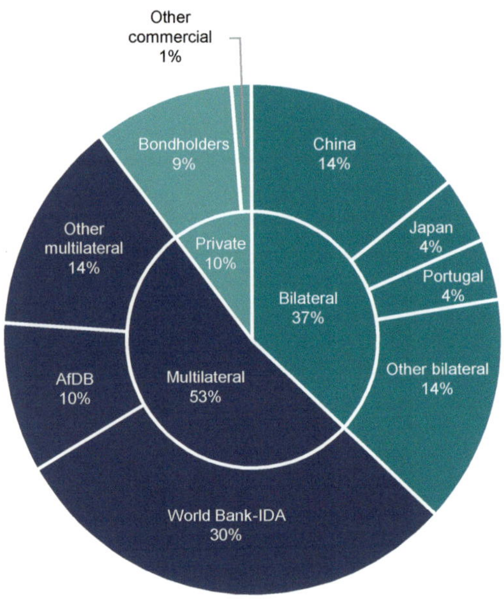

Figure 2 Average terms on new debt commitments from official and private creditors

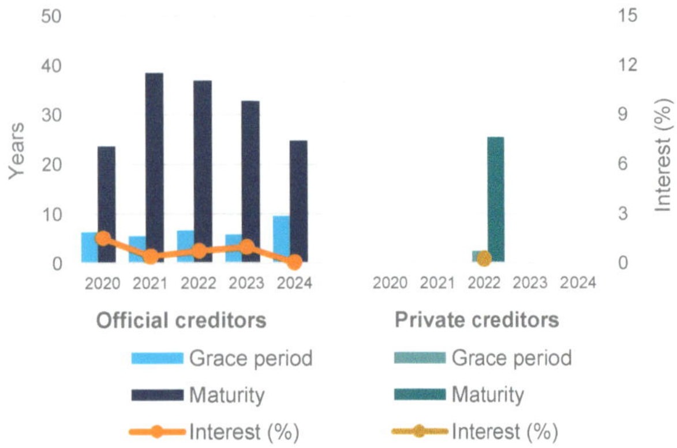

Summary External Debt Data	2010	2020	2021	2022	2023	2024
Total external debt stocks	**11,231**	**60,289**	**64,426**	**66,290**	**67,936**	**69,765**
Long-term external debt stocks	**10,263**	**57,186**	**60,903**	**63,706**	**65,444**	**67,405**
Public and publicly guaranteed debt from:	*3,263*	*11,459*	*11,282*	*10,810*	*10,125*	*9,150*
Official creditors	3,167	9,062	8,917	8,473	8,442	8,125
Multilateral	2,262	4,746	4,679	4,485	4,505	4,474
of which: World Bank	1,491	3,224	3,147	2,984	3,010	2,923
Bilateral	905	4,316	4,239	3,988	3,936	3,651
Private creditors	96	2,396	2,365	2,338	1,683	1,025
Bondholders	..	900	900	900	900	900
Commercial banks and others	96	1,496	1,465	1,438	783	125
Private nonguaranteed debt from:	*7,001*	*45,727*	*49,621*	*52,896*	*55,319*	*58,255*
Bondholders	..	..	..	..	..	..
Commercial banks and others	7,001	45,727	49,621	52,896	55,319	58,255
Use of IMF credit and SDR allocations	**357**	**689**	**947**	**1,027**	**1,071**	**1,148**
IMF credit	190	532	490	592	633	722
SDR allocations	168	157	457	435	438	426
Short-term external debt stocks	**610**	**2,415**	**2,576**	**1,557**	**1,421**	**1,212**
Disbursements, long-term	**3,810**	**4,153**	**10,083**	**6,531**	**3,256**	**3,564**
Public and publicly guaranteed sector	419	329	345	283	626	414
Private sector not guaranteed	3,391	3,824	9,738	6,248	2,630	3,150
Principal repayments, long-term	**39**	**326**	**6,176**	**3,349**	**807**	**962**
Public and publicly guaranteed sector	39	326	331	376	600	748
Private sector not guaranteed	..	..	5,844	2,973	206	214
Interest payments, long-term	**149**	**703**	**776**	**2,286**	**3,623**	**3,511**
Public and publicly guaranteed sector	47	128	111	139	114	201
Private sector not guaranteed	102	575	665	2,147	3,510	3,310

MYANMAR

(US$ million, unless otherwise indicated)

Snapshot	2024
Total external debt stocks	**11,175**
External debt stocks as % of:	
Exports	87
GNI	15
Debt service as % of:	
Exports	7
GNI	1
Net financial flows, debt and equity	694
Net debt inflows	-401
Net equity inflows	1,095
GNI	**73,153**
Population (million)	**55**

Figure 1 Public and publicly guaranteed debt, by creditor and creditor type in 2024, including IMF credit

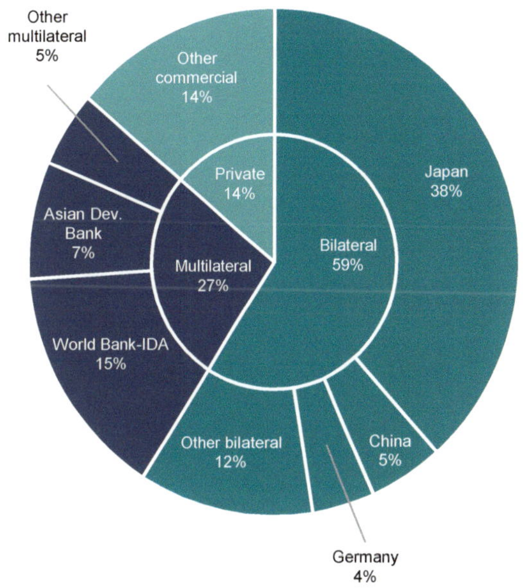

Figure 2 Average terms on new debt commitments from official and private creditors

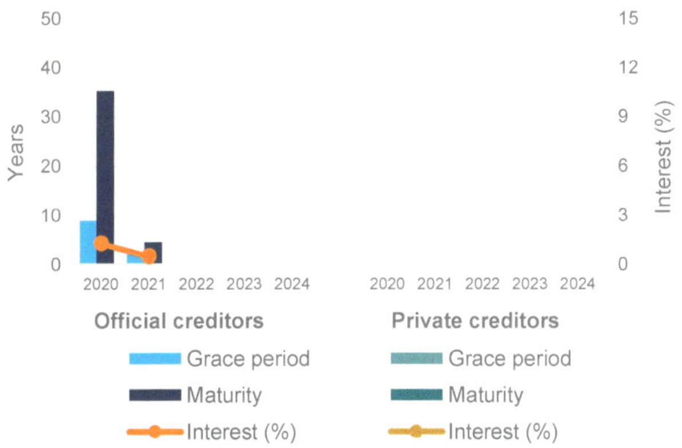

Summary External Debt Data	2010	2020	2021	2022	2023	2024
Total external debt stocks	**9,990**	**13,405**	**13,757**	**12,535**	**12,160**	**11,175**
Long-term external debt stocks	**8,433**	**12,611**	**11,964**	**10,830**	**10,486**	**9,723**
Public and publicly guaranteed debt from:	*8,433*	*12,576*	*11,803*	*10,456*	*10,034*	*9,240*
Official creditors	7,482	10,147	9,676	8,700	8,449	7,905
Multilateral	1,447	2,637	2,684	2,493	2,387	2,207
of which: World Bank	799	1,804	1,769	1,641	1,566	1,446
Bilateral	6,035	7,510	6,991	6,207	6,062	5,698
Private creditors	952	2,429	2,127	1,755	1,585	1,335
Bondholders	..	..	..	..	..	..
Commercial banks and others	952	2,429	2,127	1,755	1,585	1,335
Private nonguaranteed debt from:	..	*35*	*162*	*374*	*452*	*484*
Bondholders	..	..	..	..	..	..
Commercial banks and others	..	35	162	374	452	484
Use of IMF credit and SDR allocations	**378**	**726**	**1,761**	**1,674**	**1,630**	**1,388**
IMF credit	0	372	723	688	636	421
SDR allocations	378	354	1,037	986	994	966
Short-term external debt stocks	**1,179**	**68**	**32**	**32**	**45**	**64**
Disbursements, long-term	**714**	**1,673**	**697**	**533**	**502**	**359**
Public and publicly guaranteed sector	714	1,591	499	311	409	305
Private sector not guaranteed	..	81	199	222	93	54
Principal repayments, long-term	**201**	**488**	**721**	**753**	**642**	**560**
Public and publicly guaranteed sector	201	414	637	744	626	538
Private sector not guaranteed	..	74	84	10	16	22
Interest payments, long-term	**40**	**112**	**157**	**172**	**154**	**138**
Public and publicly guaranteed sector	40	98	150	156	140	123
Private sector not guaranteed	..	15	7	15	14	15

NEPAL

(US$ million, unless otherwise indicated)

Snapshot	2024
Total external debt stocks	**10,152**
External debt stocks as % of:	
Exports	234
GNI	23
Debt service as % of:	
Exports	12
GNI	1
Net financial flows, debt and equity	480
Net debt inflows	423
Net equity inflows	57
GNI	**43,619**
Population (million)	**30**

Figure 1 Public and publicly guaranteed debt, by creditor and creditor type in 2024, including IMF credit

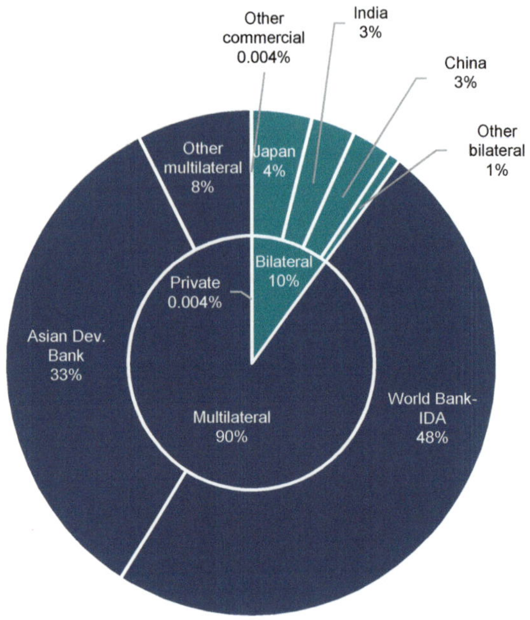

Figure 2 Average terms on new debt commitments from official and private creditors

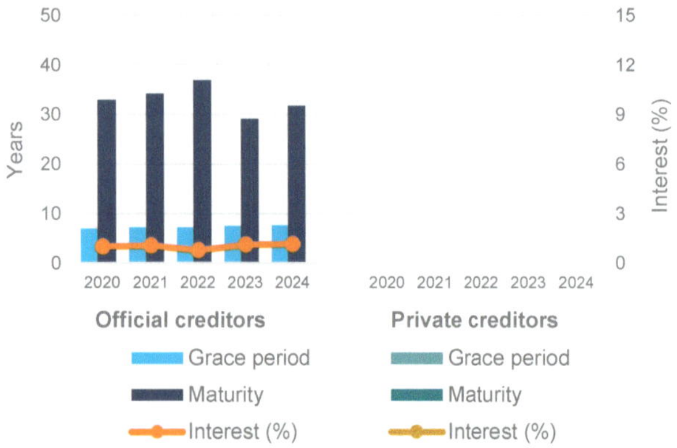

Summary External Debt Data	2010	2020	2021	2022	2023	2024
Total external debt stocks	**3,787**	**7,906**	**8,821**	**9,184**	**9,983**	**10,152**
Long-term external debt stocks	**3,507**	**7,175**	**7,926**	**8,229**	**8,832**	**8,985**
Public and publicly guaranteed debt from:	*3,507*	*7,057*	*7,759*	*7,958*	*8,619*	*8,871*
Official creditors	3,507	7,056	7,758	7,958	8,618	8,870
Multilateral	3,130	6,157	6,758	6,981	7,556	7,906
of which: World Bank	1,426	3,469	3,966	4,155	4,367	4,531
Bilateral	377	899	1,001	976	1,062	964
Private creditors	..	1	1	1	1	0
Bondholders	..	..	..	..	..	..
Commercial banks and others	..	1	1	1	1	0
Private nonguaranteed debt from:	..	*118*	*166*	*271*	*213*	*114*
Bondholders	..	..	..	..	..	..
Commercial banks and others	..	118	166	271	213	114
Use of IMF credit and SDR allocations	**219**	**370**	**560**	**633**	**733**	**744**
IMF credit	114	272	255	342	440	459
SDR allocations	105	98	306	291	293	285
Short-term external debt stocks	**61**	**361**	**335**	**322**	**418**	**423**
Disbursements, long-term	**126**	**1,158**	**1,170**	**940**	**916**	**798**
Public and publicly guaranteed sector	126	1,158	1,122	835	916	798
Private sector not guaranteed	..	..	48	105	..	..
Principal repayments, long-term	**148**	**205**	**213**	**243**	**335**	**413**
Public and publicly guaranteed sector	148	205	213	243	277	314
Private sector not guaranteed	..	..	..	..	58	99
Interest payments, long-term	**32**	**59**	**66**	**74**	**85**	**77**
Public and publicly guaranteed sector	32	54	63	65	74	70
Private sector not guaranteed	..	6	2	9	11	6

NICARAGUA

(US$ million, unless otherwise indicated)

Snapshot	2024
Total external debt stocks	**15,491**
External debt stocks as % of:	
Exports	182
GNI	83
Debt service as % of:	
Exports	21
GNI	10
Net financial flows, debt and equity	1,455
Net debt inflows	243
Net equity inflows	1,212
GNI	**18,705**
Population (million)	**7**

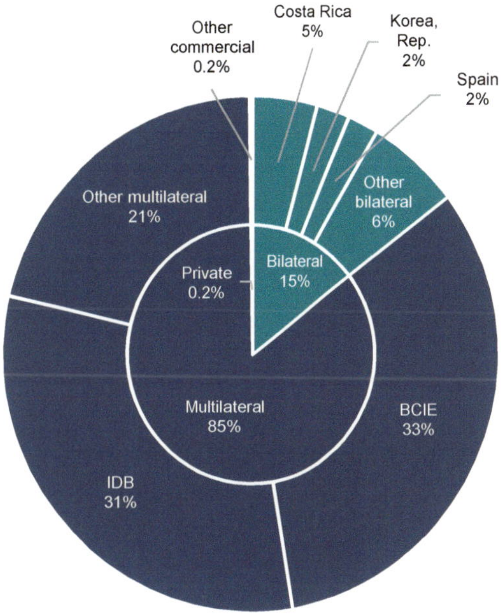

Figure 1 Public and publicly guaranteed debt, by creditor and creditor type in 2024, including IMF credit

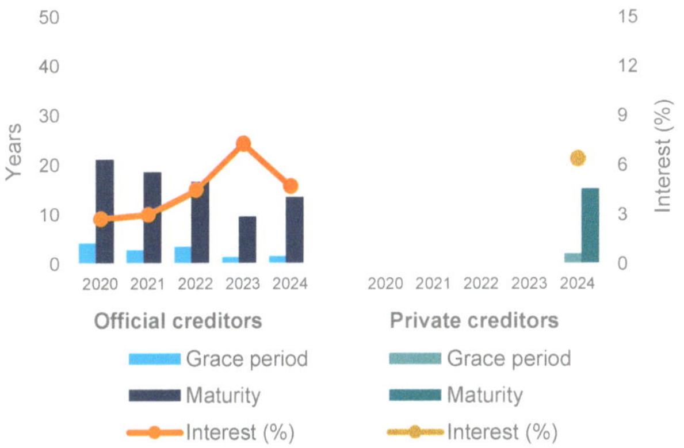

Figure 2 Average terms on new debt commitments from official and private creditors

Summary External Debt Data	2010	2020	2021	2022	2023	2024
Total external debt stocks	**7,017**	**13,840**	**14,825**	**15,131**	**15,360**	**15,491**
Long-term external debt stocks	**5,256**	**12,430**	**13,040**	**13,318**	**13,655**	**13,544**
Public and publicly guaranteed debt from:	*2,704*	*5,903*	*6,407*	*6,719*	*7,081*	*7,206*
Official creditors	2,694	5,879	6,386	6,701	7,065	7,192
Multilateral	1,661	4,653	5,193	5,550	5,929	6,122
of which: World Bank	447	771	872	886	915	974
Bilateral	1,033	1,225	1,193	1,151	1,137	1,070
Private creditors	11	25	21	18	16	14
Bondholders	..	..	..	..	..	..
Commercial banks and others	11	25	21	18	16	14
Private nonguaranteed debt from:	*2,552*	*6,527*	*6,632*	*6,599*	*6,573*	*6,338*
Bondholders	..	..	..	..	..	..
Commercial banks and others	2,552	6,527	6,632	6,599	6,573	6,338
Use of IMF credit and SDR allocations	**359**	**369**	**705**	**670**	**676**	**600**
IMF credit	167	190	182	173	174	113
SDR allocations	192	179	523	497	501	487
Short-term external debt stocks	**1,402**	**1,042**	**1,080**	**1,143**	**1,030**	**1,346**
Disbursements, long-term	**1,181**	**1,487**	**2,026**	**1,993**	**1,751**	**1,403**
Public and publicly guaranteed sector	267	652	811	660	717	530
Private sector not guaranteed	914	835	1,215	1,333	1,034	872
Principal repayments, long-term	**459**	**1,504**	**1,394**	**1,647**	**1,421**	**1,374**
Public and publicly guaranteed sector	56	230	257	295	360	357
Private sector not guaranteed	403	1,274	1,137	1,352	1,061	1,017
Interest payments, long-term	**103**	**289**	**207**	**234**	**330**	**358**
Public and publicly guaranteed sector	34	117	112	133	225	280
Private sector not guaranteed	70	171	95	101	105	79

NIGER

(US$ million, unless otherwise indicated)

Snapshot	2024
Total external debt stocks	**5,309**
External debt stocks as % of:	
Exports	264
GNI	28
Debt service as % of:	
Exports	19
GNI	2
Net financial flows, debt and equity	476
Net debt inflows	-50
Net equity inflows	526
GNI	**19,295**
Population (million)	**27**

Figure 1 Public and publicly guaranteed debt, by creditor and creditor type in 2024, including IMF credit

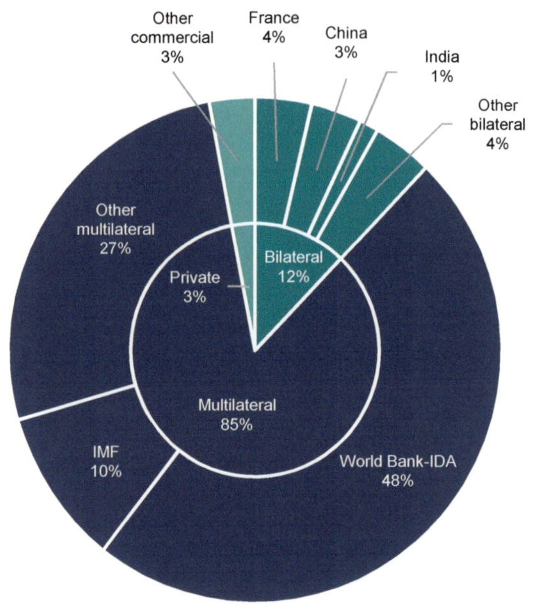

Figure 2 Average terms on new debt commitments from official and private creditors

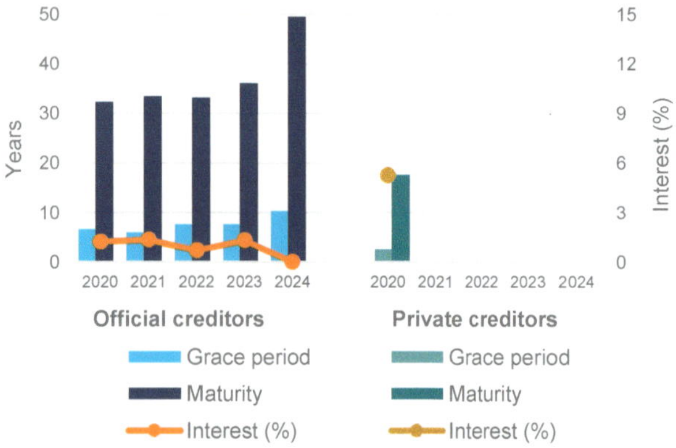

Summary External Debt Data	2010	2020	2021	2022	2023	2024
Total external debt stocks	**1,534**	**4,549**	**4,967**	**5,429**	**5,614**	**5,309**
Long-term external debt stocks	**1,206**	**4,003**	**4,238**	**4,649**	**4,834**	**4,528**
Public and publicly guaranteed debt from:	*1,206*	*4,003*	*4,238*	*4,649*	*4,834*	*4,528*
Official creditors	1,205	3,784	4,035	4,466	4,653	4,379
Multilateral	664	3,057	3,314	3,765	3,963	3,767
of which: World Bank	275	1,694	1,863	2,310	2,461	2,432
Bilateral	541	726	721	702	690	612
Private creditors	1	219	202	183	182	149
Bondholders	..	..	..	..	..	..
Commercial banks and others	1	219	202	183	182	149
Private nonguaranteed debt from:	*0*	..	..	..	..	..
Bondholders	..	..	..	..	..	..
Commercial banks and others	0	..	..	..	..	..
Use of IMF credit and SDR allocations	**158**	**498**	**687**	**737**	**736**	**752**
IMF credit	61	407	423	486	482	505
SDR allocations	97	91	265	252	254	247
Short-term external debt stocks	**170**	**48**	**42**	**43**	**43**	**30**
Disbursements, long-term	**279**	**743**	**563**	**818**	**184**	**171**
Public and publicly guaranteed sector	279	743	563	818	184	171
Private sector not guaranteed	..	..	..	..	..	..
Principal repayments, long-term	**16**	**124**	**133**	**193**	**111**	**257**
Public and publicly guaranteed sector	9	124	133	193	111	257
Private sector not guaranteed	7	..	..	..	..	..
Interest payments, long-term	**8**	**50**	**64**	**65**	**36**	**79**
Public and publicly guaranteed sector	8	50	64	65	36	79
Private sector not guaranteed	0	..	..	..	..	..

NIGERIA

(US$ million, unless otherwise indicated)

Snapshot	2024
Total external debt stocks	**108,758**
External debt stocks as % of:	
Exports	177
GNI	60
Debt service as % of:	
Exports	22
GNI	7
Net financial flows, debt and equity	10,614
Net debt inflows	7,285
Net equity inflows	3,329
GNI	**181,128**
Population (million)	**233**

Figure 1 Public and publicly guaranteed debt, by creditor and creditor type in 2024, including IMF credit

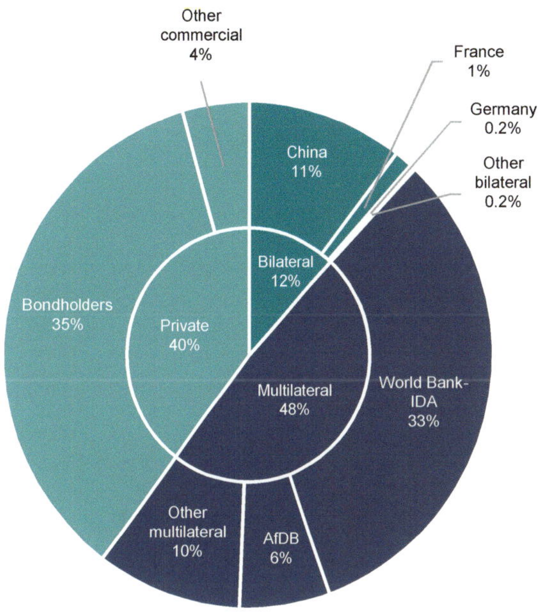

Figure 2 Average terms on new debt commitments from official and private creditors

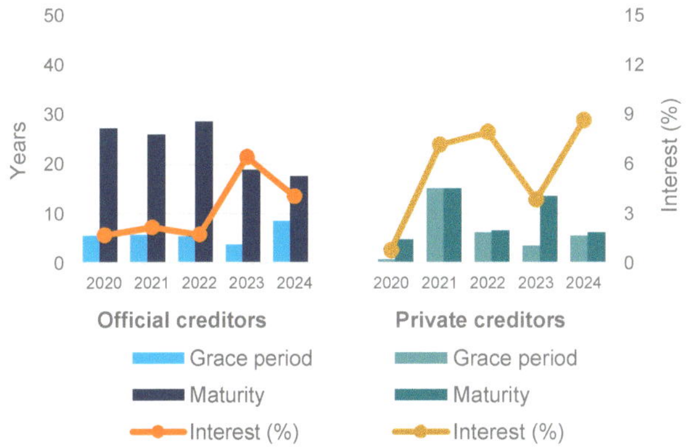

Summary External Debt Data	2010	2020	2021	2022	2023	2024
Total external debt stocks	**29,149**	**87,591**	**96,255**	**103,064**	**102,473**	**108,758**
Long-term external debt stocks	**17,128**	**63,219**	**68,608**	**72,935**	**76,305**	**80,477**
Public and publicly guaranteed debt from:	*4,686*	*32,057*	*36,150*	*39,981*	*44,040*	*50,192*
Official creditors	4,686	18,518	19,719	22,139	27,133	29,898
Multilateral	4,304	14,328	15,261	17,022	21,097	23,800
of which: World Bank	3,705	11,415	12,310	13,996	15,611	17,843
Bilateral	381	4,190	4,458	5,117	6,037	6,098
Private creditors	0	13,540	16,430	17,843	16,907	20,294
Bondholders	..	11,168	14,668	16,365	15,892	18,046
Commercial banks and others	0	2,371	1,762	1,478	1,015	2,248
Private nonguaranteed debt from:	*12,443*	*31,162*	*32,458*	*32,954*	*32,265*	*30,286*
Bondholders	..	5,817	5,900	4,550	4,200	4,200
Commercial banks and others	12,443	25,345	26,558	28,404	28,065	26,086
Use of IMF credit and SDR allocations	**2,580**	**5,948**	**9,073**	**8,627**	**7,874**	**6,053**
IMF credit	0	3,535	3,435	3,267	2,470	800
SDR allocations	2,580	2,413	5,637	5,361	5,404	5,253
Short-term external debt stocks	**9,441**	**18,424**	**18,574**	**21,502**	**18,294**	**22,227**
Disbursements, long-term	**3,370**	**7,752**	**11,708**	**10,067**	**7,498**	**11,924**
Public and publicly guaranteed sector	1,051	4,379	6,093	5,953	5,622	8,495
Private sector not guaranteed	2,319	3,373	5,615	4,114	1,876	3,429
Principal repayments, long-term	**248**	**3,250**	**5,846**	**5,046**	**4,225**	**6,952**
Public and publicly guaranteed sector	248	451	1,527	1,427	1,780	1,661
Private sector not guaranteed	..	2,799	4,319	3,618	2,445	5,292
Interest payments, long-term	**212**	**1,949**	**1,862**	**2,350**	**3,096**	**3,314**
Public and publicly guaranteed sector	59	1,115	1,118	1,485	1,788	2,199
Private sector not guaranteed	152	834	743	865	1,308	1,114

NORTH MACEDONIA

(US$ million, unless otherwise indicated)

Snapshot	2024
Total external debt stocks	**12,837**
External debt stocks as % of:	
Exports	120
GNI	81
Debt service as % of:	
Exports	14
GNI	10
Net financial flows, debt and equity	1,385
Net debt inflows	776
Net equity inflows	609
GNI	**15,818**
Population (million)	**2**

Figure 2 Average terms on new debt commitments from official and private creditors

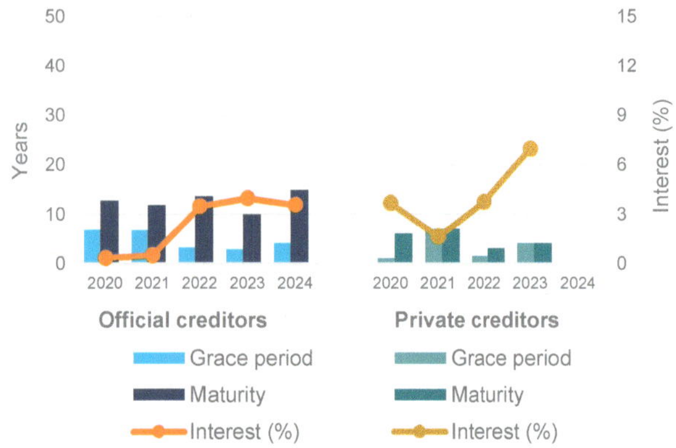

Figure 1 Public and publicly guaranteed debt, by creditor and creditor type in 2024, including IMF credit

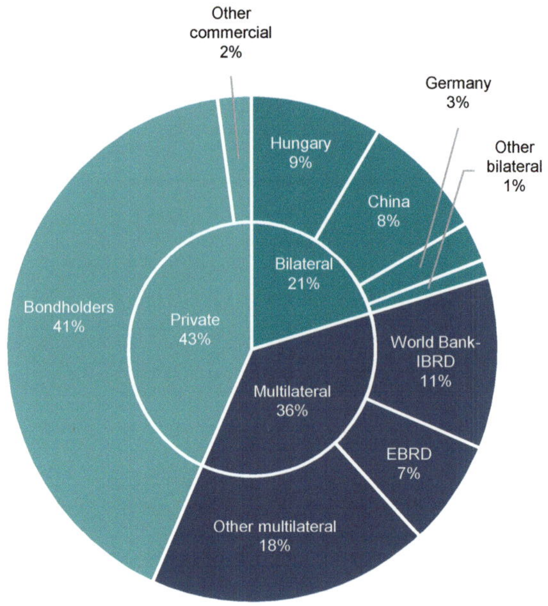

Summary External Debt Data	2010	2020	2021	2022	2023	2024
Total external debt stocks	**5,117**	**10,177**	**10,871**	**11,640**	**12,520**	**12,837**
Long-term external debt stocks	**3,798**	**7,752**	**7,955**	**7,962**	**8,857**	**9,086**
Public and publicly guaranteed debt from:	*1,880*	*5,102*	*5,092*	*5,096*	*5,655*	*5,748*
Official creditors	1,369	2,390	2,391	2,309	2,718	3,120
Multilateral	1,127	1,735	1,770	1,692	1,987	1,881
of which: World Bank	681	856	799	761	875	781
Bilateral	242	655	621	617	731	1,239
Private creditors	512	2,712	2,701	2,787	2,938	2,628
Bondholders	434	2,638	2,662	2,507	2,652	2,493
Commercial banks and others	77	74	39	280	286	135
Private nonguaranteed debt from:	*1,917*	*2,650*	*2,864*	*2,866*	*3,202*	*3,338*
Bondholders	..	8	7	6	7	7
Commercial banks and others	1,917	2,642	2,856	2,859	3,195	3,331
Use of IMF credit and SDR allocations	**101**	**297**	**476**	**565**	**523**	**572**
IMF credit	0	202	196	299	254	311
SDR allocations	101	95	280	266	268	261
Short-term external debt stocks	**1,218**	**2,128**	**2,440**	**3,113**	**3,140**	**3,179**
Disbursements, long-term	**613**	**1,806**	**1,965**	**1,153**	**1,913**	**1,694**
Public and publicly guaranteed sector	197	1,202	1,178	504	1,131	853
Private sector not guaranteed	416	605	787	649	782	841
Principal repayments, long-term	**443**	**951**	**1,241**	**787**	**1,371**	**980**
Public and publicly guaranteed sector	98	625	829	238	736	441
Private sector not guaranteed	344	326	412	549	634	540
Interest payments, long-term	**128**	**151**	**179**	**154**	**226**	**267**
Public and publicly guaranteed sector	56	112	129	107	155	199
Private sector not guaranteed	71	38	50	47	71	68

PAKISTAN

(US$ million, unless otherwise indicated)

Snapshot	2024
Total external debt stocks	**129,718**
External debt stocks as % of:	
Exports	315
GNI	36
Debt service as % of:	
Exports	40
GNI	4
Net financial flows, debt and equity	2,827
Net debt inflows	354
Net equity inflows	2,473
GNI	**364,086**
Population (million)	**251**

Figure 1 Public and publicly guaranteed debt, by creditor and creditor type in 2024, including IMF credit

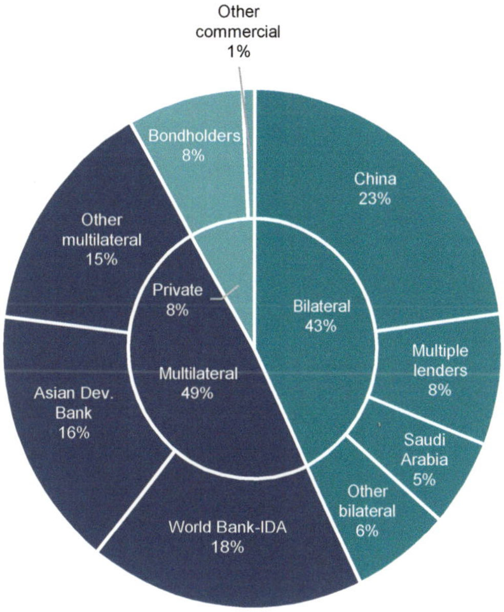

Figure 2 Average terms on new debt commitments from official and private creditors

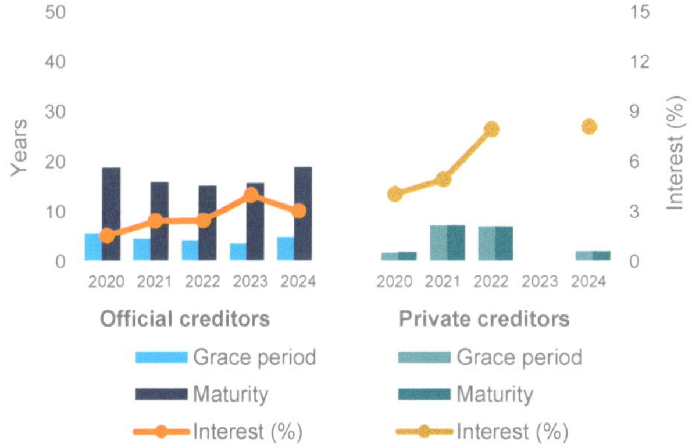

Summary External Debt Data	2010	2020	2021	2022	2023	2024
Total external debt stocks	**63,408**	**117,949**	**130,752**	**127,601**	**131,021**	**129,718**
Long-term external debt stocks	**48,483**	**101,817**	**110,838**	**107,312**	**110,548**	**107,788**
Public and publicly guaranteed debt from:	*44,010*	*86,908*	*95,293*	*91,114*	*93,096*	*89,556*
Official creditors	42,359	76,737	81,566	80,718	84,090	81,495
Multilateral	24,670	33,339	34,323	36,193	38,578	39,537
of which: World Bank	11,806	17,176	18,262	18,071	19,990	20,184
Bilateral	17,689	43,398	47,244	44,524	45,512	41,958
Private creditors	1,651	10,171	13,726	10,396	9,006	8,061
Bondholders	1,550	5,300	8,300	8,300	8,300	7,300
Commercial banks and others	101	4,871	5,426	2,096	706	761
Private nonguaranteed debt from:	*4,473*	*14,909*	*15,545*	*16,198*	*17,452*	*18,232*
Bondholders	250	12	0	..	..	..
Commercial banks and others	4,223	14,897	15,545	16,198	17,452	18,232
Use of IMF credit and SDR allocations	**10,258**	**8,902**	**10,841**	**11,522**	**11,532**	**12,321**
IMF credit	8,736	7,479	6,733	7,615	7,594	8,493
SDR allocations	1,522	1,424	4,108	3,906	3,938	3,828
Short-term external debt stocks	**4,667**	**7,230**	**9,074**	**8,768**	**8,941**	**9,609**
Disbursements, long-term	**3,960**	**14,424**	**18,997**	**11,834**	**13,248**	**7,705**
Public and publicly guaranteed sector	1,869	13,049	17,477	10,117	10,790	5,246
Private sector not guaranteed	2,091	1,375	1,520	1,718	2,458	2,459
Principal repayments, long-term	**3,046**	**7,491**	**8,880**	**12,182**	**9,751**	**9,150**
Public and publicly guaranteed sector	2,163	6,596	7,997	11,117	8,548	7,471
Private sector not guaranteed	883	895	883	1,065	1,203	1,679
Interest payments, long-term	**891**	**2,258**	**2,181**	**3,201**	**4,327**	**4,672**
Public and publicly guaranteed sector	791	1,701	1,741	2,661	3,373	3,745
Private sector not guaranteed	100	557	439	540	953	927

PAPUA NEW GUINEA

(US$ million, unless otherwise indicated)

Snapshot	2024
Total external debt stocks	**12,854**
External debt stocks as % of:	
Exports	95
GNI	42
Debt service as % of:	
Exports	43
GNI	19
Net financial flows, debt and equity	-2,120
Net debt inflows	-2,274
Net equity inflows	154
GNI	**30,689**
Population (million)	**11**

Figure 1 Public and publicly guaranteed debt, by creditor and creditor type in 2024, including IMF credit

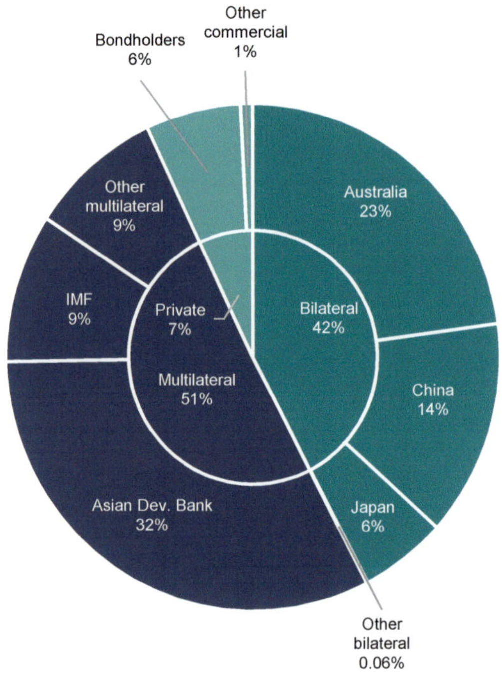

Figure 2 Average terms on new debt commitments from official and private creditors

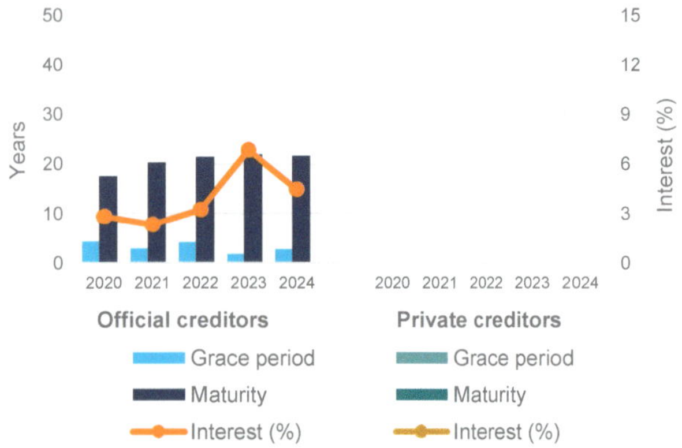

Summary External Debt Data	2010	2020	2021	2022	2023	2024
Total external debt stocks	**5,987**	**18,047**	**19,712**	**19,607**	**15,484**	**12,854**
Long-term external debt stocks	**5,380**	**17,088**	**15,905**	**15,706**	**14,428**	**11,478**
Public and publicly guaranteed debt from:	*1,042*	*5,142*	*6,047*	*6,749*	*7,142*	*7,253*
Official creditors	1,009	4,210	5,453	6,169	6,570	6,693
Multilateral	712	2,565	2,923	3,159	3,201	3,291
of which: World Bank	225	480	562	545	569	584
Bilateral	297	1,646	2,530	3,010	3,369	3,402
Private creditors	33	931	594	580	572	560
Bondholders	..	500	500	500	500	500
Commercial banks and others	33	431	94	80	72	60
Private nonguaranteed debt from:	*4,337*	*11,947*	*9,858*	*8,957*	*7,286*	*4,226*
Bondholders	..	..	..	..	..	..
Commercial banks and others	4,337	11,947	9,858	8,957	7,286	4,226
Use of IMF credit and SDR allocations	**193**	**560**	**897**	**853**	**1,037**	**1,255**
IMF credit	0	379	368	350	530	762
SDR allocations	193	181	529	503	507	493
Short-term external debt stocks	**414**	**399**	**2,910**	**3,047**	**19**	**121**
Disbursements, long-term	**3,153**	**1,538**	**2,552**	**3,060**	**3,571**	**2,571**
Public and publicly guaranteed sector	37	1,538	1,539	1,192	701	745
Private sector not guaranteed	3,116	..	1,013	1,868	2,870	1,826
Principal repayments, long-term	**758**	**2,500**	**3,716**	**3,927**	**4,952**	**5,201**
Public and publicly guaranteed sector	67	845	538	239	297	375
Private sector not guaranteed	691	1,654	3,178	3,688	4,655	4,826
Interest payments, long-term	**50**	**201**	**332**	**516**	**668**	**650**
Public and publicly guaranteed sector	16	143	107	130	219	248
Private sector not guaranteed	33	58	226	386	449	401

PARAGUAY

(US$ million, unless otherwise indicated)

Snapshot	2024
Total external debt stocks	**29,963**
External debt stocks as % of:	
Exports	168
GNI	70
Debt service as % of:	
Exports	11
GNI	5
Net financial flows, debt and equity	3,953
Net debt inflows	3,387
Net equity inflows	565
GNI	**42,964**
Population (million)	**7**

Figure 1 Public and publicly guaranteed debt, by creditor and creditor type in 2024, including IMF credit

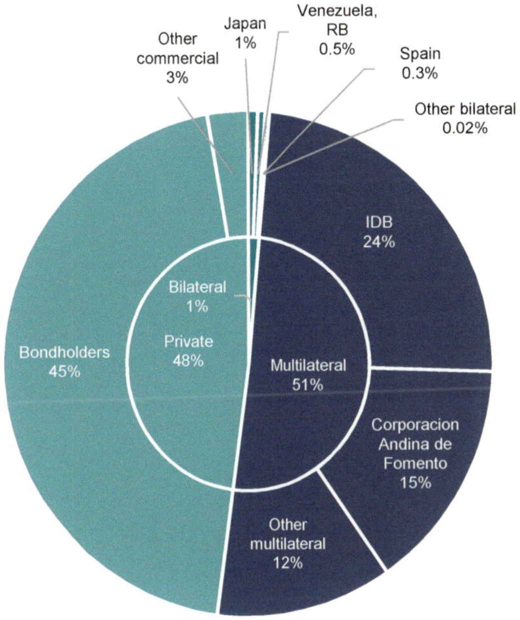

Figure 2 Average terms on new debt commitments from official and private creditors

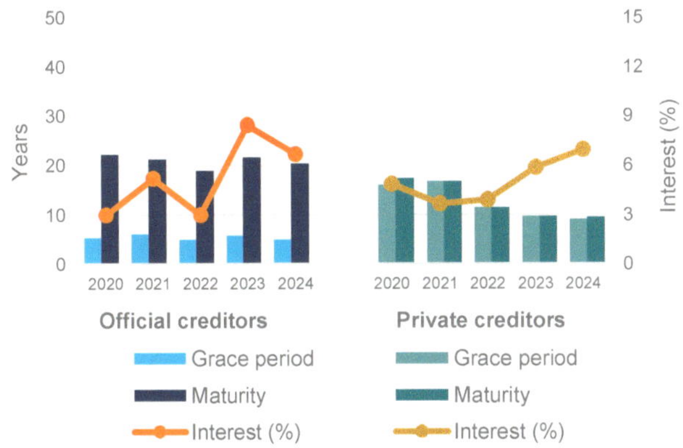

Summary External Debt Data	2010	2020	2021	2022	2023	2024
Total external debt stocks	**16,123**	**21,121**	**22,658**	**25,240**	**26,605**	**29,963**
Long-term external debt stocks	**14,951**	**19,066**	**20,383**	**22,540**	**23,455**	**26,028**
Public and publicly guaranteed debt from:	*2,390*	*10,651*	*11,811*	*13,339*	*14,353*	*15,744*
Official creditors	2,123	4,917	5,511	6,824	7,646	8,202
Multilateral	1,510	4,672	5,249	6,579	7,425	7,974
of which: World Bank	270	852	882	887	1,119	1,134
Bilateral	613	244	263	245	221	229
Private creditors	267	5,734	6,300	6,515	6,707	7,542
Bondholders	..	5,360	5,856	6,071	6,263	7,121
Commercial banks and others	267	374	443	443	443	421
Private nonguaranteed debt from:	*12,561*	*8,415*	*8,572*	*9,201*	*9,103*	*10,284*
Bondholders	..	1,150	1,450	1,150	1,150	1,150
Commercial banks and others	12,561	7,265	7,122	8,051	7,953	9,134
Use of IMF credit and SDR allocations	**147**	**137**	**403**	**384**	**387**	**376**
IMF credit	0	0	0	0	0	0
SDR allocations	147	137	403	384	387	376
Short-term external debt stocks	**1,025**	**1,918**	**1,872**	**2,316**	**2,763**	**3,559**
Disbursements, long-term	**2,076**	**4,496**	**2,082**	**2,524**	**1,597**	**3,141**
Public and publicly guaranteed sector	308	3,443	1,738	2,088	1,594	1,943
Private sector not guaranteed	1,769	1,053	344	436	3	1,198
Principal repayments, long-term	**314**	**668**	**741**	**1,359**	**675**	**549**
Public and publicly guaranteed sector	240	219	554	534	573	533
Private sector not guaranteed	75	449	188	825	102	16
Interest payments, long-term	**183**	**460**	**492**	**662**	**947**	**1,202**
Public and publicly guaranteed sector	65	359	365	456	682	910
Private sector not guaranteed	118	101	127	206	265	293

PERU

(US$ million, unless otherwise indicated)

Snapshot	2024
Total external debt stocks	**93,269**
External debt stocks as % of:	
Exports	105
GNI	34
Debt service as % of:	
Exports	17
GNI	6
Net financial flows, debt and equity	7,606
Net debt inflows	592
Net equity inflows	7,014
GNI	**272,491**
Population (million)	**34**

Figure 1 Public and publicly guaranteed debt, by creditor and creditor type in 2024, including IMF credit

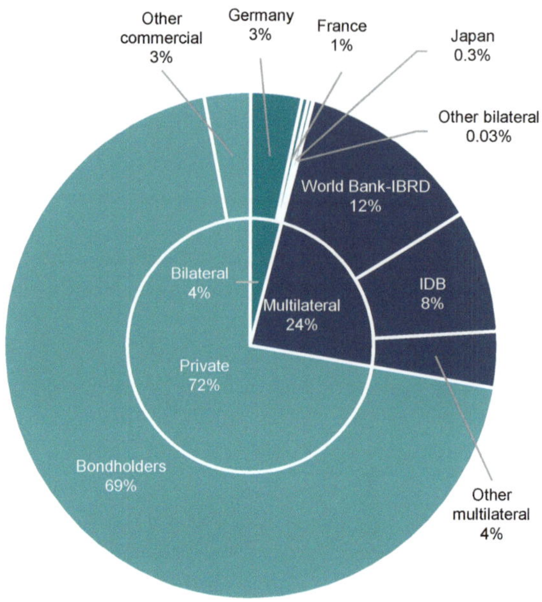

Figure 2 Average terms on new debt commitments from official and private creditors

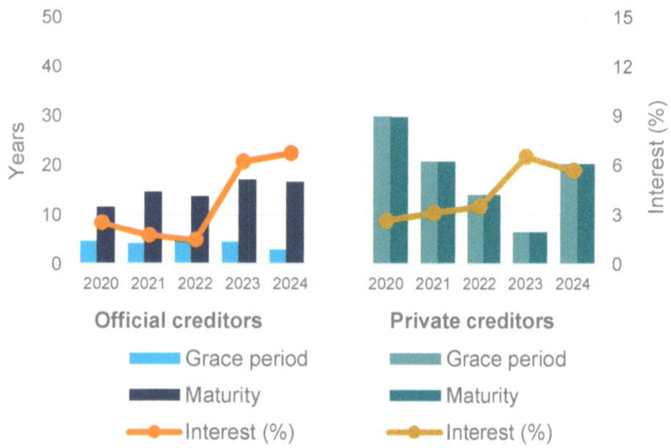

Summary External Debt Data	2010	2020	2021	2022	2023	2024
Total external debt stocks	**42,154**	**74,849**	**88,977**	**91,689**	**93,992**	**93,269**
Long-term external debt stocks	**34,822**	**63,687**	**76,048**	**78,649**	**78,735**	**80,331**
Public and publicly guaranteed debt from:	*20,009*	*30,545*	*43,720*	*45,054*	*44,867*	*47,363*
Official creditors	10,672	7,503	9,786	10,773	11,920	13,095
Multilateral	7,870	6,123	8,621	9,267	10,308	11,142
of which: World Bank	2,965	3,441	4,685	4,860	5,284	5,750
Bilateral	2,802	1,380	1,165	1,506	1,612	1,954
Private creditors	9,337	23,042	33,934	34,281	32,947	34,268
Bondholders	9,311	21,765	32,634	32,975	31,347	32,812
Commercial banks and others	26	1,277	1,300	1,306	1,600	1,455
Private nonguaranteed debt from:	*14,813*	*33,142*	*32,329*	*33,595*	*33,868*	*32,968*
Bondholders	727	17,200	16,995	16,665	15,725	17,082
Commercial banks and others	14,086	15,942	15,334	16,930	18,143	15,886
Use of IMF credit and SDR allocations	**939**	**878**	**2,644**	**2,514**	**2,534**	**2,463**
IMF credit	0	0	0	0	0	0
SDR allocations	939	878	2,644	2,514	2,534	2,463
Short-term external debt stocks	**6,393**	**10,284**	**10,285**	**10,527**	**12,722**	**10,474**
Disbursements, long-term	**5,425**	**13,663**	**19,790**	**6,347**	**7,986**	**13,022**
Public and publicly guaranteed sector	3,862	10,143	14,010	2,695	2,542	5,439
Private sector not guaranteed	1,563	3,519	5,780	3,652	5,444	7,583
Principal repayments, long-term	**4,060**	**5,811**	**6,734**	**3,390**	**8,174**	**10,183**
Public and publicly guaranteed sector	3,490	507	441	1,004	2,898	2,608
Private sector not guaranteed	570	5,304	6,294	2,386	5,276	7,574
Interest payments, long-term	**2,550**	**2,097**	**2,342**	**3,164**	**4,210**	**4,353**
Public and publicly guaranteed sector	1,096	983	1,190	1,545	2,043	2,128
Private sector not guaranteed	1,454	1,114	1,152	1,619	2,167	2,225

PHILIPPINES

(US$ million, unless otherwise indicated)

Snapshot	2024
Total external debt stocks	**137,018**
External debt stocks as % of:	
Exports	110
GNI	26
Debt service as % of:	
Exports	14
GNI	3
Net financial flows, debt and equity	17,520
Net debt inflows	14,902
Net equity inflows	2,618
GNI	**521,766**
Population (million)	**116**

Figure 1 Public and publicly guaranteed debt, by creditor and creditor type in 2024, including IMF credit

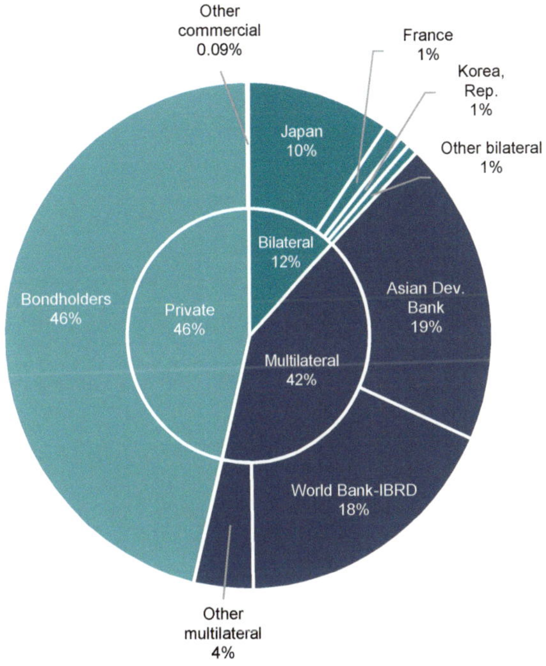

Figure 2 Average terms on new debt commitments from official and private creditors

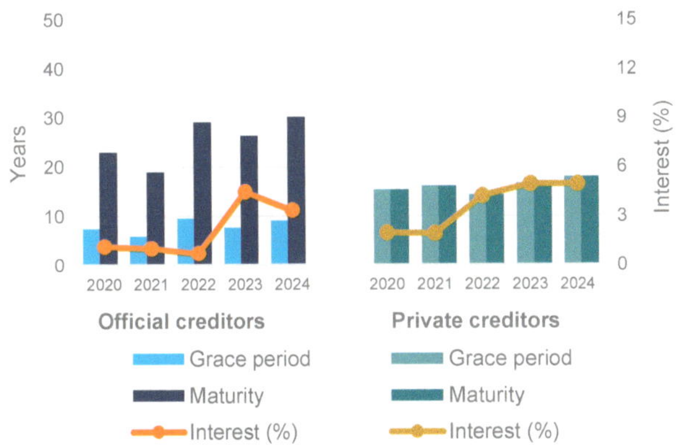

Summary External Debt Data	2010	2020	2021	2022	2023	2024
Total external debt stocks	**65,344**	**98,504**	**106,639**	**110,776**	**124,472**	**137,018**
Long-term external debt stocks	**53,542**	**83,089**	**87,636**	**90,435**	**103,625**	**112,427**
Public and publicly guaranteed debt from:	*45,080*	*56,508*	*59,696*	*62,617*	*72,914*	*80,509*
Official creditors	23,207	29,425	32,788	35,066	39,389	43,242
Multilateral	8,372	19,678	22,930	25,396	29,100	33,384
of which: World Bank	2,738	8,100	9,740	10,649	12,424	14,603
Bilateral	14,835	9,747	9,858	9,670	10,290	9,857
Private creditors	21,873	27,083	26,909	27,551	33,525	37,267
Bondholders	20,590	26,062	26,256	27,158	33,346	37,195
Commercial banks and others	1,283	1,021	652	393	179	72
Private nonguaranteed debt from:	*8,462*	*26,581*	*27,940*	*27,818*	*30,712*	*31,918*
Bondholders	1,651	8,987	10,791	9,420	7,420	7,541
Commercial banks and others	6,811	17,593	17,149	18,399	23,292	24,377
Use of IMF credit and SDR allocations	**1,290**	**1,207**	**3,913**	**3,721**	**3,751**	**3,646**
IMF credit	0	0	0	0	0	0
SDR allocations	1,290	1,207	3,913	3,721	3,751	3,646
Short-term external debt stocks	**10,512**	**14,209**	**15,090**	**16,619**	**17,096**	**20,945**
Disbursements, long-term	**10,928**	**20,996**	**15,986**	**13,231**	**24,378**	**23,093**
Public and publicly guaranteed sector	8,251	15,039	11,917	9,599	14,383	15,352
Private sector not guaranteed	2,677	5,957	4,069	3,632	9,995	7,741
Principal repayments, long-term	**8,341**	**6,869**	**9,361**	**6,278**	**9,660**	**12,041**
Public and publicly guaranteed sector	6,813	3,356	5,653	3,165	2,497	5,437
Private sector not guaranteed	1,527	3,513	3,708	3,113	7,163	6,604
Interest payments, long-term	**3,113**	**2,935**	**2,757**	**3,257**	**4,871**	**5,794**
Public and publicly guaranteed sector	2,977	2,295	2,104	2,339	3,635	4,235
Private sector not guaranteed	135	640	653	918	1,237	1,559

RWANDA

(US$ million, unless otherwise indicated)

Snapshot	2024
Total external debt stocks	**13,050**
External debt stocks as % of:	
Exports	242
GNI	94
Debt service as % of:	
Exports	8
GNI	3
Net financial flows, debt and equity	2,207
Net debt inflows	1,900
Net equity inflows	308
GNI	**13,901**
Population (million)	**14**

Figure 2 Average terms on new debt commitments from official and private creditors

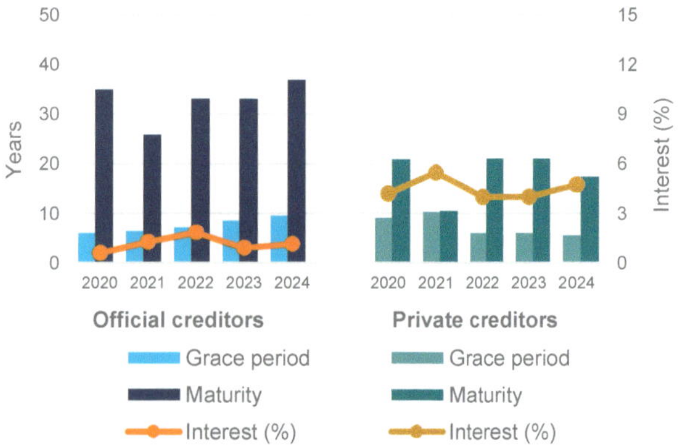

Figure 1 Public and publicly guaranteed debt, by creditor and creditor type in 2024, including IMF credit

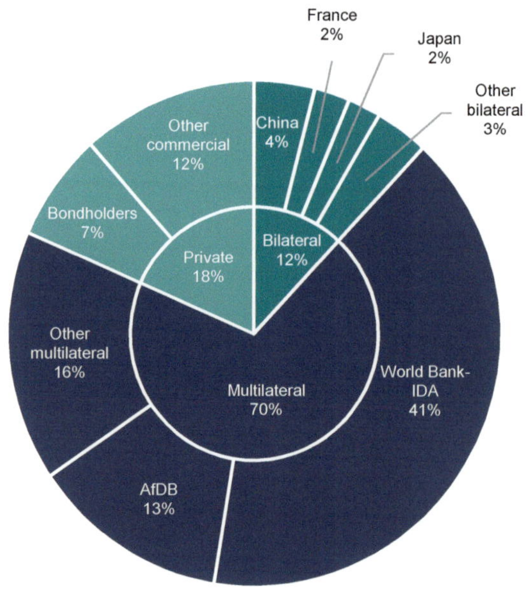

Summary External Debt Data	2010	2020	2021	2022	2023	2024
Total external debt stocks	**1,233**	**8,194**	**9,318**	**9,690**	**11,384**	**13,050**
Long-term external debt stocks	**1,086**	**7,295**	**8,226**	**8,701**	**10,127**	**11,447**
Public and publicly guaranteed debt from:	*759*	*5,122*	*5,794*	*6,145*	*7,231*	*8,346*
Official creditors	759	4,377	4,739	4,970	5,921	6,656
Multilateral	639	3,737	3,924	4,135	5,009	5,568
of which: World Bank	259	2,432	2,575	2,696	3,270	3,721
Bilateral	120	640	815	835	913	1,089
Private creditors	..	745	1,055	1,174	1,309	1,689
Bondholders	..	475	775	765	651	632
Commercial banks and others	..	270	280	410	659	1,058
Private nonguaranteed debt from:	*327*	*2,173*	*2,432*	*2,556*	*2,896*	*3,102*
Bondholders	..	..	..	..	..	..
Commercial banks and others	327	2,173	2,432	2,556	2,896	3,102
Use of IMF credit and SDR allocations	**133**	**520**	**678**	**613**	**813**	**1,102**
IMF credit	15	410	356	306	504	802
SDR allocations	118	111	322	307	309	300
Short-term external debt stocks	**14**	**378**	**414**	**376**	**443**	**501**
Disbursements, long-term	**182**	**1,368**	**1,483**	**822**	**1,654**	**1,746**
Public and publicly guaranteed sector	63	1,086	1,207	659	1,250	1,452
Private sector not guaranteed	119	282	276	163	404	295
Principal repayments, long-term	**41**	**102**	**424**	**124**	**262**	**222**
Public and publicly guaranteed sector	8	52	406	85	198	132
Private sector not guaranteed	33	50	18	39	64	89
Interest payments, long-term	**10**	**148**	**148**	**183**	**222**	**154**
Public and publicly guaranteed sector	6	61	55	81	106	113
Private sector not guaranteed	4	87	93	102	116	41

SAMOA

(US$ million, unless otherwise indicated)

Snapshot	2024
Total external debt stocks	**394.9**
External debt stocks as % of:	
Exports	97.5
GNI	37.6
Debt service as % of:	
Exports	9.0
GNI	3.5
Net financial flows, debt and equity	-21.9
Net debt inflows	-27.7
Net equity inflows	5.8
GNI	**1,051.5**
Population (thousand)	**218**

Figure 2 Average terms on new debt commitments from official and private creditors

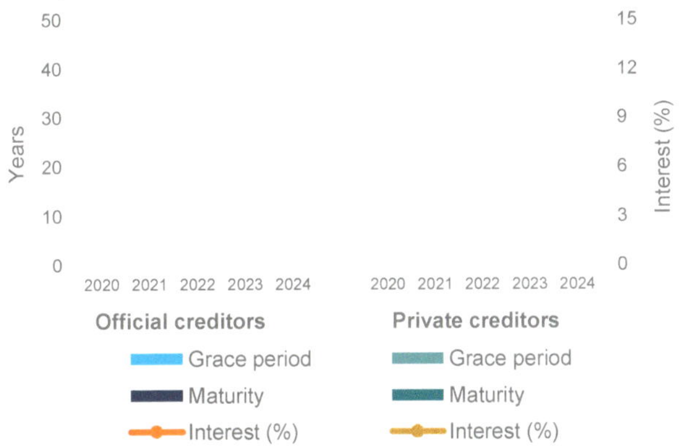

Figure 1 Public and publicly guaranteed debt, by creditor and creditor type in 2024, including IMF credit

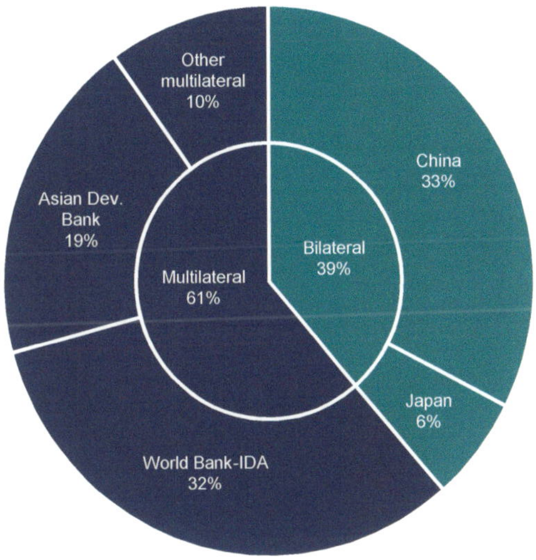

Summary External Debt Data	2010	2020	2021	2022	2023	2024
Total external debt stocks	**325.1**	**477.3**	**505.6**	**470.7**	**432.5**	**394.9**
Long-term external debt stocks	**299.1**	**395.9**	**394.6**	**341.6**	**308.6**	**270.6**
Public and publicly guaranteed debt from:	*299.1*	*393.9*	*381.0*	*328.8*	*296.2*	*258.3*
Official creditors	299.1	393.9	381.0	328.8	296.2	258.3
Multilateral	219.2	206.1	189.2	173.1	164.6	150.2
of which: World Bank	99.3	114.6	107.8	99.1	96.3	89.9
Bilateral	79.9	187.8	191.8	155.7	131.6	108.2
Private creditors	..	..	..	..	..	..
Bondholders	..	..	..	..	..	..
Commercial banks and others	..	..	..	..	..	..
Private nonguaranteed debt from:	..	*2.0*	*13.6*	*12.8*	*12.4*	*12.2*
Bondholders	..	..	..	..	..	..
Commercial banks and others	..	2.0	13.6	12.8	12.4	12.2
Use of IMF credit and SDR allocations	**26.0**	**43.5**	**62.4**	**57.8**	**57.4**	**55.8**
IMF credit	8.9	27.5	25.1	22.3	21.7	21.1
SDR allocations	17.1	16.0	37.3	35.4	35.7	34.7
Short-term external debt stocks	**0.0**	**37.9**	**48.7**	**71.3**	**66.4**	**68.5**
Disbursements, long-term	**78.9**	**3.1**	**2.3**	**3.4**	**0.9**	**0.6**
Public and publicly guaranteed sector	78.9	3.1	0.0	3.4	0.9	0.6
Private sector not guaranteed	..	0.0	2.3	..	..	..
Principal repayments, long-term	**7.2**	**18.1**	**12.0**	**29.7**	**30.9**	**30.4**
Public and publicly guaranteed sector	7.2	18.1	11.3	28.9	30.5	30.2
Private sector not guaranteed	..	..	0.7	0.8	0.4	0.2
Interest payments, long-term	**3.3**	**3.9**	**2.7**	**5.2**	**4.5**	**4.1**
Public and publicly guaranteed sector	3.3	3.8	2.6	5.2	4.5	4.0
Private sector not guaranteed	..	0.1	0.0	0.0	0.1	0.0

Note: Figure 2 shows no data values because the country did not have new commitments from 2020 to 2024.

SÃO TOMÉ AND PRÍNCIPE

(US$ million, unless otherwise indicated)

Snapshot	2024
Total external debt stocks	**326.4**
External debt stocks as % of:	
Exports	216.7
GNI	42.7
Debt service as % of:	
Exports	3.5
GNI	0.7
Net financial flows, debt and equity	40.7
Net debt inflows	18.8
Net equity inflows	21.9
GNI	**763.6**
Population (thousand)	**236**

Figure 1 Public and publicly guaranteed debt, by creditor and creditor type in 2024, including IMF credit

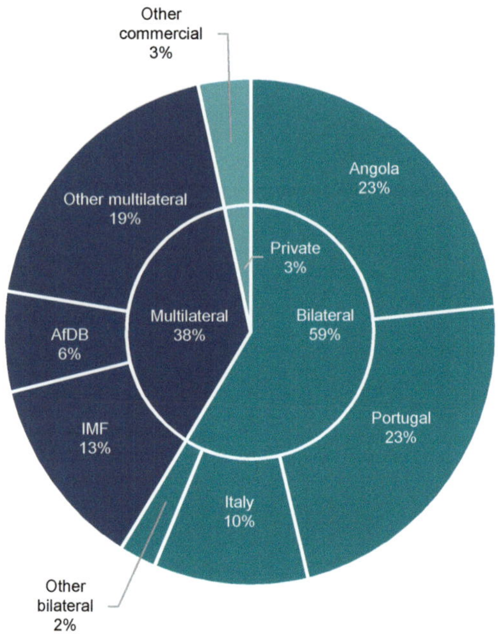

Figure 2 Average terms on new debt commitments from official and private creditors

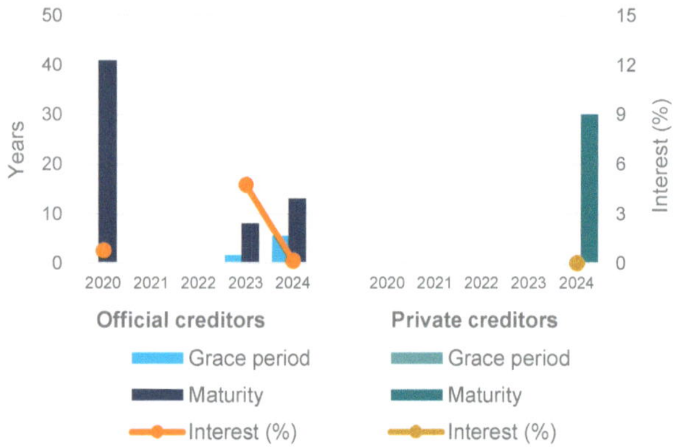

Summary External Debt Data	2010	2020	2021	2022	2023	2024
Total external debt stocks	**177.7**	**312.9**	**327.5**	**286.9**	**318.5**	**326.4**
Long-term external debt stocks	**142.3**	**252.6**	**245.6**	**218.3**	**248.8**	**254.5**
Public and publicly guaranteed debt from:	*142.3*	*252.6*	*245.6*	*218.3*	*248.8*	*254.5*
Official creditors	142.3	242.6	235.6	208.3	238.8	244.5
Multilateral	37.3	55.9	54.0	51.1	77.7	73.8
of which: World Bank	14.2	11.3	10.7	9.9	9.6	9.0
Bilateral	105.0	186.7	181.5	157.1	161.1	170.7
Private creditors	..	10.0	10.0	10.0	10.0	10.0
Bondholders	..	..	..	..	..	..
Commercial banks and others	..	10.0	10.0	10.0	10.0	10.0
Private nonguaranteed debt from:	..	..	..	..	..	..
Bondholders	..	..	..	..	..	..
Commercial banks and others	..	..	..	..	..	..
Use of IMF credit and SDR allocations	**15.9**	**37.0**	**60.5**	**62.0**	**61.5**	**63.9**
IMF credit	4.9	26.8	30.7	33.6	32.9	36.2
SDR allocations	10.9	10.2	29.8	28.3	28.6	27.8
Short-term external debt stocks	**19.6**	**23.3**	**21.4**	**6.7**	**8.2**	**7.9**
Disbursements, long-term	**19.8**	**5.9**	**2.3**	**2.6**	**27.3**	**16.6**
Public and publicly guaranteed sector	19.8	5.9	2.3	2.6	27.3	16.6
Private sector not guaranteed	..	..	..	..	..	..
Principal repayments, long-term	**1.2**	**1.3**	**2.0**	**4.8**	**2.6**	**2.2**
Public and publicly guaranteed sector	1.2	1.3	2.0	4.8	2.6	2.2
Private sector not guaranteed	..	..	..	..	..	..
Interest payments, long-term	**0.3**	**0.9**	**0.6**	**2.2**	**1.7**	**0.9**
Public and publicly guaranteed sector	0.3	0.9	0.6	2.2	1.7	0.9
Private sector not guaranteed	..	..	..	..	..	..

SENEGAL

(US$ million, unless otherwise indicated)

Snapshot	2024
Total external debt stocks	**47,146**
External debt stocks as % of:	
Exports	573
GNI	151
Debt service as % of:	
Exports	42
GNI	11
Net financial flows, debt and equity	4,886
Net debt inflows	2,870
Net equity inflows	2,016
GNI	**31,287**
Population (million)	**19**

Figure 1 Public and publicly guaranteed debt, by creditor and creditor type in 2024, including IMF credit

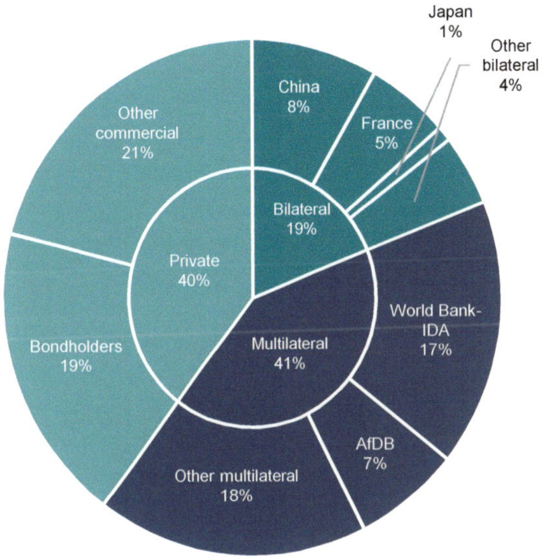

Figure 2 Average terms on new debt commitments from official and private creditors

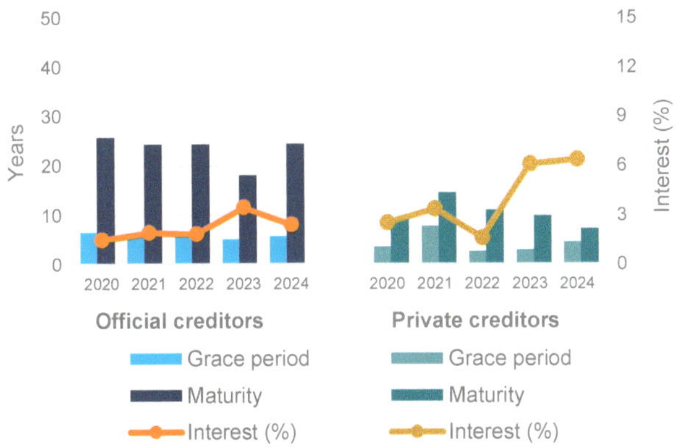

Summary External Debt Data	2010	2020	2021	2022	2023	2024
Total external debt stocks	**4,649**	**26,017**	**30,676**	**35,581**	**45,458**	**47,146**
Long-term external debt stocks	**4,197**	**23,585**	**26,498**	**30,356**	**38,334**	**40,542**
Public and publicly guaranteed debt from:	*3,150*	*16,109*	*16,924*	*17,896*	*22,415*	*25,094*
Official creditors	2,950	11,116	11,618	12,278	14,481	14,538
Multilateral	1,973	6,699	7,071	7,682	9,398	9,505
of which: World Bank	1,023	3,102	3,257	3,661	4,357	4,422
Bilateral	977	4,417	4,547	4,596	5,083	5,033
Private creditors	200	4,993	5,306	5,618	7,934	10,556
Bondholders	200	4,158	4,235	4,118	4,186	4,954
Commercial banks and others	0	835	1,071	1,500	3,749	5,602
Private nonguaranteed debt from:	*1,048*	*7,476*	*9,574*	*12,460*	*15,919*	*15,448*
Bondholders	..	..	..	..	..	..
Commercial banks and others	1,048	7,476	9,574	12,460	15,919	15,448
Use of IMF credit and SDR allocations	**451**	**689**	**1,285**	**1,609**	**2,266**	**2,034**
IMF credit	213	466	634	990	1,643	1,428
SDR allocations	238	223	651	619	624	606
Short-term external debt stocks	**0**	**1,743**	**2,894**	**3,616**	**4,858**	**4,570**
Disbursements, long-term	**1,045**	**4,335**	**4,672**	**5,071**	**8,221**	**4,844**
Public and publicly guaranteed sector	355	1,902	2,574	2,184	4,762	4,844
Private sector not guaranteed	690	2,433	2,098	2,887	3,458	..
Principal repayments, long-term	**84**	**425**	**1,033**	**507**	**691**	**1,513**
Public and publicly guaranteed sector	84	425	1,033	507	691	1,043
Private sector not guaranteed	..	..	..	..	..	470
Interest payments, long-term	**101**	**846**	**431**	**747**	**1,195**	**1,417**
Public and publicly guaranteed sector	64	397	364	393	595	862
Private sector not guaranteed	37	449	67	354	601	555

Note: Senegal's DRS data exclude external debt liabilities of state-owned enterprises.

SERBIA

(US$ million, unless otherwise indicated)

Snapshot	2024
Total external debt stocks	**51,984**
External debt stocks as % of:	
Exports	106
GNI	62
Debt service as % of:	
Exports	21
GNI	12
Net financial flows, debt and equity	7,668
Net debt inflows	3,187
Net equity inflows	4,481
GNI	**83,511**
Population (million)	**7**

Figure 2 Average terms on new debt commitments from official and private creditors

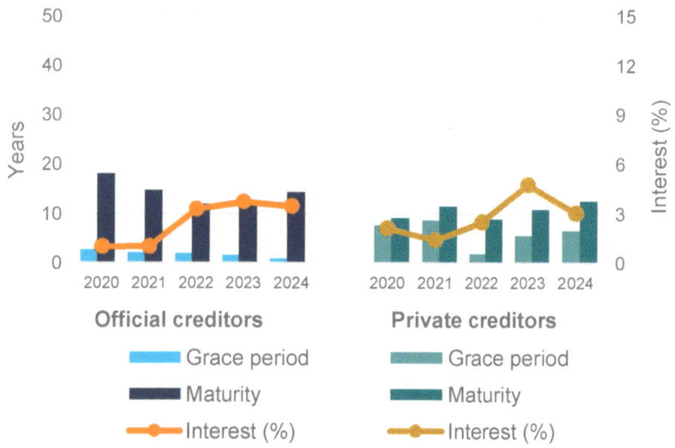

Figure 1 Public and publicly guaranteed debt, by creditor and creditor type in 2024, including IMF credit

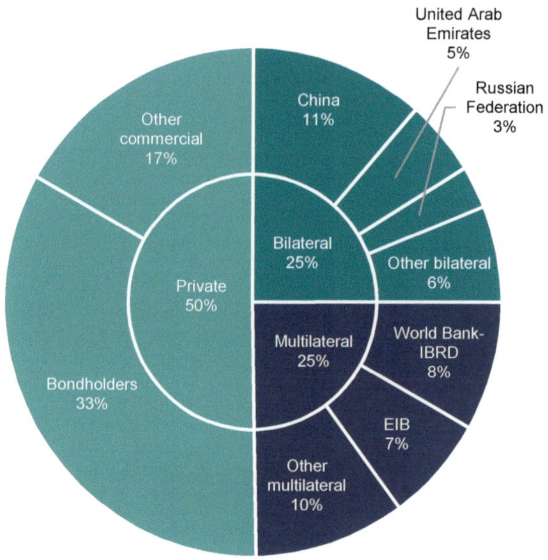

Summary External Debt Data	2010	2020	2021	2022	2023	2024
Total external debt stocks	**32,907**	**38,919**	**42,009**	**44,850**	**50,259**	**51,984**
Long-term external debt stocks	**27,389**	**36,376**	**38,514**	**39,816**	**46,576**	**48,346**
Public and publicly guaranteed debt from:	*9,477*	*19,248*	*21,461*	*22,225*	*26,388*	*27,971*
Official creditors	8,011	12,039	12,037	13,058	13,721	13,777
Multilateral	4,848	6,057	5,770	5,536	5,888	5,730
of which: World Bank	2,499	2,891	2,655	2,440	2,426	2,317
Bilateral	3,163	5,982	6,267	7,522	7,833	8,047
Private creditors	1,466	7,209	9,424	9,167	12,667	14,194
Bondholders	..	5,848	7,998	7,630	9,441	9,435
Commercial banks and others	1,466	1,361	1,426	1,537	3,226	4,758
Private nonguaranteed debt from:	*17,912*	*17,127*	*17,053*	*17,591*	*20,188*	*20,375*
Bondholders	165	..	..	..	..	..
Commercial banks and others	17,747	17,127	17,053	17,591	20,188	20,375
Use of IMF credit and SDR allocations	**2,720**	**641**	**1,501**	**2,473**	**2,713**	**2,637**
IMF credit	2,034	0	0	1,046	1,274	1,238
SDR allocations	685	641	1,501	1,428	1,439	1,399
Short-term external debt stocks	**2,798**	**1,902**	**1,993**	**2,561**	**970**	**1,001**
Disbursements, long-term	**4,594**	**9,052**	**8,328**	**7,776**	**10,473**	**11,262**
Public and publicly guaranteed sector	1,365	5,009	5,159	3,413	5,398	6,489
Private sector not guaranteed	3,230	4,043	3,169	4,363	5,075	4,773
Principal repayments, long-term	**3,431**	**4,411**	**5,213**	**5,304**	**4,050**	**8,095**
Public and publicly guaranteed sector	351	2,219	1,970	1,480	1,572	3,183
Private sector not guaranteed	3,081	2,193	3,243	3,825	2,478	4,913
Interest payments, long-term	**759**	**591**	**716**	**778**	**1,294**	**2,090**
Public and publicly guaranteed sector	321	477	426	428	825	1,080
Private sector not guaranteed	438	114	289	350	469	1,010

SIERRA LEONE

(US$ million, unless otherwise indicated)

Snapshot	2024
Total external debt stocks	**2,330**
External debt stocks as % of:	
Exports	144
GNI	31
Debt service as % of:	
Exports	9
GNI	2
Net financial flows, debt and equity	247
Net debt inflows	-27
Net equity inflows	274
GNI	**7,485**
Population (million)	**9**

Figure 1 Public and publicly guaranteed debt, by creditor and creditor type in 2024, including IMF credit

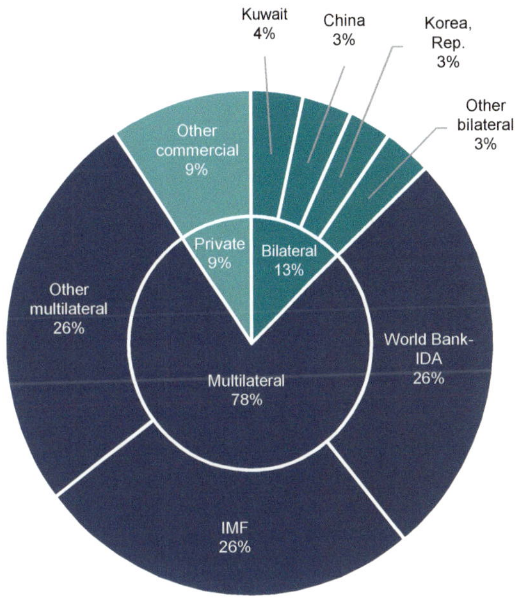

Figure 2 Average terms on new debt commitments from official and private creditors

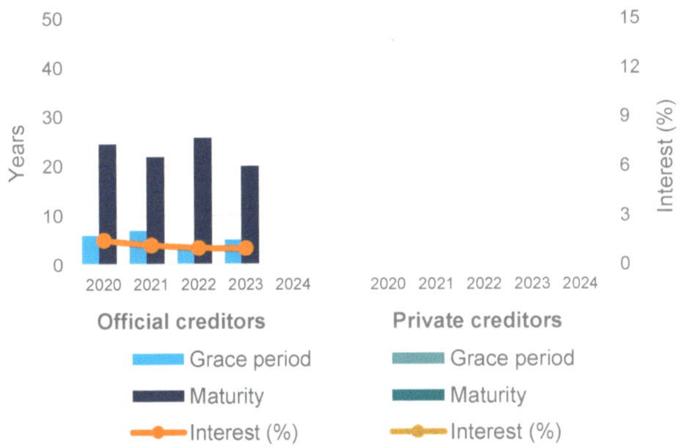

Summary External Debt Data	2010	2020	2021	2022	2023	2024
Total external debt stocks	**931**	**2,196**	**2,532**	**2,401**	**2,403**	**2,330**
Long-term external debt stocks	**661**	**1,360**	**1,387**	**1,348**	**1,364**	**1,314**
Public and publicly guaranteed debt from:	*661*	*1,360*	*1,387*	*1,348*	*1,364*	*1,314*
Official creditors	450	1,180	1,219	1,183	1,199	1,149
Multilateral	371	942	967	945	959	921
of which: World Bank	155	432	464	466	479	463
Bilateral	78	238	252	238	241	228
Private creditors	211	179	168	165	165	165
Bondholders	..	..	..	..	..	..
Commercial banks and others	211	179	168	165	165	165
Private nonguaranteed debt from:	..	..	..	..	..	..
Bondholders	..	..	..	..	..	..
Commercial banks and others	..	..	..	..	..	..
Use of IMF credit and SDR allocations	**266**	**652**	**959**	**892**	**880**	**842**
IMF credit	113	509	541	495	480	453
SDR allocations	153	143	417	397	400	389
Short-term external debt stocks	**4**	**184**	**186**	**162**	**159**	**174**
Disbursements, long-term	**66**	**135**	**100**	**51**	**69**	**27**
Public and publicly guaranteed sector	66	135	100	51	69	27
Private sector not guaranteed	..	..	..	..	..	..
Principal repayments, long-term	**5**	**46**	**51**	**56**	**58**	**57**
Public and publicly guaranteed sector	5	46	51	56	58	57
Private sector not guaranteed	..	..	..	..	..	..
Interest payments, long-term	**4**	**7**	**7**	**11**	**12**	**11**
Public and publicly guaranteed sector	4	7	7	11	12	11
Private sector not guaranteed	..	..	..	..	..	..

SOLOMON ISLANDS

(US$ million, unless otherwise indicated)

Snapshot	2024
Total external debt stocks	**596.1**
External debt stocks as % of:	
Exports	83.7
GNI	33.8
Debt service as % of:	
Exports	3.6
GNI	1.5
Net financial flows, debt and equity	102.6
Net debt inflows	76.0
Net equity inflows	26.5
GNI	**1,762.4**
Population (thousand)	**819**

Figure 1 Public and publicly guaranteed debt, by creditor and creditor type in 2024, including IMF credit

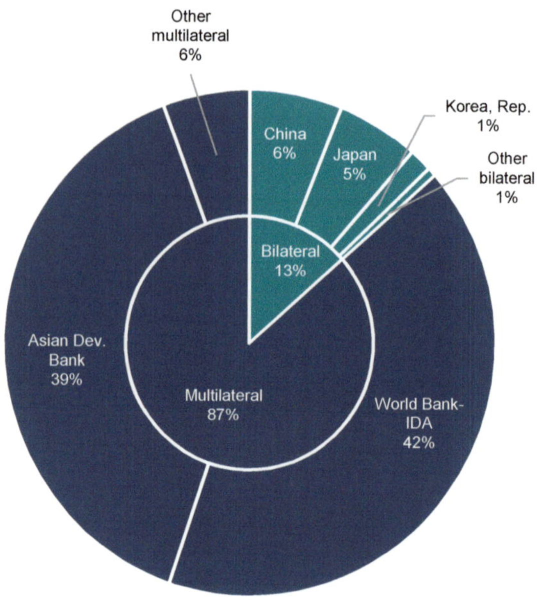

Figure 2 Average terms on new debt commitments from official and private creditors

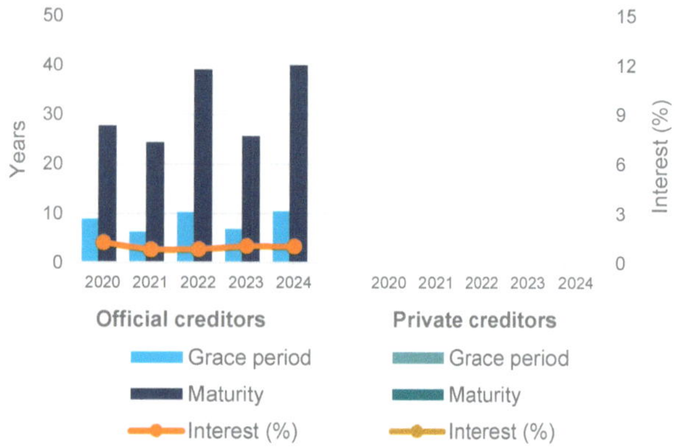

Summary External Debt Data	2010	2020	2021	2022	2023	2024
Total external debt stocks	**230.8**	**322.6**	**448.6**	**477.4**	**527.8**	**596.1**
Long-term external debt stocks	**201.9**	**270.5**	**325.3**	**350.1**	**423.4**	**514.3**
Public and publicly guaranteed debt from:	*125.3*	*124.0*	*140.8*	*154.8*	*197.6*	*284.8*
Official creditors	125.2	124.0	140.8	154.8	197.6	284.8
Multilateral	105.6	117.8	113.8	132.0	162.6	244.7
of which: World Bank	41.7	47.8	46.7	58.0	79.0	124.6
Bilateral	19.6	6.3	27.0	22.8	35.0	40.2
Private creditors	0.1	..	..	..	..	..
Bondholders	..	..	..	..	..	..
Commercial banks and others	0.1	..	..	..	..	..
Private nonguaranteed debt from:	*76.6*	*146.5*	*184.4*	*195.3*	*225.8*	*229.5*
Bondholders	..	..	..	..	..	..
Commercial banks and others	76.6	146.5	184.4	195.3	225.8	229.5
Use of IMF credit and SDR allocations	**24.9**	**25.3**	**71.7**	**67.9**	**63.6**	**52.6**
IMF credit	9.6	11.1	29.9	28.2	23.6	13.7
SDR allocations	15.3	14.3	41.8	39.7	40.0	38.9
Short-term external debt stocks	**4.0**	**26.8**	**51.7**	**59.3**	**40.8**	**29.2**
Disbursements, long-term	**36.8**	**41.8**	**66.4**	**39.0**	**93.5**	**106.9**
Public and publicly guaranteed sector	0.0	27.4	25.9	26.1	48.2	98.3
Private sector not guaranteed	36.8	14.4	40.6	12.9	45.3	8.6
Principal repayments, long-term	**17.5**	**28.9**	**7.7**	**7.0**	**19.5**	**9.8**
Public and publicly guaranteed sector	8.6	5.2	5.1	4.9	4.7	5.0
Private sector not guaranteed	8.9	23.7	2.6	2.1	14.8	4.9
Interest payments, long-term	**3.2**	**2.2**	**1.8**	**1.9**	**2.1**	**3.9**
Public and publicly guaranteed sector	1.7	1.1	1.4	1.2	1.5	1.9
Private sector not guaranteed	1.5	1.1	0.5	0.7	0.6	2.0

SOMALIA, FEDERAL REPUBLIC OF

(US$ million, unless otherwise indicated)

Snapshot	2024
Total external debt stocks	**1,799**
External debt stocks as % of:	
Exports	73
GNI	15
Debt service as % of:	
Exports	1
GNI	0
Net financial flows, debt and equity	781
Net debt inflows	16
Net equity inflows	765
GNI	**12,062**
Population (million)	**19**

Figure 1 Public and publicly guaranteed debt, by creditor and creditor type in 2024, including IMF credit

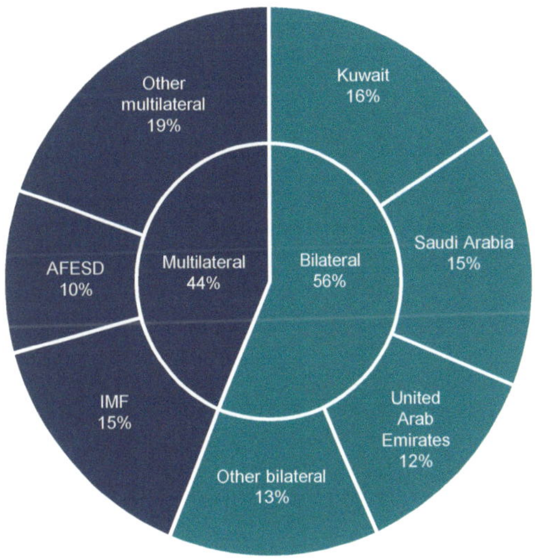

Figure 2 Average terms on new debt commitments from official and private creditors

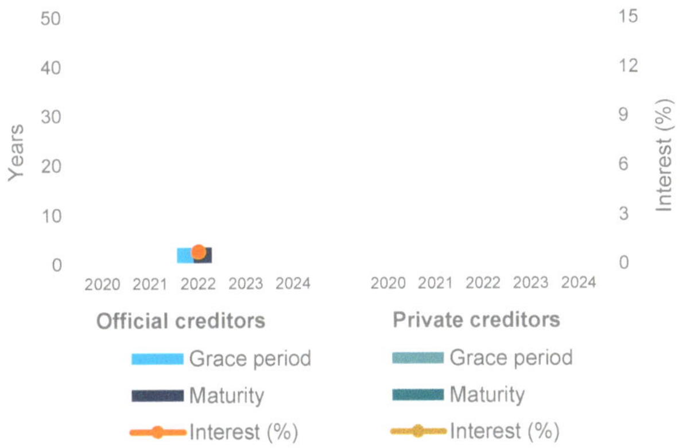

Summary External Debt Data	2010	2020	2021	2022	2023	2024
Total external debt stocks	**2,934**	**4,592**	**4,143**	**4,095**	**3,094**	**1,799**
Long-term external debt stocks	**1,879**	**2,609**	**2,313**	**2,311**	**2,019**	**664**
Public and publicly guaranteed debt from:	*1,879*	*2,609*	*2,313*	*2,311*	*2,019*	*664*
Official creditors	1,879	2,609	2,313	2,311	2,019	664
Multilateral	773	373	366	338	318	227
of which: World Bank	443	138	122	105	94	0
Bilateral	1,106	2,236	1,947	1,973	1,701	437
Private creditors	..	..	..	..	..	..
Bondholders	..	..	..	..	..	..
Commercial banks and others	..	..	..	..	..	..
Private nonguaranteed debt from:	..	..	..	..	..	..
Bondholders	..	..	..	..	..	..
Commercial banks and others	..	..	..	..	..	..
Use of IMF credit and SDR allocations	**244**	**444**	**650**	**646**	**375**	**384**
IMF credit	172	371	360	371	97	113
SDR allocations	72	73	290	276	278	270
Short-term external debt stocks	**811**	**1,540**	**1,179**	**1,138**	**700**	**752**
Disbursements, long-term	**0**	**0**	**0**	**0**	**0**	**0**
Public and publicly guaranteed sector	0	0	0	0	0	0
Private sector not guaranteed	..	..	..	..	..	..
Principal repayments, long-term	**0**	**350**	**15**	**14**	**15**	**4**
Public and publicly guaranteed sector	0	350	15	14	15	4
Private sector not guaranteed	..	..	..	..	..	..
Interest payments, long-term	**0**	**131**	**1**	**1**	**1**	**2**
Public and publicly guaranteed sector	0	131	1	1	1	2
Private sector not guaranteed	..	..	..	..	..	..

SOUTH AFRICA

(US$ million, unless otherwise indicated)

Snapshot	2024
Total external debt stocks	**175,896**
External debt stocks as % of:	
Exports	127
GNI	45
Debt service as % of:	
Exports	16
GNI	6
Net financial flows, debt and equity	9,626
Net debt inflows	10,432
Net equity inflows	-806
GNI	**392,353**
Population (million)	**64**

Figure 2 Average terms on new debt commitments from official and private creditors

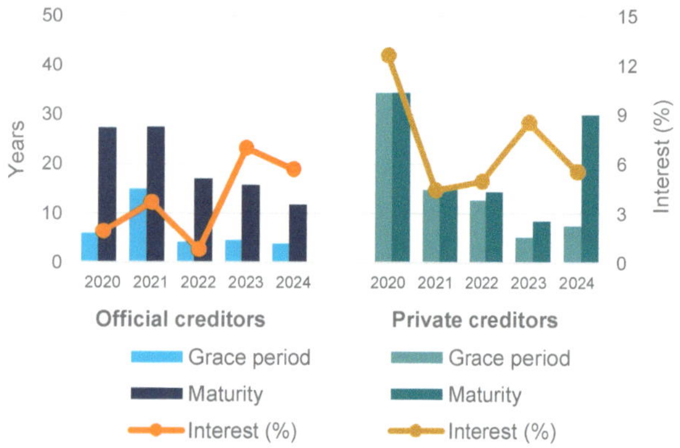

Figure 1 Public and publicly guaranteed debt, by creditor and creditor type in 2024, including IMF credit

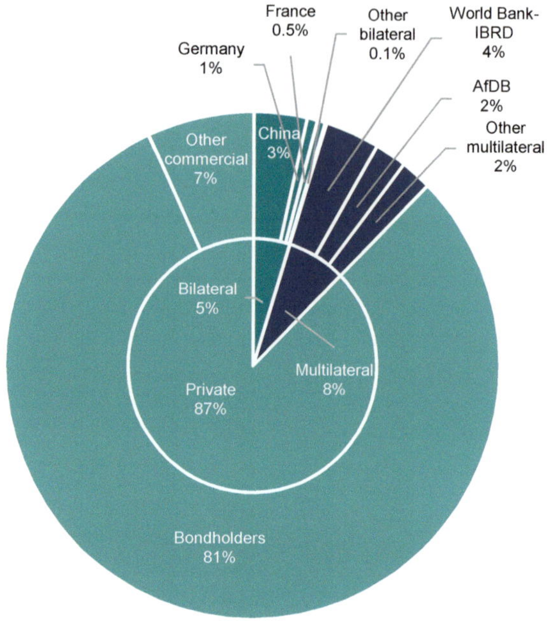

Summary External Debt Data	2010	2020	2021	2022	2023	2024
Total external debt stocks	**115,330**	**175,427**	**169,447**	**171,732**	**165,839**	**175,896**
Long-term external debt stocks	**80,508**	**131,384**	**122,293**	**118,454**	**113,719**	**121,433**
Public and publicly guaranteed debt from:	*36,338*	*99,446*	*95,187*	*91,245*	*89,526*	*97,813*
Official creditors	1,246	9,274	10,367	11,433	11,922	13,746
Multilateral	1,139	5,859	6,646	7,290	7,682	9,177
of which: World Bank	384	2,082	1,853	2,787	2,568	3,427
Bilateral	107	3,414	3,721	4,143	4,241	4,569
Private creditors	35,092	90,172	84,820	79,812	77,603	84,068
Bondholders	30,676	81,186	77,723	73,359	71,029	77,402
Commercial banks and others	4,416	8,986	7,097	6,453	6,574	6,666
Private nonguaranteed debt from:	*44,170*	*31,939*	*27,106*	*27,209*	*24,194*	*23,619*
Bondholders	8,786	2,700	2,870	2,823	1,702	1,428
Commercial banks and others	35,384	29,239	24,236	24,386	22,492	22,191
Use of IMF credit and SDR allocations	**2,750**	**6,966**	**10,862**	**10,329**	**9,901**	**7,634**
IMF credit	0	4,395	4,270	4,061	3,582	1,492
SDR allocations	2,750	2,571	6,592	6,268	6,319	6,142
Short-term external debt stocks	**32,073**	**37,077**	**36,292**	**42,949**	**42,219**	**46,828**
Disbursements, long-term	**12,114**	**12,830**	**11,103**	**19,690**	**10,087**	**20,219**
Public and publicly guaranteed sector	8,891	3,809	3,198	6,017	3,841	12,330
Private sector not guaranteed	3,224	9,020	7,905	13,673	6,247	7,889
Principal repayments, long-term	**3,474**	**20,614**	**19,848**	**20,834**	**14,769**	**12,371**
Public and publicly guaranteed sector	1,682	6,451	7,015	9,576	5,408	3,815
Private sector not guaranteed	1,792	14,163	12,833	11,258	9,361	8,556
Interest payments, long-term	**2,177**	**6,244**	**5,904**	**5,590**	**6,149**	**6,645**
Public and publicly guaranteed sector	1,559	4,664	4,317	4,103	4,600	5,117
Private sector not guaranteed	618	1,579	1,587	1,487	1,549	1,528

SRI LANKA

(US$ million, unless otherwise indicated)

Snapshot	2024
Total external debt stocks	**56,828**
External debt stocks as % of:	
Exports	280
GNI	59
Debt service as % of:	
Exports	24
GNI	5
Net financial flows, debt and equity	330
Net debt inflows	-431
Net equity inflows	761
GNI	**96,498**
Population (million)	**22**

Figure 2 Average terms on new debt commitments from official and private creditors

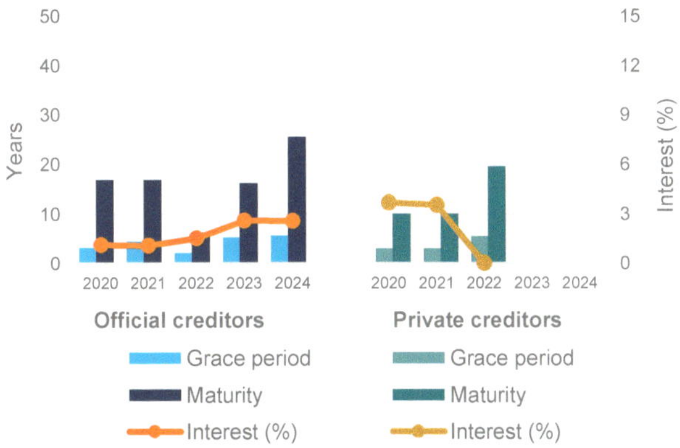

Figure 1 Public and publicly guaranteed debt, by creditor and creditor type in 2024, including IMF credit

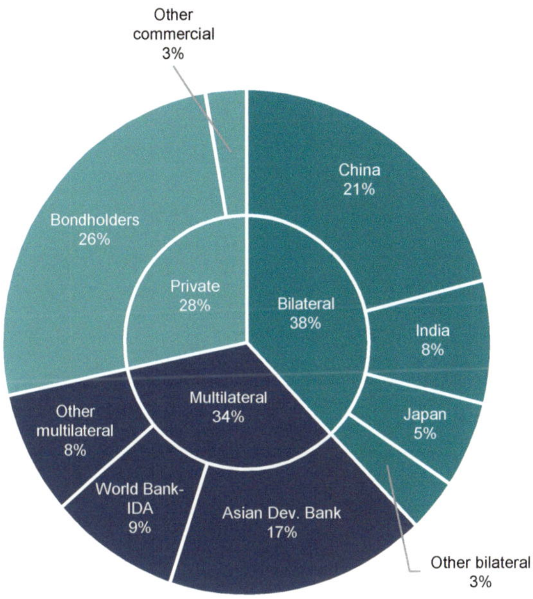

Summary External Debt Data	2010	2020	2021	2022	2023	2024
Total external debt stocks	**21,684**	**56,875**	**58,742**	**58,719**	**60,545**	**56,828**
Long-term external debt stocks	**17,349**	**46,552**	**47,523**	**47,803**	**50,394**	**48,111**
Public and publicly guaranteed debt from:	*16,430*	*37,569*	*38,491*	*38,488*	*41,392*	*39,542*
Official creditors	13,400	20,743	22,152	22,670	25,511	27,865
Multilateral	6,089	9,135	9,750	10,273	11,470	12,270
of which: World Bank	2,531	3,492	3,740	3,837	4,388	4,619
Bilateral	7,311	11,608	12,402	12,397	14,041	15,595
Private creditors	3,029	16,826	16,339	15,819	15,881	11,676
Bondholders	2,000	14,050	13,050	12,550	12,550	10,585
Commercial banks and others	1,029	2,776	3,289	3,269	3,331	1,092
Private nonguaranteed debt from:	*919*	*8,984*	*9,032*	*9,314*	*9,002*	*8,569*
Bondholders	0	175	175	175	175	175
Commercial banks and others	919	8,809	8,857	9,139	8,827	8,394
Use of IMF credit and SDR allocations	**1,920**	**1,927**	**2,593**	**2,326**	**2,854**	**2,898**
IMF credit	1,311	1,357	1,263	1,062	1,579	1,659
SDR allocations	609	570	1,330	1,265	1,275	1,239
Short-term external debt stocks	**2,416**	**8,396**	**8,626**	**8,590**	**7,297**	**5,818**
Disbursements, long-term	**3,091**	**3,392**	**4,538**	**3,330**	**4,126**	**2,513**
Public and publicly guaranteed sector	2,994	2,856	4,255	2,505	4,126	1,597
Private sector not guaranteed	97	536	283	826	..	916
Principal repayments, long-term	**727**	**3,323**	**3,043**	**2,018**	**1,378**	**3,191**
Public and publicly guaranteed sector	582	2,862	2,808	1,475	1,065	1,844
Private sector not guaranteed	145	461	235	543	313	1,348
Interest payments, long-term	**616**	**1,590**	**1,522**	**787**	**883**	**983**
Public and publicly guaranteed sector	596	1,492	1,337	540	483	876
Private sector not guaranteed	20	97	185	248	400	107

ST. LUCIA

(US$ million, unless otherwise indicated)

Snapshot	2024
Total external debt stocks	**1,194**
External debt stocks as % of:	
Exports	72
GNI	51
Debt service as % of:	
Exports	5
GNI	3
Net financial flows, debt and equity	243
Net debt inflows	104
Net equity inflows	139
GNI	**2,326**
Population (thousand)	**180**

Figure 2 Average terms on new debt commitments from official and private creditors

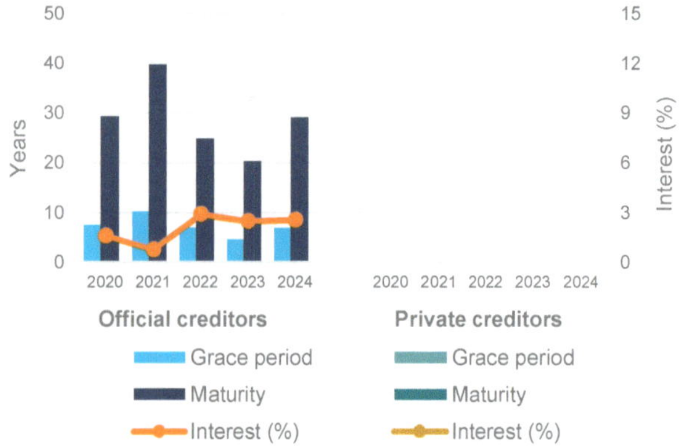

Figure 1 Public and publicly guaranteed debt, by creditor and creditor type in 2024, including IMF credit

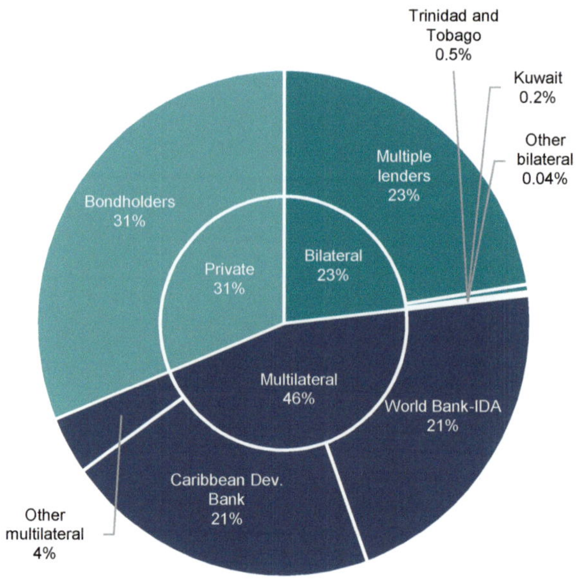

Summary External Debt Data	2010	2020	2021	2022	2023	2024
Total external debt stocks	**585**	**734**	**893**	**909**	**1,086**	**1,194**
Long-term external debt stocks	**326**	**604**	**722**	**737**	**930**	**1,041**
Public and publicly guaranteed debt from:	*326*	*604*	*722*	*737*	*930*	*1,041*
Official creditors	263	351	478	481	606	707
Multilateral	243	278	341	344	356	459
of which: World Bank	80	108	150	157	173	229
Bilateral	21	73	137	137	250	248
Private creditors	63	252	244	255	324	333
Bondholders	63	252	244	255	324	333
Commercial banks and others	..	..	..	..	..	..
Private nonguaranteed debt from:	..	..	..	..	..	..
Bondholders	..	..	..	..	..	..
Commercial banks and others	..	..	..	..	..	..
Use of IMF credit and SDR allocations	**33**	**52**	**79**	**75**	**76**	**74**
IMF credit	11	31	30	28	29	28
SDR allocations	22	21	49	47	47	46
Short-term external debt stocks	**225**	**78**	**92**	**98**	**80**	**80**
Disbursements, long-term	**36**	**94**	**148**	**29**	**146**	**127**
Public and publicly guaranteed sector	36	94	148	29	146	127
Private sector not guaranteed	..	..	..	..	..	..
Principal repayments, long-term	**30**	**18**	**19**	**21**	**23**	**23**
Public and publicly guaranteed sector	30	18	19	21	23	23
Private sector not guaranteed	..	..	..	..	..	..
Interest payments, long-term	**11**	**25**	**25**	**28**	**39**	**49**
Public and publicly guaranteed sector	11	25	25	28	39	49
Private sector not guaranteed	..	..	..	..	..	..

ST. VINCENT AND THE GRENADINES

(US$ million, unless otherwise indicated)

Snapshot	2024
Total external debt stocks	**806.4**
External debt stocks as % of:	
Exports	184.3
GNI	70.3
Debt service as % of:	
Exports	10.1
GNI	3.8
Net financial flows, debt and equity	181.6
Net debt inflows	117.3
Net equity inflows	64.2
GNI	**1,147.0**
Population (thousand)	**101**

Figure 1 Public and publicly guaranteed debt, by creditor and creditor type in 2024, including IMF credit

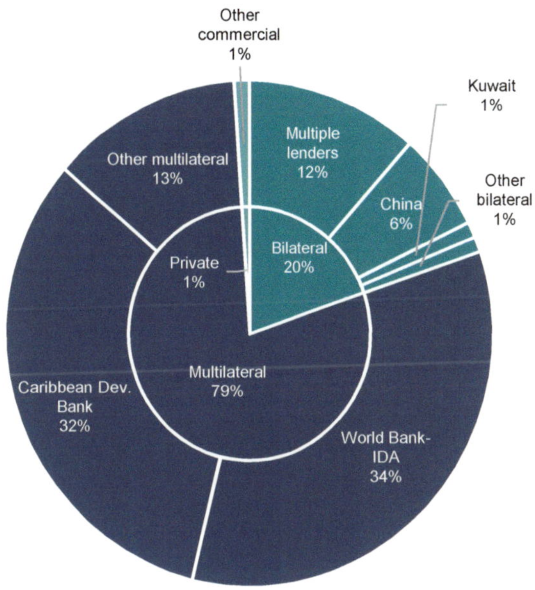

Figure 2 Average terms on new debt commitments from official and private creditors

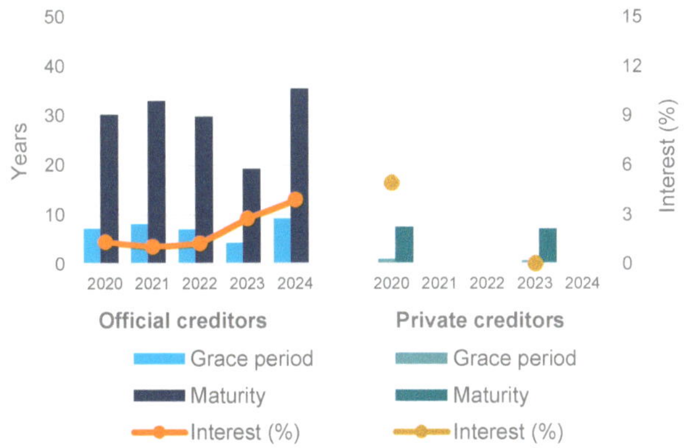

Summary External Debt Data	2010	2020	2021	2022	2023	2024
Total external debt stocks	**297.1**	**451.7**	**571.4**	**624.5**	**698.5**	**806.4**
Long-term external debt stocks	**279.1**	**366.4**	**452.6**	**504.8**	**579.3**	**690.6**
Public and publicly guaranteed debt from:	*279.1*	*366.4*	*452.6*	*504.8*	*579.3*	*690.6*
Official creditors	230.4	351.7	439.0	494.1	570.3	683.5
Multilateral	212.2	308.6	398.4	438.8	498.3	541.7
of which: World Bank	26.5	117.1	202.0	214.3	229.2	243.9
Bilateral	18.2	43.1	40.6	55.3	72.0	141.8
Private creditors	48.7	14.7	13.6	10.7	9.0	7.1
Bondholders	..	4.0	2.7	1.5	0.4	0.0
Commercial banks and others	48.7	10.7	10.9	9.2	8.5	7.1
Private nonguaranteed debt from:	..	..	..	..	..	..
Bondholders	..	..	..	..	..	..
Commercial banks and others	..	..	..	..	..	..
Use of IMF credit and SDR allocations	**17.9**	**31.3**	**56.3**	**53.0**	**52.9**	**50.9**
IMF credit	5.8	19.9	29.6	27.6	27.2	25.9
SDR allocations	12.2	11.4	26.8	25.5	25.7	24.9
Short-term external debt stocks	**0.0**	**54.0**	**62.5**	**66.7**	**66.3**	**65.0**
Disbursements, long-term	**79.3**	**70.8**	**112.1**	**80.3**	**95.3**	**144.3**
Public and publicly guaranteed sector	79.3	70.8	112.1	80.3	95.3	144.3
Private sector not guaranteed	..	..	..	..	..	..
Principal repayments, long-term	**26.0**	**32.1**	**24.2**	**23.4**	**23.2**	**25.1**
Public and publicly guaranteed sector	26.0	32.1	24.2	23.4	23.2	25.1
Private sector not guaranteed	..	..	..	..	..	..
Interest payments, long-term	**9.9**	**8.2**	**7.4**	**8.5**	**13.8**	**16.2**
Public and publicly guaranteed sector	9.9	8.2	7.4	8.5	13.8	16.2
Private sector not guaranteed	..	..	..	..	..	..

SUDAN

(US$ million, unless otherwise indicated)

Snapshot	2024
Total external debt stocks	**22,021**
External debt stocks as % of:	
Exports	..
GNI	45
Debt service as % of:	
Exports	..
GNI	0
Net financial flows, debt and equity	-167
Net debt inflows	-167
Net equity inflows	0
GNI	**48,505**
Population (million)	**50**

Figure 1 Public and publicly guaranteed debt, by creditor and creditor type in 2024, including IMF credit

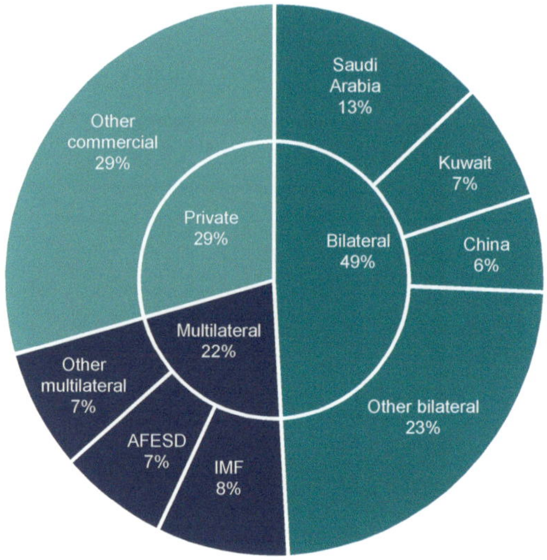

Figure 2 Average terms on new debt commitments from official and private creditors

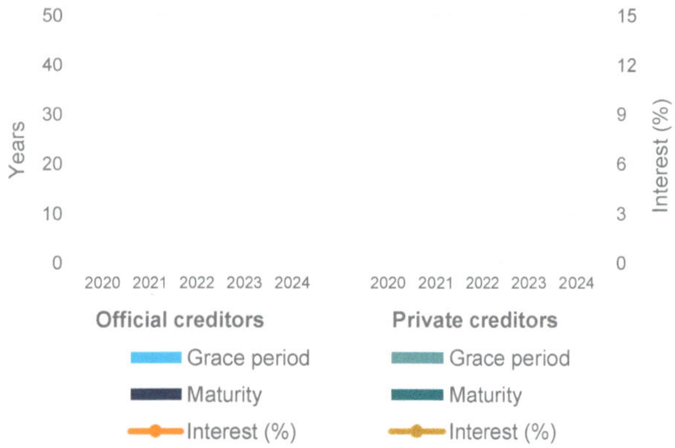

Summary External Debt Data	2010	2020	2021	2022	2023	2024
Total external debt stocks	**22,593**	**23,811**	**22,976**	**22,440**	**22,580**	**22,021**
Long-term external debt stocks	**14,638**	**17,084**	**15,611**	**15,253**	**15,364**	**14,951**
Public and publicly guaranteed debt from:	*14,638*	*17,084*	*15,611*	*15,253*	*15,364*	*14,951*
Official creditors	11,992	12,258	10,860	10,526	10,431	10,179
Multilateral	3,378	3,746	2,521	2,375	2,308	2,203
of which: World Bank	1,290	1,234	346	294	259	218
Bilateral	8,614	8,512	8,339	8,151	8,123	7,976
Private creditors	2,645	4,826	4,751	4,727	4,933	4,772
Bondholders	..	..	..	..	..	..
Commercial banks and others	2,645	4,826	4,751	4,727	4,933	4,772
Private nonguaranteed debt from:	..	..	..	..	..	..
Bondholders	..	..	..	..	..	..
Commercial banks and others	..	..	..	..	..	..
Use of IMF credit and SDR allocations	**664**	**548**	**2,505**	**2,382**	**2,401**	**2,334**
IMF credit	390	291	1,388	1,320	1,330	1,293
SDR allocations	274	256	1,117	1,062	1,071	1,041
Short-term external debt stocks	**7,292**	**6,179**	**4,860**	**4,806**	**4,815**	**4,736**
Disbursements, long-term	**935**	**8**	**4**	**0**	**0**	**0**
Public and publicly guaranteed sector	935	8	4	0	0	0
Private sector not guaranteed	..	..	..	..	..	..
Principal repayments, long-term	**400**	**111**	**1,238**	**147**	**139**	**137**
Public and publicly guaranteed sector	400	111	1,238	147	139	137
Private sector not guaranteed	..	..	..	..	..	..
Interest payments, long-term	**84**	**30**	**449**	**23**	**21**	**17**
Public and publicly guaranteed sector	84	30	449	23	21	17
Private sector not guaranteed	..	..	..	..	..	..

Note: Figure 2 shows no data values because the country did not have new commitments from 2020 to 2024.

SURINAME

(US$ million, unless otherwise indicated)

Snapshot	2024
Total external debt stocks	**4,372**
External debt stocks as % of:	
Exports	153
GNI	101
Debt service as % of:	
Exports	17
GNI	11
Net financial flows, debt and equity	294
Net debt inflows	299
Net equity inflows	-5
GNI	**4,348**
Population (thousand)	**634**

Figure 1 Public and publicly guaranteed debt, by creditor and creditor type in 2024, including IMF credit

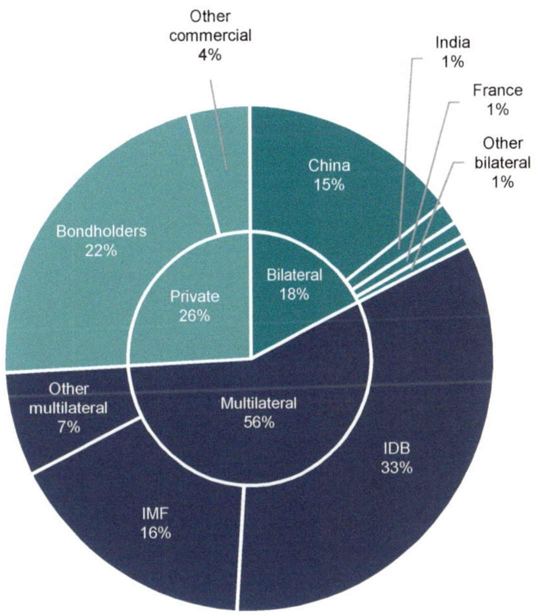

Figure 2 Average terms on new debt commitments from official and private creditors

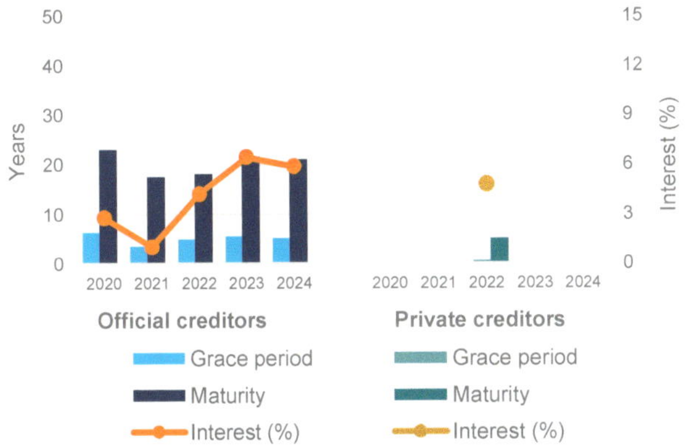

Summary External Debt Data	2010	2020	2021	2022	2023	2024
Total external debt stocks	..	**3,886**	**4,139**	**4,194**	**4,084**	**4,372**
Long-term external debt stocks	..	**3,385**	**3,280**	**3,395**	**3,285**	**3,293**
Public and publicly guaranteed debt from:	..	*2,059*	*2,031*	*2,208*	*2,394*	*2,525*
Official creditors	..	1,213	1,194	1,395	1,608	1,744
Multilateral	..	656	632	846	1,046	1,208
of which: World Bank	..	5	5	6	20	29
Bilateral	..	557	561	548	562	536
Private creditors	..	846	837	813	786	781
Bondholders	..	675	675	675	660	660
Commercial banks and others	..	171	162	138	126	121
Private nonguaranteed debt from:	..	*1,326*	*1,250*	*1,187*	*891*	*768*
Bondholders	..	2	2	2	2	2
Commercial banks and others	..	1,324	1,248	1,185	889	766
Use of IMF credit and SDR allocations	..	**148**	**351**	**387**	**548**	**777**
IMF credit	..	21	55	105	264	501
SDR allocations	..	127	296	282	284	276
Short-term external debt stocks	..	**353**	**508**	**412**	**251**	**302**
Disbursements, long-term	..	**266**	**298**	**464**	**399**	**320**
Public and publicly guaranteed sector	..	80	43	273	262	226
Private sector not guaranteed	..	186	255	191	137	93
Principal repayments, long-term	..	**306**	**318**	**319**	**513**	**297**
Public and publicly guaranteed sector	..	42	67	65	79	81
Private sector not guaranteed	..	264	251	254	433	216
Interest payments, long-term	..	**107**	**50**	**46**	**82**	**153**
Public and publicly guaranteed sector	..	58	24	19	48	127
Private sector not guaranteed	..	49	26	27	34	26

SYRIAN ARAB REPUBLIC

(US$ million, unless otherwise indicated)

Snapshot	2024
Total external debt stocks	**4,757**
External debt stocks as % of:	
Exports	..
GNI	..
Debt service as % of:	
Exports	..
GNI	..
Net financial flows, debt and equity	0
Net debt inflows	0
Net equity inflows	..
GNI	**..**
Population (million)	**25**

Figure 1 Public and publicly guaranteed debt, by creditor and creditor type in 2024, including IMF credit

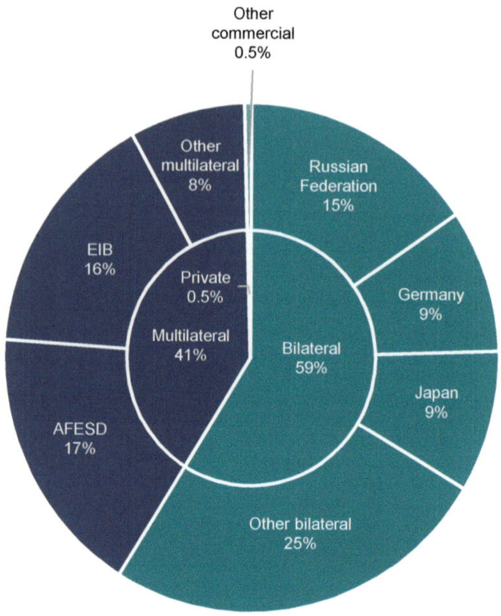

Figure 2 Average terms on new debt commitments from official and private creditors

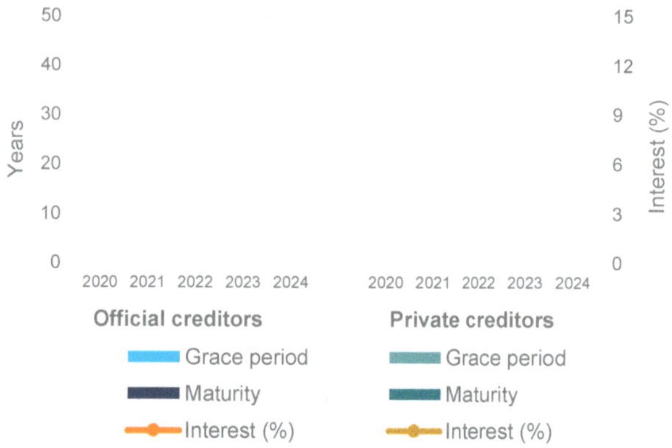

Summary External Debt Data	2010	2020	2021	2022	2023	2024
Total external debt stocks	**5,277**	**4,763**	**5,029**	**4,862**	**4,876**	**4,757**
Long-term external debt stocks	**4,284**	**3,751**	**3,632**	**3,498**	**3,502**	**3,410**
Public and publicly guaranteed debt from:	*4,284*	*3,751*	*3,632*	*3,498*	*3,502*	*3,410*
Official creditors	4,261	3,734	3,616	3,482	3,485	3,394
Multilateral	1,698	1,529	1,467	1,412	1,435	1,388
of which: World Bank	15	14	14	14	14	14
Bilateral	2,563	2,205	2,149	2,070	2,050	2,006
Private creditors	23	17	16	16	16	16
Bondholders	..	..	..	..	..	..
Commercial banks and others	23	17	16	16	16	16
Private nonguaranteed debt from:	..	..	..	..	..	..
Bondholders	..	..	..	..	..	..
Commercial banks and others	..	..	..	..	..	..
Use of IMF credit and SDR allocations	**430**	**402**	**785**	**746**	**752**	**731**
IMF credit	0	0	0	0	0	0
SDR allocations	430	402	785	746	752	731
Short-term external debt stocks	**562**	**610**	**612**	**618**	**622**	**616**
Disbursements, long-term	**286**	**0**	**0**	**0**	**0**	**0**
Public and publicly guaranteed sector	286	0	0	0	0	0
Private sector not guaranteed	..	..	..	..	..	..
Principal repayments, long-term	**509**	**0**	**0**	**0**	**0**	**0**
Public and publicly guaranteed sector	509	0	0	0	0	0
Private sector not guaranteed	..	..	..	..	..	..
Interest payments, long-term	**111**	**0**	**0**	**0**	**0**	**0**
Public and publicly guaranteed sector	111	0	0	0	0	0
Private sector not guaranteed	..	..	..	..	..	..

Note: Figure 2 shows no data values because the country did not have new commitments from 2020 to 2024.

TAJIKISTAN

(US$ million, unless otherwise indicated)

Snapshot	2024
Total external debt stocks	**6,977**
External debt stocks as % of:	
Exports	107
GNI	37
Debt service as % of:	
Exports	9
GNI	3
Net financial flows, debt and equity	772
Net debt inflows	436
Net equity inflows	336
GNI	**18,659**
Population (million)	**11**

Figure 1 Public and publicly guaranteed debt, by creditor and creditor type in 2024, including IMF credit

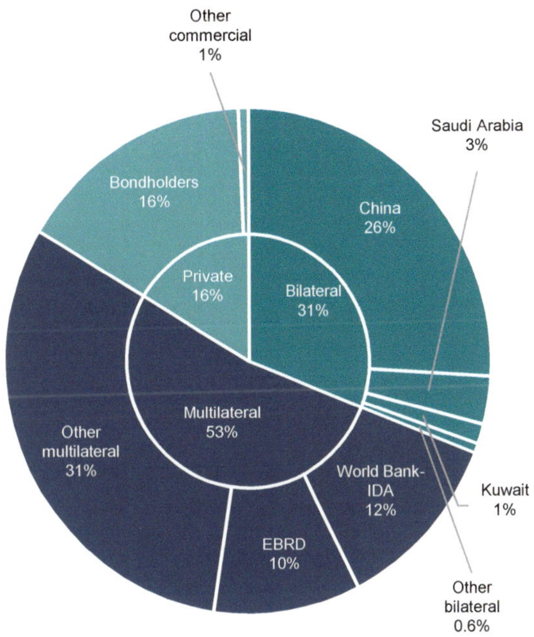

Figure 2 Average terms on new debt commitments from official and private creditors

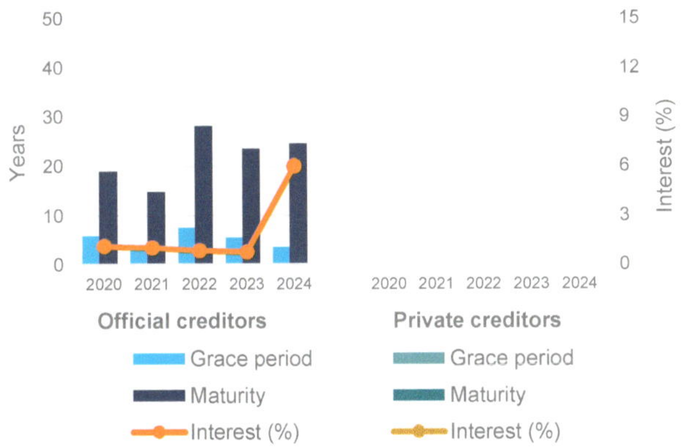

Summary External Debt Data	2010	2020	2021	2022	2023	2024
Total external debt stocks	**3,561**	**6,904**	**6,591**	**6,724**	**6,589**	**6,977**
Long-term external debt stocks	**2,733**	**5,451**	**5,538**	**5,582**	**5,666**	**5,600**
Public and publicly guaranteed debt from:	*1,806*	*3,065*	*3,142*	*3,070*	*3,090*	*2,996*
Official creditors	1,800	2,540	2,619	2,549	2,568	2,475
Multilateral	943	1,229	1,333	1,386	1,490	1,492
of which: World Bank	377	356	358	369	375	369
Bilateral	856	1,311	1,286	1,163	1,078	982
Private creditors	6	525	523	521	522	521
Bondholders	..	500	500	500	500	500
Commercial banks and others	6	25	23	21	22	21
Private nonguaranteed debt from:	*927*	*2,387*	*2,396*	*2,511*	*2,575*	*2,605*
Bondholders	..	..	..	..	..	..
Commercial banks and others	927	2,387	2,396	2,511	2,575	2,605
Use of IMF credit and SDR allocations	**227**	**330**	**545**	**516**	**521**	**506**
IMF credit	101	212	197	185	187	182
SDR allocations	126	118	348	331	334	325
Short-term external debt stocks	**601**	**1,122**	**508**	**625**	**403**	**871**
Disbursements, long-term	**924**	**484**	**513**	**394**	**470**	**337**
Public and publicly guaranteed sector	251	275	242	191	195	125
Private sector not guaranteed	673	209	271	204	275	211
Principal repayments, long-term	**631**	**228**	**373**	**353**	**390**	**369**
Public and publicly guaranteed sector	37	103	143	190	179	187
Private sector not guaranteed	593	124	230	162	210	182
Interest payments, long-term	**54**	**91**	**114**	**119**	**134**	**142**
Public and publicly guaranteed sector	23	61	77	79	87	88
Private sector not guaranteed	31	30	37	41	48	54

TANZANIA

(US$ million, unless otherwise indicated)

Snapshot	2024
Total external debt stocks	**36,343**
External debt stocks as % of:	
Exports	222
GNI	47
Debt service as % of:	
Exports	12
GNI	3
Net financial flows, debt and equity	4,774
Net debt inflows	3,056
Net equity inflows	1,718
GNI	**76,808**
Population (million)	**69**

Figure 1 Public and publicly guaranteed debt, by creditor and creditor type in 2024, including IMF credit

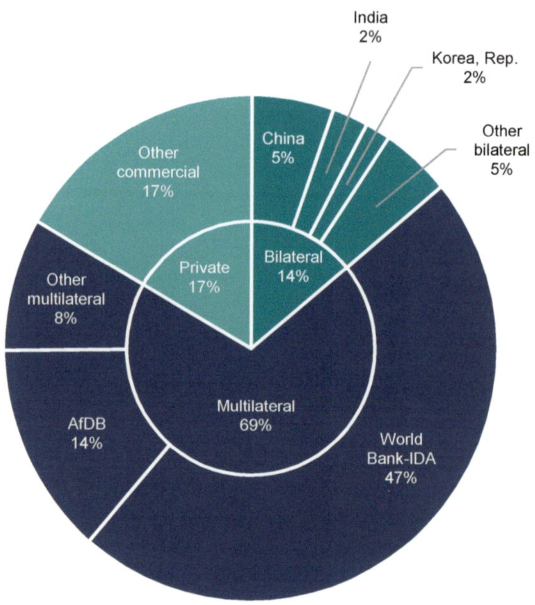

Figure 2 Average terms on new debt commitments from official and private creditors

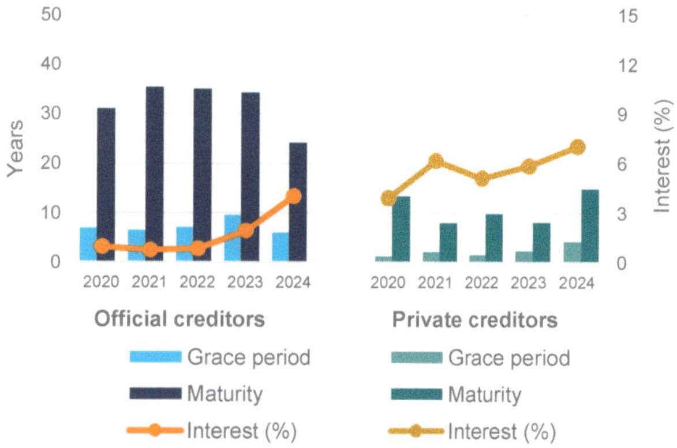

Summary External Debt Data	2010	2020	2021	2022	2023	2024
Total external debt stocks	**8,940**	**25,772**	**28,818**	**30,444**	**34,585**	**36,343**
Long-term external debt stocks	**6,904**	**22,055**	**23,589**	**24,533**	**28,271**	**30,898**
Public and publicly guaranteed debt from:	*5,680*	*17,564*	*18,938*	*19,552*	*22,386*	*24,277*
Official creditors	5,546	15,355	15,502	16,308	18,296	20,005
Multilateral	4,391	11,243	11,526	12,615	14,655	16,435
of which: World Bank	3,248	8,148	8,290	9,228	10,989	12,097
Bilateral	1,155	4,112	3,975	3,693	3,641	3,571
Private creditors	135	2,209	3,436	3,244	4,090	4,272
Bondholders	..	..	..	..	..	..
Commercial banks and others	135	2,209	3,436	3,244	4,090	4,272
Private nonguaranteed debt from:	*1,224*	*4,491*	*4,651*	*4,981*	*5,886*	*6,621*
Bondholders	..	..	..	..	..	..
Commercial banks and others	1,224	4,491	4,651	4,981	5,886	6,621
Use of IMF credit and SDR allocations	**647**	**274**	**1,357**	**1,444**	**1,760**	**2,062**
IMF credit	354	0	557	683	993	1,316
SDR allocations	293	274	800	761	767	746
Short-term external debt stocks	**1,389**	**3,442**	**3,872**	**4,467**	**4,554**	**3,383**
Disbursements, long-term	**1,361**	**1,459**	**3,049**	**3,104**	**5,200**	**4,112**
Public and publicly guaranteed sector	1,145	1,181	2,865	2,421	4,030	3,500
Private sector not guaranteed	216	279	184	683	1,171	612
Principal repayments, long-term	**134**	**984**	**1,142**	**1,533**	**1,547**	**1,204**
Public and publicly guaranteed sector	55	968	1,118	1,179	1,282	1,126
Private sector not guaranteed	79	15	25	353	266	78
Interest payments, long-term	**51**	**365**	**319**	**429**	**603**	**725**
Public and publicly guaranteed sector	34	363	315	377	547	691
Private sector not guaranteed	17	2	4	52	56	34

THAILAND

(US$ million, unless otherwise indicated)

Snapshot	2024
Total external debt stocks	**191,827**
External debt stocks as % of:	
Exports	50
GNI	37
Debt service as % of:	
Exports	5
GNI	4
Net financial flows, debt and equity	3,735
Net debt inflows	-2,493
Net equity inflows	6,228
GNI	**511,688**
Population (million)	**72**

Figure 1 Public and publicly guaranteed debt, by creditor and creditor type in 2024, including IMF credit

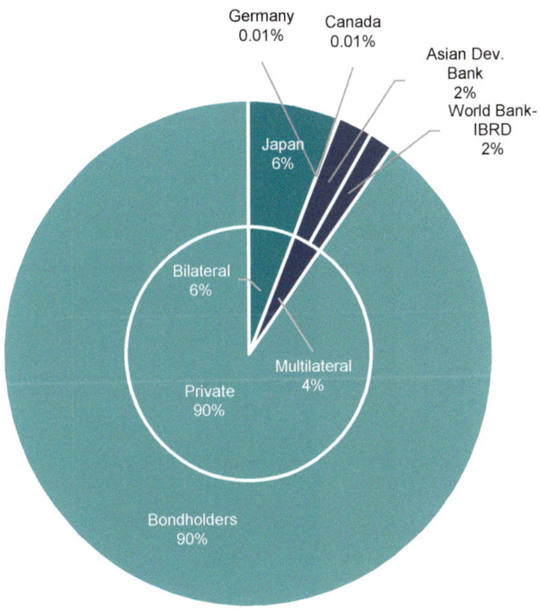

Figure 2 Average terms on new debt commitments from official and private creditors

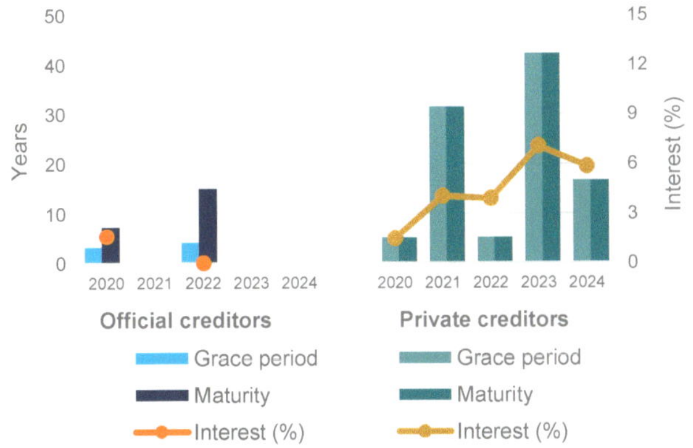

Summary External Debt Data	2010	2020	2021	2022	2023	2024
Total external debt stocks	**107,166**	**186,866**	**196,676**	**201,051**	**194,693**	**191,827**
Long-term external debt stocks	**55,015**	**120,719**	**128,241**	**127,351**	**120,420**	**117,155**
Public and publicly guaranteed debt from:	*16,737*	*35,824*	*36,815*	*35,679*	*32,419*	*31,028*
Official creditors	6,881	4,422	5,353	5,043	4,239	3,105
Multilateral	187	1,068	2,440	2,316	1,902	1,206
of which: World Bank	128	837	750	666	583	500
Bilateral	6,693	3,353	2,913	2,728	2,337	1,899
Private creditors	9,856	31,403	31,462	30,635	28,180	27,922
Bondholders	8,812	31,403	31,462	30,635	28,180	27,922
Commercial banks and others	1,045	..	..	..	..	..
Private nonguaranteed debt from:	*38,278*	*84,895*	*91,426*	*91,672*	*88,001*	*86,128*
Bondholders	4,265	15,840	17,747	17,080	14,419	12,632
Commercial banks and others	34,012	69,055	73,679	74,592	73,581	73,495
Use of IMF credit and SDR allocations	**1,494**	**1,397**	**5,667**	**5,388**	**5,432**	**5,280**
IMF credit	0	0	0	0	0	0
SDR allocations	1,494	1,397	5,667	5,388	5,432	5,280
Short-term external debt stocks	**50,657**	**64,749**	**62,768**	**68,312**	**68,841**	**69,392**
Disbursements, long-term	**17,539**	**24,053**	**25,569**	**22,136**	**28,492**	**8,132**
Public and publicly guaranteed sector	5,941	542	2,430	882	839	556
Private sector not guaranteed	11,597	23,512	23,140	21,254	27,653	7,577
Principal repayments, long-term	**9,386**	**19,995**	**14,700**	**22,587**	**35,258**	**11,176**
Public and publicly guaranteed sector	803	5,771	1,134	1,612	3,924	1,735
Private sector not guaranteed	8,582	14,223	13,566	20,976	31,334	9,441
Interest payments, long-term	**1,079**	**1,630**	**774**	**1,067**	**2,507**	**2,427**
Public and publicly guaranteed sector	202	1,059	92	276	1,788	1,769
Private sector not guaranteed	877	571	682	792	719	658

TIMOR-LESTE

(US$ million, unless otherwise indicated)

Snapshot	2024
Total external debt stocks	**296.7**
External debt stocks as % of:	
Exports	34.7
GNI	15.4
Debt service as % of:	
Exports	3.1
GNI	1.3
Net financial flows, debt and equity	226.8
Net debt inflows	-3.9
Net equity inflows	230.8
GNI	**1,930.8**
Population (million)	**1**

Figure 1 Public and publicly guaranteed debt, by creditor and creditor type in 2024, including IMF credit

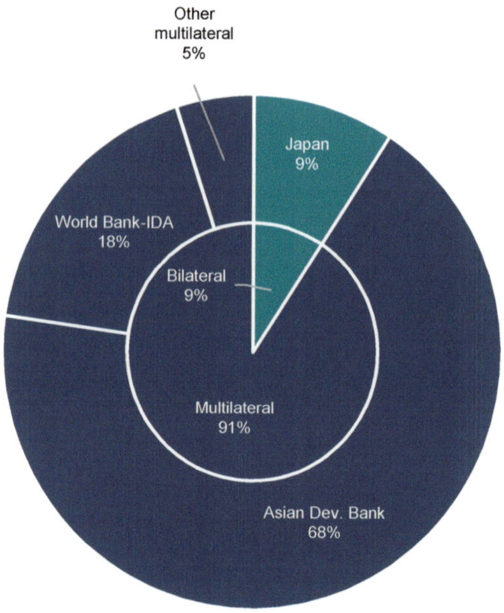

Figure 2 Average terms on new debt commitments from official and private creditors

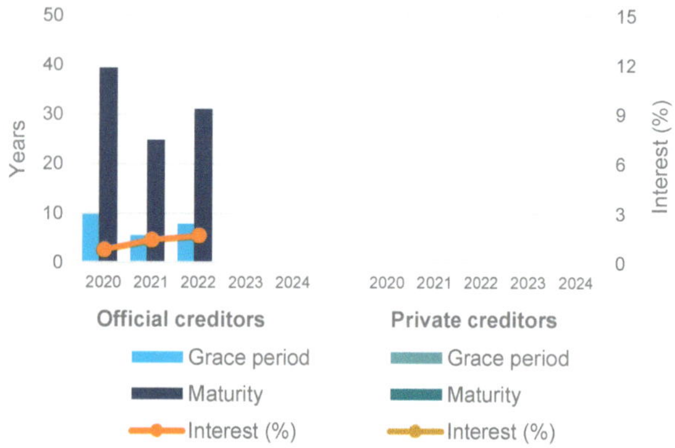

Summary External Debt Data	2010	2020	2021	2022	2023	2024
Total external debt stocks	..	**231.8**	**278.6**	**287.9**	**305.7**	**296.7**
Long-term external debt stocks	..	**220.2**	**232.4**	**244.7**	**253.1**	**253.3**
Public and publicly guaranteed debt from:	..	*220.2*	*232.4*	*244.7*	*253.1*	*253.3*
Official creditors	..	220.2	232.4	244.7	253.1	253.3
Multilateral	..	189.4	200.6	214.0	225.9	230.0
of which: World Bank	..	47.6	50.7	53.0	55.2	57.8
Bilateral	..	30.9	31.8	30.7	27.2	23.3
Private creditors	..	..	..	..	..	..
Bondholders	..	..	..	..	..	..
Commercial banks and others	..	..	..	..	..	..
Private nonguaranteed debt from:	..	..	..	..	..	..
Bondholders	..	..	..	..	..	..
Commercial banks and others	..	..	..	..	..	..
Use of IMF credit and SDR allocations	..	**11.1**	**45.2**	**42.9**	**43.3**	**42.1**
IMF credit	..	0.0	0.0	0.0	0.0	0.0
SDR allocations	..	11.1	45.2	42.9	43.3	42.1
Short-term external debt stocks	..	**0.4**	**1.1**	**0.3**	**9.3**	**1.3**
Disbursements, long-term	..	**30.1**	**22.6**	**31.0**	**24.7**	**19.1**
Public and publicly guaranteed sector	..	30.1	22.6	31.0	24.7	19.1
Private sector not guaranteed	..	..	..	..	..	..
Principal repayments, long-term	..	**3.9**	**6.4**	**12.2**	**14.6**	**14.9**
Public and publicly guaranteed sector	..	3.9	6.4	12.2	14.6	14.9
Private sector not guaranteed	..	..	..	..	..	..
Interest payments, long-term	..	**4.1**	**3.2**	**4.2**	**8.3**	**9.4**
Public and publicly guaranteed sector	..	4.1	3.2	4.2	8.3	9.4
Private sector not guaranteed	..	..	..	..	..	..

TOGO

(US$ million, unless otherwise indicated)

Snapshot	2024
Total external debt stocks	**4,294**
External debt stocks as % of:	
Exports	173
GNI	43
Debt service as % of:	
Exports	14
GNI	3
Net financial flows, debt and equity	1,055
Net debt inflows	971
Net equity inflows	84
GNI	**9,948**
Population (million)	**10**

Figure 1 Public and publicly guaranteed debt, by creditor and creditor type in 2024, including IMF credit

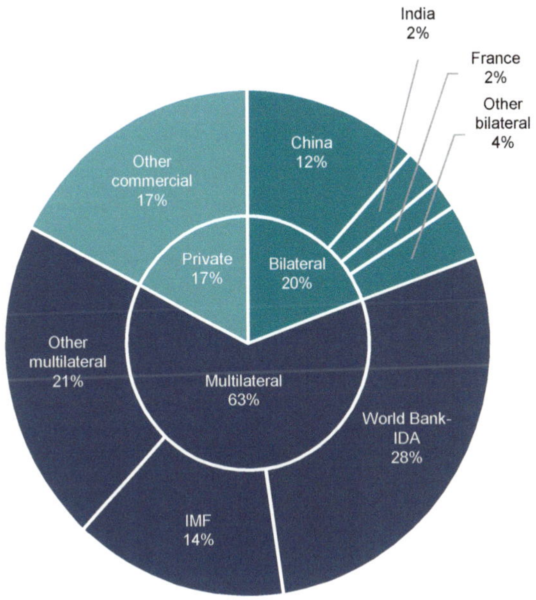

Figure 2 Average terms on new debt commitments from official and private creditors

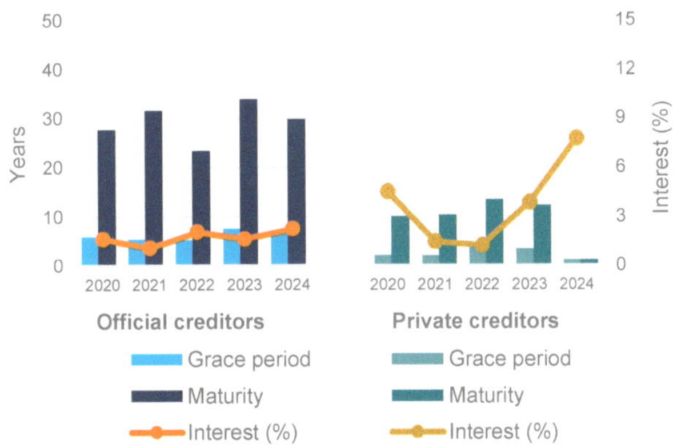

Summary External Debt Data	2010	2020	2021	2022	2023	2024
Total external debt stocks	**1,291**	**2,569**	**3,545**	**3,282**	**3,440**	**4,294**
Long-term external debt stocks	**1,010**	**1,789**	**2,501**	**2,505**	**2,744**	**3,471**
Public and publicly guaranteed debt from:	*1,010*	*1,789*	*1,851*	*1,855*	*2,094*	*2,421*
Official creditors	1,010	1,458	1,516	1,528	1,731	1,930
Multilateral	864	823	860	918	1,136	1,379
of which: World Bank	554	265	288	360	575	796
Bilateral	147	635	657	610	594	551
Private creditors	..	331	335	326	364	491
Bondholders	..	..	..	..	..	..
Commercial banks and others	..	331	335	326	364	491
Private nonguaranteed debt from:	..	..	*650*	*650*	*650*	*1,050*
Bondholders	..	..	650	650	650	1,050
Commercial banks and others	..	..	..	..	..	..
Use of IMF credit and SDR allocations	**241**	**459**	**642**	**607**	**595**	**677**
IMF credit	133	358	347	326	312	401
SDR allocations	108	101	295	281	283	275
Short-term external debt stocks	**39**	**320**	**402**	**170**	**100**	**146**
Disbursements, long-term	**94**	**376**	**853**	**240**	**338**	**995**
Public and publicly guaranteed sector	94	376	203	240	338	595
Private sector not guaranteed	..	..	650	..	..	400
Principal repayments, long-term	**28**	**55**	**74**	**148**	**141**	**170**
Public and publicly guaranteed sector	28	55	74	148	141	170
Private sector not guaranteed	..	..	..	..	..	..
Interest payments, long-term	**8**	**33**	**89**	**93**	**93**	**132**
Public and publicly guaranteed sector	8	33	37	41	41	59
Private sector not guaranteed	..	..	52	52	52	72

TONGA

(US$ million, unless otherwise indicated)

Snapshot	2024
Total external debt stocks	**173.2**
External debt stocks as % of:	
Exports	89.9
GNI	..
Debt service as % of:	
Exports	22.8
GNI	..
Net financial flows, debt and equity	-30.8
Net debt inflows	-18.7
Net equity inflows	-12.2
GNI	..
Population (thousand)	**104**

Figure 2 Average terms on new debt commitments from official and private creditors

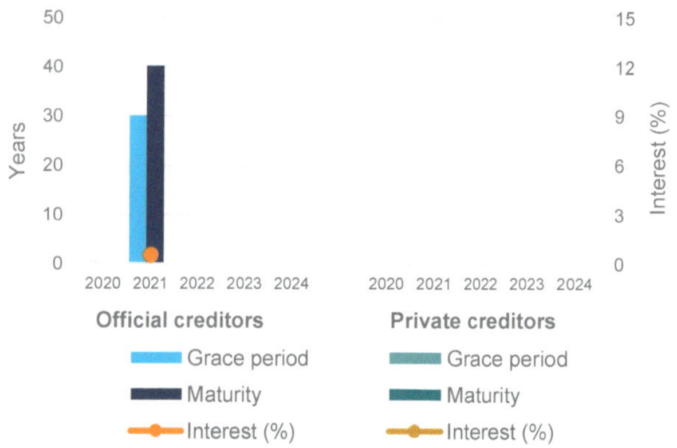

Figure 1 Public and publicly guaranteed debt, by creditor and creditor type in 2024, including IMF credit

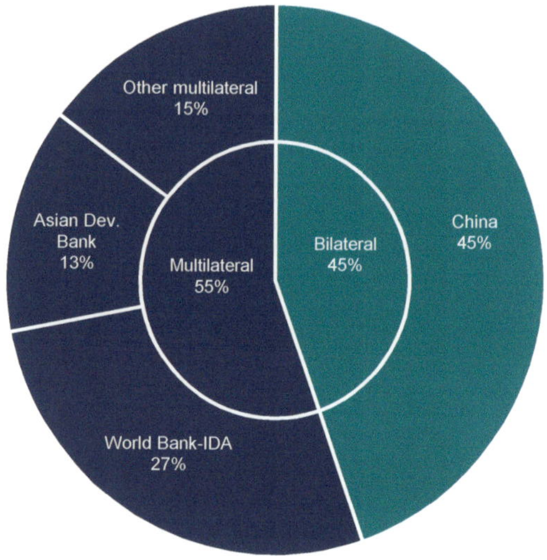

Summary External Debt Data	2010	2020	2021	2022	2023	2024
Total external debt stocks	**153.7**	**194.6**	**223.6**	**209.9**	**196.5**	**173.2**
Long-term external debt stocks	**143.5**	**185.1**	**186.2**	**165.2**	**151.4**	**129.3**
Public and publicly guaranteed debt from:	*143.5*	*185.1*	*186.2*	*165.2*	*151.4*	*129.3*
Official creditors	142.4	185.1	186.2	165.2	151.4	129.3
Multilateral	70.8	77.5	73.7	67.8	67.5	63.6
of which: World Bank	23.6	45.0	43.6	40.8	41.5	40.2
Bilateral	71.7	107.6	112.6	97.4	83.9	65.8
Private creditors	1.1	..	..	..	..	..
Bondholders	..	..	..	..	..	..
Commercial banks and others	1.1	..	..	..	..	..
Private nonguaranteed debt from:	..	..	..	..	..	..
Bondholders	..	..	..	..	..	..
Commercial banks and others	..	..	..	..	..	..
Use of IMF credit and SDR allocations	**10.1**	**9.5**	**37.4**	**44.7**	**45.1**	**43.8**
IMF credit	0.0	0.0	9.7	18.4	18.5	18.0
SDR allocations	10.1	9.5	27.7	26.4	26.6	25.8
Short-term external debt stocks	**0.0**	**0.0**	**0.0**	**0.0**	**0.0**	**0.0**
Disbursements, long-term	**40.9**	**1.3**	**1.0**	**0.3**	**1.7**	**0.8**
Public and publicly guaranteed sector	40.9	1.3	1.0	0.3	1.7	0.8
Private sector not guaranteed	..	..	..	..	..	..
Principal repayments, long-term	**2.7**	**4.7**	**2.7**	**8.1**	**14.1**	**19.5**
Public and publicly guaranteed sector	2.7	4.7	2.7	8.1	14.1	19.5
Private sector not guaranteed	..	..	..	..	..	..
Interest payments, long-term	**2.4**	**1.3**	**2.1**	**2.7**	**2.5**	**23.4**
Public and publicly guaranteed sector	2.4	1.3	2.1	2.7	2.5	23.4
Private sector not guaranteed	..	..	..	..	..	..

TUNISIA

(US$ million, unless otherwise indicated)

Snapshot	2024
Total external debt stocks	**40,460**
External debt stocks as % of:	
Exports	192
GNI	78
Debt service as % of:	
Exports	26
GNI	11
Net financial flows, debt and equity	-28
Net debt inflows	-868
Net equity inflows	840
GNI	**52,072**
Population (million)	**12**

Figure 1 Public and publicly guaranteed debt, by creditor and creditor type in 2024, including IMF credit

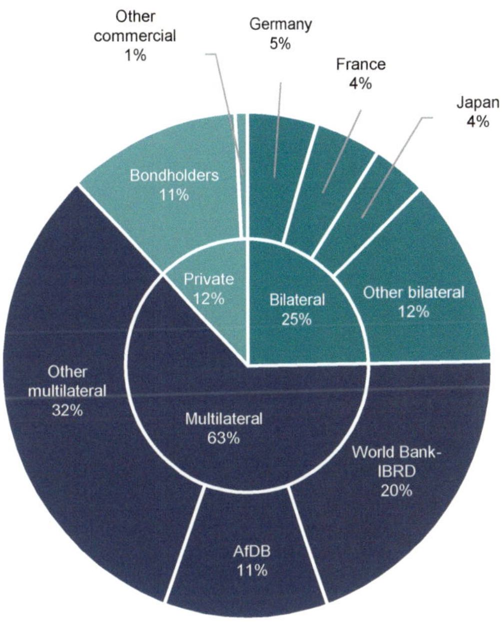

Figure 2 Average terms on new debt commitments from official and private creditors

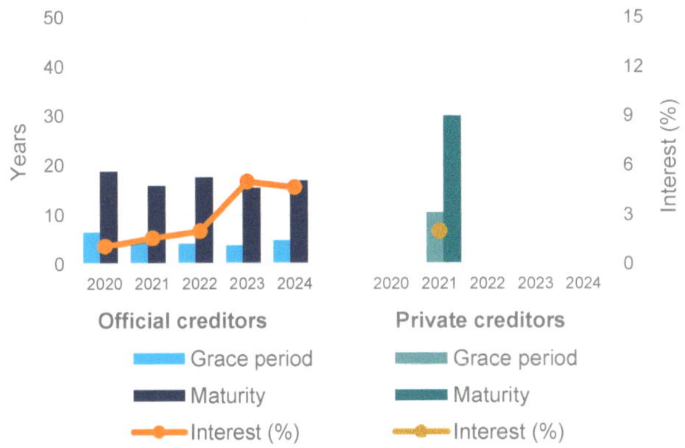

Summary External Debt Data	2010	2020	2021	2022	2023	2024
Total external debt stocks	**22,659**	**41,977**	**43,022**	**41,041**	**42,407**	**40,460**
Long-term external debt stocks	**17,260**	**28,521**	**26,137**	**24,208**	**24,091**	**22,503**
Public and publicly guaranteed debt from:	*14,858*	*25,778*	*23,152*	*21,634*	*22,062*	*20,816*
Official creditors	10,383	18,274	17,372	16,743	17,949	18,161
Multilateral	6,978	12,809	12,055	11,690	12,234	12,762
of which: World Bank	1,399	4,196	4,063	4,136	4,315	4,327
Bilateral	3,404	5,465	5,317	5,054	5,715	5,399
Private creditors	4,476	7,503	5,780	4,891	4,113	2,655
Bondholders	4,003	7,022	5,406	4,598	3,885	2,484
Commercial banks and others	472	481	374	292	229	171
Private nonguaranteed debt from:	*2,402*	*2,744*	*2,985*	*2,574*	*2,029*	*1,686*
Bondholders	..	..	..	..	..	..
Commercial banks and others	2,402	2,744	2,985	2,574	2,029	1,686
Use of IMF credit and SDR allocations	**420**	**2,824**	**3,396**	**3,109**	**2,711**	**2,027**
IMF credit	0	2,431	2,283	2,050	1,644	990
SDR allocations	420	393	1,113	1,058	1,067	1,037
Short-term external debt stocks	**4,979**	**10,632**	**13,489**	**13,724**	**15,605**	**15,930**
Disbursements, long-term	**1,671**	**2,527**	**2,327**	**2,025**	**2,192**	**2,574**
Public and publicly guaranteed sector	1,574	2,352	1,810	1,975	2,151	2,528
Private sector not guaranteed	97	175	517	50	41	47
Principal repayments, long-term	**1,631**	**2,170**	**3,452**	**2,722**	**2,704**	**3,148**
Public and publicly guaranteed sector	1,411	1,824	2,950	2,260	2,118	2,759
Private sector not guaranteed	220	346	501	461	586	389
Interest payments, long-term	**672**	**661**	**624**	**634**	**660**	**719**
Public and publicly guaranteed sector	548	583	555	530	552	647
Private sector not guaranteed	124	78	69	104	108	72

TÜRKIYE

(US$ million, unless otherwise indicated)

Snapshot	2024
Total external debt stocks	**514,989**
External debt stocks as % of:	
Exports	135
GNI	39
Debt service as % of:	
Exports	23
GNI	7
Net financial flows, debt and equity	24,446
Net debt inflows	17,925
Net equity inflows	6,521
GNI	**1,307,476**
Population (million)	**86**

Figure 1 Public and publicly guaranteed debt, by creditor and creditor type in 2024, including IMF credit

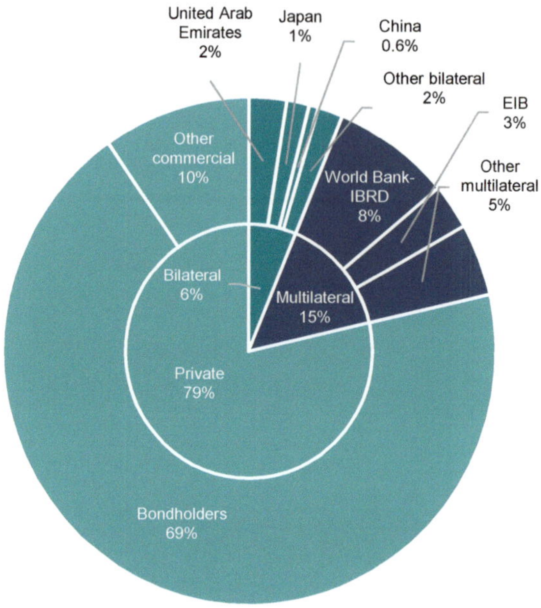

Figure 2 Average terms on new debt commitments from official and private creditors

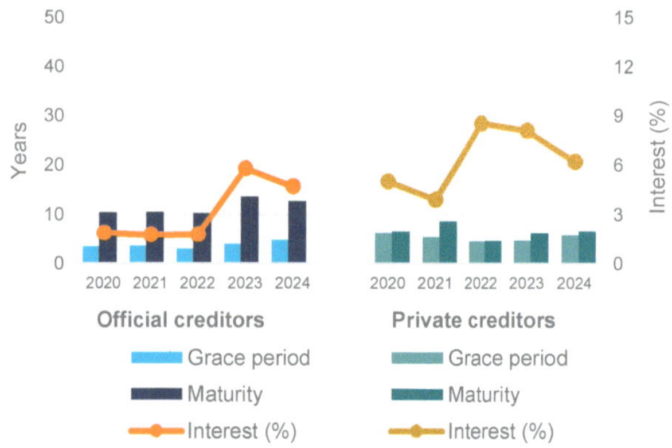

Summary External Debt Data	2010	2020	2021	2022	2023	2024
Total external debt stocks	**316,647**	**429,283**	**434,873**	**455,963**	**499,814**	**514,989**
Long-term external debt stocks	**216,369**	**316,519**	**309,090**	**300,805**	**317,529**	**329,635**
Public and publicly guaranteed debt from:	*93,289*	*138,031*	*138,016*	*139,061*	*148,508*	*157,128*
Official creditors	26,931	34,923	32,561	31,625	32,042	33,724
Multilateral	19,922	27,870	25,727	24,699	25,389	24,032
of which: World Bank	11,605	11,925	11,179	11,262	12,037	12,065
Bilateral	7,009	7,053	6,834	6,926	6,653	9,693
Private creditors	66,358	103,109	105,455	107,436	116,466	123,404
Bondholders	45,774	89,850	91,612	94,200	100,669	108,135
Commercial banks and others	20,584	13,259	13,843	13,236	15,797	15,269
Private nonguaranteed debt from:	*123,080*	*178,488*	*171,074*	*161,744*	*169,021*	*172,507*
Bondholders	6,202	34,660	34,011	27,241	27,615	34,797
Commercial banks and others	116,878	143,828	137,063	134,503	141,406	137,710
Use of IMF credit and SDR allocations	**7,277**	**1,543**	**7,749**	**7,368**	**7,428**	**7,220**
IMF credit	5,627	0	0	0	0	0
SDR allocations	1,650	1,543	7,749	7,368	7,428	7,220
Short-term external debt stocks	**93,001**	**111,221**	**118,034**	**147,790**	**174,857**	**178,134**
Disbursements, long-term	**48,825**	**59,778**	**56,421**	**47,166**	**69,258**	**77,774**
Public and publicly guaranteed sector	14,786	18,109	20,731	18,923	24,519	31,369
Private sector not guaranteed	34,039	41,669	35,690	28,243	44,739	46,404
Principal repayments, long-term	**45,504**	**68,878**	**57,487**	**51,485**	**53,598**	**63,125**
Public and publicly guaranteed sector	6,028	12,575	17,307	15,071	16,123	20,230
Private sector not guaranteed	39,476	56,303	40,179	36,414	37,475	42,895
Interest payments, long-term	**8,869**	**12,773**	**11,875**	**11,749**	**15,386**	**18,851**
Public and publicly guaranteed sector	4,693	5,749	6,073	6,312	8,149	9,428
Private sector not guaranteed	4,177	7,024	5,802	5,437	7,237	9,423

TURKMENISTAN

(US$ million, unless otherwise indicated)

Snapshot	2024
Total external debt stocks	**3,320**
External debt stocks as % of:	
Exports	..
GNI	5
Debt service as % of:	
Exports	..
GNI	2
Net financial flows, debt and equity	1,091
Net debt inflows	-553
Net equity inflows	1,645
GNI	**63,651**
Population (million)	**7**

Figure 2 Average terms on new debt commitments from official and private creditors

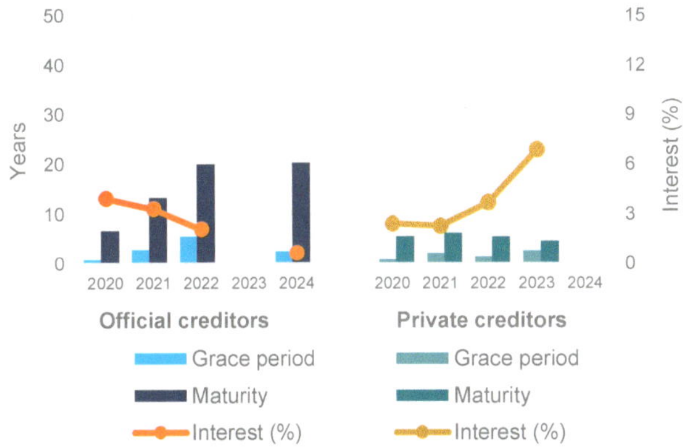

Figure 1 Public and publicly guaranteed debt, by creditor and creditor type in 2024, including IMF credit

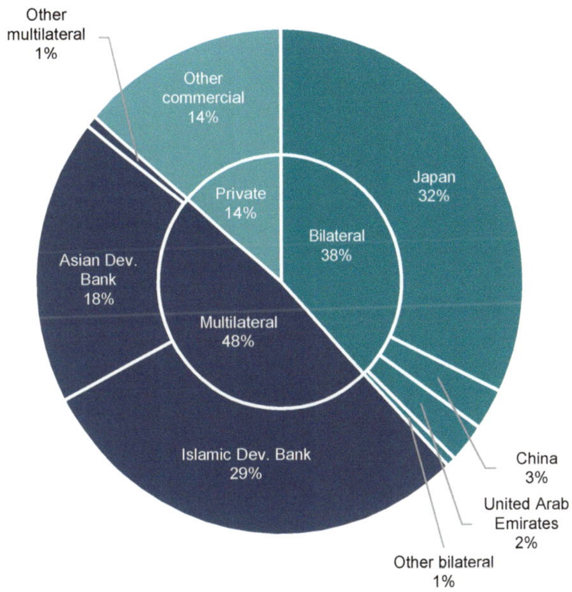

Summary External Debt Data	2010	2020	2021	2022	2023	2024
Total external debt stocks	**1,682**	**5,771**	**4,986**	**4,645**	**3,918**	**3,320**
Long-term external debt stocks	**1,520**	**5,529**	**4,569**	**4,148**	**3,517**	**2,900**
Public and publicly guaranteed debt from:	*1,513*	*5,477*	*4,522*	*4,123*	*3,502*	*2,892*
Official creditors	1,513	4,861	3,913	3,509	2,937	2,496
Multilateral	96	808	941	1,246	1,372	1,399
of which: World Bank	11	..	15	20	20	20
Bilateral	1,417	4,053	2,973	2,263	1,565	1,097
Private creditors	0	616	608	614	565	396
Bondholders	..	..	..	..	..	..
Commercial banks and others	0	616	608	614	565	396
Private nonguaranteed debt from:	*7*	*51*	*47*	*25*	*16*	*8*
Bondholders	..	..	..	..	..	..
Commercial banks and others	7	51	47	25	16	8
Use of IMF credit and SDR allocations	**108**	**101**	**418**	**397**	**400**	**389**
IMF credit	0	0	0	0	0	0
SDR allocations	108	101	418	397	400	389
Short-term external debt stocks	**54**	**142**	**0**	**100**	**0**	**31**
Disbursements, long-term	**1,051**	**747**	**552**	**611**	**313**	**189**
Public and publicly guaranteed sector	1,044	729	540	611	313	189
Private sector not guaranteed	8	18	12	..	..	..
Principal repayments, long-term	**148**	**1,850**	**1,446**	**943**	**935**	**774**
Public and publicly guaranteed sector	135	1,839	1,423	919	924	766
Private sector not guaranteed	13	11	23	24	11	8
Interest payments, long-term	**50**	**240**	**205**	**185**	**210**	**183**
Public and publicly guaranteed sector	50	239	204	184	210	183
Private sector not guaranteed	0	1	1	0	0	0

UGANDA

(US$ million, unless otherwise indicated)

Snapshot	2024
Total external debt stocks	**20,534**
External debt stocks as % of:	
Exports	184
GNI	39
Debt service as % of:	
Exports	14
GNI	3
Net financial flows, debt and equity	3,828
Net debt inflows	676
Net equity inflows	3,152
GNI	**52,361**
Population (million)	**50**

Figure 1 Public and publicly guaranteed debt, by creditor and creditor type in 2024, including IMF credit

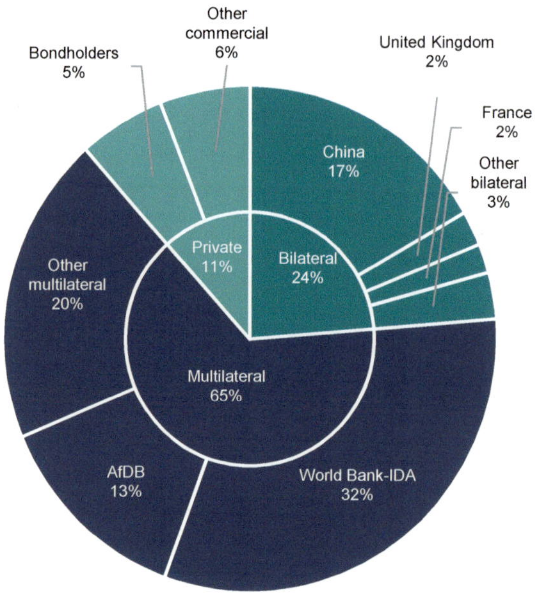

Figure 2 Average terms on new debt commitments from official and private creditors

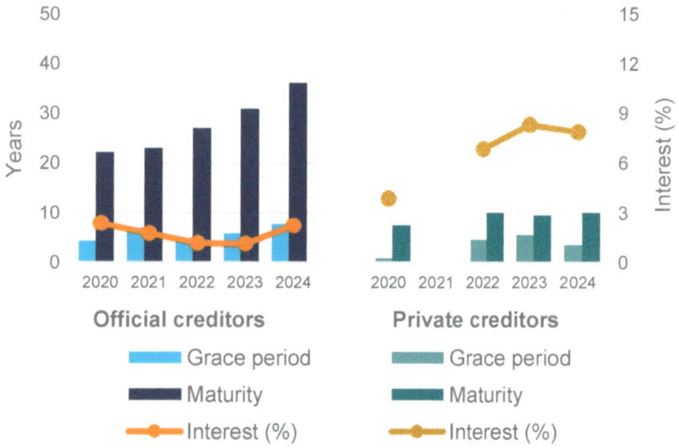

Summary External Debt Data	2010	2020	2021	2022	2023	2024
Total external debt stocks	**2,975**	**17,702**	**20,671**	**21,041**	**20,285**	**20,534**
Long-term external debt stocks	**2,673**	**15,741**	**17,415**	**17,786**	**17,892**	**18,044**
Public and publicly guaranteed debt from:	*2,673*	*11,830*	*12,725*	*12,589*	*14,050*	*14,100*
Official creditors	2,673	10,846	11,542	11,547	12,114	12,314
Multilateral	2,416	7,242	7,888	7,887	8,489	8,662
of which: World Bank	1,682	4,300	4,453	4,464	4,675	4,899
Bilateral	257	3,604	3,654	3,660	3,625	3,652
Private creditors	0	984	1,183	1,043	1,936	1,785
Bondholders	..	464	697	633	888	874
Commercial banks and others	0	519	487	410	1,048	912
Private nonguaranteed debt from:	..	*3,911*	*4,690*	*5,197*	*3,842*	*3,944*
Bondholders	..	..	..	..	..	..
Commercial banks and others	..	3,911	4,690	5,197	3,842	3,944
Use of IMF credit and SDR allocations	**275**	**769**	**1,484**	**1,532**	**1,907**	**1,972**
IMF credit	9	520	758	841	1,211	1,295
SDR allocations	267	249	726	691	696	677
Short-term external debt stocks	**26**	**1,191**	**1,772**	**1,724**	**485**	**519**
Disbursements, long-term	**489**	**2,494**	**2,119**	**1,382**	**1,742**	**1,268**
Public and publicly guaranteed sector	489	2,494	1,341	875	1,742	1,167
Private sector not guaranteed	..	..	778	507	..	102
Principal repayments, long-term	**40**	**403**	**342**	**469**	**1,992**	**746**
Public and publicly guaranteed sector	40	172	342	469	638	746
Private sector not guaranteed	..	231	..	..	1,354	..
Interest payments, long-term	**21**	**340**	**495**	**479**	**670**	**758**
Public and publicly guaranteed sector	21	215	367	312	426	534
Private sector not guaranteed	..	125	128	166	244	224

UKRAINE

(US$ million, unless otherwise indicated)

Snapshot	2024
Total external debt stocks	**193,492**
External debt stocks as % of:	
Exports	296
GNI	101
Debt service as % of:	
Exports	16
GNI	5
Net financial flows, debt and equity	31,420
Net debt inflows	27,873
Net equity inflows	3,547
GNI	**191,071**
Population (million)	**38**

Figure 2 Average terms on new debt commitments from official and private creditors

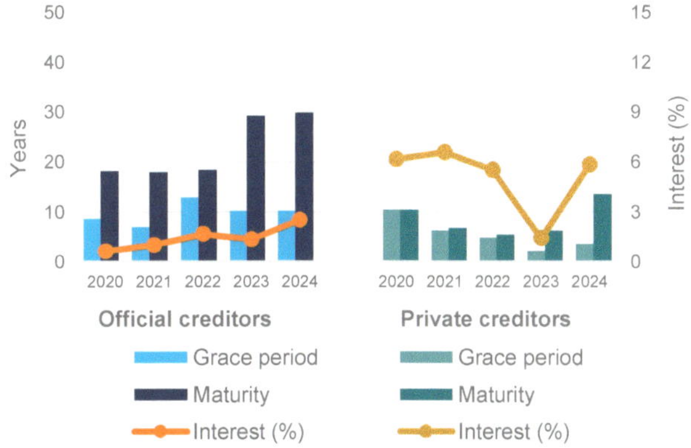

Figure 1 Public and publicly guaranteed debt, by creditor and creditor type in 2024, including IMF credit

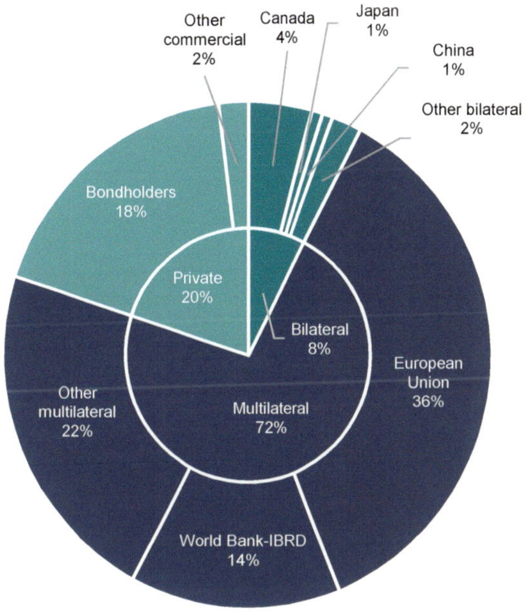

Summary External Debt Data	2010	2020	2021	2022	2023	2024
Total external debt stocks	**124,527**	**133,406**	**136,908**	**143,391**	**178,989**	**193,492**
Long-term external debt stocks	**81,001**	**96,426**	**99,159**	**112,690**	**141,396**	**156,251**
Public and publicly guaranteed debt from:	*25,327*	*42,529*	*44,918*	*61,592*	*89,734*	*105,180*
Official creditors	14,961	14,920	15,942	32,447	60,482	81,233
Multilateral	13,560	12,404	13,551	26,541	52,676	72,096
of which: World Bank	3,212	5,741	6,623	8,773	13,584	22,470
Bilateral	1,400	2,516	2,391	5,906	7,806	9,138
Private creditors	10,366	27,609	28,976	29,145	29,252	23,947
Bondholders	9,058	25,613	26,944	26,655	26,822	21,654
Commercial banks and others	1,308	1,996	2,031	2,490	2,430	2,293
Private nonguaranteed debt from:	*55,674*	*53,897*	*54,241*	*51,098*	*51,661*	*51,070*
Bondholders	4,313	5,294	4,833	4,654	4,666	4,010
Commercial banks and others	51,361	48,603	49,409	46,444	46,995	47,060
Use of IMF credit and SDR allocations	**16,262**	**12,824**	**14,505**	**14,434**	**16,477**	**18,916**
IMF credit	14,245	10,938	9,974	10,125	12,133	14,694
SDR allocations	2,017	1,886	4,531	4,309	4,344	4,222
Short-term external debt stocks	**27,264**	**24,156**	**23,243**	**16,266**	**21,116**	**18,326**
Disbursements, long-term	**32,240**	**16,500**	**12,820**	**19,842**	**29,263**	**27,587**
Public and publicly guaranteed sector	7,969	7,056	6,373	18,524	27,621	26,292
Private sector not guaranteed	24,272	9,444	6,447	1,318	1,642	1,296
Principal repayments, long-term	**22,885**	**12,445**	**8,992**	**4,791**	**2,230**	**4,035**
Public and publicly guaranteed sector	1,446	4,987	2,940	1,129	968	2,156
Private sector not guaranteed	21,439	7,458	6,052	3,662	1,262	1,879
Interest payments, long-term	**3,532**	**3,372**	**3,649**	**1,901**	**1,512**	**2,307**
Public and publicly guaranteed sector	594	1,893	2,126	1,197	881	1,456
Private sector not guaranteed	2,938	1,479	1,523	704	631	851

UZBEKISTAN

(US$ million, unless otherwise indicated)

Snapshot	2024
Total external debt stocks	**70,256**
External debt stocks as % of:	
Exports	221
GNI	61
Debt service as % of:	
Exports	36
GNI	10
Net financial flows, debt and equity	10,836
Net debt inflows	9,136
Net equity inflows	1,700
GNI	**116,100**
Population (million)	**36**

Figure 2 Average terms on new debt commitments from official and private creditors

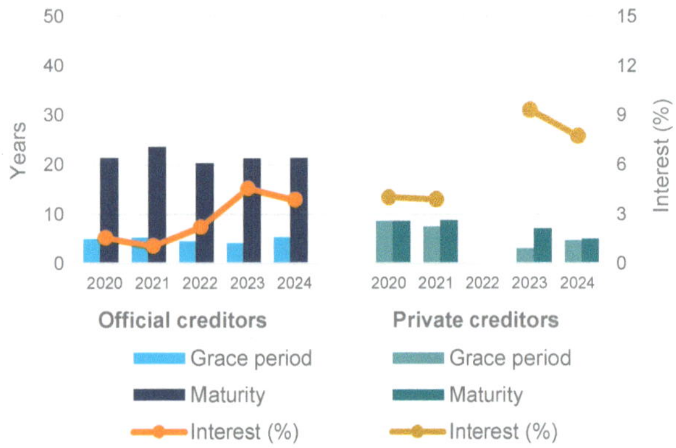

Figure 1 Public and publicly guaranteed debt, by creditor and creditor type in 2024, including IMF credit

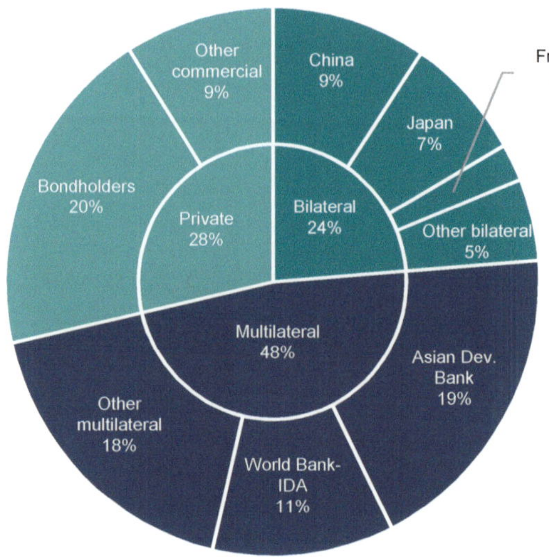

Summary External Debt Data	2010	2020	2021	2022	2023	2024
Total external debt stocks	**7,986**	**37,154**	**44,872**	**53,593**	**61,570**	**70,256**
Long-term external debt stocks	**7,159**	**34,003**	**39,817**	**45,896**	**53,267**	**63,346**
Public and publicly guaranteed debt from:	*3,428*	*22,173*	*25,955*	*29,258*	*32,991*	*39,165*
Official creditors	3,203	17,445	19,486	22,245	24,846	27,927
Multilateral	1,210	9,787	10,760	13,691	15,987	18,567
of which: World Bank	373	3,734	4,328	5,571	6,615	7,679
Bilateral	1,992	7,658	8,726	8,554	8,859	9,360
Private creditors	226	4,728	6,469	7,013	8,144	11,238
Bondholders	..	2,548	3,883	3,883	4,391	7,704
Commercial banks and others	226	2,181	2,587	3,131	3,753	3,534
Private nonguaranteed debt from:	*3,730*	*11,829*	*13,862*	*16,637*	*20,276*	*24,181*
Bondholders	..	600	900	900	1,000	1,284
Commercial banks and others	3,730	11,229	12,962	15,737	19,276	22,897
Use of IMF credit and SDR allocations	**405**	**775**	**1,493**	**1,420**	**1,370**	**1,212**
IMF credit	0	397	386	367	308	180
SDR allocations	405	378	1,107	1,053	1,061	1,032
Short-term external debt stocks	**423**	**2,376**	**3,562**	**6,278**	**6,933**	**5,699**
Disbursements, long-term	**1,191**	**10,814**	**11,213**	**12,751**	**14,532**	**18,399**
Public and publicly guaranteed sector	455	7,092	5,144	4,996	5,815	9,343
Private sector not guaranteed	736	3,722	6,069	7,755	8,717	9,056
Principal repayments, long-term	**493**	**2,402**	**3,938**	**6,124**	**7,056**	**7,911**
Public and publicly guaranteed sector	370	559	988	1,144	1,978	2,698
Private sector not guaranteed	123	1,842	2,950	4,980	5,078	5,213
Interest payments, long-term	**118**	**860**	**957**	**1,282**	**2,325**	**3,039**
Public and publicly guaranteed sector	63	407	481	662	1,231	1,719
Private sector not guaranteed	55	453	476	619	1,095	1,320

VANUATU

(US$ million, unless otherwise indicated)

Snapshot	2024
Total external debt stocks	**519.9**
External debt stocks as % of:	
Exports	129.4
GNI	39.2
Debt service as % of:	
Exports	6.5
GNI	2.0
Net financial flows, debt and equity	95.1
Net debt inflows	66.2
Net equity inflows	28.9
GNI	**1,327.5**
Population (thousand)	**328**

Figure 1 Public and publicly guaranteed debt, by creditor and creditor type in 2024, including IMF credit

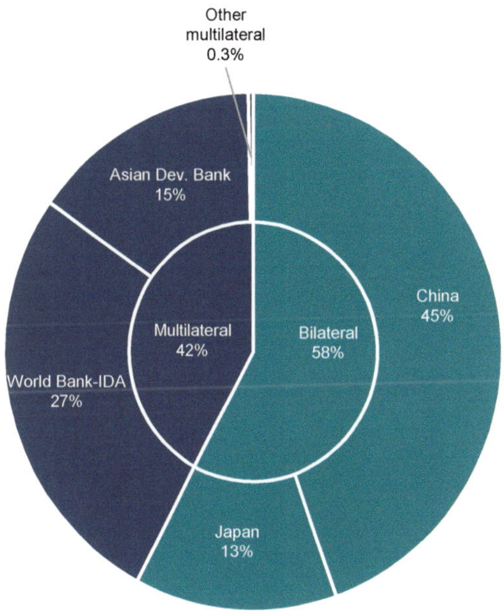

Figure 2 Average terms on new debt commitments from official and private creditors

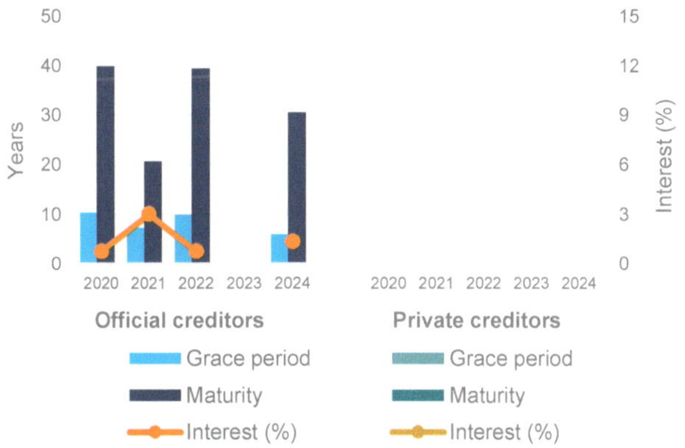

Summary External Debt Data	2010	2020	2021	2022	2023	2024
Total external debt stocks	**177.7**	**439.9**	**476.7**	**463.4**	**470.7**	**519.9**
Long-term external debt stocks	**102.6**	**367.1**	**373.9**	**374.0**	**362.3**	**352.9**
Public and publicly guaranteed debt from:	*102.6*	*367.1*	*373.9*	*374.0*	*362.3*	*352.9*
Official creditors	102.6	367.1	373.9	374.0	362.3	352.9
Multilateral	68.8	145.2	148.4	151.1	153.4	148.4
of which: World Bank	11.7	91.6	97.9	98.2	96.0	95.5
Bilateral	33.8	221.9	225.4	222.9	208.9	204.5
Private creditors	..	..	..	..	..	..
Bondholders	..	..	..	..	..	..
Commercial banks and others	..	..	..	..	..	..
Private nonguaranteed debt from:	..	..	..	..	..	..
Bondholders	..	..	..	..	..	..
Commercial banks and others	..	..	..	..	..	..
Use of IMF credit and SDR allocations	**25.1**	**34.4**	**63.0**	**57.7**	**55.9**	**52.1**
IMF credit	0.0	11.0	8.3	5.7	3.4	1.1
SDR allocations	25.1	23.4	54.7	52.0	52.4	51.0
Short-term external debt stocks	**50.0**	**38.4**	**39.9**	**31.8**	**52.5**	**114.9**
Disbursements, long-term	**3.3**	**10.7**	**25.5**	**46.0**	**11.3**	**17.0**
Public and publicly guaranteed sector	3.3	10.7	25.5	46.0	11.3	17.0
Private sector not guaranteed	..	..	..	..	..	..
Principal repayments, long-term	**3.6**	**8.1**	**10.5**	**13.8**	**13.6**	**10.9**
Public and publicly guaranteed sector	3.6	8.1	10.5	13.8	13.6	10.9
Private sector not guaranteed	..	..	..	..	..	..
Interest payments, long-term	**1.6**	**4.1**	**4.2**	**4.6**	**4.5**	**4.4**
Public and publicly guaranteed sector	1.6	4.1	4.2	4.6	4.5	4.4
Private sector not guaranteed	..	..	..	..	..	..

VIET NAM

(US$ million, unless otherwise indicated)

Snapshot	2024
Total external debt stocks	**132,907**
External debt stocks as % of:	
Exports	31
GNI	29
Debt service as % of:	
Exports	8
GNI	7
Net financial flows, debt and equity	11,583
Net debt inflows	-7,170
Net equity inflows	18,753
GNI	**460,695**
Population (million)	**101**

Figure 1 Public and publicly guaranteed debt, by creditor and creditor type in 2024, including IMF credit

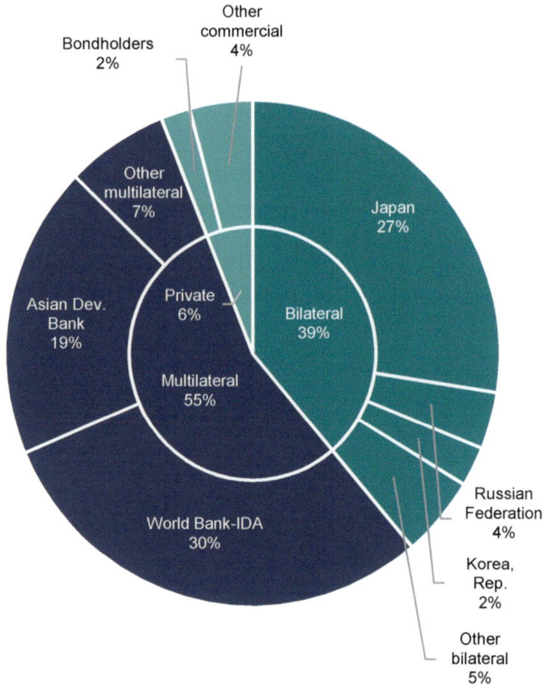

Figure 2 Average terms on new debt commitments from official and private creditors

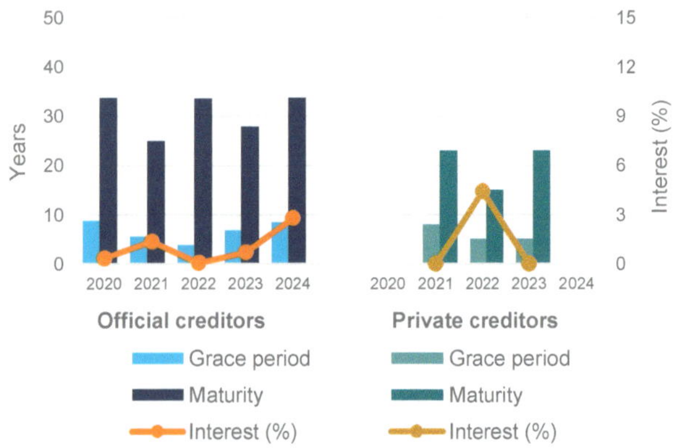

Summary External Debt Data	2010	2020	2021	2022	2023	2024
Total external debt stocks	**45,022**	**129,479**	**139,853**	**146,622**	**141,845**	**132,907**
Long-term external debt stocks	**37,560**	**102,422**	**104,632**	**106,578**	**104,824**	**93,968**
Public and publicly guaranteed debt from:	*32,805*	*55,651*	*51,374*	*46,460*	*43,883*	*38,450*
Official creditors	27,320	49,185	45,796	41,567	39,721	36,124
Multilateral	12,573	25,383	24,656	23,344	22,658	21,193
of which: World Bank	7,743	16,378	16,008	15,109	14,532	13,585
Bilateral	14,746	23,802	21,140	18,223	17,063	14,931
Private creditors	5,485	6,467	5,578	4,893	4,163	2,326
Bondholders	2,020	756	751	746	741	737
Commercial banks and others	3,465	5,711	4,827	4,147	3,421	1,589
Private nonguaranteed debt from:	*4,755*	*46,771*	*53,258*	*60,118*	*60,941*	*55,518*
Bondholders	..	1,094	1,444	1,769	1,734	1,734
Commercial banks and others	4,755	45,677	51,814	58,349	59,208	53,784
Use of IMF credit and SDR allocations	**529**	**453**	**1,987**	**1,890**	**1,905**	**1,852**
IMF credit	45	0	0	0	0	0
SDR allocations	485	453	1,987	1,890	1,905	1,852
Short-term external debt stocks	**6,932**	**26,604**	**33,233**	**38,154**	**35,115**	**37,087**
Disbursements, long-term	**6,965**	**17,327**	**23,264**	**28,470**	**21,833**	**19,592**
Public and publicly guaranteed sector	5,643	2,124	1,746	1,778	1,643	1,065
Private sector not guaranteed	1,322	15,202	21,518	26,692	20,190	18,527
Principal repayments, long-term	**1,055**	**14,389**	**18,779**	**23,494**	**22,971**	**28,734**
Public and publicly guaranteed sector	1,055	4,116	3,751	3,665	3,605	4,784
Private sector not guaranteed	..	10,273	15,028	19,829	19,366	23,950
Interest payments, long-term	**699**	**2,020**	**1,595**	**2,017**	**4,191**	**3,923**
Public and publicly guaranteed sector	554	995	756	739	1,041	1,067
Private sector not guaranteed	145	1,025	839	1,278	3,150	2,856

YEMEN, REPUBLIC OF

(US$ million, unless otherwise indicated)

Snapshot	2024
Total external debt stocks	**7,087**
External debt stocks as % of:	
Exports	..
GNI	..
Debt service as % of:	
Exports	..
GNI	..
Net financial flows, debt and equity	-120
Net debt inflows	-120
Net equity inflows	..
GNI	..
Population (million)	**41**

Figure 2 Average terms on new debt commitments from official and private creditors

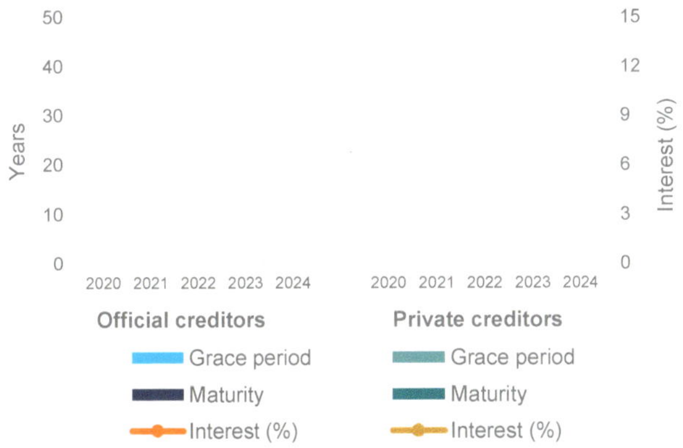

Figure 1 Public and publicly guaranteed debt, by creditor and creditor type in 2024, including IMF credit

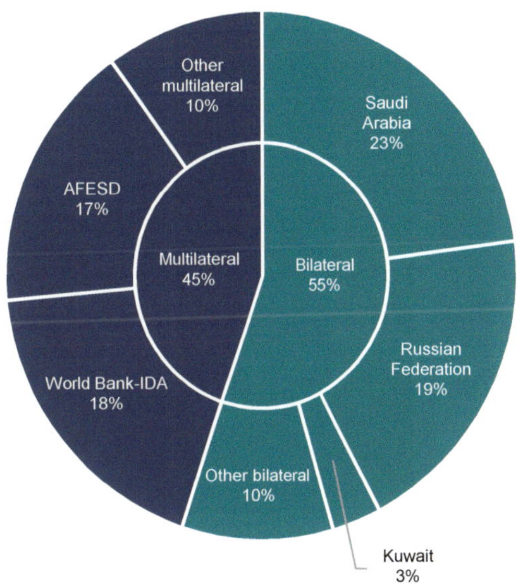

Summary External Debt Data	2010	2020	2021	2022	2023	2024
Total external debt stocks	**6,504**	**7,121**	**7,602**	**7,351**	**7,283**	**7,087**
Long-term external debt stocks	**5,945**	**6,251**	**6,108**	**5,896**	**5,815**	**5,665**
Public and publicly guaranteed debt from:	*5,945*	*6,251*	*6,108*	*5,896*	*5,815*	*5,665*
Official creditors	5,941	6,251	6,108	5,896	5,815	5,665
Multilateral	3,294	3,027	2,910	2,739	2,669	2,541
of which: World Bank	2,180	1,488	1,368	1,225	1,155	1,042
Bilateral	2,647	3,224	3,198	3,157	3,146	3,124
Private creditors	3	..	..	..	..	..
Bondholders	..	..	..	..	..	..
Commercial banks and others	3	..	..	..	..	..
Private nonguaranteed debt from:	..	..	..	..	..	..
Bondholders	..	..	..	..	..	..
Commercial banks and others	..	..	..	..	..	..
Use of IMF credit and SDR allocations	**436**	**410**	**1,021**	**956**	**951**	**912**
IMF credit	78	75	43	26	13	0
SDR allocations	358	335	978	930	938	912
Short-term external debt stocks	**124**	**460**	**473**	**499**	**517**	**511**
Disbursements, long-term	**297**	**38**	**13**	**9**	**0**	**0**
Public and publicly guaranteed sector	297	38	13	9	0	0
Private sector not guaranteed	..	..	..	..	..	..
Principal repayments, long-term	**155**	**75**	**80**	**78**	**79**	**82**
Public and publicly guaranteed sector	155	75	80	78	79	82
Private sector not guaranteed	..	..	..	..	..	..
Interest payments, long-term	**74**	**11**	**11**	**9**	**9**	**8**
Public and publicly guaranteed sector	74	11	11	9	9	8
Private sector not guaranteed	..	..	..	..	..	..

Note: Figure 2 shows no data values because the country did not have new commitments from 2020 to 2024.

ZAMBIA

(US$ million, unless otherwise indicated)

Snapshot	2024
Total external debt stocks	**28,118**
External debt stocks as % of:	
Exports	219
GNI	114
Debt service as % of:	
Exports	30
GNI	16
Net financial flows, debt and equity	893
Net debt inflows	-333
Net equity inflows	1,226
GNI	**24,621**
Population (million)	**21**

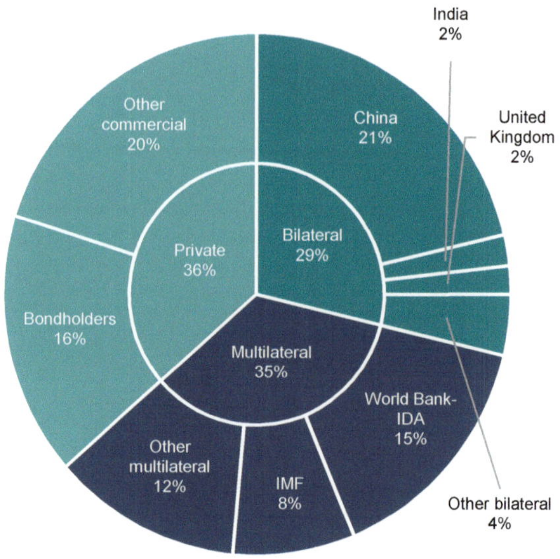

Figure 1 Public and publicly guaranteed debt, by creditor and creditor type in 2024, including IMF credit

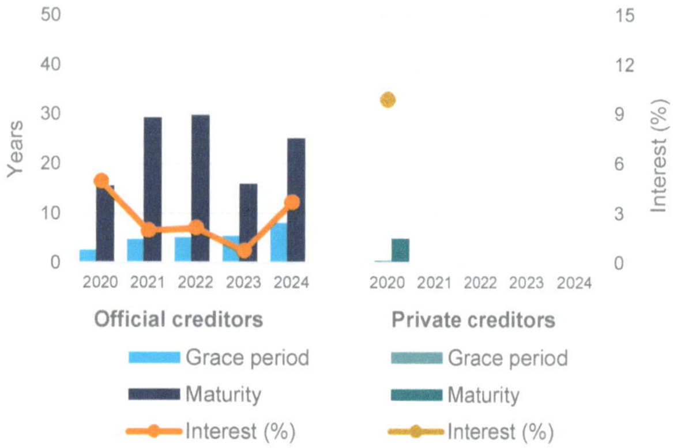

Figure 2 Average terms on new debt commitments from official and private creditors

Summary External Debt Data	2010	2020	2021	2022	2023	2024
Total external debt stocks	**4,321**	**29,531**	**26,943**	**28,423**	**29,077**	**28,118**
Long-term external debt stocks	**2,054**	**28,123**	**23,559**	**23,641**	**23,217**	**22,196**
Public and publicly guaranteed debt from:	*1,259*	*15,058*	*15,258*	*15,719*	*15,385*	*15,473*
Official creditors	1,203	7,855	8,099	8,789	8,936	9,353
Multilateral	872	3,082	3,186	3,911	4,123	4,534
of which: World Bank	430	1,296	1,377	2,047	2,221	2,510
Bilateral	331	4,772	4,914	4,877	4,812	4,819
Private creditors	56	7,203	7,159	6,930	6,449	6,120
Bondholders	..	3,000	3,000	3,000	3,000	2,739
Commercial banks and others	56	4,203	4,159	3,930	3,449	3,382
Private nonguaranteed debt from:	*794*	*13,066*	*8,301*	*7,922*	*7,832*	*6,723*
Bondholders	..	..	..	..	..	..
Commercial banks and others	794	13,066	8,301	7,922	7,832	6,723
Use of IMF credit and SDR allocations	**1,117**	**678**	**1,969**	**2,058**	**2,450**	**3,129**
IMF credit	395	3	0	186	563	1,295
SDR allocations	722	676	1,969	1,872	1,887	1,835
Short-term external debt stocks	**1,150**	**730**	**1,416**	**2,724**	**3,409**	**2,792**
Disbursements, long-term	**251**	**3,272**	**496**	**1,428**	**590**	**2,592**
Public and publicly guaranteed sector	224	2,130	496	997	340	684
Private sector not guaranteed	27	1,143	..	431	250	1,907
Principal repayments, long-term	**92**	**1,556**	**1,471**	**1,158**	**608**	**3,496**
Public and publicly guaranteed sector	52	368	237	349	269	479
Private sector not guaranteed	40	1,188	1,234	809	339	3,017
Interest payments, long-term	**31**	**467**	**232**	**221**	**166**	**265**
Public and publicly guaranteed sector	12	335	104	89	81	208
Private sector not guaranteed	18	132	127	132	85	57

ZIMBABWE

(US$ million, unless otherwise indicated)

Snapshot	**2024**
Total external debt stocks	**14,404**
External debt stocks as % of:	
Exports	..
GNI	33
Debt service as % of:	
Exports	..
GNI	3
Net financial flows, debt and equity	559
Net debt inflows	-38
Net equity inflows	597
GNI	**43,679**
Population (million)	**17**

Figure 2 Average terms on new debt commitments from official and private creditors

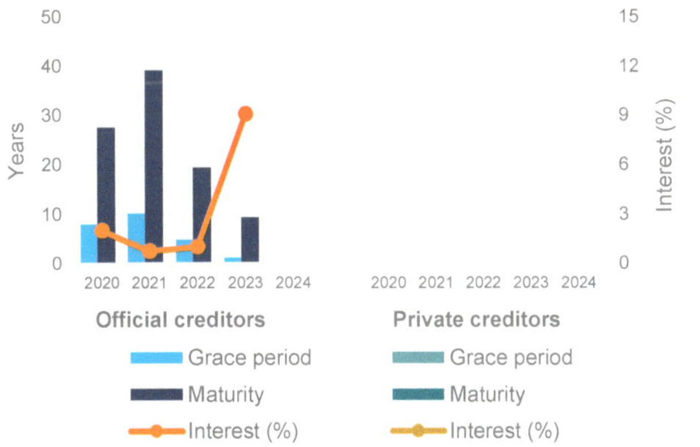

Figure 1 Public and publicly guaranteed debt, by creditor and creditor type in 2024, including IMF credit

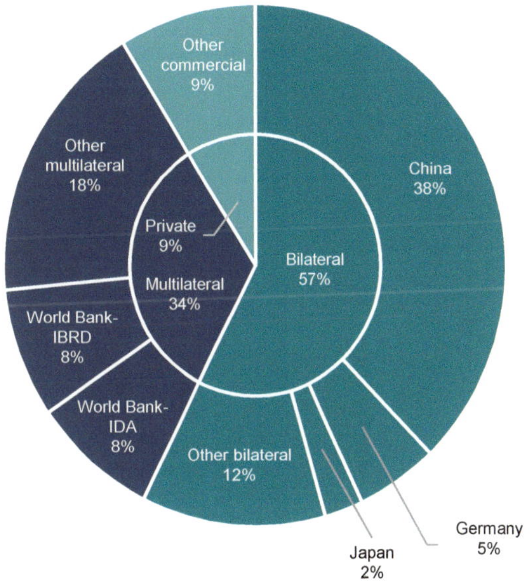

Summary External Debt Data	**2010**	**2020**	**2021**	**2022**	**2023**	**2024**
Total external debt stocks	**7,050**	**13,034**	**14,111**	**14,121**	**14,549**	**14,404**
Long-term external debt stocks	**4,692**	**8,692**	**8,951**	**8,793**	**9,249**	**9,112**
Public and publicly guaranteed debt from:	*4,087*	*4,860*	*4,880*	*4,969*	*5,400*	*5,314*
Official creditors	3,518	4,318	4,369	4,492	4,910	4,846
Multilateral	1,900	1,529	1,498	1,464	1,850	1,797
of which: World Bank	976	910	893	867	869	855
Bilateral	1,618	2,788	2,872	3,028	3,059	3,049
Private creditors	569	542	510	476	490	468
Bondholders	0	0	0	0	0	0
Commercial banks and others	569	542	510	476	490	468
Private nonguaranteed debt from:	*605*	*3,832*	*4,072*	*3,825*	*3,849*	*3,798*
Bondholders	..	..	..	..	..	..
Commercial banks and others	605	3,832	4,072	3,825	3,849	3,798
Use of IMF credit and SDR allocations	**529**	**488**	**1,422**	**1,352**	**1,363**	**1,325**
IMF credit	110	0	0	0	0	0
SDR allocations	419	488	1,422	1,352	1,363	1,325
Short-term external debt stocks	**1,830**	**3,855**	**3,738**	**3,975**	**3,936**	**3,967**
Disbursements, long-term	**847**	**906**	**914**	**316**	**1,425**	**913**
Public and publicly guaranteed sector	4	60	209	295	478	73
Private sector not guaranteed	843	845	706	20	947	839
Principal repayments, long-term	**338**	**934**	**551**	**290**	**994**	**946**
Public and publicly guaranteed sector	2	25	85	23	72	55
Private sector not guaranteed	336	910	466	266	922	891
Interest payments, long-term	**32**	**22**	**29**	**45**	**308**	**301**
Public and publicly guaranteed sector	14	17	25	12	49	34
Private sector not guaranteed	18	5	4	32	259	267

APPENDIX

Data Sources

The principal source of information for the tables in *International Debt Report 2025* is the International Debt Statistics database, which is based on reports to the World Bank through the World Bank's Debtor Reporting System (DRS) from member countries that have received either International Bank for Reconstruction and Development loans or International Development Association credits. The DRS has its origin in the World Bank's need to monitor and assess the financial position of its borrowers. Since 1951, borrowers have been required to provide statistics on their public external debt and private sector debt that benefit from a public guarantee. Reporting countries submit reports on the annual status, transactions, and terms of the long-term external debt of public agencies and that of private ones guaranteed by a public agency in the debtor country. The DRS maintains these records on a loan-by-loan basis. In 1973, coverage of the DRS was expanded to include private sector nonguaranteed borrowing; however, for this category of debt, data are provided by borrowers in aggregate rather than loan by loan.

Data submitted to the DRS are processed in the World Bank External Debt system, along with additional information received from the African Development Bank, the Asian Development Bank, the European Bank for Reconstruction and Development, the Inter-American Development Bank, the International Monetary Fund, and institutions of the World Bank Group (International Bank for Reconstruction and Development and International Development Association). The World Bank External Debt is an internal system of the World Bank. Among its outputs is the International Debt Statistics database, from which the tables and data visualizations in this publication and the online database are produced.

Data on exports and imports (on a balance of payments basis), international reserves, current account balances, foreign direct investment on equity, portfolio equity flows, and primary income on foreign direct investment are drawn mainly from the International Monetary Fund, supplemented by UN Trade and Development reports and country data. Balance of payments data are presented according to the sixth edition of the International Monetary Fund's *Balance of Payments Manual.* Official aid flows come from data collected and published by the Development Assistance Committee of the Organisation for Economic Co-operation and Development. Short-term external debt data are as reported by debtor countries or are estimates based on the Bank for International Settlements quarterly series of commercial banks' claims on low- and middle-income countries. For some countries, estimates were prepared by pooling creditor and debtor information. Data on the gross national income of most low- and middle-income countries are collected from national statistical organizations or central banks by visiting and resident World Bank missions.

Every effort has been made to ensure the accuracy and completeness of the external debt statistics. Coverage has been improved through the efforts of the reporting agencies and close collaboration between the World Bank and its partners, the Commonwealth Secretariat and UN Trade and Development, which provide debt recording and reporting systems across the globe, as well as through the work of the World Bank missions, which visit member countries to gather data and to provide technical assistance on debt issues. Nevertheless, quality and coverage vary among debtors and may also vary for the same debtor from year to year. Data on long-term external debt reported by member countries are checked against, and supplemented by, data from several other sources. Among these sources are the statements and reports of several regional development banks, government lending agencies, and official government websites.

Country Groups

Regional Groups

East Asia and Pacific
Cambodia (A)
China (P)
Fiji (A)
Indonesia (A)
Lao PDR (A)
Mongolia (A)
Myanmar (A)
Papua New Guinea (A)
Philippines (A)
Samoa (A)
Solomon Islands (A)
Thailand (A)
Timor-Leste (A)
Tonga (A)
Vanuatu (A)
Viet Nam (A)

Europe and Central Asia
Albania (A)
Armenia (A)
Azerbaijan (A)
Belarus (E)
Bosnia and Herzegovina[a] (A)
Georgia (A)
Kazakhstan (A)
Kosovo (A)
Kyrgyz Republic (A)
Moldova (A)
Montenegro (A)
North Macedonia (A)
Serbia[a,b] (A)
Tajikistan (A)
Türkiye (A)
Turkmenistan (A)
Ukraine (A)
Uzbekistan (A)

Latin America and the Caribbean[c]
Argentina (A)
Belize (A)
Bolivia (A)
Brazil (A)
Colombia (A)
Dominica (A)
Dominican Republic (A)
Ecuador (P)
El Salvador (A)
Grenada (A)
Guatemala (A)
Haiti (A)
Honduras (A)
Jamaica (A)
Mexico (A)
Nicaragua (A)
Paraguay (A)
Peru (A)
St. Lucia (A)
St. Vincent and the Grenadines (A)
Suriname (A)

Middle East, North Africa, Afghanistan, and Pakistan
Afghanistan (E)
Algeria (A)
Djibouti (A)
Egypt, Arab Rep. (A)
Iran, Islamic Rep. (E)
Iraq (A)
Jordan (A)
Lebanon (E)
Morocco (A)
Pakistan (A)
Syrian Arab Republic (E)
Tunisia (A)
Yemen, Rep. (P)

South Asia
Bangladesh (A)
Bhutan (A)
India (A)
Maldives (A)
Nepal (A)
Sri Lanka (A)

Sub-Saharan Africa
Angola (A)
Benin (A)
Botswana (A)
Burkina Faso (A)
Burundi (A)
Cabo Verde (A)
Cameroon (A)
Central African Republic (A)
Chad (P)
Comoros (A)
Congo, Dem. Rep. (A)
Congo, Rep. (A)
Côte d'Ivoire (A)
Equatorial Guinea (A)
Eritrea (E)
Eswatini (A)
Ethiopia (A)
Gabon (A)
Gambia, The (A)
Ghana (A)
Guinea (A)
Guinea-Bissau (A)
Kenya (A)
Lesotho (A)
Liberia (A)
Madagascar (A)
Malawi (A)
Mali (A)
Mauritania (A)
Mauritius (A)
Mozambique (A)
Niger (A)
Nigeria (A)
Rwanda (A)
São Tomé and Príncipe (A)
Senegal (A)
Sierra Leone (A)
Somalia, Fed. Rep. (A)
South Africa (A)
Sudan (E)
Tanzania (A)
Togo (A)
Uganda (A)
Zambia (A)
Zimbabwe (A)

Source: World Bank Debtor Reporting System.
Note: Letters in parentheses indicate Debtor Reporting System reporters' status: (A) as reported, (P) preliminary, and (E) estimated. The status "as reported" indicates that the country was fully current in its reporting under the Debtor Reporting System and that World Bank staff are satisfied that the reported data give an adequate and fair representation of the country's total public debt. "Preliminary" data are based on reported or collected information; however, because of incompleteness or other reasons, an element of staff estimation is included. "Estimated" data indicate that countries are not current in their reporting and that a significant element of staff estimation has been necessary in producing the data tables.
a. For Bosnia and Herzegovina, total debt before 1999, excluding International Bank for Reconstruction and Development and International Monetary Fund obligations and short-term debt, is included under Serbia.
b. Data before 2006 include Montenegro.
c. Guyana's data are reported and included in this report because the country is eligible for International Development Association resources. However, because it is classified as a high-income country, its data are excluded from the regional aggregates.

Income Groups

Low-income countries	*Middle-income countries*		
Afghanistan	Albania	Gabon	Nigeria
Burkina Faso	Algeria	Georgia	North Macedonia
Burundi	Angola	*Ghana*	Pakistan
Central African Republic	Argentina	Grenada	Papua New Guinea
Chad	Armenia	Guatemala	Paraguay
Congo, Dem. Rep.	Azerbaijan	*Guinea*	Peru
Eritrea	*Bangladesh*	*Haiti*	Philippines
Ethiopia	Belarus	*Honduras*	*Samoa*
Gambia, The	Belize	India	*São Tomé and Príncipe*
Guinea-Bissau	*Benin*	Indonesia	*Senegal*
Liberia	*Bhutan*	Iran, Islamic Rep.	Serbia
Madagascar	Bolivia	Iraq	*Solomon Islands*
Malawi	Bosnia and Herzegovina	Jamaica	South Africa
Mali	Botswana	Jordan	*Sri Lanka*
Mozambique	Brazil	Kazakhstan	St. Lucia
Niger	Cabo Verde	Kenya	St. Vincent and the Grenadines
Rwanda	*Cambodia*	*Kosovo*	Suriname
Sierra Leone	Cameroon	*Kyrgyz Republic*	*Tajikistan*
Somalia, Fed. Rep.	China	*Lao PDR*	*Tanzania*
Sudan	Colombia	Lebanon	Thailand
Syrian Arab Republic	*Comoros*	*Lesotho*	Timor-Leste
Togo	Congo, Rep.	*Maldives*	*Tonga*
Uganda	*Côte d'Ivoire*	*Mauritania*	Tunisia
Yemen, Rep.	*Djibouti*	Mauritius	Türkiye
	Dominica	Mexico	Turkmenistan
	Dominican Republic	Moldova	Ukraine
	Ecuador	Mongolia	Uzbekistan
	Egypt, Arab Rep.	Montenegro	*Vanuatu*
	El Salvador	Morocco	Viet Nam
	Equatorial Guinea	*Myanmar*	*Zambia*
	Eswatini	*Nepal*	Zimbabwe
	Fiji	*Nicaragua*	

Source: World Bank.
Note: Low-income countries are those with a GNI per capita of US$1,135 or less in 2024. Middle-income countries are those with a GNI per capita equal to or more than US$1,136 but equal to or less than US$13,935. Italicized countries are IDA-only countries as of July 1, 2025; IDA-only excludes blend and IBRD countries. Ethiopia has a temporary status of unclassified according to the FY2026 income classification, but for this publication it has been retained under its FY2025 status as a low-income country and is included in this report and the International Debt Statistics database. The World Bank still considers Ethiopia as an IDA-only country, so there is no change to the terms and conditions of Bank financing for the country. Guyana is classified as a high-income country as of July 1, 2025, so it does not appear in this table or in the low- and middle-income countries' aggregates; however, as an IDA-only country, its data are included in this report. República Bolivariana de Venezuela is unclassified according to the World Bank FY2026 income classification owing to a lack of available data; thus, it is not included in this report or the International Debt Statistics database. FY = fiscal year; GNI = gross national income; IBRD = International Bank for Reconstruction and Development; IDA = International Development Association.

Glossary

This list provides general descriptions, not precise legal definitions, of the terms commonly used in this report. However, the descriptions include legal and policy elements relevant to how these terms are understood and applied in practice.

Base year is the period against which quantities and prices of a given period are compared.

Bilateral currency swap line is an agreement between two central banks to exchange a cash flow in one currency against a cash flow in another currency according to predetermined terms and conditions.

Blue bond is a debt instrument issued by governments, development banks, or other entities to raise capital from impact investors to finance marine and ocean-based projects that yield positive environmental, economic, and climate benefits.

Bonds are debt instruments issued by public and publicly guaranteed or private debtors with durations of one year or longer. Bonds usually give the holder the unconditional right to fixed money income or to contractually determined, variable money income.

Central bank is a country's financial institution that exercises control over key aspects of the financial system. It carries out activities such as issuing currency, managing international reserves, transacting with the International Monetary Fund, and providing credit to deposit-taking corporations.

Commitments (of public and publicly guaranteed debt) constitute the total amount of new long-term loans to public sector borrowers or to borrowers with a public sector guarantee extended by official and private lenders and for which contracts were signed in the year specified.

Common Framework for debt treatment beyond the Debt Service Suspension Initiative is an initiative launched in 2022 and endorsed by the Group of Twenty, designed to support, in a structural manner, low-income countries with unsustainable debt.

Concessional debt conveys information about the borrower's receipt of aid from official lenders at concessional terms as defined by the World Bank, that is, loans with an original grant element of 35 percent or more. The World Bank classifies loans from major regional development banks—the African Development

Bank, Asian Development Bank, and Inter-American Development Bank—as concessional.

Debt buyback is the repurchase by a debtor of its own debt, either at a discount price or at par value. In the event of a buyback of long-term debt, the face value of the debt bought back will be recorded as a decline in stock outstanding of long-term debt, and the cash amount received by creditors will be recorded as a principal repayment.

Debt distress, as defined under the Debt Sustainability Framework, is caused by unsustainable debt, wherein a country is unable to fulfill its financial obligations and debt restructuring is required.

Debt-distressed is when a country's debt and debt service ratios significantly and persistently breach established thresholds, indicating an inability to meet its financial obligations. It is the most severe risk category in the International Monetary Fund–World Bank Debt Sustainability Framework (DSF) for low-income countries.

Debt-for-climate swaps are agreements that convert debts into commitments related to climate activities.

Debt-for-development swaps are agreements that convert debts into commitments related to a specific development goal, such as nature conservation, climate action, education, nutrition, or support for refugees.

Debt-for-equity swaps are agreements that convert debts into commitments related to equity investments.

Debt-for-nature swaps are agreements that convert debts into commitments related to conservation activities.

Debt restructurings are revisions to debt service obligations agreed on by creditors and debtors. Such agreements change the amount and timing of future principal and interest payments. Debt restructuring is a complex process that requires the agreement of domestic and foreign creditors and involves burden sharing between different parties (for example, between residents and banks in most restructurings of domestic debt).

Debt service is the sum of principal repayments and interest paid on total long-term debt (public and publicly guaranteed debt and private nonguaranteed debt).

Debt Service Suspension Initiative (DSSI) took effect on May 1, 2020, and allowed 73 eligible countries to apply for a temporary suspension of debt service payments owed to official bilateral creditors. The suspension period, originally set to end on December 31, 2020, was extended through December 2021.

Debt service-to-export ratio is the ratio of total debt service (principal repayments and interest payments) to the value of exports of goods and services and receipts of primary income from abroad.

Debt service-to-GNI ratio is the ratio of total debt service (principal repayments and interest payments) to gross national income (GNI).

Debt sustainability is the condition under which a country (or its government) does not, in the future, need to default or renegotiate or restructure its debt, or make implausibly large policy adjustments.

Debt swap (conversion) is an exchange of debt—typically at a discount—for a nondebt claim (such as equity) or for counterpart funds that can be used to finance a particular project or policy. In essence, public sector debt is extinguished and a nondebt liability created in a debt conversion.

Debt-to-export ratio is the ratio of outstanding external debt to the value of exports of goods and services and receipts of primary income from abroad.

Debt-to-GNI ratio is the ratio of outstanding external debt to gross national income (GNI).

Debt transparency results in readily available data on public debt, allowing governments to make informed decisions about macroeconomic policy and debt sustainability.

Disbursements are drawings during the year specified on loan commitments contracted by the borrower.

Disinflation is the slowdown or fall in the annual rate of inflation.

Eurobond is a type of bond that governments or corporations issue outside of their home country and is denominated in a currency different from that of the issuer. Typically, Eurobonds are long-term debt instruments and are commonly denominated in US dollars. They can also be denominated in other currencies such as the euro, pound, Japanese yen, and Swiss franc.

External debt flows are debt-related transactions during the year specified. They include disbursements, principal repayments, and interest payments.

External debt stocks comprise public and publicly guaranteed long-term external debt, private nonguaranteed long-term external debt, use of International Monetary Fund credit and special drawing rights allocation, and short-term external debt.

Fiscal sustainability refers to the future implications of current fiscal policies and, more precisely, to the question of whether the government can continue to pursue its set of budgetary policies without endangering its solvency.

Foreign direct investment refers to direct investment equity flows in the reporting economy. It is the sum of equity capital, reinvestment earnings, and other capital. Direct investment is a category of cross-border investment associated with a resident in one economy having control or a significant degree of influence on the management of an enterprise that is resident in another economy. Ownership of 10 percent or more of the ordinary shares or voting stock is the criterion for determining the existence of a direct investment relationship.

Fragile and conflict-affected situations (FCS) are countries with high levels of institutional and social fragility, identified using indicators that measure the quality of policy and institutions, and manifestations of fragility, and/or are countries affected by violent conflict, identified using a threshold number of conflict-related deaths relative to the population.

The Group of Seven (G-7) is the collection of seven industrialized countries—Canada, France, Germany, Italy, Japan, the United Kingdom, and the United States—that meets annually to discuss issues such as global economic governance, international security, and, most recently, artificial intelligence.

The Group of Twenty (G-20) is the collection of the world's largest economies—Argentina, Australia, Brazil, Canada, China, France, Germany, India, Indonesia, Italy, Japan, the Republic of Korea, Mexico, the Russian Federation, Saudi Arabia, South Africa, Türkiye, the United Kingdom, and the United States—along with the African Union and the European Union, established to discuss international economic and financial stability.

Grace period is the time between the date on which a loan is committed and the date on which the first principal payment is due. The information presented in the International Debt Statistics database is the average grace period on all public and publicly guaranteed debt committed during the specified period.

Grants are legally binding commitments that obligate a specific value of funds available for disbursement for which there is no payment requirement. They include debt forgiveness grants and grants from bilateral and multilateral agencies (such as the International Development Association).

Green bonds are bonds that finance green projects and provide investors with regular or fixed income payments.

Gross domestic product is the sum of gross value added by all resident producers in the economy, plus any product taxes and minus any subsidies not included in the value of the products.

Gross national income is the sum of value added by all resident producers, plus any product taxes (less subsidies) not included in the valuation of output, plus net receipts of primary income compensation of employees and property income from abroad. Yearly average exchange rates are used to convert gross national income from local currency to US dollars.

Heavily Indebted Poor Countries (HIPC) Initiative is a program of the World Bank and the International Monetary Fund to provide debt relief to qualifying countries with unsustainable debt burdens.

IDA-eligible countries are the countries that are eligible to receive International Development Association (IDA) resources. Eligibility for IDA support depends on a country's relative poverty, defined as gross national income per capita below an established threshold, which is updated annually.

Inflation is the rate of increase in prices over a given period in an economy.

Interest payments are the amounts of interest paid in foreign currency, goods, or services in the year specified.

Interest payment-to-GNI ratio is the ratio of interest payment to gross national income.

Interest rate is the interest rate applicable to a loan commitment as specified in the loan contract. The information presented in the International Debt Statistics database is the average interest on all public and publicly guaranteed debt committed during the specified period.

Long-term external debt is debt that has an original or extended maturity of more than one year and that is owed to nonresidents by residents of an economy and is repayable in currency, goods, or services.

Maturity is the date on which the final principal repayment on a loan is due. It is the sum of the grace and repayment periods. The information presented in the International Debt Statistics database is the average maturity on all public and publicly guaranteed debt committed during the specified period.

Monetary policy is used by central banks to manage economic fluctuations and achieve price stability, with low and stable inflation. Central banks conduct monetary policy by adjusting the supply of money, usually through buying or selling securities in the open market. When central banks lower interest rates, monetary policy is easing. When they raise interest rates, monetary policy is tightening.

Multilateral Debt Relief Initiative (MDRI) is a program of the World Bank, the International Monetary Fund, the Inter-American Development Bank, and the African Development Bank that provides additional debt relief to countries that have completed the Heavily Indebted Poor Countries Initiative process.

Multilateral official creditors are official agencies owned or governed by more than one country that provide loan financing. They include international financial institutions such as the World Bank, regional development banks, and other intergovernmental agencies.

Multilateral-to-external debt stock is the ratio of the stock of debt owed to multilateral creditors to total external debt.

Net debt flow is gross disbursements minus principal payments.

Net transfers on external debt are net flows minus interest payments during the year; negative transfers show net transfers made by the borrower to the creditor during the year.

Official creditor committee is a group formed to represent the collective interests of creditors during the debt restructuring or bankruptcy process of a debtor, typically a corporation or sovereign entity.

Official creditors are governments or other bilateral public entities (such as export-import agencies or development agencies) and multilateral financial institutions (such as the World Bank and regional development banks).

Paris Club is an informal group of official creditors whose role is to find coordinated and sustainable solutions to the payment difficulties experienced by debtor countries. Paris Club creditors provide appropriate debt treatment as debtor countries undertake reforms to stabilize and restore their macroeconomic and financial situations.

Principal repayments are the amounts of principal (amortization) paid in currency, goods, or services in the year specified with respect to long-term external debt.

Private creditors are bondholders, commercial banks, and other trade-related lenders.

Private nonguaranteed debt is debt owed by private sector borrowers to external creditors on loans that do not benefit from a public sector guarantee by the debtor country.

Public and publicly guaranteed debt comprises public debt (an external obligation of a public debtor, such as the general government or agency, the central bank, a political subdivision or agency, or an autonomous public body) and publicly guaranteed external debt (an external obligation of a private debtor that is guaranteed for repayment by a public entity).

Public debt is an external obligation of a public debtor, including all levels of government, the central bank, state-owned enterprises, public corporations, development banks, and any other autonomous public bodies of government.

Public domestic debt comprises debt liabilities owed by public sector entities to other resident units of the same economy.

SDR allocations are reserve-related liabilities, distributed to member countries in proportion to their quota shares at the International Monetary Fund. The SDR (special drawing right) allocations are included in the gross external debt position and classified as long-term special drawing rights.

Short-term external debt has an original maturity of one year or less. Available data permit no distinctions among public, publicly guaranteed, and private nonguaranteed short-term external debt.

State-owned enterprise is a corporate entity recognized by law that is at least partially owned by the government.

Treasury bonds are long-term debt securities with a maturity period of 20 or 30 years. They are considered low-risk and are generally free of risk when held until maturity.

Variable-rate loans are loans for which the interest fluctuates according to changes in market interest rates.

www.ingramcontent.com/pod-product-compliance
Ingram Content Group UK Ltd.
Pitfield, Milton Keynes, MK11 3LW, UK
UKHW060016051026
15591UKWH00002B/235
* 9 7 8 1 4 6 4 8 2 2 6 2 9 *